Party Systems in Latin America

Based on contributions from leading scholars, this study generates a wealth of new empirical information about Latin American party systems. It also contributes richly to major theoretical and comparative debates about the effects of party systems on democratic politics, and about why some party systems are much more stable and predictable than others.

Party Systems in Latin America builds on, challenges, and updates Mainwaring and Timothy Scully's seminal *Building Democratic Institutions: Party Systems in Latin America* (1995), which reoriented the study of democratic party systems in the developing world. It is essential reading for scholars and students of comparative party systems, democracy, and Latin American politics. It shows that a stable and predictable party system facilitates important democratic processes and outcomes, but that building and maintaining such a party system has been the exception rather than the norm in contemporary Latin America.

Scott Mainwaring is the Jorge Paulo Lemann Professor for Brazil Studies at the Harvard Kennedy School. His research interests include democratic institutions and democratization; authoritarian and democratic regimes; and political parties and party systems. His book with Aníbal Pérez-Liñán, *Democracies and Dictatorships in Latin America: Emergence, Survival, and Fall* (Cambridge University Press 2013) won prizes for the best book awarded by the Comparative Democratization section of the American Political Science Association and the Political Institutions section of the Latin American Studies Association. He was elected to the American Academy of Arts and Sciences in 2010.

(*continued*)

PDC	Christian Democratic Party	*Partido Democrata Cristão*
PDS	Democratic Social Party	*Partido Democrático Social*
PDT	Democratic Labor Party	*Partido Democrático Trabalhista*
PFL	Party of the Liberal Front	*Partido da Frente Liberal*
PHS	Humanist Party of Solidarity	*Partido Humanista da Solidariedade*
PL	Liberal Party	*Partido Liberal*
PMDB	Party of the Brazilian Democratic Movement	*Partido do Movimento Democrático Brasileiro*
PMN	Party of National Mobilization	*Partido da Mobilização Nacional*
PP	Progressive Party	*Partido Progressista*
PPB	Brazilian Progressive Party	*Partido Progressista Brasileiro*
PPR	Reform Progressive Party	*Partido Progressista Reformador*
PPS	Popular Socialist Party	*Partido Popular Socialista*
PR	Party of the Republic	*Partido da República*
PRB	Brazilian Republican Party	*Partido Republicano Brasileiro*
PRN	Party of National Reconstruction	*Partido da Reconstrução Nacional*
PRONA	Party of the Reconstruction of the National Order	*Partido da Reedificação da Ordem Nacional*
PROS	Republican Party of Social Order	*Partido Republicano da Ordem Social*
PRS	Party of Social Reforms	*Partido das Reformas Sociais*
PSB	Brazilian Socialist Party	*Partido Socialista Brasileiro*
PSC	Social Christian Party	*Partido Social Cristão*
PSD	Social Democratic Party	*Partido Social Democrático*
PSDB	Brazilian Social Democratic Party	*Partido da Social Democracia Brasileira*
PSL	Social Liberal Party	*Partido Social Liberal*
PSOL	Party of Socialism and Liberty	*Partido Socialismo e Liberdade*
PT	Workers' Party	*Partido Dos Trabalhadores*
PTB	Brazilian Labor Party	*Partido Trabalhista Brasileiro*
PTN	National Labor Party	*Partido Trabalhista Nacional*
PTR	Renewal Labor Party	*Partido Trabalhista Renovador*
PTdoB	Labor Party of Brazil	*Partido Trabalhista do Brasil*
PV	Green Party	*Partido Verde*
REDE	Sustainability Network	*Rede Sustentabilidade*
SD	Solidarity	*Solidariedade*
UDN	National Democratic Union	*União Democrática Nacional*

Chile

–	Amplitude	*Amplitud*
–	Coalition of Parties for Democracy/New Majority (coalition)	*Concertación de Partidos por la Democracia /Nueva Mayoría*
–	Alliance/Alliance for Chile (coalition)	*Alianza/Alianza por Chile*
AN	National Advance	*Avanzada Nacional*
FN	National Falange	*Falange Nacional*
PC	Communist Party	*Partido Comunista de Chile*
PDC	Christian Democratic Party	*Partido Demócrata Cristiano*
PN	National Party	*Partido Nacional*
PPD	Party for Democracy	*Partido por la Democracia*
PRI	Independent Regionalist Party	*Partido Regionalista de los Independientes*
PRO	Progressive Party	*Partido Progresista*
PRSD	Social Democratic Radical Party	*Partido Radical Socialdemócrata*
PS	Socialist Party	*Partido Socialista de Chile*
RN	National Renewal	*Renovación Nacional*
UDI	Union of Independent Democrats	*Unión Demócrata Independiente*

Colombia

–	Social Party of National Unity (U Party)	*Partido Social de Unidad Nacional (Partido de la U)*
–	Democratic Center	*Centro Democrático*
AD-M19	M-19 Democratic Alliance	*Alianza Democrática M-19*
ALAS	Alas-Team Colombia	*Alas-Equipo Colombia*
CC	Citizen's Convergence Party	*Convergencia Ciudadana*
CR	Radical Change Party	*Cambio Radical*
FSP	Social and Political Front (coalition)	*Frente Social y Político*
PC	Colombia First	*Primero Colombia*
PCC	Colombian Conservative Party	*Partido Conservador Colombiano*
PDA	Democratic Alternative Pole	*Polo Democrático Alternativo*
PLC	Colombian Liberal Party	*Partido Liberal Colombiano*
UP	Patriotic Union	*Unión Patriótica*

Costa Rica

PLN	National Liberation Party	*Partido Liberación Nacional*
PUSC	Social Christian Unity Party	*Partido Unidad Social Cristiana*

Mexico

FDN	National Democratic Front (coalition)	*Frente Democrático Nacional*
MC	Citizen Movement	*Movimiento Ciudadano*
MORENA	Movement for National Regeneration	*Movimiento Regeneración Nacional*
PAN	National Action Party	*Partido Acción Nacional*
PANAL	New Alliance Party	*Nueva Alianza*
PCM	Mexican Communist Party	*Partido Comunista de México*
PMS	Mexican Socialist Party	*Partido Mexicano Socialista*
PMT	Mexican Workers' Party	*Partido Mexicano de los Trabajadores*
PNR	National Revolutionary Party	*Partido Nacional Revolucionario*
PRD	Party of the Democratic Revolution	*Partido de la Revolución Democrática*
PRI	Institutional Revolutionary Party	*Partido Revolucionario Institucional*
PRM	Party of the Mexican Revolution	*Partido de la Revolución Mexicana*
PRT	Revolutionary Workers Party	*Partido Revolucionario de los Trabajadores*
PST	Socialist Workers Party	*Partido Socialista de los Trabajadores*
PSUM	Unified Socialist Party of Mexico	*Partido Socialista Unificado de México*
PT	Labor Party	*Partido del Trabajo*
PVEM	Green Party	*Partido Verde Ecologista de México*

Peru

–	Let's Advance	*Avancemos*
AAP	Alliance for Progress	*Alianza para el Progreso*
AP	Go on Country	*Avanza País*

(continued)

AP	Popular Action	*Acción Popular*
APRA	American Popular Revolutionary Alliance	*Alianza Popular Revolucionaria Americana*
C90-NM	Change 90-New Majority	*Cambio 90/Nueva Mayoría*
CR	Radical Change	*Cambio Radical*
FA	Broad Front (coalition)	*Frente Amplio*
FIM	Independent Moralizing Front	*Frente Independiente Moralizador*
FP	Popular Force	*Fuerza Popular*
FS	Social Force	*Fuerza Social*
IU	United Left	*Izquierda Unida*
MNI	New Left Movement	*Movimiento Nueva Izquierda*
OBRAS	Public Works	*Movimiento OBRAS*
P2000	Peru 2000	*Perú 2000*
PH	Humanist Party	*Partido Humanista*
PNP	Nationalist Party	*Partido Nacionalista del Perú*
PP	Possible Peru	*Perú Posible*
PPC	Popular Christian Party	*Partido Popular Cristiano*
PPK	Peruvians for Change	*Peruanos por el Kambio*
PS	Socialist Party	*Partido Socialista*
PSN	National Solidarity Party	*Partido Solidaridad Nacional*
RN	National Restoration	*Restauración Nacional*
SP	We are Peru	*Somos Perú*
UNO	Odriísta National Union	*Unión Nacional Odriísta*
UPP	Union for Peru	*Unión por Perú*
VV	Let's Go Neighbor	*Vamos Vecino*

Venezuela

ABR	Fearless People's Alliance	*Alianza Bravo Pueblo*
AD	Democratic Action	*Acción Democrática*
BR	Red Flag	*Bandera Roja*
CD	Democratic Coordinator (coalition)	*Coordinadora Democrática*
Convergencia	National Convergence	*Convergencia Nacional*
COPEI	Social Christian Party	*Comité de Organización Política Electoral Independiente (Partido Socialcristiano)*

(*continued*)

GPP	Great Patriotic Pole (coalition)	*Gran Polo Patriótico*
LCR	The Radical Cause	*La Causa Radical*
MAS	Movement toward Socialism	*Movimiento al Socialismo*
MBR 200	Revolutionary Bolivarian Movement-200	*Movimiento Bolivariano Revolucionario 200*
MEP	People's Electoral Movement	*Movimiento Electoral del Pueblo*
MUD	Democratic Unity Roundtable (coalition)	*Mesa de la Unidad Democrática*
MVR	Fifth Republic Movement	*Movimiento Quinta República*
PCV	Communist Party of Venezuela	*Partido Comunista de Venezuela*
PJ	Justice First	*Primero Justicia*
PODEMOS	For Social Democracy	*Por la Democracia Social*
PPT	Fatherland for All	*Patria Para Todos*
PRVZL	Project Venezuela	*Proyecto Venezuela*
PSUV	United Socialist Party of Venezuela	*Partido Socialista Unido de Venezuela*
UNT	A New Era	*Un Nuevo Tiempo*
VP	Popular Will	*Voluntad Popular*

Introduction

Scott Mainwaring*

Party systems vary on many attributes. This book focuses on one of the most important: the level of institutionalization. Party systems in democracies vary hugely in how stable and predictable they are, and this variance has important implications for democratic politics.

The book examines why party system institutionalization (PSI) is important and what explains changes in levels of institutionalization. It addresses these issues by exploring the recent Latin American experience. Because of the extraordinary diversity of outcomes in the region, Latin America provides a fertile ground for the broader theoretical and comparative discussion of PSI, deinstitutionalization, and collapse. Latin American party systems span most of the spectrum among the world's democracies in PSI, from institutionalized to highly inchoate cases. We aim to advance broader theoretical and comparative knowledge by refining the concept of party system institutionalization, presenting new empirical indicators for it, and contributing to understanding its consequences and causes.

The book has five objectives: reconceptualizing PSI; creating measures that reflect this reconceptualization; adding to the knowledge about the effects of PSI; contributing toward understanding why party systems become more institutionalized or experience deinstitutionalization; and generating new empirical knowledge about Latin American party systems.

In our 1995 edited book, *Building Democratic Institutions: Party Systems in Latin America* (Stanford University Press), Timothy Scully and I introduced the concept of PSI.[1] We argued that PSI varies hugely across cases and that this variance has important consequences for democratic politics. For understanding differences among and dynamics of party systems in the world's democracies and semi-democracies, the level of institutionalization is at least as important as earlier

* I am grateful to Fernando Bizzarro, Ryan Carlin, James Loxton, Ana Petrova, Richard Price, and Samuel Valenzuela for helpful comments.
[1] We subsequently became aware of Bendel's (1993) work on PSI. Another precursor was Welfling (1973). An important reference point on related issues was Sartori (1976).

ways of classifying party systems, such as the number of parties and the degree of ideological polarization. *Building Democratic Institutions* made the case for why PSI was a useful concept, and it offered some empirical measures. In the intervening two decades, dozens of scholars who study the post-Communist countries, Africa, Asia, and Latin America have analyzed PSI.

Party Systems in Latin America: Institutionalization, Decay, and Collapse builds on this earlier book with Timothy Scully, as well as the large literature on PSI that has appeared since then. This literature now spans many regions of the world, especially Africa (Weghorst and Bernhard 2014; Kuenzi and Lambright 2001; Lindberg 2007; Riedl 2014), Asia (Croissant and Völkel 2012; Hicken and Kuhonta 2015a), Latin America (Torcal 2015), and the post-Soviet countries (Moser and Scheiner 2012).[2]

Theoretically, the book repeats the claim in Mainwaring and Scully that institutionalization is one of the most important attributes along which party systems vary. Institutionalized party systems are stable, and parties and other political actors believe that they are fairly predictable into the near to medium-term future. Weakly institutionalized systems are less stable and less predictable. These conditions generate less certainty, which in turn affects the logic of major actors in the system.

For the broad theoretical and comparative analysis of PSI, Latin America is a fertile region. The Latin American countries cover most of the huge range in institutionalization among the world's party systems in democratic and semi-democratic regimes, from fairly high (Uruguay, Mexico, and Chile) to very low institutionalization (Guatemala and Peru). They include countries of increased institutionalization over time (Brazil and El Salvador) and of significant deinstitutionalization (Argentina and Colombia), and most of the world's rare cases of party system collapse (Bolivia, Ecuador, Peru, and Venezuela).

WHY STUDY PARTIES IN THE DEVELOPING WORLD?

Before I turn to the core of this volume, a few words about why parties should remain a central part of the agenda in studying democracies and possible democratic transitions in the developing world are in order. The short answer is that parties continue to be central actors in democratic politics.

First, parties and party leaders are often the most important actors in democratic transitions. Among Latin American cases in the post-1978 wave of democracy, I would argue that parties were the most important actors in the transitions in Brazil (1974–85), Chile (1987–90), Mexico (1977–2000), and Uruguay (1981–84), among other cases. Parties were the lead actors for a shorter time in Argentina, but after the military's defeat in the Falklands/Malvinas war (June 1982), they became the main actors in negotiating the transition with the armed forces,

---

[2] A partial list of 111 books, published articles, and Ph.D. dissertations on party system institutionalization appears in the online Appendix 0.1.

culminating in the October 1983 elections and the December 1983 inauguration of President Raúl Alfonsín. In earlier democratic transitions, parties were the central actors in the transition from the oligarchic republic of the late eighteenth and early nineteenth centuries to a system of competing parties with universal white adult male enfranchisement in the US (Hofstadter 1969), and in democratic transitions in Sweden (Rustow 1955), Colombia in 1958 (Hartlyn 1988), and Venezuela in 1959 (Levine 1973).

Second, historically parties have usually been among the most important actors in democratic breakdowns. Scully (1992) and Valenzuela (1978) portrayed parties as the main protagonists in the breakdown of democracy in Chile in 1973. Linz (1978) and Payne (2006) viewed parties as the main players in the Spanish breakdown of 1936, and Lepsius (1978) focused on parties (and their paramount leaders) as key players in the German breakdown of 1930–33. Parties can polarize and act intransigently in ways that make democracies vulnerable to breakdown, or they can manage conflict in ways that can sustain democracy even in difficult times and places (Varshney 1998).

Third, in democracies, parties remain the primary way through which politicians gain access to state power. In most democracies, outsiders running on new party labels have scant chances to become head of government. The primary route to state power, and hence the primary way to effect political and social change, is by winning elections through political parties. For this reason, parties and their leaders are usually the main actors in democratic politics (Sartori 1976). They set the broad policy parameters of democratic politics. Social movements, interest groups, lobbyists, and other actors affect democratic politics, but they do so from outside the state.

Fourth, parties remain important vehicles by which citizens express their preferences regarding who should govern. Citizens have a panoply of mechanisms for expressing their interests and articulating their demands, but with unusual exceptions (independent candidates, recall referenda), they choose the rulers through parties.

Fifth, in democracies, parties are almost always the primary basis for organizing support and opposition to governments in the legislature (Aldrich 1995). What parties do in government has significant consequences for policy outcomes, which, in turn, shape long-term societal trajectories (Grzymala-Busse 2007).

Sixth, parties offer information short cuts to voters (Downs 1957). Relatively few voters invest time in researching a wide range of issues. Rather, they take cues from trusted organizations and leaders, almost all of which have strong partisan predilections.

Finally, parties help shape citizen identities. To take one example, class is an objective reality, but the way class is mobilized politically depends on how parties and other actors politicize class or take it off the agenda. In the 1990s, class voting was muted in most or all of Latin America. By the second half of the 2000s, strong class voting had appeared in most countries with leftist or left-of-center presidents or strong presidential contenders. These presidents and presidential candidates, and their parties, had a strong impact in mobilizing class identities. In contrast, in countries without strong leftist presidential candidates, there was very little class voting. Class voting depends on the partisan mobilization of latent identities (Mainwaring *et al.* 2015; Przeworski and Sprague 1986; Sartori 1969). Likewise, religion, ethnicity, and nationality do not automatically constitute political identities. The degree to which they become political identities hinges on political mobilization through concrete historical actors, including very prominently parties.

Although these points hold for almost all democracies, there is variance in the degree to which the final five points are true. This variance corresponds to the extent to which parties and the interaction among them have stable and predictable patterns. Because parties are important actors in democratic politics, the level of PSI is a central issue for democracy.

RECONCEPTUALIZING PARTY SYSTEM INSTITUTIONALIZATION

While building on Mainwaring and Scully, this volume conceptualizes PSI in a different way than they did. Coauthored by Mainwaring, Fernando Bizzarro, and Ana Petrova, Chapter 1 defines and reconceptualizes PSI. We define an institutionalized party system as one in which a stable set of parties interacts regularly in stable ways. Actors develop expectations and behavior based on the premise that the fundamental contours and rules of party competition will prevail into the foreseeable future. An institutionalized party system shapes the future expectations and behavior of political elites, masses, and other actors.

Mainwaring and Scully (1995a) posited that the concept has four dimensions: (1) stability of inter-party competition; (2) strong party roots in society; (3) the major actors accord legitimacy to the electoral process and to parties; and (4) solid organizations. Many subsequent works followed this conceptualization. In contrast, our revised definition focuses exclusively on the first of the four previous dimensions – but on an expanded understanding of it. The reason for shedding the second, third, and fourth previous "dimensions" of PSI is that by definition, institutionalization necessarily entails that a stable set of parties interact regularly in relatively stable ways, but it does not intrinsically require the other three previous dimensions. These three previous dimensions are underpinnings that facilitate PSI but are not defining features of it.

While narrowing the operationalization of PSI to one of the four previous dimensions, we expand our understanding of this dimension. More than previous work on PSI, we emphasize the stability of the membership of the party system, i.e., the parties that constitute the system. A system in which new significant contenders frequently emerge and major old contenders fade into oblivion is weakly institutionalized. Finally, we consider relative stability in parties' ideological positions a feature of institutionalized systems. If major parties veer sharply in one direction or another, it affects not only the stability and predictability of that particular party, but also systemic competition.

Because its patterns of electoral competition are stable, an institutionalized system is predictable. The parties themselves, voters, and other organized actors expect patterns to continue prevailing into the future. Conversely, in a weakly institutionalized or inchoate system, parties and voters are less clear about future patterns.

MEASURING PARTY SYSTEM INSTITUTIONALIZATION

A second goal of this volume is to contribute to measuring PSI. Since the publication of Mainwaring and Scully, many scholars have measured PSI. This volume contributes to that ongoing discussion. Chapter 2 presents measures of PSI that stem directly from the conceptual discussion in Chapter 1 and that are easily replicable across time and space.

Consistent with the theoretical and conceptual discussion in Chapter 1, the elements I use to assess PSI are: (1) stability in the membership of the party system; (2) stability in parties' vote shares; and (3) stability in parties' ideological preferences. With few exceptions (Sánchez 2009), previous scholarship has not paid much attention to stability in the membership of party system as a defining feature of PSI, yet it is implied by the notion of institutionalization. If significant new contenders emerge with some frequency while others vanish from the scene, a system is weakly institutionalized. In such circumstances, the supply of parties from which the electorate chooses changes substantially.

Electoral volatility, long a familiar indicator to scholars who work on party systems and elections, measures the degree to which parties win even vote shares over time. I supplement it with two other measures: *cumulative* electoral volatility since 1990 (based on comparing election results in the most recent election with those circa 1990) and the vote share in the most recent election won by parties that existed in 1990. Both of these measures assess electoral stability over the medium term, whereas electoral volatility as conventionally assessed is based on change from one election to the next.

The final measure of PSI is stability of parties' programmatic positions, an important measure in a region that has frequent party shifts from left-of-center to right-of-center, and vice versa. Systemic stability and predictability hinge on the stability and predictability of individual components thereof. If parties undergo sharp ideological shifts, it diminishes systemic level stability and predictability.

All of these indicators are logical implications of the reformulated core concept. All travel seamlessly to different regions of the world, within the context of democratic or semi-democratic regimes. Chapter 2 also examines PSI in contemporary Latin America. It demonstrates great variance across cases both in levels of institutionalization and in trends since 1990. It also suggests one of the democratic paradoxes and deficits of the third wave of democratization in Latin

America: although PSI facilitates important positive outcomes, establishing and maintaining institutionalized systems has been an elusive reality in most countries.

PARTY SYSTEM INSTITUTIONALIZATION, PREDICTABILITY, AND DEMOCRACY

A third goal of this volume is to advance knowledge about why PSI is important for democratic outcomes and processes. Chapter 3 shows that PSI is associated with several important democratic outcomes. Although it focuses empirically on Latin America, the arguments should travel beyond this region.

Institutionalized systems have more predictable electoral outcomes, and they create high barriers for political outsiders. In inchoate systems, political outsiders can more easily win power. Weakly institutionalized systems are the breeding grounds for populist outsiders who have sometimes used their ascent to power to dismantle democratic institutions (for example, Alberto Fujimori in Peru, Hugo Chávez in Venezuela, and Rafael Correa in Ecuador). In turn, political outsiders are (1) less accountable to their parties; (2) less likely to engage in party building; (3) more likely to have severe conflict with the legislature; and (4) more likely to attempt to undermine democracy.

Second, inchoate systems produce less experienced politicians (see Levitsky's chapter on Peru in this volume). In turn, less experienced politicians are less likely to be unconditionally supportive of democracy and less likely to believe that parties are essential for democracy.

Third, as Flores-Macías (2012) and O'Dwyer and Kovalcik (2007) show, policy stability tends to be greater in institutionalized systems. This is in part because outsiders do not win presidential elections in highly institutionalized systems, and outsiders are more likely to favor radical policy change. In addition, well-established parties have commitments to some constituencies, making radical policy change less likely (Berman 1998; Kitschelt 1994: 207–79; Przeworski and Sprague 1986: 119–26).

Fourth, fluid party systems are associated with shorter time horizons (Lupu and Riedl 2013), with more frequent radical changes in the rules of the game, with less effectual provision of public goods, and with greater propensity to corruption. Finally, electoral accountability is easier in institutionalized systems because voters probably have greater knowledge about what the parties represent. Voters have more difficulty in behaving strategically in weakly institutionalized systems (Moser and Scheiner 2012). Effective democratic representation and electoral accountability are less likely in the absence of a relatively institutionalized party system. With the weak and often ephemeral and personalistic parties that characterize inchoate systems, it is more difficult for voters to grasp parties' programmatic positions (Kitschelt *et al.* 2010). Electoral rules have different, more consistent and more predictable effects in institutionalized party systems (Moser and Scheiner 2012).

The argument that weak PSI is usually associated with some negative outcomes does not imply that PSI suffices to ensure good democratic outcomes. Institutionalized systems are sometimes embedded in democracies that do not function well. Venezuela had an institutionalized party system from 1968 to 1988, but its democracy was racked by corruption scandals and plagued by poor economic results from the late 1970s until 2003 (Coppedge 1994; Morgan 2011). Likewise, voters in Italy by the early 1990s began to see an institutionalized system as sclerotic and the parties as corrupt. An ideal type "perfectly" institutionalized system would have serious democratic deficits associated with excessive stultification. The argument in Chapter 3 is not that high levels of institutionalization are always good, but that weak institutionalization is associated with democratic shortcomings.

EXPLAINING INSTITUTIONALIZATION AND DEINSTITUTIONALIZATION

A fourth goal of this volume is to contribute to the scholarship that explains institutionalization and deinstitutionalization. If a reasonably institutionalized party system is associated with more positive democratic outcomes than an inchoate system, then understanding why some systems institutionalize while others erode is an important theoretical task, with real world implications.

Institutionalizing party systems in new democracies in an era of mass television and newer electronic media is challenging. In democracies created after 1978, it has been the exception rather than the norm. Politicians today can win an election without making time demanding investments in organization building (Hale 2006; Mainwaring and Zoco 2007; Schmitter 2001). Wrenching economic transformations and crises battered many parties in Latin America and the post-Soviet region, leading to erosion of party systems (Bernhard and Karakoç 2011; Lupu 2016; Roberts 2014). Nevertheless, another lesson, seen in the chapters on Brazil and Mexico as well as in the case of El Salvador, is that institutionalization is possible even in difficult contexts for party building.[3]

The literature that attempts to explain why some systems institutionalize while others deinstitutionalize is thin, notwithstanding important recent contributions by Lupu (2016), Morgan (2011), Riedl (2014), Roberts (2014), and Seawright (2012), among others. Chapter 4, by Scott Mainwaring and Fernando Bizzarro, examines the conditions that on average were associated with higher and lower PSI in Latin America from 1990 to 2015. Systems with solid party organizations tend to be more institutionalized.[4] Bad government performance, as almost all Latin American countries have periodically experienced, can make governing parties vulnerable to steep electoral losses and therefore result in lower party system stability. Bad performance by multiple governing parties can make the

---

[3] For a related argument, see Levitsky *et al.* (2016a).   [4] Along related lines, see Tavits (2013).

entire system vulnerable (Morgan 2011; Seawright 2012). Conversely, as the Brazilian case from 1995 to 2011 suggests, solid economic performance can promote institutionalization. Although most of the recent literature has turned against arguments about the effect of institutional rules, in some cases, rules have fostered PSI or its reverse (see the chapters on Brazil and Colombia). Against expectations, neither the year when democracy was born nor the longevity of democracy have had a statistically measurable association with PSI.

THE DIVERSITY OF PATHWAYS IN LATIN AMERICA

A final goal of this book is to generate new empirical knowledge about Latin American party systems. Empirically, the book explores the stunning diversity of PSI in Latin America and the remarkably different pathways that Latin American party systems have experienced since the 1990s. It also offers some explanations for these different pathways.

If we focus on institutionalization, Latin American party systems have evolved in very different directions since 1995. We can usefully delineate five patterns, with variations within each category. Uruguay and Chile had institutionalized systems in 1995 and still do today, although the Chilean system has experienced an erosion of partisanship. This pattern is *persistent institutionalization*. Honduras also had a highly institutionalized system in 1995, and it remained institutionalized until the 2009 coup that overthrew President Manuel Zelaya.

Second, four systems became more institutionalized. Brazil, whose system we classified as inchoate in 1995, is an example of a country with greater institutionalization until 2014. Between 1988 and 2000, Mexico gradually moved from an institutionalized hegemonic party system (and an authoritarian political regime) to an institutionalized party system under democracy. El Salvador and Panama are also cases of institutionalization since 1994. I call this pattern *increasing institutionalization*.

Third, in a few systems that were institutionalized in 1995, at least one of the traditional major parties has declined steeply, with no clear sign of consolidation of a new competitor, or else both traditional parties have eroded deeply. These systems are markedly less institutionalized today than they were in 1995. In Argentina, the Radical Party, created in 1890 and the country's governing party during seven presidencies (1916–22, 1922–28, 1928–30, 1958–62, 1963–66, 1983–89, 1999–2001), has shriveled.[5] In Colombia, the Conservative and Liberal parties, the two great contenders that always dominated elections from the 1880s until 1991, have weakened greatly, although not quite as steeply as the Argentine Radicals. I call this third pattern *deep erosion*. In Costa Rica, the Social Christian Unity Party (PUSC), for generations one of the two contenders for

---

[5] This does not count Roberto Ortiz (1938–42), who was president during the "infamous decade" from 1932 to 1943. Ortiz was a member of the UCR, but his election was vitiated by fraud.

presidential power, has become irrelevant. Costa Rica is an intermediate case, with less stability than Chile and Uruguay but less seismic change than Argentina, Colombia, and Venezuela.

Fourth, in Peru in the 1990s, and Ecuador, Bolivia, and Venezuela in the 2000s, *all* of the old parties that dominated political life since redemocratization disappeared or were reduced to minor party status with almost no prospect of revival. I call this pattern *collapse*. The three "Bolivarian" cases of collapse (Ecuador, Bolivia, and Venezuela) subsequently led to asymmetrical institutionalization, in which the governing party attempted to institutionalize hegemonic party systems in competitive authoritarian regimes or semi-democratic regimes.

Finally, other countries have had *persistently low institutionalization*. Guatemala was a paradigmatic case of very weak institutionalization in 1995 and has remained so ever since (Sánchez 2008, 2009). Since the restoration of democracy in 2001, Peru has been a case of persistently low institutionalization, as Steven Levitsky argues in his chapter in this volume. Paraguay also has a relatively weakly institutionalized system – although not to the same degree as Guatemala and Peru.

Many of these changes were surprising. In the early 1990s, nobody foresaw that major parties that had existed for generations and had often governed – the Radicals in Argentina; the MNR and MIR in Bolivia; *Acción Democrática* and COPEI in Venezuela – would largely disappear.

The established literature underscored the indispensability of parties for modern representative democracy and implicitly seemed to suggest that if democracy survived, solid parties would have to be a solid underpinning for it. E. E. Schattschneider famously wrote in 1942 that "Political parties created modern democracy and democracy is unthinkable save in terms of the parties" (p. 1). In contemporary Latin America, this conventional wisdom might not fully hold. Some countries (e.g., Peru) combine democracy with very weak parties, as Levitsky shows in his chapter in this volume.

Party Systems in Latin America documents and attempts to explain these changes. To a surprising degree in light of how many scholars have become interested in PSI, there have been few efforts to analyze these questions. Lupu (2011, 2016, this volume), Morgan (2011), Seawright (2012), Tanaka (1998, 2006), and Zoco (2007) have written on party or party system collapse, and Roberts (2014) offers an important explanation for why some systems experienced greater upheaval than others. We lack comparably good analyses that examine why a few systems remained persistently institutionalized or became more institutionalized.

Party Systems in Latin America focuses on democratic and semi-democratic regimes, although we include a chapter on Venezuela, whose political regime has become competitive authoritarian (Levitsky and Way

TABLE 0.1 *Case Selection Criteria*

Country	Type of case	Population rank within Latin America
Chile	I. Persistent institutionalization	7
Brazil	II. Increased institutionalization	1
Mexico	II. Increased institutionalization	2
Colombia	III. Deep erosion	3
Argentina	III. Deep erosion	4
Venezuela	IV. Collapse between 1998 and 2000; asymmetrical institutionalization since 2000	6
Peru	IV and V. Collapse in the 1990s; persistently weak institutionalization since 2001	5

2010).[6] We exclude patently authoritarian regimes in which the governing party buttresses the regime but does not hold elections with uncertain outcomes. In such cases, stability in the patterns of party competition tends to be artificial, reflecting the effects of repression, state patronage, and an uneven playing field as much as, or more than, stable sincere support for the regime. If the authoritarian incumbents open the regime, their support might quickly dissipate. This makes it difficult to compare indicators of system institutionalization across democratic and authoritarian regimes (Lindberg 2007; Mainwaring 2015). Contemporary Latin America has only one openly authoritarian regime (Cuba).

The book features seven chapters focused on specific countries. I used two criteria to select country cases. The more important criterion is theoretical. I included at least one country that exemplifies the five broad patterns set out above. The case studies also focus on the larger countries. Table 0.1 indicates the seven countries and how they fit these two criteria. Serendipitously, for contemporary Latin America, it is possible to choose cases on theoretical grounds *and* include the largest countries.

The country studies focus on PSI. They provide insights into the countries they analyze and generate ideas that contribute to a broader understanding of PSI, decay, and collapse.

In Chapter 5, Samuel Valenzuela, Nicolás Somma, and Timothy Scully address one of the region's two cases of persistent institutionalization: Chile

[6] Chapters 2, 3, and 4 give data for the region as a whole except Haiti and Cuba. We include Nicaragua, whose regime has also become competitive authoritarian. Some scholars also view Bolivia and Ecuador as cases of competitive authoritarianism.

(Uruguay is the other). They argue that the party system's overall stability has largely been the product of enduring voter attachments to underlying and persistent political tendencies (a religious/secular divide and divisions over socioeconomic policies). They recognize declining interest in parties, elections, and politics, and argue that the system is stable but not ossified.

In Chapter 6, Mainwaring, Power, and Bizzarro analyze Brazil, by far the largest country in Latin America and until 2014 one of only four cases in the region of increased PSI. After the party reform passed by the military dictatorship in 1979, Brazil's party system went through a tumultuous fifteen-year period. However, since 1994, the main contenders have been stable, electoral volatility has diminished sharply, and the competition for the presidency has consistently been between the same two parties, the PT and PSDB.

In Chapter 7, Greene and Sánchez Talanquer analyze Mexico, another case of increased PSI. Mexico's PRI, which has governed the country since 2012, has long been a highly institutionalized party. In the early 1990s, the hegemonic party system in transition did not fit squarely on a continuum of indicators for PSI under democratic regimes. Building on the party system that emerged late during the authoritarian period, an institutionalized democratic party system has taken hold. Greene and Sánchez Talanquer analyze this smooth transition from the late authoritarian era to the democratic period.

Colombia and Argentina are cases of deep party system erosion. In 1995, both countries had institutionalized systems, though both, especially the Colombian, were evincing clear signs of impending change. In Chapter 8, Juan Albarracín, Laura Gamboa, and Scott Mainwaring document this transition from an institutionalized to a much more volatile system.

In Chapter 9, Carlos Gervasoni analyzes the growing "fragmentation, denationalization, factionalization, personalization, and fluidity" (to borrow from his subtitle) of the Argentine party system. From 1946 until 1994, the competition between the Peronist Party, officially known as the Justicialist Party (PJ), and the Radical Party (*Unión Cívica Radical*) dominated electoral politics. Today, the old system is not recognizable. The main Peronist party is now called the *Frente para la Victoria*, headed by President Néstor Kirchner (2003–07) and his wife, President Cristina Fernández de Kirchner (2007–15). The Radical Party has been reduced to a shadow of its former self. A dizzying plethora of new parties has emerged; many are important at the provincial level, in only one or two provinces. The system's deinstitutionalization is illustrated by the fact that a new party, Mauricio Macri's PRO, headed the alliance that won the 2015 presidential election.

The final two country cases, Venezuela and Peru, involved party system collapse, in 2000–05 in the former case and 1995 in the latter. While they are similar in this important regard, they are different in others. In Chapter 10, Jana Morgan analyzes the Venezuelan case, focusing both on the collapse of the old system and the post-collapse system. She explains the collapse of the old system by emphasizing the erosion of the three kinds of linkage that held it together: programmatic, group, and clientelism (Morgan 2011). The new system began to emerge in 1998 with the election of Hugo Chávez and the precipitous electoral decline of the traditional parties in the presidential contest. The Chavista party has become quite institutionalized; in contrast, most of the parties in the opposition coalition are organizationally flimsy.

In Chapter 11, Steven Levitsky analyzes the Peruvian party system since the restoration of democracy in 2001. His title, "Peru: The Institutionalization of Politics without Parties," reveals the core argument: sixteen years after the restoration of democracy, Peruvian parties are extraordinarily weak. Levitsky examines the causes and consequences of party system decomposition. Post-Fujimori politicians "developed alternative strategies and technologies that enabled them to succeed without parties, thereby weakening incentives for party building. The difficulties of party rebuilding were exacerbated by state weakness." Levitsky argues that extreme party weakness has had negative consequences for the quality of Peruvian democracy.

The standard wisdom in political science was that parties offered huge advantages to politicians (Aldrich 1995) and provided indispensable information shortcuts to voters (Downs 1957; Hinich and Munger 1994) and hence were essential to democratic politics (Schattschneider 1942). In some Latin American countries today, party labels have become a hindrance to many politicians and irrelevant to most voters. These cases raise new and important questions about how (and how well) democratic politics can function with very weak parties – an issue that Levitsky takes up (Chapter 11).

COMPARATIVE ANALYSES

Four comparative analyses follow the country cases. Noam Lupu (Chapter 12) addresses "Party Brands, Partisan Erosion, and Party Breakdown." Building on his previous work, he argues that the combination of brand dilution and bad governing performance is fatal to parties. Parties can dilute their brand by engaging in sharp policy switches or by moving ideologically close to the competition. His chapter extends the scope of his analysis beyond the cases he covered in his recent book.

Jason Seawright (Chapter 13) writes on individual-level underpinnings of PSI, based on survey data. He addresses trends over time and variance across countries in partisanship, participation in parties, and attitudes toward parties (trust in parties and agreement with the statement that parties are necessary for democracy). He argues that solid links between citizens and parties provide an important underpinning for PSI. He shows that partisanship, participation in parties, and supportive attitudes are related in quite different ways to country-level potential explanatory variables. Thus, they do not seem to form a unified consistent form of citizen connections to party systems.

Gustavo Flores-Macías (Chapter 14) addresses some macro-level consequences of variance in PSI. Based on a quantitative analysis of seventeen Latin American countries, he shows that on average, more institutionalized systems are associated with less volatility in rates of economic growth.

Two scholars with deep expertise on PSI in other regions of the world provide a cross-regional perspective in Chapter 15. Rachel Beatty Riedl is an expert on Africa, and Allen Hicken works on South and Southeast Asia. Both have authored books on PSI (Hicken and Kuhonta 2015a; Riedl 2014). Their chapter focuses on where the African and Asian experiences mesh with the Latin American cases, and where there are striking cross-regional differences. How do the Latin American cases (in all of their diversity) inform understanding of Africa and Asia, respectively, and how might the African and Asian cases (also in all of their diversity) inform understanding of Latin America?

undergone decay or collapse than institutionalization. Likewise, the number of institutionalized democratic party systems in Asia, Africa, and the post-communist world is limited.

Although parties hold center stage in this volume, this does not imply a party centric view of democracy. Other mechanisms of citizen participation – social movements, NGOs, labor unions and owners' associations, protests, referenda, and other mechanisms of direct democracy – can make democracy more vital. However, parties occupy a unique position in democratic politics (Sartori 1976; Schattschneider 1942). Through elections, parties can achieve positions in government and hence usually shape political outcomes more than other vehicles of citizen participation. Parties are both critical vehicles of representation and of shaping the political system (Sartori 1976) – though to degrees that vary according to the system's level of institutionalization.

2

Party System Institutionalization in Contemporary Latin America*

Scott Mainwaring

This chapter has three purposes. First, I develop indicators of party system institutionalization (PSI) that reflect the reconceptualization in Chapter 1. Despite the proliferation of work on PSI, advances in measurement have not kept up with theoretical and other empirical contributions. Chapter 2 presents thirteen indicators of party system stability to measure the three different attributes of PSI discussed in Chapter 1 (stable membership, stable inter-party competition, and stable party linkages to society). These indicators stem directly from the theoretical discussion in Chapter 1. They are straightforward, informative, easy to operationalize, and comparable across cases and over time. They can be used for analyses of party system change and stability in all regions of the world.

Second, the chapter lays out the data for these measures for eighteen Latin American countries – all but Cuba and Haiti – and the United States as a benchmark case among the advanced industrial democracies. It begins with six measures for the stability of the *membership* of Latin American party systems. These party systems differ dramatically on all six measures.

The chapter then presents six measures for the stability of inter-party competition, beginning with the most widely used: electoral volatility, which I calculated for both presidential and lower chamber elections. I also created two indicators to measure cumulative change or stability in inter-party competition: cumulative electoral volatility since 1990, and the vote share in the most recent elections of parties that existed by 1990 for both presidential and lower chamber elections. Again, these party systems vary widely on all of these measures.

* I am grateful to Michael Coppedge, María Victoria De Negri, Laura Gamboa, Carlos Gervasoni, Frances Hagopian, Noam Lupu, Ana Petrova, Guillermo Trejo, and Samuel Valenzuela for comments and to Fernando Bizzarro, Rodrigo Castro Cornejo, María Victoria De Negri, Lauran Feist, Laura Gamboa, Jenny Ng, Richard Price, and Adriana Ramírez Baracaldo for research assistance.

TABLE 2.3 *Stability in the Membership of the Party System: Z-Scores, Latin America, and the US*

	Vote share of new parties		Stability of significant contenders, election-to-election		Stability of significant contenders, medium term		Average of Z-scores
	Presidential	Lower chamber	Presidential	Lower chamber	Presidential	Lower chamber	
Uruguay	0.95	1.11	1.31	0.78	2.06	1.47	1.28
Mexico	0.75	0.64	1.31	0.78	2.06	1.34	1.15
United States	0.74	1.47	0.88	0.78	0.82	1.47	1.03
Dominican Republic	0.89	1.00	1.02	0.52	1.44	1.26	1.02
Chile	0.99	1.15	0.37	0.63	0.43	1.35	0.82
Brazil	0.91	0.72	0.32	0.32	0.13	0.14	0.42
Honduras	0.40	-0.10	1.31	0.78	0.20	-0.12	0.41
Nicaragua	0.79	1.26	0.26	-0.51	-0.03	-0.32	0.24
Costa Rica	0.55	-0.36	0.98	0.24	-0.05	-0.34	0.17
El Salvador	0.13	-0.19	0.79	0.20	0.20	-0.36	0.13
Panama	0.54	-0.47	-0.66	0.08	-0.59	-0.28	-0.23
Paraguay	-0.09	-0.53	-0.66	-0.19	-0.42	-0.28	-0.36
Bolivia	0.07	-0.03	-0.91	-1.16	-0.63	-0.82	-0.58
Ecuador	-0.99	-0.51	-0.46	-0.56	-0.66	-0.76	-0.66
Colombia	-1.35	-1.11	-0.91	0.35	-0.97	-0.42	-0.73

TABLE 2.3 (*continued*)

	Vote share of new parties		Stability of significant contenders, election-to-election		Stability of significant contenders, medium term		Average of Z- scores
	Presidential	Lower chamber	Presidential	Lower chamber	Presidential	Lower chamber	
Argentina	-0.35	–	-1.47	–	-1.16	–	-0.99
Peru	-1.06	-1.49	-0.87	-1.40	-0.59	-1.01	-1.07
Venezuela	-1.43	-1.43	-1.44	-1.01	-1.10	-1.15	-1.26
Guatemala	-2.43	-1.12	-1.19	-0.63	-1.14	-1.18	-1.28

with the Z-scores in Table 2.3 is −0.48).[11] Low volatility and ideological stability tend to be mutually reinforcing.

SUMMARY SCORES FOR PARTY SYSTEM INSTITUTIONALIZATION FOR 1990–2015

For synthetic purposes, it might be useful to have a summary score for PSI. To create this score, I averaged the Z-scores for the thirteen indicators used in this chapter. The third aspect of PSI, stability in party linkages with society, has only one indicator, so it is weighted much less than the other two characteristics of PSI (1/13 of the total). All of these indicators capture different aspects of PSI, and there is no clear theoretical or empirical rationale for weighting any one more than the other. Where necessary, Z-scores are inverted so that high stability yields a high score. Table 2.6 shows the results.

To facilitate looking at the three attributes of PSI in one table, Table 2.6 also includes the summary Z-scores for each of them. As noted previously, because these scores represent the number of standard deviations above and below the mean for the 19 countries, a score of 0 represents a volatile system compared to the mean for the advanced industrial democracies.

Based on Table 2.6, the US (an average Z-score of 1.27), Uruguay (1.16), Mexico (1.09), and Chile (0.90) had on average the most institutionalized systems for the 1990–2015 period. All four systems had high stability in the main contenders, high electoral stability, and average (Uruguay) to high (Mexico and Chile) continuity in parties' ideological positions.

The Dominican Republic (0.72), Honduras (0.55), Brazil (0.48), and El Salvador (0.42) also had institutionalized systems compared to the average. However, in the 2013 elections, the Honduran system showed signs of deep erosion in the wake of the 2009 coup. Costa Rica (0.09), Nicaragua (0.08), Panama (−0.13), and Paraguay (−0.19) scored around the mean. For generations, Costa Rica had an institutionalized system, but the collapse of the Social Christian Unity Party, the emergence of *Acción Ciudadana* in 2002 as an important new contender, high cumulative electoral volatility from 1990 to 2015, and high perceived ideological instability (from 5.57 to 8.29) for the country's largest party, the PLN, from the 2002–06 legislature to the 2006–10 legislature lowered the PSI score.

The party systems of Guatemala (−1.28), Peru (−1.16), Venezuela (−1.15), Bolivia (−0.85), and Argentina (−0.81) ranked as the least institutionalized according to Table 2.6. These scores have face validity. Peru's ranking is consistent with Steven Levitsky's analysis in Chapter 11 (see also Meléndez 2015). Guatemala has persistently had a very inchoate party system (Sánchez 2008, 2009). Peru, Venezuela, Ecuador, and Bolivia all experienced party

---

[11] The *p* values are 0.07 and 0.04, respectively. As Online Appendix 2.1 shows, ideological change correlates with the other twelve indicators at a lower level than the rest.

TABLE 2.6 *Summary Score for PSI for Latin America and the US, 1990–2015 (Z-scores)*

Country	Stability of members of the party system	Stability in inter-party electoral competition	Stability of parties' ideological positions	Overall PSI score
United States	1.10	1.50	–	1.27
Uruguay	1.35	1.10	0.07	1.16
Mexico	1.21	0.81	1.63	1.09
Chile	0.88	0.73	1.95	0.90
Dominican Republic	1.07	0.54	−0.90	0.72
Honduras	0.46	0.68	0.50	0.55
Brazil	0.45	0.41	1.04	0.48
El Salvador	0.14	0.76	0.75	0.42
Costa Rica	0.18	0.15	−0.80	0.09
Nicaragua	0.21	−0.14	0.21	0.08
Panama	−0.23	−0.13	0.61	−0.13
Paraguay	−0.38	0.31	−1.42	−0.19
Colombia	−0.72	−0.56	−1.11	−0.69
Ecuador	−0.71	−0.89	−0.73	−0.78
Argentina	−0.99	−0.72	−0.30	−0.81
Bolivia	−0.67	−1.24	−0.25	−0.85
Venezuela	−1.34	−1.24	0.59	−1.15
Peru	−1.18	−1.05	−1.54	−1.16
Guatemala	−1.34	−1.39	−0.32	−1.28

system collapses in the 1990s or 2000s. In the latter three cases, new systems might be institutionalizing, but under regimes that have become less democratic over time.

In most cases, the three attributes of PSI worked in tandem, but with a few exceptions. Costa Rica and the Dominican Republic had above average scores for the stability of membership in the system and stability of inter-party electoral competition, but below average stability in parties' ideological positions. Panama had the reverse pattern: average stability of main contenders and stability of electoral competition, but higher than average ideological stability. In such cases, the summary score for PSI should not obscure the more differentiated scores for the different attributes of institutionalization.

CHANGE IN INSTITUTIONALIZATION SINCE THE 1990S

When Tim Scully and I (1995a) wrote the introduction to *Building Democratic Institutions*, nobody foresaw the extraordinary upheavals that would face so many Latin American party systems. We expected – and the world history of democracy until the 1990s supported this expectation – that most countries with relatively institutionalized party systems would remain in that category. Some classic works suggested that democratic longevity would favor PSI (Converse 1969). The decades since 1995 have dashed these expectations.

To assess change in PSI since 1995, I first present data about countries' mean PSI from 1970 to 1995, again using a twenty-five-year period. Of the thirteen indicators used to assess PSI for 1990–2015, for the 1970–95 period, I reproduce only six – the vote share of new parties in presidential and lower chamber elections, electoral volatility in lower chamber and presidential elections, and the two short-term indicators for continuity in main contenders. The six medium-term indicators do not work well for comparing data points from roughly 1970 to points from roughly 1995 because only Colombia, Costa Rica, and Venezuela had competitive political regimes during that entire period. The data for measuring ideological change from the mid-1990s to 2015 do not exist before the mid-1990s. Because the correlations among the thirteen indicators were mostly very high for the 1990–2015 period, most likely, using only six of them for 1970–95 will produce estimates of PSI that would be close to estimates based on all thirteen.

Table 2.7 shows the vote share of new parties, electoral volatility, and stability of the main contenders in presidential and lower chamber elections and the mean Z-scores for the 1970–95 period.[12] Because the means (based on averaging the scores for the nineteen countries) for all six variables are very close for 1970–95 and 1990–2015, the Z-scores for the two periods are almost comparable.

The ordering of the ten countries that had clearly established competitive political regimes by the early 1990s matches Mainwaring and Scully's (1995a) two main categories (institutionalized and inchoate party systems). They classified Argentina, Chile, Colombia, Costa Rica, Uruguay, and Venezuela as having institutionalized systems. All of them had average Z-scores above the mean for 1970–95. They classified Bolivia, Brazil, Ecuador, and Peru as having inchoate systems. All four countries had less stable systems than the mean for 1970–95.

For purposes of showing more clearly how countries changed over time, Figure 2.8 shows the mean Z-scores for the 1990–2015 period (from Table 2.6) and the average Z-scores for 1970–95 (from Table 2.7). Since 1995, Argentina and Colombia shifted to inchoate systems, and the Venezuelan system collapsed only to later partially reinstitutionalize under a competitive authoritarian regime. As Carlos Gervasoni (on Argentina), Juan Albarracín *et al.*

---

[12] The beginning point was all democratic elections that took place in 1970 or thereafter. The last election was 1995 or the one immediately before 1995.

TABLE 2.7 *Summary Scores for PSI, 1970–95*

Country	Average vote share of new parties, presidential elections	Average vote share of new parties, lower chamber elections	Average electoral volatility, presidential elections	Average electoral volatility, lower chamber	Stability from one election to the next, presidential elections	Stability from one election to the next, lower chamber	Average of 6 Z scores, 1970–95
Honduras	0.0	0.0	7.0	7.0	1.00	1.00	1.08
United States	5.3	0.1	11.5	3.6	1.00	1.00	1.00
Uruguay	0.3	3.0	12.6	13.9	1.00	1.00	0.89
Dominican Republic	2.5	4.4	18.3	20.6	1.00	1.00	0.70
Mexico	3.9	6.7	15.7	19.9	1.00	1.00	0.67
Chile	0.0	3.2	20.38	25.7	0.80	0.88	0.41
Argentina	17.3	3.3	28.7	18.4	1.00	0.92	0.37
Costa Rica	4.6	7.8	18.9	23.6	0.87	0.87	0.35
Colombia	11.0	5.5	25.5	15.8	0.77	0.94	0.32
Venezuela	8.7	7.4	24.1	21.8	0.83	0.85	0.22
Paraguay	24.6	0.0	37.3	34.3	1.00	1.00	0.14
El Salvador	14.9	14.9	29.6	22.5	0.80	0.86	-0.08
Bolivia	15.7	11.4	36.6	34.3	0.86	0.92	-0.12

Ecuador	23.2	7.2	43.1	23.8	0.58	0.76	-0.45
Brazil	6.6	6.1	60.7	27.1	0.50	0.75	-0.49
Nicaragua	3.6	2.8	48.7	47.0	0.50	0.50	-0.72
Panama	19.2	39.2	38.3	57.2	1.00	0.50	-1.23
Guatemala	44.2	10.7	59.1	37.6	0.50	0.64	-1.30
Peru	32.4	17.6	61.1	57.1	0.38	0.44	-1.77
Average for 19 countries	12.5	8.0	31.4	26.9	0.8	0.8	

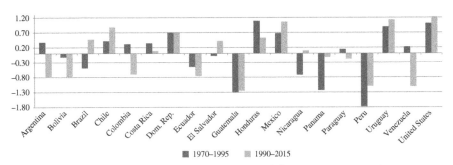

FIGURE 2.8 Average Z-Scores in Latin America and the US, 1970–95 and 1990–2015

(on Colombia), and Jana Morgan (on Venezuela) describe in their chapters in this volume, all three systems unraveled quickly and dramatically within years after the publication of *Building Democratic Institutions*. They are among the few cases of democracies with institutionalized party systems that experienced such profound change in such a short time.

Today, Chile and Uruguay still have institutionalized party systems. Costa Rica is an intermediate case, with greater stability in the main contenders and in electoral competition than the mean, but with moderately high ideological instability. Its system is less institutionalized than it was in the 1990s, but it has not radically de-institutionalized.

Three of the four systems that we regarded as inchoate in 1995 – Bolivia, Ecuador, and Peru – were subsequently among the uncommon cases of party system collapse. Conversely, Brazil, El Salvador, and Mexico are cases of increasing institutionalization. Contrary to Converse (1969), institutionalization in these cases did not take generations. Panama shifted from a weakly institutionalized system to being close to the Latin American average.

In 1995, Mexico and Paraguay had hegemonic party systems in transition. Some aspects of these systems needed to be de-institutionalized before a democratic party system could be built. Subsequently, Mexico became a textbook case of a party system that emerged under authoritarian rule and institutionalized under democracy. In this respect, it is similar to the Taiwanese case (Cheng and Huang 2015), and it lends support to scholars who have argued that solid parties built under authoritarian rule can become an asset for PSI under democracy (Hicken and Kuhonta 2015a; Loxton forthcoming; Riedl 2014). The Paraguayan system is a case of intermediate institutionalization compared to the mean for the nineteen countries.

Contrary to my expectations and contrary to the impression that the collapse of many erstwhile major parties and four party systems could generate, for the region on average, the data do not support the idea of a tendency toward de-institutionalization. For the eighteen Latin American countries, the (country) mean vote share of new parties *decreased* from 12.9% for 1970–95 to 12.4%

for 1990–2015 in presidential elections and from 8.4% to 7.7% in lower chamber elections. Mean (at the country level) volatility in presidential elections increased from 32.5% for 1970–95 to 34.0% for 1990–2015, but mean volatility in lower chamber elections *declined* from 28.2% (1970–95) to 26.3% (1990–2015).

Figure 2.9 shows Latin American means (leaving out the US) by decade for the vote share of new parties, electoral volatility, and the short-term stability of main contenders for both presidential and lower chamber elections.[13] In contrast to the scores in the previous paragraph, which were based on country means, the means in Figure 2.9 are for electoral periods. Because three countries with institutionalized party systems were the only stable democracies in the 1970s and therefore had more electoral periods than the other countries, the data based on electoral period means in Figure 2.9 show a slightly different picture than the data based on country means.

The vote share of new parties in presidential elections peaked at 16.0% in the 1990s. Subsequently, it declined to 12.1% in the 2000s and 11.0% in the 2010s. Since the peak in the 1990s (8.0%), the vote share of new parties has also declined slightly in lower chamber elections (to 7.6% in the 2000s and 7.0% in the 2010s). In presidential elections, the stability of main contenders has declined steadily since peaking in the 1980s, but it is the only one of the six indicators that follows this pattern of increasing instability. The stability of main contenders in lower chamber elections in the 2010s (0.83) is only marginally lower than it was for the entire period from the 1970s to the 2010s (0.86). In both presidential and lower chamber elections, electoral volatility has been stable at high levels since the 1990s. Overall, then, against expectations, the data do not show a regional trend toward deinstitutionalization.

PATH DEPENDENCE, CHANGE, AND PARTY SYSTEM INSTITUTIONALIZATION

Much of the literature on parties and party systems has looked at long-term patterns and predicted that change would be gradual after an initial period of democracy. In Lipset and Rokkan's (1967) analysis, party systems in Western Europe formed as a result of conflicts that occurred over centuries (see also Bartolini and Mair 1990). After the incorporation of the working class, these

---

[13] For purposes of calculating averages for each decade, I assigned all electoral periods to the second election of that period. I included all electoral periods from 1970 on for all competitive regimes. For Mexico 1985–88 and Brazil 1982–86, I counted the first election of the new competitive regime as the starting point; the first electoral period includes the last election of the authoritarian regime. The last congressional elections (1985 and 1982, respectively) under patently authoritarian regimes were competitive and reasonably fair. The party that supported the Brazilian government won only 43% of the lower chamber vote in 1982.

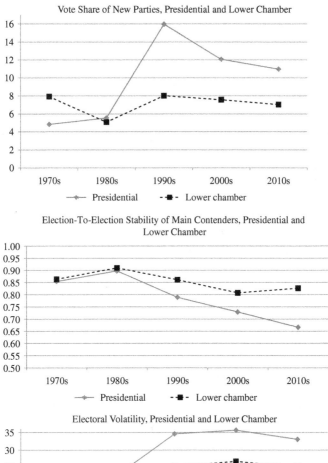

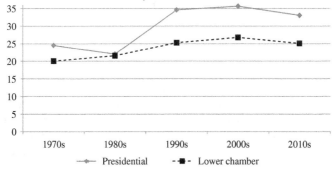

FIGURE 2.9 Vote Share of New Parties, Election-to-Election Stability of Main Contenders, and Electoral Volatility in Latin America – Regional Mean by Decade, 1970–2010

systems remained stable for generations. Converse (1969) argued that it took a few generations for voters to identify with parties in large numbers; in turn, partisan identification was the micro foundation of party system stability. Shefter (1994) argued that long historical patterns of state and party building shape the degree to which parties engage in clientelism. Kitschelt *et al.* (2010) asserted that the development of programmatic competition in Latin America hinged on long historical processes. Some literature on party system change in the advanced industrial democracies links it to slow, gradual processes such as secular changes in values (Inglehart 1990).

The Latin American experience raises questions about these long-term approaches for understanding this region in this time. These approaches might be right for the advanced industrial democracies, but they presume contexts of less severe stress on institutions and more solid institutions than exist in most of Latin America. More than the social science and historical literature anticipated, extraordinary stress dramatically and quickly undermined major parties (Argentina and Colombia) and even entire party systems (Bolivia, Ecuador, Peru, and Venezuela) that had been bedrocks of democratic politics, for decades (Ecuador) or generations (Argentina, Bolivia, Colombia, Peru, and Venezuela). Conversely, the transformation from an inchoate party system to an unevenly institutionalized one in Brazil also occurred over a few electoral cycles rather than generations.

In political science, sizable literature on path dependence and PSI emerged in the 1990s. They share an important commonality; both concepts rest on self-reproducing mechanisms once a system or a set of institutions has been consolidated.

Levi (1997: 28) defined path dependence as meaning that "once a country or region has started down a track, the costs of reversal are very high." Events in one historical moment greatly alter the distribution of possible and probable outcomes into the medium- and/or long-term future.[14] The two decades since the publication of *Building Democratic Institutions* undermined strong claims of path dependence in PSI in Latin America. Three systems (Argentina, Colombia, and Venezuela) became dramatically less institutionalized. The Honduran system has more recently moved in the direction of much less institutionalization. Conversely, three systems (Brazil, El Salvador, and Panama) became more institutionalized. The fact that seven countries underwent deep changes in PSI might call into question whether the concept is meaningful for Latin America and call into question how much the past shapes the present.

At the extreme, if countries' PSI fluctuated rapidly in random ways from one moment in time to the next, the concept would not be useful. A country's score for PSI in past elections would not help predict its score for the next. Systemic predictability and stability would be extremely low (o in the event that a score

---

[14] For a similar definition, see Pierson (2004: 20–22).

for PSI in one election did not correlate at all with its score in the previous elections). Such randomness is the opposite of institutionalization.

To look at whether indicators of party system stability have predictive capacity, I turned to the large dataset on electoral volatility that Mainwaring *et al.* (2016) developed based on sixty-seven countries and 618 electoral periods that met a threshold of democracy in the period since 1945. This dataset includes all major world regions. The question is whether earlier measures (at $T-1$) of the dependent variables help to predict the dependent variable at time T. To test this, I used, in addition to the dependent variable in the previous electoral period ($T-1$), the same covariates as Mainwaring *et al.* (2016): per capita GDP growth, inflation (logged), the effective number of parties, district magnitude (logged), the Birth Year of Democracy (logged), Age of Democracy (logged), and per capita GDP (logged). Because electoral volatility measures change (from one election to the next) rather than level, in principle, the value at $T-1$ is independent from the value at T. Mainwaring *et al.* used GEE (General Estimating Equations) models, which are appropriate for estimating coefficients for entire samples; cases need not be independent.

The results (Models 1 and 2 in Table 2.8) show that the previous score for total volatility is highly statistically significant. Volatility at $T-1$ is by far the most statistically significant covariate, and it has a powerful substantive effect. Every increase of 1% point in volatility at $T-1$ is associated with a predicted increase of 0.51% at T. Results are very similar in the OLS model with panel corrected standard errors (PCSE), which Beck (2001) recommended as a possible alternative approach to analyzing panel data. In this model, the substantive effect is slightly greater; every increase of 1% volatility at $T-1$ is associated with an increase of 0.56% at T. Results with Latin American data, based on a much smaller number of countries and electoral periods, are similar (Models 3 and 4 in Table 2.8). Electoral volatility varies in systematic ways.

In contrast, with the Mainwaring *et al.* dataset for sixty-seven countries, the vote share of new parties at $T-1$ has no predictive power for the vote share at T (Models 1 and 2 in Table 2.9). Thus, the vote share of new parties varies randomly for this broader sample of countries. For the Latin American sample, the vote share of new parties at $T-1$ is strongly associated with the vote share of new parties at T in the GEE model (Model 3) but not in the OLS-PCSE model (Model 4). Strikingly, *no* covariates are statistically significant in the Latin American sample in the OLS-PCSE model.

Perhaps this lack of impact of extra-system volatility at $T-1$ on the same variable at T is because even in weakly institutionalized party systems, major new parties do not come along every day. They make their entrance, and in the next election, the emergence of a major new party in the previous election does not increase the probability of yet another major new contender. Although the vote share of new parties varied randomly from one electoral period to the next, for the Latin American cases, it was integrally related to other aspects of PSI.

TABLE 2.8 *Effect of Electoral Volatility (T–1) on Electoral Volatility (T) – Lower Chamber*

	Model 1 GEE (Robust GE) World	Model 2 OLS (PCSE) World	Model 3 GEE (Robust GE) Latin America	Model 4 OLS (PCSE) Latin America
Volatility (T–1)	0.509***	0.561***	0.478***	0.509***
	(0.053)	(0.094)	(0.062)	(0.083)
District magnitude (ln)	−0.044	−0.030	−0.013	−0.228
	(0.324)	(0.235)	(0.877)	(1.040)
ENP	0.978**	0.877*	0.195	0.087
	(0.354)	(0.344)	(0.543)	(0.381)
GDP growth PC	−0.636**	−0.604**	−1.034*	−1.112**
	(0.223)	(0.222)	(0.430)	(0.389)
Inflation (ln)	0.032	0.077	−0.241	−0.232
	(0.414)	(0.402)	(0.625)	(0.633)
GDP PC (ln)	−2.153**	−1.904*	−1.656	−1.042
	(0.725)	(0.842)	(1.989)	(1.849)
Age of democracy (ln)	3.293**	3.045***	6.303***	5.836**
	(1.023)	(0.876)	(1.620)	(1.824)
Birth of democracy (ln)	−6.947***	−6.225***	−6.692**	−6.655*
	(1.651)	(1.401)	(2.517)	(2.622)
Type of government (ln)	0.492	0.436	33.640	30.042
	(0.997)	(0.891)	(18.626)	(18.348)
Constant	42.201***	37.173***	0.478***	0.509***
	(8.499)	(10.379)	(0.062)	(0.083)
r2		0.603		0.442
N	544	544	140	140

Notes: Robust standard errors in parentheses * significant at 10%; ** significant at 5%; *** significant at 1%.
R2 is not reported because this statistic is not defined for GEE models.
ENP = effective number of parties.

TABLE 2.9 *Effect of Extra-System Electoral Volatility (T–1) on Extra-System Electoral Volatility (T) – Lower Chamber*

	Model 1 GEE (Robust GE) World	Model 2 OLS (PCSE) World	Model 3 GEE (Robust GE) Latin America	Model 4 OLS (PCSE) Latin America
Extra-system vol. (T–1)	0.079	0.079	0.224***	0.120
	(0.063)	(0.149)	(0.063)	(0.137)
District magnitude (ln)	0.202	0.004	0.668	0.776
	(0.493)	(0.330)	(0.901)	(0.607)
ENP	1.599**	1.347***	−0.203	−0.137
	(0.515)	(0.386)	(0.273)	(0.442)
GDP growth PC	−0.417	−0.398	−0.608*	−0.586
	(0.215)	(0.217)	(0.283)	(0.338)
Inflation (ln)	−0.170	−0.021	0.429	0.396
	(0.383)	(0.449)	(0.398)	(0.414)
GDP PC (ln)	−2.401*	−2.554**	−0.816	−0.919
	(1.013)	(0.860)	(1.622)	(1.522)
Age of democracy (ln)	2.349*	3.157***	3.421*	3.417
	(1.120)	(0.648)	(1.670)	(1.909)
Birth of democracy (ln)	−5.397***	−5.821***	−2.694	−2.424
	(1.527)	(1.029)	(2.509)	(2.784)
Type of government (ln)	−1.259	−0.482		
	(1.549)	(0.911)		
Constant	36.187***	37.137***	11.398	11.592
	(9.178)	(7.371)	(16.071)	(15.689)
r2		0.212		0.081
N	544	544	140	140

Notes: Robust standard errors in parentheses * significant at 10%; ** significant at 5%; *** significant at 1%.
R2 is not reported because this statistic is not defined for GEE models.

TABLE 2.10 *Correlations between Party System Institutionalization Indicators at T–1 and T, 1970–95 and 1990–2015 (p values in parentheses if p<0.10)*

	1970–95		1990–2015	
	Correlation (Pearson)	p value (2-tailed)	Correlation (Pearson)	p value (2-tailed)
Vote share of new parties, presidential elections	0.26	–	0.25	0.02
Vote share of new parties, lower chamber	0.30	0.02	0.22	0.02
Electoral volatility, presidential elections	0.76	0.00	0.64	0.00
Electoral volatility, lower chamber	0.73	0.00	0.67	0.00
Stability of main contenders, presidential elections	0.19	–	0.41	0.00
Stability of main contenders, lower chamber	0.23	0.09	0.46	0.00
Ideological stability, lower chamber	Nd	nd	0.04	–

Table 2.10 shows the Pearson bivariate correlations between scores at $T–1$ and T for all seven electoral period-specific variables used in this chapter for both 1970–95 and 1990–2015. Correlations for electoral volatility are consistently high for both presidential and lower chamber elections. Systems with high volatility at one time tend to continue exhibiting high volatility, and vice versa. Consistent with the regression results in Table 2.9, correlations for the vote share of new parties are much lower.

For 1990–2015 but not 1970–95, systems that had stable (or unstable) main contenders in one electoral period tended to have stability (or instability) in the next one. Finally, ideological stability varied randomly. When party systems experienced pronounced ideological shifts from one election to the next, they were not more likely to undertake another pronounced shift in the subsequent election.

In terms of institutionalization, party systems, including in Latin America, are neither immutable nor do they vary randomly. Several Latin American cases underwent deep change in PSI between the 1990s and 2015, but Table 2.8 shows

that deep change in some cases is compatible with a high predictive capacity of PSI for total volatility and, to a lesser degree, the stability of main contenders.

Although levels of institutionalization tend to persist, the Latin American experience suggests shortcomings of strong claims about path dependence in contexts of weak institutions. Some of the literature on historical institutionalism overstated path dependence and assumed that institutions are strong (Levitsky and Murillo 2005, 2014). A central point of this volume is that the institutionalization of party systems in Latin America (and around the world, as can be seen in Mainwaring *et al.* 2016) varies greatly. High and low levels of institutionalization *tend* to be self-reinforcing, but party systems do not always get stuck in immutable patterns.

CONCLUSION

This chapter had three goals. First, building on the reconceptualization of PSI proposed in Chapter 1, I created indicators to measure the three attributes of the concept. These indicators are logically derived from the concept; they measure phenomena that are by definition a part of PSI. They travel seamlessly across time and space. Most of these indicators are new, and they can fruitfully be used for studying other world regions and other historical periods.

Second, I provided data for PSI for eighteen Latin American countries for the period from 1990 to 2015 and for the US as a benchmark. On almost every indicator, the range in country means across cases was huge. Most Latin American party systems are not well institutionalized, but Mexico, Chile, Uruguay, El Salvador, Brazil, and Honduras until 2013 were exceptions. At the low end of the spectrum, Peru stood out for its low PSI in a democracy that has registered many successes since 2001 (see Levitsky's chapter). Guatemala stands out for persistently low institutionalization (Sánchez 2008, 2009), and Venezuela for a party system collapse in the wake of an institutionalized system from 1968 to 1988 (Morgan 2011, and this volume; Seawright 2012). Most Latin American party systems are not well institutionalized, and that has been true for a long time, but there is great variance across countries.

Third, in light of the fact that three systems (Argentina, Colombia, and Venezuela) that were once institutionalized underwent severe erosion or collapse, and that three countries (Brazil, El Salvador, and Panama) that once had weakly institutionalized systems became more stable, I addressed whether PSI in Latin America is so transitory as to make the concept useless. The answer is a resounding no. Countries do not remain forever at the same level of institutionalization, but PSI does not fluctuate randomly. These differences in institutionalization have important consequences for democratic politics, as I show in Chapter 3.

3

Party System Institutionalization, Predictability, and Democracy

Scott Mainwaring*

This chapter focuses on consequences of differences in the level of party system institutionalization (PSI) for democracy. The reason for producing this volume is that party systems function in very different ways depending on their level of institutionalization. In one of the most famous quotes in the history of political science, Schattschneider (1942: 1) wrote that "Political parties created modern democracy and modern democracy is unthinkable save in terms of the parties." Many other prominent scholars have likewise emphasized that parties are essential for modern representative democracy (Downs 1957; Sartori 1976). What happens, then, in contexts where parties are weak, so much so that Levitsky (Chapter 11) speaks of democracy without parties in Peru? If the history of modern democracy is built on political parties, then democracy will function differently with weakly institutionalized party systems. This chapter addresses some of these differences.

I begin with some theoretical, deductively derived implications of PSI for democracy. Institutionalized party systems provide stability and predictability to important democratic outcomes and processes. [1] Greater predictability means that actors can be more confident about the range of likely future outcomes and that time horizons are typically longer. In these systems, parties serve as a major gateway to elected political office; help organize the legislature; and provide critical information cues to voters. These outcomes and processes are less stable

* Fernando Bizzarro, Jaimie Bleck, Omar Coronel, Sarah Zukerman Daly, María Victoria De Negri, Laura Gamboa, Tahir Kilavuz, Steve Levitsky, Noam Lupu, Sean McGraw, Kristin McKie, Gabriela Ippolito O'Donnell, Ana Petrova, George Tsebelis, and Samuel Valenzuela offered valuable comments. I thank Rodrigo Castro Cornejo, María Victoria De Negri, Lauran Feist, Krystin Krause, Ana Petrova, and Adriana Ramírez Baracaldo for research assistance.
[1] A different literature discusses why party institutionalization is important for authoritarian regimes. See Brownlee (2007); Geddes (1999); Hicken and Kuhonta (2015b); Smith (2005). Our volume addresses this issue only in passing.

and predictable in fluid party systems.[2] Although the empirical evidence in the chapter is limited to Latin America, the theoretical expectations about the consequences of weak PSI should hold for other regions of the world.

The chapter then presents some empirical evidence. First, institutionalized systems create high barriers for political outsiders. In weakly institutionalized systems, political outsiders can more easily win power. In turn, political outsiders are less accountable to their parties and less likely to engage in party building. They are more likely initially to be elected with weak congressional support, and, as a result, they are more likely to have severe conflict with the legislature. By temperament, they are more likely to attempt to undermine democracy.

Second, even beyond the presidency, less institutionalized party systems produce less experienced politicians. In turn, less experienced politicians are less likely to be unconditionally supportive of democracy and less likely to believe that parties are essential for democracy.

Third, as Flores Macías (2012) and O'Dwyer and Kovalcik (2007) show, policy stability tends to be greater in institutionalized party systems. This is in part because outsiders do not win presidential elections in institutionalized party systems, and outsiders are more likely to favor radical policy change. In addition, well-established parties have strong commitments to some constituencies and to programmatic positions, making radical policy change unlikely.

Fourth, weak institutions, of which fluid party systems are a prime example, are associated with shorter time horizons, with more frequent changes in the rules of the game, with less effective provision of public goods, and with greater propensity for corruption. Fifth, electoral accountability is easier in institutionalized systems because the electoral environment is more stable, allowing for clearer cues for voters. And, finally, weak PSI tends to have corrosive effects on the quality of democracy.

Institutionalized party systems do not guarantee good outcomes. Nor does weak institutionalization always produce bad outcomes. Although ever-greater institutionalization is not a blessing for the quality of democracy, the high degree of openness and instability and the low predictability of inchoate systems tend to produce some problems for democracy.

INSTITUTIONALIZED PARTY SYSTEMS, PREDICTABILITY, AND DEMOCRACY: THEORY

Institutionalized party systems give structure to the democratic competition for power. They give citizens stable and predictable vote options; actors and voters have a sense that future patterns are predictable. In inchoate party systems, past

---

[2] Levitsky and Murillo (2014) make the broader point that democratic politics functions differently in contexts of weak institutions. Along related lines, see O'Donnell (1993, 1994).

stability is lower, and actors and voters have less clarity about the likelihood of future patterns.

Because politicians win elected office through parties, and because elected politicians govern in democratic regimes,[3] institutionalized systems generate stability regarding who is likely to govern and what the range of policies is likely to be.[4] The boundaries of who is likely to govern are relatively clear. In the United States, voters and politicians can be almost certain that the next president will be a Republican or Democrat and that this president will probably adhere reasonably closely to the median position within her party or the median position in the congress. In 2016, Donald Trump flabbergasted many pundits by winning the Republican nomination despite holding positions outside the mainstream on some issues, including free trade and a few social issues such as same sex marriage. However, even this unconventional candidate hewed closely to mainstream Republican positions on most issues (for example, taxes, abortion, gun control) and depended heavily on the Republican coalition. In the US, months ahead of the actual election, skilled pollsters can predict the results of presidential elections within a few percentage points[5] – and they know with near certainty who the strongest two contenders will be.

Likewise, in the United Kingdom, voters and politicians have long known that the next prime minister would be from the Conservative, Labour, or (much less likely) the Liberal Democratic parties. In Western European countries with institutionalized but fragmented party systems, it is often not clear which party will lead a coalition government, but the general contours of policy have been fairly consistent and predictable. Change occurs within bounds established by the party system. Dramatic surprises in who holds executive power are unlikely.[6] As a result, dramatic surprises in policy are uncommon (Flores Macías 2012; O'Dwyer and Kovalcik 2007).

In weakly institutionalized party systems, there is greater uncertainty over electoral outcomes and more flux during the campaign. The turnover from one party to others is higher, and the entry barriers to new parties are lower, resulting in greater uncertainty about who will govern and what policy direction the country will take. Sometimes candidates who look strong a year

---

[3] This is not to deny the important governing powers of administrative and regulatory agencies or, in the case of the European Union, of supranational entities.

[4] In contexts of high polarization, highly divergent policy options are feasible even in institutionalized party systems. For example, in Chile, before the 1970 presidential election result was decided, it was evident that policy choices would be very different depending on who won a tight contest. However, an institutionalized system, in which it was evident that the socialist left, a left-of-center Christian Democratic party, and the right all had reasonable chances of winning, made this fact clear. With lower institutionalization, the potential variability itself is less clear.

[5] In fact, this was the case in the 2016 US presidential election. Many people were surprised by the outcome, but the 538 website accurately anticipated a close race.

[6] Przeworski (1986) famously argued that democratic elections are characterized by uncertain outcomes. This is true, but outcomes are far more predictable in institutionalized party systems.

before the election fade into oblivion, and candidates who were not on the radar screen experience a meteoric rise and win the presidency (Baker *et al.* 2006; Castro Cornejo forthcoming). For example, in December 1997, Irene Sáez, an independent presidential candidate, led Venezuelan public opinion surveys with around 40% of preferences, followed by AD dissident Claudio Fermín with 35%. Both candidates had plummeted in the polls – Sáez to 18% and Fermín to 6% – by April 1998 (McCoy 1999: 66) as outsider and former coup leader Hugo Chávez and later Henrique Salas Römer rose. Ultimately, Sáez won only 2.8% of the vote, and Fermín withdrew when his support collapsed. Chávez seemingly came from nowhere in 1997 to capture 56.2% of the vote, while Salas Römer won 40.0%.

Weak institutions reduce time horizons, increase policy instability, and make inter-temporal agreements and commitments more difficult (Garay 2016; Levitsky and Murillo 2005; Lupu and Riedl 2013; O'Donnell 1994; Simmons 2016; Spiller and Tommasi 2005, 2008). These findings presumably apply to inchoate party systems, which are defined by weak parties, sharp changes in the power of different actors (because some parties lose a high vote share while others gain it), uncertainty about future electoral prospects, and occasional profound change in who the key actors are. These systems are also more likely to experience radical change in the rules of the game.

In institutionalized systems, party labels are important to politicians and to many citizens. Attachments to institutionalized parties extend temporal horizons because politicians want to preserve the value of the party brand. With unusual exceptions under extenuating circumstances of deep crisis (Stokes 2001),[7] institutionalized parties do not abruptly radically switch positions for electoral gain (Berman 1998; Downs 1957: 103–11; Kitschelt 1994: 254–79). They function with one eye toward protecting their reputations and maintaining connections with key constituencies. Party labels, connections to key groups, and ideological commitments constrain change and hence promote predictability and longer time horizons. Politicians with strong attachments to their parties are less willing to risk burning the party label in order to eke out a short-term personal gain. In systems in which they owe their election win to the party, politicians are accountable to the organization, hence cannot act as freewheeling agents.

In personalistic parties, the organization is subordinate to the whims of the leader. The party brand is useful only insofar as it promotes the leader's agenda. Because electoral outcomes vary more from election to election, and because there is much more space for new parties and outsiders and less policy stability, it is more difficult to gauge who will be important players and what the range of likely outcomes is. Under these circumstances, time horizons shorten (O'Dwyer 2006; Simmons 2016).

In contexts of weak institutions, the absence of binding rules creates uncertainty about outcomes and reduces actors' time horizons (Flores-Macías

---

[7] See also Lupu (this volume, 2016); Roberts (2014); Weyland (2002a).

TABLE 3.1 *Outsider Presidents, Electoral Volatility, and Delegative Democracy Scores*

	Successful election	Electoral volatility when they were elected	Electoral volatility in previous electoral period	Mean delegative democracy score	Change in delegative democracy score
Evo Morales	Bolivia, 2005	66.3	56.2	6.0	+6
Fernando Collor	Brazil, 1989	–	–	8.0	+2
Lucio Gutiérrez	Ecuador, 2002	58.7	43.6	8.0	+6
Rafael Correa	Ecuador, 2006	39.0	58.7	7.0	+4
Violeta Chamorro	Nicaragua, 1990	48.7	–	–	–
Fernando Lugo	Paraguay, 2008	51.8	37.0	6.0	0
Alberto Fujimori	Peru, 1990	68.0	50.4	7.2	+3
Alejandro Toledo	Peru, 2001	62.1	44.1	2.0	+1
Ollanta Humala	Peru, 2011	43.4	51.9	–	–
Hugo Chávez	Venezuela, 1998	99.4	52.8	8.0	+3
Mean		59.7	49.3	6.70	+3.1

Note: In Brazil 1989 and Nicaragua 1990, there was no previous electoral period under the new competitive regimes. Electoral volatility scores are for presidential elections. Mean delegative democracy score is based on country years, not on presidents. Change in delegative democracy score shows the change from the last year of the previous president to the first year of the outsider. *Source for delegative democracy scores:* González (2014)

Consequences of Outsider Presidents

Weak PSI paves the way for outsider presidents, who, in turn, frequently undermine democracy. Outsiders promise and deliver different styles of conducting politics. The ten outsiders who were elected under competitive political regimes railed against the establishment and promised to change the status quo in radical ways.

Outsider presidents have important consequences for presidential accountability to their parties, party building, legislative/executive relations, and democracy. As Samuels and Shugart (2010) argue, the ways in which heads of government are elected have important consequences for their relationships with their parties and for how they govern. Because they are elected by popular

vote rather than chosen by their party peers, presidents generally have greater authority over and autonomy from their parties than prime ministers. Presidents are not agents of the party, but of voters.

The incentives and opportunities for presidents to have dominant authority over and autonomy from their parties are exceptionally strong with outsiders, who are not even minimally beholden to their parties. These parties emerged because of the outsider candidates, and in almost all cases were created as personalistic electoral vehicles.[11] These parties have neither the desire nor the capability to monitor these presidents, increasing the likelihood of loose cannon presidents who often have deleterious effects on democracy.

Most insider presidents care about their party brand. They have built their political careers through their party, and they need their parties' support to accomplish their legislative agendas. They usually cannot be oblivious to their party.[12] In contrast, outsider presidents have almost no incentive, and usually no disposition, to prioritize party building, at least initially.

Because they won election without a previously existing party, many outsider presidents initially see little utility to building an organization. Some view a party as more of a limitation than an asset, and they might want to reduce the probability of having a viable rival emerge within the party by keeping the organization weak. Few outsider presidents initially engage in party building, leading to the possibility of a vicious cycle: they are elected in a context of weak PSI, and they proceed to undermine the existing parties. All four cases of party system collapse in contemporary Latin America (Peru in the 1990s, Venezuela between 1998 and 2005, and Ecuador and Bolivia in the 2000s) occurred during the presidencies of full outsiders (Fujimori in Peru, Chávez in Venezuela, and Correa in Ecuador) or a partial outsider (Morales in Bolivia).

For example, Alberto Fujimori repeatedly undermined his own party and opposition parties. He ran in 1990 on the *Cambio 90* (Change 90) label. He forged a new label, NM-C90, *Nueva Mayoría-Cambio 90* (New Majority, Change 90), for the 1992 elections for a constituent assembly. Conaghan (2000: 268) summarizes, "The NM-C90 majority in the CCD (constitutional congress) exhibited no signs of being anything other than an executor of presidential directives." Fujimori never delegated power to party leaders, nor did he build an organization.

In light of the dependence of parties on outsider presidents, one would expect that when these presidents leave the scene, their parties would be vulnerable to

---

[11] MAS in Bolivia is an exception. Created in 1998, it had strong roots in Bolivia's labor movement. But even so, Evo Morales has always been the party's supreme leader.

[12] Under the stress of dire economic crises in the 1980s and 1990s, a few Latin American presidents turned their backs on their parties. See Corrales (2002); Roberts (2014); Stokes (2001); Weyland (2002a).

rapid electoral decline. This expectation is often borne out. After Fernando Collor de Mello's impeachment in 1992, his party (the *Partido de Reconstrução Nacional*, PRN) nearly vanished. In 1994, the PRN presidential candidate won 0.6% of the vote. It never fielded a presidential candidate after that. The party won only 0.4% of the vote for the Chamber of Deputies in 1994 and has never reached 1% since then. Likewise, Alberto Fujimori's party in Peru suffered a huge electoral defeat in 2001 – Fujimori had fled the country the year before. It won only 4.8% of the lower chamber vote and did not field a presidential candidate. His daughter, Keiko Fujimori, has subsequently built a party (see Steven Levitsky's chapter in this volume; Meléndez 2015), but if it were not for her, *Fujimorismo* would have evanesced. Fernando Lugo in Paraguay left almost no party legacy when he was removed from office in 2012. After Alejandro Toledo won the presidency in Peru in 2001, his party (*Perú Posible*) was not able to field a presidential candidate in 2006, and it won only 4.1% of the vote for the Chamber of Deputies. It recovered somewhat in 2011 when Toledo ran for the presidency again,[13] but as Levitsky notes in his chapter on Peru, *Perú Posible* remains closely tethered to and highly dependent on Toledo. Violeta Chamorro's UNO coalition splintered in 1992 in her second year in office in Nicaragua, never to be resurrected again.

Evo Morales and Hugo Chávez are partial exceptions to the norm that outsiders do not invest in party building. Because of its origins as a party based in a social movement that he spearheaded, from the outset, Morales was committed to building the *Movimiento al Socialismo* (Movement Toward Socialism, MAS). Chávez initially kept his party at arm's length. Later he realized that a party could be a useful way of mobilizing support. In 2007, he rebranded his party, after a merger with some minor allied parties, as the United Socialist Party of Venezuela (*Partido Socialista Unido de Venezuela*, PSUV). Although it remained strictly subordinated to Chávez, the PSUV developed some organizational capacity, as Jana Morgan shows in her chapter in this volume.

The origin of outsider presidents is likely to generate conflictual congressional/ executive relationships, with potential adverse effects on democracy. In their initial successful bid, outsider presidents' coattails are rarely long enough to generate a massive vote on behalf of their congressional candidates. Table 3.2 shows the percentage of seats their parties and coalitions won in their first successful election. On average, their parties won only 18.8% of lower chamber seats and 19.4% of Senate seats. Five of the ten outsiders came to power with parties that controlled less than 10% of the seats in the lower chamber. Governing without a party (Correa and Chamorro) or with very small parties (Lugo, Collor, and Gutiérrez) is taxing. Only one of the ten outsiders – Chamorro – had a majority coalition in both chambers of congress (or in the unicameral chamber) – and it did not last for long.

[13] The coalition of which *Perú Posible* was part won 14.8% of the congressional vote.

TABLE 3.2 *Outsider Presidents' Share of Seats in the National Congress*

	Successful election	President's party	Party's % of seats in lower or unicameral chamber	Party's % of seats in upper chamber	Other parties in initial cabinet	Coalition's % of seats in lower or unicameral chamber	Coalition's % of seats of in upper chamber
Evo Morales	Bolivia, 2005	MAS	56	44	None	56	44
Fernando Collor	Brazil, 1989	PRN	5	5	PMDB, PFL	49	55
Lucio Gutiérrez	Ecuador, 2002*	PSP	7	unicameral	MUPP-NP PSC	41	unicameral
Rafael Correa	Ecuador, 2006*	Movimiento Alianza PAIS/PS-FA	0	unicameral	*Izquierda Democrática* (ID); *Partido Sociedad Patriótica* (PSP)	9	unicameral
Violeta Chamorro	Nicaragua, 1990*	None	0	unicameral	UNO: (APC, MDN, PALI, PAN, PC, PDCN, PLC, PLI, PNC, PSD, PSN)	55	unicameral
Fernando Lugo	Paraguay, 2008	Christian Democratic Party	2.5	0	*Partido Liberal Radical Auténtico,* Popular Movement Tekojoja (MPT), Democratic Progressive Party (PDP)	37.5	33

that the process was unconstitutional, leading to a sharp confrontation with Correa. The Supreme Electoral Court (*Tribunal Superior Eleitoral*) terminated the mandates of fifty-seven deputies who had voted against the constitutionality of the constituent assembly. The Supreme Court declared the decision of the Supreme Electoral Court unconstitutional, but the government proceeded with the constitutional assembly anyhow.

Unlike most outsider presidents, Evo Morales came to power with solid congressional backing, but he, too, experienced severe conflict with congress during the constitutional assembly of 2006–08. The MAS approved a new constitution only by violating an agreement it had reached with the opposition that two-thirds of the constitutional assembly would need to approve the new charter before it was submitted to a popular referendum. Lehoucq (2008) called this move a coup.

Outsider presidents are far more likely to govern in a "delegative" style (O'Donnell 1994) in which the president claims legitimacy because he was popularly elected, but regards mechanisms of horizontal accountability (legislatures, courts, and oversight agencies) as nuisances to be circumvented. González (2014) coded the degree to which eleven Latin American countries approximated a delegative democracy or its opposite ideal type, a representative democracy, for every year from 1980 or the establishment of a competitive regime, whichever came later, until 2010. Based on expert surveys, the scores range from zero (representative democracy) to eight (delegative democracy).[15] The eleven countries in his sample include all countries in Table 3.1 except for Nicaragua and all outsider presidents except Chamorro and Humala, who took office in 2011. The average score for forty-three country years for the eight outsider presidents was 6.70. The average score for all 243 country years under other presidents was 2.70.[16] Outsiders are much more likely to promote presidential supremacy and to steamroll mechanisms of horizontal accountability.

Impact on Democracy

Because political outsiders were never previously in leadership positions in the democratic process, they are likely to be less committed to preserving democracy if doing so entails sacrificing some policy preferences. They were not socialized under democratic politics, and some railed against liberal democracy before taking power. Moreover, their relative isolation in congress and other seats of power creates a situation of initial institutional weakness that generates incentives to work against established institutions. Many outsiders (such as Fujimori, Chávez, Morales, and Correa) are indifferent or hostile to democratic checks and balances in principle, and their initial institutional isolation reinforced this indifference. In contrast, insiders develop political

---

[15] I am grateful to Lucas González for sharing his data.
[16] The difference between these two means is significant at $p = 0.000$.

careers under liberal democracy. In the post-Cold War west, except in minor extremist parties, most insiders are loyal to democratic rules of the game.

A distinction between the eight outsider presidents who won election in the context of existing competitive political regimes and the two (Chamorro and Toledo) who won the foundational elections of new competitive regimes is useful here.[17] Chamorro and Toledo were outsiders, but they came to power with a goal of building liberal democracy where it had not existed.

All eight outsiders who came to power in the contexts of competitive regimes attempted to undermine democratic checks and balances. Chávez and Gutiérrez established their fame by leading high profile military coups (in 1992 and 2000, respectively) that, if successful, would have resulted in democratic breakdowns. This willingness of outsiders to undermine democracy is especially likely when they have radical policy agendas that could be thwarted by the establishment.

Five of the ten outsider presidents (and five of the eight elected under competitive regimes) deliberately undermined liberal democracy. They presided over some of the most important democratic erosions in contemporary Latin America. Alberto Fujimori overthrew Peruvian democracy, dismissing the congress and courts in April 1992 in a palace coup. Evo Morales (2006–present), Rafael Correa (2007–present), and Hugo Chávez (1999–2013) presided over regimes that undermined opposition rights, expanded presidential powers, and extended presidential terms. Very early in their terms, all three began efforts to circumvent the obstacles created by congressional oppositions and the judiciary. They dismantled democratic checks and balances and attacked what remained of the old party systems. All three made extensive use of state resources to create uneven electoral playing fields.[18]

Lucio Gutiérrez (2003–05) also undermined democratic checks and balances. After breaking with the left-of-center coalition that initially supported him in 2002, in December 2004 Gutiérrez unconstitutionally replaced the Supreme Court and packed it with his supporters. In April 2005, he was forced to step down in the middle of his term amidst great public dissatisfaction and mobilization, an opposition vote in congress to remove him from office, and the withdrawal of support from the armed forces.

An earlier outsider president who dismantled democracy was Juan Perón in his first presidency in Argentina (1946–55). Perón closed opposition newspapers, tolerated the destruction (by fires and bombings) of opposition organizations, changed the rules of the game so that he could run for reelection in 1951, jailed prominent political opponents, harassed the opposition,

---

[17] Although the Sandinista regime in Nicaragua allowed for elections in 1984, part of the opposition abstained. The 1990 presidential election was the first since the downfall of the authoritarian Somoza regime (1936–79) to include all opposition forces. Likewise, the 2001 presidential election in Peru was the first free and fair election since Fujimori closed congress in 1992.

[18] On the authoritarian turn in Ecuador, see de la Torre (2013) and Basabe Serrano *et al.* (2010). On Venezuela, see Corrales and Penfold (2011) and Gómez Calcaño *et al.* (2010). On all three countries, see Mayorga (forthcoming), Mazzuca (2014), and Weyland (2013). On Venezuela and the contrast with Colombia under Alvaro Uribe, see L. Gamboa (2016).

terminated the mandates of elected opposition politicians, removed judges who were not favorable to his cause and packed the courts, and changed the electoral rules to favor his party.

The ability of political outsiders to win presidential elections in weakly institutionalized party systems, and their frequent willingness to undermine democratic checks and balances, is probably one reason why Pérez-Liñán and Mainwaring (2013) found that higher democratic PSI before 1978 helps predict higher post-1978 levels of democracy in Latin America. This pattern of outsider presidents undermining democracy is not unique to Latin America, as the examples of Boris Yeltsin (1991–99) and Vladimir Putin (2000–08, 2012–present) in Russia show.

INCHOATE PARTY SYSTEMS, POLITICAL EXPERIENCE, AND DEMOCRACY

Even beyond the presidency, fluid party systems produce less experienced politicians. Outsiders are more likely to win elections, and by definition, they have less political experience. New parties are more electorally successful in less institutionalized systems, and they are more likely to bring in fresh politicians than established parties. Some new parties campaign on the basis of shaking up the political system, and this message is likely to attract newcomers. Established parties are more likely to fade, often ending the political career of veteran politicians. Moreover, institutionalized party systems tend to generate different incentives for politicians. Because party labels and organizations endure, there is a greater prospect of having a political career through the party.

Thus, deductively, it seems likely that Steven Levitsky's argument about amateur politicians in Chapter 11 should be generalizable. Levitsky argues that one consequence of weak parties in Peru has been the rise of amateur politicians, with pernicious consequences on some democratic processes. Amateur politicians are less able to build a strong congress; they lack the know-how and usually the interest. If they are not going to pursue political careers, they have little reason to invest in institution building. Because strong legislatures foster robust democracies (Fish 2006), and because a solid core of experienced legislators is almost a *sine qua non* for a strong legislature (Jones *et al.* 2002), indirectly, a large flock of amateur legislators is likely to make it more difficult to construct a robust democracy. Because they typically have short political horizons, amateurs are likely to be less committed to serving the public and more interested in using office for personal gain. If professional politicians are members of long-established parties and if their electoral and political prospects depend partly on the party label, they have incentives to pay attention to good public policy and to the medium term (Garay 2016; Simmons 2016).

Consistent with this deductive reasoning and with Levitsky's argument about Peru, the linkage between more experienced politicians and PSI holds up in a cross-national sample of seventeen Latin American legislatures (all but Cuba, Haiti, and Venezuela).[19] Fluid party systems have less experienced members of congress. In turn, less experienced members of congress are less likely to support democracy unconditionally and less likely to believe that parties are necessary for democracy.

Surveys of lower chambers (or unicameral legislatures) conducted by the University of Salamanca asked deputies about their political experience. Based on the survey questions, I constructed three variables to measure deputies' political experience. The first variable is Lower Chamber Novice, operationalized as a deputy who was serving his/her first term in the national lower chamber (see the final column of Table 3.3). The percentage of lower chamber novices was over 50% in fifteen of seventeen countries. Leaving aside Costa Rica and Mexico, which have strict term limits that ban deputies from running for reelection and therefore should exclusively have Lower Chamber Novices (Carey 1996), the countries with the highest percentage of Lower Chamber Novices had weakly institutionalized party systems. For the fifteen countries that allow reelection and for which data are available, the correlation between the summary PSI score in Table 2.6 and the percentage of Lower Chamber Novices was -0.72 ($p = 0.00$). As hypothesized, inchoate party systems have legislatures with less experienced members.

The second variable is Elected Novice, operationalized as a deputy who was serving in his/her first term and who had never previously held elected office. Elected novices can have held a party post or an appointed position in the past. For the same fifteen countries, the correlation between the PSI score in Table 2.6 and the percentage of elected novices is -0.46 ($p = 0.08$), consistent with expectations.

A political amateur is a deputy who was serving his/her first term in the national assembly *and* had no prior experience in an elected public position, an appointed public position (such as Minister or Vice-Minister), or an official party position. As Table 3.3 shows, with this stringent definition, most countries had a low percentage of political amateurs. For the seventeen countries,[20] a high summary score for PSI is modestly associated with a lower percentage of political amateurs (the Pearson's bivariate correlation is -0.33 ($p = 0.19$), based on the Z-scores in Table 2.6). Although this correlation is not statistically significant, higher PSI is weakly associated with fewer political amateurs.

Levitsky hypothesizes in Chapter 11 that political amateurs probably have pernicious effects on democracy. This seems likely. To function well, legislatures

[19] This wave was not conducted in Haiti and Cuba, and data are not available for Venezuela because the sample was not representative.
[20] For this variable, there was no clear reason to exclude Costa Rica or Mexico.

TABLE 3.3 *Prior Political Experience of Members of Lower Chamber, Latin American Countries*

Country	Number of interviews	Legislature	Political amateur (%)	Elected novice (%)	Lower chamber novice (%)
ARG	70	2007–11 and 2009–13	8.7	35.7	72.5
BOL	97	2010–13	32.0	56.7	90.7
BRA	129	2007–10	3.1	11.6	35.7
CHI	86	2010–14	10.5	25.6	44.2
COL	91	2010–14	11.0	20.9	64.8
CR	56	2010–14	9.1	55.4	82.1
Dom. Rep.	78	2010–16	5.3	49.3	57.3
ECU	95	2009–12	17.9	51.6	81.1
ELS	68	2009–11	10.3	39.7	55.9
GUA	97	2008–12	5.2	51.5	63.9
HON	91	2010–14	30.8	46.2	63.7
MEX	98	2009–11	12.4	41.2	89.6
NIC	69	2007–11	2.9	34.8	63.8
PAN	64	2009–13	15.6	54.7	62.5
PAR	72	2008–13	25.0	51.4	72.2
PER	93	2011–16	27.8	55.9	72.5
URU	79	2009–14	3.8	29.5	51.3
Mean			13.6	41.9	66.1

Notes: "Political novice": A deputy who (1) was serving in the lower chamber (or the unicameral chamber) for the first time; and (2) had no previous experience in an elected political position, as an appointed public official (Minister, Viceminister, etc.), OR in an official party position. "Elected novice": A deputy who (1) was serving in the lower chamber (or the unicameral chamber) for the first time; and (2) had no previous experience in an elected political post. "Lower chamber novice": Operationalized as a deputy who was serving in the lower chamber (or the unicameral chamber) for the first time. Source for lower chamber novice: TR3 of the PELA surveys ("Is this the first legislature in which you were elected deputy/representative?"); sources for Political Novice and Elected Novice: TR3 and TR5 of the PELA surveys (wave of 2007 to 2011) (TR3: "Is this the first legislature in which you were elected deputy/representative?"; TR5: "Have you ever served as an elected public official (mayor, city council) in addition to your current position as deputy/representative?" "Have you ever served in an appointed public position (Minister, Vice-minister, etc.)?" "And have you served in an official party position (secretary general, delegate, etc.)?"); Source for mean number of years as party member: TR2 of the PELA surveys.
Source: Elites Parlamentarias de América Latina Project (PELA). Universidad de Salamanca, Manuel Alcántara, director. Wave of 2007–11.

need members who are committed to the assembly and who have the experience to help make it run.

To test two attitudinal aspects of Levitsky's hypothesis for seventeen Latin American countries, Tables 3.4, 3.5, and 3.6 show the relationship between deputies' prior political experience and their attitudes toward democracy and political parties. Consistent with Levitsky, deputies with less political experience are less likely to unconditionally support democracy and more likely to believe that democracy is possible without parties.

Table 3.4 compares Lower Chamber Novices versus all deputies on unconditional support for democracy and on whether parties are necessary for democracy. For the region as a whole, Lower Chamber Novices were much more likely to question that parties are essential for democracy (the means are 3.59 versus 3.26 on the 4-point scale). On average, Lower Chamber Novices were almost twice as far from the maximum value (0.74 away from it compared to 0.41) as deputies who had previously served in the lower chamber. The two means are statistically different at $p = 0.000$. Lower Chamber Novices score about the same on unconditional support for democracy; this is the only finding that does not support the hypothesis that less experienced politicians have less democratic attitudes.

Table 3.5 compares Electoral Novices to all others on these same questions, with similar results. For the region as a whole, Electoral Novices voice less unconditional support for democracy (the two samples are statistically different at $p = 0.005$) and show more willingness to believe that democracy is possible without parties (the two means are statistically different at $p = 0.000$).

Table 3.6 compares Political Amateurs to all other politicians on these same questions. For the region as a whole, 7.7% of political amateurs and only 2.4% of politicians with prior experience did not unconditionally support democracy. Although both percentages are low, the difference between the two samples is significant at $p = 0.000$. Likewise, politicians with prior experience were more likely to strongly agree that "Without parties there can't be democracy" ($p = 0.001$).

Kenney (1998: 62) reports a similar finding for an earlier Peruvian legislature (1990–95). The equivocal attitudes about liberal democracy and the indispensability of political parties for democracy found among less experienced politicians are likely to be associated with more instrumental attitudes toward democracy.

Although the percentage of deputies who question that "Democracy is always the best form of government" is low regardless of whether or not they have political experience, given social desirability bias in favor of democracy, especially among legislators in democracies, it is remarkable

TABLE 3.4 *Political Experience and Attitudes toward Democracy and Parties –*
Lower Chamber Novices versus Others

Country	Democracy is preferable (% yes)			No democracy without parties (mean)		
	Lower chamber novices	Others	*P* value if *p*<0.10	Lower chamber novices	Others	*P* value if *p*<0.10
ARG	100	100		3.76	3.65	
BOL	97.7	100		2.63	3.33	0.021
BRA	97.8	98.8		3.22	3.69	0.011
CHI	100	100		3.58	3.6	
COL	98.3	100		3.41	3.56	
CR	100	90	0.030	3.61	4.00	0.001
DOM. REP.	95.2	100		3.63	3.81	
ECU	98.7	100		3.03	3.78	0.001
ELS	84.2	93.1		3.08	3.43	
GUA	91.9	85.7		3.08	3.34	
HON	96.5	96.9		3.54	3.58	
MEX	94.2	100		2.73	2.64	
NIC	100	95.8		3.45	3.52	
PAN	97.5	95.8		3.43	3.58	
PAR	94.2	100		3.56	3.5	
PER	97	96.3		3.22	3.69	0.014
URU	100	100		3.63	3.70	
Total	97.4	96.7		3.26	3.59	0.000

Notes: "Democracy is preferable." The question is "With which of the following statements do you
agree more?" (1) Democracy is preferable to any other form of government. (2) In contexts of economic
crisis and political instability, an authoritarian government might be better.
"No democracy without parties." The question is "Some people say that without parties there can't
be democracy. How much do you agree with that statement?" (4) a lot; (3) somewhat; (2) a little; (1)
not at all.
Source: Elites Parlamentarias de América Latina Project (PELA), Universidad de Salamanca. Wave
of 2007–11.

that there are statistically significant differences on this question between
amateur politicians and more experienced politicians. Likewise, it is
notable that less experienced politicians express less support for the
statement that there can be no democracy without parties.

TABLE 3.5 *Political Experience and Attitudes toward Democracy and Parties –
Electoral Novices versus Others*

Country	Democracy is preferable (% yes)			No democracy without parties (mean)		
	Electoral novices	Others	P value if $p<0.10$	Electoral novices	Others	P value if $p<0.10$
ARG	100	100		3.68	3.76	
BOL	96.3	100		2.73	2.64	
BRA	93.3	99.1	0.088	3.07	3.58	0.085
CHI	100	100		3.55	3.61	
COL	94.7	100	0.050	3.21	3.53	
CR	100	96		3.68	3.68	
DOM. REP.	94.4	100		3.57	3.84	
ECU	97.9	100		2.90	3.46	0.015
ELS	77.8	95	0.033	3.07	3.34	
GUA	90	89.4		3.20	3.15	
HON	95.2	97.9		3.50	3.60	
MEX	95	94.7		2.65	2.77	
NIC	100	97.7		3.50	3.47	
PAN	97.1	96.6		3.37	3.62	
PAR	94.6	97.1		3.51	3.57	
PER	96.2	97.6		3.37	3.32	
URU	100	100		3.70	3.65	
Total	95.3	98	0.005	3.26	3.45	0.000

Notes: "Democracy is preferable." The question is "With which of the following statements do you agree more?" (1) Democracy is preferable to any other form of government. (2) In contexts of economic crisis and political instability, an authoritarian government might be better.

"No democracy without parties." The question is "Some people say that without parties there can't be democracy. How much do you agree with that statement?" (4) a lot; (3) somewhat; (2) a little; (1) not at all.

Source: Elites Parlamentarias de América Latina Project (PELA), Universidad de Salamanca. Wave of 2007–11.

POLICY STABILITY AND STABLE RULES OF THE GAME

Institutionalized party systems tend to generate longer time horizons, greater policy stability and predictability, and greater stability in the rules of the game. In these systems, the main actors in democratic politics are stable, and their positions are

TABLE 3.6 *Political Experience and Attitudes toward Democracy and Parties – Political Novices versus Others*

Country	Democracy is preferable (% yes)			No democracy without parties (mean)		
	Political novices	Others	P value if p<0.10	Political novices	Others	P value if p<0.10
ARG	100	100		3.33	3.76	
BOL	100	96.9		2.58	2.74	
BRA	75	99.2	0.000	3.00	3.54	0.000
CHI	100	100		3.56	3.60	
COL	90	100	0.004	3.10	3.51	
CR	100	98		3.40	3.70	
DOM. REP.	100	97.2		3.25	3.74	
ECU	94.1	100	0.032	2.82	3.24	
ELS	42.9	93.3	0.000	2.86	3.28	
GUA	80	90.2		2.00	3.24	0.014
HON	92.9	98.4		3.64	3.52	
MEX	91.7	95.3		2.92	2.69	
NIC	100	98.5		4.00	3.46	0.000
PAN	90	98.1		3.40	3.50	
PAR	94.4	96.3		3.44	3.57	
PER	92	98.5		3.32	3.45	
URU	100	100		3.33	3.68	
Total	92.3	97.6	0.000	3.15	3.41	0.001

Note: "Democracy is preferable." The question is "With which of the following statements do you agree more?" (1) Democracy is preferable to any other form of government. (2) In contexts of economic crisis and political instability, an authoritarian government might be better.
"No democracy without parties." The question is "Some people say that without parties there can't be democracy. How much do you agree with that statement?" (4) a lot; (3) somewhat; (2) a little; (1) not at all.
Source: Elites Parlamentarias de América Latina Project (PELA), Universidad de Salamanca. Wave of 2007–11.

relatively stable. This stability and predictability favor longer time horizons that partially counteract the short-term electoral incentives that necessarily also drive politicians' behavior. In institutionalized parties, politicians have incentives to protect and strengthen the party label. Their own fortunes rise and fall partly on the fortunes of their party.

This is less true in inchoate systems. Mechanisms of electoral accountability are easily vitiated; politicians can escape accountability by shifting from one party to another (Zielinski *et al.* 2005). Even major parties are subject to steep electoral losses, so politicians might jump ship for opportunistic reasons. Politics is more of an amateur affair, and, for political amateurs, developing long time horizons makes little sense.

As Flores-Macías (2012) showed, an institutionalized party system favors greater policy stability than an inchoate system for two reasons.[21] First, it is easier for outsiders to win the presidency in weakly institutionalized systems. In turn, many outsider presidents favor radical policy change. For example, Collor and Fujimori on the right and Chávez, Correa, and Morales on the left were committed to radical reform.

Second, presidents from well-established parties are typically more constrained than outsiders or other presidents from weak parties. Well-established parties make it more difficult to implement radical reforms, as Carlos Andrés Pérez's (1989–93) presidency and impeachment in Venezuela showed (Corrales 2002: 121–27, 131–68). Pérez wanted to implement far-reaching neoliberal economic change, but his party, *Acción Democrática*, did not go along with this, partly because of programmatic objections, helping to sink his reform agenda and ultimately his presidency.

The prior history of ideological and programmatic commitments, connections to organized interests, the existence of experienced leaders within the party, and organizational structures in established parties constrain presidents and prime ministers. In institutionalized systems, parties generally remain faithful to long-established ideological and programmatic principles (Berman 1998; Downs 1957: 103–11; Kitschelt 1994: 254–79). Radical change tends to be costly electorally because parties would risk losing the support of organized interests, activists, and voters. The interests of funders, activists, and organized groups limit change. They hold influence within the party and contribute time, money, organizational capacity, talent, and votes. Going against these stakeholders entails potentially high costs. Established parties in institutionalized systems are usually loath to risk losing large numbers of partisans by undertaking radical shifts.

In contrast, new parties exercise little constraining effect. Political outsiders create party labels to run for the presidency, but they are not beholden to the party. To the contrary, the party owes its existence to the outsider president. Inchoate party systems "undermine political parties' ability to prevent the president from conducting drastic changes to the status quo" (Flores-Macías

[21] O'Dwyer and Kovalcik (2007) make a similar argument for Postcommunist Europe and O'Donnell (1994) did for delegative democracies. For a diverging perspective, see Campello (2015), who argues that more institutionalized parties did not block left-of-center presidents from implementing market-oriented economic policies and that high electoral volatility likewise did not affect the probability that presidents would announce one program as candidates and pursue another in office.

2012: 5). Programmatic principles are not yet strongly established in many young parties, so the cost of radical change is lower. The parties generally have weaker connections to organized interests, few committed activists, and fewer fund raisers and funders. Funders and organized interests are usually less attached to specific parties and more willing to support candidates of different parties. Fewer voters are partisans, so radical party shifts do not disrupt long-established bonds between the party and a strong core of partisans.

Because they were not tethered by their parties' established ties and ideological commitments, outsiders who took power in the context of inchoate party systems – Alberto Fujimori in Peru (1990–2000), Hugo Chávez in Venezuela (1999–2013), Evo Morales in Bolivia (2006–present), and Rafael Correa in Ecuador (2007–present) – were able to undertake radical change in economic policy. Conversely, leftist presidents who took office in the context of institutionalized party systems – Ricardo Lagos (2000–06) and Michelle Bachelet in Chile (2006–10, 2014–present), Luis Inácio da Silva (2003–11) and Dilma Rousseff (2011–16) in Brazil, Mauricio Funes in El Salvador (2009–14), and Tabaré Vázquez (2005–10 and 2015–present) and José Mujica in Uruguay (2010–15) – implemented modest reforms. In Latin America, stronger institutions in general, including more institutionalized party systems, helped provide greater policy stability and averted radical policy change that often proved ill-advised (O'Donnell 1994).[22]

Although policy stability is not always normatively desirable, high instability often has costs (O'Donnell 1994; Spiller and Tommasi 2005). It induces uncertainty among investors and citizens, with negative economic effects. For investors, policy instability is anathema. It makes it difficult to plan future courses of action, including decisions about investment and employment. It could raise the specter of erratic policy making and radical anti-business policies. For citizens and consumers, too, policy instability has high costs. It makes it difficult to plan major expenses and investments such as education, and it makes it difficult to figure out how to save money for the future.

In some situations, major policy change might be in order. Strong formal institutions generally, and institutionalized party systems specifically, tend to stifle radical change, which means that the possibility of radical political innovation is low. Accordingly, Coppedge (1994) warned of the perils of "partyarchy," and Schedler (1995) of the potential costs of over-institutionalization. The argument here is not that stability is always good, but rather that chronic instability shortens actors' time horizons and reduces the probability of good collective outcomes.

---

[22] An institutionalized party system does not preclude the possibility of sharp policy change. Sharp change is more likely if the main parties are programmatically polarized. In such circumstances, a change of government can produce significant policy change even in an institutionalized system. The argument here rests on an "all other things equal" clause.

Institutionalized systems also favor maintaining stable rules of the game. The set of actors is stable, and new actors are more likely than established ones to seek a radical change of the rules of the game. They might be ideologically committed to radical change in the rules, and they often have strategic reasons to change the rules. They often railed against these rules as part of the decayed and corrupt establishment. To maintain their political standing with their constituents, they want to follow through on these clamors to radically change the system. Outsider presidents typically come to power with weak congressional support, so they have strong incentives to seek to get rid of the sitting congress and to secure new rules that would help them consolidate power and weaken the old establishment forces.

One of the most radical forms of changing the rules is a new constitution. Corrales (2014) and Negretto (2013) identified twelve new constitutions in Latin America in the post-1980 period: El Salvador 1983, Guatemala 1985, Nicaragua 1987, Brazil 1988, Colombia 1991, Paraguay 1992, Peru 1993, Argentina 1994, Ecuador 1998, Venezuela 1999, Ecuador 2008, and Bolivia 2009. Four of the twelve occurred under the first president of a new democratic or semi-democratic period (Guatemala 1985, Nicaragua 1987, Brazil 1988, and Paraguay 1992) and a fifth shortly before a transition to a competitive regime (El Salvador 1983). Because the presidents in these five cases inaugurated (or were on the verge of doing so) new competitive regimes, there is no score for electoral volatility for the year when they were elected. The other seven presidents who presided over new constitutions governed in already existing competitive regimes.

Based on these seven presidents, radical constitutional change is more likely in inchoate party systems, consistent with the hypothesis that the rules tend to be more stable in institutionalized systems. Mean presidential electoral volatility when these seven presidents were elected was 54.3 compared to 31.3 for 118 elections of presidents who did not oversee the writing of new constitutions in the post-1978 period. The difference between means is statistically significant at $p<0.06$ notwithstanding the small number (seven) of presidents who were elected and then oversaw the writing of new constitutions.

Four of the ten full outsider presidents mentioned earlier – Fujimori, Chávez, Morales, and Correa – presided over the establishment of new constitutions that enabled them to concentrate power and move toward competitive authoritarian regimes. These presidents account for every single new constitution since 1983 that expanded constitutional presidential powers according to Corrales's (2014) index. In light of Fish's (2006) evidence that strong legislatures are good for democracy, the fact that these outsiders bolstered their own powers at the expense of congress was a bad portent. The other six new constitutions that Corrales (2014) coded, introduced by insider presidents, all reduced presidential powers. All four outsiders who produced new constitutions with expanded presidential powers were impatient with the normal checks and

balances of democratic politics. They sought and achieved constitutions that ended the ban on consecutive presidential terms. All ran for and won reelection. Partly because of their expanded presidential powers, they presided over the emasculation of democratic checks and balances.

EXTENDING TIME HORIZONS AND LIMITING CORRUPTION

Institutionalized party systems generate stability and predictability in electoral competition; in linkages with voters, organized interests, and the state; and in broad contours of policy. As a result, they lengthen time horizons. Conversely, more is up for grabs in weakly institutionalized systems. Parties structure the political process less than with institutionalized systems. As a result, predictability is lower and time horizons tend to be shorter (O'Donnell 1994), easily leading to policy myopia (Simmons 2016; Spiller and Tommasi 2005, 2008). Policies that pay off in the long term but not the short term, such as inclusionary and non-discretionary social policies (Garay 2016) and technology policies (Simmons 2016) are more likely with well-established parties. More generally, programmatic politics is more likely with well-established parties (Kitschelt and Kselman 2013).[23]

Although some institutionalized parties have made widespread use of clientelism, on deductive grounds, there is reason to hypothesize that institutionalized systems might be associated with less clientelism. Because institutionalized parties breed longer time horizons that are associated on average with more focus on policies that generate long-term development, they might focus less on clientelistic provision (Kitschelt and Kselman 2013). Parties have less incentive to focus on building programmatic brands in inchoate systems; they might not have the time to do so. Because less institutionalized systems have more amateur politicians with short-term horizons, they might be more conducive to clientelistic exchange. Because institutionalized systems on average feature more programmatic competition (Kitschelt *et al.* 2010), parties might rely less on clientelistic linkages. Weak formal institutions make for bastions of strong informal ones, and they more often than not protect the interests of the powerful.

If weak PSI reduces actors' time horizons and is associated with clientelistic practices, then it might correlate with a high perception of corruption because the particularistic exchange of favors that characterizes clientelism is rife with opportunities for corruption. The widely used Worldwide Governance Indicators include a measure of perception of a government's capacity to control corruption. The scores for a given country–year are the number of standard deviations above or below the world mean for a specific country in a specific year. Figure 3.1 shows the scores for Latin America for 2014. Except

---

[23] The data in Chapter 4, however, do not show an association between programmatic linkages and more institutionalized party systems.

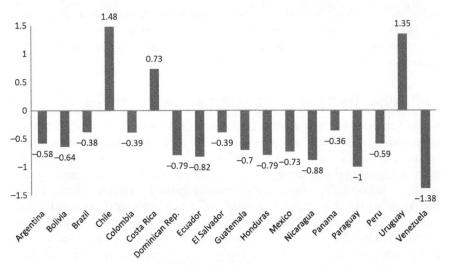

FIGURE 3.1 Perception of Control of Corruption, 2014: Worldwide Governance Indicators
Source: Worldwide Governance Indicators (2015).

Chile, Costa Rica, and Uruguay, Latin American countries scored below the world mean in 2014. Consistent with the hypothesis, institutionalized party systems are associated with better perception of control of corruption. The summary PSI score in Table 2.6 is correlated at 0.52 (p = 0.03) with the 2014 World Governance Indicator for perception of control of corruption, based on eighteen countries (all but Cuba and Haiti).

It also seems likely that, consistent with Garay (2016) and Simmons (2016), the longer time horizons that result from institutionalized party systems are conducive to a better provision of public goods. Consistent with this hypothesis, the correlation between the summary score for PSI in Table 2.6 and the 2014 World Governance Indicator for perception of government effectiveness is 0.55 (significant at p = 0.02). Of course, this correlation is merely suggestive and far from conclusive. Factors beyond an institutionalized party system (for example, a solid state and good policies) also affect government effectiveness.

THE EMERGENCE OF PARTISANSHIP AND THE POSSIBILITY OF ELECTORAL ACCOUNTABILITY

This chapter has until now focused on the effects of weak institutionalization on politicians and elite actors. Weakly institutionalized party systems also provide different environments for voters. In institutionalized systems, voters face a stable electoral landscape. The set of actors, electoral results, and

parties' ideological positions are stable. As a result, it is easier for voters to get a clear sense of what the options are and which is best for them (Marinova 2016). The information environment is more stable and clearer.

The electoral environment is less stable and predictable for voters in inchoate systems. The entrance of major new parties and the exit or sharp decline of major old parties make for changing electoral alternatives. Electoral volatility is higher, so it is less predictable who the winners and losers will be. Sometimes, candidates for executive office experience meteoric rises and declines in a short time (Baker *et al.* 2006). Lower ideological and programmatic stability of the main parties make it less clear how different parties are positioned relative to one another.

For these reasons, weak PSI is inimical to partisanship. Converse (1969) argued that partisanship emerged over time as voters came to more clearly identify the main parties and what they stood for (see also Dinas 2014). In inchoate systems, the main actors change with some frequency, and the parties are less fixed ideologically. Assuming that Converse's and Dinas's arguments are correct, we should have different expectations for the emergence of partisanship in inchoate systems. Voters will not bond to ephemeral organizations; new parties are likely to take time to develop a large contingent of partisans. Voters' attachments to established parties are likely to be disrupted if those older organizations become minor contenders or undertake deep programmatic changes. The instability of the main contenders and their ideological positions creates hurdles for building partisans.[24]

This argument reverses the normal claim about partisanship, namely that partisanship is a foundation for stabilizing party systems (Converse 1969; Green *et al.* 2002). This is not to argue that the causal arrow works in only one direction or that Converse's and Green *et al.*'s classic claim is wrong. Weak partisanship makes the institutionalization of a party system more difficult and subjects it to greater future uncertainty, and it makes party systems more vulnerable to radical change (Lupu 2016; Seawright 2012).[25]

---

[24] The time series on party identification is not long enough or consistent enough to statistically test the hypothesis that lower PSI is associated with lower partisanship. A test of this hypothesis would require a measure of partisanship for the year immediately following an electoral period. Otherwise, the time gap between the data on partisanship and the electoral period is too great for a causal mechanism about the effect of PSI on partisanship to be convincing. For most Latin American countries, only one or two data points meet these criteria. Moreover, region-wide surveys often did not use the same questions about partisanship, weakening the comparability of different data points over time.

[25] The country correlation between the summary PSI score in Table 2.6 and the percentage of survey respondents who said that they sympathized with a political party in the 2014 AmericasBarometer survey was modest at 0.33 ($p = 0.19$). However, the AmericasBarometer question is not ideal for tapping partisanship because it asks about respondents' *current* partisan identification. Partisanship is better assessed by questions that ask about respondents' identification regardless of the immediate situation. See Castro Cornejo (forthcoming).

Other things equal,[26] low PSI might also be unfavorable to electoral accountability (Mainwaring and Torcal 2006; Moser and Scheiner 2012; O'Dwyer 2006; Zielinski *et al.* 2005). In most democracies, parties are the primary mechanism of electoral accountability.[27] In turn, electoral accountability is core to the very practice of representative democracy, whose promise hinges on the contract between voters and elected politicians. In principle, politicians should work to further the interests of voters and of the public good, and they should be voted out of office for failure to live up to this contract. Voters use parties as information short cuts to help understand what individual politicians stand for. For electoral accountability to work well, then, voters must be able to identify in broad terms what the main parties are and what they stand for (Aldrich 1995: 3; Downs 1957; Hinich and Munger 1994). In contexts where parties disappear and appear with frequency and where personalities often overshadow parties as routes to executive power, the prospects for effective electoral accountability diminish. Getting elected politicians to faithfully represent voters is challenging under the best of circumstances (Przeworski *et al.* 1999) – all the more so with weakly institutionalized systems.[28]

For electoral accountability and political representation to function well, citizens need effective information cues that enable them to vote in reasoned ways without spending inordinate time to reach these decisions.[29] In institutionalized systems, parties provide an ideological reference that gives some anchoring to voters. Voters can reduce information costs, thus enhancing electoral accountability. The limited stability of less institutionalized systems reduces the information cues that they offer voters (Moser and Scheiner 2012). The weaker information cues hamper the bounded rationality of voters, undercutting the potential for electoral accountability based on a somewhat informed evaluation of policies, governments, and leaders. Where electoral accountability is vitiated, the ideal of representative democracy, that elected politicians will serve as agents of the voters to promote good policy or public goods or to advance the interests of specific constituencies, may break down (Luna and Zechmeister 2005).

---

[26] If an institutionalized system is exclusionary or collusive, such as the Colombian system from 1958 to 1990, electoral accountability suffers for different reasons.

[27] Even in democracies in which the personal vote is important, such as the US, partisan cues and identities can be highly important (Bartels 2000; Green *et al.* 2002).

[28] Torcal and Lago (2015) correctly argue that the relationship between electoral volatility and accountability is not linear. An ideal type hyper-institutionalized party system would afford little or no accountability because vote shares would be stable regardless of how well or poorly governments performed. Accountability rests on the capacity of citizens to change their votes if they are not satisfied with the government.

[29] This paragraph comes from Mainwaring and Torcal (2006).

PARTY SYSTEM INSTITUTIONALIZATION AND THE QUALITY OF DEMOCRACY

For theoretical reasons already suggested in this chapter, we can hypothesize that low PSI would be associated with lower quality democracy. Weakly institutionalized systems make it easier for political outsiders to win power. Outsiders usually have a cavalier attitude toward representative democracy, and many attempt to undermine it. Weakly institutionalized systems have less experienced politicians, who tend to be less committed to democracy and to parties. Fluid party systems are associated with greater corruption, which can have corrosive effects on democracy. Inchoate systems hinder electoral accountability.

I leave more rigorous tests about the impact of PSI on democratic quality to subsequent scholarship and to already published work (Pérez-Liñán and Mainwaring 2013),[30] but the hypothesis holds up in a simple preliminary test of correlation. The Pearson bivariate correlation between the summary score for PSI (Table 2.6) and Freedom House scores for 2015 (based on the 2016 *Freedom in the World*) is 0.48 (p = 0.04).[31] The bivariate correlation between the summary score for PSI and *mean* Freedom House scores for 1990–2015 is 0.55 (p = 0.02).

The five cases of democratic erosion in Latin America in the new millennium have been Venezuela, Ecuador, Bolivia, Nicaragua, and Honduras (Mainwaring and Pérez-Liñán 2015). In all five countries (and in Mexico), Freedom House scores were at least two points lower in 2014 compared to their highest score during the post-1978 wave of democratization.

In Venezuela, Ecuador, and Bolivia, democratic erosion was causally connected to weak PSI (Mazzuca 2014). The election of political outsiders and the sharp erosion of the traditional party systems paved the way for the ensuing erosion of democracy. The demise of the traditional parties removed obstacles to the path from representative democracy to competitive authoritarianism in Venezuela and to a degraded representative democracy that borders on competitive authoritarianism in Ecuador and Bolivia. The absence of solid party oppositions enabled presidents with hegemonic aspirations to trample over mechanisms of accountability. All three countries had weakly institutionalized systems in the run-up to the election of the outsider presidents. All three systems show signs of becoming institutionalized in the wake of party system collapse – but under the aegis of presidents with hegemonic aspirations.

---

[30] For an interesting paired comparison along these lines, see Corrales (2001).
[31] I inverted the Freedom House scores so that a high score indicates a high quality democracy. The inverted scores range from 0 (extremely authoritarian) to 12 (very democratic). The correlation between the summary PSI score and the most recent (as of August 2016) Varieties of Democracy score for liberal democracy was 0.41 (p = 0.09) (Coppedge *et al.* 2016a).

Nicaragua's party system is fairly weakly institutionalized (its score for PSI in Table 2.6 was slightly above the Latin American average), but in its case, the relationship between weak PSI and democratic erosion is less clear-cut. The Honduran case reverses the causal direction between PSI and democratic erosion. The 2009 coup and its aftermath provoked a degradation of democracy, and subsequently a previously highly institutionalized party system eroded.

Most Latin American countries with highly institutionalized party systems have high quality democracies. According to the summary score in Table 2.6, Uruguay, Mexico, and Chile have the most institutionalized systems in the region. According to Freedom House and V-Dem, Chile, Uruguay, and Costa Rica have the highest quality democracies in Latin America. The Mexican case underscores that PSI does not ensure good democratic outcomes.

What about the relationship between change in the level of institutionalization and change in the quality of democracy? The three countries (Brazil, El Salvador, and Mexico – the latter with the qualifications discussed in Chapter 2) that experienced a clear increase in PSI since the publication of *Building Democratic Institutions* became higher quality democracies (Brazil and El Salvador) or became democratic (Mexico). The countries that maintained highly institutionalized systems, Chile and Uruguay, are high quality liberal democracies. Bolivia, Ecuador, and Peru, the cases of inchoate systems circa 1993 that later culminated in party system collapse, moved in divergent directions in the quality of democracy. Bolivia and Ecuador have experienced some erosion of democracy. Peru's party system collapse was also associated with a democratic breakdown when President Fujimori shuttered the Peruvian congress and part of the court system in 1992. Today Peru has a democracy, though as Levitsky argues (Chapter 11), not a robust one. Argentina, Colombia, and Costa Rica are cases of party system erosion without collapse, although one major party in Argentina (the Radicals) shrivelled and one in Costa Rica (the Social Christian Unity Party, PUSC) collapsed. Democracy has remained robust in Costa Rica and troubled in Colombia, with no major net gain or loss in the quality of democracy.

Overall, then, increasing PSI has been associated with increases in the quality of democracy; persistently high PSI has usually been associated with high quality democracy; and party system collapse has consistently been associated with dips in the quality of democracy – sometimes profound ones, as in Peru in the 1990s and Venezuela in the 2000s.

Notwithstanding the solid association between PSI and higher quality democracy, citizens in Latin America are not enthusiastic about parties even in institutionalized systems. Trust in parties is low in Latin America and most of the democratic world. The AmericasBarometer survey regularly asks, "How much confidence (*confianza*) do you have in political parties?" The scale ranges

from 1 (no confidence at all) to 7 (a lot of confidence). In 2014, the country mean for the eighteen Latin American countries in the survey (all but Cuba and Haiti) was 2.90,[32] well below the mid-point (4) on the scale (LAPOP 2014). The country-level correlation between mean confidence in parties (based on the 2014 AmericasBarometer survey) and average PSI from 1990 to 2015 (based on Table 2.6) was modest (0.35 (p = 0.16)). High system institutionalization has not rescued parties from widespread negative citizen sentiment. Citizens do not share the enthusiasm of most political scientists for institutionalized party systems.

CONCLUSION

PSI has important consequences for democratic politics. The chapter has highlighted six usually negative effects of weakly institutionalized party systems. They increase electoral uncertainty and make it easier for political outsiders to win the presidency, often with deleterious consequences for democracy; they are associated with more political amateurs; they increase policy instability and instability of the rules of the game; they shorten actors' time horizons and are associated with political systems more permeated by corruption; they make electoral accountability more challenging; and, on average, they are associated with lower quality democracies.

Institutionalized party systems are not a panacea, as countless historical and contemporary cases show. When it is based on exclusion and restricted options (e.g., Colombia from 1958 until 1990), high PSI has high democratic costs. Inchoate systems do not doom a country to bad results on all dimensions, as the Peruvian example today shows (see Levitsky's chapter in this volume). High levels of PSI do not necessarily produce better democratic processes or outcomes than moderate levels. Moreover, throughout most of the region, citizens seem to dislike parties regardless of how institutionalized the system is. However, inchoate party systems are generally associated with the problematic outcomes discussed in this chapter and with lower quality democracy. A major challenge for contemporary democratic politics in Latin America and beyond is that citizens are becoming less attached to parties and more skeptical and even disdainful of them, but they remain essential agents of democratic representation and accountability

---

[32] This excludes non-respondents.

4

Democratization without Party System Institutionalization: Cross-National Correlates

Scott Mainwaring and Fernando Bizzarro*

For generations, a conventional wisdom in political science was famously captured by Schattschneider's (1942: 1) dictum that "Political parties created democracy, and modern democracy is unthinkable save in terms of the parties." By Schattschneider's logic, it is difficult to imagine a democracy without solid parties (see also Aldrich 1995: 295–96). Many other scholars have seen parties – and implicitly, institutionalized party systems – as essential underpinnings of modern representative democracy (Sartori 1976; Stokes 1999).

But as post-transition experiences in Latin America, Africa, the post-communist countries, and parts of Asia make clear, the solidity of parties and party system institutionalization (PSI) vary greatly across cases and over time. Rather than being the norm, institutionalized party systems have been the exception in third and fourth wave cases of democratization. What explains the extraordinary variance in institutionalization?

A complete answer to this question would require a different book devoted primarily to that analysis. This chapter has a more modest objective. It offers insights into average patterns for the most recent episodes of democratization in eighteen Latin American countries. Rather than exploring the process by which individual cases evolved, we search for the "average" quantifiable factors associated with variations in levels of PSI.

The chapter outlines five theoretical approaches to explaining PSI, presents hypotheses that derive from these theoretical approaches, and offers quantitative analyses that assess how compatible the results are with these theoretical approaches and hypotheses. The quantitative analysis is a crucial test of which theoretical approaches and specific hypotheses are likely to offer explanatory leverage for Latin America. Without it, it would be difficult to assess which

* We are grateful to Sarah Zukerman Daly, Steve Levitsky, Tarek Masoud, Daniel Ziblatt, and participants at the MIT Latin American politics seminar for comments and to María Victoria De Negri for helpful research assistance and comments.

in this volume and 2012; Kitschelt and Kselman 2013; Levitsky this volume; Levitsky and Murillo 2005; Lupu and Riedl 2013; O'Donnell 1994; Simmons 2016; Spiller and Tommasi 2005). Short-term horizons favor clientelistic practices and work against the effective provision of public goods (Hicken 2015; O'Donnell 1994; O'Dwyer 2006; Simmons 2016).

With inchoate party systems, uncertainty is not limited to outcomes. As some parties fade into oblivion and others experience meteoric ascents, there is also more uncertainty about who the players will be.

PARTY SYSTEM INSTITUTIONALIZATION, ELECTORAL UNCERTAINTY, AND OUTSIDERS

Weakly institutionalized party systems make it easier for outsiders to win power. In principle, outsiders could be good for democracy, but, in practice, they more often have pernicious effects. In inchoate systems, the turnover from one party to another is high, the entry barriers to new parties are low, and the likelihood that outsiders can become the head of government is higher than in institutionalized systems. In presidential systems with inchoate party systems, new contenders can burst on the scene and win executive power (Carreras 2012; Flores-Macías 2012; Linz 1994: 26–29; Samuels and Shugart 2010: 62–93). Once powerful parties sometimes fade into oblivion.

Presidential systems usually have more personalized parties than parliamentary systems because presidents are chosen by voters and cannot (except under extraordinary circumstances such as impeachment) be removed by their parties, whereas prime ministers are chosen by, and can be removed by, their parties. Because they do not need to develop long careers within the organization to become the party leader, it is easier for outsiders to win power in presidential systems (Linz 1994: 26–29; Samuels and Shugart 2010: 62–93). Presidents are directly accountable to voters; prime ministers to their parties.

Among presidential systems, there is also a difference between institutionalized and inchoate party systems. Political outsiders do not win the presidency in institutionalized systems. In contrast, in weakly institutionalized systems, outsiders can pop up and immediately become major contenders for executive posts.

Latin American experience is rife with examples of outsiders bursting on to the scene and winning presidential elections in the context of weak party systems. Carreras (2012) developed a dataset of outsider presidential candidates in Latin America from 1980 to 2010. Sixteen of them won the presidency, including eight "full outsiders" – candidates who had never run for office before *and* who ran on new political parties: Fernando Collor de Mello in Brazil (1989),[8] Lucio

---

[8] Collor de Mello should be coded as a partial outsider – a political "maverick" in Carreras's lexicon. He had previously served as appointed mayor of the city of Maceió (1979–82) and as a federal deputy (1983–87), and governor of the state of Alagoas (1987–89), but he created a new

Gutiérrez (2002) and Rafael Correa in Ecuador (2006), Violeta Chamorro in Nicaragua (1990), Fernando Lugo in Paraguay (2008), Alberto Fujimori (1990) and Alejandro Toledo in Peru (2001), and Hugo Chávez in Venezuela (1998). In addition, Evo Morales ran in Bolivia in 2002 as a full outsider and came in second, and then ran again in 2005 and won; and Ollanta Humala ran in 2006 as a full outsider in Peru and came in second and ran again in 2011 and won. All ten outsiders ran in the context of weakly institutionalized party systems.

Table 3.1 lists these ten presidents and shows the electoral volatility when they were elected and in the previous electoral period. Mean volatility when these presidents were elected was extraordinarily high (59.7%). Because they helped produce the extraordinary party system change, volatility in the election when they won office is not an antecedent, independent measure of PSI. Therefore, Table 3.1 also shows the level of volatility in the electoral period before they won. Although the sample is limited to eight of the winning outsider candidates,[9] mean volatility was extremely high (49.3%). Even the lowest volatility in the previous period, 37.0%, is very high. No full outsider has been elected in the context of a moderately institutionalized party system.

Carreras also coded "political mavericks" – presidential candidates who had previously run for elected office but were running on new parties. Four political mavericks in his dataset successfully ran for the presidency: Álvaro Uribe in Colombia (2002), Sixto Durán Ballén in Ecuador (1992), Ricardo Martinelli in Panama (2009),[10] and Rafael Caldera in Venezuela (1993). With the partial exception of Caldera in 1993, these mavericks were elected in the context of weakly institutionalized or eroding party systems. Ecuador and to a lesser degree Panama had long had weakly institutionalized party systems. In Venezuela, Caldera's election in 1993 made visible the rapid erosion of the party system that led to collapse by 2000. The linchpins of the system, AD and COPEI, had already weakened significantly when Caldera was elected. In Colombia, the long-standing two-party system that dominated political life from 1910 to 1991 was greatly eroded in the 1990s (see Chapter 8 in this volume). Uribe's election in 2002 and the aftermath dealt it a deathblow, but the prior erosion was a necessary condition for his victory.

party to run for the presidency in 1989. Whether we code him as a full or partial outsider ("maverick") has no impact on the analysis that follows.

[9] In Brazil in 1989 and Nicaragua in 1990, there was no antecedent electoral period under the current competitive regime. Fernando Collor de Mello was elected in 1989 in the first popular presidential election since 1960. The first presidential election under Sandinista's rule took place in 1984. Elections under the Somoza regime (1936–79) were too controlled to be a reasonable basis for determining volatility in 1984.

[10] Martinelli was a maverick in 2004, when he first ran for the presidency on his new party label and won only 5.3% of the valid vote. He ran successfully in 2009.

Alberto Fujimori	Peru, 1990	*Cambio 90*	18	23	IU-IS	29	38
Alejandro Toledo	Peru, 2001*	*Perú Posible*	37.5	unicameral		37.5	unicameral
Ollanta Humala	Peru, 2011*	*Gana Peru*	36	unicameral		36	unicameral
Hugo Chávez	Venezuela, 1998	MVR	26	25	MAS, PPT	37	35
Mean			18.8	19.4		38.7	41.0

Notes: Presidents' coalitions are defined by the parties that had cabinet positions.

*Brazil 1989: Presidential and congressional elections were not concurrent. Data for cabinet composition and congressional seat shares are from Collor's inauguration in March 1990.

Ecuador 2006: Correa's party, *Alianza País*, did not run any congressional candidates.

Nicaragua 1990: Violeta Chamorro was elected with a coalition of fourteen parties, but she was not a member of any party.

Peru: From 1979 to 1992, the Congress of Peru was bicameral. Since 1995, it has been unicameral.

Sources: See Online Appendix 3.1.

Because most outsider presidents initially have weak support in congress, they face a dilemma. They can either cultivate support among the established parties, accept limitations in accomplishing their legislative agendas, or try to circumvent congress to pursue their agendas. On the campaign trail, most outsiders railed against the existing parties. Most are reluctant to do an abrupt about face and bring them on board as partners in government,[14] and many are ideologically hostile to them. Of the ten outsider presidents listed in Table 3.1, only Gutiérrez, Toledo, and Humala from the outset cultivated the establishment parties. Nor, given their harsh criticisms of the status quo and in many cases their desire to implement radical change, are outsider presidents likely to accept protracted legislative/executive deadlock. Instead, a frequent path of outsider presidents has been to attack congress and the establishment parties and to attempt to expand presidential powers (Carreras 2014; Corrales 2014; Negretto 2013).

Eight of the ten outsiders (all but Toledo and Humala) experienced severe conflict with congress. Three (Collor in 1992, Gutiérrez in 2005, and Lugo in 2012) were removed from office by congress – an extraordinary number even in an era of a fair number of impeachments and other forms of presidential removals (Pérez-Liñán 2007). The Peruvian Chamber of Deputies nearly voted to remove Fujimori from office in December 1991 (Kenney 2004: 186), and the Ecuadoran congressional opposition attempted to impeach Gutiérrez in November 2004 before removing him the following year.

Other outsiders attacked the legislature because of difficulty working with them. Fujimori shuttered the Peruvian congress in April 1992, producing a democratic breakdown, because of his inability to win support for some proposals (Kenney 2004: 171–210). Violeta Chamorro ran into difficulties when the conservative parties within her broad electoral coalition jumped to the opposition because of her conciliatory policies toward the Sandinistas. Her own vice president, the head of the national assembly, and most of her initial coalition moved into the opposition, leading to fractious conflict within the congress and between Chamorro and the legislature (McConnell 1997).

Almost immediately after taking office, Hugo Chávez and Rafael Correa announced their desire to hold constitutional congresses to create new constitutions. The constitutional congresses diminished the capacity of the sitting congresses, and in Venezuela it replaced the existing congress. In Venezuela, the new constitution greatly expanded presidential powers, helping allow Chávez to eventually dismantle the system of checks and balances and install a competitive authoritarian regime.

Correa also experienced severe conflict with the sitting congress. When he became president, Correa announced his intention to hold a referendum to convene a constitutional assembly. The legislature voted against it on the grounds

---

[14] Lucio Gutiérrez in Ecuador (2003–05) was an exception, but his turn to the establishment parties led to a rapid rupture with the coalition that elected him and eventually led to him being ousted.

theoretical approaches and hypotheses are most fruitful for further exploration. It is also perhaps the best way to consider a wide array of alternative hypotheses.

The most striking finding is the degree to which many statistical associations defied expectations and ran counter to the established literature. Neither a country's past history of democracy nor the longevity of the current semi-democratic or democratic regime had an association with PSI. In Latin America, on average, the latest wave of democratization has not induced PSI, contrary to the experience of the early democratizing countries (Lipset and Rokkan 1967) and to southern Europe after 1974. A venerable literature has postulated that in mass representative democracy, parties offer great advantages to politicians (Aldrich 1995) – but in Latin America, either politicians are not investing much in party building (see Levitsky's chapter on Peru; Hale 2006), or those investments are failing. In several party systems, outsider presidents purposefully crippled the established parties as a way of bolstering their own power (e.g., Alberto Fujimori in Peru, Hugo Chávez in Venezuela, Rafael Correa in Ecuador, Evo Morales in Bolivia).

Converse (1969) argued that as democracy survived for a longer time, voters would be more likely to develop partisan identifications, which, in turn, would stabilize electoral markets. Downs (1957) expected that electoral markets would stabilize as parties built reputations and voters learned which parties best represented their interests. But these expectations, too, have been dashed. Mainwaring *et al.* (2016) and Mainwaring and Zoco (2007) showed that electoral volatility and the vote share of new parties were on average much lower in democracies that were born a long time ago. But contrary to these two works based on a broader sample of countries, in Latin America, countries with a long prior legacy of democracy did not on average have more institutionalized party systems than countries with little history of democracy prior to the third wave. On average, democracy or semi-democracy has now lasted for two generations without PSI.

A second key finding is that, despite these and other counterintuitive null results, PSI and erosion do not occur randomly. The most important "positive" findings are associations between PSI and other party or party system characteristics. After testing the argument advanced by Zucco (2015) and Luna and Altman (2011) that PSI can occur even in the absence of programmatic connections between voters and parties and of organizationally strong parties, we find support for the first part of this argument, but not for the second. Institutionalization is much more likely when parties have strong national organizations. It is also more likely where party systems are less fragmented (i.e., where there are fewer parties).

Third, government performance has had a surprisingly weak association with PSI in Latin America. Economic growth and inflation had weak correlations with PSI. This is surprising in light of the magnitude of economic crisis and change in Latin America since the beginning of the great debt crisis in 1982, and also in light of the weight some previous literature has placed on

economic distress as the major cause of party system upheaval in Latin America and the post-Soviet region.

The analysis in this chapter has several limitations. We do not offer a parsimonious theory that purports to explain PSI, but rather spell out the major theoretical approaches that might explain variance in outcomes and provide empirical tests about them. Given that the data are observational, we refrain from causal claims.

The chapter examines the plausibility of competing theories and hypotheses about PSI. It considers five different theoretical approaches to understanding PSI and twenty specific hypotheses associated with those theoretical approaches. We give evidence about theoretically important correlates that scholars have hypothesized to have a causal impact on PSI.

The chapter proceeds as follows. The first section describes the dependent variables and explains the case selection of electoral periods. The second section describes five theoretical approaches to understanding party system change, presents twenty hypotheses that correspond to these theoretical approaches, describes the operationalization of the variables, and discusses results. The third section discusses the model and presents results. The conclusion reviews the findings and their limitations.

DEPENDENT VARIABLES AND CASE SELECTION

We test for the associations between PSI and its hypothesized determinants in eighteen Latin American party systems.[1] We included all presidential and all lower chamber elections (in separate regressions) belonging to the contemporary electoral regime (as of 2015). We define an electoral regime as a continuous period in which countries score 2 or more in the Polity2 index. This criterion includes fifteen Latin American countries since (re)democratization during the third wave and the region's only three countries that democratized before the third wave and remained democratic or semi-democratic until the 2000s – Costa Rica, which has been democratic since 1953; Colombia, democratic or semi-democratic since 1958; and Venezuela, which was democratic from 1959 until the 2000s, before descending to competitive authoritarianism. We also include elections under three competitive authoritarian regimes that began as democracies or semi-democracies but then eroded: the Peruvian elections during Alberto Fujimori's presidency (1990–2000), the Venezuelan elections since 1958 despite the erosion to competitive authoritarianism in 2009, and the Nicaraguan elections since 1990 despite the erosion around 2010. In all three cases, the electoral process remained uninterrupted and elections remained highly contested except for Venezuela in 2005, when the opposition abstained.

---

[1] Coverage for Argentina's lower chamber does not extend past 2001 because of problems of data availability. As we noted in Chapter 2, after 2003 the Argentine data are available at the provincial level but not at the national level.

The unit of observation for the quantitative analyses is country electoral periods – that is, each electoral period in each country. Chapter 2 included seven indicators of PSI for which data are available for each electoral period: the vote share of new parties, the stability of the main contenders, and electoral volatility, for both presidential and lower chamber elections, and ideological change at the system level in the lower chambers of national congresses.[2] We did not include ideological stability in the analyses in this chapter because the coverage of data for this measure was more limited.

Table 4.1 reports the electoral periods included for each country and the basic descriptive statistics for the dependent variables. The 148 electoral periods for the lower chamber and 113 electoral periods for the presidency in the dataset encompass a huge range of scores for the dependent variables and most of the independent variables. This is the longest time series that has been used in quantitative analyses of electoral volatility and the vote share of new parties for Latin America.

THEORETICAL EXPECTATIONS, HYPOTHESES, AND MEASUREMENT
OF VARIABLES

The literature on party system change, stability, and collapse, and party collapse contain a wide range of theoretical approaches and hypotheses. Ex-ante and post-facto, we found it difficult to adjudicate among these different theoretical approaches and hypotheses. No extant parsimonious theory satisfies us on empirical grounds, and party system change and stability are influenced by a multiplicity of variables that are difficult to boil down to a parsimonious theory. For these reasons, we tested several major theoretical approaches and included many potentially important variables at the expense of sacrificing theoretical parsimony.

The institutionalization of a party system reflects an equilibrium between the supply side (the creation, splits, mergers, and disbanding of parties by politicians; the formation and dissolution of coalitions; and defections by individual politicians from one party to another) and voters' choices. Five theoretical approaches in the literature on stability and change in parties and party systems might help explain why such an equilibrium emerges, exists, or becomes disrupted: formal rules of the game, features of parties and party systems that are not directly associated with PSI, government performance,

---

[2] We do not include the six indicators of change over a generation (1990–2015) or the summary country measures of PSI because they would limit us to cross-sectional analysis, with only seventeen or eighteen observations (countries). This is not enough observations for multivariate regression analysis with many independent variables. As a result, the dependent variables in this chapter capture only part of PSI – short-term, but not medium-term change and stability. Because of the high correlations between the six dependent variables in this chapter and the medium-term (1990–2015) values for these same indicators, the findings here should offer some guidance about the medium-term correlates of PSI.

TABLE 4.1 *Dependent Variables, Descriptive Statistics*

Country	Elections included	Lower chamber elections				Presidential elections			
		No. of EP	Volatility	New parties	Main party stab.	No. of EP	Volatility	New parties	Main party stab.
Argentina	1983–2011	9	20.7	3.5	89.0	7	46.9	10.2	67.6
Bolivia	1980–2009	8	39.9	8.7	67.5	7	42.1	11.5	62.9
Brazil	1986–2010	7	17.5	3.7	90.0	6	31.0	1.3	77.8
Chile	1989–2009	6	15.1	1.6	96.7	5	28.8	0.4	80.0
Colombia	1958–2010	18	16.4	6.4	96.8	10	33.1	20.7	71.7
Costa Rica	1953–2010	15	25.7	8.3	85.6	15	25.3	8.6	85.6
Dom. Republic	1978–2008	8	20.0	3.0	95.9	9	18.5	1.4	96.3
Ecuador	1979–2009	12	29.0	9.4	79.9	9	44.2	22.4	61.9
El Salvador	1984–2012	10	14.4	7.7	90.1	6	19.9	8.9	88.9
Guatemala	1985–2011	8	40.5	12.7	65.8	7	56.6	40.3	47.6
Honduras	1981–2009	8	12.6	5.8	100.0	8	11.5	5.5	100.0
Mexico	1988–2012	8	16.8	3.3	100.0	4	19.2	2.2	100.0
Nicaragua	1984–2006	5	31.4	1.1	66.6	5	32.0	2.7	76.7
Panama	1989–2009	5	29.0	9.5	76.8	5	43.4	5.6	70.0
Paraguay	1989–2008	5	26.0	9.8	81.8	5	42.1	13.0	70.0
Peru	1980–2006	7	47.1	12.9	53.6	7	54.9	21.0	50.0
Uruguay	1984–2009	6	12.0	1.6	100.0	6	10.8	0.7	100.0
Venezuela	1958–2012	12	34.1	14.0	78.3	12	32.6	17.7	72.9

Note: Country means. No. EP = Number of electoral periods. New Parties = Vote share of new parties. For Argentina, data for legislative elections extend to only 2003.

the political regime, and societal features. These theoretical approaches have deductive merit and have found empirical support in some studies on related issues.

H1. Open formal rules of the game are associated with lower PSI. Formal rules of the game affect the strategic incentives of politicians and voters, which, in turn, might affect their behavior and as a final result impact PSI. Rules of the game that either facilitate the entrance of new actors or that provide few incentives to stop voters changing their vote choice between elections are more likely to create the conditions for greater party system change (Carreras 2012; Cox 1997; Madrid 2005; Mainwaring *et al.* 2016; Roberts and Wibbels 1999; Su 2015; Tavits 2005). Open institutional arrangements facilitate greater supply-side changes in the party system, decreasing the system's predictability. Conversely, where rules help close systems, for example by making it harder for new parties to enter the system and become major contenders, we should see greater institutionalization.

H1a. Higher district magnitudes (the average number of seats per district) should make it easier for new parties to establish an electoral toehold in lower chamber elections (Cox 1997; Tavits 2006, 2008). Conversely, low district magnitudes might reduce volatility and set high barriers for new entrants. The effects of district magnitude operate partly through their impact on the number of parties (H2a), but district magnitude might have an independent effect on volatility.

We calculate district magnitude as the average number of seats per electoral district of a country, *District Magnitude (Log)*. We logged district magnitude because we expect a log-linear relationship between the average number of seats and PSI: if district magnitude has an effect on PSI, these effects should decrease as the average number of seats becomes larger.

H1b. Concurrent presidential and congressional elections should be associated with greater institutionalization. With concurrent presidential and legislative elections, members of congress have more at stake in the outcomes; their own political careers are immediately on the line. When presidential elections are not held concurrently with congressional elections, other politicians from the same party and coalition have weaker incentives to participate in the campaign (Cox 1997). Their own political careers are less directly tied to the outcome of the presidential election. This situation makes it easier for political outsiders to fare well (Carreras 2012) and might boost electoral volatility. This variable, *Concurrent*, is coded 1 if elections in both the first-round presidential and the lower chamber elections occurred on the same day, and 0 if otherwise.

H1c. Rules that allow candidates and parties to purchase TV and radio ads are associated with less institutionalization. If candidates can purchase TV and radio time, it makes it easier for outsiders and new parties to enter the system and expand. If they may not purchase TV and radio time, new parties have more

difficulty getting their message out, which could favor the survival and stability of already established parties. *Buy TV* is an indicator of whether candidates and parties can buy television and radio ads to broadcast campaign advertising or whether ads are allocated by the state. It takes the value of 1 when candidates and parties cannot independently buy air time on national media and 0 if they can't.

H1d. Regulations that grant parties exclusive access to elected positions (and that bar independents) are associated with higher PSI. In forty-four of the legislative elections we include and forty-eight of the presidential elections, independent candidates could run without being nominated by a political party. When such a regulation is in place, non-partisan candidates can challenge the existing parties, potentially decreasing PSI. The variable *Independents can run* assumes the value of 1 when this regulation exists and of 0 when it does not. We include *Independents can run (presidential elections)* in presidential elections only; we include *Independents can run (lower chamber)* in lower chamber elections only.

H1e. More difficult registration requirements for forming a new party are associated with greater PSI. Some laws make it more difficult to create new parties, possibly increasing PSI. A high required number of signatures makes it difficult to register a new party, which might favor the existing parties and limit party system change. Consistent with this theoretical intuition, Su (2015) found that a high number of signatures favored lower electoral volatility in Latin America. We follow Su (2015) and measure the NSPR, i.e., the number of signatures required, to form a new political party. Our variable follows Su's rules, converted to a 0 to 1 scale, where 0 means that no signatures are required to register a party, and 1 is the highest value registered on Su's original scale. All intermediate values are calculated as a percentage of the highest value on Su's scale.

H1f. If public funding is generous, and if it is allocated primarily on the basis of party size, and if there is a high threshold for receiving public funding, these conditions favor the main contenders and should help stabilize the party system. This variable is calculated as the interaction between the per capita amount of public funding (in US dollars) times the allocation rule times the threshold.[3] It captures the degree to which rules for public funding favor the main contenders and make it harder for new parties to emerge and for small parties to grow. A high score means that public funding of parties is generous, that it is distributed almost exclusively based on the size of the parties and hence favors large parties, and that small parties are not eligible to receive it. A low score results from little public funding, or from allocating the public funds in a way that favors small parties. *Public Funding* is scaled from 0 to 1, where 0 is the

---

[3] For details of the construction of this variable, see Online Appendix 4.1.

lowest score of any case in the dataset, 1 is the highest score, and all intermediate scores are linear interpolations based on the original scale.

H2. Some party and party system characteristics are associated with higher PSI. Following a large literature, we test several hypotheses arguing for the association between some characteristics of the party system and of the parties with greater or lower institutionalization.

H2a. A higher effective number of parties is associated with lower PSI. In many previous studies, a higher number of parties has led to increased electoral volatility; this has been one of the most consistent findings in this literature (Bartolini and Mair 1990: 131–45; Madrid 2005: 10; Mainwaring and Zoco 2007; Mainwaring *et al.* 2016; Remmer 1991; Roberts and Wibbels 1999; Tavits 2005, 2008). A more open party system, as expressed by a higher effective number of parties, might make it less daunting for politicians to form new parties, and might particularly increase extra-system volatility for this reason. It could also affect voters' logic. If the system has many parties, the ideological difference between any two contiguous parties tends to be smaller, so that citizens might more readily switch parties from one election to the next. Moreover, voters have more options to which they can defect. Conversely, if a system affords few options, voters might be less inclined to switch to a different party.[4]

Our measure is the effective number of parties (ENP) in the lower chamber (one divided by the sum of the squares of the share of each party) (Laakso and Taagepera 1979) in the first election of an electoral period when the dependent variable is measured using legislative elections results. When the dependent variable comes from presidential elections, we use the effective number of presidential candidates (ENPC). We use the logged version because we expect diminishing effects on the dependent variables as ENP increases, *EN Parties (Log)*.

H2b and H2c test the impact of what we called underpinnings of PSI in Chapter 1. In Mainwaring and Scully (1995a), these were two dimensions of PSI.

H2b. Systems in which large numbers of voters identify with a party should be more institutionalized. Where large numbers of voters identify with a party, this party should have a stable electoral base (Green *et al.* 2002; Lupu 2016; Seawright 2012), and a large swath of voters will vote for the same party consistently over time. In turn, this should generate stability at the aggregate level. There are fewer floating voters. This is why Lupu's (2016) theory about

---

[4] The effective number of parties is conceptually completely independent from electoral volatility and the vote share of new parties. The latter two variables measure electoral change at $T+1$. In contrast, the effective number of parties is based on parties' vote shares (i.e., it is a variable about levels, not about change) measured at T. Empirically, many party systems are fragmented but stable, and some erstwhile two-party systems can unravel and experience high instability (e.g., Colombia after 1990).

party system collapse hinges critically on a prior decrease in the share of partisans.

We collected information on the percentage of respondents to Latinobarometer surveys between 1997 and 2003 and the AmericasBarometer between 2006 and 2012, which reported sympathizing with a political party (Latinobarometer 2015; LAPOP 2016). Because the years when the surveys were conducted and election years did not match exactly, we used the most recent survey conducted within an electoral period.

H2c. Systems with solid party organizations should be more institutionalized. Solid party organization is a fairly proximate explanatory variable that might help explain why some systems institutionalize and others do not. Solid organizations should help politicians connect in more stable ways to voters, thus reducing volatility (Samuels and Zucco 2015; Tavits 2013; Van Dyck 2016).

We use V-Dem data to measure the strength of party organizations (one year lag). V-Dem's *National Party Organizations* variable asks coders to report the share of parties in a country that have permanent national organizations.[5] Answers in the questionnaire range from "no parties" to "all parties."[6] Using a Bayesian IRT (Item Response Theory) model, these answers are translated into a continuous scale. In theory, this indicator could vary from minus infinity to plus infinity. In reality, values range from around –3 to 3. Higher values indicate countries where all parties have permanent organizations.

H2d. Countries with more programmatic linkages between parties and voters tend to have more institutionalized systems. Some scholars have posited that programmatic linkages are likely to be more stable than clientelistic or personalistic linkages (Hanson 2010; Kitschelt *et al.* 2010; Mainwaring and Torcal 2006). Clientelistic linkages involve an exchange: a voter gives a politician her vote in exchange for some selective or club goods (a job; access to health care, education, or retirement benefits; a local school, a paved road or street). But voters can easily defect, and in competitive political markets, they might conclude that another politician's offer is better. In contrast, programmatic linkages are built on voters' belief that a party's programmatic offer is the best available. Voters' programmatic preferences tend to be fairly stable.

We used V-Dem data to measure the types of connections between voters and parties. V-Dem asked coders to describe the predominant types of

---

[5] The V-Dem survey defines what coders should understand by "permanent organizations": "A permanent organization connotes a substantial number of personnel who are responsible for carrying out party activities outside of the election season" (Coppedge *et al.* 2016b: 125)

[6] The full text of the question is: "Question: How many political parties for national-level office have permanent organizations? Responses: 0: No parties. 1: Fewer than half of the parties. 2: About half of the parties. 3: More than half of the parties. 4: All parties" (Coppedge *et al.* 2016b: 125).

linkages established by the main parties in a polity, explicitly mentioning "clientelistic," "local collective," and "programmatic" linkages.[7] Higher values in the *Programmatic Linkages* variable indicate parties with predominantly programmatic connections between parties and voters. Scores for Programmatic linkages vary from around −3 to 3.

H2e. *More polarized party systems are associated with higher PSI.* With greater polarization, voters might see greater differences among parties, increasing the cost of changing options between elections. This hypothesis is consistent with recent work on Latin America. Lupu (2016) argued that programmatic or ideological convergence among parties can lead to brand dilution, which, in turn, can weaken partisanship and make parties vulnerable to collapse if they perform badly in government. If his argument applies broadly to understanding party system change and stability rather than only to party collapse, greater polarization should be associated with greater stability. Roberts (2014) argued that party systems were more stable after the neoliberal period if erstwhile left-of-center parties during the neoliberal period did not renounce their pasts by governing to the right of center. Because left-of-center parties migrating to the right would have led to reduced party system polarization, if Roberts's argument for the post-neoliberal era was applied broadly (rather than being limited to the post-neoliberal period), we would expect less polarization to be associated with greater system upheaval. We measured polarization following Singer's formula,[8] using the electoral results and ideological scores of parties in the first election of every electoral period. Values range from approximately 0.1 to 8.3, with higher values corresponding to more polarization.

H3. *Poor government performance is associated with lower institutionalization.* Many works have found that party systems are more likely to institutionalize when governments perform well. Bad government performance could increase politicians' willingness to abandon the governing parties and to create new parties. Poor performance might also weaken voters' support for the governing party or coalition, consistent with theories of retrospective voting.

H3a. *High positive and negative rates of GDP growth are associated with less institutionalization.* Some studies have found that lower rates of economic growth or high inflation are associated with higher electoral volatility – and,

---

[7] The question is: "Among the major parties, what is the main or most common form of linkage to their constituents?" Clarification: A party-constituent linkage refers to the sort of 'good' that the party offers in exchange for political support and participation in party activities. Responses: 0: Clientelistic. Constituents are rewarded with goods, cash, and/or jobs. 1: Mixed clientelistic and local collective. 2: Local collective. Constituents are rewarded with local collective goods, e.g., wells, toilets, markets, roads, bridges, and local development. 3: Mixed local collective and policy/programmatic. 4: Policy/programmatic. Constituents respond to a party's positions on national policies, general party programs, and visions for society" (Coppedge *et al.* 2016b: 126).
[8] We thank Yen-Pin Su for sharing the data.

we expect, by extension to lower PSI (Remmer 1991, 1993; Roberts and Wibbels 1999).[9] We do not expect a direct relationship between poor economic performance and an increase in within-system volatility. Positive growth can increase instability by causing large shifts toward the governing coalition. Assume a simple two-party system consisting of governing party A and opposition party B. In its first term in office, A presides over a per capita GDP growth rate of 3%, generating high public approval and producing a vote shift of 10% in its favor in the next election. In its second term, per capita GDP declines by 3% per year, producing a vote shift of 10% against it in the subsequent election. Both good and very bad growth rates (+3% versus −3%) produce the same volatility. Diametrically opposed growth rates lead to the same prediction: greater instability.

H3b. Long-term economic growth increases institutionalization. We expect that sluggish growth over an extended time will lead to dissatisfaction with existing parties and open the doors to new contenders. Political outsiders and new parties might be more able to capitalize on public dissatisfaction. Conversely, good government performance could deter the creation of new parties.

We measure economic performance with short-term and medium-term per capita GDP growth. The short-term variable, *Growth 1 year,* records the rate of GDP per capita growth in the year prior to the second election of an electoral period. To test for the non-linear association described above, we replace the linear term by the absolute value of GDP Growth (*Growth 1 year (Absolute)*). The medium-term variable for per capita growth is calculated for periods of up to ten years, *GDP Growth (10 years)* – starting 11 years before the second election of an electoral period and finishing the year before the second election of an electoral period.[10]

H3c. Higher inflation is associated with lower institutionalization. This hypothesis again follows the logic that bad government performance is associated with lower PSI. We measure inflation with the logged rate of inflation in each country prior to the second election of an electoral period.[11] The source of data on inflation and growth is The Maddison Project (2013) for 1953–2010 and IMF data for the subsequent years (IMF 2012).

---

[9] In Roberts and Wibbels's analysis, this was true in lower chamber elections, but not presidential elections.

[10] The only exceptions for this rule are for the few observations of elections between 1945 and 1955. In these cases, the averages are over the number of years between 1945 and the year previous to the second election in an electoral period.

[11] It is not possible to calculate a log from a negative value. To minimize the number of missing observations, we assumed that inflation below 1% per year including deflation has an impact on electoral volatility that is indistinguishable from that of an inflation rate of 1%. We recorded all such cases as having a logged inflation of 0.

H3, we report results for the absolute measure of GDP Growth in the year prior to the election, the measure of long-term GDP growth (average over a ten year period), corruption, and state capacity measured with immunization records.

Online Appendices 4.3 to 4.8 report alternative specifications using the GEE estimator. The first and third model in each table replace our absolute measure of economic growth by the linear measure and inflation, respectively. The model in the fourth column replaces the measure of state capacity we used in the benchmark model (Immunization), by the second measure of state capacity we analyzed (Schooling). Finally, the fifth column replaces the Prior democracy indicator by the Stock of previous democracy indicator mentioned above.

Using a large number of covariates can sometimes suppress the coefficients of some of them, thus potentially obscuring statistically significant results. In order to confirm the findings, Online Appendices 4.9 and 4.10 report the coefficients for the bivariate regression of the dependent variables for each independent variable listed above.The main conclusions derived from the model reported below are supported by the analysis of bivariate associations.

Many hypotheses that were well grounded in previous work did not pan out. Moreover, a few covariates were statistically significant in the "wrong" direction. These results suggest more randomness in patterns of PSI and erosion than we expected, along the lines of what Powell and Tucker (2014) reported for electoral volatility in the post-communist countries.

Excellent work on related subjects (Lupu 2016; Morgan 2011; Riedl 2014; Roberts 2014; Seawright 2012; Tanaka 1998) provided reasonably parsimonious theoretical accounts about the causes of change in Latin American party systems. Our results do not mesh well with any of these accounts. To be clear, we did not directly test any of these theories, nor do any of these works – except Riedl's and perhaps Roberts's – focus on the same dependent variable (PSI) as we do. Still, our results speak to some ideas in these theories.

Are Some Institutional Rules Associated with Greater PSI?

For lower chamber elections, the answer is no; none of fifteen coefficients for these rules was significantly different from 0 at $p<0.05$. In presidential elections, three coefficients suggest that variations in PSI are associated with variations in the rules of the game. As hypothesized, PSI was higher on average, with less volatility and a lower vote share for new parties, where public funding was more generous and more concentrated on the main parties. A one-unit change in the measure of public funding, i.e., a comparison between the electoral period with the lowest and highest levels of public funding, was associated with a 19.9% (in absolute terms)

decrease in electoral volatility and a huge 28.4% decrease in the vote share of new parties.

Contrary to expectations, if independents could run for the presidency the predicted vote share of new parties was 9.13 percentage points lower. One plausible interpretation is that if independents can run, they might see less need to form new parties.

The result for the number of signatures required (NSPR) index is also statistically different from 0. Comparing countries with the most stringent rules for new party formation to countries with the least stringent rules shows that, on average, the former had 13.5 percentage points less volatility and 17.1 percentage points lower vote share for new parties. All these results are robust to different specifications of the GEE models and to the substitution of the GEE estimator by the OLS with random effects.

The null associations for other specific institutional rules do not necessarily mean that the rules of the game do not matter for PSI. It is impossible in the cross-national analysis to systematically test for the effects of country-specific rules. Some institutional rules, for example, the de facto single non-transferable vote in Colombia, the fact that lists rarely elected more than a single candidate for the national congress, and the extraordinarily high rotation among different politicians of a single seat in the national congress created powerful incentives for politicians to act as free-wheeling individuals. As Chapter 8 argues, these rules contributed to weakening the party system.

The Connection between Party System and Party Institutionalization

Consistent with expectations, results show a consistent positive association between party organizational strength and system institutionalization in both lower chamber and presidential elections. For every unit more in the strength of party organizations, volatility was 5.9% lower in lower chamber elections and 10.2% lower in presidential elections. New parties had on average 3% fewer votes (although the coefficient was statistically significant only for lower chamber elections); and the stability of main contenders was 12.8% higher in lower chamber elections and 17% higher in presidential elections – by far the largest substantive associations in our models.

These results support the conclusions of Samuels and Zucco (2015), Tavits (2013), and Van Dyck (2016) regarding the capacity of solid organizations to stabilize individual parties' vote shares and, as a result, to help institutionalize the system. Solid organizations are no panacea; AD and COPEI in Venezuela once had dense organizations. But they give parties a way of connecting to voters and building networks of activists. They can help buffer parties from the electoral effects of bad government performance, corruption scandals, and other challenges.

TABLE 4.2 (*continued*)

	Legislative			Presidential		
	1	2	3	4	5	6
Ethnic fractionalization	26.36**	1.14	−25.65*	14.12	17.09*	−10.01
	(8.81)	(3.24)	(12.50)	(9.13)	(7.85)	(10.61)

Notes: + $p<0.10$, * $p<0.05$, ** $p<0.01$, *** $p<0.001$
Estimator: GEE. Robust standard errors in parentheses. Models 1 and 4; Volatility is the dependent variable (DV). Models 2 and 5: The Vote share of new parties is the DV. Models 3 and 6: The Stability of the main parties is the DV. For Legislative elections: Observations = 157, Countries = 18. For Presidential elections: Observations = 133, Countries = 18.

Party organizations	−5.90**	−3.07**	12.80***	−10.22**	−3.01	17.01***
	(2.13)	(1.18)	(2.41)	(3.41)	(2.63)	(4.08)
Programmatic linkages	2.10	0.20	−3.68	5.12*	1.51	−8.77*
	(1.55)	(0.98)	(2.21)	(2.14)	(2.64)	(3.80)
Polarization	−0.49	−1.10	−0.81	−1.61	−0.94	0.09
	(0.95)	(0.98)	(1.55)	(1.18)	(1.13)	(1.23)
GDP growth 1 year (absolute)	0.65**	0.23	−0.65	1.23***	0.35	−2.13**
	(0.25)	(0.23)	(0.66)	(0.37)	(0.73)	(0.77)
GDP growth 10 years	−1.25	−0.57	0.75	−0.59	−0.96	0.30
	(0.82)	(0.51)	(1.01)	(0.78)	(1.09)	(1.12)
Corruption	2.22	−0.28	−3.96*	12.16	16.84*	−24.72*
	(1.58)	(0.80)	(1.62)	(7.67)	(7.50)	(11.01)
State capacity	14.76	−0.84	−24.25+	22.64+	14.47	−20.92+
	(9.18)	(5.18)	(13.66)	(11.46)	(14.13)	(11.69)
Prior democracy	4.87	−4.11	3.25	−0.37	5.15	−1.04
	(6.87)	(4.00)	(8.68)	(6.20)	(6.04)	(7.60)
Age of democracy	0.59	2.52+	3.82	1.87	1.99	−5.29
	(2.00)	(1.46)	(2.82)	(1.43)	(1.96)	(3.46)
GDP per capita	0.71	1.99	−0.96	0.31	0.57	−1.65
	(3.75)	(1.89)	(4.19)	(2.12)	(2.93)	(3.19)

H3d. High corruption is associated with lower PSI. Other forms of poor government performance could also affect PSI. Seawright (2012) argued that corruption scandals can destabilize party systems, and Pavão (2015) argued that corruption generates political disaffection, which could lead to greater volatility in party systems. We expect that voters are more likely to punish incumbents in contexts of more government corruption and to support new parties entering the system when corruption is rampant. Indicators of PSI, therefore, should be inversely associated with indicators of corruption.

We measure perception of corruption using two variables in the V-Dem project (Coppedge *et al.* 2016a). For legislative electoral periods, we use *Legislative Corruption*, measured in the year immediately before the second election for an electoral period. For presidential elections, we use V-Dem's *Executive Corruption* index, again measured in the year before the second election of an electoral period.[12] V-Dem indicators of corruption are more accurate and reliable than alternative measures and cover a much larger sample of country–years (McMann *et al.* 2016).

H3e. Greater state capacity is associated with higher PSI. Governments are more likely to succeed in policy implementation when state capacity is greater. State capacity is difficult to operationalize, but we follow a measure proposed by Soifer (2015), namely, the percentage of children between two and twenty-three months who were vaccinated against measles.

H4. An early history of democracy and longer-lasting democracy favor higher PSI.

H4a. An early and deeper history of democracy favors greater party system stability. Parties in long-established democracies developed strong organizations with deep connections to voters and organized interests, whereas most third and fourth wave democracies lack strong parties. Past democratic periods could have allowed for the development of many facilitators of PSI that come back to life once redemocratization happens. Some of those facilitators are the parties themselves, more robust civil societies, a population more used to voting and participating in representative democracy, or more responsive state institutions. The Uruguayan experience illustrates this argument: many organizations – including the parties – emerging during the process of redemocratization were built upon pre-existing networks and loyalties, most dating back from the democratic period that preceded the dictatorship of 1973–84. In light of these experiences, we could expect that where those organizations had more time and freedom to develop, they

---

[12] *Executive Corruption* is an index that ranges from 0 to 1, where 0 means less corrupt and 1 means more corrupt. In the original V-Dem dataset, *Legislative Corruption* varies from around −3 to 3, with lower values indicating more corruption. In order to facilitate comparisons, we multiply the values for the *Legislative Corruption* indicator by −1, so both vary in the same direction (from less to more corrupt).

facilitate PSI once redemocratization happens. Consequently, we expect that countries with a democratic past would be more likely to see greater levels of PSI contemporaneously.

We measure past experience with democracy in two ways. First, we count the number of years that countries were democratic or semi-democratic (i.e., scored at least 2 on the Polity IV scale) from 1900 until the beginning of their current electoral regime and divide by the total number of years from 1900 to the beginning of the current electoral regime. This measure emphasizes time under democracy (Prior Democracy). Alternatively, one could argue that it is not as much the time spent under democracy but the degree to which countries were democratic that allows for the development of the features that correlate to higher contemporaneous levels of PSI. Following Gerring *et al.* (2012), we measure the "stock" of previous democracy countries have. We sum the values of Polity IV scores for all years between 1900 and the year prior to the start of the current electoral regime (with an early depreciation rate of 1%). Higher values indicate countries with previous democratic experiences that were intense and long. Intermediate values indicate either short-term very democratic experiences or long-term semi-democratic histories. Low values indicate countries where authoritarianism prevailed.

H4b. Party system stability increases over time as a democracy ages. Converse (1969) argued that it takes time for voters to understand what different parties represent and therefore to identify with a party. In the early stages of a democracy, he expected a large number of floating voters who have not yet identified with a party. In turn, a large number of floating voters should generate considerable electoral volatility (Dalton and Weldon 2007). Over time, more citizens should identify with a party, leading to greater aggregate stability. Likewise, political elites might over time become more committed to party building, leading to tighter connections between voters and parties and greater PSI.[13]

Age of democracy is the number of years since the inauguration of the current "electoral regime." The expectation of a log-linear relationship between this variable and the outcomes of interest justifies the usage of the logged version of this variable.

H5a and H5b focus on the impact of societal features on PSI. Some societal features might make it more likely that voters will establish strong connections

---

[13] With cross-regional samples, however, Mainwaring and Torcal (2006), Mainwaring and Zoco (2007), and Mainwaring *et al.* (2016) argued against this hypothesis, showing that electoral volatility did not decrease over time if *Birthyear of Democracy* was also in the equation. Nevertheless, the hypothesis that stabilization occurs over time might hold for our Latin American sample. Tavits (2008) found that the vote share of new parties first decreased and then increased.

to parties, leading to more institutionalized systems. For this reason, we add two control variables.

H5a. A higher level of development is associated with greater party system stability. Wealthier countries might have more stable party systems for a variety of reasons. We treat this possibility as a control variable. Per capita GDP proxies this variable. Data come from the Maddison Project (2013) (logged).

H5b. Greater ethnic fractionalization is associated with lower party system institutionalization. Madrid (2005) argued that Latin American party systems with greater indigenous populations were beset by greater volatility because parties never established connections with the indigenous peoples, disposing them to shift support to new parties once parties that actively courted indigenous votes emerged. Arguments about ethnicity have also figured in some accounts of African party systems. We test arguments about the impact of ethnicity using a common measure of *Ethnic Fractionalization.*

The coverage of data for some variables is limited. Their overlap is even more restricted, which would make jointly testing for associations of each of these variables almost impossible; with list-wise deletion, we would end up with too few observations for statistical analysis. To circumvent this problem, we used multiple imputation to estimate values for the missing observations in the independent variables using the Amelia II software (Blackwell *et al.* 2015), estimating values for all electoral periods described above.

ESTIMATION AND RESULTS

To test for the relationship between PSI and its hypothesized covariates we use a Generalized Estimation Equations model with an AR-1 correlation structure, which is appropriate for contexts in which the dependent variable may not be independent over time from its previous values. We clustered standard errors by country. Overall, this makes for a very demanding estimation setting; it is difficult to obtain statistically significant results, and statistically significant results are probably not spurious. Given that we use ten multiply imputed datasets to overcome problems of missing data, regression results shown below are coefficients that aggregate over all datasets using the rules described by Rubin (1975).

Robustness tests (Online Appendix 4.2) use random effects with standard errors clustered by countries. These estimation strategies are in line with previous analyses of similar data (Mainwaring *et al.* 2016; Weghorst and Bernhard 2014). Results for these robustness checks mimic the conclusions of the GEE models.

Table 4.2 reports results that test most of the hypotheses listed above. We concentrate on a model that tests the hypotheses that we consider theoretically most relevant, and report results testing the other hypotheses in the Online Appendix. Below, we include all variables listed under H1, H2, and H5. From

TABLE 4.2 *Benchmark Regression Results*

	Legislative			Presidential		
	1	2	3	4	5	6
District magnitude	0.09	1.53	-1.39			
	(1.65)	(0.94)	(2.21)			
Runoff				0.27	-0.40	2.97
				(3.31)	(4.16)	(6.08)
Concurrent	3.80	3.12	-5.24	-8.06	-9.63	9.61
	(2.49)	(2.12)	(3.34)	(5.88)	(7.55)	(6.53)
Buy TV	-4.89	-4.26	16.86+	-4.53	-10.63+	-1.36
	(5.35)	(3.53)	(8.88)	(4.53)	(5.44)	(6.10)
Independents can run	-0.32	-1.03	5.90+	-1.70	-9.13**	2.58
	(3.53)	(2.11)	(3.06)	(3.01)	(3.44)	(4.30)
NSPR	-6.64	-0.65	-7.02	-13.56+	-17.18*	5.99
	(5.96)	(3.83)	(9.79)	(7.79)	(6.77)	(10.40)
Public funding	-7.86	-11.39	-23.52	-19.89*	-28.44*	16.48
	(10.13)	(7.29)	(14.26)	(9.71)	(11.35)	(18.30)
EN parties (log)	3.44	1.40	-12.08*	25.21***	8.32	-41.05***
	(4.81)	(2.30)	(4.68)	(5.34)	(5.32)	(7.02)
Party ID	0.90	0.59	-4.49	8.45	-10.96	-14.08
	(8.19)	(6.54)	(12.45)	(11.32)	(10.47)	(16.44)

How Are Other Party and Party System Characteristics Associated with PSI?

One of the most puzzling results was for programmatic linkages. Contrary to the findings of Kitschelt *et al.* 2010 and Mainwaring and Torcal 2006, systems that had a perception of stronger programmatic linkages were associated with increased electoral volatility and lower stability of the main parties – though the substantive effects were modest (a one unit increase in programmatic linkages was associated with a 5.1% increase in electoral volatility and a 8.7% decrease in the stability of main contenders). In the 2000s, in cases such as Bolivia, Ecuador, and Venezuela, the new radical left developed programmatic connections, but also in the short-term profoundly disrupted the established party systems. The combination of programmatic linkages and profound disruptions of party systems in these three cases is emblematic of the broader pattern detected in the statistical analysis.[14] In lower chamber elections, there was no statistically significant association between levels of PSI and programmatic competition.

Contrary to the expectations of the comparative literature (Converse 1969; Dalton and Weldon 2007) and some work on Latin America (Lupu 2016; Seawright 2012), higher aggregate levels of partisan identification were not associated, on average, with greater PSI. Coefficients were all over the place and standard errors were huge, indicating major across-country variation in the association between Party ID and indicators of PSI.

The high individual-level instability of party identification in some countries, including Brazil and Mexico, suggests one possible reason: if partisanship is not a strong and stable social identity, it will not form a reservoir of electoral support for individual parties. In that case, parties might be vulnerable to steep electoral declines, even if they have meaningful numbers of partisans. The PT's electoral setback in Brazil in 2016 supports this hypothesis, especially if confirmed by subsequent results. Another possibility is that partisanship might buffer individual parties from precipitous electoral decline, but that other parties in the system, without the benefit of many partisans, are still subject to the withering effects that batter many parties in third and fourth wave democracies. As a result, the system could still be unstable.

Consistent with many previous studies, the effective number of parties in legislative and presidential elections had a negative association with PSI: a higher effective number of parties was correlated with greater volatility and more votes for new parties, and lower stability of the main contenders. These results were particularly pronounced in presidential elections. For visualization, we plotted (Figures 4.1 and 4.2) the expected levels of each dependent variable at different (exponentiated) values of EN Parties (Log), with other variables in

---

[14] To ensure that the measure was capturing relevant dimensions of party systems in Latin America, we regressed the indicator of ideological stability of Latin American party systems discussed in Chapter 2 on the Programmatic linkages variable (results not shown). We found a strong and positive effect, indicating that as expected parties' ideological stability is higher where linkages between voters and parties are based on programmatic grounds.

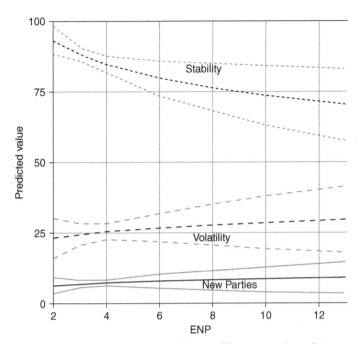

FIGURE 4.1 Predicted Value of DVs at Different Effective Number of Parties – Lower Chamber
Note: 95% confidence intervals in shaded lines.

the regression kept at their means. On average, electoral periods with three presidential parties had 10% more volatility (33%) than systems with two parties (23%) – a meaningful substantive association.

Once again against expectations, results do not show a statistically significant association between PSI and party system polarization. The works by Lupu (2016) on how brand differentiation fosters partisanship and serves as an inoculation against party collapse, by Morgan (2011) and Seawright (2012) on how gaps in programmatic representation make established parties vulnerable to collapse, and by Levitsky *et al.* (2016b) on the positive effects of sharp conflict on party building suggest that more polarized systems might anchor voters more to their parties and create greater systemic stability and predictability. The absence of statistically significant differences is robust even if we exclude some potential confounders of polarization, such as the measure of programmatic connections between parties and voters.

In sum, results show a close association between PSI and the set of parties that form the system. This is not surprising: party system characteristics such as the level of institutionalization should be highly associated with the nature and features of the parties themselves. These associations are probabilistic, not deterministic: on average parties that have stronger organizations, and party

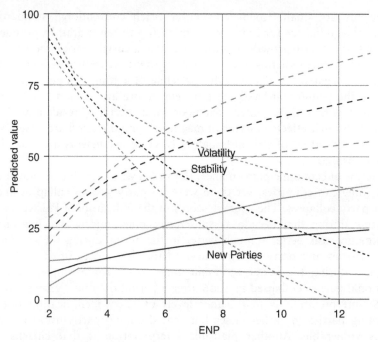

FIGURE 4.2 Predicted Value of DVs at Different Effective Number of Parties – Presidential
Note: 95% confidence intervals in shaded lines.

systems with fewer parties are more institutionalized, but that is not always the case. On average, PSI in Latin America was not greater where more party–voter linkages were more programmatic, where a larger number of voters identified with parties, and where polarization was higher. These negative findings are more surprising than the positive ones.

Is Better Government Performance and State Capacity Associated with Higher PSI?

Economic crisis has figured prominently in previous accounts of party system volatility (Roberts 2014), party system collapse (Morgan 2011; Seawright 2012; Tanaka 1998), and party collapse (Lupu 2016) in Latin America – although all of these authors had sophisticated interactive arguments. Moreover, the extensive literature on economic voting suggests that economic downturns or high inflation could disrupt party systems. In light of this previous literature, the relationship between economic crisis and PSI in Latin America has been surprisingly weak.

In both lower chamber and presidential elections, the association between per capita GDP growth and PSI is consistent with expectations, but the coefficients are small. Coefficients never reach conventional standards of statistical significance for long-term growth (up to ten years). In presidential elections, short-term growth volatility exhibited a curvilinear relationship with indicators of PSI, predicting lower PSI when growth was either strongly positive or sharply negative. A 1% growth or decline of a country's per capita GDP between the penultimate and the last year before an election is on average associated with 0.65% (lower chamber) and 1.23% (Presidential) higher volatility. Similar effects in terms of magnitude and direction are observed for the other indicators of PSI, although only some coefficients are statistically different from 0.

In terms of economic performance, the 1980s was a terrible decade in most Latin American countries, yet there were no party system collapses and no major party collapses. The average scores in the indicators of PSI were about the same during that decade as subsequent ones, during which economic performance was better – much better in the 2000s during the commodity boom. Parties and party systems survived the deep crises of the 1980s but collapsed during the better economic times later; for example, Ecuador's traditional parties collapsed in 2006 after a period of robust growth. Lupu's (2016) interpretation is that higher levels of party identification buffered governing parties in earlier crises but that declining partisanship left these parties vulnerable. Another plausible interpretation is that citizens were willing to stick to the traditional parties for a while, but then, as economic malaise extended or returned, they punished parties (Pop-Eleches 2010). The data make clear that an economic explanation of party system upheaval is woefully inadequate; other factors contributed to the extraordinary upheaval of party systems during this time.

The results of economic performance on PSI here are weaker than those reported by Mainwaring *et al.* (2016) in a cross-regional analysis of sixty-seven countries and 618 electoral periods. In the Mainwaring *et al.* (2016) sample, each increase of 1% in the GDP growth rate was associated with 0.9% lower electoral volatility ($p<0.01$) and 0.8% lower extra-system volatility ($p<0.01$) in lower chamber elections compared to 0.6% ($p<0.01$) for total volatility and 0.2% for extra-system volatility for our Latin American sample. At times, Latin American party systems endured brutal recessions and hyperinflation without massive upheaval. If they had been affected as much by bad performance as the average case in the Mainwaring *et al.* dataset, volatility would have been even higher. In sum, economic performance affected PSI during this time period, but on average, the impact was modest. The interesting question is why bad economic performance had a weak impact on PSI.

Alternatively, we tested whether inflation rates were associated with greater PSI. Results are in Tables A4.3–A4.8 in the Online Appendix and show that PSI is smaller where inflation is larger, but substantive effects are weak. This association is more often substantively different from 0 in presidential elections than in lower chamber elections.

Seawright (2012) emphasized corruption scandals as a major factor in party system breakdown in Peru and Venezuela. The regressions here show a connection between PSI and corruption – particularly between greater corruption in the executive and lower institutionalization of presidential party systems. On average, presidential electoral periods that had greater levels of executive corruption also had a higher vote share of new parties and less stability in the main contenders (consistent with Seawright). A one-unit increase in executive corruption is associated with an average increase of 16.8% in the vote share of new parties and a drop of 24.7% in the stability of main contenders. However, a one-unit change in executive corruption is a comparison between the least corrupt (a value of 0) and the most corrupt country in the world (a value of 1). Although there are a few instances in which Latin American electoral periods assumed values close to those extremes (Chile has values close to 0, while Venezuela has values around 0.9 in recent years), most of the cases are around the center of the scale, implying that differences in terms of how corruption and PSI are associated are moderate. Legislative corruption was associated with PSI in legislative elections to a lesser degree, with coefficients pointing in the right direction when tested against volatility and the stability of the main parties, with just the latter being statistically different from 0.

Surprisingly, the regressions show that PSI tends to be lower in electoral periods with a higher score for state capacity, but the substantive association is weak. Results in Table 4.2 above measured state capacity as the percentage of children between two and twenty-three months who were vaccinated against measles. In a comparison between a country where no children are vaccinated versus a country where 100% of children are vaccinated (variable scaled 0 to 1), the latter tend to have higher electoral volatility, new parties perform better, and stability is lower. The associations are weaker because during the time of our sample, Latin America was highly urbanized and a basic education had been universalized in many of the countries. The mean for the sample is that 80% of the children were in school, with a standard deviation of 17%, implying that a standard deviation difference in state capacity between two countries is associated with 3.8% more volatility in presidential elections in the country with more state capacity.

This is a counterintuitive result because countries with the greatest state capacity in Latin American have institutionalized party systems (Chile, and Uruguay, for example). However, this result in Tables A4.1 and A4.2 in the Online Appendix holds in bivariate tests. Results are similar (and more often statistically different from 0) in the tables in the appendix that replace state capacity (immunization) with state capacity (schooling).

In sum, although better government performance tends to be associated with PSI, average differences in levels of institutionalization in countries with better and worse performance tend to be small. This raises doubts about theoretical accounts that focus on economic performance as a major driver of party system change in Latin America.

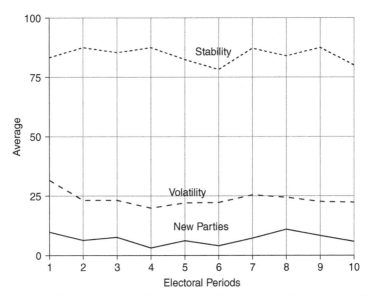

FIGURE 4.3 Evolution of PSI Indicators over Electoral Periods – Lower Chamber Elections
Note: Number of electoral periods since the establishment of democracy or semi-democracy.

Has Party System Institutionalization Increased as Democracies Aged in Latin America?

Figures 4.3 and 4.4 provide convincing evidence against this hypothesis. We plotted regional averages for each indicator of PSI in lower chamber and presidential elections. Despite important within-country variations, there has been no clear trend toward greater institutionalization over time in the region. This is not a new finding: Roberts and Wibbels (1999) motivated their contribution by stating that electoral volatility in Latin America did not fall as expected during the 1990s.

Regression results confirm this conclusion. No matter how we measure the passage of time (number of electoral periods, number of years since democratic transition, and number of years since democratic transition logged), there was no tendency toward increasing PSI over time. Coefficients in Table 4.2 are usually in the opposite direction from the one hypothesized, but standard errors are large, usually larger than the coefficients themselves. On average, countries had similar levels of PSI no matter how many elections/years they experienced. These results reproduce the findings of Mainwaring and Torcal (2006), Mainwaring and Zoco (2007) and Mainwaring *et al.* (2016) who, with cross-regional samples, showed that electoral volatility

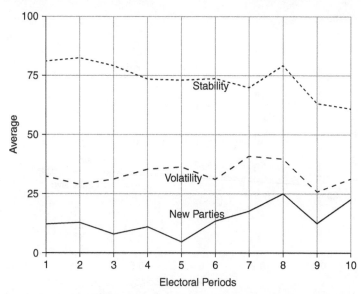

FIGURE 4.4 Evolution of PSI Indicators over Electoral Periods – Presidential Elections
Note: Number of electoral periods since the establishment of democracy or semi-democracy.

did not decrease over time. On average, the forces that have led to party system erosion have been as strong as those that have favored institutionalization.

The results underscore a major democratic paradox in the third wave of democratization in Latin America: party systems remain important for facilitating important democratic processes and outcomes, but the path to institutionalization is tenuous and is not secure even once it is seemingly achieved. In the last decade, some of the most discernible movement toward institutionalization has occurred under regimes that are increasingly autocratic. Enduring party weakness is among the factors that have hampered Latin America's democratization in the third wave.

Does an Early History of Democracy Favor Greater Party System Stability?

Some scholars argued that early democracies were more favorable to the development of strong parties (Gunther 2005; Mainwaring and Zoco 2007; Mainwaring *et al.* 2016; Schmitter 2001). Along related lines, Roberts and Wibbels (1999) showed that volatility was lower in Latin American democracies with parties that were established earlier. Our results are not consistent with these previous arguments.

There are multiple ways to model the effects of the democratic past. One approach is to concentrate on early elections. If past democratic experiences

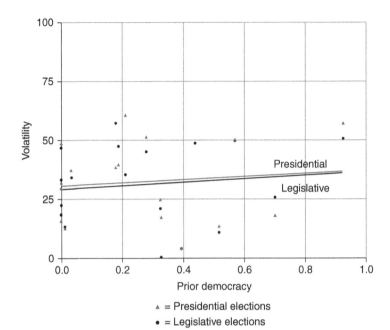

FIGURE 4.5 Electoral Volatility in the First Electoral Period by % of Previous Years under Democracy

facilitate the emergence of institutionalized party systems once democracy returns, countries with more democratic pasts should have greater PSI after their first electoral period. This is not the case. The data in Figure 4.5 show no clear association between previous democratic experience and volatility measured in the first electoral period for the new electoral regime. Similar results derive from the evaluation of the relationship between the "stock" of past democracy and PSI in the first electoral period (not shown). Although the lines that summarize the linear association are slightly tilted upward, statistical estimation of confidence intervals suggests that the association is not significantly different from 0.

Alternatively, the effects of a democratic past might not be time specific, but resonate over the whole contemporaneous experience with democracy. Realizing how hard it has been to institutionalize party systems in the region, we could hypothesize that the contemporaneous effects of past democracy consist of moving levels of PSI up or down on average for all elections. Modeling the linear association between past democratic experiences and PSI over the whole time series of data tests this hypothesis. Again, results show no significant association as seen in Table 4.2. Coefficients are small and standard errors are large, indicating that there is major variation in the observations. These null findings are robust to different specifications of the benchmark model and to the replacement of the *Age of democracy* variable by the stock measure of democracy (see tables in the Online Appendix).

In sum, longer and more democratic previous regimes are not associated with higher levels of PSI in contemporary Latin America. During the third wave, countries with long histories of democracy were no more likely to have an institutionalized party system than countries that had almost no democratic experience prior to the third wave.

The consistent finding here that *Prior Democracy* had no association with PSI runs counter to the finding in Mainwaring and Zoco (2007) and Mainwaring *et al.* (2016) that early democracy was favorable to institutionalized party systems. The earlier findings were based on broader cross-national samples and for somewhat different time periods (beginning as early as 1945 and ending in 2006). The difference in results suggests the possibility that an important general finding has not held for Latin America, and it raises the question of why this is the case.

One speculation about this result: the quarter century analyzed in this volume was one of such painful transitions in Latin America that some "normal" average tendencies (such as the general tendency of a long democratic tradition being favorable to PSI) were wiped out. Many of the scores on the dependent and independent variables in our analyses were extraordinary outliers. Many Latin American countries in the third wave experienced profound change in the membership of the party system and exceptionally high electoral volatility. Most experienced hyperinflation and long periods of economic retrenchment. It is not surprising that regression results that include the advanced industrial democracies as a basis for a majority of the electoral periods do not consistently mesh with Latin American results during a highly turbulent era.

The most exceptional outliers relative to the finding in Mainwaring and Zoco (2007) and Mainwaring *et al.* (2016), i.e., the countries with long democratic traditions that experienced massive party system dislocations from 1990 to 2015, are Venezuela and Colombia. From 1978 to 2003, Venezuela had one of the worst rates of economic growth in the world, and its growth performance was almost uniquely bad – excluding countries that experienced civil war. In much of the 1990s, Colombia had the highest homicide rate in Latin America and one of the highest in the world, a massive problem of kidnapping, and the world's largest population of displaced people. The crises in both countries were severe, and they lasted for decades. For an extended time, voters turned to the establishment parties for solutions, but eventually large numbers defected. It is not surprising that extraordinary crises of such magnitudes and durations helped shatter the positive institution-building consequences one would expect from protracted experiences with democracy.

Do Levels of Development or Ethnic Fractionalization Correlate with PSI?

Finally, we tested whether levels of development or ethnic fractionalization were associated with PSI. While we did not find support for the first argument in any specification of our model, there was a robust association between ethnic fractionalization and the indicators of PSI. Those findings were robust to the different specifications of the model and to the replacement of the GEE estimator by the random effects estimator. However, the effects are small: a standard deviation difference between two countries in ethnic fractionalization (0.17, similar to the difference between Venezuela and Peru) tends to be associated with 4.48 percentage points more volatility and 4.3 percentage points less stability of the main parties in lower chamber elections, and 2.9 percentage points more votes for new parties. Results for the other dependent variables are not statistically significant.

CONCLUSIONS

This analysis has several limitations. We have largely avoided causal claims based on the results. The results are correlational, and limits to causal inference remain even after this cautionary note is included. We employed a demanding estimation strategy – estimating clustered standard errors and AR1 correlations costs many degrees of freedom – which limits how much we can say with these models.

Caution is also in order due to potential endogeneity problems. For example, given that institutional arrangements are endogenous to political systems, some of the rules of the game here described as potentially increasing PSI could be caused by them. The literature on the cartelization of party systems in Europe (Katz and Mair 1995) suggests that this is indeed the case: strong parties may manipulate rules and increase the availability of public resources to reinforce their dominant position. Positive associations might derive not from the fact that certain rules help party systems to institutionalize but rather because institutionalized party systems are more likely to put those regulations in place.[15] The measures of the rules are always temporally antecedent to the six indicators used as dependent variables in this chapter, which diminishes but does not resolve the problem of endogeneity. Likewise, in principle, solid party organizations could help party systems to institutionalize, but the reverse is also true: a stable and predictable institutional environment creates more incentives for politicians to develop the longer time horizons that are conductive to investing in party building.

Our ability to test for complex interactions was limited, in part because of statistical limits stemming from degrees of freedom. Yet the processes that promote PSI or erosion probably involve complex interactions. The major works on related issues in Latin American party systems (e.g., party system collapse, party collapse, profound party system change) all invoke interactions (Lupu 2016; Morgan 2011; Roberts 2014; Seawright 2012; Tanaka 1998).

---

[15] For Latin America in this period, this particular endogeneity problem is not too worrisome because the results were mostly not significant.

Finally, the quantitative testing is based on electoral periods as the unit of analysis,[16] but our abiding theoretical interest is explaining country outcomes. Still, results based on electoral periods reveal useful information about the factors associated with PSI and erosion.

The results in this chapter suggest two critical questions for future research. Why do so many results defy expectations and results from previous work based on different sets of countries and time periods? For example, why was earlier history of democracy not an asset to PSI during most episodes of democratization, contrary to the findings of Mainwaring and Zoco (2007) and Mainwaring *et al.* (2016) for broader sets of countries? Second, given the large number of null and weak findings, are we missing some explanations and variables that are important for understanding PSI in contemporary Latin America?

Despite these limitations, we can draw some conclusions. First and foremost, PSI does not occur randomly. It is associated with the survival of organizationally strong parties that anchor the system and stabilize patterns of electoral competition. Although in principle patterns of interaction could stabilize without strong parties, party systems tend to be more institutionalized where parties are organizationally stronger.

On average, party systems were more institutionalized when parties were more organized, when governments enjoyed better economic performance, when formal rules of the game made it more difficult for new parties to enter, and where there were fewer parties.

The results indicate that more theorizing about the causes of PSI is needed. While all hypotheses build on well-established theoretical approaches to understanding party system change and stability, only a few found empirical support in contemporary Latin America. Either the routes to institutionalization and erosion in Latin America are more idiosyncratic than expected based on existing theories, or else we have not been able to capture them with the approach here.

One important factor that has been under-theorized in work on party system change and stability is the impact presidents can have in shaping and reconfiguring party systems. Because they are elected independently, have great power in most democracies, and are not subject to removal by legislatures except in cases of impeachment or other extraordinary circumstances, presidents typically have more power than prime ministers over parties.[17] In contexts of crisis-ridden democracies, they can sometimes dramatically and purposefully weaken parties, seeing them as obstacles to their routes to delegative democracy (O'Donnell 1994) or to competitive authoritarianism. Social science correctly prioritizes systematic explanation, but we should not overlook the profound

---

[16] Some of the covariates (for example, prior history of democracy) are based on long sweeps of time, so the analysis is not limited to short-term effects.

[17] A major work on this issue is Samuels and Shugart (2010).

impact some presidents have had in effecting deep change in party systems. In Venezuela, Hugo Chávez purposefully overthrew Venezuela's old parties. They had eroded considerably from their heyday of the 1960s through the 1980s, but they did not collapse in 1998 when he was first elected. Their collapse occurred later, after they had been subjected to several electoral cycles of machinations. The presidents of Bolivia (Evo Morales, 2006–present), Ecuador (Rafael Correa, 2007–present), and Honduras (Manuel Zelaya, 2005–09) attempted to follow Chávez's path. Morales and Correa encouraged and presided over the collapse of the party systems in their countries, thus accounting for, along with Chávez, three of the four cases of party system collapse in contemporary Latin America (Peru in the 1990s is the other). The coup that ousted Zelaya, whom the Honduran military, court system, and political elite feared was trying to follow in the path of Chávez, Morales, and Correa, led to the destabilization of what had been the region's most institutionalized party system. In the period after Chávez assumed power, these four countries have been responsible for some of the most dramatic changes in party systems in world democratic history.

Associations between some factors and PSI have been robust within some regions, while they disappear when the sample changes. If regional boundaries provide scope conditions for some of the theories advanced in the literature, those scope conditions have not yet been fully articulated and deserve close examination. We agree with Crabtree and Golder (2016), who called for further investment in theoretical development in this area.

The case studies that follow offer insights about why the party systems in Latin America's seven biggest countries followed their unique trajectories. They are essential complements to this chapter, just as this chapter is an essential complement to the case studies.

PART II

COUNTRY CASES

5

Resilience and Change: The Party System in Redemocratized Chile

J. Samuel Valenzuela, Nicolás Somma, and Timothy R. Scully

A party system with clearly defined issue polarities has been a long-standing feature of Chile's political life, and Mainwaring and Scully (1995a) considered it one of the few "institutionalized" systems in Latin America.[1] If parties are formed, strengthened, and sustained both through the creation of like-minded political groups in legislatures as well as through regular and repeated electoral contests, Chile constitutes a textbook case. Its legislative institutions date back to the dawn of the Republic, and their membership was generated through electoral contests held at least once every three years since 1823. From the 1890s, six to eight major parties and a variable number of smaller ones have competed in national elections, and the great majority of presidents, congressmen, and mayors have been associated with them.

The breakdown of Chilean democracy in 1973, as General Augusto Pinochet, with the complicity of the Nixon administration, deposed the government of Salvador Allende (1970–73), created the greatest crisis the nation's parties have ever faced. Pinochet closed the congress and outlawed those that had supported Allende's coalition (Socialists, Communists, Radicals, and minor Christian Left and Social Democratic groups). He also "suspended" the activities of the Christian Democratic Party (PDC)[2] and of the rightist National Party – the label adopted by the Conservative and Liberal parties of nineteenth-century origin and a smaller rightist group when they merged in 1966. In March 1977, Pinochet banned all party activities with the purpose of dismantling those of the PDC. Nonetheless, centrist and leftist party activists reemerged as important players when massive monthly protests began against the Pinochet regime in May of 1983 (Valenzuela and Valenzuela 1986). Although the protests did not dislodge Pinochet from power, he lost a 1988

[1] Our appreciation to the Luksic program of academic exchanges between the University of Notre Dame and the Pontificia Universidad Católica de Chile, which provided funding for this collaborative research. Our thanks as well to Millicent Bader, who served as our research assistant.
[2] We use Spanish language acronyms for all party labels. They appear in Table 5.1.

plebiscite that was intended to give him a further eight years in office following the dictates of "transitory articles" in the 1980 Constitution that he himself had enacted. Under such circumstances, the same constitutional provisions required holding open presidential and congressional elections within a year. Having relabeled itself the Concertation of Parties for Democracy, the coalition of center and leftist parties, created to defeat Pinochet, also won the 1989 elections while running against the candidates of an alliance of the right.[3] The leaders of the right had tried to form a single party, but they emerged from the dictatorship divided into two main forces, the National Renewal (RN) and the Union of Independent Democrats (UDI). Given that the Chilean transition did not create a *new* democracy as the Christian Democrat Patricio Aylwin assumed the presidency in March of 1990 for a four-year term, but consisted, instead, of a process of *re*democratization, the Chilean polity rapidly reacquired a key component of consolidated democratic regimes: the notion that electoral processes were to be, once again, the "only means" to reach positions of governmental power.[4] This characteristic is also a central feature of PSI (Mainwaring and Scully 1995a: 14).

Chile's party system has been largely structured since the return of competitive politics around the two coalitions that were formed to support or oppose Pinochet's bid to continued rule. This coalitional arrangement was powerfully reinforced by a "binomial" electoral formula imposed by the dictatorship on party leaderships in May 1989 for congressional elections. It created districts that elected only two representatives, obligated partisan lists to run only two candidates per district, and assigned both seats to the winning list only if it obtained twice the vote of the runner up list.[5] As a result, parties had strong incentives to run their candidates as part of two larger inter-party agreements whose lists elected almost all members of congress in the post-transition period. Nonetheless, smaller parties and movements have presented candidates in all elections since 1989, even congressional ones, capturing between a tenth and a quarter of the vote. And after municipal elections were reinstated through a constitutional amendment in 1992, the main parties that form part of the Concertation have usually created two pacts to put forward their candidates for municipal council seats.

In this chapter, we examine the recomposition of the party system during the Pinochet years and its characteristics after the quarter of a century that has elapsed since the return to elected government in 1990. A key feature of a party system's institutionalization is the relative stability of electoral outcomes.

---

[3] This coalition has changed its name, but not its main composition, several times. Its longest lasting one was "Alliance for Chile." For the sake of clarity, we refer to it as the "Alliance" here.
[4] See J. S. Valenzuela (1985: 31–34) for a discussion of the importance of this notion for democracy.
[5] This is equivalent to applying a D'Hondt proportional representation formula with a district magnitude of two. And yet, a D'Hondt system does not necessarily require, as did the binomial mechanism, that the parties present only two candidates per district.

Hence, a main focus of this chapter is to explain this phenomenon. We also address scholarly debates on the post-dictatorship configuration of the party system, the determinants of voter choices, the consequences of the abrogation of obligatory voting in 2012, and the effects of the binomial electoral system. We draw much of our evidence from a survey conducted through face–to-face interviews applied to 1,470 respondents with a random sample of major urban areas of the country in January and February 2014, soon after the conclusion of the second round of the 2013 presidential election.[6]

CONTINUITIES IN VOTER OPTIONS

If a main feature of a party system's institutionalization is the relative stability of the vote for its various ideological and programmatic tendencies, then this characteristic has not only been an attribute of the Chilean party system since the 1930s, but it also leapfrogged Pinochet's nearly seventeen years of dictatorial rule. Thus, during the 1937 to 1973 period the average right, center, and left proportions of the vote in lower house legislative elections were 29.6%, 30.4%, and 24.2%, respectively.[7] The same vote shares in the elections between 1992 and 2016 – as can be seen in Table 5.1 – were 32%, 25.5%, and 25.9%. Moreover, the sum of the vote for the major parties that make up these three tendencies both before and after the dictatorship has been about the same with an average of a little over 80% of the total.[8] We resort to the municipal elections in the period after the return to democracy for these calculations because the binomial rules used in the post-transition legislative elections do not provide an accurate view of the actual levels of electoral support for the parties. By compelling the parties to join larger inter-party electoral pacts that could only field two candidates per district, such rules prevented them from freely

[6] The survey was concluded in February 2014, and administered by the Institute of Sociology of the Pontifical Catholic University of Chile. It is representative of the nation as a whole, as only about 10% of Chileans live in rural areas.

[7] Calculated from legislative election results in A. Valenzuela (1985: pp. 58–61). We omit the left's vote in 1949, 1953, and 1957 given that it was weakened by a cold war era removal of members of the Communist Party from the electoral rolls, and a ban on the presentation of candidates under its party label.

[8] "Major parties" are those that received on average more than 5% of the vote and presented candidates in all of the elections in each period (albeit discounting the results of the left in the years noted in the previous footnote). During the 1937 to 1973 period, we consider both the National Party and the *Falange Nacional* to be "major parties" on the right and center, respectively; the first as an extension of the Conservatives and Liberals, and the second as a precursor of the PDC. It is difficult to estimate the size of the social Christian and traditionalist Conservative votes before 1957, although the former should be classified as centrist and the latter rightist. Hence, the averages for the 1937 to 1973 period are, strictly speaking, approximations. The Socialist vote before 1973 adds all Socialist factions to the left total when they ran separately. In the post-1992 period, the leftist tendency includes the votes for the Party for Democracy. The party labels on the right are different between the two periods, but they share the same overall tendency. The Radical Party label changed partially after 1994.

TABLE 5.1 *Vote Share for Major Parties Divided into Right, Center, and Left Tendencies in Municipal Council Elections: Chile, 1992–2016*

Parties	1992	1996	2000	2004	2008	2012	2016	Average
RIGHT:								
UDI	13.2	12.8	16.0	18.8	15.1	17.1	16.1	15.6
RN	16.4	18.5	15.5	15.1	16.1	15.7	17.7	16.4
Total	*29.6*	*31.3*	*31.5*	*33.9*	*31.2*	*32.8*	*33.8*	*32.0*
CENTER:								
PDC	28.9	26.0	21.6	20.3	14.0	15.1	12.8	19.8
PRSD	4.9	6.5	5.2	4.6	5.2	5.7	7.4	5.7
Total	*33.8*	*32.5*	*26.8*	*24.9*	*19.2*	*20.8*	*20.2*	*25.5*
LEFT:								
PPD	9.2	11.7	11.4	10.0	8.5	9.9	8.8	9.9
PS	8.5	10.7	11.3	10.9	11.2	12.2	10.7	10.8
PC	6.6	5.1	3.2	4.9	5.0	6.4	5.4	5.2
Total	*24.3*	*27.5*	*25.9*	*25.8*	*24.7*	*28.5*	*24.9*	*25.9*
Total Major Party Vote	87.7	91.3	84.2	84.6	75.1	82.1	78.9	83.4

Notes: The figures include the percentage of the vote obtained by "independents" only if they were associated to major party lists, as defined in footnote 8. The party labels are: UDI, Union of Independent Democrats. RN, National Renewal. PDC, Christian Democratic Party. PRSD, Social Democratic Radical Party. PPD, Party for Democracy. PS, Socialist Party. PC, Communist Party. *Source:* Calculated from Chilean Electoral Service figures (for the 1992–2012 elections, see SERVEL 2014; for the 2016 results, see SERVEL 2016).

presenting their own choices everywhere they wanted to do so, and led them to receive the votes of their coalitional partners in those districts where their own militants did appear on the ballot.[9] By contrast, the D'Hondt proportional formula used in the post-transition municipal elections, which have district magnitudes of 6, 8, or 10, is comparable to the one used in the legislative elections prior to 1973. Table 5.1 also shows that the electoral results for each one of the parties have been quite consistent over time since 1992, with the significant exception of the PDC vote – an issue to which we return below.

Another indicator of a party system's level of institutionalization is the relative consistency of voter options as they are expressed in different electoral contests that take place simultaneously. Again, in this respect the Chilean system scores highly as well. For instance, on November 17, 2013,

[9] Carey (2002: 228) warned against using Chilean legislative elections for calculating party vote shares given the binomial rules.

parliamentary and regional council elections were held together with the first round of the nation's presidential contest. The eventual winner of the presidential election, Michelle Bachelet, won 46.7% of the vote in the first round, while her coalition candidates obtained 47.7% in lower house contests and 46.7% (exactly the same score as Bachelet's!) in the regional council elections. These results did not occur as people simply voted down-ballot following the same column on a single sheet of paper, because each race had its own ballot and the names of the presidential candidates did not appear on the parliamentary or regional council ones. Moreover, the lack of cross-over voting did not result from the dearth of alternative candidacies. There were eight additional lists, mainly leftist ones, in addition to those of the two major coalitions in both the legislative and regional council campaigns. Bachelet also won 62.2% of the vote in the second round, a percentage that is basically equal to the 62.6% of the vote obtained by all the candidates in her coalition – relabeled "New Majority" (NM) after the parties of the Concertation formally added the Communists to their fold – plus those of all other lists with center and leftist programmatic positions in the lower house elections.

The candidate of the rightist Alliance for Chile, Evelyn Matthei, under-performed in the first round of the 2013 presidential election, receiving only 25% of the vote while her coalition obtained 36.2% in the lower house election and 32.3% in the regional council one. This was exceptional. Her candidacy got a late start because two prior rightist candidates had to withdraw from the race under a cloud due to, in the first case, financial irregularities, and, in the second, mental health problems. But Matthei did recover the right's share of the parliamentary vote in the second round of the presidential contest by obtaining 38.3%.

PARTY IDENTITIES AND MEMBERSHIPS

Following pioneering studies of American electoral behavior in the post-war decades, analysts have long associated relatively constant patterns of voting with high proportions of voters who identify with specific parties. As a result, party identity questions became standard tools in the political polling repertoire deployed in all democracies. But acquiring and maintaining a sense of identification with a specific party is likely to be more infrequent in multi-party rather than two-party systems, especially in relatively homogeneous national societies, such as the Chilean one, in which individual parties rarely obtain more than a quarter of the votes.

The national surveys of the Santiago-based *Centro de Estudios Públicos* (CEP) have regularly asked Chileans whether they "identify," "sympathize," or "feel close" to a specific party. While many democracies have shown declining levels of party identification for reasons that are unclear (Angell 2007: 200–01), the results of the CEP surveys raise eyebrows. They show that identification with parties in Chile dropped from a high of nearly 80% in

December 1993 to a low of about 35% in October of 2013,[10] and yet the bulk of this decline resulted from a decrease in the number of respondents who said that they identified with the PDC (Navia and Osorio 2015: 815–16). The levels of partisan identity for the other parties remained quite low and mostly stable.

Many among the 45% of voting-age respondents who "identified" with the PDC in the December 1993 CEP survey must, however, have interpreted the party identity question in ways that did not relate to their voting preferences. Voting was then compulsory, and PDC candidates obtained only 27.1% of the vote in congressional elections that took place that very same month. If more people "identify" with a party than vote for it, then a standard party identification question can hardly provide a reliable guide for the stability of voting patterns. The CEP's question at that time most probably captured the appreciation many Chileans felt for President Aylwin's leadership of the then still recent transition from the dictatorship.

In discussing Chilean party identity data from 1957 to 2012, Navia and Osorio dismissed the over-inflated numbers that favored the PDC in the immediate post-transition years as well as those that were registered in the politically polarized late 1960s and early 1970s, and concluded that the claim that the nation's parties have "always enjoyed high levels of identification is not supported by public opinion data" (2015: 823). Still, the Latin American Political Opinion Project (LAPOP) 2010 survey question on this dimension – which showed that only 11.6% of Chileans identified with parties (Luna and Zechmeister 2010: 170) – did generate an excessively low estimate. The low level of this result stems perhaps from the inappropriate wording of the question ("[A]t this moment, do you sympathize with a political party?"), given that party identities are supposed to refer to considerably longer-term attachments.[11] Luna and Altman (2011) used this figure to characterize the nation's party system as being "uprooted" while at the same time recognizing, but being unable to explain, the stability of its voting trends.

In our survey, we avoided asking a straightforward party identity question. Instead, we asked respondents whether "during the last twenty years" their "sympathies" had leaned more toward the center/left or the center/right coalition, "with one or the other … or with neither?" The two coalitions were mentioned by 44.6%, while 7.9% noted that their sympathies had varied over time and 34.1% said that they did not sympathize with either one. We also asked which party they would favor if voting were to become legally obligatory once again, but they did not know any of the candidates. Half of all respondents (49.7%) indicated they would vote for a party – with 45.7%

---

[10] We have examined all CEP surveys, four yearly, over this period.
[11] For a discussion of the difficulties of translating the American party identification question and the importance of the time frame it conjures up among survey respondents in a different political context – the French – which shares many similarities with the Chilean case, see Converse and Pierce (1986: 72–77).

choosing a specific one from a non-exhaustive list. In sum, while these answers are more robust than those recorded by the LAPOP survey (Luna and Zechmeister 2010), it would still seem that a clear sense of party identity may well explain only partially the stability of voting patterns in Chile, limited as it probably is in general to the most militant portions of the population.

And such militancy does surely exist. In August 2017, after a year-long process of government-mandated renewal of all party memberships, the Chilean Electoral Service reported that 1.2 million individuals had registered as such.[12] This figure represents about 8.5% of the total voting age population (registration to vote is currently automatic at age eighteen). It also represents an increase in party memberships of nearly 579,000 since 2006.[13] Moreover, about 62% of the party members are in the seven principal parties (including the Communists) that have formed part of the two main national coalitions that have dominated Chile's political life since the return to democracy. Other registrants are in parties that have small proportions of the vote, some of which are active only in specific regions of the country. An indication of the relative vitality of this aspect of party life in Chile can be appreciated by the fact that in long-established European democracies, the average proportion of party members over all *registered voters* (not the total voting age population) had declined to only 5.7% circa 2008 (Van Biezen *et al.* 2012: 29, 33).

VOTER PERCEPTION OF CHILEAN PARTY SYSTEM TENDENCIES

Exceptionally in the Americas, the Chilean party system developed out of historically determined symbolic, cultural, religious, programmatic, and ideological differences of the same sort that configured what Klaus von Beyme called "spiritual families" in European politics (Ware 1996: 21–47). An awareness among voters of these differences can be seen as adding a deeper layer of identities that contribute to the relative stability of the nation's voting patterns. As a high school teacher said emphatically as we pressed her to reveal her voting preferences, "Look: I will never vote for the right!"[14] The process leading from such meta-attachments to specific polling day choices can lead some voters, like this high school teacher, to sort through what they view as the more palatable candidates (for whatever reason) within the spectrum of opinion they favor. The relative stability of voter choices may actually mask, therefore, the fact that some voters oscillate to and from kindred parties in different directions, and this would also explain, at least in part, why low levels of identification with specific parties do not affect that stability. A general sense of voter self-placement within the scaffolding of party system divisions therefore contributes to a deeper social rootedness of the system that is easily

[12] Figure provided by the SERVEL at the authors' request.
[13] The 2006 figure appears in *El Mercurio*, February 22, 2015, D9.
[14] J. S. Valenzuela's interview in Concepción, December 2008.

overlooked by analysts. Navia and Osorio's (2015: 834) conclusion that "ideology" has been "an important determinant of political identification in Chile" aims in the right direction, although it falls short of capturing the much broader scope of what underlies the nation's political divisions. Rather than being based narrowly only on ideologies, such divisions are more akin to shared political sensibilities, even sub-cultures, based on a broad spectrum of identities built on family legacies, social belongings, and perceptions of the nation's history that set boundaries to voter choices.

The historical configuration of the Chilean party landscape was a result of conflicts that reflected a religious versus secular divide, as well as programmatic differences over socioeconomic, welfare, and labor policies (Scully 1992; J. S. Valenzuela 1985, 1995). The Conservative, Liberal, and Radical parties all emerged in the mid-nineteenth century over different conceptions of the proper role of the Catholic Church and its teachings in the state and society, while the Communist party (PC) and various Socialist parties (PS) were formed during early decades of the twentieth century with industrial strife and the emergence of labor as well as entrepreneurial organizations.

With the rise of the second set of parties related to what was called the "social" as opposed to the "religious question," the older ones also had to position themselves in what then became the new left–right axis in the party system. Its first issues were whether or not to legalize unions and collective bargaining. The Radicals opted to identify more closely with white collar workers, public sector employees, and teachers, becoming active in the leadership of their associations. The Liberals drifted further to the right in socioeconomic policies as well as to a discreet proximity to the Catholic Church after they spearheaded the separation of church and state. And the Conservatives split into two factions: a rightist "traditional" and a centrist "social Christian" one. The latter actively participated in shaping the nation's labor laws as its militant circles sponsored mutual aid societies, educational programs, and even some unions (Valenzuela and Valenzuela 2000). This division of the Conservative Party generated breakaway groups, most notably the National Falange, created by its youth wing in the mid-1930s. The party finally broke apart in 1957 as its president, who identified with the social Christian faction, joined other such groups (including the National Falange) to form the PDC. The members of the "traditionalist" faction retained the Conservative Party label in what became both a much more rightist party in terms of the socioeconomic axis of division, as well as more conservative in its understanding of the Catholic social doctrine. Similarly, the new parties of the left that emerged over the "social question" had to define their views along the older Catholic/secular axis. They assumed starkly secular positions.

All these parties were formed in association with party generative social cleavages in the sense that they were linked to conflicts that also involved important organized segments of civil society. While this is evident in terms of the religious/secular as well as the socioeconomic policy divisions, it is also true of the conflict between the conservative traditionalists and social Christians. It evolved as a set of opposing policy positions over property rights, markets, social welfare measures, and the rights of workers, peasants, and their unions, and expressed itself through many organizations linked to Church networks in different social strata. Traditionalist conservatives also expressed doubts about the wisdom of mass suffrage in the 1920s (Valenzuela and Valenzuela 2000: 218), and in the 1960s right-wing Catholic groups, such as the Society for the Defense of Tradition, Family, and Property, assigned greater importance to property rights than to democratic institutions. These differences also spilled over into scriptural interpretations and conceptions of Catholic social doctrine. They influenced the choices middle- and upper-class Chilean Catholics made regarding which parish to attend and which religious schools to choose for their children. The traditionalist versus social Christian division sharpened under the PDC government of Eduardo Frei Montalva (1964–70) as it sponsored an agrarian reform, a rural worker unionization law, and health programs that facilitated access to contraceptives. Frei's administration coincided with the rise of a more progressive post-Conciliar Chilean Church that favored the PDC (Scully 1992: 149–50; Smith 1982: 115).

As parties and party factions emerged through these conflicts, they also reinforced the overall matrix of political-ideological choices in the country. Given the fact that the issue polarities pertaining to religious and class-based party-generative cleavages may display various gradations between their most extreme positions – and that the religious pole is bifurcated into progressive and conservative inclinations – the resulting matrix of political and symbolic positionings combining all three dimensions of division has always been complex. Some of these possible combinations are unlikely to correspond to any viable parties. This would be the case with, for instance, a combination between leftist socioeconomic programs and very conservatively orthodox religious views. However, the opposite combination, namely rightist socioeconomic views with secular stances on value-laden social issues, is quite possible. While it has not been expressed as clearly in the post-transition configuration of the party system as it was in previous ones, *Amplitud* – a new party formed in 2014 – hopes to fill this void by calling itself both "liberal" and "of the center-right."

Political leaders often remind the public of the connection between their parties and specific positionings in the overall symbolic and ideological matrix that undergirds the party system. They do so by referring to their progressive, secular, liberal, or "laic" (in the French sense of this term) positions – or their Christian inspiration – as well as their left, center, or right (and combinations thereof) orientations. Such references provide cues to voters regarding party positions that do not need to be elaborated fully.

If Chilean electoral stability does stem partly from voter attachments to the political tendencies formed by the historic divisions that shaped the party system from its beginnings, then voters should be aware of the differences between the parties along these lines of differentiation. To examine this, our survey asked respondents to indicate on a scale from 1 to 7 how close – or distant – they thought the seven major parties were to "the rich" and to "the Catholic Church." These simple indicators reflect the main class and religious versus secular cleavages. Table 5.2 summarizes the results by showing which paired relationships between the parties' average scores on both scales generated statistically significant differences between them, and which did not. It is based on survey respondents who said they voted in the second round of the 2013 presidential election.

Regarding the Church, survey respondents correctly viewed the UDI, the RN, and the PDC as the parties that were closest to it. Thus, the paired contrasts between the average scores assigned to them all failed to reach statistical significance. The same is true with the scores on the opposite side of this polarity assessing the relationships between the Church and the Radical, Socialist, and Communist parties. And – as expected – the differences between the scores across these two sets of parties were all statistically significant. The

TABLE 5.2 *Statistical Significance of the Differences between the Mean Scores Given by Survey Respondents to the Parties on a 7-Point Scale Measuring Their Proximity or Distance from the Rich and from the Catholic Church*

	UDI	RN	PDC	PPD	PS	PRSD	PC
UDI	Rich \ Church	ns	s	s	s	s	s
RN	ns	Rich \ Church	s	s	s	s	s
PDC	ns	ns	Rich \ Church	s	s	s	s
PPD	s	s	s	Rich \ Church	ns	s	s
PS	s	s	s	s	Rich \ Church	ns	s
PRSD	s	s	s	s	ns	Rich \ Church	s
PC	s	s	s	s	ns	ns	Rich \ Church

$N = 691$.

Note: The letter "s" signifies statistical significance *at least* at the 0.05 level, and "ns" non-significance. The section of the table below the bold face diagonal refers to perceptions of the relative proximity or distance of the parties to the Church, and the one above it refers to the same regarding the rich. For a listing of party labels, see Table 5.1.

one result that stands out is that the Party for Democracy's (PPD) average score is statistically significant when paired with that of all the other major parties. This has to do with the recent formation of the PPD during the transition back to democracy – a process we analyze below. It therefore does not have a prior history associating it with anti-clericalism (which explains why its distance from the secularist parties is significant), and yet it is also seen as more secular given its proximity to the so-called "progressive" sub-group of parties (for which its average score is sufficiently distant from that of the PDC, the RN, and the UDI to trigger statistical significance as well).

The results regarding the relative proximity of the parties to the rich show that survey respondents view the two parties of the right as closest to them, with average scores for each whose differences are not statistically significant. Conversely, respondents viewed the parties of the left as distant from the rich, with scores that fail to reach statistical significance when contrasting the PPD and the PS, and the PS and the PSRD. All the other paired contrasts were significant. This is not surprising regarding the differences between the scores of the parties of the right and those in the Concertation, nor those of the Communists with all other parties. However, it is noteworthy that the perception of the position of the Christian Democrats with respect to the rich produced an average score that is also statistically significant when paired with that of all the other parties. Hence, with their middling score, the Christian Democrats are viewed as a more centrist party than the social democratic PS and the PPD, and even than the Radicals.[15] This result helps explain the dwindling support for the PDC over the years shown in Table 5.1. Given that its alliances have been with secular parties that are also to its left, this isolates the party like no other within the matrix of symbolic positionings that buttresses the party system, thereby limiting its ability to obtain occasional support from the soft vote of its coalition partners. At the same time, it also makes the PDC more vulnerable to defections to the right by some of its leaders and supporters, given both their religious commitments as well as their occasional uneasiness with the more leftist discourse of the party's coalition partners. In recent years, for example, the PDC lost votes as a breakaway group joined a small party, the *Partido Regionalista de los Independientes* (PRI) (del Pozo *et al.* 2012: 151–63). At present, the PRI takes part in the rightist coalition, although the key PDC leader who led the breakaway group died and others have returned to the center-left coalition as independents.

In sum, Chilean voters do perceive the differences between the major parties along the two historic party generative dimensions. And new parties that emerge are also quite readily located by commentators and the general public

---

[15] In Table 5.1 we placed the Radicals as a centrist party given its historic trajectory and the references of its leaders to this positioning. The lack of statistical significance of their average score with that of the Socialists has to do with the latter's currently much more moderate leftist profile.

within the two quadrants of the party system's divisions, where they therefore compete mainly with other parties in the same spectrum of opinion.

A NEW AND BI-POLAR PARTY SYSTEM?

The notion that the Chilean party system has more continuities than discontinuities with its pre-dictatorship past (Scully and Valenzuela 1993) has been disputed by other analysts. Tironi and Agüero (1999) noted that the party system's old divisions are no longer salient, having been subsumed under a new democracy versus authoritarian "cleavage" that replicates the pattern first established by the 1988 plebiscite. Their analysis inspired a significant body of literature discussing whether the post-transition party system does indeed have a new dual morphology or not.[16] And, more recently, James Loxton (2016a: 6–7) has argued that the Chilean right has undergone a fundamental transformation. Its parties are new, he notes – in particular the UDI – having been created by officials of the Pinochet dictatorship in order to preserve its legacy.

The fact that our survey respondents clearly differentiate the parties according to their relative proximity or distance from both the Church and the rich does indicate that there is something more to the party system in people's perceptions than just an authoritarian versus democratic divide. But we return to this matter below. What follows is a process-tracing analysis of how the parties, especially those of the right, and the party system reacted to and changed under the military regime. The focus here is, of course, on party leadership and militant actions: there were no elections for representative bodies of any kind during the dictatorship.

Parties since the Breakdown of Democracy

Severely repressed by the dictatorship, the two main parties of the left evolved in opposite directions. The Socialists abandoned their revolutionary 1960s discourse in favor of a commitment to social democracy and forged an alliance with the PDC (Lagos 2013: 390; Ortega Frei 1992; Walker 1990), while the Communists turned away from their long-standing opposition to the use of violence in politics. This change of direction by the PC and its initial resistance to join efforts to register voters for the 1988 plebiscite, cost it the loss of many militants and followers (Lagos 2013: 573, 585) and about half its electorate. By contrast, the PS was better able to retain the loyalty of its

---

[16] See, among others: Angell (2007: Chapters 8–9); Gamboa *et al.* (2013); Joignant and López (2005); López and Morales (2005); Navia and Saldaña (2009: Chapters 2, 7, 8, 10); Raymond and Barros Feltch (2014); Torcal and Mainwaring (2003); Toro *et al.* (2011); Valenzuela (1999); and Valenzuela *et al.* (2007).

militants and voters (Lagos 2013: 391–96), and its mean electoral support approximates the 12% it obtained on average prior to 1973.[17]

The PPD arose as a result of the impossibility of legally registering the PS and the PC as parties before the 1988 plebiscite, given that they were framed as upholding "totalitarian" doctrines. Following the terms of the dictatorship's 1987 law on political parties, such legal registration was, however, a prerequisite for party leaders to have access to television messaging during the plebiscite campaign as well to place poll observers on voting day. Hence, working with a PS faction, the then future President Ricardo Lagos (2000–06) led an effort to gather the signatures that were needed to register an "instrumental party" for all opponents of the dictatorship to participate fully in the plebiscite with a single legal vehicle in order to defeat it (Lagos 2013: 582–83, 588–93).

If the plebiscite had really been a founding moment for a new authoritarian versus democratic divide, Lagos' effort, which barely succeeded, would not have had such difficulty. The enactment of the law on parties stimulated a resurgence of pre-existing party identities among Pinochet opponents (Lagos 2013: 591–95), not a rush to unite under a single venue, as might have occurred in a country without such long-standing party profiles. Thus, Christian Democrats and Radicals, whose principles were deemed to be acceptable by the authorities, rapidly took advantage of the 1987 law to legally register their own parties, while the Communists used Lagos' initiative for several months to reactivate their base in opposition to it and to the plebiscite. And with their ban lifted after President Aylwin's election, the PS and the PC quickly registered legally with their own labels.

But after becoming a legally registered party before the plebiscite, the PPD gradually became a political home – not just an "instrumental" tool – for militants who had previously been in small Christian left and social democratic groups, and for former Socialists, Communists, Radicals, and even a few former rightists (Lagos 2013: 592, 597–99). It therefore did not dissolve as the old parties of the left obtained their legal status. Hence, in 1992 the PS leadership forced its militants who were also in the PPD from its earliest days to choose between the two parties. As a result, the PS retained closer links than the PPD to the labor movement and a higher proportion of secular-leaning militants derived from its historic factions. Thus, on a 5-point scale of ascending religiosity, PS members of the 2001–05 legislature ranked 1.5, while those of the PPD scored 2.27 (Ruiz Rodríguez 2006: 93).

The Radical Party divided twice over its decisions to join – and then to remain – within Allende's Popular Unity coalition, thereby losing half of its late 1960s electorate by 1973. In 1994, the core party group reunited with the second one of its former breakaways, adding the Social Democratic qualifier to

---

[17] The average party vote shares here and in subsequent paragraphs have been calculated from A. Valenzuela (1985: 58–61). The same means for the 1992–2016 period appear in Table 5.1.

its name – hence its PRSD acronym. The party's discourse remains attached to its sesquicentennial history with a secularist orientation. Its average vote share since 1992 is slightly above that of all three of its splinters in the 1973 lower house election.

After its leaders disagreed over their response to the military coup, the PDC came together as an opposition force, generating defections by its rightist factional militants and figures. Key party members were sent into exile, and former President Frei Montalva was assassinated by agents of the dictatorship. The party's average vote share since 1992 has been about 9% lower than that which it received in legislative elections from 1961 to 1973, when its center-right component was larger.

Having clamored for a military intervention to depose Allende, the right willingly "suspended" the National Party's activities as demanded by the newly formed governing junta. The party consisted of an uneasy combination of traditionalist conservatives, liberals, and other smaller groups, and with the cessation of its activities it splintered into different social networks linked to entrepreneurial associations, think tanks, newly formed private universities, and conservative religious circles. With the exception of a few short-lived ministers, Pinochet drew from the ranks of right-wing politicians to fill only minor government positions. The right's electorate had dipped during the 1960s as the Christian Democrats had surged – a tendency that had mostly reverted by 1969. After the return to democracy, the right's electoral support hovered around its historic averages of the 1930–60 period.

After assuming the "presidency" of the military junta, Pinochet sought someone to devise a legitimating framework for his unprecedented regime. He found that person in Jaime Guzmán, who became "the principal ideologue and political inspiration" of the military regime (Allamand 1999: 38). Guzmán wrote Pinochet's key speeches during the 1970s, and was "the principal architect" of the permanent articles of the 1980 Constitution (Fontaine 1991: 253).

At age twenty-seven, in 1973 Guzmán was already an important political figure. An orthodox Catholic and an admirer of Franco's regime in Spain, his maternal grandfather had been a Conservative Party senator from a prominent landholding family. Guzmán joined the party's youth wing at age thirteen (Guzmán 2008: 139, 143) when it was reduced to its Traditionalist faction. He was viscerally opposed to the Frei Montalva government – particularly its agrarian reform. He held the post-Conciliar Church in disdain, wrote articles for right-wing magazines, and sparred publicly with the progressive-leaning Cardinal-Archbishop of Santiago, Raúl Silva Henríquez, who later confronted the dictatorship over its human rights violations.

Guzmán did not join the National Party with his fellow Conservatives. Instead, he started his own political group and ran successfully for the presidency of the Catholic University Student Federation in 1967. The following year he became the key rightist commentator in a television program devoted to political affairs (Huneeus 2000: 332–36). He argued at the time that democracy had to be "protected" in underdeveloped countries because its voters could be "manipulated" by Marxists.

Guzmán's views had no chance of ever being supported by more than a minority of Chileans. The military regime gave him, therefore, a unique opportunity to try to reshape the nation's political institutions following his precepts. Guzmán's early proximity to the dictatorship allowed him to place many of his like-minded associates in official positions – a move facilitated by the National Party's recess (Allamand 1999: 49, 54–56; Huneeus 2000: 328–32). In the late 1970s, he began to consider founding a new political party with them (Montecinos *et al.* 2001: 66). At the time, the prospect of easing into a five-year transition out of military rule, as envisioned in non-permanent articles added to the constitution by a "Council of State" led by former President Jorge Alessandri (1958–64), a senior mentor to Guzmán, appeared to be likely. However, Pinochet and his advisors substituted all such articles with new ones that named him "President" for an additional eight years at the helm of a regime that was designed to remain essentially the same with the exception of a new constitutional tribunal (Valenzuela 1998: 154–62). Alessandri bitterly rejected this substitution, and relations between Guzmán and Pinochet also became distant.

Protests against the military regime began in May 1983, leading Pinochet to name Sergio Onofre Jarpa, the former head of the National Party, as minister of the interior in what was seen as an "opening." This reactivated partisan organizing on the right. Andrés Allamand, a leader of the National Party's youth at the time of the coup, began working with Jarpa to create a party that would be called "National Union". In turn, Guzmán returned to the idea of forming his own party with the UDI label, while *Avanzada Nacional*, a small group that Pinochet seemed to prefer, also resurfaced (Allamand 1999: 35, 56–57). Although Jarpa's political initiatives were unsuccessful, Guzmán continued thereafter to speak publicly as a leader of the UDI (see Avetikian 1986: 19–23, 28–30, 65–67), and Allamand did the same, invoking the National Union label.

Discussions to form a single party of the right were rekindled by the enactment of the 1987 law on parties, and its various leaders (except those in *Avanzada Nacional*) agreed to unite under the RN label. However, as internal party elections were taking place later that year with two lists that reflected the split between Guzmán's associates and the rest, he suddenly asked for a co-equal federation between the two groups and derailed the electoral process. This led to Guzmán's expulsion from RN (Allamand 1999: 142–47). Consequently, the right came out of the dictatorship with two main parties with new labels, neither one of which was sponsored by Pinochet.

Guzmán reactivated his connection with Pinochet during the campaign for the 1988 plebiscite (Huneeus 2000: 155, 331). The application of the permanent articles of the constitution was supposed to begin at that point, and by supporting the "yes" Guzmán was, strictly speaking, defending his own – not Pinochet's – constitutional creation and legacy. Guzmán had added anti-democratic provisions to the permanent articles that reflected his long-standing notion that democracy had to be "protected." He probably hoped that they would help retain his impact on Chilean institutions well into the future.

While the UDI's commitment to the 1980 Constitution was unwavering, this was not so with RN. Its leaders had signed a "National Accord" in 1985 with the Christian Democrats and other parties opposed to Pinochet. It called for the formation of a provisional government and for the election of a constituent assembly (Godoy 1999: 90–91). And after Pinochet's defeat, RN joined the parties that backed the "no" in a partially successful effort to remove the most egregiously anti-democratic provisions from the constitution through negotiations with the military regime. Moreover, Sebastián Piñera, the most important RN leader after the return to democracy, voted "no" in the 1988 plebiscite while publicly defending this option at the time. The UDI did, nonetheless, eventually alter its position on the undemocratic features that remained in place after the post-plebiscite changes to the constitution. Its legislators joined those of all other parties in supporting reforms proposed by President Lagos in 2005 that eliminated all such features.[18]

Although RN claims to draw inspiration from "Christian humanism," it has been open to a variety of center-right tendencies – much like the pre-1973 National Party. By contrast, Guzmán sought to anchor the UDI firmly in religiously orthodox principles. For instance, in 1988 he wrote that "the defense of the right to life of the unborn child constitutes for the UDI a fundamental principle that we will defend with all our might in the upcoming democracy" (cited in Santoni 2013: 209). And to this end, Guzmán prevailed on Pinochet in 1989 to substitute legislation that had permitted abortion for "therapeutic" reasons with language that banned it in all circumstances – even when a woman's pregnancy threatened her life.[19] On the 5-point ascending religiosity scale mentioned above, UDI congressmen in the 2001–05 legislature averaged 3.71, while those in RN averaged 3.00. By comparison, PDC legislators rated 3.22 (Ruiz Rodríguez 2006: 93).

New appointments in the Church under John Paul II turned it in a conservative direction, and Opus Dei and the Legionnaires of Christ expanded their influence among well-off Chileans who were generally supportive of the Pinochet regime (Mönckeberg 2003; Thumala Olave 2010). These changes helped to invigorate the UDI, which followed the lineage of the traditionalist segment of the Conservative Party that Guzmán had identified with during his youth. Consequently, not only did a left to right and a secular versus religious division remain in place as underlying sources of differentiation

---

[18] Guzmán would perhaps have hindered this evolution, but he was assassinated in 1991.
[19] As Guzmán wrote in 1974, "a mother must have her child ... even if in carrying it, she dies" (cited in Hormazábal 2015).

in the party system among its militants, but also a conservative/progressive distinction within its religiously inclined quadrant.[20]

Determinants of Voter Choices

If the overall continuity of Chilean electoral outcomes is largely explained by the enduring effects of the divisions that have long framed the party system, then the perceptions of party positions in relation to the rich and the Church encapsulated in Table 5.2 should indeed help shape voter options. However, the figures in that table may simply reflect what survey respondents think they know about the parties while, as the Tironi and Agüero (1999) thesis would have it, a division between those who preferred authoritarianism and those who remained committed to democracy may have a much stronger effect on how they vote. In what follows, we put these alternatives to statistical tests with different segments of our survey's subjects.

If our survey respondents view the parties of the right as being "closer to the rich" and, therefore, by implication, those of the left as closer to the poor, we can venture that those who see themselves as relatively richer or poorer will choose to vote in accordance with this perception. Hence, we used survey respondents' socioeconomic positions as measured by a combination of their income and educational attainment as an indicator for this dimension, even though we are aware of the fact that many people who are well off materially may also be leftist, and vice versa.

Similarly, if some parties are perceived to be closer to the Church than others, then survey respondents who are themselves more religious can be assumed to vote more for such parties than those who are thoroughly secular – and vice versa. For this purpose, we developed a religiosity index based on questions in our survey regarding religious beliefs and practices. All respondents, even self-identified atheists, were asked a set of basic questions, to which we added others that reflect levels of religiosity in different traditions. We then standardized the resulting scores on a single scale from 0 to 1.[21]

---

[20] Although this distinction plays out in socioeconomic policies, it also affects choices related to value-laden social issues. During the Lagos government, PDC legislators rewrote the Chilean civil marriage law, legalizing divorce. This was opposed by UDI and part of RN. President Piñera proposed a new law on civil unions for gay and other non-traditional couples. All parties except the UDI approved it. And legislation proposed by Bachelet's government to decriminalize abortion to save the life of the mother, when extra-uterine life cannot be sustained, and in cases of rape or incest, has been opposed by UDI and RN, while PDC congressmen have been divided over the issue (Hormazábal 2015). The PDC's declaration of principles opposes abortion, but it also calls for drafting guidelines to deal with "complex medical" situations that may arise (see the PDC's 2007 Fifth Programatic Congress).

[21] The indicators and their values to construct the religiosity index may be examined in the *Kellogg Institute Working Papers* series (no. 416, December 2016, pp. 34–35) version of this paper.

To test for the effects of attitudes toward democracy and authoritarianism we posed a question (number 47) that attempts to capture this distinction in an abstract, value judgment sense. It asked respondents to indicate their agreement with one of three points: first, "a democracy is the best form of government;" second, "it is better to have a government with strong authority that will be subjected neither to elections nor to popular pressures;" and, third, "such forms of government make no difference." We followed this question up with another one (number 48) that aims at capturing attitudes towards the two types of regimes in a historically contingent sense. It asked respondents to indicate "regardless of what you think in general about the forms of government," whether it is better to "always maintain a democracy" even if there is "a profound political crisis," or whether in such cases it is better "to resort to an authoritarian government."

Table 5.3 presents the results of logistic regressions with support for the main parties of the two coalitions as the dependent variable. We draw the data for this table from the above-mentioned question regarding voting preferences for the nation's parties in case voting were to become, once again, obligatory. It includes only those respondents who chose a party that belongs to one of the two major coalitions, regardless of whether they voted or abstained in the 2013 election. Its control variables are gender (women equal 1), age (as a continuous variable), and religious identity (whether respondents self-identified as Protestants or as irreligious, with Catholics as the reference category).

The results in Table 5.3 show that socioeconomic position, religiosity, and attitudes toward democracy – as reflected in both pertinent questions – all have effects in the expected directions on voter choices for the parties as they are aggregated to reproduce the two major coalitions. Options for the New Majority parties are more prevalent among individuals who have lower socioeconomic status, lower religiosity, and seemingly more pro-democratic attitudes – and vice versa. All of these results easily meet the highest level of statistical significance. Model 4 in the table also shows that voters who agree with the notion that having a democratic or an authoritarian regime "makes no difference" are more likely to support the parties of the Alliance than those of the New Majority, although this relationship is weaker than that between opting for the Alliance and expressing support for the notion that authoritarian regimes are better than democracies. Running model 4 with a fictitious coalition of the right that has the Christian Democrats in it, while leaving only the parties of the left in the New Majority coalition, weakens all of the significant results (model not shown here). This outcome indicates that PDC voters line up better with the parties of the left than those of the right: creating the fictitious coalition reduces the sharpness of the distinctions between the two actual ones. Still, the religiosity index produces less robust results than the two other variables given that the New Majority includes the more religiously inclined PDC voters with the more secular ones of the left. Gender and age have no effects, and being Protestant or irreligious does not have any influence beyond those captured by the religiosity index.

TABLE 5.3 *Chile: Determinants of Voting Preferences for Party Coalitions*

	(1)	(2)	(3)	(4)
Women	0.400	0.263	−0.034	0.033
	(0.230)	(0.246)	(0.273)	(0.264)
Age	0.002	-0.003	0.003	0.001
	(0.00661)	(0.00757)	(0.00802)	(0.00798)
SES	0.444***	0.501***	0.774***	0.665***
	(0.117)	(0.131)	(0.152)	(0.152)
Protestant		0.109	0.095	0.072
		(0.350)	(0.370)	(0.330)
Irreligious		0.346	0.237	0.134
		(0.366)	(0.436)	(0.416)
Religiosity index		2.355***	2.846***	2.657***
		(0.566)	(0.636)	(0.580)
Keep democracy[1]			−2.528***	
			(0.337)	
Question 47[2]				
– prefer authoritarian rule				1.941***
				(0.387)
– makes no difference				1.333***
				(0.390)
N	579	527	505	523
pseudo R2	0.04	0.08	0.25	0.18

Notes: Binary logistic regressions with UDI/RN = 1, and DC/PPD/PRSD/PS/PC = 0. Standard errors in parenthesis. * $p < 0.05$; ** $p < 0.01$; *** $p < 0.001$.
[1]Question 48. Reference category: install authoritarian rule in a crisis.
[2]Reference category: prefer democracy.

Table 5.4 also addresses the determinants of voting for the center-left versus the right, but it does so with the reported voting options of our survey respondents in the presidential election of 2013. Models 1 and 2 draw from the results of the primary election in June, and capture the differences between the profiles of voters who selected Michelle Bachelet from the field of candidates in the New Majority coalition, and those – added together – who participated in the competition between the RN and the UDI candidates. This was the first time primary elections for the presidency were held under the direct control of the Electoral Service, and a quarter of the electorate participated in them. Bachelet

Party Systems in Latin America

TABLE 5.4 *Chile: Determinants of Voter Choices in the Presidential Election of 2013*

	(1)	(2)	(3)	(4)
Women	−0.419	−0.613	0.103	−0.044
	(0.310)	(0.331)	(0.243)	(0.259)
Age	−0.006	−0.001	−0.003	0.003
	(0.0101)	(0.0105)	(0.00796)	(0.00891)
SES	0.799***	0.907***	0.848***	1.009***
	(0.184)	(0.201)	(0.148)	(0.165)
Protestant	0.041	−0.342	0.426	0.267
	(0.411)	(0.423)	(0.309)	(0.348)
Irreligious	0.353	0.599	0.188	0.224
	(0.485)	(0.542)	(0.394)	(0.456)
Religiosity index	2.313***	2.731***	1.767***	2.015***
	(0.637)	(0.716)	(0.496)	(0.536)
Keep democracy[1]		−2.256***		−2.002***
		(0.361)		(0.298)
N	436	413	617	586
pseudo R2	0.13	0.26	0.12	0.223

Notes: Binary Logistic Regressions with Bachelet = 0, and her opponents = 1. Models 1 and 2: A contrast between Bachelet (PS) voters, and those for Allamand (RN) plus Longueira (UDI), in the June primary elections. Models 3 and 4: Second-round voting in December between Bachelet (New Majority) and Matthei (Alliance).
Standard errors in parentheses. * p <0.05, ** p <0.01, *** p<0.001.
[1]Question 48; reference category: install authoritarian rule in a crisis.

easily won the New Majority nomination, while the candidate of the UDI narrowly won among voters of the Alliance. He then had to step aside for health reasons, as noted earlier, and was replaced by Evelyn Matthei of the same party. Models 3 and 4 draw from the results of the second round of voting in December between Bachelet and Matthei. The variables in Table 5.4 are the same as those in Table 5.3, except for the omission of our abstract survey question on the democratic versus authoritarian regime distinction. Its coefficients basically repeat those given by the contingent one.

The results in Table 5.4 are very similar to those of Table 5.3. A significant finding shown by the models in both tables is that the strength of the metrics for the socioeconomic and religious factors tends to increase slightly, not diminish, with the introduction of the variables that capture the distinction between what seem to be the pro-democratic or authoritarian views. In sum, the tables show that survey respondents choose the parties they support to a significant extent given personal socioeconomic status characteristics and degrees of religiosity that dovetail with the differences that they perceive among the parties (see Table 5.2), and that their views regarding the value, intrinsic or instrumental, of the two types of regimes also have an impact on such choices.

This exercise seemingly confirms, therefore, both alternative theses. And yet, what does the democratic versus authoritarian divide really mean? If its terms do really reorganize the Chilean party system in a new way, then why did a majority of the voters of the "authoritarian" segment opt to support Piñera – the leader who voted for the pro-democratic "no" side at what was supposedly the founding moment of this polarity – over the "yes" advocate Joaquín Lavín of the UDI in the first round of the presidential election of 2005? Similarly, why did *all* legislators of the right vote in favor of discarding Guzmán's "protective" institutions from the constitution in 2005 in order to make it fully compatible with a democratic regime?[22] These actions by the leaders of the right are in fact quite compatible with the Chilean public's current opinion of the Pinochet years. A 2013 Barómetro CERC survey showed that only 9% of its respondents viewed them as "good or only good." And when asked whether Pinochet was "a dictator" or "one of the best heads of state of the twentieth century," 76% chose the former while only 9% opted for the latter (CERC 2013).

Our evaluative and contingent regime preference questions elicited from *all* respondents to our survey basically the same overall level of support for the democratic options (71% and 73.2%, respectively) and low levels of agreement with the authoritarian ones (11% and 17.7%, respectively). And a bivariate crossing of the two questions showed that 92.7% of all respondents who preferred a democratic form of government insisted on keeping it under a "severe crisis," while 84.3% of the minority of respondents opting for an authoritarian regime thought that it should be maintained under such circumstances.[23] These are, overall, solid numbers expressing a preference for democracy, and the responses to the second, contingent question, are quite consistent with the first one. But both Tables 5.3 and 5.4 are not drawn, as noted, from the overall sample of respondents, which includes slightly more than half of subjects who did not vote in 2013. They stem, instead, from sub-groups that have higher levels of politicization, whose opinions are therefore more sharply divided in ways that express in starker terms the country's political divisions.

---

[22] The three votes against the 2005 reforms were cast by designated senators who had been former commanders of the armed forces. They lost their seats because of them.

[23] Respondents who saw no difference between the two regime forms split roughly into thirds – including those who opted to say they did not know which one to choose – when asked which regime would be preferable in times of "severe crisis."

Given Evelyn Matthei's poor performance in the first round of the presidential election of 2013, her votes were probably drawn disproportionately from people who were strongly committed to the right. Their views on our two questions regarding regime types are therefore instructive, because they can be expected to be among the most favorable to the authoritarian options. And yet a majority, 59% of our survey respondents, who said that they backed Matthei in the first round of voting opted for democracy in answering the first, evaluative question on the two regime types, while 51.7% chose to retain democracy as well in times of crisis. By contrast, Bachelet supporters and those of the other leftist candidates in that same round of the election backed the democratic options in both questions by an average of 83.5%. There is a clear difference between these answers, but it lies in the size of the majorities in favor of the democratic options. And it is this gap, not a polarity between the views of pro-democratic and pro-authoritarian supporters, that produces the results shown in Tables 5.3 and 5.4. While this does not support the notion that there is indeed a new democratic versus authoritarian cleavage in Chilean party politics, the difference in the size of the pro-democratic *majority* between rightist voters and the rest requires an explanation.

Questions about democracy or authoritarianism are not abstract ones for the Chilean public. Even the most unsophisticated voters can be expected to be aware of how the political tendency they or their families usually identify or identified with reacted to the "worst crisis" scenario faced by the country when its democracy collapsed. Normally, if the two questions are understood correctly, the first one would be answered only with an abstract value judgment, without also thinking of the Chilean crisis which the second one, when posed, will inevitably conjure up in the respondents' minds. However, it is unlikely that all respondents will only think abstractly even when answering the first question. The specter of the past will also color, to an unknown degree, an abstract democracy versus authoritarian question in Chile in ways that do not occur in countries without such a vivid experience of democratic regime collapse and dictatorship. Moreover, every Chilean voter knows that the Pinochet regime was one of the right: it implemented the right's market driven economic and social policies against a state-centered socialist model pursued by Allende. And when center to leftist Chileans answer the regime preference questions, both their support for democracy in an abstract, evaluative sense, and their rejection of the military coup of 1973 as a "solution" to Chile's worst crisis, aggregate to produce among the highest preferences for democracy in the world. By contrast, for right-leaning Chileans their preference for democracy is tempered by an awareness of the fact that the parties they support have their base in the sector of opinion that was most militantly in favor of forcibly displacing the Allende government. This means that the operative antecedent date for this difference of opinion harks back to the Chilean crisis of 1973 – and not to the "yes" or "no" option in the 1988 plebiscite that purportedly generated the new "authoritarian versus democratic" cleavage. This is confirmed by data in the same 2013 Barómetro CERC survey mentioned previously that recorded the rock-bottom levels of assessment of Pinochet himself and of his dictatorship's years in power (CERC 2013). Its subjects were asked to choose between the following two phrases referring to the military coup of 1973: "it liberated Chile from Marxism" or it "destroyed democracy": 69% of the UDI and 53% of RN supporters chose the first, while 79% of the PDC, 87% of the PPD, and 85% of PS supporters opted for the second.

This result also suggests that for Chilean rightist opinion, the 1973 crisis was essentially a dispute over socioeconomic policies, not the value of democracy itself. Hence, the support of rightist voters for a presidential candidate who cast a "no" in the 1988 plebiscite and the agreement of rightist legislators to the 2005 constitutional reforms that fully redemocratized Chilean institutions *de jure* were not anomalies. Moreover, the "protective" mechanisms to safeguard those socioeconomic policies through the constitution no longer had the same effect when center-leftist governments could start to appoint designated senators and army commanders. And they seemed moot, anyway, given the fact that the scope of disagreement over socioeconomic policies had narrowed since the late 1960s.

RECENT CHANGES IN ELECTORAL INSTITUTIONS

Two important changes in electoral laws with potential implications for the future of the party system and the stability of electoral results have been enacted in recent years. The first is a change to voluntary voting, and the second is the abrogation of the binomial electoral system.

The Impact of Voluntary Voting

This reform, introduced at the onset of Sebastián Piñera's government, instituted an automatic process of voter registration with a voluntary vote, substituting the voluntary registration but obligatory voting left in place by the dictatorship. It accelerated a drop in the number of voters as a percentage of those aged eighteen and over who had already been dwindling as many in the new age cohorts opted not to register. The first election held with the new norms was the municipal one of 2012, when voter participation declined by 9.2%. A further 23.8% drop occurred in the next such contest held in 2016.[24] And the first parliamentary election, held in 2013, under the new voting rights law recorded 7.8% fewer votes than the previous one in 2009.[25]

[24] About 35% of *all* Chileans aged over eighteen voted in 2016. This is equivalent to the turnout among *registered voters* in the 2014 municipal council elections in the United Kingdom.
[25] We include valid, blank, and annulled votes in these percentages. Chilean electoral results are available at www.electionresources.org/cl/deputies.php?election=2013, and pertinent variations thereof.

Changing from obligatory to voluntary voting may increase the volatility of electoral results – and create even more variation in the composition of legislatures and councils given the small margins of victory in many contests – as voters who are aligned with different segments of opinion feel differentially motivated, given the circumstances of the moment, to show up at the voting booth.

The drop in the number of voters during the 2013 congressional election furnished an important indication of this effect. Bachelet's reelection to the presidency, which occurred at the same time, motivated center-left supporters to go to the polls while the listless Matthei campaign discouraged those who normally support the center-right. Bachelet's NM coalition increased the size of the center-left's representation in the 120-seat lower house from fifty-seven to seventy (including three seats for "independents" linked to it, two of whom were former student leaders who gained prominence during recent demonstrations in favor of tuition-free tertiary education).[26] By contrast, the number of seats controlled by the right dropped from fifty-eight to forty-eight. All these losses were sustained by the UDI, while the RN gained a seat.

The number of valid votes cast in the congressional election of 2013 declined by nearly 400,000 in comparison to the previous contest, but this figure conceals the extent of the electorate's reshuffling. Extrapolating from the voting options of our survey respondents in 2009 and 2013, the addition of those who voted in 2009 but abstained in 2013, and of those who did not vote in 2009 but did do so in 2013, is equal to about a fifth of the total number of 6,616,000 valid votes cast in 2009. And, unlike the larger prior losses of valid votes between 1993 and 1997 as new generations of Chileans opted in greater numbers to not register to vote, the decline in the number of votes between 2009 and 2013 was not evenly distributed: the Alliance *lost* 620,900 votes while the New Majority *gained* 33,500.[27] Crossing our survey's question regarding which parties respondents would choose if voting "became obligatory once again" with another asking whether or not they had voted in the congressional election of 2013, shows that 33.4% of those who chose the UDI and the RN had abstained from voting in 2013, while the same figure for PDC, PPD, and PS supporters was 26.5% – a nearly 7% difference. If the Alliance's rate of abstention had been equal to that of the New Majority according to these figures, it would have been able to retain nearly 200, 000 more of its 2009 votes in 2013 than it did. The survey also indicates that those who voted after having abstained in 2009 were nearly four times as likely to be supportive of the New Majority rather than the Alliance. Moreover, those who switched their support from one coalition to another between 2009 and 2013

[26] Two other young former student leaders, members of the Communist Party, were also elected.
[27] Smaller parties outside the two major coalitions gained nearly 102,000 votes, in part by taking advantage of free publicity given by the state to their first-round presidential candidates.

did so in favor of the New Majority by a factor of about ten to one – although their numbers were only about 3% of all valid votes in 2009.[28]

The 2016 municipal election also produced a small asymmetrical change, but in the opposite direction, in the partisan composition of those who voted. While the number of valid votes for the seven major parties declined by 13.2% in relation to the previous municipal election, the NM coalition accounted for nearly three quarters of that drop. This was enough to give the right a slight advantage in the number of mayors, although the NM retained its majority of seats in the municipal councils. And, yet, voters who abstain from casting ballots do not necessarily change their inclination to vote one way or the other. Hence, the increase in volatility that stems from voluntary voting does not necessarily reflect shifts in the overall political attachments of the population. This can normally be seen over several electoral cycles as former abstainers who vote, and former voters who abstain, even out the expression of political preferences.

Among the factors that may discourage voter turnout for parties are allegations of corruption in their leadership ranks. The first legal norms regarding campaign funding were enacted in Chile in 2003, establishing some public funding for them, regulating donations, and setting spending limits (Fuentes 2011). During the last three years, revelations of illicit funding for parties and campaigns have resulted in judicial investigations that have been at the forefront of news reports. Top UDI leaders, as well as the head of a new Progressive Party that has drawn votes from the center-left, were indicted before the 2016 municipal contest. However, such proceedings did not impact the electoral support obtained by these parties.

The Electoral Regime

The binomial electoral system congealed the party alliances that supported the "yes" and "no" in the 1988 plebiscite. Critics of this unusual system have argued that it was designed to favor the rightist coalition by disproportionately enhancing its congressional representation (Polga-Hecimovich and Siavelis 2015). However, this effect was small. Leaving aside the abnormal 1989 election, in the six lower house elections from 1993 to 2013 the ratio of seats to votes for the Concertation/NM was on average 1.08, and for the Alliance 1.13.[29] Both coalitions' positive results were of course generated at the expense of the minor lists that also fielded candidates.

Given the binomial system's stricture limiting candidate lists to only two per district, the relative proportionality of the vote to seat allocations for individual

---

[28] Using communal socioeconomic data, Morales (2015) noted that the UDI support dropped more heavily in poorer urban areas, although this cannot be interpreted as referring to individual characteristics.

[29] Our calculations with SERVEL data. More than 1 equals over-representation – and vice versa.

parties in the two major coalitions played out differently. With a few exceptions for minor parties, the Alliance could basically list a candidate from each one of its two principal parties in most districts, and therefore an over-representation of the party that obtained the most votes was unavoidable. In the first three elections beginning in 1989, this effect worked in favor of the RN (with a seat to vote ratio of 1.31), and in the last three it worked in favor of the UDI (with the same ratio at 1.32).[30] The 2001 election was a draw.

By contrast, with four major parties – or five in the New Majority – plus a variable number of smaller ones, no single party in the center-left coalitions could present its candidates everywhere. As a result, the process of creating the lists of candidates for congressional offices had to become a key mechanism to manage inter-party relations within the center-left. This meant in practice that the proportionality of the distribution of seats in congress for the center-left voting block was manufactured by party leaders, not voter choices.[31] And all these negotiations and compromises resulted in over-representing the parties with the fewest votes – that is, the opposite effect of what occurred in the Alliance. This meant that the parties with the larger vote share, in particular the Christian Democrats, had to bear a greater cost in terms of lost representation and local party activation in order to sustain the center-left coalition. This may also have contributed to the slow attrition of its electoral support over the years.

These different outcomes can be illustrated by calculating how many deputies the parties in the two main coalitions would have elected if the 2013 regional council election had been that year's legislative one. Both elections were held at the same time, and the legislative districts aggregate to fit exactly into the regional council ones. The council elections were conducted with a D'Hondt proportional formula with full slates of candidates per party in each district, and their magnitudes can be assumed to be the sum of all the deputies each region elects – a number that ranges from two, to thirty-two. As expected, this simulation showed that, within the Alliance, the UDI would have lost five seats – an indication of its over-representation – and RN would have gained four. In turn, the NM would have lost eight seats, overall, to candidates from other lists. Two would have gone to the Alliance thereby increasing its representation, while six would have gone to other lists that claim to be "progressive." Those losses would have affected only the Radicals and the Communists – that is, the smallest vote getters in the NM coalition, thereby revealing their relative over-representation. While both of these parties elected six deputies each with the binomial system in 2013, the Radicals would have obtained only one, and the Communists three.

---

[30] Our calculations with SERVEL data. More than 1 equals over-representation – and vice versa.
[31] Hence, proportionality indexes such as Gallagher's are misleading when applied to Chilean legislative elections. For analysis of how the candidacies were determined in the Concertation, see Siavelis (2005).

What worked well for coalition management from a national political perspective for the center-leftist parties was detrimental, however, for local district party organizations and militants because more than half of them were unable to work for their own party's candidates in legislative contests. Moreover, the national game plan of distributing target numbers of seats to the different parties in the coalition often led to pairing strong candidates, frequently the incumbents – who have more than an 80% rate of reelection and an outsized influence in their parties – with weaker ones (Siavelis 2005). This further discouraged local party activation in favor of candidates who were expected to lose. These practices have probably contributed to raising public disaffection with politics.

The binomial regime was finally eliminated in 2015 after years of attempts to do so fell short of the constitutionally required four-sevenths majority needed in both houses of congress for this purpose (Campos 2009). The key vote to reach that majority in the senate was provided by *Amplitud*, the breakaway party from the RN. The new electoral law introduces an open list proportional representation system using a D'Hondt formula much like the one Chile had before 1973, except that voters will not be able to opt, as was formerly the case, for a straight party list vote. All parties will be able to present one more candidate than there are seats to be filled.

The senate will have fifty seats distributed among the nation's fifteen regions, each one of which will elect between two and five senators depending on their population. This means that Metropolitan Santiago will continue to be under-represented. The lower house will be composed of 155 seats distributed among twenty-eight districts, each one of which will elect between three and eight deputies. The parties may form electoral pacts, which will be treated as a single party in a first round of seat allocations, with the specific winners within them to be determined in a second D'Hondt formula distribution. Only up to 60% of all candidates presented nationwide on a party's lists may be of the same gender.

Given the relatively low district magnitudes, the effects of the D'Hondt formula will be muted. There will still be some electoral advantage to fielding candidates for the lower house of congress through inter-party ones, but they are unlikely to take the form of only two main coalitions as has been the case since 1990. Indeed, the PDC has formed its own congressional candidate lists for the November 2017 elections – a first since the return to democracy. But even if only two main coalitions were formed, voters would still have a greater choice among candidates linked to the seven major parties given the fact that they will all be able to list candidates in every district. This will probably favor the reactivation of party life across the board. The new electoral law also lowers the number of signatures needed to form a new party to just 0.25% of the total number of votes in the previous electoral cycle, thereby facilitating the creation of new parties.

CONCLUSIONS

Despite its suppression by an anti-party dictatorship, the Chilean party system reemerged after the return to democracy much like it had been before: a multi-party system with a similar number of core parties – seven presently – and many smaller ones – about two dozen at this point. And it retained a characteristic stability, overall, in the distribution of electoral support for its major political tendencies and parties, a central feature of institutionalized systems.

The resilience of this stability – which endured long years of electoral closure – reflects the long-standing divisions in Chilean society along religious and class lines that created the party system. After emerging, party and party faction leaders reinforced, through their pronouncements and policy choices, what eventually became sets of partially overlapping as well as exclusive political sub-cultures among voters, each with historically tinged symbols and narratives. The relative stability of the intergenerational continuities of Chilean electoral results stem to some degree from a straightforward sense of party identification among some voters, but more generally it results from an on-going process of matching between the predispositions of different segments of the electorate as defined by their sub-cultural sensibilities, with candidates who seek to channel them into votes for their parties. This matching generates a form of social rootedness of the Chilean party system that extends beyond the various parties' links to civil society associations. And it can occur – not that it always does – at a level that is beyond many voters' conscious awareness – as in-depth qualitative interviews are best suited to reveal. For instance, voters often explain their choices by noting that they focus on the personal qualities of the candidates. But after conducting a long interview with one such voter, the owner of a small business in a town in Southern Chile, a clear pattern emerged: he had always simply voted for RN candidates at all levels, and yet he was utterly surprised to come to realize this, even though his clearly rightist programmatic inclinations and low religiosity did indeed best coincide with support for the RN.[32]

This explanation for the stability of voting patterns is consistent with the fact that our survey respondents answered so readily our questions regarding the closeness of each of the major Chilean parties to the Church and to the rich. Nowhere else in the Americas could *both of these questions* be asked generating such high response rates and clarity in the results. And this reflects as well the notion that the party system was not recomposed by the impact of the military regime following a pro-democratic and pro-authoritarian divide. While our statistical models registered a differential impact of pro-authoritarian attitudes on voting options, it bears repeating that this stems from rightist voters' awareness of the fact that they, or their forebears and families, generally opted to support the coup against President Allende. Hence, the difference in attitudes toward what appear to be regime types reflect instead a

---

[32] Interview by J. S. Valenzuela, December 2008, in Santa Bárbara.

strand of historical memory in the rightist sub-culture that refers to the political contingencies of 1973 – not to a new divide in the party system generated by the 1988 plebiscite. Moreover, the Pinochet regime reinforced the deeper cultural sub-structure embedded in the party system's long history by simply being the expression of the most rightist and religiously conservative force in the nation's politics. For those who supported this tendency it was their government, executing their economic policies after "saving" the country from "a Communist dictatorship."

A partial exception to the stability of voting patterns has been the secular decline of support for the PDC. But as the largest party in the Concertation and in its successor New Majority coalition, it shouldered the primary costs of what we referred to as coalition maintenance by not running candidates in many legislative districts due to the strictures of the binomial formula. Thus, the PDC leadership has not only been in a long-standing alliance with secular leaning parties to its left, but has also repeatedly and unavoidably forced some of its local constituencies to vote for congressional candidates from such parties. This scenario was likely to foster a constant leakage of regular but soft PDC voters to the right, a notion reinforced by the fact that crossover voting between the two coalitions, though small, has occurred with greater frequency between the parties of the right and the PDC (Navia and Saldaña 2009). The new electoral law may assist the PDC in recovering its losses by permitting the party to present its own full slates of candidates in all lower house legislative districts, thereby allowing it to better reassert its identity whatever coalition it creates with other parties. And yet the electoral gains from the party's ability to better project its identity may be limited by growing levels of secularization in Chilean society, and by its weaker links to a more conservative Catholic Church.

Despite having a similar morphology in terms of its composition and family identities to its pre-dictatorial past, the current party system is, nonetheless, quite different from what it was before. It has changed primarily because much of the left has become a social democratic force with a strong commitment to democracy and a clear acceptance of the operation of an open market economy. In sum, the party system is no longer polarized by the shadow of the cold war hanging over the nation's politics.

6

The Uneven Institutionalization of a Party System: Brazil*

Scott Mainwaring, Timothy J. Power, and Fernando Bizzarro

Along with El Salvador and Panama, Brazil is one of the few Latin American countries that have more institutionalized party systems today than a generation ago. When the Mainwaring and Scully (1995a) volume was published, Brazil's party system was characterized by high electoral volatility, the steep electoral tailspins of the parties that governed the country from 1982 until 1992, the meteoric rise and subsequent fall of a populist who won the 1989 presidential election, frequent party switching by politicians, and weak linkages between voters and parties. In recent years, the party system has enjoyed stability in presidential and lower chamber elections. Two parties, the leftist Workers' Party (PT, Partido dos Trabalhadores) and the center-right Brazilian Social Democratic Party (PSDB, Partido da Social Democracia Brasileira), have dominated the last six presidential elections (1994–2014), providing structure and stability to the system, including in programmatic terms. In contrast to the sharp policy shifts (Stokes 2001) that many Latin American parties pulled in the 1980s and 1990s, obfuscating traditional ideological divisions and diluting party brands (Lupu 2016), the *relative* positions of Brazilian parties have been stable – even though the PSDB and PT both shifted to the right after winning the presidency in 1994 and 2002, respectively. During a generation of the collapse of many major parties and the weakening of party systems in several Latin American countries, the Brazilian case was a counter example of increasing institutionalization from 1994 to 2014.

This institutionalization, however, is uneven and thin, and the PT's woes over the last few years have dealt a crushing blow to one of the system's pillars. Institutionalization is uneven in the sense that electoral stability has been high

* We are grateful to Oswaldo Amaral, Mariana Borges, José Antonio Cheibub, Michael Coppedge, Ann Mische, Lucas Novaes, Gabriela Ippolito O'Donnell, Bruno Reis, Guilherme Russo, David Samuels (on two occasions), and Thiago Silva for comments; to Andréa Freitas, Oswaldo Amaral, Rachel Meneguello, and the Center for Studies in Public Opinion, UNICAMP, for providing access to data; and to María Victoria De Negri for research assistance.

for the presidency and the Chamber of Deputies, but not for gubernatorial contests. Institutionalization is thin in that individual-level and organizational underpinnings of systemic-level stability are modest and are uneven across parties.[1] The PT had strong roots in society until 2014, with many party identifiers and a strong, penetrating organization. The other parties have weaker roots in society, far fewer party identifiers, and less robust organizations. Thus, at the level of individual parties, there was a gap between the solidity of the PT and the rest. This fact has important consequences for system-level stability: until 2016, the position of the PT as one of the main actors in the system was safer than that of the other parties. While PT identifiers formed a group large and loyal enough to give it a competitive edge in presidential elections, no other party had a similar contingent of partisans. Systems that are not grounded in strong partisanship and solid party organizations are more vulnerable to deinstitutionalization (Lupu 2016; Morgan 2011; Seawright 2012).

This chapter documents the change from an inchoate to a relatively institutionalized party system and then attempts to explain why it happened. Notwithstanding burgeoning scholarly interest in party system institutionalization (PSI) since 1995, there have been relatively few efforts to explain how institutionalization occurs. In part, this is because there are few clear-cut cases of the institutionalization of democratic party systems in third and fourth wave democracies; in contrast, there are several good books on the opposite phenomenon: party system collapse (Morgan 2011; Seawright 2012) and/or party collapse (Lupu 2016).

Our explanation of growing PSI focuses on three factors. First, in Brazil, economic stabilization fostered party system institutionalization. Between 1980 and 1994, chronic triple and quadruple inflation that peaked at 2948% in 1990 and no net economic growth led to massive defections of politicians and huge electoral losses for three successive governing parties and coalitions: the Democratic Social Party, PDS (Partido Democrático Social), 1979–85; the Party of the Brazilian Democratic Movement, PMDB, 1985–90; and the Party of National Reconstruction (PRN), 1990–92. The massive setbacks of these parties opened doors for others and provoked a profound reorganization of the party system. Economic stabilization in 1994 and some subsequent positive policy results under the governments of the PSDB (1995–2003) and the Workers' Party (PT) (specifically from 2003 to 2010) positioned these two parties as the major players in the system. Socioeconomic advances helped bring about greater institutionalization.

Second, changes in the formal rules of the game have supported PSI. Some early changes (just after the 1988 constitution was approved) boosted party discipline relative to the constitutional congress of 1987–88 (Figueiredo and Limongi 1999). Greater discipline helped build more cohesive party identities and loyalties. The 1995 Law of Political Parties vastly increased public funding,

---

[1] Zucco (2015) makes a similar argument; he speaks of "stabilization without roots."

enabling parties to build more solid organizations. It also altered the criteria for allocating free television and radio campaign time in a way that strongly favors established parties. The change from non-concurrent to concurrent presidential and congressional elections in 1994 increased hurdles for political outsiders. In 2002, a law abolished the birthright candidate rule (*candidato nato*), by which any elected politician automatically had the right to run for reelection. The birthright candidate law meant that incumbent politicians did not need the support of parties to run for reelection, and hence they could more easily turn their backs on the leadership. These institutional changes promoted PSI.

Third, institutionalization benefitted from the consistent presence of viable contenders with clearly contrasting programmatic preferences. These programmatic differences gave voters a sense that they could choose something different within the system if other options failed them. Programmatic differentiation thereby lowered the risk of systemic collapse.

We close the chapter with some reflections on the PT's steep decline of partisans, the repudiation of the party throughout much of Brazilian society, and its steep electoral losses in 2016, and on what this augurs for the system's institutionalization. The PT was not just any old party. It won the presidency four times in a row, and in all seven presidential elections since redemocratization, it came in first or second. It gained far more partisans than other parties, and it was more organized. In important ways, it was a central pillar of the system.

BRAZIL'S CONTEMPORARY PARTIES

After twenty-one years of military rule (1964–85), Brazil returned to democracy in March 1985. The first nine years of democracy were characterized by a new Constitution (1988), years of three and four-digit inflation rates, an impeached president (Fernando Collor de Mello in 1992), and ongoing upheaval in the party system. From the successful economic stabilization plan in 1994 until the political and economic crisis that erupted in 2015, the country enjoyed a deepening of democracy, a reduction of poverty, an amelioration of long-standing stark inequalities, and more stability in the party system.

Since 1990, the congressional party system has been extremely fragmented. As of 2015, thirty-two parties were registered with the Electoral Justice[2] and at least another dozen have petitioned for formal recognition.[3] Twenty-six have at least one representative in the Chamber of Deputies (as of November 2016).

Created in 1980, the Workers' Party (PT, *Partido dos Trabalhadores*) was initially spearheaded by leftist activists and politicians; the "new" union movement that emerged in the late 1970s in greater São Paulo, mainly in the automobile industry; and grassroots Catholic activists. It was initially a small,

---

[2] www.tse.jus.br/partidos/partidos-politicos
[3] https://pt.wikipedia.org/wiki/Lista_de_partidos_pol%C3%ADticos_no_Brasil

ideological socialist party with somewhat radical tendencies, with roots primarily in the state of São Paulo.[4] It enjoyed steady electoral growth from its first election in 1982 until 2002, when Luis Inácio (Lula) da Silva was elected president. It also expanded its organization. Building upon the mobilization of a series of grassroots networks, the PT became a fully national organization by the end of the 1990s, with more than two thousand local branches across Brazil (Hunter 2010).

Even though it was still a small party, in 1989, when the first popular elections for president since 1960 took place, PT candidate Lula came in second place and made it to the runoff, where he lost with 47% of the valid vote. Lula also finished second in presidential voting in 1994 and 1998. Over time, the PT became more pragmatic, more willing to form electoral alliances that it once spurned, and more moderate. The 2002 election was an inflection point; in order to enhance his chances of winning and governing successfully, Lula moved toward the center during his campaign (Meneguello and Amaral 2008; Hunter 2010).

Lula served two terms as president, from 2003 through 2010. During his presidency, Brazil achieved considerable success in reducing poverty and inequality. During these years, the PT's social base changed toward the poor states and toward poor and less educated voters (Hunter and Power 2007; Soares and Terron 2008). Whereas previously it had fared best in the country's most developed states and among the more educated, since 2006 the PT has fared best in the poor northeastern and northern states and among the less educated.

In 2010, PT candidate Dilma Rousseff was elected president, winning decisively (56% to 44%) in the second round over PSDB candidate José Serra. She was reelected in 2014, again winning against a PSDB candidate (Aécio Neves, former governor of Brazil's second largest state, Minas Gerais) in the closest presidential election in Brazil's history (51.6% to 48.4%). In her second term, she presided over an endless stream of corruption revelations about past PT practices and over Brazil's deepest recession in decades. She was removed from office on May 12, 2016 and succeeded by her Vice-President, Michel Temer of the PMDB (*Partido do Movimento Democrático Brasileiro*, Party of the Brazilian Democratic Movement), who had defected to the opposition and worked in favor of her impeachment.

Since 1994, the PSDB has either won the presidency (1994 and 1998) or finished second and made the runoff (2002–14). It emerged in 1988 as a center-left splinter from the PMDB. In 1994, it moved to the center or center-right (Power and Zucco 2009: 230) to enhance presidential candidate Fernando Henrique Cardoso's chances of winning – which he did in a first-round landslide. Cardoso repeated the first-round landslide in 1998. The PSDB fared best among better-educated and wealthier voters and in larger cities in the

---

[4] On the PT's early years, see Keck (1992) and Meneguello (1989).

2002–14 period and in the 1989 presidential election and 1990 congressional elections. During Cardoso's presidency, from 1994 until 2002, it had strong support from the poorest areas of the country (Zucco 2008), while the educated middle class tended to vote for Lula.

The PMDB was created in 1966 as the official opposition party to the military government. From 1966 to 1980, it was known as the *Movimento Democrático Brasileiro* (MDB, Brazilian Democratic Movement). It spearheaded growing opposition to the military, paving the way for the transition to democracy in 1985. The PMDB swept to landslide victories in the 1986 congressional and gubernatorial elections, but scores of members of congress elected on the party's label in 1986 defected to other parties in the next few years. It diluted its brand, strongly associated with redemocratization, by the end of José Sarney's government (1985–90), and it governed during a period of hyperinflation and economic turmoil. Sarney's disastrous economic policies severely impacted the party's electoral fortunes. The failure of Ulysses Guimarães's candidacy in the 1989 presidential elections, when he received 4.5% of the vote, the decrease in the party's support in lower chamber elections between 1986 and 1990 (from 48.1% to 19.3%),[5] and the steep decline in the number of PMDB partisans were consequences of a poor governing record and brand dilution.[6]

The PMDB has never fielded a competitive presidential candidate, but it remains one of the country's largest parties in the national congress and in winning state gubernatorial posts. Since the 1990s, it has fared best in the northeast and north and among poorer voters. Ideologically, the PSDB and PMDB have been largely indistinguishable since 1994 (Lucas and Samuels 2010), anchoring the center or center-right of the spectrum. Current President Temer has been a PMDB member since the 1980s, and was the party president from 2001 to 2016.

For the first two decades of the democratic regime, there was a fourth major party, the Democrats (DEM). This party was founded with the name *Partido da Frente Liberal* (Party of the Liberal Front, PFL) in 1984–85, when many leaders of the party that had supported the military dictatorship defected. By casting their votes for opposition presidential candidate Tancredo Neves in 1985, the PFL helped bring about an orderly end to the dictatorship. A conservative party with traditional strongholds in northeastern Brazil, the PFL formed a coalition with the PSDB in the 1994 and 1998 presidential elections (both won by Cardoso of the PSDB) and again in 2006 and 2010.[7] After Cardoso left power

---

[5] Georgetown Political Database for the Americas, 1990 Legislative Elections for the Chamber of Deputies. [Internet]. Georgetown University and Organization of American States, see http://pdba.georgetown.edu/Elecdata/Brazil/legis1990.html.

[6] Mainwaring (1999) reports that in 1978, 61% of the voters in the city of São Paulo identified with the [P]MDB. By 1989, this number had fallen to 14%.

[7] On the PFL, see Ferreira (2002: 47–134), R. Ribeiro (2014), and Tarouco (1999).

and the PT began to displace the PFL in the Northeast, in 2007, the party changed its name to DEM (Democrats) and transitioned to a younger leadership in Lula's second term in office. As recently as 2006, it was still the fourth largest party in congressional elections, but its erosion has accelerated in recent years.

In national legislative and sub-national elections, these four parties collectively win about half of the vote. There is also a large and diverse group of medium-sized parties, which we operationalize as parties receiving from 3% to 8% of the seats in the Chamber of Deputies and winning governorships in at least one state in recent elections. These parties stand at both the right and at the left of the ideological spectrum.[8] On the right are the PP (Progressive Party), PTB (Brazilian Labor Party), PR (Party of the Republic), PSD (Social Democratic Party), and PSC (Social Christian Party). The first three date to the initial years of the democratic regime and have since gathered important electoral support in specific areas of the country. The PSD is a political machine that was created in 2011 as a pro-government party to accommodate politicians who had previously been members of parties that opposed the PT. After the impeachment of Dilma Rousseff in 2016, the party remained in the cabinet of Michel Temer. The PSC is the most successful of the parties of the new Brazilian right, with strong roots in neoPentecostal churches and other new actors such as radio announcers and police officers.

The importance of medium-sized parties is mirrored on the left side of the political spectrum. The Brazilian Socialist Party, PSB, enjoys strong electoral support in the northeast of the country, where it absorbed many of the voters and the elites of more traditional parties, such as the PFL/DEM (R. Ribeiro 2014). The *Partido Popular Socialista* (Popular Socialist Party, PPS) and *Partido Verde* (PV, Green Party) are center-left parties that have systematically won more than a dozen representatives in the country's legislature and have played important roles in presidential elections. The PV had a viable presidential candidate in 2010 with Marina Silva.[9] Marina won 19.3% of the votes in the first round (until 2014, the best performance of any third-place presidential candidate since 1955) and was largely responsible for preventing an outright victory by Dilma Rousseff in the first round. She joined the PSB and became its presidential candidate in 2014, again running third behind the PT and PSDB candidates.

Appendix 6.1 lists the parties that are currently represented in the Chamber of Deputies, the lower chamber of the national congress. Table 6.1 shows the ten most important parties, which together win approximately three-quarters of the vote in PR contests. We rank their electoral potency according to their average performance in the most recent elections for federal deputy (2014)

---

[8] This ideological ordering of Brazilian parties follows Zucco (2011).
[9] Marina Silva is a historical leader of environmental movements in the Amazon forest. She was Lula's Environment Minister until 2008 and left the government and the PT to run for president in 2010.

TABLE 6.1 *Electoral Performance, Main Brazilian Parties, 2014–16*

Party	2014 Chamber of Deputies (%)	2016 City Councils (%)	Mean of 2014 and 2016 (%)	Rank
PMDB	11.0	9.4	10.2	1
PSDB	11.4	8.5	10.0	2
PT	13.9	5.5	9.2	3
PP	6.6	5.7	6.2	4
PSD	6.1	6.2	6.2	5
PSB	6.4	5.8	6.1	6
PR	5.8	4.4	5.1	7
PDT	3.6	5.7	4.7	8
DEM	4.2	4.5	4.4	9
PTB	4.0	4.4	4.2	10
Total	73.0	60.1	66.6	–

Note: Percentages refer to party's share of total valid votes cast.
Source: Tribunal Superior Eleitoral.

and municipal councils (2016). Of these ten parties, two were founded under military rule (the PMDB and PP, which trace their roots to 1966) while six date to the democratic transition between 1980 and 1985 (PT, PDT, PTB, and PSB, plus arguably the PR, which is heir to the defunct Liberal Party). The PSDB was born during the constitutional assembly of 1987–88. As befits an institutionalized system, only one of the ten leading parties is a true newcomer: the PSD. Table 6.1 shows the extreme fragmentation of the party system in proportional elections. The two largest parties each win only a tenth of the national vote in municipal council elections.

STABILITY IN THE MEMBERSHIP OF THE PARTY SYSTEM

In institutionalized party systems, the main contenders are stable over time. Chapter 2 of this volume proposed six indicators to assess the stability of the membership of a party system. The first two are the vote share of new parties in presidential and congressional elections. These indicators reflect the system's openness, or to put it conversely, the barriers to new contenders. In both presidential and lower chamber elections, since 1990, in Brazil new parties have had negligible electoral impact. In presidential elections, Brazil had the third lowest mean vote share for new parties for the 1990–2014 period (1.3%), among the nineteen countries included in Figure 2.1. Brazil had the seventh lowest average vote share for new parties in lower chamber elections (3.7%).

In 1980, the PT, PTB, and PDT formed. The membership of the party system changed profoundly from 1980 through 1990. In 1985 (the PFL) and 1988 (the PSDB), important new parties emerged. In contrast, no new party created after 1990 has won more than 6.2% of the lower chamber vote (the PSD in 2014). Except for the PSD and the PSDB (created in 1988), all major parties were born in the first half of the 1980s or earlier (the PMDB dates from 1966). In 2011, the PSD became the fourth largest party in the Congress, taking many of its new leaders from the Democrats and the PSDB.

In lower chamber elections, new parties won 13.8% in 1982, 26.3% in 1986, and 11.5% in 1990. Since 1994, the main contenders have been stable, as is seen in the precipitous drop in the vote share of new parties (the bottom row of Table 6.2). Except for 2014 because of the PSD, the vote share of new parties has consistently been very low.

Tables 2.2 and 2.3 in Chapter 2 displayed four indicators for the stability of the significant contenders. Election-to-election stability (Table 2.2) is the percentage of times that a party that won at least 10% of the vote surpassed that threshold again in the next election. Brazil has had high election-to-election stability of significant contenders in both presidential and lower chamber elections. Of the twenty-four times that a party won at least 10% of the lower chamber vote from 1990 to 2010, that party remained a significant contender in the following election on twenty-one occasions. Of the fourteen times that a party won at least 10% of the presidential vote from 1994 until 2010, it reached that threshold eleven times in the following election.

The indicator for medium-term stability is the number of times that all parties that ever reached the 10% threshold from 1990 to 2014 did so again as a percentage of all the times that they could have (Table 2.3). For medium-term stability, Brazil had the fifth highest score for lower chamber elections and the eighth highest for presidential elections. In sum, by all four indicators, Brazil has had relatively stable main contenders. Moreover, these indicators do not capture one of the most salient features of Brazil's party system: the stability of the main two contenders for the presidency in the last six elections (1994–2014): the PT and the PSDB.

THE STABILIZATION OF ELECTORAL COMPETITION

Another defining feature of an institutionalized party system is that the vote share of parties is relatively stable over time. This section describes the stabilization of electoral competition in presidential and lower chamber elections and notes the ongoing high levels of volatility in elections for governors. We also note the concentration of the vote on two parties in presidential elections, the exceptional fragmentation of the party system in the lower chamber, and the intermediate situation in gubernatorial elections: low fragmentation at the state level but high fragmentation when we aggregate to the national level. The differences in the party system across these three levels are so great that it

TABLE 6.2 *Presidential Election Results (% of 1st Round Valid Vote) and Effective Number of Presidential Candidates, 1989–2014*

Year	1989	1994	1998	2002	2006	2010	2014
PRN	30.5	0.6					
PT	17.2	27.0	31.7	46.4	48.6	46.9	41.6
PDT	16.5	3.2			2.6		
PSDB	11.5	54.3	53.1	23.2	41.6	32.6	33.5
PDS	8.9	2.8					
PL	4.8						
PMDB	4.7	4.4					
PRONA		7.4	2.1				
PCB/PPS	1.1		11.0	12.0			
PSB				17.9			21.3
PSOL					6.9		1.5
PV	0.2		0.3			19.3	0.6
Others	4.8	3.1	1.9	0.5	0.3	1.2	1.4
Total	100.0	100.0	100.0	100.0	100.0	100.0	
ENPC	5.45	2.65	2.53	3.17	2.41	2.75	3.02
Electoral volatility	–	60.7	17.6	33.8	30.4	19.5	24.2
Vote share new parties	51.1	0.0	0.7	0.0	7.0	0.0	0.0

Source: IPEADATA and *Tribunal Superior Eleitoral.*

makes sense to distinguish between the presidential and the congressional party systems. Alternatively, one could argue that Brazil has had a bifurcated party system: exceptionally fragmented in the national congress yet with low fragmentation in presidential voting (Meneguello 2011). As we explain later in this chapter, the impressive fragmentation of the legislature is not incompatible with our broad argument of uneven institutionalization of the party system.

Presidential Elections

The presidency is by far the most powerful position in Brazil, so we analyze it in greater detail than the congressional party system. Our discussion of presidential elections emphasizes a shift from high volatility (1989–94), high fragmentation (1989), and the electoral victory of an outsider populist in 1989 to the stabilization of electoral tendencies, the concentration of the vote on two leading candidates, and the consistent dominance of the PT and PSDB from 1994 through 2014. The second and third points have been closely linked in Brazil since 1994, but they are discrete in principle and usually in reality; in highly fragmented congressional party systems, voting for the presidency is usually concentrated on two or three leading candidates but these candidates do not always come from the same two or three parties.

From High Volatility (1989–94) to Stabilization (1994–2014). The president and the other most powerful political positions in Brazil – state governors and mayors of cities with at least 200,000 registered voters – are elected in majority runoff systems. For these posts, two candidates get to the second round if nobody wins a majority of the valid vote in the first round.

Table 6.2 shows the results of first-round presidential voting, organized by the party of the candidate who spearheaded different coalitions. The table includes only parties that won at least 5% of the vote on at least one occasion. The second row from the bottom shows the sharp drop in electoral volatility, from 60.7% (extremely high) for the 1989–94 electoral period to an average of 25% in the five elections since then, with a high of 33.8%. The top two contenders have always been from the same parties since 1994.

From Fragmentation to Concentration of the Vote. The third row from the bottom of Table 6.2 shows the effective number of presidential candidates. This number is calculated in the same way as the effective number of parties: by squaring each candidate's percentage of the vote, summing these squares, and dividing one by the sum of the squares. The 1989 presidential election was marked by fragmentation of the first-round vote. The effective number of presidential candidates was 5.45%. Populist Fernando Collor de Mello, who created a party (the PRN, *Partido da Reconstrução Nacional*) to run for office, won 30.5% of the valid vote, and Lula came in second with 17.2%.

The fragmentation of the vote for the presidency declined sharply after 1989. The average has been 2.70% in the five subsequent elections, and the numbers

TABLE 6.3 *Results of Presidential Elections, 2nd Round, 1989–2014*

Party	1989	2002	2006	2010	2014
PRN	Collor 53.0%	-	-	-	-
PT	Lula 47.0%	Lula 61.3%	Lula 60.8%	Dilma 56.0%	Dilma 51.6%
PSDB	-	Serra 38.7%	Alckmin 39.2%	Serra 44.0%	Neves 48.4%

Note: No runoff election was necessary in 1994 or in 1998.

have fluctuated little, from a low of 2.41% in 2006 to a high of 3.17% in 2002 – another component of the stabilization of presidential elections.

From Outsider Victory to PT/PSDB Duopoly. The third important change, also associated with increasing institutionalization, is that the same two parties, the PT and PSDB, have consistently come in first or second in the last six presidential elections. The route to the presidency has been through these same well-established parties, in sharp contrast to what occurred in 1989.

The PSDB candidate won in the first round in 1994 and 1998 and lost in the runoff in 2002, 2006, 2010, and 2014. The PT was the runner-up in 1994 and 1998 (as well as 1989) and won in 2002, 2006, 2010, and 2014. The two parties' candidates won 81% (1994), 85% (1998), 70% (2002), 90% (2006), 80% (2010), and 75% (2014) of the first-round presidential vote in the last six elections. Table 6.3 shows the second-round results of presidential voting.

Except in 2002, the gap between the PT and PSDB, on the one hand, and third place finishers, on the other, has been large: 19.6% in 1994, 20.7% in 1998, 5.3% in 2002, 34.7% in 2006, 13.3% in 2010, and 12.2% in 2014. There has been no major outsider candidate since Collor won in 1989. In 1994, outsider Enéas Carneiro won 7.4% of the valid vote; since then no outsider has come close to Enéas's percentage.

This combination of an exceptionally fragmented party system in congress and the consistent dominance of the same two parties over many (six) presidential elections is rare and perhaps unique in the history of presidential democracies. In other presidential democracies with highly fragmented congressional party systems, no set of two parties has consistently dominated presidential elections.

This duopoly in presidential competition is a contrast to Brazil's democracy of 1946–64. During that earlier period of democracy, the party system was much less fragmented in congress, *and* four different parties (the PSD, the PTB, the UDN, and the PDC) either won the presidency or came a close second at least one time. Each of the three largest parties had at least one winning presidential

TABLE 6.4 *Coalitions Running Presidential Candidates, 1994–2014*

1994	1998	2002	2006	2010	2014
	PSDB/PFL/			PSDB/DEM/	PSDB/ PMN/SD/
PSDB/PFL	PPB/PTB/	PSDB/ PMDB	PSDB/PFL	PTB/PPS/PMN/	DEM/PEN/ PTN/PTB/
	PSD			PTdoB	PTC/PTdoB
PT/PSB/ PCdoB/ PPS/PV/ PSTU	PT/PDT/ PSB/ PCB/ PCdoB	PT/PL/ PCdoB/ PMN/PCB	PT/PRB/ PCdoB	PT/PMDB/PDT /PCdoB/PSB/ PR/PRB/ PTN/ PSC/PTC	PT/PMDB/ PSD/ PP/PR/PROS/ PDT/ PCdoB/PRB
PMDB/PSD	PPL/ PL/PAN	PPS/PDT/ PTB	PSOL/PCB/ PSTU	PV	PSB/PRP/PPS/ PPL/PHS/PSL
Prona	PTdoB	PSB/PGT/ PTC	PSL	PSDC	PSOL
PDT	PMN	PSTU	PDT	PRTB	PSC
PPR	PSDC	PCO	PSDC	PSOL	PV
PRN	PSN			PCO	PRTB
PSC	PTN			PSTU	PSTU
	PSC				PSDC
	PSN				PCB
	Prona				PCO
	PV				

Source: Tribunal Superior Eleitoral.

candidate (if we count Jânio Quadros's party in 1960 as the UDN), and each was unable to field its own candidate on at least one occasion.

It is not only the consistent dominance by the PSDB and the PT that stabilized the system. As Limongi and Cortez (2010) noted, party coalitions in presidential elections have also been fairly stable. The PT and other leftist and center-left parties have always anchored one coalition, augmented since the 2002 election with at least one center-right party in every contest. In four of the last five presidential elections, all except for 2002, the PSDB and PFL/Democrats have spearheaded the other coalition. Among the four parties profiled in the first section of this chapter, the PMDB has been the only one outside this generally stable set of coalitions. After dismal showings by its own candidates in 1989 and 1994, the PMDB sat out the 1998 and 2006 presidential contests and joined the PSDB coalition in 2002 and the PT coalition in 2010 and 2014. Table 6.4 shows the coalitions in presidential elections.

LOWER CHAMBER ELECTIONS: STABILIZATION WITH EXTREME
FRAGMENTATION

Our discussion of the party system in the lower chamber emphasizes the plunge
in electoral volatility starting in 1994 combined with extreme fragmentation.
Table 6.5 shows the results in votes for the main parties in lower chamber
elections, 1982–2014. In the 1980s, electoral volatility in voting for the
Chamber of Deputies was very high: 35.4% for the 1982–86 electoral period
and 35.6% for 1986–90. The 1980s were a decade of turmoil in the party
system.

Since 1994, mirroring the stabilization of presidential elections, Brazil has
had low electoral volatility for the Chamber of Deputies. For these last six
elections, Brazil's electoral volatility has been close to the average for the
advanced industrial democracies and well below average for Latin America.

The congressional party system is extraordinarily fragmented – the most
fragmented in the history of Latin America and perhaps beyond. The effective
number of parties in votes for the Chamber of Deputies has increased
monotonically since 1982, reaching 14.1 in 2014. Since 1990, the largest vote
share that any party has won for the Chamber of Deputies was the PMDB's
20.3% in 1994. In 2014, the largest party was the PT, with only 13.9% of the
vote. Brazil's effective number of parties in 2014 was much higher than any
election in the 618 electoral periods in sixty-seven countries in the Mainwaring/
España/Gervasoni dataset on electoral volatility (Mainwaring *et al.* 2016).

For state assemblies and the Chamber of Deputies, voting at the state level
results in a high effective number of parties in all twenty-seven states (Ferreira
et al. 2008: 443–46). In 2010, the least fragmented state assembly was Santa
Catarina with an effective number of parties (ENP) of 7.2, and the unweighted
mean for all twenty-seven states was 11.4 (Rebello 2012). At the state level, there
has been a huge contrast in party system fragmentation between gubernatorial
results and proportional elections (state assembly and the Chamber of Deputies).
The combination of low electoral volatility and extremely high fragmentation is
unusual; high fragmentation tends to be associated with high electoral volatility
(Mainwaring *et al.* 2016; Roberts and Wibbels 1999).

PARTY COMPETITION FOR STATE GOVERNORS: PERSISTENTLY
HIGH VOLATILITY

State governors – especially those of large and wealthy states such as São Paulo,
Minas Gerais, Rio de Janeiro, and Rio Grande do Sul – are powerful actors in
Brazil. Next to the presidency, these are the most powerful elected positions. Brazil
is a federal country, and states have ample resources and legal competencies.

In contrast to what has occurred in presidential and lower chamber elections,
gubernatorial contests continue to be marked by persistently high electoral

TABLE 6.5 *Vote Share of Brazilian Main Parties, Lower Chamber Elections since 1982*

Party	Founded	1982	1986	1990	1994	1998	2002	2006	2010	2014
PP[1]	1966	43.2	7.8	8.9	9.4	11.3	7.8	7.1	6.5	6.6
PMDB[2]	1966	43.0	48.1	19.3	20.3	15.2	13.4	14.5	13.0	11.1
PDT	1979	5.8	6.5	10.0	7.2	5.7	5.1	5.3	5.0	3.6
PTB	1979	4.5	4.5	5.6	5.2	5.7	4.6	4.7	4.2	4.0
PT	1979	3.6	6.9	10.2	12.8	13.2	18.4	14.9	16.9	13.9
DEM[3]	1985		17.7	12.4	12.9	17.3	13.4	10.9	7.5	4.2
PR[4]	1985		2.9	4.3	3.5	2.5	4.3	4.4	7.5	5.8
PSB	1985		0.9	1.9	2.2	3.4	5.3	6.2	7.0	6.4
PSDB	1988			8.7	13.9	17.5	14.3	13.7	11.9	11.4
PSD	2011									6.1
Others		0.0	4.7	18.8	12.6	8.2	13.4	18.3	20.5	26.9
ENPv[5]		2.6	3.6	9.8	8.5	8.1	9.3	10.6	11.2	14.1
Volatility		–	35.4	35.6	18.0	15.3	14.9	10.4	11.2	17.6
Vote share, new parties		13.8	26.3	11.5	0.3	0.6	0.0	1.4	0.0	11.9

[1] *Aliança Renovadora Nacional* (ARENA)/*Partido Democrático Social* (PDS)/*Partido Progressista Reformador* (PPR)/ *Partido Progressista* (PP).
[2] *Movimento Democrático Brasileiro* (MDB)/*Partido do Movimento Democrático Brasileiro* (PMDB).
[3] *Partido da Frente Liberal* (PFL)/*Democratas* (DEM).
[4] *Partido Liberal* (PL)/*Partido da República* (PR). The PR is result of the merger between the PL and PRONA.
[5] Effective number of parties, in votes.
Source: Data from the *Tribunal Superior Eleitoral.*

volatility. In this respect, the institutionalization of the party system has been uneven. Mean electoral volatility for the twenty-seven states was 67.8% from 1990 to 1994, 56.3% from 1994 to 1998, 48.8% from 1998 to 2002, 52.1% from 2002 to 2006 (Melo 2010: 27), and 48.8% for 2006–10. Party switching by major gubernatorial candidates accounts for an important share of this volatility (Cortez 2009: 130; Melo 2010: 29).

At the aggregate national level, many parties compete for and win state governorships.[10] Table 6.6 shows the number of state governorships won by party since 1982. Since 1990, in every election at least six different parties have captured at least one state. During this time, no party has ever won more than nine of twenty-seven states. Thus, the near duopoly that has existed on the presidency since 1994 does not exist at the country-wide level in the competition for governors. The bottom row shows the "effective number of governors" at the national level; the number is consistently much higher than the effective number of presidential candidates. The PT and PSDB combined have never won more than 37.7% of the vote; this zenith occurred, oddly, in 2002, when the two parties had a lower share of the first-round presidential vote than in any election since 1989. The PSB, PMDB, and PFL/Democrats, the latter two of which have never fielded a major presidential candidate and have not even presented a candidate since 1994 and 1989, respectively, win a meaningful number of states. In 2014, the PMDB won seven states, more than any other party, and the PSB won three.

Coalitions are the rule in gubernatorial elections. Presidential coalitions shape gubernatorial elections; state-level coalitions for gubernatorial elections tend to follow the same lines as the presidential coalitions. The PSDB and PFL frequently join forces, as do the PT, PSB, PDT, and PC do B (Limongi and Cortez 2010: 32–35). This consistency in coalitions between the presidential election and gubernatorial elections stems in part from ideological compatibility and in part from strategic bargaining: Coalition Partner A, realizing it is unlikely to field a competitive presidential candidate, supports Coalition Partner B in the presidential election; B support A's gubernatorial candidates in some states.

At the state level, consistent with what has occurred in presidential elections since 1994, fragmentation in gubernatorial elections has been modest (Cortez 2009). Melo (2010: 26) reports a mean effective number of gubernatorial candidates of 2.57 from 1990 to 2006. In the 2010 elections, the mean was 2.36, and in 2014, it was 2.55. Thus, the high dispersion of seats and votes for governors at the national level results exclusively from federal aggregation; low fragmentation in each state coexists with high fragmentation when results are aggregated to the national level.

---

[10] For analyses of party competition for state governorships, see Cortez 2009; Limongi and Cortez (2010); and Melo (2010: 24–35).

TABLE 6.6 *State Governors Elected by Party (N) and Effective Number of Governors, 1982–2014*

Party	1982	1986	1990	1994	1998	2002	2006	2010	2014
ARENA/ PDS/ PPR/PPB/PP	12	0	1	3	2	0	1	0	1
PMDB	9	22	7	9	6	5	7	5	7
PT	0	0	0	2	3	3	5	5	5
PSDB	–	–	1	6	7	7	6	8	5
PSB	–	–	0	2	2	4	3	6	3
PFL/DEM	–	1	9	2	6	4	1	2	0
PDT	1	0	3	2	1	1	2	0	2
PTB	0	0	2	1	0	0	0	0	0
PTR	–	–	1	–	1	1	–	1	0
PRS	–	–	1	–	1	1	1	–	0
PSC	–	–	1	0	0	0	0	0	0
PSL	–	–	–	–	0	1	0	0	0
PPS	–	0	0	0	0	2	2	0	0
PMN	–	1	0	0	1	0	0	1	0
PSD	–	1	1	1	0	1	1	–	2
PCdoB	–	1	0	0	0	0	0	0	1
PROS	–	1	–	–	1	1	1	–	1
Total	22	23	27	27	27	27	27	27	27
No. of parties that won at least one state	3	2	10	8	7	8	8	6	9
Effective No. of Governors	2.1	1.1	4.8	5.1	5.2	6.0	5.7	4.7	6.1

Source: Nicolau 1996 and *Tribunal Superior Eleitoral*.

180 *Party Systems in Latin America*

STABILITY OF IDEOLOGICAL POSITIONS

Stable ideological positions of the main parties characterize institutionalized systems. The main Brazilian parties have shown remarkable consistency in terms of their ordinal left–right ideological placement. The left has been anchored by the PT, the center and center-right by the PMDB and PSDB, and the right by the PFL/DEM until 2010. Although the ordinal placement of parties has been stable, the system has seen increasing ideological moderation accompanied by a gradual shift to the right. Table 6.7 shows the reputational left–right placement of each of the main parties as recorded in the Brazilian Legislative Surveys, which have been carried out in each legislature under democracy. The PFL/DEM has held a consistent position on the right, and most other parties have been drawn closer to it (Power and Zucco 2012). Both the PSDB and PT shifted sharply to the right after they won the presidency in 1994 and 2002, respectively. The net result has been a narrowing of the ideological range of the party system and a reduction in the ideological distances between the key power contenders, especially the PSDB and PT. On the 10-point ideological scale, the gap between the furthest left (always the PT) and the furthest right party fell sharply from 6.99 in 1990 to 4.39 in 2013.

TABLE 6.7 *Reputational Ideology: Left–Right Placements of the Major Parties, 1990–2013*

Party	1990 placement (BLS Wave 1)	2001 placement (BLS Wave 4)	2013 placement (BLS Wave 7)	Total movement relative to 1990
PT	1.51	2.27	3.86	2.35 right
PMDB	5.10	6.19	6.19	1.09 right
PSDB	3.98	6.30	6.32	2.34 right
PSB	2.23	2.85	4.12	1.89 right
PDS/PPB/PP	8.50	8.65	7.55	0.95 left
PL/PR	7.20	6.94	6.98	0.22 left
DEM	8.02	8.59	8.25	0.23 right
PDT	3.15	3.46	4.21	1.06 right
PTB	6.88	6.96	6.52	0.36 left
PSD	–	–	6.65	–

Notes: Parties are placed by non-members only on an ideological scale where 1 is left and 10 is right.
Source: Brazilian Legislative Surveys, http://thedata.harvard.edu/dvn/dv/zucco (accessed November 2016).

CONNECTIONS BETWEEN VOTERS AND PARTIES

In this volume, we moved away from conceptualizing party roots in society as a dimension of PSI. Nevertheless, as many scholars have argued (Lupu 2016;

Seawright 2012), strong connections between voters and parties generally underpin stable electoral competition. Although "stabilization without roots" (Zucco 2015) is empirically plausible and is a reasonable characterization of the Brazilian case, PSI is likely to be more secure if parties have deep roots in society.

Although there is fairly broad agreement among scholars that the Brazilian party system has institutionalized, there is disagreement about the strength of connections between voters and parties. Most scholars agree that these linkages are weak (Ferreira *et al.* 2008; Limongi and Cortez 2010; Samuels and Zucco 2014; Zucco 2015). Others, however, argue that they are stronger than skeptics have posited (Braga and Pimentel 2011; Braga *et al.* 2016).

We largely agree that Brazilian parties do not have deep roots in society; to put it conversely, most voters do not have strong attachments to parties. Party identification has recently dropped to low levels, and voters evince cynicism about parties (Pavão 2015). However, we qualify this conventional wisdom in two ways. First, at least until 2015, the PT was an exception to the idea that parties have weak roots in society. It developed strong connections to a sizable constituency. From early on, it forged deep roots in society, both among its voters (although they were relatively few in number until 1989) and among labor unions, grassroots Church groups, and organized social movements. Its huge advantage in party identifiers from 2002 until 2015 supported its consistent competitiveness in presidential elections, which, in turn, helped stabilize the party system.

Figure 6.1 shows the PT's gaping advantage in party identification from 2002 until 2015. In 2012, 27% of survey respondents identified with the PT. During the 2000s, the PT diluted its brand and still boosted the number of party identifiers – perhaps surprisingly in light of Lupu's (2016) findings about brand differentiation and partisanship. All other parties combined accounted for only 19%, and the PMDB was second with only 5%. In a context of great party system fragmentation and few identifiers beyond the PT, 27% of party identifiers constituted a large advantage.

From 2002 to 2014, the PT's substantial and fairly stable base of partisans gave it a sizable advantage in presidential elections. Dilma Rousseff's election in 2010 supports this argument. She had never run for elected office previously, and she had a non-populist profile. She won because of her party and Lula's support. The PT's strong roots in society qualify the claim that stabilization at the aggregate level has occurred despite weak party roots in society.

The second qualification to the claim that parties have weak roots in society is that many voters have relatively stable preferences about the parties, leading to an individual-level underpinning of systemic institutionalization that is not captured by party identification.[11] Braga and Pimentel (2011) advanced this argument by turning from the traditional question about spontaneous party

---

[11] Valenzuela, Somma, and Scully make a similar argument in Chapter 5 regarding the Chilean case.

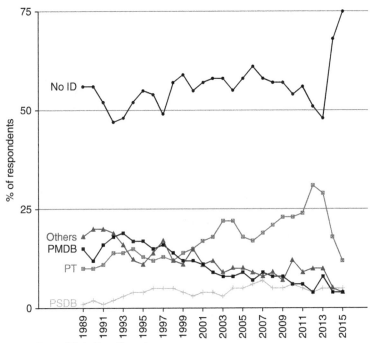

FIGURE 6.1 Party ID in Brazil, 1989–2015
Source: Kinzo (2005) with data from *Datafolha*; from 2003 to 2010, annual average of
party ID reported in *Datafolha* surveys compiled by Braga, Ribeiro and Amaral (2016).
Data for 2011–15 extracted from *Datafolha* website (http://datafolha.folha.uol.com.br/).

identification to a newer question, asked in the 2002, 2006, and 2010 Brazilian
post-election surveys, about how much voters "liked" the main parties (*gostar
de*). A voter might not state that he or she identifies with a party yet still might be
strongly disposed for or against it. Using this question, they showed that how
much voters "like" different parties has a powerful association with their vote.
We build on this insight by modifying their models to control for party
identification. By including partisanship as a control variable, we test their
argument that voters might have latent sympathies or antipathies toward
parties, and that traditional measures of partisanship often do not capture
these affective orientations.[12]

The survey response scale to this question runs from 0 (the respondent does
not like the party at all) to 10. Table 6.8 shows the results. The dependent variable
is the respondent's presidential vote in 2002, 2006, and 2010. In Models 1, 3, and
5, we regress vote choice in the first round of the three elections. In Models 2, 4,
and 6, we do the same with second-round vote choices. To facilitate comparison,

---

[12] We did not include the 2014 elections in our analysis because the question about how much
citizens like parties was not included in that year's survey.

TABLE 6.8 *Presidential Vote Choice and How Much Respondents Like Parties (Logistic Regression Models)*

	2002		2006		2010	
	1st round	2nd round	1st round	2nd round	1st round	2nd round
Difference (like PT minus like PSDB)	0.041***	0.045***	0.049***	0.053***	0.044***	0.052***
	(0.002)	(0.002)	(0.004)	(0.004)	(0.004)	(0.003)
Age	-0.001	-0.002	-0.002	-0.001	0.001	0.001
	(0.001)	(0.001)	(0.001)	(0.001)	(0.001)	(0.001)
Some High School	-0.050	-0.040	-0.066	-0.036	-0.057	-0.002
	(0.026)	(0.025)	(0.039)	(0.039)	(0.043)	(0.042)
Some college	-0.071	0.023	-0.157**	-0.152**	-0.251***	-0.074
	(0.042)	(0.038)	(0.057)	(0.058)	(0.052)	(0.073)
Woman	-0.029	-0.027	-0.085**	-0.058	-0.056	0.003
	(0.023)	(0.022)	(0.032)	(0.032)	(0.038)	(0.035)
PT Partisan	0.248***	0.134***	0.142***	0.083**	0.135*	0.120**
	(0.03)	(0.025)	(0.03)	(0.032)	(0.055)	(0.042)
PSDB Partisan	-0.074	-0.156**	-0.050	-0.050	-0.056	-0.149**
	(0.041)	(0.053)	(0.077)	(0.073)	(0.052)	(0.055)
Intercept	0.481***	0.638***	0.729***	0.698***	0.385***	0.443***
	(0.041)	(0.041)	(0.060)	(0.060)	(0.071)	(0.071)
Pseudo R-squared	0.310	0.313	0.318	0.329	0.325	0.386
N	1637	1633	732	714	1411	1398

Notes: * $p < 0.1$, ** $p < 0.05$, *** $p < 0.001$. Estimator: Logit, using survey weights. Standard errors in parentheses.

vote choice for the PT's candidates is always coded as 1. In models 1, 3, and 5, we assign o to all other candidates. In models 2, 4, and 6, only the PSDB candidate is assigned a o.

The main independent variable for all models is the difference in the levels of how much respondents like the PT and the PSDB. This variable captures both a strong positive identification with a party, and a negative orientation – for example, a voter who does not identify as a PT partisan but consistently votes for it and reports liking it, or a voter who does not identify as a PSDB partisan but maintains a clear anti-PT position. We subtracted the respondents' answer about the PSDB from the same value for the PT. On average, this difference was 1.4 points in favor of the PT in the three surveys. We control the effects of our main independent variable by adding respondents' age, sex, level of education,[13] and partisanship.[14]

The results are substantively and statistically powerful, suggesting that the way citizens view parties is strongly associated with their vote even after controlling for partisanship. The more respondents liked the PT and disliked the PSDB, the more likely they were to vote for Lula in 2002 and 2006 and Dilma in 2010. The key variable of interest (how much the respondent liked the PT minus the PSDB) is far more significant than being a partisan of either the PT or the PSDB. Indeed, surprisingly, the variable for PSDB partisans is not consistently significant. Figures 6.2 and 6.3 present the predicted probabilities for voting for the PT's candidate in the first and second rounds of the three elections, respectively.

PARTY ORGANIZATION

Solid organizations should facilitate PSI. For this reason, we briefly analyze the growing solidity of party organizations.

In the period of great turbulence in Brazil's party system, 1982–94, the major parties except for the PT were comparatively loose federations of free-wheeling politicians. Party switching was rampant among members of the catch-all parties, reflecting low allegiance of politicians to their party.[15] Many politicians of the catch-all parties had a long history of switching from one

---

[13] A three-category variable. The reference category is "Less than high school." The only way to make the measurement of educational level comparable across the three waves of the survey was by using three different categories (no high school, some high school, some college). The reference category is "no high school."

[14] We thank David Samuels for suggesting this design. We included two dummies to control for partisanship with the PT and the PSDB. Respondents answering PT/PSDB to the question "Would you say that some party represents how you think?" were coded as 1, while all other respondents were coded as o.

[15] Analyzing data for the state of São Paulo, Meneguello and Bizzarro (2012) found that more than 50% of all candidates in the 1982–86 elections ran again under a different party label in the 1988–96 period.

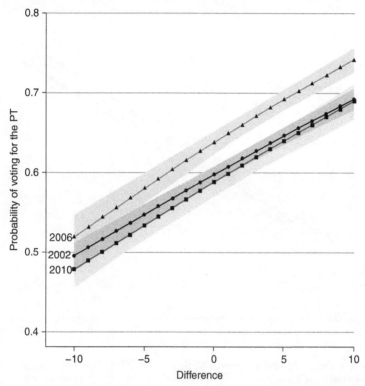

FIGURE 6.2 Predicted Probabilities of Voting for the PT by Difference in Liking the PT and the PSDB (1st Round)

party to another; some had been members of five or six parties. Party switching remained rampant until 2007 (on average 29.7% of federal deputies changed parties at least once in each legislature). Pervasive party switching indicated that individual politicians, not party organizations, were the key actors.

During the constitutional congress of 1987–88, party discipline was low except on the left (Mainwaring and Pérez-Liñán 1997). Again, this indicated considerable autonomy of politicians with respect to their parties. Except during electoral campaigns, local party organizations in most medium and small municipalities were listless. Parties were generally bereft of financial resources and very limited in their activities; campaign donors primarily gave to individual candidates rather than to parties. Elected politicians reigned supreme in the catch-all parties; neither the national leadership of the parties nor local-level members and activists had de facto decision-making authority.

The catch-all organizations have experienced changes over the last two decades, all in the direction of greater cohesion, organizational density, and resources. Because of changes in institutional rules, party discipline became

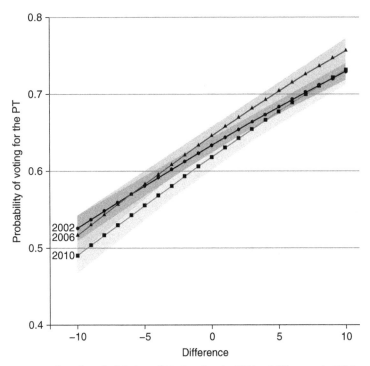

FIGURE 6.3 Predicted Probabilities of Voting for the PT by Difference in Liking the PT and the PSDB (2nd Round)

tighter after the constitutional congress of 1987–88 (Figueiredo and Limongi 1999: 73–100). The 1995 Organic Law of Political Parties sharply increased public financing of parties, enabling them to carry out more activities. It also provided them with other resources, such as guaranteed free access to television and radio advertising every year.

The 1995 law and the scope and constancy of Brazilian elections in the period have created incentives for the main parties to nationalize their local bases (Speck and Campos 2014). From 1982 to 2016, the main parties listed above became national organizations, with extensive territorial penetration. Figure 6.4 shows information about the territorial penetration of six of Brazil's main parties, two from each side of the ideological spectrum (Right: DEM, PP; Center: PMDB, PSDB; Left: PT, PSB) to demonstrate this point. In 2016, on average they had local organizations in 82.2% of the 5,570 municipalities in the country[16] (an average of 4,579 local organizations). Ribeiro (2014) and Meneguello *et al.* (2014), relying on two different surveys

---

[16] Measured by the number of cities in which the parties run at least one candidate to the cities' councils. Samuels and Zucco (2015) also use this measure.

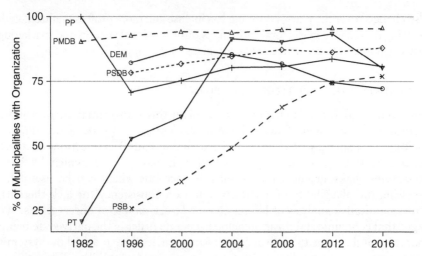

FIGURE 6.4 Municipalities with Local Organization (% of Total)
Source: IPEADATA and *Tribunal Superior Eleitoral.*
Note: Parties are identified with their current names.

conducted in the state of São Paulo with party rank-and-file members and party middle-level elites, respectively, demonstrated that overwhelming majorities of party activists reported the existence of regular activities at the local level in the main parties, particularly the PT and the PSDB. As Samuels and Zucco (2015) demonstrated, the establishment of local units had positive impacts on parties' electoral results, suggesting that those units are a partisan resource for candidates during electoral races.

The PT has long been an exception to the organizational norms of the other Brazilian parties (Meneguello 1989). The party demanded and received strong allegiance from its politicians. On several occasions, it expelled PT members of congress because they refused to toe the line on important issues. Party switching among elected PT officials was rare. Elected PT officials contributed a substantial part of their salaries to the party to help finance the organization. Party discipline was ironclad. Whereas the catch-all parties were created top-down by politicians, the labor movement, Catholic Church activists, and other local-level activists played a major role in forging the PT. Local organizations were often the site of intense discussions and extensive grassroots involvement.

Despite its programmatic moderation over time, the PT retained considerable organizational distinctiveness. Local PT branches for a long time engaged civil society and were sources of real involvement in the party. A high percentage of PT members also participate in social movements.[17] However, this involvement has

---

[17] Roma (2009: 163, Table 4) reports that according to one survey, in 1997, 84% of PT members also participated in a social movement.

also changed over the years, becoming less intense and more professionalized, with growing dominance in electoral campaigns of professional surveys and marketing firms as opposed to the activist-led campaigns of the 1980s (Hunter 2010).

EXPLAINING INSTITUTIONALIZATION

Our second goal in this chapter is to explain this transformation to a more institutionalized system. Our explanation rests mostly on process tracing, i.e., looking at sequences of change and examining causal connections in these sequences. It rests secondarily on comparing across cases, which by itself constitutes shaky grounds for causal inference but which can be useful for assessing the plausibility of arguments, and on consistency (or lack thereof), with quantitative analysis of PSI based on a larger sample of observations. We argue that economic stabilization helped generate order in the party system and that rules of the game that advantage existing parties have reduced the system's openness to new contenders and conversely enhanced its stability. When things went badly, programmatic differentiation gave voters options within the system; therefore, they did not need to turn to outsiders.

The timing of change provides useful information about the causes of institutionalization. Many indicators of institutionalization registered a clear change in 1994. The vote share of new parties dropped precipitously in 1994 for both the presidency (from 51.1% in 1989 to 0% in 1994) and the lower chamber (from 11.5% in 1990 to 0.3% in 1994). Electoral volatility for the lower chamber dropped sharply in the 1990–94 electoral period (from 35.6% in 1986–90 to 18.0% in 1990–94). The year 1994 also marked the beginning of the PT/PSDB duopoly in presidential competition.

This timing supports the assertion that one key to the shift from an inchoate party system in the 1985–94 period to greater institutionalization since then was economic stabilization. From 1980 until 1994, the Brazilian economy lurched from one crisis to the next, and chronically high inflation plagued the country. Bad economic performance pummeled the approval ratings of presidents João Figueiredo (1979–85), José Sarney (1985–90), and Fernando Collor de Mello (1990–92). Brazil experienced fourteen consecutive years (1981–94) of triple and quadruple digit inflation, peaking at 2,948% in 1990.[18] During this long period, in net terms the economy was stagnant (though with sharp year-to-year fluctuations); according to the World Bank estimates, per capita GDP (in 2010 constant US dollars) was essentially unchanged in 1994 ($8,269) compared to 1980 ($8,247) (World Bank 2016).

Bad economic performance helps explain the fracturing of the PDS in 1984 and its steep electoral demise in 1986, the dismal electoral results of the PMDB and PFL presidential candidates in 1989, the sharp electoral decline of the

---

[18] Estimates of the World Bank. Variable: Inflation, consumer prices (annual%) (World Bank 2016).

PMDB/PFL coalition in 1990, and the near disappearance of the PRN after 1992. The sharp decline of these governing parties contributed greatly to party system upheaval. Almost all of the decline side of the high electoral volatility for the Chamber of Deputies in 1986 and 1990 came from the PDS (1986) and the PMDB/PFL coalition (1990), respectively. Figueiredo's government (1979–85) triggered massive defections by politicians from the PDS to the PFL, and Sarney's government catalyzed massive defections away from the PMDB. Pinto (2013) demonstrated that presidential popularity varied to a large degree due to changes in the country's economic performance (rates of inflation, unemployment, and public debt) in the 1995–2010 period.

Given its nodal position in the Brazilian political system, the presidency is always a potential source of systemic instability (Lima 1999), and during the 1986–94 period it increased the fluidity of the party system. A clear contrast between the two periods is seen in Table 6.2 above. Consider the share of votes cast for the parties of the first two presidents of the post-1985 democracy in the next election. Ulysses Guimarães, the PMDB's candidate in 1989 four years into the disastrous Sarney government, and Carlos Antonio Gomes, the 1994 candidate of Fernando Collor's 1989 party, the PRN, two years after Collor's impeachment received only 4.6% and 0.6% of the votes in 1989 and 1994, respectively. Fernando Henrique Cardoso was reelected in 1998 with 53.0% of the vote and José Serra, the PSDB's presidential candidate in 2002, received 23.2% of the vote. Although the decrease in Cardoso's popularity in his second term led voters to punish the PSDB in 2002, this punishment was far more moderate than the one observed before economic stabilization. This PSDB was the first post-1985 party to govern the country reasonably well, making it a stable option for the country's government in the views of a large number of voters.

In contrast to what occurred in many Latin American countries, economic stabilization led to significant short-term increases in real wages in 1994 – a fact that helps explain the vast popular support for the stabilization plan (Mendes and Venturi 1994) and the dramatic turn toward Cardoso in the 1994 electoral campaign. Economic stabilization occurred simultaneously with the beginning of markedly lower electoral volatility. Rather than defecting from the governing parties of the 1994–2014 period, voters stuck with them, fostering the institutionalization of the party system. For the 1994–98 electoral period, presidential electoral volatility plummeted.

Economic stabilization catapulted Cardoso to the presidency in 1994 and 1998, and it put the PSDB on the map as a major player. After fifteen years of chronically high inflation (1979–94) and thirteen years of no net growth (1981–94), stabilization under the PSDB government gave the party a leg up over other contenders in presidential elections. If the stabilization plan had failed, it is highly unlikely that Cardoso would have won a landslide reelection and that the PSDB would have consistently been one of the top two contenders in subsequent presidential elections.

In turn, the consistent domination by the PT and PSDB in presidential elections fostered the institutionalization of other dimensions of the party system. The presidency is the cornerstone of the political system. Because of the dominance of the PT and PSDB in presidential elections, the dynamics of electoral competition since 1994 have focused primarily on their rivalry (Cortez 2009; Limongi and Cortez 2010; Melo 2010). The presidential competition influenced congressional and gubernatorial elections because the PT and PSDB coordinated strategies across different levels of elections in order to maximize their presidential candidates' prospects (Cortez 2009).

In some Latin American countries, including Argentina and Peru, economic stabilization in the wake of hyperinflation did not lead to PSI. In Peru, economic stabilization occurred shortly before party system collapse; President Fujimori (1990–2000) oversaw economic stabilization and purposefully fostered the collapse of the party system (Tanaka 1998). In Argentina, stabilization in the 1990s splintered the Peronist party because President Menem's (1989–99) policies diverged radically from the party's historical programmatic commitments and produced massive unemployment from 1995 onwards. A continuation of Menem's economic policies led to a crushing repudiation of the failed government of 1999–2001. The Brazilian experience diverged from these other cases in two critical respects. First, in the short term, stabilization in Brazil helped boost income, especially of the poor, so it was very popular. As already noted, stabilization was critical in Cardoso's election in 1994 and his reelection in 1998. For this reason, economic stabilization helped solidify the PSDB's position. Second, economic stabilization in Brazil was not accompanied by a muting of programmatic differences in the party system.

In sum, economic stabilization had a profound effect in institutionalizing Brazil's party system. Subsequent economic growth, poverty reduction, and income redistribution under Lula (2003–10) solidified the PT's pivotal role in presidential competition and in the party system. It helped boost PT party identification. The counterfactual is what would have happened if Lula's presidency had been a failure. Given that the 2006 election was competitive even after four years of significant economic growth, income redistribution, and poverty reduction, it is unlikely that an underperforming Lula would have won reelection. Moreover, it is uncertain that the PT would have solidified its position as part of a duopoly that dominated presidential elections, and the doors for other contenders to become competitive in presidential elections would have opened. It is unlikely that the system would have achieved the level of institutionalization that it did without the PT's success under Lula.

Programmatic Differentiation. In combination with reasonably successful PSDB and PT governments, clear programmatic differentiation between the PT and the PSDB-led coalition helped foster PSI (Hagopian *et al.* 2009). In Brazil, voters who became disaffected with the coalition that implemented stabilization had a clear and viable option within the system – the PT. The combination of economic stabilization without economic distress *and* clear programmatic differentiation distinguished Brazil from all cases of deep party system erosion and collapse.

In countries in which programmatic distinctions among the major parties became blurred, voters were more likely to become disgruntled with the entire system in periods of economic distress (Lupu 2016; Morgan 2011; Roberts 2014; Seawright 2012). In Bolivia from 1985 on and Peru after 1990, voters who repudiated the economic policies associated with orthodox stabilization lacked an alternative within the system. In both countries, differences among the main parties were obfuscated by structural adjustment. Voters flocked en masse to new contenders, destabilizing the old party systems. In Colombia, likewise, the programmatic blurring among parties after 1958 ultimately was an important ingredient in discrediting the traditional parties (see the chapter by Albarracín, Gamboa, and Mainwaring).

Programmatic differentiation did not ensure institutionalization, nor does sharp programmatic differentiation by itself explain increasing institutionalization in Brazil after 1994. In Brazil, the party system offered voters very distinctive choices from 1982 on, yet high volatility and considerable turmoil prevailed until 1994. But sharp programmatic divisions in conjunction with the fact that the PT, the most important opposition to the PSDB government, did not govern at the national level until 2003, meant that dissatisfied voters did not turn against the entire system. Consistent programmatic differentiation distinguishes all contemporary Latin American cases of fairly high institutionalization (Brazil, Chile, El Salvador, Mexico, Uruguay) from all cases of party system collapse (Bolivia, Ecuador, Peru, and Venezuela) and from most cases of deep deinstitutionalization (Colombia and Argentina).

Changes in Formal Institutional Rules. In the 1980s and 1990s, an extensive literature on Latin America emphasized the impact of formal rules of the game on actors' behavior and, as a result, on political outcomes (Linz and Valenzuela 1994). In the last decade, a new literature has questioned this earlier work, emphasizing that formal rules often do not have their anticipated consequences and that informal institutions are often more salient in political life (Helmke and Levitsky 2006; Levitsky and Murillo 2014; Weyland 2002b). However, formal rules sometimes have deep consequences, especially when political actors *must* follow the rules of the game, either because otherwise outcomes would be stacked against them or because enforcement mechanisms would punish them.

Several changes in formal rules helped foster PSI in Brazil. The constitutional congress of 1987–88 passed measures that led to higher party discipline on roll-call votes from 1989 on (Figueiredo and Limongi 1999: 73–100). Except for the PT, party discipline on roll-call votes never reached comparatively high levels, but it rose significantly relative to the constitutional congress. These changes made the political system more manageable, and they paved the way for building more solid party identities.

As mentioned above, in 1995, the Law of Political Parties greatly increased public funding for parties and gave them ample free television time during electoral campaigns. Parties became well funded. In 2015, the value of public funds distributed to the parties was 811 million reais (more than US$200 million).[19] In addition, parties have access to free television and radio time for political advertising. In values of 2014, the price paid by the government for this time (with tax waivers) was estimated at 850 million reais.[20] Combining these two figures with the value of the *Fundo Partidário* for 2014 (310 million reais), in the 2014–15 period, public funding for parties was nearly two billion reais.[21]

With more resources, party organizations became more robust. The distribution of public funding supports the "cartelization" of the party system: 99% of the resources are distributed proportionally, based on a party's share of seats in the Chamber of Deputies in the last election, and 1% is distributed evenly to all parties. Moreover, the parties have free office space in the national congress, plus mailing and telephone privileges for these offices. Brazilian parties have changed from being resource poor to resource rich. These changes allowed parties to establish and maintain regular bureaucracies at the national and sub-national levels.

Since 1995, the laws regulating access to campaign time on television and radio have favored the main parties and coalitions at the expense of political outsiders and coalitions or parties with few seats in congress. No candidate may buy time for political ads on television or radio; the only legally permissible TV and radio ads are those allocated for the free campaign time. In 2014, this was substantial: an hour and forty minutes (fifty minutes, twice a day) during the first round on TV and an hour and forty minutes on radio for six weeks (August 19 to October 2). Every TV and radio station in Brazil must broadcast the campaign ads during this period. During the runoff round for the presidential and gubernatorial elections, television and radio stations reserved an hour and twenty minutes (forty minutes twice a day) for campaign ads for three weeks.

TV and radio time is allocated mostly on the basis of the size of a party or coalition's delegation in the Chamber of Deputies as of the previous election. Without access to television or radio, political outsiders would be very hard pressed to campaign effectively for the presidency or for governorship in a large state. The current rules for access to free TV and radio time are more favorable to established parties than they were in 1989, when the allocation of time was based on the share of seats in the Chamber of Deputies one year before the election. The current rules benefit those parties that existed a full four years earlier. Thus, an outsider cannot gain access to substantial TV and radio time by virtue of members of congress switching to his/her party as the presidential election approaches.

---

[19] Source: www.justicaeleitoral.jus.br/arquivos/tse-distribuicao-do-fundo-partidario-duodecimos-2015-1429900293402 (accessed December 2016).
[20] Source: www.contasabertas.com.br/website/arquivos/8075 (accessed December 2016).
[21] Source: www.justicaeleitoral.jus.br/arquivos/tse-distribuicao-do-fundo-partidario-duodecimos-2014 (accessed December 2016).

The 1995 Law of Political Parties also established moderately demanding criteria for creating a new party. The most difficult hurdle is the gathering and authentication of signatures. The threshold, which is 0.5% of the number of valid votes cast in the previous Chamber of Deputies election, with at least 0.1% of the valid vote in at least nine states, changes every four years based on the previous results. After the 2010 elections, 484,169 signatures were needed to form a new party. The authentication requirement stopped Marina Silva from registering a new party in 2013. The local electoral authorities rejected 95,000 of her signatures, denying the registration of her party.

In March 2015, a new law was passed that prohibits any two parties from merging unless they have existed for five years. It also stipulates that any party switching into "merged" parties (*fusão*) cannot be used to determine allocations for public funding or for free TV and radio campaign time. These measures have added disincentives to creating new parties.

In 1997, congress approved a constitutional amendment that allowed for immediate presidential reelection once, shortened the presidential term from five to four years, and made presidential and congressional (and also gubernatorial and state assembly) elections concurrent. The change from non-concurrent to concurrent elections was favorable for PSI. With non-concurrent elections, as occurred in the 1989 presidential contest, governors, gubernatorial candidates, members of congress and candidates for congress, and state legislators and candidates had weaker incentives to invest heavily in the campaign. Their own political positions were not at stake. With concurrent elections, almost everyone in the party machines has a high stake in the presidential outcome. Moreover, with concurrent elections, there are economies of scale in investing time and resources into campaigns across different levels. As Carreras (2012) showed, the meteoric rise of a political outsider such as occurred with Fernando Collor in 1989 is less likely with concurrent elections.

In 2002, the Supreme Court effectively overturned a rule known as the *candidato nato* (birthright candidate). Under this rule, every incumbent politician had the right to run for his or her same position in the next election. Politicians who were not aligned with the party leadership in their states had the right to become candidates, formalizing a situation in which politicians had considerable autonomy and the party leaders (except in the PT) were in a weak position. The abolition of the birthright candidate rule gave party leaders more power over the rank-and-file politicians.

In 2007, the Supreme Electoral Court (*Tribunal Superior Eleitoral*, the country's highest electoral court) changed its interpretation of the 1995 parties statute and started stripping the mandate from elected officials who changed parties. With this new legal ruling, politicians had powerful incentives to change their behavior. This change increased the leverage of the party leadership over rank-and-file elected politicians; the latter could no longer flaunt their independence because of their ability to switch parties. Constant party switching reduces the value of party labels, and, thus, it should make it harder to build party labels in the electorate. A subsequent (2011) Supreme Electoral Court ruling allowed elected politicians to form a new party without losing their mandate, softening the effect of the end of the birthright candidate rule. Still, forming a new party takes collective action, whereas party switching was an individual decision. In this respect, the change in rules made it more costly to leave the label on which a politician was elected. Although it is not a change in the rules, in Brazil candidates for elected offices must run on a party label, making it harder for outsiders to challenge the system.

In and of themselves, these changes in institutional rules might not have produced huge effects on PSI. Most of the changes in rules post-dated the early signs of a shift to a more stable party system, so they cannot fully explain institutionalization. But these reforms reinforced the effects created by economic stabilization and growth and by programmatic differentiation. Their net effect has been to establish fairly high barriers to outsider presidential candidates and to major new parties.

These arguments about institutionalization in Brazil are consistent with our broader explanatory effort in Chapter 4. The growing institutionalization of Brazil's party system shows a process that mirrors the dynamics of party system deinstitutionalization and collapse, providing support for the argument in Chapter 4 that processes of institutionalization and deinstitutionalization have symmetrical causes. Economic stabilization fostered party system stability – in contrast to the Venezuelan and Peruvian experience where economic failure led to massive support for political outsiders (Lupu this volume; Morgan 2011; Seawright 2012). The relative economic success of the policies implemented both by the PSDB and the PT kept voters "within the system," avoiding the search for political outsiders. Similarly, the PSDB and PT provided clear alternative programmatic options to voters, again sustaining partisan actors as the main political alternatives in national elections.

THE CRISIS OF THE PT AND ITS IMPLICATIONS FOR THE SYSTEM

In its early years, the PT was a highly idealistic party, willing to shun alliances to preserve ideological principles. However, Lula's victory in the 2002 presidential election sealed a turn toward greater pragmatism (Baker *et al.* 2016). The party agreed to a pre-electoral coalition with the conservative PL in 2002, and, once in government, formed the most ideologically heterogeneous coalition in Brazil's democratic history (Pereira *et al.* 2016), ranging from the Communist Party of Brazil to small clientelist right-wing parties. Managing this coalition was costly, though. One of the biggest corruption scandals in Brazil's history erupted in 2004–05, when the media, based on information from public officials and members of congress, reported that the PT was systematically paying conservative members of congress a sizable bribe to vote for PT proposals. The scandal led to a jail term for Lula's chief of staff, José Dirceu, among others. However, probably because of economic growth and the government's social policies, Lula and the PT emerged largely unscathed.

The party was less fortunate when arguably the most publicized corruption scandal in world democratic history emerged during Dilma Rousseff's government. Investigators uncovered a massive corruption network involving the country's largest company, the publicly owned Petrobras, several huge construction firms, many PT leaders, and other politicians. The PT siphoned funds from Petrobras to pay for political campaigns, and it took bribes from construction firms for the same purpose and to pay off political allies. Former President Lula faces multiple criminal investigations. Many prominent PT politicians, as well as prominent politicians from other parties and business leaders, have gone to jail or face criminal charges. President Rousseff experienced the fallout from the scandal and from Brazil's worst recession in decades.

Even before this scandal erupted, the PT was hemorrhaging partisans, in part because of the economic downturn. In the 2016 municipal elections, it suffered large reversals. Many politicians exited the party, some to avoid the stigma of its label, others dismayed because of the corruption scandal. The party fielded only 1,004 mayoral candidates compared to 1,779 in 2012 (a decline of 43%), and 22,259 candidates for municipal assemblies compared to 38,784 in 2012 (a decline of 42%). After electing 655 mayors in 2012, the PT elected only 256 in 2016. The party suffered big setbacks in almost all of Brazil's largest cities.

Given that the PT was one of its linchpins, the party system seems less predictable now than it was from 1994 until 2014. The massive corruption scandal on top of a long and bruising economic recession has left few parties unscathed. It has exacerbated voter cynicism and anger, conditions that in the past have been favorable to political outsiders.

Nevertheless, we do not expect radical deinstitutionalization, much less a collapse. Established parties, not new organizations or outsiders, were the winners in 2016. Of the eight parties that won the largest number of mayoral positions in 2012, only the PT and the PSB won fewer *prefeituras* in 2016. The PSDB won 15.6% more mayoral positions than in 2012 (793 versus 686, respectively), including winning Sao Paulo, Brazil's largest city. These results suggest that even if citizens repudiate the existing parties, they have little choice but to vote for existing organizations because the rules of the game create high barriers to new parties and outsiders. These barriers to entry remain salient and meaningful even while fragmentation in the national legislature has soared.

CONCLUSION

From 1994 to 2014, Brazil's party system became more institutionalized even as systems in many other Latin American countries experienced partial deinstitutionalization (Argentina, Colombia) or collapse (Bolivia, Venezuela, Ecuador, and Peru). Electoral competition became much more stable from 1994 on. The system changed from one in which multiple new parties emerged on the scene and became important contenders (1980–89) to one in which new parties have enjoyed scant success (1990–present); from one in which governing parties suffered huge defeats and defections (1984–94) to one in which three consecutive presidents won reelection attempts (Cardoso, Lula, and Dilma); from one in which a populist outsider created a party and captured the presidency (1989) to one in which presidential contests have been dominated by two solid parties (1994–2014). In a historically unprecedented manner, two parties established a regular (though potentially fragile) duopoly in presidential elections. Party organizations are more solid today than they were in the 1980s and early 1990s. Party discipline increased; party switching decreased; parties enjoyed a substantial infusion of public funding, enabling them to undertake far more activities than they could between 1985 and 1994.

But institutionalization occurred somewhat unevenly and with generally thin roots, as Zucco (2015) argued. Stabilization occurred even though only one party, the PT, developed strong roots in society. Institutionalization was also uneven across party organizations; the PT developed a more robust organization than other parties.

Economic stabilization fostered the institutionalization of the Brazilian party system. Unlike in many countries, the initial phase of stabilization was not associated with economic hardship – much to the contrary. In the 2000s, moderate economic growth, steep declines in poverty, and some income redistribution helped further cement the PT and PSDB's positions in the system.

Consistent programmatic differentiation helped preserve the system from the fate suffered in several cases in which there were no meaningful differences among the main contenders: system collapse (Bolivia, Ecuador, and Venezuela), party collapse, or the sharp demise of one of the traditional major parties (Argentina and Colombia). Voters disappointed with the PMDB and the PFL in the 1980s could turn to the PSDB in 1994. It offered a different programmatic and ideological profile. Voters who subsequently became disenchanted with the PSDB/PFL coalition could move to the PT, whose positions differed significantly from those of the previous governing parties. To get change, voters did not need to turn from the entire system.

Changes in institutional rules also helped foster institutionalization. These changes fostered greater party discipline; increased the barriers for political outsiders; increased the funding and other material advantages and the campaign advantages of existing parties; helped make it easier for parties to build solid organizations; made it costly for politicians to switch parties once they were elected on a given label; and strengthened the hand of party leaders in relation to individual members of congress.

As of this writing (August 2017), Brazil is in turbulent waters, with a deep and long recession, a massive corruption scandal, and an unpopular, unelected president who has also been severely tarnished by accusations of improbity, among other woes. These new challenges raise questions about whether a moderately institutionalized party system can be sustained despite the country's downturn and despite uneven and thin institutionalization. Our cautious answer is that it probably can.

APPENDIX 6.1

Brazilian Political Parties in 2016

Party	Seats (2016)	Orientation and background	Ideology score (2013)
Party of the Brazilian Democratic Movement (PMDB), founded 1966	67	Party opposing military regime of 1964–85; currently centrist, decentralized, functions as catchall support party for Lula and Dilma governments; party of President Michel Temer	6.19
Workers' Party (PT), founded 1980	58	Prior to 2002: left-wing; grew out of labor unrest in late 1970s; strong support from intellectuals, workers, state employees; best organized party in Brazilian history. Since 2003: centrist turn, alliances with right parties, pragmatic economic policy, expanding support in Northeast	3.86
Party of Brazilian Social Democracy (PSDB), founded 1988	50	Progressive faction of PMDB 1988–94 originally Western European-style social democratic; champion of 1990s pro-market reforms; supports parliamentarism; principal force of the modernizing center-right	6.32
Progressive Party (PP), founded 1966, renamed 2003	47	Conservative: formerly ARENA and then PDS, the pro-military party in 1964–85; shrank drastically in 1980s; has changed names four times	7.55
Party of the Republic (PR), founded 2006	42	Center-right, based on merger of former Liberal Party (PL) and PRONA party. Founded as PL in 1985.	6.98
Social Democratic Party (PSD), founded 2011	35	Center-right party created (mostly from DEM, but some from PTB, PP, PSDB) by politicians who wanted to support the then PT government	6.65

(*continued*)

Party	Seats (2016)	Orientation and background	Ideology score (2013)
Brazilian Socialist Party (PSB), founded 1985	32	Center-left party, generally supported PT governments until 2013; strong base in Northeast	4.12
Democrats (DEM), founded 1984, renamed 2007	27	Formerly PFL; conservative, pragmatic, clientelistic "party of power"; supported every president from 1964 to 2002, military or civilian; usually allies with PSDB	8.25
Brazilian Republican Party (PRB), founded 2005	22	Christian and conservative; founded by Lula's vice president José Alencar (1931–2011) with support from pastors linked to Universal Church of the Kingdom of God (IURD)	NA
Democratic Labor Party (PDT), founded 1980	19	Center-left; created by Leonel Brizola (1922–2004); on-again, off-again partner of PT in 1980s and 1990s	4.21
Brazilian Labor Party (PTB), founded 1980	18	Center-right; clientelistic; "party for rent" that supports most presidents; after 2003, grew as repository for opportunistic center-right politicians wishing to support Lula	6.52
Solidarity (SD), founded 2013	14	Pragmatic center-left party, linked to *Força Sindical* labor central, allied with PSDB against PT government	NA
National Labor Party (PTN), founded 1995	13	Center-Left, claims connection to the homonymous PTN of the previous democratic period (1945–66)	NA
Communist Party of Brazil (PC do B), founded 1962	11	Defected from PCB in 1962 during Sino-Soviet split, later pro-Albanian until end of Cold War; after 1989 mostly satellite of PT; dominated national student union. Since 2003: centrist turn and pragmatic ally of PT presidents	2.86

(continued)

Party	Seats (2016)	Orientation and background	Ideology score (2013)
Popular Socialist Party (PPS), founded 1922, renamed 1992	8	Descended from Moscow-line Brazilian Communist Party (PCB); abandoned Leninism and supported Gorbachev in 1980s; later center-left; in Lula years moved rightward to ally with PSDB-led opposition	4.72
Social Christian Party (PSC), founded 1985	7	Center-right "party for rent" loosely linked to Christian doctrine and to Assembly of God churches; identified with socially conservative causes	NA
Republican Party of Social Order (PROS), founded 2013	7	Opportunistic, centrist "party for rent," supported by Pentecostal pastors	NA
Humanist Party of Solidarity (PHS), founded 1996	7	Center-right, associated with traditional religious movements	NA
Green Party (PV), founded 1986	6	Center-left, pragmatic environmentalists	4.63
Party of Socialism and Liberty (PSOL), founded 2004	4	Former radical left faction of PT, founded by dissidents unhappy with centrist policies; key leaders were expelled from PT in 2003	1.73
Sustainability Network (REDE), founded 2015	4	Center-left party movement created and led by Marina Silva, environmentalist leader and two-time presidential candidate	NA

Note: "Seats" refers to seats in Chamber of Deputies as of October 2016. The 18 parties shown here comprise 498 of 513 chamber seats (97%), with some small parties excluded from the table. Reputational ideology: in surveys of Congress, parties are placed (by non-members only) on an ideological scale where 1 is left and 10 is right. Ideology data from Brazilian Legislative Survey 2013 (7th wave), http://thedata.harvard.edu/dvn/dv/zucco [accessed November 2016].

7

Authoritarian Legacies and Party System Stability in Mexico

Kenneth F. Greene and Mariano Sánchez-Talanquer

Mexico's political party system is remarkably institutionalized compared to other new democracies in Latin America and around the world. The formation of the two main opposition parties during the authoritarian period starting in 1929 and the survival of the long-dominant Institutional Revolutionary Party (PRI) yielded a three-party system at the onset of fully competitive democracy in 2000. These three parties have continued to align politicians and a majority of voters during the three general and three mid-term elections since. We discuss initial signs of change, principally affecting parties on the left, in the conclusion. These potential shifts notwithstanding, Mexico stands out as a paragon of party system institutionalization (PSI).

Institutionalized party systems are more likely to provide voters with clear and distinct platforms that permit electoral mandates, channel political conflict in system-supporting ways, and facilitate electoral accountability. The concept of PSI is closely connected to multiple aspects of well-functioning representative democracy (Mainwaring and Scully 1995a: 20). Indeed, where party systems are fragile, party–voter linkages tend to rest on personalist appeals, maverick outsiders are more likely to win high office, ordinary citizens are less able to influence public policy, and mandates are less easily interpreted and more easily violated.

As described in other chapters in this volume, many new democracies suffer challenges associated with unstable party systems. In our view, institutionalization under democracy requires solving two key problems. First, parties must solve a *representation problem* by offering meaningful policy choices that collectively stand for majoritarian voter interests. When parties instead converge on similar platforms (Roberts 2014), often violating their mandates (Stokes 2001) and weakening their partisan brands (Lupu 2014), they can cause voter dealignment that propels new parties (Hug 2001; Mainwaring *et al.* 2006) and, in the most extreme cases, lead to party system breakdown as in Peru and Venezuela (Morgan 2011; Seawright 2012). We recognize that stability without representation under democracy is possible where clientelism dominates (Kitschelt and Wilkinson

2007a; Riedl 2014); however, even the most clientelist parties in contemporary Latin America campaign on program and performance, and voting behavior in many countries in the region revolves substantially around issue representation (Baker and Greene 2015; Luna and Zechmeister 2005).

Second, parties must solve a *coordination problem* by aggregating local political elites into national-level parties (Chhibber and Kollman 2004; Cox 1997; Duverger 1954; Sartori 1968) and investing in enduring organizations capable of commanding politicians' continuing allegiance. Failure to coordinate across space can spawn many local parties that form temporary and unstable alliances to compete for national offices, a problem that has recently bedeviled Peru (Meléndez 2012a) and Colombia (Albarracín, Gamboa, and Mainwaring, this volume). Failure to coordinate behind labels that endure over time can generate fleeting and often personalistic campaign vehicles that contribute to chronic instability in the party system. Systems that solve both the representation and coordination problems achieve institutionalization because they diminish "bottom-up" challenges that could come from defecting voters and "top-down" challenges that could emerge from defecting politicians.

Mexico's democratic party system has solved these key problems despite having a number of the conditions that plausibly cause instability. It is a country with large and persistent regional, ethnic, and socioeconomic disparities that could fuel many parties. It has a federal system that could encourage a plethora of local parties rather than a few national-level ones. It has experienced episodes of deep economic crisis and mandate violations through the "bait and switch" adoption of free-market economic policies that has been associated with party system instability elsewhere. It experienced decades' long authoritarian rule that has been associated with political fragmentation in other new democracies (Remmer 1989). In addition, Mexico's new democracy has three main parties, a configuration that the formal theory literature views as especially unstable (McKelvey 1986). The country has been plagued by rapid increases in violent crime that demonstrated the state's inability to provide basic security and even spurred the rise of autonomous citizen militias (Shirk and Wallman 2015). Citizens have surprisingly low levels of effective partisanship (Greene 2011; McCann and Lawson 2003), they are dissatisfied with democracy (Crow 2010), and they chafe at chronic public corruption.[1] A variety of forces would thus seem to yield space for new parties and political outsiders.[2] Yet, the party system remains remarkably stable.

---

[1] Since 2000, an average 25% of Mexicans have been very or somewhat satisfied with democracy. In 2015, just 19% were satisfied, placing Mexico lowest in Latin America (Latinobarometer). See Online Appendix 7.3.

[2] Since 2000, an average of just 20% of Mexicans trust the parties a lot or somewhat, making parties the least-trusted political or social institutions queried. In 2015, just 2% trusted parties a lot (Latinobarometer 2015).

In this chapter, we argue that Mexico's institutionalized democratic party system results from its authoritarian past. We build on our past work (Greene 2007a) and the recent literature on "authoritarian legacies" (Flores-Macías forthcoming; Hicken and Martinez-Kuhonta 2011; Loxton 2015; Riedl 2014). In our view, biased but competitive elections under dominant-party authoritarian rule blunted the potentially fragmenting effects of social cleavages and federalism, and instead encouraged partisan elites to invest in nationally oriented parties, craft differentiated economic policy platforms, and establish tight links to core electoral constituencies. Subsequent negotiations between the then-dominant PRI and its two primary challengers over electoral rules and party finance regulations locked in advantages for these existing parties at the onset of fully competitive democracy, helping them survive and dissuading potential new competitors. The dynamics of contestation under Mexico's brand of dominant-party authoritarianism thus created the conditions for solving the representation and coordination problems under democracy, yielding a robust three-party system. Whereas new democracies exiting harsher forms of authoritarian rule have experienced instability because they stunted genuine and independent opposition parties before the onset of competitive elections, Mexico's dominant-party authoritarian regime retarded democratization but bequeathed it the bases for an institutionalized party system.

The first section portrays Mexico's stable party system. The second and third sections discuss the limitations of existing theories that could plausibly explain party system institutionalization and present our own argument that highlights the legacies of authoritarian rule. The fourth and fifth sections present empirical evidence in favor of our argument, focusing on how authoritarian legacies conditioned elite investments in parties as well as the (endogenous) design of electoral rules that enhanced party system institutionalization under democracy. We conclude by discussing some initial signs that the stability of Mexico's party system may be eroding.

MEXICO'S INSTITUTIONALIZED DEMOCRATIC PARTY SYSTEM

Mexico's party system ranked as the second-most institutionalized in Latin America from 1990 to 2015, slightly behind Uruguay (see Table 2.6, this volume). In this section, we describe the main elements of these stable alignments, drawing on the authoritarian past to characterize party system institutionalization under Mexico's current democracy.

During most of the twentieth century, the PRI and its predecessors presided over the most durable dominant-party authoritarian regime in the world. It won the presidency from 1929 to 2000, the majority in the Congress until 1997, every gubernatorial election until 1989, and the vast majority of local contests. Opposition parties were permitted to form and compete in regularly held elections that included universal adult suffrage, but, despite this minimal openness, tremendous biases in favor of the incumbent party (Greene 2007a) and episodes of electoral fraud (Simpser 2013) helped dominant-party rule endure. The openness of Mexico's prior authoritarian regime meant that its main parties significantly pre-dated the onset of fully competitive democracy in 2000. Whereas transitions from fully closed authoritarian rule in countries such as Argentina, Uruguay, Chile, and Soviet states required elite pacts or regime breakdown, Mexico's protracted transition to multi-party competition advanced as the PRI's hyper-incumbency advantages diminished and the partisan playing field leveled (Greene 2007a). Democratization thus involved continuity in the main parties but shifts in their vote shares.

The PRI traces its roots to the settlement among warring elites organized by President Plutarco Elías Calles following the Revolution of 1910–17. Initially formed as the National Revolutionary Party (PNR) in 1929, it was later transformed into the Party of the Mexican Revolution (PRM) by President Lázaro Cárdenas in 1938, and finally renamed the PRI in 1946. The dominant party represented a large, heterogeneous, and carefully balanced coalition of diverse social and political interests. It incorporated the formal labor sector, the peasantry, and urban government- and service-sector workers into three hierarchical corporatist organizations that formed the backbone of the party and served both to represent and suppress citizens' demands. At the same time, the party also represented conservative interests, including regional elites, an industrial bourgeoisie, a relatively small middle class, and a largely depoliticized military (Collier and Collier 1991; Garrido 1982). From the 1930s to the 1980s, it managed to balance this "contradictory alliance" (Collier 1992) through a state-led model of development that produced decades of strong economic growth and furnished regime allies with protection from foreign competitors, the conditions for business to grow, and inducements to the lower classes, such as land, rising wages, and social benefits. During this period, its ideology shifted within the broad center, leaning relatively leftist in the 1930s and 1970s, centrist in the 1940s, 1950s, and 1960s, and rightist in that aftermath of the 1982 debt crisis as it adopted free-market economic reforms.

The main opposition parties grew on the dominant party's flanks when it opened political space either on the right or on the left (Greene 2007a). The National Action Party (PAN) emerged in 1939 as a conservative reaction to President Cárdenas' pro-labor policies, expansion of socialist and anti-clerical public education, and land redistribution program that threatened capital and Church interests (Shirk 2005). The PRI's centrist policy shift in the 1940s undercut the PAN's market-oriented appeal, making it into a small and marginalized confessional party that "wandered in the electoral wilderness for 40 years" (Loaeza 1999). When the PRI shifted policy back toward the left in the 1970s and early 1980s to mollify rising leftist movements, the PAN once again attracted business people, known as *neopanistas*, as well as middle-class pro-democracy groups. From this point on, the PAN combined pro-market and socially conservative core constituencies, not unlike the US Republican Party.

The third major party, the leftist Party of the Democratic Revolution (PRD), emerged in 1989 following the PRI's adoption of free-market economic policies; however, this new party combined older elements, including PRI-defectors led by Cuauhtémoc Cárdenas – the son of former President Lázaro Cárdenas – under the banner of the Democratic Current, and members of former communist and socialist parties, as well as intellectual cliques and social movements (Bruhn 1997; Garrido 1993). Ideologically, the PRD took over the commitment to economic nationalism and social justice the PRI had largely abandoned, attracting poor people's movements, dissident labor organizations, and civic groups representing diverse progressive causes. The party buttresses its redistributive economic policy platform with a call for more participatory democracy.

At the onset of fully competitive democracy in 2000, then, all three major parties had long histories and clear programmatic identities among political elites.[3] They also had fairly clear profiles in the electorate. The PRI continued to draw the most heterogeneous electoral base from across the entire country. The PAN and PRD benefited from tight links to narrow core constituencies in the electorate and looser links to a larger group of weakly partisan and non-partisan voters who floated among the parties from election to election.

Figure 7.1 helps appreciate the protracted nature of Mexico's regime transition as votes reshuffled among the main competitors. In congressional elections, the PRI's vote share started to decline after the 1976 general elections, when its presidential candidate ran unopposed. The decline accelerated after the 1982 debt crisis and the subsequent adoption of free-market economic policies, due to a combination of dissatisfaction with the PRI's performance in office (Magaloni 2006), decreases in its ability to politicize public resources to bias elections in its favor (Greene 2007a), and a deep sense of mandate violation by the leftist elements of its coalition (Bruhn 1997). This opposition vote fed both the PAN and the PRD, temporarily forestalling the PRI's defeat until the opposition broke through by claiming the majority of the legislature in 1997 and the PAN won the presidency with Vicente Fox in 2000.

Electoral shifts among the main parties transformed Mexico's regime, but regime transformation did little to change membership in Mexico's party system. Both before and after democratization, the three main parties have nearly closed out the electoral market in presidential elections. As depicted in Figure 7.2, they accounted for an average of 94.1% of the valid vote in the 1988, 1994, and 2000 presidential elections that were held under PRI rule, and 94.3% in the 2006 and 2012 elections. The type of political outsiders, mavericks, or upstarts backed by ephemeral political organizations that have risen to prominence and

---

[3] Dating the PRD to its official founding in 1989 yields the three parties' average age in 2000 as forty-seven years. On average, Mexico's main parties are older than those in all but five of the region's twelve largest countries (Mainwaring and Scully 1995a: 15).

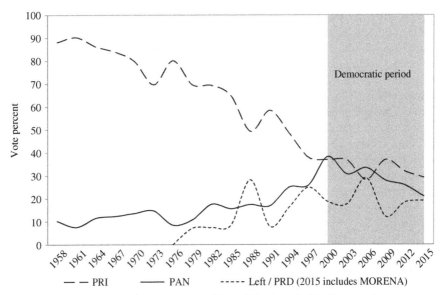

FIGURE 7.1 Party Vote Shares in Lower House Elections in Mexico, 1958–2015
Note: For 1979–85, left parties include the Mexican Communist Party (PCM), the Socialist Workers Party (PST), the Unified Socialist Party of Mexico (PSUM), the Revolutionary Workers Party (PRT), and the Mexican Workers Party (PMT). In 1988, the left party is the National Democratic Front (FDN). For 1988–2012, the left party is the PRD alone; for 2015, it also includes MORENA.
Source: Prepared by the authors based on Nohlen (2005) and INE (2016).

won the presidency in some other Latin American countries have claimed no electoral space in Mexico.

In congressional elections, the three main parties have also accounted for the overwhelming majority of votes. Federal congressional elections feature a two-tier design. In constituency elections, candidates campaign with their name in addition to their party label and the plurality winner takes the seat. Since the 1988 general elections, 300 of the 500 seats in the lower house are filled through plurality rules in single-member constituency elections. The other 200 seats are filled through proportional rules in five forty-member regional districts that cross state lines. The candidates for these multi-member district elections are selected by the parties and presented to the voters as ordered and closed lists. Voters cast a single vote for both tiers. As a result, candidates competing for proportional representation seats campaign under the party label, if they campaign at all. Smaller parties might prosper in lower house constituency elections where districts are of manageable size and voters may respond to candidate traits. Yet even in these elections, also depicted in Figure 7.2, the three major parties accounted for an average of 90.1% of the vote in the five elections before the PRI lost the presidency (1988–2000) and

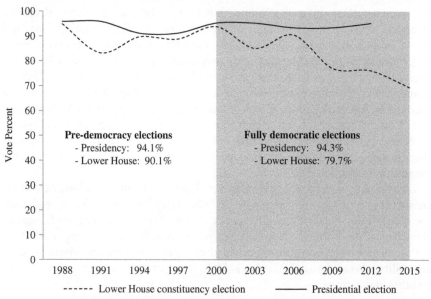

FIGURE 7.2 Cumulative Vote Share of Mexico's Main Political Parties, 1988–2015
Note: The solid line shows the cumulative vote share of the three main parties' presidential candidates. Lower house votes tallied for coalitions are credited equally to member parties, except for 2000–06 when coalition members' votes were not reported and thus votes are attributed to the largest party. MORENA is included in the PRD's vote in 2015.
Source: Prepared by the authors based on Nohlen (2005) and INE (2016).

79.7% in the five elections since (2003–15). We will return to the recent advances of smaller parties in lower house elections in the last section of this chapter.

Since democratization in 2000, Mexico has experienced low levels of electoral volatility. Among post-democratization legislative elections in seventeen Latin American countries, Mexico ranks third lowest (1.2 standard deviations below the mean) using the Pedersen Index (1983) of overall volatility that summarizes an aggregate shift in vote shares across parties from election to election. The index is lower only in Uruguay (and then only in the third decimal place) and Honduras. Volatility is nearly five times higher in Peru, the region's most volatile party system.[4]

Yet low aggregate volatility hides a key characteristic of Mexico's stable democratic party system: stability is not mainly due to hardened voter attachments to the major parties. The parties do enjoy solid core constituencies

---

[4] Greene (2015). Argentina was not scored.

that support them in each election; however, only 49.4% of the electorate identified with a party at the start of the 2012 general election campaigns, and even this level of partisanship overstates the case.[5] Self-reported partisanship is tremendously unstable (McCann and Lawson 2003) and only about 16% of the electorate has *effective* partisanship that insulates it from the persuasive effects of campaigns in the mass media (Greene 2015). On average, Mexico's voters are much more susceptible to campaign influences than are voters in the United States and Western European countries where partisanship is on more solid footing (Greene 2011). Narrower and shallower partisanship leads to more fluidity in vote choices across election cycles as well as less predictability in the vote during the run-up to election day.

Low levels of effective partisanship, high levels of dissatisfaction with democracy and, as we describe in the next section, strong regional, socioeconomic, and ethnic differences across Mexico, recent performance debacles, a theoretically fragile three-party system, and a long period of authoritarian rule seem as though they could underwrite party system instability. What causes Mexico's high level of democratic party system institutionalization?

EXISTING ARGUMENTS ABOUT PARTY SYSTEM STABILITY

Existing arguments about the sources of party system stability can be divided into two camps. Classic arguments in the sociological, institutional, spatial theory, and behavioral traditions predict that Mexico's democratic party system should be less institutionalized than it is. We show that these arguments stumble because they discount the impact of authoritarian rule on subsequent democratic party systems. In contrast, most recent arguments that focus on authoritarian legacies correctly predict Mexico's institutionalized party system. However, whereas they focus on the continuing salience of regime divides even in the democratic era, we argue that partisan competition over non-regime issues during authoritarian rule is key to institutionalization in subsequent democratic party systems. Thus, whereas classic arguments assume a legacy of too much democracy, the newer authoritarian legacies arguments assume too little pre-democratic competition.

Classic Arguments about Party System Institutionalization

In one of the most enduring statements about party system configurations, Lipset and Rokkan (1967) argue that parties represent the political demands of groups that emerge around major social cleavages associated with class,

[5] Mexico 2012 Panel Study, Wave 1. Including leaners yields 61.1% partisans. Partisanship has not solidified since 2000 as theory predicts (Converse 1969; Roberts and Wibbels 1999). Biennial LAPOP surveys show party sympathy at 49.2% in 2006, 31.7% in 2008, 28.5% in 2010, 36.1% in 2012, and 27.7% in 2014 (LAPOP 2016).

region, religion, and urban–rural divides. Subsequent work also emphasizes ethnicity (Birnir 2007). Analysts argue that several major social divisions produce multi-party systems as in West European countries (Charlesworth 1948; Cox 1997: 15) and milder divisions lead to a two-party system as in the United States (Key 1964). This approach claims that party systems rooted in social group distinctions are more stable than those that are not.

Mexican society is sharply divided along ethnic, regional, cultural, and economic lines, and thus has sufficient raw ingredients for structuring partisan competition along social cleavages. The northern population tends to be whiter, more affluent, pro-business, and modern, with major industrial centers and mechanized privately owned farms whose fortunes are tied to trade with the United States. The central-western Bajío region contains Mexico's Bible belt, where conservative Catholic religious tradition holds greater sway. In centrally located Mexico City and adjacent areas, a large and marginalized urban informal sector coexists with wealthy elites and a socially liberal middle class. The southern population tends to be poorer, less educated, and more rural, with uneven landholding and collectively farmed *"ejido"* lands that typically lack modern technology. Distant from the northern border and mired in rigid socioeconomic hierarchies inherited from the past (Trejo 2012), this region's fortunes rely more on state protection from market forces. Its population is also more indigenous and propels Mexico to the fourth highest level of indigenous self-identification in Latin America (Madrid 2016).

Yet Mexico's stable democratic party system is only weakly rooted in these social divisions. Statistical models using data from the Mexico Panel Studies in 2000, 2006, and 2012 (Greene 2013; Lawson *et al.* 2001, 2007) show that demographics (gender, age, education, and income), religiosity, and location of residence (region and degree of rurality) predict less than half of voters' choices in presidential elections. Clearly, something more than social profiles influences citizens' voting behavior.[6]

Much of the (limited) explanatory power in the sociological models comes from respondents' location of residence, including region and degree of urbanity. Aggregate voting patterns depict something similar to red vs blue state differences in the United States. But Mexico's parties are far from the full-throated voices of regional cleavages found in other countries. The PRI draws support from constituencies across the country. The PAN prospers more in the north and conservative Bajío regions, but since the mid-1980s its electoral base is broader than that of a confessional or regionalist party. It seeks to patch together free-market interests, social conservatives, and constituencies invested in modern, transparent government. The leftist PRD seeks to represent social interests adversely affected by market liberalization, including segments of industrial labor, poor people's movements, and rural southern interests, but

---

[6] Models are multinomial logistic regressions with two-level random effects to account for nested observations within states. Results appear in Online Appendix 7.1.

also the liberal urban middle class. The PAN and PRD are not catchall parties; rather, they are niche parties that represent left- and right-wing interests defined mainly by their economic policy preferences (Greene 2016). During electoral periods, they also strive to attract the large group of floating voters.

Democratic Mexico has fewer and more stable parties than social cleavages theory would predict. Despite strong links to core constituencies in the electorate, the plurality of voters remain unidentified and thus each party draws a heterogeneous voting bloc from election to election. We argue that biased elections under authoritarian rule muted the effects of social cleavages and encouraged elites to form parties that expressed their preferences on economic policy, rather than a host of other potentially salient social divisions.

Arguments about the impact of electoral district magnitude in the tradition of Duverger (1954) and Cox (1997) provide a maximum number of sustainable party labels based on the notion that elites or voters strategically abandon weaker competitors. But magnitude only exerts meaningful downward pressure when something else would push the number of competitors up. Using Beck and colleagues' (2001) counting rules, Mexico's electoral system could accommodate a maximum of 17.7 competitive parties (see also Cox 1997), and thus magnitude provides no leverage in understanding why politicians coordinate on three main labels. This approach also struggles to explain why the same parties endure over time and why local political entrepreneurs coordinate on national-level labels (Chhibber and Kollman 2004; Cox 1997; Hicken 2009; Sartori 1968). We argue below that party formation under authoritarian rule provided initial solutions to these coordination problems and that negotiation over other institutional rules beyond district magnitude solidified this coordination since the onset of fully competitive democracy.

Mexico's party system is also more stable than spatial theory arguments predict. Whereas competition between a small number of parties produces equilibrium conditions in theoretical work and less vote volatility in empirical work (Mainwaring *et al.* 2016), formal theorists consider three-party competition as a special case. If competition occurs on a single dimension such as left versus right, equilibrium is elusive because the center party's attempts to avoid being squeezed by parties to its left and right generate a cycle of leapfrogging (Cox 1990). In more than one dimension, there is virtually never a Nash equilibrium, and this "chaos" (McKelvey 1986) implies constant opportunities for new parties to enter competition and adopt winning platforms.[7] Yet Mexico's three main parties have maintained consistent platforms and successfully deterred new party entry.

---

[7] Greene (2007b) shows that there was no median in all directions in Mexico's 2006 election and thus no Nash equilibrium in two-dimensional competition.

Mexico's party system is also more stable than recent arguments about the negative effects of "mandate violations" would suggest (Stokes 2001). Lupu (2014) argues that partisanship erodes when parties adopt platforms that contradict their historical issue positions. Roberts (2014) pushes the argument further by claiming that incumbent labor-based or leftist parties that abandon their core constituencies by adopting free-market policies cause party system instability and possibly breakdown if no other leftist party gives voters an outlet for their dissent.[8] A similar logic links performance failures (economic, public security, corruption) to increases in system-level instability where citizens perceive lack of competent or honest alternatives (Seawright 2012).

The PRI acted as a clear mandate violator when it shifted Mexico's political economy from an inward-looking import-substitution model to an export-oriented market model beginning in 1984 (Lustig 1992). In response, identification with the then dominant party declined; however, votes flowed primarily to an increasingly unified left and the process culminated in a three-party system, not an unstable multi-party system or a populist backlash. Similarly, performance failures by the PRI in 1994 (the "Peso Crisis") and the PAN from 2007 to 2012 (a dramatic public security crisis and an economic downturn in 2009) have fueled turnover but not party system instability.

The stability of Mexico's party system is not due to voter alignments propelled by social cleavages, electoral district magnitude, or strong and generalized partisan attachments. Stability owes more to elite identities and sustained coordination than it does to committed voters. One way to appreciate this difference is to decompose the Pedersen Index (1983) of volatility into the portion contributed by parties entering or exiting competition and the portions contributed by voters moving around among the continuing parties (Mainwaring *et al.* 2016; Powell and Tucker 2014). Since 2000, volatility in Mexico's federal elections due to party entry and exit is one-twelfth the level in Peru and less than one-fifth the level in Brazil. Just 28% of total Pedersen volatility comes from party entry and exit in Mexico, whereas the region's average is just over 50%, putting Mexico 0.9 standard deviations below the mean. Strikingly, over 68% of volatility in Chile, a country that analysts often consider a paragon of party system stability, comes from party entry and exit. Thus, whereas much of the volatility in party systems across Latin America comes from the actions of partisan elites, Mexico's parties have created durable elite alignments.[9]

---

[8] In Roberts (2014), Mexico differs from the rest of the region because the PRD formed quickly enough to give leftists who were abandoned by the PRI's market-oriented shift a partisan alternative before instability took hold. In our view, the formation of the PRD (and the opposition PAN) as separate forces contesting economic policy issues is key to party system institutionalization in Mexico. Our argument accounts for these outcomes.

[9] Data come from Greene (2015). Argentina was not scored.

Recent Arguments about Party System Institutionalization

A more recent wave of scholarship ties PSI in new democracies to the legacies of prior authoritarian rule. One set of arguments highlights the destabilizing effects of having experienced longer autocratic rule (Geddes and Frantz 2007; Remmer 1989). Yet, Mexico's institutionalized democratic party system emerged from the world's most durable dominant-party authoritarian regime. Another set of arguments takes this endogeneity as its point of departure, arguing that strong authoritarian incumbent parties (that nevertheless lose power) paradoxically enhance the prospects for stable democratic party systems. We build on this important insight, but we disagree with these arguments' explanation linking legacies to party system outcomes.

In works on several countries in Asia (Hicken and Martinez-Kuhonta 2011) and Africa (Riedl 2014), analysts argue that strong authoritarian incumbents encourage opposition forces to invest in party organizations and coordinate against the regime. As a result, party systems are structured around pro- and anti-regime camps. If authoritarian parties survive the transition to democracy – a prospect that is more likely when they benefit from continuing resources (Flores-Macías forthcoming; Loxton 2015) – new party systems consolidate into two stable blocs consisting of an authoritarian successor party and its opposition. In these cases, the issues that animated authoritarian and anti-authoritarian unity under autocratic rule continue to structure partisan competition under democracy. This argument runs into two difficulties.

First, although anti-authoritarian coalitions may help end competitive authoritarian rule (Howard and Roessler 2006), they do not resolve the representation problem and can thus yield fragile democratic party systems. Having achieved democracy, the regime cleavage that stitches the opposition together usually disappears or greatly diminishes in salience. Unless the coalition is bound by other commitments, such as clientelism or shared positions on non-regime dimensions of contestation, it typically fragments. For instance, in five of the seven democratizing competitive authoritarian regimes examined by Howard and Roessler (2006) in which the opposition coordinated, coalitions came apart after helping open competition. In these cases, measures associated with party system instability worsened.[10]

Second, competitive authoritarian regimes with the strongest ruling parties often generate party systems that are not organized around the regime cleavage. Rather than rely on repression or electoral fraud that help unite challengers in opposition to the regime, powerful incumbents can use their policy appeals and

[10] Opposition coalitions fragmented in Croatia, Kenya, Nicaragua, Romania, and Serbia, and possibly fragmented in a sixth case, Senegal. The number of competitive parties increased after coalitions fragmented in all of these cases. Vote volatility also increased, if we score party name changes as new parties. We are insufficiently expert on these systems to apply more sensitive scoring standards. The opposition did not fragment and the number of competitive parties did not increase in Ghana.

patronage to divide and demobilize challengers (Greene 2007a). For instance, challengers to dominant parties in Mexico, Taiwan, Senegal, and Botswana were animated more by their economic policy concerns than anti-regime ones. Similarly, challengers in Malaysia and Taiwan mobilized on ethnic and national identity issues and typically refused to coalesce in broader opposition coalitions. Partisan coordination thus occurred on durable non-regime cleavages.

In sum, party systems organized around regime issues do not solve the representation problem or the coordination problem in newly democratic party systems. Systems structured in this way instead tend toward fragility. We agree with recent authors that the strongest authoritarian dominant parties, including Mexico under PRI rule, bequeathed the most propitious conditions for institutionalized party systems under democracy; however, we argue that they did so precisely because non-regime cleavages structured partisan competition.

AUTHORITARIAN RULE AND MEXICO'S INSTITUTIONALIZED DEMOCRATIC PARTY SYSTEM

This section details our argument that authoritarian rule helps generate institutionalized democratic party systems when it allows challenger parties to form but divides them on non-regime issues. Authoritarianism that permits (at least) minimally open election contests encourages opposition elites to form parties designed to win power through the ballot box rather than social movements or revolutionary organizations dedicated to reforming or overthrowing the regime. Severe biases against these parties diminish their probability of winning elections and thus drive donors, career-oriented politicians, and voters seeking material benefits away from them. As a result, their main tools for attracting support are their platforms, through which they try to win hearts and minds. Under these conditions, opposition elites have incentives to build independent parties and craft programmatic identities that are strictly differentiated from that of the incumbent authoritarian party.

In our view, solving the representation and coordination problems requires that parties differentiate their platforms on non-regime issues that voters care about once democracy is achieved. Such issues include economic development policy, ethnic representation, or orientations toward national sovereignty, to name a few. Challenger parties adopt such positions when democratization is not their overriding priority, as it tends to be in harsher authoritarian regimes that rely strongly on repression and outcome-changing election fraud. In these cases, if opposition forces build parties, they often create grand coalitions animated by anti-authoritarianism. As we discussed above, such coalitions typically fragment after democratization, creating less stable party systems.

Newly democratic party systems are more likely to be institutionalized when parties solve the representation and coordination problems under prior authoritarian rule. If party systems start with high levels of fragmentation, electoral volatility tends to persist (Mainwaring *et al.* 2016; Powell and Tucker 2014). Institutional mechanisms are unable to rein in the many incentives in democracies for voters to move among the existing parties and for politicians to create new parties or abandon failing ones (Meléndez 2012a; Moser 2001). As a result, systems that start with fragmenting opposition coalitions or those exiting fully closed authoritarian regimes where opposition forces were unable to form parties have less institutionalized party systems than those exiting more open authoritarian rule with competition that divided challenger parties on non-regime issues.

Yet, even where relatively open competition under authoritarianism yields initial alignments, they are likely to be fragile. Social cleavages suppressed under autocracy will seek expression in new regional, ethnic, class, or religious parties after democratization. In addition, disgruntled insiders may capitalize on new competitive opportunities by defecting from existing parties to run under new labels. Unless mechanisms are present to reproduce partisan alignments that were forged under authoritarianism, initial elite coordination may break down due to the expanded opportunities for political entrepreneurs and the political expression of social identities under open competition.

We argue that electoral rules crafted during the pre-democratic era can offset these pressures toward fragmentation and thus support democratic party system stability. Stability-enhancing arrangements advantage existing parties and, in particular, bestow national leaders with power over affiliated politicians. Such control can come in a variety of ways, but principal among them are unique access to political finance and nomination power. Financial advantages for existing parties diminish the incentives for new parties to form. Centralized nomination power can channel politicians' efforts into competing for power inside existing parties, as opposed to primaries that encourage them to amass power in society, and can yield independent candidacies or a new party.

Such rules are most likely to emerge from negotiations between challengers and the incumbent party during managed transitions to democracy. In the shadow of fully open democratic elections, existing parties have strong incentives to lock in advantages for themselves. Autocratic incumbents prefer to write rules that help their party survive democratization rather than dilute their electoral presence by distributing resources widely. Challenger parties that become strong enough to extract concessions from the incumbent naturally prefer rules that deconcentrate resources but stop short of funding new rivals.

In our view, successful oligopolistic negotiations help structure newly democratic party systems; however, they also carry significant risks. Club-like deals between insufficiently representative parties can create "partyarchy" (Coppedge 1994) or cartels (Katz and Mair 1995) that fuel voter dissatisfaction and precipitate outsider challenges, even leading to party system implosion.

Concerns over representational failure are enhanced by successful negotiations that naturally help autocratic incumbent parties survive democratization. Thus, parties must solve both the representation and coordination problems simultaneously, and this carries significant trade-offs. Determining the equilibrium conditions that support these simultaneous solutions and push in favor of democratic party system stability is beyond the scope of this chapter. Instead, we draw out the particular solutions to these problems for Mexico in the sections that follow.

ELITE INVESTMENTS AND INITIAL PARTISAN ALIGNMENTS IN MEXICO'S NEW DEMOCRACY

Mexico arrived at its first fully competitive democratic elections in 2000 with a well-formed three-party system that included the formerly dominant PRI in the center, the PAN on the right, and the PRD on the left. In this section, we substantiate our argument that the party system's characteristics at the onset of democracy were endogenous to prior authoritarian rule. The dynamics of open but biased competition encouraged opposition elites to form a small number of parties with differentiated platforms on the underlying economic policy cleavage, instead of a more fragile opposition front. In so doing, the system produced a durable solution to the representation problem.

Like other authoritarian regimes that permitted inter-party competition (Levitsky and Way 2010, Schedler 2013), the dominant PRI preferred to win power through regular but biased elections rather than close the electoral arena or run sham contests. The incumbent party sought popular support through elections for three reasons. First, the toll of the Revolution (1910–17), uprisings throughout the 1920s and 1930s, the bloody Church-backed Cristero Rebellion (1926–29), and violent class conflicts during the early stages of industrialization (Aguilar and Meyer 1993; Carr 1992; Meyer 1976) convinced regime insiders that it was more effective to cede minority space to (largely ineffectual) challengers than to risk armed insurgency and rely on the widespread repression required to maintain fully closed authoritarian rule. Second, regular elections helped the PRI portray itself as the legitimate institutional expression of the nation and champion of the social justice values that helped spark the Revolution (Bartra 1989). Finally, regular elections created a mechanism for succession that helped stabilize relations among aspiring leaders because it encouraged them to compete for power within the party rather than raise armies to fight for it from the outside (Castañeda 1999).

The PRI's multi-class constituency limited its ideological elasticity. Adopting relatively centrist policies helped balance the interests in the party's "contradictory alliance" (Collier 1992). Moving policy too far to the left or right encouraged internal challengers and external opposition to mobilize against the regime, typically provoking a shift back toward the center. For instance, periods of labor mobilization, aided by the communist party (PCM) in the 1930s encouraged President Lázaro Cárdenas (1934–40) to adopt labor-friendly policies; however, a strong reaction from conservative forces, including the formation of the National Action Party (PAN) in 1939, generated more pro-business policies in the following administration of President Manuel Avila Camacho (1940–46). Similarly, leftist mobilization associated with the student movement of 1968 and the emergence of revolutionary organizations and radical intellectual cliques in the 1970s encouraged Presidents Luis Echeverría (1970–76) and José Luis López Portillo (1976–82) to increase social spending and tax the wealthy. Yet, the subsequent conservative reaction that included capital flight and renewed electoral mobilization through the PAN, combined with a crushing debt burden and pressure from international lenders, encouraged President Miguel de la Madrid (1982–88) to privatize public enterprises and reduce social spending. Bruhn's analysis of the PRI's published platforms from 1940 to 2000 shows that despite shifts to the left and right over time, its policies remained within the broad center until the mid-1980s (Bruhn and Greene 2009).

Why did Mexico's brand of authoritarianism generate opposition parties to the left and right? In our view, challenger party ideology was endogenous to dominant-party authoritarian rule. Drawing on literature about party affiliation decisions (Aldrich 1983; Schlesinger 1991) and decisions to participate in social movements (Chong 1991; Olson 1965), as well as in-depth interviews with party personnel in Mexico, Greene (2007a) argues that prospective candidates and activists value the probability of winning, expressing a platform with which they agree, and the costs of participation. Opposition parties in authoritarian regimes with inter-party competition face a low probability of victory because elections are severely biased in favor of the incumbent party's candidates (see also Magaloni 2006; Simpser 2013). Such actors also face high costs of participation because authoritarian regimes constantly threaten to use the repressive apparatus of the state against them, with sanctions ranging from jailing on trumped-up charges, to beatings by regime-allied thugs, enforcement of tax laws, and even death (Carr 1992; Martínez Verdugo 1985; Shirk 2005). Facing low and uncertain benefits as well as high and nearly certain costs, the only citizens willing to join opposition parties were those with ideological preferences that deviated markedly from the incumbent's policies. As a result, if opposition parties form, they form on the ideological fringes when the authoritarian incumbent's advantages are high (see Greene 2007a).

Analysts of political parties in fully democratic settings typically expect volunteer lower-level activists to hold relatively extremist views relative to status quo policies (Aldrich 1983) and candidates and party leaders to focus on electability and thus prefer moderation (May 1973). Mexico's experience contrasts sharply. Challenger parties faced such a low probability of victory that the only prospective candidates and party elites willing to join them rather than compete for nominations inside the PRI were those with even more radical ideologies than lower-level activists. Figure 7.3 shows that, in contrast to

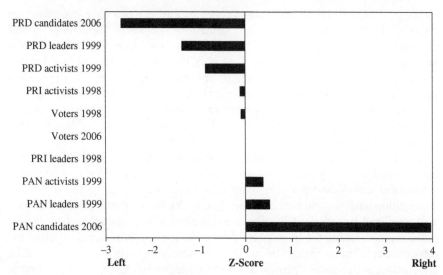

FIGURE 7.3 Economic Policy Preferences of Voters, Activists, Leaders, and Congressional Candidates in Mexico
Sources: Prepared by the authors, based on several data sources: Data on activists and leaders come from the Mexico Party Personnel Surveys 1998–99 using questions on privatization, social welfare, and capital controls (Greene 2007a). Data on candidates come from the Mexico 2006 Candidate Surveys, using questions on privatization, social welfare, and trade with the United States. Data on voters come from the Mexico 2006 Panel Study, Wave 1, using questions on privatization and social welfare (Lawson *et al.* 2007). A similar figure appears in Greene (2016).

standard theory, higher-level personnel held less centrist ideologies than lower-level activists and voters.[11] The figure also shows that voters and both leaders and activists in the PRI located in the center of the space.

This array of platform preferences inside the then challenger parties could have produced centrist parties that favored an opposition coalition (and thus failed to solve the representation problem) if intra-party democracy had allowed the more numerous lower-level activists to override the more radical vision of candidates and party leaders. Nevertheless, higher-level personnel prevailed because they created hierarchical parties with relatively closed membership structures and demanding advancement procedures (Bruhn 1997; Greene 2007a; Loaeza 1999). Opposition parties could not offer their members electability, salaries, or other side-payments, and activism risked state repression. As a result, these parties were in constant danger of abandonment. A key way to retain members was to offer them an identity based on strong

---

[11] Bruhn and Greene (2009) also show candidate ideologies were extreme relative to each party's identified voters.

ideological beliefs. Identities become more powerful when they provide crisp dividing lines between "ins" and "outs" or between "opposition" and "incumbent" (Chong 1991). The best way to hone and protect this ideological identity was to ensure that only the most committed and longest suffering members had access to the levers of power. As a result, opposition organizations became "niche parties" that restricted intra-party voting rights to small groups selected through somewhat opaque procedures and imposed a combination of formal and informal requirements for affiliation and advancement (Greene 2016).

The ideological and organizational profiles of challengers to the PRI, which helped resolve the representation and elite coordination problems in Mexico's subsequent democratic party system, were thus endogenous to the degree of competition under authoritarian rule. These challenger party profiles are not well predicted by standard theories. As described above, spatial theory derives indeterminate results for three-party competition; arguments based on electoral rules predict a higher maximum number of competitors and give no leverage in understanding deviations below that upper bound; social cleavages theory cannot determine why region, class, ethnicity, and other identities did not form the basis for parties; and even authoritarian-legacies arguments that focus on splits between the incumbent and opposition cannot explain the creation of two ideologically polarized challengers instead of a single broad centrist coalition. In our view, open but biased competition created recruitment incentives for prospective politicians and activists that yielded unified challengers to the left and right of a relatively centrist dominant party. These differentiated platforms provided an initial solution to the representation problem. We believe that the representation problem would not have been resolved and the party system would have been unstable under democracy if (1) authoritarian rule had generated more numerous and less cohesive challenger parties or an ideologically heterogeneous anti-authoritarian opposition coalition, or (2) the PRI had not survived the transition to fully competitive democracy. We address each of these issues in turn.

First, why were there only two main opposition parties, despite the presence of multiple social cleavages and a sufficiently open electoral arena that could have propelled more competitors? In fact, the 1950s to mid-1980s saw the formation of many small parties on both the right and left; however, these proto-parties either folded or threw their lot in with the PAN or PRD by the late 1980s (Bruhn 1997; Greene 2007a). Part of the reason for opposition coordination concerns the hyper-concentration of power in the presidency during the authoritarian era. Not only did pursuing the presidency encourage the formation of larger, nationally oriented parties (Cox 1997), but ousting the PRI from the presidential palace was viewed as necessary for democratization. Lacking access to fungible resources that would help them to mount mass media campaigns, opposition forces found it easier to rally activists behind fewer labels with identifiable platforms. Platforms that were weakly differentiated from the incumbent's would not have inspired enough citizens to risk the costs of voicing their political dissent publicly. At the same time, broader platforms recruited more activists and lowered the perceived costs of opposition. We offer no theory of how challenger parties navigated between the opposing incentives of differentiation and breadth, except to note that the process unfolded for parties on the left and right over decades of struggle.[12] By the late 1980s, challengers on both the right and left had created larger and more unified parties with solid organizations capable of launching competitive presidential candidates, winning sub-national contests, and maintaining a local presence in substantial parts of the country. The ideological value of their labels was the glue that held them together, not only in a single election, but also over time.

Second, why did coordination stop with leftist and rightist platforms rather than unify both partisan groupings into a broad anti-authoritarian front, as the legacies existing authoritarian arguments would predict? Public opinion polls and voting patterns suggest that such a coalition could have ousted the PRI from the presidency sooner. In addition, other competitive authoritarian regimes were more likely to have experienced "liberalizing electoral outcomes" when opposition parties unified (Howard and Roessler 2006). In Mexico, whereas a plurality of voters and more moderate party personnel preferred an opposition front, the most leftist and rightist leaders in the PRD and PAN, respectively, were strongly against it. Having established hierarchically controlled parties, they were able to block such a coalition (see Greene 2007a for an account of the failed alliance).

Paradoxically, the absence of intra-party democracy that blocked the creation of a broad anti-authoritarian coalition likely helped create a stable democratic party system, even if it retarded democratization. In most cases, such coalitions are formed by parties that disagree on a primary dimension of competition, such as the PAN and PRD, but temporarily ignore those differences to coalesce against an authoritarian incumbent. If they succeed, their reason for existence erodes and they fragment, as argued above. The recalcitrant insiders that blocked the formation of an anti-PRI coalition likely helped infuse Mexico's newly democratic party system with more structure and representativeness than it otherwise would have enjoyed.

Finally, we argue that the PRI survived the transition to fully democratic competition for three reasons, the first two of which are associated with our argument. First, the very dynamics of authoritarian rule with competition that generated opposition parties on the right and left also yielded expanded space for a party to occupy the center. Had the PRI not benefited from dramatic advantages over opposition forces or had an opposition coalition formed, challenger parties might have vied more successfully for space in the center; however, their non-centrist ideological profiles allowed the PRI to close ranks and campaign as a responsible and moderate option. Because this platform continued to resonate with citizens, the PRI maintained the plurality of identified voters and therefore also retained the loyalties of office-seeking

---

[12] As discussed below, ballot access requirements also pushed challengers to create larger and nationally oriented parties.

politicians across the country. Theoretically, the PRI could have been replaced by a similarly centrist successor party; however, the second reason it survived, as we describe below, concerned its deft management of the transition that traded its prior access to illicit public resources for licit ones during the 1990s. In other words, it anticipated and prepared for fully open elections by substituting key elements of its authoritarian advantages for democratic resources during the protracted transition. Finally, the PRI also maintained control over clientelistic networks and many state and local governments, which proved useful in supporting its national-level comeback (Flores-Macías forthcoming; Langston 2003).

Mexico thus arrived at the onset of fully competitive democracy in 2000 with initial partisan alignments around three parties with identities and platforms that were shaped by prior authoritarian rule and the protracted transition to democracy. However, fully open competition with a level playing field changed the calculations for prospective politicians. Now, their choice was not between a centrist dominant party with a high probability of winning or a non-centrist challenger with a low probability, but between working inside existing parties with inherited platforms and relatively equal probabilities of winning or forming a new party with its own identity. Regional, ethnic, religious, sectoral, and generational cleavages, some of which were under-represented and some of which struggled for representation inside existing parties, could now hypothetically form the basis for new parties. The PAN could have split into a party of fiscal conservatives joined by center-right pro-market PRI members and another of social conservatives based in the Bajío region. The PRD could have split into an ethno-populist party representing southern indigenous groups, a socially liberal middle-class party, and an urban poor people's party. Yet, not only did the three main parties remain intact, small new parties either disappeared quickly or have survived through temporary and often shifting alliances with the major parties, without disturbing the system's stability.

HOW ELECTORAL RULES AND PRACTICES HELP MEXICO'S STABLE DEMOCRATIC PARTY SYSTEM ENDURE

Why did elite coordination around the three main parties forged during the authoritarian era persist in democratic Mexico? We argue that electoral rules and practices inherited from the authoritarian era reinforced elite coordination around three distinct partisan options. The relevant rules were designed to address problems of single-party dominance and its decline starting in the late 1970s. In mediating these problems, they created high barriers to new party entry, granted financial advantages to larger existing parties, and concentrated nomination power with party leaders. As a result, politicians typically had greater incentives to maintain allegiance to the existing parties rather than create new ones, even in the face of growing anti-party sentiment among voters, electoral losses, and bitter intra-party disputes.

We focus on electoral rules for two reasons. First, rules exerted strong influence on Mexico's democratic party system because an initial solution to the representation problem was already in place. Where parties are not already well established, new rules rarely engineer institutionalized party systems, as the Peruvian experience shows (Meléndez 2012a). Second, although formal rules certainly do not tell the whole story of inter-party competition, they significantly advantaged the three main parties over potential new competitors that could have destabilized the system, and thus helped reproduce initial partisan alignments inherited from the prior process of party building.[13]

Electoral Rules and the Emergence of a Three-Bloc Party System

Authoritarian regimes with competition risk tilting the partisan playing field so significantly in their favor that opposition forces turn away from parties and instead form revolutionary organizations or social movements. Whereas rulers in fully closed authoritarian regimes might prefer to fragment the opposition in this way, incumbents in authoritarian regimes that permit competition derive legitimacy from holding regular and at least semi-open elections (Levitsky and Way 2010).

Mexico's PRI faced a legitimacy crisis in 1976 when its presidential candidate ran unopposed. The left had fragmented with elements going underground following episodes of bloody repression (Carr 1992), and the PAN failed to nominate a candidate due to doubts the PRI could be ousted through elections (Loaeza 1999). In response, the government used electoral law to ease the barriers for challenger parties. The scheme had a complex goal: encourage opposition forces to compete through parties but stop short of helping them coordinate on a broad anti-PRI front.

The 1977 reform encouraged dissidents to organize through parties in three ways. First, it lowered the barriers to registration to 1.5% of the vote in their first federal election, a low threshold by international standards (Dalton *et al.* 2011). Active organizations that represented a significant "current of opinion" could also obtain "conditional registration" for one electoral cycle. Second, the threshold of representation was lowered by increasing the number of seats in Congress from 237 to 400 and raising the proportion of seats allocated through proportional representation criteria from 17.3% in 1976 (forty-one seats) to 25% (100 seats). Finally, parties were permitted access to some (unspecified) amount of public financing and free access to mass media (see Middlebrook 1986 and Online Appendix 7.2).

The reform not only encouraged opposition groups to channel their grievances through parties, it also gave incentives to coordinate on larger parties. The allure

---

[13] Formal rules play a similar role in Riedl's (2014) argument.

of maintaining national registration by amassing votes was significant by itself. Local politicians were encouraged to throw their support behind bigger parties because nationally registered ones could automatically run candidates in all subnational contests. The reforms also enhanced the power of party leaders by giving them control over public finances. Combined with closed-list proportional representation seats and the prohibition on consecutive reelection inherited from the Revolution, party leaders had effective nominating power and could thus control politicians' career paths.

With these new incentives on the table, many of the fragmented and fragile leftist parties and movements subsumed their ideological differences and coalesced into the Unified Socialist Party of Mexico in 1981 (Bruhn 1997: 323; Rodríguez and Sirvent 2005). This degree of coordination had not existed on the left since the Mexican Communist Party (PCM) lost its registration in 1946. A further unification occurred with the formation of the Mexican Socialist Party (PMS) in 1987; however, this party never competed because it threw its support behind Cuauhtémoc Cárdenas's presidential bid in 1988 and was later folded into an even broader coalition with the formation of the PRD in 1989. Opposition forces on the right had suffered less repression (Shirk 2005) and had formed major tenets of its ideology around Catholic doctrine. Thus, the right was significantly more unified than the left, facing only minor competition from rural fascist parties until the late 1990s. Nevertheless, the opportunities created by the reform positioned the PAN to incorporate market-oriented elites who believed that the PRI's shift toward the left in the 1970s bordered on a socialist project (Loaeza 1999: 303).

Although the reform encouraged opposition unity on the PRI's flanks and thus a three-bloc system, it did not encourage a grand opposition front. Such a broad coalition would have been based on opposing the PRI and a shared desire for democracy. Challenger parties did fight for democracy, but the process of party formation in opposition to a relatively centrist PRI created ideologically polarized parties that preferred the incumbent's policies to those of their further-flung ideological rivals (Greene 2007a).

Public Party Financing and the Institutionalization of a Three-Party System

The 1977 reforms helped set the stage for a party system with three blocs that eventually coalesced into the PAN on the right, the PRI in the center, and the PRD on the left. Subsequent reforms, born of economic crisis and negotiations between the regime and its challengers, created a complex system of public finances that reinforced the three parties' advantages over potential new entrants before and after democratization in 2000.

Following the 1982 debt crisis, the PRI's nearly unbridled access to politicized public resources declined dramatically. It was not the debt crisis itself, but the government's orthodox economic response after 1984 that privatized state-owned enterprises and moved toward a free-trade model that diminished government revenue (Lustig 1992). After the government burned through the capital raised from privatizations, the public budget was substantially smaller than it had been. Finance minister, Pedro Aspe, sent a memo to the president of the PRI in 1992 informing him that the central government could no longer finance the party and, as a result, the party would have to make up for the "estimated $1 billion in government funds that was wire transferred every year to the party's headquarters" (Oppenheimer 1996: 88).

The government's response to economic crisis had three major effects on the party system. First, it deprived the PRI of much of the public resources that other authoritarian successor parties such as Taiwan's KMT have used to remain competitive after democratization (Loxton 2015). Second, it encouraged the PRI to establish a public party finance system for its own benefit. Finally, it made further electoral reform a major intermediate target for opposition parties on the road to democratization (Schedler 2002).

The combination of a dramatically smaller public sector and rising political competition meant that the PRI could scarcely raid the public budget as it had before. Hypothetically, legacy resources could have come from private sources, and indeed the PRI initially turned to crony capitalists who had benefited from the initial privatization process, raising US$750 million in contributions (Oppenheimer 1996). Although temporarily useful, the business community proved a fickle friend. As more of the economy was privatized, capital interests became less dependent on the large state and thus less willing to fund its official party.

The PRI then turned to an expanded system of public financing. The first notable increase was adopted in 1986 when the PRI used its electoral dominance to allocate all funds based on vote and seat shares in the prior election. But, by 1996, three processes forced the regime to concede resources to the opposition. First, challenger parties had accumulated notable electoral support. By 1995, the PAN and PRD together held 40% of congressional seats, the PAN held four governorships, and opposition parties together controlled about 14% of the country's municipalities. Of particular importance, the PRI needed the PAN's congressional votes to pass economic reforms. Second, the government faced an insurgency in Chiapas that was small but initially generated broad social support. High-profile assassinations inside the PRI also wrested confidence from the party. Finally, just months after winning the 1994 presidential elections, a short-term liquidity problem spurred by the start of NAFTA and inflamed by an overvalued peso, caused a currency crisis. The crisis was short-lived but caused serious pain, especially for the emerging middle-class and debt-holding businesses that saw interest rates on loans skyrocket.

The PRI's vulnerability gave the opposition the opening it sought. Three-party negotiations produced a new election law in 1996 that consequentially leveled the playing field. It increased public party financing 600%, making Mexico's elections among the most expensive per capita in the world. It also shifted allocation in favor of the opposition by distributing 70% of public resources by vote share and 30% equally across registered parties, a formula that remains in force today. Private contributions were now restricted to just 10% of total public subsidies. In addition, the independent Federal Electoral Institute (IFE) assumed sweeping power to audit spending and sanction transgressions. Although the parties continued to use illicit resources, two elements of the new system advantaged existing parties over potential entrants. First, due mainly to public financing, the three main parties accounted for 83% of total licit funding in the 1997 elections and 78% in 2000, with the remainder spread across numerous small competitors (Lujambio 2001). Second, as a result of these parties' financial advantages and thus the likelihood they would continue to dominate elections, potential illicit donors would do better to contribute to these parties rather than upstarts. Finally, the auditing system made it difficult for small parties to receive the bulk of their funding from illicit sources.

The three parties' financial dominance similarly gave politicians continuing incentives to fight for nominations and other posts inside the existing parties rather than invest in overcoming the barriers to creating new parties. To make matters more difficult for upstarts, the 1996 law raised these barriers. Conditional party registration adopted in 1977 was eliminated, the threshold for registration grew to 2% of the vote, and new parties needed membership totaling 0.13% of all registered voters, with 3,000 members in at least ten of the thirty-two states or 300 members in at least 100 of 300 single-member electoral districts.

Overall, the legacy of election law reforms under authoritarian rule generated important incentives for elite coordination. Hypothetically, these system-reproducing rules could have changed after democratization. Yet rather than opening the system to more actors, reforms since 2000 have typically pushed in the opposite direction. Membership requirements for new parties were doubled in 2003. A 2007 reform dramatically shortened the official campaign period for federal offices, restricted new party entry to once every six years, and prohibited parties, candidates, and private citizens from purchasing political advertising in the mass media. Instead, registered parties receive free airtime, distributed using the same formula in place for public funding since 1996, both of which privilege major competitors. Legislation in 2014 further raised the threshold of party registration to 3% of the national vote.

During the period of authoritarian single-party dominance, opposition movements on the left and the right emerged organically in opposition to the incumbent PRI. The regime preferred for challenger movements to organize through parties where dissident social interests could be controlled and defeated electorally; thus, it encouraged the formation of two opposition blocs in the 1977 reform. Economic crisis and free-market reforms in the 1980s pushed the PRI toward a generous public funding system, from which challenger parties slowly wrested support. Once privileged by various aspects of the electoral code, none of the three players wanted to open the system to new entrants. As a result, the reforms were designed to reinforce initial coordination on the existing parties.

CONCLUSION: IS MEXICO'S PARTY SYSTEM BECOMING LESS INSTITUTIONALIZED?

Authoritarian legacies endowed Mexico's new democracy with an institutionalized party system, but few legacies last forever, and the party system now shows some signs of weakening. As mentioned above, citizens trust parties less than a gamut of other political and social institutions. There is plenty of fuel for this dissatisfaction, including a bloody wave of criminal violence that has claimed some 70,000 lives since 2007 (Dell 2015), related human rights violations (IACHR 2015), persistent poverty and inequality (Esquivel 2015), widespread corruption (Morris 2009), and meager economic growth (Moreno-Brid and Ros 2009). Public mood is primed for change.

In our view, such change could come from three sources, none of which currently poses more than a vague threat to the existing system. First, the PRD's two-time presidential candidate, Andrés Manuel López Obrador, recently created the Movement for National Regeneration (MORENA). Our best guess is that this new party will absorb much of the PRD's voter base but maintain similar ideological inclinations to the existing left. We do not view name changes by themselves as a threat to party system stability.

Second, despite the system-reinforcing effects of most elements of election law, smaller parties have wrested some vote share from the traditional parties. Figure 7.2 shows that whereas the three main parties accounted for 89% of the congressional vote in 1997, their share fell to 75% in 2015.[14] The five surviving parties (not counting MORENA) face significant obstacles. We see five main ways they can grow. First, they can establish regional strongholds such as the Workers' Party (PT) that grew from a social movement in the state of Durango. Second, they can attract politicians seeking to capitalize on discontent with the major parties. For instance, the Citizen Movement (MC) won the plurality in Jalisco state, carrying Guadalajara with a candidate formerly linked to both the PRI and PRD. Third, they can cozy up to major media outlets. The Green Party (PVEM) is closely aligned with Televisa, the country's leading broadcasting company, and thus benefits from clever "earned" media advertising that otherwise eludes small parties. Fourth, they can link to previously organized groups, such as the New Alliance Party (PANAL) that enjoys close ties to the powerful teachers' union. Finally, they can form strategic preelection alliances with the main parties. In the shadow of a divided Congress, small parties are

---

[14] Sixty-one per cent if we consider MORENA to be a new party.

often pivotal and thus can negotiate handsome rewards for their votes. Hypothetically, parties could use one or more of these strategies to bootstrap themselves from minor players into major competitors, but their success is uncertain at best.

Finally, threats to stability could come from two reforms adopted in 2014 that permit independent candidates and term-limited consecutive reelection for federal and state legislators, as well as mayors. These provisions hypothetically weaken national party organizations because candidates can threaten defection if party leaders do not (re)nominate them and political outsiders can launch campaigns that are independent of the established parties. The first major success came quickly with a former PRI member turned-independent, Jaime Rodríguez Calderón (nicknamed "El Bronco"), winning the governorship of the wealthy northern state of Nuevo León in 2015 with a 25-point lead over the traditional parties. Several well-known politicians have entertained the possibility of running for high office as independents in 2018, but it is unclear that voters are willing to follow.

In our view, independent candidates' success depends on four sets of conditions. First, rules governing campaign finance and political advertising are stacked against them (see Online Appendix 7.2). At present, they may raise more of their funding from private sources than can parties; however, independents will receive little from the current public-finance and mass-media distribution systems. They can increase their share of public funds by coordinating on a small number of candidates. But coordination, our second condition, is difficult to fulfill without a party organization and nomination procedures designed for this purpose. Third, independents will likely prosper where they make deft use of the internet and social media, a media mechanism that is not highly regulated to date. Finally, in light of their disadvantages, independents will do best where they enjoy name recognition before the campaigns begin, where performance debacles or corruption scandals have weakened the traditional parties' images, and where voters are urban, informed, and online. Most of these conditions favored "El Bronco." He competed as the only independent candidate in a prosperous state with recent corruption scandals, he used social media aggressively, and his previous positions in the PRI bestowed name recognition. His relatively prosperous constituents tuned in. Whether his experience will generalize, however, is far from clear. Public discontent may instead fuel democratic alternation among the main parties without producing major party system change.

Our best guess is that Mexico's party system will remain stable in the face of recent new parties and independent candidates, but there is certainly a chance that conditions will conspire to turn its edifice of stability into sand. As with all legacies, time will tell!

8

Deinstitutionalization without Collapse: Colombia's Party System

Juan Albarracín, Laura Gamboa, and Scott Mainwaring*

Since the 1990s, Colombia's party system made a transition from an institutionalized party system, as it was classified in *Building Democratic Institutions* (Mainwaring and Scully 1995a), to a deinstitutionalized one. Although the change was not as dramatic as the collapse of party systems in Bolivia, Ecuador, Peru, and Venezuela, the members of the party system have changed profoundly, with new important entrants and the decline of the two traditional parties. The system has also exhibited high electoral volatility. Levels of partisan attachment are low, and party organizations have weakened. In this chapter, we describe this process of deinstitutionalization and examine its causes.

Many countries in Latin America have experienced collapses of major parties, party system deinstitutionalization, and even party system collapse since the early 1990s. In this sense, Colombia is not unusual. The Colombian case is distinctive in that both of the traditional parties suffered major electoral and organizational erosion but still remain important actors. The closest counterpart among the cases examined in this volume is Argentina, whose party system has also experienced deinstitutionalization, growing fragmentation, and decreasing nationalization, but in which one of the traditional parties, the Peronists, was dominant from 2003 to 2015.

Unlike most of the other cases in which once institutionalized systems either collapsed or seriously frayed, Colombia did not experience traumatic bursts of hyperinflation or severe economic downturns (Lupu 2016 and Chapter 12 in this volume; Roberts 2014). The decomposition of Colombia's traditional party system occurred in relative economic tranquility compared to the massive upheaval so many other Latin American countries experienced. The economic distresses that were pivotal in undermining traditional parties in Argentina, Peru,

* We are grateful to Sandra Botero, Eduardo Dargent, Gustavo Flores-Macías, Steve Levitsky, Noam Lupu, Juan Pablo Milanese, Jana Morgan, Monika Nalepa, Timothy Power, and Samuel Valenzuela for comments.

and Venezuela are not central to the Colombian story of party system deinstitutionalization.

In the Colombian case, the mismanagement of the security situation by both traditional parties and a severe security threat in the early 2000s fostered deep change in the competition for the presidency and altered national party competition. In the midst of an increasing disconnect between regional and national party politics, these changes did not have the same effect sub-nationally. Local patronage and clientelistic structures allowed the two traditional parties, particularly the Liberal Party, to survive. Although some regional politicians switched to new parties, the pace of change in regional politics was slower. The Liberal and Conservative parties remained relevant actors in municipal and regional elections. Consequently, even though Colombia's party landscape changed substantially after the early 1990s, the system did not collapse.

THE MAIN PARTIES

Liberal and Conservative Parties

The Liberal and Conservative parties are the oldest in Colombia and among the oldest major parties in the world. They emerged in the late 1840s as parties of notables, and they dominated elections continuously from 1849 until 2002. With the exception of a few short-lived military dictatorships, a Liberal or Conservative president governed Colombia continuously from 1900 until 2002. Moreover, these two parties thoroughly dominated congress and sub-national political offices. Until 1991, Colombia usually had one of the purest two-party systems in the world, though in some presidential elections, a splinter candidate emerged and divided the vote of one of the two traditional parties.

These parties started with different programs. The Conservatives supported a centralized administration, economic protectionism, and involvement of the Catholic Church in state affairs. The Liberals supported federalism and free-trade policies, and they opposed involvement of the Catholic Church in state affairs (Delpar 1981; Dugas 2000; Latorre 1974; Posada-Carbó 1997; Roll 2002). Throughout the second half of the nineteenth century, the parties fought several civil wars over these differences, generating deep partisan attachments and antipathies. The civil wars created "hereditary hatreds" that outlived the parties' ideological differences. During the first half of the twentieth century, people were born either Liberal or Conservative and it was unthinkable to switch (Dugas 2000; Gutiérrez 2007; Hartlyn 1988; Pérez 1989).

The turn of the century brought an end to the civil wars of the 1800s. Political stability generated economic growth and with it a small working class. Although keeping its commitment to the interests of economic and political elites (landowners, coffee growers, merchants, industrialists, and bankers), the Liberals incorporated the working class (Archila 1991). When universal male suffrage was re-instituted in 1936,[1] they became a dominant party, thus changing the nature of political competition. Unable to defeat them at the polls, during the late 1940s the Conservatives used state violence against Liberals, who formed rural guerrillas and fought back. A blood bath ensued. Between 1948 and 1953, both parties engaged in armed conflict over the control of the state, a time referred to as "La Violencia."

After a military dictatorship (1953–58), the Liberal and Conservative parties agreed to distribute public offices equally amongst themselves for sixteen years as a way of promoting power sharing and avoiding the polarization that had led to civil war. Liberal and Conservative presidents would alternate, and all public elected and non-elected offices would be equally divided. Although the National Front, the name given to this period (1958–74), stopped inter-party violence, it excluded all other parties from meaningful political participation (Hartlyn 1988). In the aftermath of the Cuban revolution, the restricted nature of Colombian democracy provided a setting for the emergence of revolutionary movements, such as the *Fuerzas Armadas Revolucionarias de Colombia* (FARC) and the *Ejército de Liberación Nacional* (ELN) in 1964, and the *Movimiento 19 de Abril* (M-19) in 1970. Liberals and Conservatives colluded to marginalize other parties and also on policy grounds. Both became pragmatic, clientelistic machines, with minor policy and ideological differences between them. The National Front promoted intra-party competition, demobilized Liberal and Conservative partisans, and encouraged state-led patronage (Gutiérrez 2007; Leal Buitrago and Dávila 1990), thus gradually weakening parties and party labels.

Institutional reforms in the late 1980s and early 1990s opened the system (Bejarano 2011), and they accelerated organizational weakness and the electoral vulnerability of the two traditional parties (Pizarro Leongómez 2002, 2006; Dargent and Muñoz 2011). Political and economic decentralization, larger district magnitudes in the Senate, and lower electoral thresholds stripped national Liberal and Conservative leaders of control over party members and devalued party labels (Pizarro Leongómez 2006). In the absence of strong partisan attachments, by the end of the 1990s running for the Liberal or Conservative Party was not an asset and, in many cases, it was a liability. Party labels became less meaningful. With the growth of drug traffic and the paramilitary right, office-seekers had access to illegal resources that allowed them to campaign and feed clienteles even if they did not run on the Liberal or Conservative labels (Gutiérrez 2007).

---

[1] During the nineteenth century, there were periods in which male universal suffrage was instituted but later withdrawn. Women were given the right to vote in 1957, very late by comparative standards.

The Emergence of New Parties

The 2002 presidential and congressional elections marked a watershed in Colombia's political history. Some prominent Liberal politicians defected to the coalition of the Liberal dissident presidential candidate, Álvaro Uribe. The Conservatives did not run a presidential candidate in 2002 or 2006, and most Conservatives supported Uribe. This exodus from the traditional parties accelerated with Uribe's unprecedented triumph over the Liberal Party's candidate and the Liberals' decision to not join the government coalition (Gutiérrez 2002, 2007). The epoch of traditional party hegemony abruptly ended with Uribe's victories in 2002 and 2006. In 2006, Uribe was reelected with 62% of the vote compared to 22% for his closest rival (Carlos Gaviria of the center-left *Polo Democrático Alternativo*) and 12% for the Liberal Party candidate. His landslide victory stemmed from his success in pushing back the guerrilla forces, greatly improving the country's security situation, as well as Colombia's international standing and its economic performance. Uribe was not a party builder; he ran his presidential campaigns in 2002 and 2006 with his personalistic movement, *Primero Colombia* (Colombia First).[2] Some of his supporters coalesced into new parties, particularly after an electoral reform in 2003 fostered the creation of larger parties rather than the personalized electoral movements that were common at the end of the 1990s (Botero and Rodríguez-Raga 2008).

Many Liberal Party dissidents and so-called "independents" formed the *Partido Social de Unidad Nacional* (Social Party of National Unity), commonly known as *Partido de la U* (U Party), in a clear reference to President Uribe. This party is a coalition of politicians with strong regional political machines, as well as figures of national reputation who can attract policy-oriented voters. Although Uribe never formally joined this party, *Partido de la U* legislators composed the largest part of his coalition in congress.

In 2010, the *Partido de la U's* founder and a former Minister of Defense under Uribe, Juan Manuel Santos, won the presidency on Uribe's coattails. The Conservative and Liberal presidential candidates in 2010 experienced crushing defeats. They won only 6.1% and 4.4% of the vote, respectively, confirming their decline. However, conflict between Santos and Uribe led to a division in the coalition that brought them to power. Santos remains the leader of the U Party, but he has revived his old ties to the Liberal Party, while Uribe created a new personalistic party, *Centro Democrático*. In the 2014 elections, *Centro Democrático* became the second largest party in the Senate with former president Uribe heading the list, and it fielded the strongest candidate (Oscar I. Zuluaga) in opposition to Santos's successful reelection bid and the peace

[2] *Primero Colombia* was created with the sole purpose of supporting Uribe's presidential candidacy. It did not field candidates in any other election, and it barely existed in between elections. Uribe used it again to run for reelection in 2006.

agreement between the state and the FARC that the president started negotiating in 2012. The latter was the central axis of party competition in the 2010s. As the negotiations progressed, the conflict between Uribe and Santos deteriorated.

Several small parties were also part of Uribe's coalition: *Cambio Radical, Alas-Equipo Colombia*, and *Convergencia Ciudadana*. Many politicians in this group had strong ties to paramilitaries (right-wing extra-official militias that usually had strong connections to the military and/or to former military officials). In April 2010, two-thirds of the hundreds of politicians accused of connections to paramilitaries were part of Uribe's coalition (López 2010).

Parties of the Left
Historically, the Colombian left consisted of several parties and tendencies. Until recently, it remained a marginal force in electoral (legal) politics. For a long time, part of Colombia's left, with its social-democratic tendencies, was a faction within the Liberal Party. With the end of the National Front and the initiation of peace processes with guerrilla groups in the 1980s and early 1990s, many parties of the left emerged. Two of them, the Unión Patriótica (UP) and Alianza Democrática M-19 (AD-M19), enjoyed ephemeral electoral success. The UP was formed in the midst of the peace talks between the Betancur's government (1982–86) and guerrilla movements such as the FARC. It experienced short-lived electoral gains. However, hundreds of militants, including presidential candidates Jaime Pardo Leal (1986) and Bernardo Jaramillo Ossa (1990), were assassinated by right-wing paramilitaries and members of the Colombian Armed Forces in 1987 and 1990, respectively (Romero 2003). The AD M-19 emerged as the political party of the demobilized M-19 guerrilla in the early 1990s. With 27% of the seats, it was a powerful force in the Constitutional Assembly that wrote the 1991 Constitution, but it collapsed soon after.

In the 2002 presidential election, several forces of the left supported Luis Eduardo Garzón of the *Frente Social y Político* (Social and Political Front). After coming in third with 6% of the vote, this leftist coalition won the mayorship of Bogotá[3] with Garzón as a candidate in 2003 and developed into a party, the *Polo Democrático Alternativo* (PDA, Democratic Alternative Pole). It became the main partisan opposition to the Uribe government and gained 22% of the vote in the 2006 presidential election, an unprecedented level of electoral support for a leftist party in Colombia. After retaining the mayorship of Bogotá in the 2007 local elections, the PDA's reputation was stained by corruption scandals, and it declined after the 2010 presidential election. A new leftist party, *Progresistas* (Progressives), elected its candidate, former PDA senator Gustavo Petro, mayor of Bogotá from 2011–15, but the fact that he did not run with his old party indicates that the left was once again fragmented.

---

[3] The mayorship of Bogotá is the second most important elected position (after the Presidency).

DEINSTITUTIONALIZATION OF THE COLOMBIAN PARTY SYSTEM

Institutionalized party systems are characterized by having (1) stability in the significant contenders; (2) low electoral volatility; and (3) stability in the ideological or programmatic positions of the main parties (see Chapter 1 of this volume). With the dramatic weakening of the traditional parties, as well as the rise of new parties and independents, Colombia's party system has shifted rapidly from being fairly highly institutionalized throughout most of the twentieth century to weakly institutionalized. As Chapter 2 showed, it exhibits deinstitutionalization in most measures.

New Contenders and Increasing Volatility

Since 1990, the membership of Colombia's party system has undergone frequent changes with the emergence of several important new contenders, the near disappearance of one (the M19), the emergence and weakening of another (the *Polo Democrático*), and the significant decline of the Conservatives and Liberals. New parties have captured large vote shares. In 2002, a dizzying plethora of new parties that had never before competed – forty-six – captured 32.9% of the vote for the lower chamber. In 2006, five other new parties won 21.2%. In the Colombian case, the increase in instability is due more to extra-system volatility (new parties) than to within-system volatility. Gutiérrez (2007) suggests that there is little movement from the Liberal Party to the Conservative Party or the other way around. Instead, voters flocked from both traditional parties into newer movements that did not exist before 1991.

   According to four of the six indicators of stability in the membership of the party system in Chapter 2, Colombia has registered high instability. For the 1990–2015 period, it had the third highest mean vote share of new parties in presidential elections (27.6%), only behind Guatemala (41.8%) and Venezuela (28.5%). This is in sharp contrast to most of the twentieth century. For example, in the first three elections after the National Front, new parties won only 1.4%, 12.1%, and 0.6% of the presidential vote in 1978, 1982, and 1986, respectively. For 1990–2015, Colombia also had the second highest mean vote share of new parties for the lower house of the national congress, at 15.7%. Again, this is in sharp contrast to the very low capacity of new parties to win votes from 1960 through 1990; the mean for eleven lower chamber elections was 2.7%.[4] Colombia also had a low score for election-to-election continuity for significant contenders in presidential elections (0.53, higher only than Venezuela, Argentina, and Guatemala). This indicator measures the percentage of cases in which the significant contenders (parties with at least 10% of the vote) in one election were also significant contenders in the next (see Chapter 2 for details). It had one of the lowest scores for medium-term stability in presidential contenders (0.18, only slightly higher than Guatemala,

---

[4] From 1958 until 1970, lower chamber elections were held every two years.

Venezuela, and Argentina). This indicator shows the percentage of times that a significant contender in any election between 1990 and 2015 was also a significant contender in all the other elections.

Colombia's electoral results shifted from very stable in most of the twentieth century to highly volatile since 2002. Until 1990, the party system had consistently low electoral volatility. The Conservative and Liberal parties always dominated elections, and they won a similar percentage of votes every election. Starting in the 1990s, however, the picture changed significantly. In congressional elections, the first inkling of the change occurred with the 1991 elections for congress, which resulted in a shattering defeat for the Conservatives, who garnered only 17% of the vote for the lower chamber and a meager 7% for the Senate. Minor parties fared much better than they had historically, resulting, in combination with the Conservatives' poor showing, in a volatility score of 27%. In 1998, volatility increased to 30% in the lower chamber. It was even much higher, 45% in 2002 and 53% in 2006, as the Liberals and Conservatives were eclipsed – and in the case of the Conservatives, decimated. The Conservatives won only 11.4% in 2002 and 15.7% of the votes in 2006; the Liberals garnered 31.7% and 30.5%, respectively. Volatility remained very high for both the Senate and the lower chamber in 2006, followed by a decline to 23% (Senate) and 27% (Lower House) in 2010. In 2010, the Conservatives rebounded to 21.4%, while the Liberals declined steeply to 19.3% of the votes in the Lower House elections. For the presidency, volatility increased earlier, to 23.1% in the 1982–86 electoral period, the highest since the restoration of competitive elections in 1974. Since then, it has consistently been high: 38.0% for 1986–90, 36.7% for 1990–94, 29.4% for 1994–98, 60.5% for 1998–2002, 27.0% for 2002–06, 38.3 for 2006–10 (counting Santos's party, the *Partido de la U*, as a continuation of Uribe's *Primero Colombia*), and 48.6% for 2010–14 (Figure 8.1).

Colombia also scores above the very high regional mean for cumulative electoral volatility in lower chamber elections from 1990 until 2015, and it has one of the highest scores for cumulative volatility in presidential elections (Table 2.6). In the 2014 elections, parties that existed in 1990 won only 36.8% of the lower chamber vote and 16.5% of the presidential vote. In sum, since the 1980s, party competition has become dramatically less stable. The traditional parties have entered into steep decline, and it is not certain whether stable new parties are emerging. Finally, largely because of the entrance of so many new parties, Colombia has exhibited a high score for change in ideological positions at the party system level (Table 2.8).

Party Roots in Society: Party Identification

Historical accounts suggest that before the 1980s, most people used to strongly identify as Liberal or Conservative (Gutiérrez 2007). Civil wars and violence in the nineteenth and early twentieth century fueled Liberal and Conservative inherited partisan affiliations up until the 1960s (Hartlyn 1988; Latorre 1974;

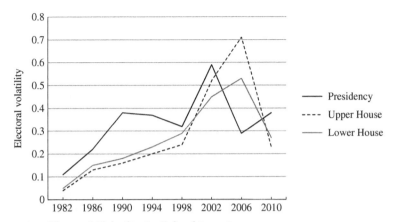

FIGURE 8.1 Electoral Volatility in Colombia, 1982–2010
Note: The year on the horizontal axis refers to the second election of an electoral period.
Source: Prepared by the authors.

Pécaut 2001). During the National Front (1958–74), however, the dynamics of alternation and power sharing between these parties caused partisanship to wither. By the end of the 1980s, the Liberal and Conservative parties were clientelistic machines with small programmatic differences between them (Hoskin 1990; Pécaut 2006; Pizarro Leongómez 2006). This lack of brand differentiation (Lupu 2016) opened up the space for independent candidates, including Antanas Mockus (1995) and Enrique Peñalosa (1997), to win important elected offices such as Bogotá's mayoralty.

Today, few people identify with a party and, those who do, do not associate consistently with a single party. Parties no longer have strong roots in Colombian society. In 2014, according to LAPOP, only 28% of the respondents sympathized with a party (see Figure 8.2). Because of the paucity of survey data before 1996, it is difficult to assess exactly when and how levels of partisanship began to decline. Survey data from Latinobarometer (1996, 1997, 2003) suggest that in the 1990s party identification was already low. In 1996, only 37% of people sympathized with a party. In 1997 that number increased to 42%, but in 2003 it receded to 32%.[5] Partisanship has decreased even more since then.

According to LAPOP data (2005–14), the parties with which most people sympathize are the Liberal Party and the _Partido de la U_, followed by the Conservative Party and the PDA (see Figure 8.3). Partisan identification has been volatile across time. The Liberal Party started with the highest percentage

---

[5] The Latinobarometer question "Which political party do you feel close to?" had four responses: "very close," "fairly close," "just a sympathizer," and "not close." The percentages for 1996, 1997, and 2003 correspond to respondents who answered "very close," "fairly close," or "close."

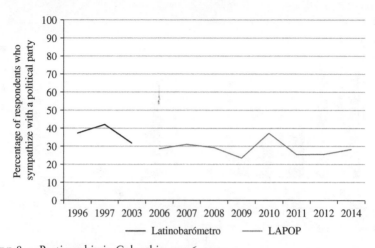

FIGURE 8.2 Partisanship in Colombia, 1996–2012
Note: Question Latinobarometer: "With respect to the political parties, do you feel very close, fairly close, just a sympathizer, or not close to any political party?" Question LAPOP: "At this time, do you sympathize with a political party?"
Source: Latinobarometer (1996, 1997, 2003) and LAPOP (2006–14).

of sympathizers in 2005, lost considerable support in the late 2000s, regained some sympathizers in 2011 and 2012, but lost them again in 2014. The *Partido de la U* has followed the opposite pattern. It won supporters from 2008 until 2010 but lost sympathizers in 2011, 2012, and 2014. The Conservative Party has had a steadier pattern of support. It won sympathizers in 2009 but lost them in 2010. The PDA had roughly the same support until 2008, when it won many supporters. Its success, however, was short lived. The rapid declines and increases in identifiers of specific parties show that for many, party identification in Colombia is not a strong political identity, contrary to the situation in the United States (Green *et al.* 2002).

Despite the limitations of the data, the trend is clear. Parties' roots in society have weakened greatly. Partisanship, which is a key measure of party roots in society, is low.

Party Organization

Solid party organizations facilitate PSI. The Colombian experience suggests that the reverse is also true: weaker organizations facilitate party system deinstitutionalization. The traditional parties in Colombia underwent rapid organizational decomposition in the 1990s, especially in their ability to control nomination procedures and command loyalty from elected officials. These are key functions of solid party organizations. For generations, Colombia's traditional parties had organizations that were able to mobilize

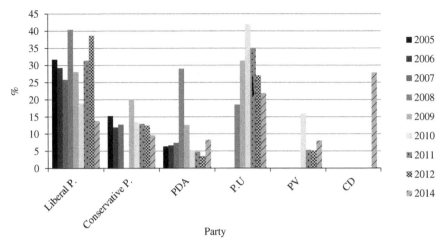

Party

FIGURE 8.3 Party ID in Colombia According to LAPOP, 2005–12
Note: Question (2005–07): "Do you consider yourself a member or sympathizer of the
Conservative Party, the Polo Democrático, the Liberal Party, or some other political
movement? Or do you consider yourself an independent or without a party?"
Question (2008–12): "Which political party do you sympathize with?"
*Starting in 2008 this question has a filter. They only ask the Party ID question to those
respondents that in an earlier question respond they do sympathize with a party.
Source: LAPOP (2005–14)

parts of the population and, at times, to engage in acts of violence. However, the
ability of the traditional parties to mobilize the electorate and the strong sense
of partisan identification did not mean that they were centralized and
bureaucratized organizations (Hoskin and Swanson 1974). They were highly
decentralized. Institutionalized factions within the parties were the core of
electoral and congressional activity (Losada 2005; Pizarro Leongómez 2002).
The level of autonomy enjoyed by partisan factional organizations led Pizarro
Leongómez (2006) to argue that the Liberals and Conservatives were better
understood as political sub-cultures rather than parties.

Starting in the 1990s, party endorsements and labels lost their value, and
institutionalized factions lost their control over the electoral process. Rules that
lowered the requirements to register a new party, combined with an electoral
formula that benefited new parties, and increasingly weak labels and
partisanship decreased the incentives to stay in the Liberal or Conservative
parties. Under the new rules, politicians could move into newer, smaller
parties, avoid the fight for endorsements, and still win elections. Party leaders
lost control over nomination procedures and with it their ability to control
members (Pizarro Leongómez 2002, 2006). Local political bosses could form
their own party list, and the parties had no real ability to control these lists. As a
result, the number of party lists proliferated wildly. In 2002, the Liberal Party

had 148 lists running for 100 seats in the Senate. The total number of party lists in the 2002 senate elections was 321, of which only three elected more than one senator (Pizarro Leongómez 2006).

From 2002 to 2006, parties' ability to structure parliamentary activity eroded. Although most parties fulfill certain formalities (they have formal statues, regional offices, internal proceedings etc.), few of their members live by those rules. Since 1990, the parties have no longer been able to act as gatekeepers in the legislative arena; the number and particularistic nature of proposed bills was staggering. Between 1998–99, 354 bills and thirty-five constitutional amendments were proposed (Bejarano *et al.* 2001, cited in Pizarro Leóngomez 2006: 91). Support for a bill was the outcome of individual transactions between the bill sponsor (usually the president) and each member, via the committees that distributed pork barrel to other members of congress in order to pass different projects (Cárdenas *et al.* 2006; Milanese 2011; Pachón 2003).

One important indicator of organizational loyalty is party switching, that is, the extent to which politicians switch from one party to another. Gutierrez (2007) suggests that party switching was not common until the late 1990s and early 2000s. In recent years, it has been rampant (Illera and Buchely 2015). Using data from the National Registrar, we examined party switching between 2002 and 2006 in the Senate. Of a total of 3,726 candidates in the 1998, 2002, and 2006 senate elections combined, only 217 (6%) candidates ran in more than one election, and only forty-nine (1%) ran in all three. Of the 217 candidates who ran in two or more elections, 129 (59%) switched parties at least once. Of the candidates who ran all three times, thirty-seven (76%) switched parties at least once, and twenty-one (45%) switched parties twice. Among the 168 candidates who ran in two of these three elections, more than half, ninety-two (55%) switched parties.

This information underestimates party switching.[6] Partisan loyalties, which in the past were so deep that they led to civil wars, have severely eroded. Levels of incumbency are very low, and incumbents who try to keep their seat usually run for reelection on a different label. Moreover, because most politicians do not run for reelection, politics has become a field for the inexperienced, in stark contrast to the portrait that Wilde (1978) painted as politics being dominated by "conversations among gentlemen." Even though parties are well structured in terms of rules, proceedings, and presence throughout the country, they are not well organized. Party leaders have little control over their members, who come and go from organizations as they please both in and between elections.[7]

---

[6] We tracked party switching between elections, but within a legislative period party switching can and did occur.

[7] Since 2007, this might have changed due to the "Bancadas Law," which mandated that all legislators had to vote with their party and created stronger penalties for party switching. However, the law had serious loopholes that might have reduced its effectiveness. Without data beyond 2006, it is difficult to assess its impact.

FRAGMENTATION AND DECREASING NATIONALIZATION

In Colombia, as also occurred in Argentina (see Chapter 9 by Carlos Gervasoni), party system deinstitutionalization happened in tandem with two other phenomena: increasing fragmentation and decreasing nationalization. For generations, there were only two serious contenders in the country. Starting in 1990, the number of parties increased sharply until 2006. The number of parties participating in presidential elections increased from three in 1978 to seven in 2010 (Jaramillo and Franco-Cuervo 2005; data from the Colombian National Registrar). The number of parties participating in senate elections jumped from five in 1978 to sixty-four in 2002, and from five in 1978 to seventy-three in 2002 for the lower chamber. This was the "atomization of the party system" (Pizarro Leongómez 2002).

The effective number of parties (Laakso and Taagepera 1979) shows the dramatic change from a relatively pure two-party system in 1978 to a highly fragmented one by the 2000s. As Figure 8.4 shows, for congressional elections, the effective number of parties (ENP) trended upwards during the 1980s and 1990s, gradually increasing from around 2 in both the Chamber of Deputies and the Senate in 1978 to around 3.5 in the lower chamber and 4 in the Senate in 1998. These numbers spiked in 2002, as the old two-party system was definitively shattered. In the lower chamber, the ENP jumped to 7.7 in 2002 and kept increasing until 2010, when it declined to 6. In the Senate, the ENP jumped to 8.5 in 2002 and went down to 6.8 in 2010. The ENP in 2002 was among the highest in contemporary Latin America (though lower than Brazil). Fragmentation has been much lower in presidential elections.

As the party system became much more volatile and fragmented, it also became much less nationalized. Jones and Mainwaring (2003) conceptualized party nationalization as the degree to which a party wins a uniform percentage of the vote across the primary sub-national units of a country (states, provinces, departments, etc.), and they measured it with an inverted Gini index (that is, 100-Gini). A score of 0 means that a party won all of its votes in one sub-national unit, and a score of 100 means that it won an equal percentage of the vote in every sub-national unit. A highly nationalized *system* is one in which the main parties win an even vote share across the sub-national units. The nationalization score for the system weights the nationalization score of each party by its vote share. The data show the decrease in nationalization in Colombia both of the system (see Figure 8.5) and of the traditional parties.[8] The change in a short time is stunning. Colombia's party system in 1978 was more nationalized than that of almost

---

[8] Throughout the twentieth century, either the Conservative or Liberal party had solid and stable electoral majorities in many municipalities and regions (Hoyos 2007; Pinzón de Lewin 1989), but both parties were present across the Colombian territory.

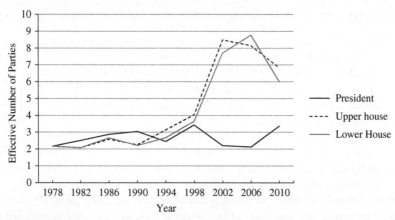

FIGURE 8.4 Effective Number of Parties in Colombia, 1978–2010
Source: Prepared by the authors.

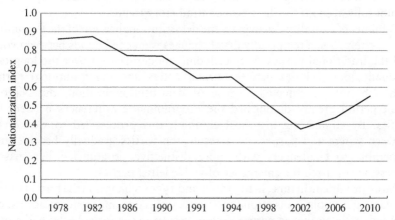

FIGURE 8.5 Nationalization of the Colombian Party System
Note: For the nationalization index, 0 = Poorly Nationalized, and 1 = Very Nationalized.
Source: Batlle and Puyana (2011) (using Jones and Mainwaring's (2003) nationalization index).

all of the seventeen western hemisphere countries included in Jones and Mainwaring's analysis. From 1998 through 2010, its system was *less* nationalized than all seventeen countries in this earlier analysis (though more nationalized than Argentina's system has been since 2003). Moreover, the new parties are also weakly nationalized (Batlle and Puyana 2011). Thus, the contemporary system is characterized by very high fragmentation and very low nationalization; the traditional system (until the 1990s) had very low fragmentation and high nationalization.

CAUSES OF PARTY SYSTEM DEINSTITUTIONALIZATION

In recent years, some scholarship, including important works produced by scholars who contributed to this volume, has appeared on party system collapse (Morgan 2011; Seawright 2012; Tanaka 1998, 2006) and party collapse (Lupu 2016). Other work is starting to appear on party building in third wave democracies (Levitsky *et al.* 2016b). Presumably, these works on related issues should help explain deinstitutionalization that falls short of party system and party collapse. In recent works, lack of programmatic differentiation among the main parties ("brand dilution") coupled with bad economic performance have been highlighted as causes of party system and party collapse (Lupu 2016; Morgan 2011; Seawright 2012).

In studying Colombia, we have a double challenge. We must account for deinstitutionalization and also explain why the Colombian party system did not collapse. Unlike in Bolivia, Ecuador, Peru, and Venezuela, the traditional parties in Colombia remained key political players especially at the subnational level, although they declined considerably. Previous explanations cannot fully account for these two contradictory trends.

A funnel of causality can explain the deinstitutionalization of the Colombian party system. Some temporally distal changes weakened bonds between voters and the traditional parties. Socioeconomic modernization over the long term gradually loosened ties between urban voters and the traditional parties. Although not an immediate cause of deinstitutionalization, the National Front period greatly diminished the programmatic differences between the parties. By eliminating historical enmities, this process led to weaker ties between voters and parties. As a result, the parties gradually became more vulnerable to challengers with more distinctive programs – but massive repression thwarted the emergence of viable leftist parties.

More proximate in time, in the 1980s and 1990s, changes in the formal rules of the game gave politicians strong incentives to become independent agents, and they indirectly weakened parties. These changes in the formal rules had a more direct impact on politicians and parties than the more distal influences. They weakened the traditional parties, but they were in place for several electoral cycles before the seismic changes that occurred in 2002. While these structural and institutional changes increased the odds that the traditional parties would over the long haul experience some electoral erosion and face new challengers, in and of themselves they do not explain rapid deinstitutionalization in the 1990s and 2000s.

In 2002, these multiple sparks combusted, leading to change in the party system, including a profound electoral erosion of the traditional parties. The exacerbation of an already severe security crisis during the Pastrana administration (1998–2002), coupled with the Liberal Party's failure to produce a viable alternative security policy and the appeal of Álvaro Uribe based on a hard line stance against the left-wing guerrilla insurgencies made possible his 2002 victory. A deep change in national party politics resulted.

Subsequently, choices made by President Uribe thwarted the institutionalization of a new party system at the national level. His policy choices splintered the traditional parties. At the sub-national level, however, entrenched forms of local patronage and clientelism have so far ensured the ongoing vitality of the Liberals and Conservatives.

Structural Change

Socioeconomic Modernization and Demography

Throughout the twentieth century, socioeconomic factors and violence increased migration to the cities. This movement out of the countryside into the cities, plus increased access to education during the National Front and the consequent secularization of society disrupted party–voter linkages and created a largely urban, more policy-oriented constituency. Although their impact was distal, these changes took a toll on the traditional parties' support in the late 1980s and early 1990s when more policy-oriented independent candidates and new parties with different clientelistic networks were better able to capture these discontented, disconnected voters.

Throughout the twentieth century, Colombia underwent huge structural transformations. The economy diversified and became less reliant on agricultural commodities. In the 1930s, 71% of the population lived in the countryside. By the end of the century, the rural–urban proportion had been inverted completely.

These structural changes slowly impacted the party system. Migration to the cities, secularization, and increased education uprooted people from their traditional networks and created a more policy-oriented constituency to which the traditional parties found it hard to appeal. By the 1990s, the Colombian electorate was much more complex and diverse than during the National Front. Forms of political intermediation successfully used by the traditional parties then (see the discussion about clientelism below) did not captivate middle-class, policy-oriented urban residents, whose numbers expanded greatly in the second half of the twentieth century. The traditional parties reacted slowly to this change, leaving a space that dissident movements and independent candidates exploited. Not by coincidence, since the 1990s, several large cities, including Bogotá, have elected mayors from small political movements at the expense of the traditional parties.

Intense violence during the civil war (1948–58) as well as the post-1980s conflict between state, paramilitaries, and insurgents aided this process. Escaping from violence, people moved in large numbers to urban areas. Colombia held the sad distinction of having one of the current highest numbers of internally displaced persons in the world (more than 6.9 million internally displaced people by the end of 2015) (UNHRC 2016: 57).

Mass migration further uprooted people from their partisan networks, which were mostly local in nature. In the absence of party organizations that could reintegrate them to political life through partisan channels in their new homes in cities (mostly in urban slums), they became clients of the new political organizations characteristic of "market clientelism" in which patron–client relationships are non-ideological, particularistic, and horizontal. These relationships do not link the local, regional, and national levels, but rather rely on the politician's individual skill at providing goods and services (Dávila and Delgado 2002).

These structural changes were incremental and long term, while party system change occurred rapidly and did not seem visible until 1991. The structural changes were not sufficient to cause party system change, but by disrupting linkages between parties and voters, they paved the way for it.

The drug trafficking business also changed party competition in Colombia (Gutiérrez 2006; López 2010). Organized crime injected huge sums of money to politicians at the national level and even more so at the regional level. Drug money provided a source of funding for regional politicians, some of them new to the political arena, independent of their partisan affiliation. This allowed these politicians to create political organizations that were not connected to national-level partisan structures. It thereby contributed to the growing fragmentation and decreasing nationalization of the party system.

Institutional Change

The excellent recent analyses of party and party system collapse have not focused on formal rules of the game. Nonetheless, to explain the rapid deinstitutionalization of the Colombian party system, changes in formal institutional rules as well as changes in informal institutions are important.

In the last decades of the twentieth century, Colombia experienced several institutional changes. It modified its electoral rules, promoted decentralization, and saw changes in the nature of patron–client relationships. These changes created incentives for politicians to act as independent agents, and, in turn, they helped weaken parties. Nevertheless, these rules cannot entirely explain changes in volatility and fragmentation.

One frequent explanation for the system's fragmentation and high electoral volatility were the rules that structured Colombia's electoral competition between 1991 and 2003. A series of reforms in the late 1980s and early 1990s, such as a larger district magnitude in the Senate, a new system of congressional substitutes that allowed members of the list to replace the elected member of congress at any point in time, and the simplification of the requirements to win recognition as a party by the National Electoral Council created incentives for parties to become personalistic, and therefore weak (Pizarro Leongómez 2002). Party endorsements became costless, leading politicians to leave big parties for new smaller organizations, increasing party system fragmentation, and electoral volatility.

Institutional factors help explain change in Colombia's party system. From the end of the National Front until 2003, Colombia had a system of closed-list proportional representation in legislative elections. Each party could present multiple lists of candidates in each electoral district (i.e. each region –"departamento"), and there was no vote pooling among these lists. Seats were awarded to lists and not by the total number of votes obtained by a party, so that one list competed with others from the same party. This system generated strong intra-party competition.

Until 2003, legislative seats were distributed according to the Hare quota largest remainders formula, which divided the number of valid votes by the number of seats. The number of seats assigned to a sub-party list equaled the number of times that list reached the quota. The remaining seats were assigned in descending order to the lists that won the largest remainders. Accordingly, seats won with remainders were "cheaper" than those won with quotas. This system provided incentives for Liberal and Conservative party leaders to promote many small lists rather than one unified large list (the so-called "wasp" strategy – *operación avispa*) (Pizarro Leongómez 2002).

Together, proportional representation, the ability of parties to present as many lists as seats available, and the Hare electoral formula generated strong incentives to present multiple lists per party, which, in turn, increased intra-party competition. As the number of lists of the same party increased throughout the 1980s and 1990s, the system came to resemble a single non-transferable vote (SNTV) (Cox and Shugart 1995; Pizarro Leongómez 2002). Politicians had incentives to campaign based on their personal reputation rather than on party appeal, which depreciated party labels and made Colombia's electoral system one of the most candidate-centered in the world (Carey and Shugart 1995).

Initially, this quasi-SNTV system benefited the traditional parties. By perfecting the so-called "wasp" strategy, these parties gained a larger share of seats than their share of votes. Third parties were systematically under-represented. This success, however, did not endure. The 1991 Constitution reduced the thresholds to create new parties to encourage new forces to enter the electoral arena and democratize the political system. From 1991 to 2003, only 50,000 signatures or the same number of votes in past elections were needed to gain legal recognition as a party (or political movement) and thereby win access to public funding.[9] These reforms lowered the costs of building new parties. Together with the Hare electoral formula, they created incentives to leave large organizations in order to join smaller ones, in which nominations were easier to attain, and being elected to a seat was almost guaranteed.

---

[9] In 1985, party registration was regulated by law for the first time. The law required a party to gather 10,000 signatures and present party platforms and statutes to electoral authorities (Moreno 2005).

As the costs of being in a large party remained the same and the benefits of party labels declined due to intra-party competition, the electoral rules ended up hindering the traditional parties and fostering extremely small parties that profited from personalistic competition (Shugart *et al.* 2007). The combination of a personalistic electoral system, the ability to switch parties with little or no penalty, and low registration thresholds enabled Liberal and Conservative politicians to leave their old organizations and create micro-parties as personalistic electoral vehicles, thus contributing to the fragmentation and volatility of the system (Moreno 2005; Pizarro Leongómez 2002).

This problem was worse as the district magnitude increased. In the Colombian Senate, the fragmentation was worsened with the creation in 1991 of one national district to elect all 100 senators.[10] Initially created as a mechanism to strengthen policy-oriented politicians to the detriment of clientelistic regional machines (Crisp and Ingall 2002), the high magnitude district combined with quasi-SNTV electoral rules enabled candidates to win a seat with a small number of votes. For example, in the 2002 election, the last list to win a seat needed only 40,460 votes or 0.42% of the national vote. Instead of fostering policy-oriented, "new" political forces, this institutional design enabled politicians with parochial interests to win seats.

In sum, the institutional rules from 1991 on provided great incentives for weak party organizations, growing fragmentation, the birth of new parties, personalistic politics, and parochial perspectives. They contributed to the steep demise of the traditional parties.

Decentralization

Starting in the 1980s, Colombia underwent a process of political, fiscal, and administrative decentralization that affected the party system. Political decentralization introduced elections for executive positions at the regional (governors, 1992) and local (mayors, 1988) levels. Concomitant fiscal and administrative decentralization gave regional and local governments more fiscal resources and increased competencies in the regulation and provision of public goods and services (Eaton 2004; Falleti 2005).

Decentralizing reforms were expected to democratize Colombia's political system by allowing new political forces to enter the political arena (Eaton 2004). While in the past governors and the mayor of Bogotá were appointed by the president, and mayors by the governors, electoral competition allowed new political forces to compete for and win public offices that used to be firmly in the hands of traditional parties. Regional and local elections became spaces for new political forces to develop and gain experience in government. In

---

[10] Two indigenous senators are elected in a separate indigenous electoral district. Thus, the Colombian upper chamber has 102 senators. For simplicity, we will henceforth refer only to the election of senators in the regular electoral districts.

Bogotá and other big cities, independent candidates won elections and gained national recognition (Gilbert 2006).

In addition, the loss of valuable sources of patronage by traditional parties enabled Liberal and Conservative politicians to use these new spaces to gain more autonomy *vis-à-vis* national party leaders (Dargent and Muñoz 2011; Leal Buitrago and Dávila 1990). Political decentralization changed the means of access to patronage positions, and local and regional governments gained more fiscal resources and administrative competencies. Control of these governments gave politicians resources and more autonomy from already weak party organizations (Dargent and Muñoz 2011). While the centralization of patronage provided the incentives to keep ambitious politicians loyal to traditional parties, decentralization in a context of weak organizations led to an increasing atomization of partisan competition into personalistic micro-parties (called "microempresas electorales" by Pizarro Leongómez).[11] These micro-parties became useful vehicles for politicians only because a substantive source of patronage became de-linked from national parties. Micro-parties were as much a result of decentralization as of electoral rules.

Understanding the decentralization process offers a broader view of the institutional framework that constrains politicians in Colombia and allows us to understand why the emergence of micro-parties and new political forces was possible and why the progressive denationalization of the party system occurred. It also helps explain why, despite a major electoral reform in 2003, the system remained fragmented and continued to denationalize.

Changes in Forms of Clientelism

Changes in the nature of clientelistic linkages are important to understand the transformation of the party system. Although clientelism, that is, the provision of goods in exchange for political support (Stokes 2007), has been a widespread practice since the inception of the two-party system in the mid-nineteenth century, the way it has been organized changed over time. Initially, clientelistic relationships were dominated by rural (partisan) oligarchs who provided goods to local peasants in exchange for electoral support. Ties between these patrons and their clientele were long-standing and included socialization through intense partisan identification. These captive electorates were the source of power of regional elites, who themselves supported national elites (*jefes naturales*) in exchange for control of local offices. This form of clientelism provided the link between national and regional-level partisan politicians in the absence of effective formal partisan organizations (Archer 1990; Leal Buitrago and Dávila 1990).

The growth of the Colombian state in the mid-twentieth century and the end of partisan violence with the National Front led to changes in the form of clientelism

---

[11] Pizarro Leongómez (2002) refers to "micro-empresas electorales" to describe small lists. The head of the list takes a leave of absence from congress in order to allow those who followed on the list to use the seat to get patronage and offer resources to clienteles.

246 *Party Systems in Latin America*

(Archer 1990; Leal Buitrago and Dávila 1990). Professional politicians replaced local oligarchs as the central actors of political intermediation. State resources and, later, money from the drug trade became the basis undergirding clientelistic exchanges. During the National Front, the absence of inter-party competition increased intra-party competition. Because the Liberal and Conservative parties did not compete against each other and the rules dictated whether the president was Liberal or Conservative beforehand, competition moved inside each organization. The power-sharing pact therefore increased intra-party competition and with it the fragmentation of traditionally large party factions (Gutiérrez 2007; Leal Buitrago and Dávila 1990).

The restrictions to competition in the National Front greatly reduced partisan sectarianism but, in turn, led to a decline in partisan identification.[12] Leal Buitrago and Dávila (1990) argued that if partisan identification survived, it was for the most part because joining the Conservative or Liberal Party was the only way to gain access to political office and patronage during the National Front and its immediate aftermath. The increasing factional fragmentation and the progressive weakening of national party leaders notwithstanding, linkages between local politicians and national elites subsisted because patronage positions were still controlled by Bogotá (Dávila and Delgado 2002).

The increasing access to resources from the drug trade and decentralizing reforms in the late 1980s severed bonds between local politicians and national elites, inducing new transformations in patron–client relationships. As mentioned earlier, decentralization eroded the control by national elites over local public officials (Leal Buitrago and Dávila 1990). Ambitious politicians no longer needed an affiliation with the Conservative or Liberal parties to gain access to patronage (Dargent and Muñoz 2011). Moreover, decentralization, coupled with access to the money from the drug cartels, gave local politicians resources not controlled by national party elites. As a result, clientelistic networks became more decentralized and atomized. The proliferation of politicians running their own networks increased the competition among them and fostered less stable and durable relationships with voters. Vote buying practices, involving a short-term exchange of political support (vote) for material goods on the eve or day of elections, largely replaced the long-term bonds between client and patron that had characterized Colombian clientelism until the 1970s.

In short, local and regional direct access to state resources changed the nature of clientelism. The links between local and national-level politics are now less hierarchical and institutionalized (Dávila and Delgado 2002). Politicians no longer depend on resources allocated to them by the national executive in order to maintain their clientele, nor do they foster partisan appeals within their

---

[12] This is consistent with Lupu's argument (2016, Chapter 12 in this volume) about the importance of brand differentiation for creating party identification.

more "volatile" network. The changing character of clientelistic relationships, therefore, also explains a part of the changes experienced by the Colombian party system.

Security Crisis, the Erosion of Party Brands, Agency, and the Weakening of the Traditional Parties

These longer-term processes and the changes in formal rules are distal explanations of party system deinstitutionalization, but they do not explain the dramatic inflexion point of 2002 when Álvaro Uribe won the presidency. The grave public security crisis in Colombia, combined with the failure of the traditional parties to offer compelling and distinctive answers to it, made possible Uribe's successful outsider challenge.[13] In turn, as also occurred in the aftermath of the election of outsider presidents in Peru (Alberto Fujimori in 1990), Venezuela (Hugo Chávez in 1998), and Ecuador (Rafael Correa in 2006), Uribe's election further weakened the party system.

As occurred in many other Latin American cases, the erosion of programmatic differences between the two traditional parties in Colombia coupled with bad governing performance was an important ingredient in their decline. In many Latin American countries, parties that renounced their historical positions on the center-left to implement market-oriented economic policies lost their brand differentiation and eventually their voters. After long and storied histories, several such parties – *Acción Democrática* in Venezuela, the MIR (*Movimiento de Izquierda Revolucionaria*) and the MNR (*Movimiento Nacionalista Revolucionario*) in Bolivia – have largely disappeared. In some cases, including AD and the MNR, the combination of diminished brand distinction and failed governments was crippling.

The deinstitutionalization of the Colombian party system followed a similar story but with one major difference. Lack of programmatic differentiation between the Conservatives and Liberals during the National Front and its aftermath is central to understanding diminished partisan enmities, polarization, and identification. But the rapprochement between the Liberals and Conservatives took place in the late 1950s, so reduced brand differentiation is a distal explanation of the deinstitutionalization of the party system in the 1990s and 2000s.

Bad governing performance is an essential though not sufficient explanation for the decline of many Latin American parties (for example, the Argentine Radical Party, UCR) and for the collapse of the Peruvian and Venezuelan party systems in the 1990s and early 2000s (Lupu 2016; Morgan 2011; Seawright 2012). Colombia was among the few countries in Latin

---

[13] Álvaro Uribe had belonged to the Liberal Party in the past. However, in 2002 he ran as an independent.

America that avoided severe economic crises in the 1980s and 1990s,[14] but it faced appalling government performance – in the security realm. The country's severe security problems undermined citizen support for the traditional parties.

Despite mounting security challenges in the 1980s and 1990s (the fight against the Medellín and Cali cartels, as well as against guerrillas and paramilitaries), no party consistently grabbed the mantle of law and order. Both Liberal and Conservative governments engaged simultaneously in policies of appeasement and repression of illegal armed actors. All presidents from Belisario Betancur (1982–86) to Andrés Pastrana (1998–2002) pursued peace negotiations with guerrillas, as well as episodes of military action. In this sense, on the most important issue facing the country, both parties were indistinguishable and offered inconsistent signals regarding their policy preferences.

The security situation worsened in Andrés Pastrana's administration (1998–2002). During the late 1990s, violence skyrocketed (Echandía Castilla and Bechara Gómez 2006). Kidnappings increased from 1122 in 1990 to 3306 in 2002 (195%); massacres from fifty-eight in 1990 to 149 in 2002 (156%); terrorist attacks from two in 1989 to twenty-one in 2002 (950%); civilian casualties in armed confrontations from 60 in 1990 to 218 in 2002 (263%) (Centro de Memoria Histórica 2013). At this time, Colombia had one of the highest rates of homicide and kidnappings in the world. In this context, the Liberal dissident candidate, Álvaro Uribe, who had made a name for himself as a security hardliner as governor of Antioquia, used his law and order discourse to disrupt the traditional competition for the presidency between Liberals and Conservatives, won the presidency, and induced a change in electoral competition (Wills Otero 2014).

During Uribe's administration, the security cleavage was the central organizing dimension of politics. Leftist and rightist politicians offered distinct policy recommendations to deal with Colombia's armed conflict. Public opinion perceived these alternatives and aligned accordingly (Albarracín 2013). However, as we will discuss in the next section, the reluctance by key actors, particularly President Uribe, to build strong parties around this cleavage, did not allow for the institutionalization of a new system. Rather, Colombia's system remained somewhere between full-fledged collapse and institutionalization.

Actor's Choices and PSI

Except for Tanaka's (1998, 2006) accounts of party system collapse in Peru, which underscored the role of Alberto Fujimori, the recent literature on party

[14] Colombia's peak inflation rate in the 1980s and 1990s was 30% in 1991, compared to 7482% for Peru in 1990, 3080% for Argentina in 1989, and 100% for Venezuela in 1996 (World Bank 2016). Notwithstanding recessions in the early 1980s and late 1990s, Colombia eluded the severe and protracted declines in national income that afflicted Argentina (1984–90 and 1998–2002), Peru (1981–83 and 1987–92), and Venezuela (1977–90 and 1992–2003).

and party system collapse has not invoked actor-centered explanations. However, President Uribe had a major impact on the process of party system deinstitutionalization. His election and subsequent governing policies and style, by which he coopted important factions of the Conservatives and Liberals, destabilized the old parties. His decision to avoid building a new organization is an important component in the lack of new strong parties.

Uribe ran as an independent in 2002. Even though a myriad of parties – including the Conservative Party – backed him, he never recognized any of them as his own. Instead, he distributed government offices and cabinet positions across parties of his coalition and astutely played parties against each other. When he ran for reelection in 2006, he did so with the movement *Primero Colombia*, whose sole purpose was to serve as a vehicle for his presidential campaigns.

Uribe positioned himself above parties and partisan competition. While the party system was weak before he came to power, his personalistic and anti-politics discourse gave it another blow. By splitting the Liberal Party and coopting the Conservatives, Uribe weakened both, while failing to strengthen alternative parties. The Conservative Party's alliance with Uribe proved detrimental to its future, despite a short-lived electoral rebound in 2010. Its unconditional support for Uribe thwarted emerging Conservative leadership and hindered programmatic appeals beyond support for Uribe's policies. The fact that Uribe did not recognize the Conservative party as his own eventually divided it between *Uribistas* and non-*Uribistas*.

Uribe's presidency was costly for the Liberal Party (LP) as well. When Uribe won the presidency in 2002, several Liberal members of congress jumped ship and joined the various *Uribista* parties. Instantaneously, the LP lost several important leaders and the networks they controlled. Moreover, throughout Uribe's presidency the LP had little access to the state resources. This diminished its ability to feed clienteles and attract office-seeking politicians. Although their alliance with the Santos administration has helped the Liberals recover, it is highly unlikely that they will come back to what they were.

The decline of the traditional parties did not result in new strong parties. The *Uribista* parties won overwhelming legislative majorities, but they never consolidated into one label or created robust organizations. They remained loose associations of sub-national politicians. Moreover, Uribe did not foster the emergence of prominent national-level leaders in these parties, and he had tense relationships with politicians who tried to become leaders without his approval. As the presidential succession came up in early 2010, the field was crowded with politicians who claimed to be Uribe's heir; however, there was no mechanism to select among them. Only at the end, when Santos remained the only viable *Uribista* candidate, did Uribe support him.

Party Competition in Legislative Elections: Change and Continuity

In this section we examine changes in party competition for the national Congress and for regional offices. While national political competition for the presidency changed radically in 2002, changes in sub-national competition were more complex. In the 2002 congressional elections, many new parties won seats in Congress and fragmentation reached an all-time high, but competition for regional offices (such as regional assemblies) did not initially change as much. The Liberals and Conservatives used their strength in regional politics to survive the changes in national politics.

The level of party system fragmentation in the 2002 national congressional elections reached historic levels, prompting calls for political reform. The traditional parties had lost control over the nomination process and could no longer profit from the electoral system through the "wasp" strategy. Increasingly, national political leaders viewed the political system as dysfunctional. This sense of crisis contributed to a profound change in the electoral and party rules in 2003 (Shugart *et al.* 2007). Political reform was seen as the only way to rationalize an extremely fragmented party system and personalistic electoral competition (Botero and Rodríguez-Raga 2008). Accordingly, in 2003, congress approved reforms that included the introduction of electoral thresholds to reduce party system fragmentation,[15] the D'Hondt seat distribution formula to favor larger parties, open single-party lists,[16] stricter thresholds for registering parties,[17] a prohibition of dual party membership, and mechanisms to induce discipline of party caucuses in Congress.

These reforms had differential effects depending on district magnitude and administrative level. They contained party system fragmentation in elections with large district magnitudes such as the Senate (Botero and Rodríguez-Raga 2008), but fragmentation increased in the 2006 lower chamber elections in districts with few seats (Pachón and Shugart 2010) and in local elections (Albarracín and Milanese 2012). Moreover, the reform did not reduce personalistic electoral competition (Albarracín and Milanese 2016), in part due to the introduction of open lists, which give strong incentives for intra-party competition because the winning candidates within a party are those who attract the most personal votes. Particularly in large electoral districts, what had previously been intense personalistic competition between lists of the same or different parties became instead personalistic intra-party competition among candidates of the same list. The reform did, however, create incentives for minimal cooperation and

---

[15] Parties need to win at least 2% of the vote in order to win a seat in the Senate, and 50% of the simple quotient for seats in the House.
[16] Unlike in most electoral systems, in Colombia the party decides if, for a particular election, its list is open or closed.
[17] In order to maintain their registry, political parties must obtain at least 2% of votes in either Senate or House elections nationwide.

coordination between politicians of the same party (Pachón and Shugart 2010). It reduced the number of parties that competed in both chambers of the national legislature by bringing together regional politicians aspiring for national office into fewer parties. Parties are confederations of these politicians rather than strong centralized and hierarchical organizations.

Changes in regional and local party politics were generally slower. The institutional and structural changes described earlier increased the autonomy of local and regional politicians *vis-à-vis* national political actors and thus allowed for a disconnect in the logic of electoral competition between the national and regional or local levels. In contrast to the situation at the national level, the traditional parties, particularly the Liberal Party, remained a powerful force. In 2003, it remained the largest party in nineteen out of the thirty-two regional assemblies; in sixteen in 2007; and in thirteen in 2010 (Gamboa 2012).

This survival may have resulted from the persistence of established patronage and clientelistic networks. Local politicians are important gatekeepers who provide access to regional and local state bureaucracies. They indirectly provide access to local state services in exchange for votes. These gatekeepers were, for the most part, established Liberal politicians. Since their political fate did not depend on access to national resources, they were insulated from changes in national politics and thus had no real incentive to switch to the new parties (Gamboa 2012).

This does not mean that the dynamics of party competition at the sub-national level remained static. After the political reforms of 2003, progressive fragmentation and growing levels of intra-party competition occurred at the local level (Milanese *et al.* 2014). Even though the traditional parties no longer control party politics at the sub-national level, their slow decline (compared to their national counterparts) gave them a lifeline that avoided their collapse.

Consequences for Democratic Governance

The deinstitutionalization of the party system in Colombia opened up the door for outsiders with both positive and negative consequences for democracy. In some cases at the sub-national level, the weakening of the traditional parties allowed the election of democratically oriented mayors who were political outsiders – for example Antanas Mockus (1995–97 and 2001–03) in Bogotá and Sergio Fajardo (2003–07) in Medellín. They leveraged their independence from traditional political machines and implemented creative and innovative public policies that improved these cities in areas such as security, traffic, and education.

At the national level, deinstitutionalization of the party system allowed Álvaro Uribe to attain power. Uribe's security policy was, by many measures, successful. Unaccountable to any party, Uribe used his popularity to try to coopt courts and oversight agencies, undermine checks and balances, and stay in power (Gamboa 2017). While outsiders can provide new inputs to the political processes and introduce policy innovations that result in good governance, their election is a gamble. They run a high risk of legislative deadlock, their policy positions in many areas are vague or unknown, and they rarely build parties that can carry on their legacies (see Chapter 3).

Deinstitutionalization can also have negative effects on electoral accountability. Electoral accountability is severely limited in a context of extensive party switching and renaming of party labels, as has been the case in Colombia. If party labels lose or never have any meaning (as is the case of many new parties in Colombia), they cannot serve as cognitive shortcuts for voters. Vote choice can become volatile, governed by other shortcuts such as candidate attributes or personalistic appeals (Marinova 2016). Furthermore, changing party labels can undermine the ability of voters to punish politicians (Zielinski *et al.* 2005). For example, one of the parties most closely associated with paramilitaries changed its name three times (*Convergencia Ciudadana* to *Partido de Integración Nacional* and recently to *Opción Ciudadana*) and thus made it harder for voters to associate this party with the illegal dealings of its members. Finally, the increasingly disjointed logic of national and sub-national party competition exacerbates the informational problems that voters face. Not only is the party label a poor cognitive shortcut, but its content can vary from region to region.

Deinstitutionalization also hindered elite accountability in Colombia. Strong parties check politicians' behavior. Politicians in strongly institutionalized systems where parties have meaningful labels have incentives to take care of the party brand. Because they depend upon that brand to attain office, politicians will sanction programmatically or ethically deviant behavior from fellow party members. The depreciation of party labels in Colombia decreased the incentives to take care of the party brand and in doing so it hindered this elite accountability. Due to volatility, fragmentation, and weak party organization, politicians in Colombia do not have the incentives or the means to sanction other party members whenever they deviate.

Notwithstanding the negative consequences of party system deinstitutionalization, the fact that the Colombian system did not collapse had positive consequences. The survival of the traditional parties helped protect democracy during Uribe's government (2002–10). Party system collapse often entails a temporary delegitimation of normal democratic politics. In countries where traditional parties collapse, such as Venezuela, traditional politicians become symbols of ineffectiveness and corruption, and people often think that electioneering, legislating, or litigation are not good ways to get things done. Consequently, party system collapse not only opens the door to outsiders, but also encourages those who oppose them to resort to extra-institutional, often undemocratic tactics, to fight them.

In Colombia, the Liberal and Conservative parties survived. Even if voters no longer supported the traditional parties, many still had confidence in some traditional politicians and believed that the existing institutions were functional even if they moved slowly. Consequently, politicians were less likely to support undemocratic mechanisms to fight Uribe's rule, and more willing to trust traditional politicians, such as César Gaviria,[18] who opposed Uribe. These politicians were key to preventing the erosion of democracy. They had worked through formal political institutions before and understood how they work. In the 2000s, they used congress and the courts to thwart Uribe's attempts to weaken mechanisms of accountability and stay in power (Gamboa 2017).

CONCLUSIONS

The Colombian party system underwent a drastic decrease in institutionalization since the publication of *Building Democratic Institutions*. The more than century-long dominance of the Conservatives and Liberals ended. Major new parties came on the scene, and electoral volatility increased sharply. However, in contrast to what occurred in the party systems in Venezuela, Ecuador, Peru, and Bolivia, the system did not collapse, as the traditional parties remained important, albeit diminished, political actors.

The deinstitutionalization of the Colombian system is more similar to what occurred in Argentina and Costa Rica than to the cases of collapse (Bolivia, Ecuador, Peru, and Venezuela) or those that maintained a high level of institutionalization (Uruguay and Chile). In Argentina as in Colombia, the party system became less institutionalized, less nationalized, and more fragmented (see Chapter 9). Deinstitutionalization was more symmetrical in Colombia than in Argentina and Costa Rica: it affected both of the traditional parties in roughly even ways, whereas in Argentina, the Radical Party (*Unión Cívica Radical*) underwent severe erosion while the Peronists maintained electoral dominance until 2015. Likewise, in Costa Rica, one of the traditional parties, the PUSC (*Partido Unidad Social Cristiana*) collapsed, but the PLN (*Partido Liberación Nacional*) has continued to be a leading contender – it won the presidential elections of 2006 and 2010 and reached the runoff round in 2014.

We explained party system deinstitutionalization with a funnel of causality. Some temporally distant causes (long-term modernization and the deep erosion of brand differentiation brought about by the National Front) weakened bonds between voters and parties. These temporally distant causes, however, did not bring about deinstitutionalization until the 1990s, in part because repression thwarted the emergence of leftist partisan challengers in the 1980s. Voters were less attached to parties, but repression of the left blocked the emergence of a new alternative.

---

[18] Gaviria was President between 1990 and 1994, leader of the Liberal Party between 2005 and 2009, and one of the more visible members of the opposition to Uribe.

Changes in institutional rules in the 1980s and 1990s in response to the widespread perception that Colombian democracy was too restricted generated strong incentives for politicians to become individualistic entrepreneurs. Parties became decentralized federations of individual politicians. The changes in the rules of the game dramatically weakened party organization and hierarchy; parties became "electoral microenterprises" (Pizarro Leongómez 2006). We thus agree with other scholarly works that have emphasized the impact of institutional rules on politicians' behavior and hence ultimately on parties and party systems. Rules of the game intended to strengthen parties do not necessarily have that effect, but rules that create powerful incentives to weaken parties are likely to do so.

Increasing dissatisfaction with the traditional parties and the lack of brand differentiation between them made them vulnerable to new challengers in the 1990s, first especially at the sub-national level. A more temporally proximate cause of deinstitutionalization was the Pastrana administration's (1998–2002) inept handling of the severe security crisis in tandem with the fact that the Liberal Party failed to offer a credible alternative to his policies. As occurred in Latin American countries that experienced severe economic crises, a profound crisis in Colombia delegitimized the traditional parties and led voters to seek alternatives. However, in Colombia the grave challenge arose not from economic crisis but from the extraordinary violence that beset the country in the 1980s, 1990s, and 2000s. Widespread alarm about the massive wave of homicides, kidnappings, extortions, threats, and displaced people provided an environment in which a dissident with a hard line security agenda won the presidency in 2002 and definitively shattered the earlier (1886–1990) logic of political competition at the national level.

However, changes in competition for legislative offices were more complex. While congressional elections were characterized by fragmentation and denationalization of the party system, the persistence of local structures of clientele allowed traditional parties to remain relevant at the sub-national level and survive, thus averting the collapse of the system.

Even though Colombia's security situation has improved considerably, it is uncertain whether the party system will re-institutionalize in the future. The Uribe–Santos rift over the 2016 peace agreement is not leading to party system stabilization. If anything, the system might become less institutionalized in the 2018 elections. The Partido de la U declared that it will not file candidates for the 2018 presidential elections, and candidates associated with major parties such as the Partido de la U, the Liberal party, the Conservative Party, Cambio Radical, and the PDA are collecting signatures to run as independents. In the short term, the party system looks like Humpty Dumpty after his great fall: after profound deinstitutionalization, it is challenging to put the system together again in a stable constellation.

9

Argentina's Declining Party System: Fragmentation, Denationalization, Factionalization, Personalization, and Increasing Fluidity

Carlos Gervasoni*

Argentina's party system has changed significantly since 1993, the last year covered by James McGuire's chapter in *Building Democratic Institutions* (Mainwaring and Scully 1995a). In fact, it was about to enter an extended period of turbulence that started with the *Pacto de Olivos* and the 1994 constitutional reform, and that has not yet ended. This chapter describes these changes in terms of five interrelated processes: (1) fragmentation, (2) denationalization, (3) factionalization, (4) personalization, and (5) increasing fluidity. The common theme behind these trends is a transition from a relatively simple and stable party system to one that is very complex and volatile. Argentina's party system was reasonably institutionalized in the period covered by *Building Democratic Institutions*, but it is now a case that justifies adding the word "decay" to the title of this new volume. If the defining feature of Party System Institutionalization (PSI) "is the stability of patterns of electoral competition" (Mainwaring et al., Chapter 1 of this volume), so that the main contenders tend to be the same (and to obtain fairly similar vote shares) over time, Argentina has clearly deinstitutionalized since 1993. So much so that Mauricio Macri's PRO – the party that headed the *Cambiemos* alliance[1] that won the 2015 presidential election – was created only a decade earlier and had never competed for the presidency before.

This process of deinstitutionalization, however, has stopped short of party system collapse. In contrast to other cases analyzed in this volume such as Peru

* I thank Paula Clerici, Facundo Galván, Scott Mainwaring, Ana María Mustapic, Steve Levitsky, Sybil Rhodes, Gerardo Scherlis, Javier Zelaznik and the participants of the conference "Party Systems in Latin America: Institutionalization, Decay, and Collapse" (Kellogg Institute. University of Notre Dame, June 1–3, 2014) for their useful suggestions and comments on earlier versions of this chapter.
[1] *Cambiemos* was formed in 2015 and includes the following parties (main leaders between parentheses): PRO (Mauricio Macri), UCR (Ernesto Sanz), CC-ARI (Elisa Carrió), Unión por la Libertad (Patricia Bullrich), and FE (Gerónimo Venegas).

and Venezuela, in which all of the traditional parties disappeared or became insignificant, Argentina's two main historical parties – the PJ and the UCR– are still important players, although the former much more than the latter.

By 1993, the system was clearly dominated by the *Partido Justicialista* (or PJ, sometimes called *Partido Peronista*) and the *Unión Cívica Radical* (or UCR, sometimes called *Partido Radical*). Other small national parties existed and a few local parties ruled or were important contenders in some of the twenty-four provinces.[2] Although, as McGuire pointed out (1995: 223), there was no clear ideological cleavage separating the PJ and the UCR, their historical rivalry and their different social bases (more socioeconomically lower class and geographically peripheral in the case of the PJ) made them well-separated forces with clear identities. An important development changed this picture after the 2001–02 political and economic crisis: the UCR lost its status as one of the main contenders for the presidency, losing voters and leaders to many different forces. A cause and/or consequence of this was the emergence or strengthening of a number of parties that occupied the political space previously dominated by the UCR. Some of these parties are actually its splinters (GEN, *Coalición Cívica-ARI*), some are more properly new parties (PRO), and some are old parties (*Partido Socialista*). The PJ quickly adapted to the post-crisis context and accepted the new leadership and statist outlook of Néstor and Cristina Kirchner (as it had adapted to neoliberalism and accepted *menemismo* in the 1990s), but in the process lost a group of significant leaders collectively known as *Peronistas disidentes* (in the same way that it had lost a center-left faction – which went on to form the *Frente Grande* – after its neoconservative turn in the early 1990s).

A semantic clarification – *Peronismo* and *Radicalismo* – are loosely used in Argentina to refer both to political parties and to political identities. It is not uncommon that a politician who formally belongs to a party other than the PJ call him/herself a *Peronist*. This ambiguous distinction between party and identity muddles both the political and academic debate. The point is well illustrated by the 2011 presidential elections: the official PJ candidate was the incumbent Cristina Kirchner, but two of her competitors were very prominent PJ dissidents (former President Eduardo Duhalde and former governor Alberto Rodríguez Saá), who ran using other party labels. For analysts, journalists, and voters, there were three *Peronist* candidates, but there was only one PJ option on the ballot. In the rest of this chapter, I use *Peronist/Peronism* and *Radical/ Radicalism* to refer to the identities and PJ and UCR to refer to the parties.

A second clarification: if all parties are to some extent actors in and of themselves and, to some extent, complex and not-so-coherent conglomerates of factions and individuals, the post-2001 Argentine parties are much closer to the latter description. Therefore, readers should avoid "reifying" the references below to "the PJ," "the UCR," or any other party. These labels tend to overstate

[2] I treat the Ciudad Autónoma de Buenos Aires as a province.

the extent to which these entities are tight organizations with clear identities, leaders, members, rules, programs, and strategies. Contemporary Argentine parties are more accurately described as loose groupings of poorly coordinated politicians and factions, with quite diverse ideologies, weak *esprit de corps*, easily by-passed formal rulers and rules, few loyal members, and few or no shared goals and strategies.[3]

The chapter proceeds as follows: The first section provides a description of the main actors of the Argentine party system. The following section describes the significant changes it has undergone since the redemocratization of the country in 1983, and the consequent high complexity of the resulting system. The third section assesses the current-level PSI and compares it with the past. The final section introduces a tentative set of causal explanations for the changes documented in the previous two.

A DESCRIPTION OF THE MAIN PARTIES: ENTERING THE NEW COMPLEXITY OF ARGENTINA'S SYSTEM

Identifying political parties in Argentina is not easy, and this is in and of itself an indication of the complex current state of affairs. The main party is clearly the PJ but, paradoxically, this label is difficult to find on Argentine ballots. The ruling force from 2003 to 2015 was the *Frente para la Victoria* (FpV), the PJ-led alliance with which Néstor Kirchner and his wife won the presidency three consecutive times. The FpV includes several minor parties, typically left-leaning, some of which vary from election to election and from province to province.[4] In most sub-national units, the FpV is basically the local (provincial or municipal) PJ, perhaps in alliance with small forces but clearly dominated by the PJ elites that pre-existed *kirchnerismo*. In the same way that the PJ (including Santa Cruz governor Néstor Kirchner) supported the neoliberal policies and right-leaning alliances carried out by menemismo (1989–99), the party largely accompanied kirchnerismo's populist-statist turn and its left-leaning alliances. Presidents Néstor (2003–07) and Cristina Kirchner (2007–15), chose not to use the labels *Justicialista* or *Peronista*, however, and they hardly ever used these words in their speeches. They were able to impose a telling change in political jargon: the incumbent force in Argentina after 2003 was generally known as *kirchnerismo* (instead of *Peronismo*) and its electoral label as *Frente para la Victoria* (instead of PJ). These rhetorical choices reflected the Kirchners' disregard for their party, which was given little say in

---

[3] Interestingly, politicians themselves have changed their way of speaking about their organizations. The often fleeting groupings that they use to run for office are often referred to as "*espacios*" rather than "*partidos*."

[4] Parties that have frequently been part of the FpV in both national and provincial elections include the following: Comunista, Conservador Popular, De la Victoria, Frente Grande, Humanista, Intransigente, and Kolina.

government decisions and was often overshadowed by other (non-party) supporters such as *piquetero* movements, human rights organizations, unions, and youth groups.[5] The Kirchners, even more so than Menem before them, gave few cabinet and other important appointments to the main party leaders, privileging instead relatives, friends, aides from their previous provincial administration, and party outsiders chosen on technical or ideological grounds. Appointments were used to control the bureaucracy, to attract allies from other parties and social organizations, and to reshape the PJ's leadership from above, much more than to reward the main party leaders or reinforce the existing party organization (Scherlis 2012).

The FpV, then, is more than the PJ, but it is also less: because Argentina's party system is federal, provincial party branches can break away from the national leadership. Thus, the PJ and the FpV have actually competed against each other in some provincial elections. In these cases, the FpV was made up just of the small allied parties mentioned above. This happened most famously in the 2005 senatorial election in the province of Buenos Aires, where, after failing to reach an agreement on who the party candidates would be, former president and Buenos Aires PJ boss Eduardo Duhalde controlled the official party ticket (headed by his wife "Chiche") and President Kirchner launched a FpV list (headed by his wife Cristina); other examples include La Rioja in 2005, Córdoba in 2013 (where the PJ-led alliance supported by governor de la Sota defeated the FpV), and San Luis in several elections during the period. At other times, Peronist dissidences were expressed through splinters in which former PJ leaders started their own parties or joined existing ones.

The leftist/populist orientation of kirchnerismo did not bode well for important Peronist leaders who placed themselves in the center and the center-right. The hegemonic ambitions of the Kirchners, who in all likelihood planned to succeed each other to circumvent the constitutional two-consecutive-terms limit, also alienated party leaders with their own presidential ambitions. In fact, some of the FpV's most important challengers in the 2007, 2011, and 2015 presidential elections were "identitarian" Peronists and prominent former PJ leaders (such as Duhalde, Rodríguez Saá, Roberto Lavagna, and Sergio Massa). Moreover, two of the most consequential electoral defeats suffered by kirchnerismo – both in legislative elections in the province of Buenos Aires – were at the hands of self-proclaimed Peronists (Francisco De Narváez in alliance with former PJ governor Felipe Solá in 2009, and Massa in alliance with several PJ mayors in 2013). Rebellions from within or without the party, however, have

[5] *"Piqueteros"* refers to well-organized groups of unemployed and poor people who often resort to street blockades to press their demands. Some important *kirchnerista* leaders have been *piqueteros* (e.g., Luis D'Elía, Emilio Pérsico, and Milagro Sala), leaders of human rights organizations (Hebe de Bonafini, Estela de Carlotto, and Juan Cabandié), union bosses (Hugo Yasky and Edgardo de Petri) and members of the state-sponsored youth organization *La Cámpora* (Eduardo de Pedro, Andrés Larroque, and Mariano Recalde).

not been the norm. The Kirchners were able to subordinate most of the PJ, and to become the *de facto* national party leaders.

Néstor and Cristina Kirchner's political strategies further downplayed their party by incorporating non-PJ and/or non-Peronist leaders and political forces into their ruling and electoral coalitions, often under specific political frameworks such as "Transversalidad" and "Concertación Plural" (on these political initiatives, see Zelaznik 2011a). Thus, many FREPASO[6] politicians joined the ranks of kirchnerismo[7] (an unsurprising move, given that this party was to a large extent made up of center-left Peronist leaders who broke away from the official PJ in the 1990s), as did the recently formed *Nuevo Encuentro*, led by Martín Sabatella, a former FREPASO mayor. More unexpected was the incorporation of many and important UCR officials (the so-called "Radicales K"), especially governors and mayors, including Cristina Kirchner's first vice-president Julio Cobos (a former governor of Mendoza). The FpV also attracted politicians from other non-Peronist forces such as ARI (Graciela Ocaña) and the Partido Socialista (Oscar González, Jorge Rivas).

All in all, and partly hidden under the new FpV label, the PJ remained Argentina's most important party throughout the period, commanding at all times a majority of governorships and municipalities, and a majority or plurality of legislative seats in Congress. In fact, it is difficult to distinguish the party from the offices it controls. Its dominance of national and sub-national governments since 1983 has pushed the PJ in the direction of the "agent of the state" type of party (Katz and Mair 1995), and also allowed the Kirchners to build a somewhat new political force, the FpV, on the basis of plentiful appointments and other state resources. Throughout its policy and leadership changes, the electoral bases of the PJ have remained relatively stable. Historically the party did better among the lower classes and in the smaller and more remote provinces of the interior (Mora y Araujo 1980), a pattern that did not change radically even during Menem's neoconservative turn in the 1990s (Gervasoni 1998; Gibson and Calvo 2000; Levitsky 2003). Néstor and Cristina Kirchner were elected with stronger support from the interior (as shown in Figure 9.4) and from less wealthy and less educated voters. Survey data also show that, in spite of the official rhetoric emphasizing progressive values and deemphasizing the party label, PJ sympathizers were – other things being equal – more likely to vote for Néstor and Cristina Kirchner, while leftist voters were not (Tagina 2012). Its control of many offices and its stable electoral base have made the PJ very attractive for ambitious politicians. A very prominent PJ (but anti-kirchnerist) leader, José Manuel de la Sota, sees his own party as follows: "Peronism does not work today. Ideas are not debated.

[6] More on FREPASO and its main constituting party, the Frente Grande, below (see specially Table 9.1 and footnote 11).
[7] Among others, former Vicepresident Carlos Alvarez, former Buenos Aires mayor Aníbal Ibarra, Juan Manuel Abal Medina, Diana Conti, and Nilda Garré.

Peronism is not a party today. It is just an electoral seal. A machine for candidacies" (Sehinkman 2014).

The UCR, on the other hand, suffered an acute decline after its historical electoral victory in 1983. It remained the second largest party in terms of governorships and legislators (after the 2015 elections on par with PRO), but this is mostly due to the fragmentation and low level of nationalization of other parties. As of the writing of this chapter (2016), and even after winning (as a member of the *Cambiemos* alliance) the 2015 presidential elections, the UCR controls only eight senators (11%) and thirty-nine deputies (15%) in Congress,[8] and only three of twenty-four provincial governments (13%; Corrientes, Jujuy, and Mendoza, and does so in alliance with other forces), clearly below its numbers in the 1980s and 1990s. More strikingly, although the party was able to win the presidency in 1983 (with Raúl Alfonsín) and in 1999 (with Fernando de la Rúa, in an alliance with FREPASO), its performance in presidential elections over the last fifteen years has been dismal: the UCR ticket (sometimes allied with other parties) obtained 2% in 2003 (sixth place), 17% in 2007 (third place), 11% in 2011 (third place), and 3% in the 2015 open and mandatory primaries (sixth place).[9] Possibly as a consequence of its discrediting, the UCR has also tended to hide its party label, often running under alliances that do not include the word "Radical" in their names (for example, "Una Nación Avanzada," "Acuerdo Cívico y Social," "UNEN"). Even in the few provinces that remained under its control after 2001, the UCR chose to compete using alternative labels.[10]

The very robust UCR of the 1980s was weakened by a number of blows: the hyperinflationary crisis that ended (early) the presidency of Raúl Alfonsín in 1989; the 1993 *Pacto de Olivos* between Menem and Alfonsín to reform the constitution and permit the former to run for reelection,which produced strong tensions within the party and cost it many voters; the 2001 political and economic crisis that ended (again early) the presidency of Fernando de la Rúa; and, more recently, a very incoherent political line that has left its potential voters confused or disgruntled. Many important leaders left the party to found their own (most notably Elisa Carrió, Ricardo López Murphy, and Margarita Stolbizer), while others were lured by existing parties. Those who stayed in the party have been quite divided, both ideologically and in terms of their stance regarding kirchnerismo and PRO.

The UCR's incoherence is well illustrated by its behavior in the 2007 presidential elections: the party presented its own ticket, but it was ironically headed by a Peronist, Roberto Lavagna, who had served as economics minister

---

[8] These figures include the legislators from the *Frente Cívico de Catamarca*, a provincial UCR-led alliance.
[9] The UCR ticket Sanz-Llach lost by a landslide to PRO's Macri-Michetti ticket in the *Cambiemos* primary.
[10] For example, "*Alianza Concertación para el Desarrollo*" in Río Negro.

for President Kirchner (UCR senator Gerardo Morales was his running mate). At the same time, the UCR governors and other *"Radicales K"* supported the official FpV ticket led by Cristina Kirchner and their own Julio Cobos. It was challenging for voters (and even for scholars) to decide whether the UCR supported or opposed the ruling FpV. Things did not improve in the 2011 or 2015 elections. The UCR initially sought an alliance with the center-left and non-Peronist *Partido Socialista*, but ended up striking deals with *Unión Celeste y Blanco* (a center-right and self-proclaimed Peronist outfit created by tycoon Francisco de Narváez) in 2011 and with also center-right PRO in 2015. These inconsistencies are not entirely new. The UCR was always ideologically heterogeneous and internally factional, and suffered traumatic divisions in the past (such as those between Yrigoyenistas and anti-personalistas in the 1920s). From 1983 to 2001, however, it remained united and, until 1993, was generally perceived as *the* rival of the PJ. The *Pacto de Olivos*, the recent haphazard pattern of alliances, and its inconsistent stance with respect to kirchnerismo strongly diluted the party image and severely compromised its credibility as a check on the PJ.

The UCR's material bases have shrunk severely, as over the last fifteen years it lost control of the presidency and several governorships. It is still in charge of many municipal governments, but these command far fewer fiscal and human resources than their provincial and national counterparts.

Describing the rest of the main parties requires establishing a threshold of relevance. I only consider parties that (1) are nationally significant (leaving out important provincial parties), and (2) obtained more than 10% of the vote in a presidential election since 1983. The parties that meet both criteria (besides the PJ and the UCR) are those in Table 9.1.

Several patterns emerge. First, with the exception of the *Partido Socialista*, all of the relevant "third parties" are recent creations. Although there were a few relatively significant third parties in the first years of the current democratic period (such as Oscar Alende's *Partido Intransigente*, Arturo Frondizi's *Movimiento de Integración y Desarrollo*, Álvaro Alsogaray's *Unión del Centro Democrático*, and Francisco Manrique's *Partido Federal*), all of them ended up becoming electorally irrelevant within a few years. The new parties created in the 1990s, *Frente Grande/FREPASO*[11] and AR (*Acción por la República*), met a similar fate – after some significant electoral gains, they collapsed together with the *Alianza* government in which they participated.[12] Of those parties created in the early 2000s, one has also become irrelevant

---

[11] *Frente Grande* was created in 1993 as an alliance of center-left Peronists (who left the PJ in dissidence with President Menem's conservative orientation) and several pre-existing small center-left forces (for details, see Abal Medina 2009).

[12] An important party in the 1990s not listed in Table 9.1 was MODIN, a nationalistic, hard-on-crime, personalistic vehicle created by Aldo Rico, a colonel who rebelled against President Alfonsín and his trials against officers accused of human rights violations during the 1976–83 military government.

TABLE 9.1 *Relevant National Third Parties, Argentina 1983–2015 (from oldest to newest)*

Party	Origin	Leaders	Presidential elections >10% vote	Years of national relevance	Current status
Partido Socialista (often under the "Frente Amplio Progresista" label)	Created "from below" in the late nineteenth century	Hermes Binner, Rubén Giustiniani, Antonio Bonfatti, Miguel Lifschitz	2007 (allied with ARI) and 2011 (allied with GEN)	2007–present	Ruling party in the province of Santa Fe (allied with UCR).
Frente Grande-Frente por un País Solidario (FREPASO)	Created in 1993 by center-left PJ dissidents and several minor center-left parties	Carlos Álvarez, José Bordón, Graciela Fernández Meijide, Aníbal Ibarra	1995 and 1999 (in the latter year allied with the UCR)	1994–2001	FREPASO disappeared; Frente Grande still exists but is very weak
Acción por la República (AR)	Created in 1997 by Menem's former minister Domingo Cavallo	Domingo Cavallo	1999	1997–2001	Inactive
Coalición Cívica (CC)-Afirmación para una República Igualitaria (ARI)	Created in 2002 by center-left dissident UCR leader Elisa Carrió	Elisa Carrió	2003, 2007 and (allied with UCR & PRO) 2015	2002–present	Weak. Minor member of Macri's Cambiemos alliance.
Recrear para el Crecimiento	Created in 2002 by UCR's center-right dissident leader Ricardo López Murphy	Ricardo López Murphy	2003	2002–03	Does not exist. It merged with PRO in 2009. López Murphy left the party.

Propuesta Republicana (PRO)	Created in 2003 by businessman Mauricio Macri	Mauricio Macri, Gabriela Michetti, Marcos Peña, Horacio Rodríguez Larreta, María Eugenia Vidal	2015 (allied with UCR & CC-ARI)	2007–present	Main member of the Cambiemos ruling alliance. Controls presidency and governorships of city and province of Buenos Aires
Frente Renovador[1]/ Unidos por una Nueva Alternativa (UNA)[2]	Created in 2013 by dissident FpV leader Sergio Massa	Sergio Massa, José Manuel de la Sota	2015	2013–present	Strong in provinces of Buenos Aires and Córdoba. Obtained the 3rd place in the 2015 elections.

[1] Strictly speaking not a national party but an alliance of minor parties in the Province of Buenos Aires.
[2] UNA is a national alliance created by Massa and de la Sota to compete in the 2015 presidential elections.
Source: Author's elaboration based on journalistic sources and Tow 2016.

(*Recrear*), one remains active but is electorally weak (CC-ARI), and one has consolidated (PRO) after winning the government of the city of Buenos Aires for three consecutive terms (from 2007 to 2019) and, allied with the UCR and the CC-ARI, obtaining the presidency (plus the key governorship of the province of Buenos Aires) in the 2015 elections. The general rule, however, is that after some good electoral showings, Argentina's national minor parties fade away.

A second pattern is the personalistic nature of these parties. Most of them revolved around a single, high-profile leader. This was clearly the case of the parties started by former ministers Cavallo and López Murphy, by Deputy Elisa Carrió, by former Chief of Cabinet Sergio Massa, and by businessman Mauricio Macri.[13] FREPASO was a more collective creation, but its driving force was the media-based popularity of its main leaders (listed in Table 9.1), who enjoyed very high levels of leadership autonomy in the context of a party that was very weakly institutionalized (Abal Medina 2009).

Third, most of these parties are to some extent splinters from the major ones. FREPASO's main member, the *Frente Grande*, was founded by a group of dissident PJ legislators in the 1990s. Its presidential ticket in 1995 was made up of two mainstream PJ politicians, José Octavio Bordón (a PJ senator and former governor of Mendoza) and Carlos "Chacho" Álvarez (a PJ deputy). The *Frente Renovador* emerged from inside of the Kirchner administration, led by its former Chief of Cabinet Sergio Massa and joined by many PJ mayors and legislators. It formed the national electoral alliance UNA to compete in the 2015 presidential elections by incorporating the PJ governor of Córdoba, José Manuel de la Sota. AR was less clearly a PJ splinter, but it was created by former minister Domingo Cavallo, who had won significant popularity for his macroeconomic successes in the early 1990s (serving under Menem). Parties were also formed as a result of UCR dissidences: after the collapse of the UCR-FREPASO (*Alianza*) administration headed by President de la Rúa, a center-left faction led by Deputy Elisa Carrió founded ARI, while a center-right faction led by former Minister Ricardo López Murphy started *Recrear*. The exception to this pattern are the *Partido Socialista* (founded "from below" by workers, professionals and immigrant groups in the 1890s) and the PRO, which was founded by Macri from scratch (but incorporating several politicians from the PJ, the UCR, *Recrear*, etc.).

A fourth pattern not shown in Table 9.1 is that "national" third parties have been geographically limited. They have tended to thrive in the city of Buenos Aires and in the main cities of the Pampas region, having little success in the smaller provinces of the North, West, and South. Even if doing well in presidential elections, they systematically fail to win Senate seats or governorship in

---

[13] Macri was also very well-known because of his successful stint as president of Boca Juniors, the country's most popular soccer team. Many politicians start or support their careers as leaders of soccer clubs (see Levitsky 2003: 63–64).

the interior. The starkest illustration of this point is FREPASO's electoral performance in 1995. In spite of winning almost 30% of the vote for the presidency, it elected only one senator[14] (for the city of Buenos Aires) and no governors. From 1983 to 2015, third parties controlled just between zero and three senators and between zero and one governors (only those of the city of Buenos Aires – PRO – and the province of Santa Fe – PS –). Even after winning the presidency in 2015, Macri's PRO only captured one additional district (even if the most important one, the province of Buenos Aires) and three additional Senate seats (for a total of six, or 8% of all senators). This difficulty to expand territorially is due to several factors: (a) *de facto* majoritarian electoral institutions in the smaller provinces (low district magnitudes compounded by staggered legislative elections), (b) lack of extended on-the-ground political machines (which only the PJ and to some extent the UCR have),[15] and (c) the hegemonic economic and political control that incumbents in "rentier provinces" (those heavily subsidized by federal transfers from Buenos Aires; see Gervasoni 2010) exercise over their districts. The effects of this failure to reach deep into the territory are amplified by the over-representation of the smaller districts: Argentina has one of the highest levels of malapportionment in the world (Samuels and Snyder 2001). Therefore, third parties typically win considerably smaller proportions of legislators than their share of national votes would suggest.

Argentina has many more parties. As of 2016, there were forty-two national parties (most of them electorally irrelevant) and many more district parties (i.e., those legally recognized only in one or a few provinces). Some of the latter are significant in their districts, including the *Movimiento Popular Neuquino* (which has governed Neuquén since 1983), Luis Juez's *Frente Cívico* in Córdoba, and Gerardo Zamora's *Frente Cívico* in Santiago del Estero (an alliance of many small parties led by former UCR and PJ leaders that has dominated the province for a decade). These local parties have some influence beyond their province's boundaries: they form alliances with national forces for presidential elections and negotiate the support of their national legislators with the president.

The increasing complexity of Argentina's party system cannot be easily reduced to one or a few clear cleavages. Peronism–antiperonism was the main political divide in the second half of the twentieth century. However, it has been losing significance since 1983, in part because of the notorious ideological about-face of the PJ, which left the Peronist identity devoid of clear content. Most voters, who did not live through the heyday of Juan Perón,

---

[14] This is partly due to the staggered election of Senators. After the 1994 constitutional reform, senators are elected in one-third of the provinces every two years.
[15] These machines are funded by (and difficult to distinguish from) the government offices these parties control, especially national, provincial, and municipal executives.

do not feel as strongly – positively or negatively – about it as previous generations. The left–right axis is present but weak: the main parties are ideologically quite heterogeneous and very inconsistent over time (especially the PJ), and even the parties that express more clear positions (for example, the PS or the PRO) tend to play down this cleavage in favor of personalistic, performance, or valence appeals.[16] Analyses of roll call votes in Congress reveal a single but not very informative dimension: government vs opposition (Jones *et al.* 2009). Between 2003 and 2015, the FpV and small allies anchored the government side of this cleavage, while the opposition side included very diverse parties such as the UCR, the CC-ARI, the PRO, the PS, and dissident Peronists. Few things united them except their opposition to kirchnerismo. Although not as polarizing, this cleavage was similar to the chavismo vs anti-chavismo divide in Venezuela (Morgan, Chapter 10 of this volume).

THE NEW COMPLEXITY: FRAGMENTATION, DENATIONALIZATION, FACTIONALIZATION, PERSONALIZATION AND INCREASING FLUIDITY

Argentina's party system is considerably less institutionalized than in the first decade of democracy (1983–93), because of a number of trends that became evident after *Building Democratic Institutions* was published. They can be summarized under five labels: fragmentation, denationalization, factionalization, personalization, and increasing fluidity. These concepts isolate analytically the most prominent trends over the last two decades, but are in reality very much intertwined because of some definitional overlap and because of empirical relationships of correlation and causality. Fragmentation and denationalization, for example, are likely to reinforce each other: Jones and Mainwaring (2003: 159) report a correlation of 0.87 for indicators of these two variables in a sample of eighty-five elections in seventeen Western Hemisphere countries. Analyzing Colombia, another case that was "institutionalized" in the 1980s and 1990s, Albarracín, Gamboa and Mainwaring (Chapter 8 of this volume) write: "party system deinstitutionalization happened in tandem with two other phenomena: increasing fragmentation and decreasing nationalization" of the party system.

The common thread unifying these five trends is a movement from simplicity to complexity, or from a relatively stable system with a few well-defined parts to a volatile and fluid system made up of many diffuse actors.

---

[16] An exception is the *Partido Obrero*, a small but well-organized Trotskyite party that has been a significant presence since 1983. In the 2013 elections, it formed an alliance with other small leftist parties, obtaining a modest but record number of deputies (three over 128 elected that year).

The party system is now more difficult for scholars to describe and for voters to make sense of. An important caveat: I take as the reference point the 1983–93 period analyzed in *Building Democratic Institutions*. In historical perspective, however, that decade of relatively high institutionalization largely dominated by two established parties is more the exception than the rule. Some of the deinstitutionalizing changes I stress below imply, from a long-term viewpoint, the reemergence of party system features that were common in the short stints of democracy Argentina enjoyed between 1916 and 1976.

Fragmentation

Fragmentation has been a prominent trend in the post-1993 period (Mustapic 2013). Argentina's relevant actors were few in the 1980s – two large national parties and a few provincial parties of local prominence[17] – there are many more now.

Figure 9.1 shows national ENP trends since 1983. The new democracy started with slightly more than two presidential and legislative parties. Already in the 1985 legislative elections, the number of parliamentary parties grew to three and remained approximately at that level until 1995. Over the next ten years, the figure grew to slightly over four parties, reaching a record of six in 2009 (because of a high loss of FpV deputies in mid-term elections at the hands of many parties) and of five in 2015 (when a similar loss was capitalized mainly by PRO and UNA). The overall trend reflects both the increasing success of third national forces and of new provincial parties. The share of the seats in the lower house controlled by third parties tells a similar story: it ranged between 5.5% and 17.9% in the 1983–94 period, jumped to 20.2–30.4% for the 1995–2002 period, leaped again to 31.5–49.4% for the 2003–09 period (Mustapic 2013: 275), and has hovered around 50% since then.

In fact, (legislative) fragmentation has been considerably lower in terms of seats – shown in Figure 9.1 – than in terms of votes because of a combination of low district magnitudes in most provinces and of the over-representation of these (smaller) provinces in Congress. These two features give the main parties (mostly the PJ but also the UCR) a majoritarian seat bonus (Calvo 2014). Without them, the level of legislative fragmentation would have grown still more than it did.

Fragmentation in elections for the presidency also grew after 1983. The imperfections of the ENP mask the fact that the 1995 presidential election

---

[17] Such as the *Pacto Autonomista-Liberal* (Corrientes), the *Movimiento Popular Neuquino* (Neuquén), and the *Partido Bloquista* (San Juan), all in control of their respective governorships in the 1980s.

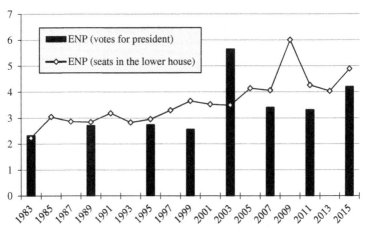

FIGURE 9.1 Effective Number of Parties: Executive (Votes for President) and Legislative
(Seats in Chamber of Deputies), 1983–2015
Note: The ENP for president was calculated using the primaries (PASO) results in 2011
and 2015.
Sources: ENP president: Author's calculations based on data available from Tow 2016;
ENP Legislative: Author's calculations based on lower house seats data from Molinelli
et al. (1999) for 1983 to 1997, Zelaznik (2011b) for 1999 to 2011, and Paula Clerici's
calculations based on data from www.diputados.gov.ar for 2013 and 2015.

was substantively more fragmented than the previous ones and the following
one: it contained not two but three significant contenders, the PJ (50% of
the vote), the UCR (which came third, with 17%), and the newly created
FREPASO (the runner up with 29%). The two latter parties joined forces for
the legislative elections of 1997 and the general elections of 1999 (under the
label *Alianza para el Trabajo, la Justicia y la Educación*), which led to a
temporary reduction in fragmentation in 1999. However, the 2001–02 crisis
had a large impact on the party system, shattering it into many pieces in
the presidential elections of 2003. That year, Argentines were able to choose
among three different Peronist candidates and three different Radical ones. The
presidential ENP declined significantly (to about 3.4) in the following two
elections, marked by the dominance of the FpV, only to rebound in 2015.
Beyond these ups and downs, however, presidential fragmentation in the new
century has remained well above the figures of the 1980s and 1990s.

One important element has persisted throughout this process of increasing
fragmentation, helping stabilize the system. The PJ has remained a central actor
both at the national and sub-national levels. This "anchor," however, is not as
firm as it could be, due to the abrupt changes the PJ has suffered both in
membership (for example, factions that break away from the party) and
programmatic orientation. The UCR, on the other hand, quickly lost the
remarkable electoral strength with which it started the new democratic

period, regressing to the position it had had in the 1950s, 1960s, and 1970s as a weaker national party, not as well implanted throughout the territory as the PJ.

Denationalization

Denationalization refers to the transition from a system in which "the major parties' respective vote shares do not differ much from one province to the next" to one in which "the major parties' vote shares vary widely across provinces" (Jones and Mainwaring 2003: 149).[18] At the extreme, it even means that some political forces are strong or even dominant in one province but are irrelevant or non-existent elsewhere (Peru approaches this situation, see Levitsky in Chapter 11 of this volume). Much recent work on Argentine parties has documented and attempted to explain increasing levels of denationalization since the beginning of the new century (Calvo and Escolar 2005; Clerici 2015; Leiras 2010).

Figure 9.2 shows the evolution of the Party System Nationalization Score (PSNS) (Jones and Mainwaring 2003) for Argentina, plus the individual nationalization scores for the PJ and the UCR (*Alianza UCR-FREPASO* for 1997–2001, and *Cambiemos* for 2015). The PSNS starts at a rather high level in 1983 and declines moderately until 1991. It then recovers during the second half of the 1990s, only to plummet in the first elections of the twenty-first century, after the collapse of the *Alianza* administration. Most of the post-2001 figures (ranging from 0.38 to 0.64) are in fact lower than the minimum of 0.47 recorded for the 1985 elections in seventeen countries studied by Jones and Mainwaring (2003), which makes clear how far denationalization has advanced over the last fifteen years. The recovery in the PSNS in the 2015 elections is largely due to the increased nationalization of the two main political forces and to their higher combined share of the total vote. However, the high PNS for the UCR-PRO-CC alliance masks significant regional disparities in the electoral support of each of these parties across the provinces. It is not yet clear whether this recovery of the PSNS marks the beginning of a durable reversal of previous denationalization trends or merely reflects the peculiarities of the 2015 elections.

Figure 9.2 also shows that this acute denationalization is only partly driven by the major parties. Even if not as territorially homogeneous as in the 1980s, the PJ and the UCR remained national parties during most of the period. The PSNS, however, is always lower than the scores of these parties, and stays low even after 2007, when the UCR recovers previous nationalization levels. The diverging trends (until 2013) of the national score and the PJ and UCR scores reflect the emergence and consolidation of parties that are strong in one or a couple of significant districts and weak or non-existent in the rest of the country. Prominent examples are the PRO, the PS, and the FR.

---

[18] This definition implies referring to what the literature has called the "static" and "horizontal" dimensions of party nationalization.

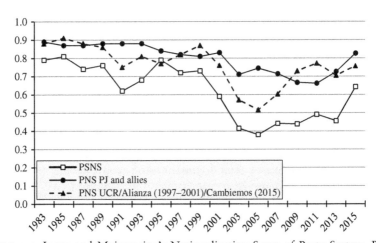

FIGURE 9.2 Jones and Mainwaring's Nationalization Score of Party System, PJ and Allies, and UCR and Allies, 1983–2015
Source: Jones and Mainwaring (2003) from 1983 to 2001; Paula Clerici's calculations based on data from Tow 2016 from 2003 to 2013, and from elecciones.gov.ar for 2015.

Argentina has a tradition of strong local parties in some provinces, but since the 1980s the phenomenon has become more prevalent: in the 1983 elections, the PJ and the UCR were the top contenders for the governorship in nineteen of twenty-two provinces (86%); in 2011 and 2015 the figure had fallen to eleven and twelve of twenty-four provinces (46% and 50%), respectively. Figure 9.3 shows the percentage of gubernatorial elections in which the PJ (solid line) and the UCR (dashed line) – alone or in alliances dominated by them – were among the top two contenders. The ascending thick line shows a similar indicator – the percentage of the two top vote-getters for gubernatorial elections that are *not* the PJ or the UCR (or alliances led by them). Only six of the eighty-eight (7%) winners or runner-ups for governor in 1983 and 1987 were local parties (those mentioned in footnote 17). The figure more than doubles during the 1990s (with the rise of local parties in districts such as Salta, Tucumán, and the city of Buenos Aires), and doubles again to reach more than 30% in 2007, 2011, and 2015, with the emergence of significant local forces in the provinces of Buenos Aires, Córdoba, Misiones, and Santiago del Estero,[19] among others.

The PJ also denationalized. The party was already geographically heterogeneous before 1983, in particular showing better electoral performances in the small and remote provinces than in the central Pampas region (Mora y Araujo 1980). Gibson and Calvo (2000) documented that the politics of

---

[19] Misiones and Santiago del Estero are ruled by complex alliances of existing parties and/or factions of existing parties, especially the PJ and the UCR.

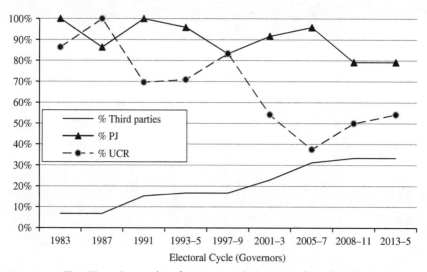

FIGURE 9.3 Top Two Contenders for Provincial Governorships, by Electoral Cycle, 1983–2015: PJ, UCR, and Local Parties
Source: Author's calculation based on official electoral results (given the complexity of some provincial alliances, decisions about what counts as a local force not affiliated with the PJ or UCR were made by the author on the basis of case information).

economic reform in the 1990s made the electoral support for President Menem more peripheral. This pattern in fact deepened sharply during the Kirchners' years. Figure 9.4 shows boxplots of the PJ presidential vote share in each province divided by region: the "center" (city and province of Buenos Aires, Córdoba, Entre Ríos, Mendoza, and Santa Fe) and the "interior" (the other eighteen provinces). The PJ starts in 1983 with a moderate "peripheral" bias, which actually disappears in the election of 1989 in which the PJ wins with Menem. By Menem's reelection in 1995, the graph shows an increased peripheral bias in the PJ vote, which is maintained in 1999 (when Duhalde lost to De la Rúa) and 2003 (considering Néstor Kirchner as the PJ candidate among the three Peronist competitors, given that he was sponsored by PJ interim president Duhalde). This moderate regional gap widens sharply after 2003. The difference between the median PJ vote in the interior and the center was 3% in the first democratic election of 1983, 6% in 1995, and 7% when Kirchner won in 2003, but it skyrocketed to 17% in 2007 and 19% in 2011, the years of the election and reelection of Cristina Kirchner (it fell to 14% in 2015, still well above pre-2007 levels). In other words, the *kirchnerista* version of the PJ has been significantly more peripheral than previous versions.

In sum, the territorially homogeneous distribution of parties that characterized the early years of democracy has been replaced by a highly diverse party landscape across the country. The PJ remains a significant contender in most provinces, but the UCR has been losing out to a myriad of different parties and

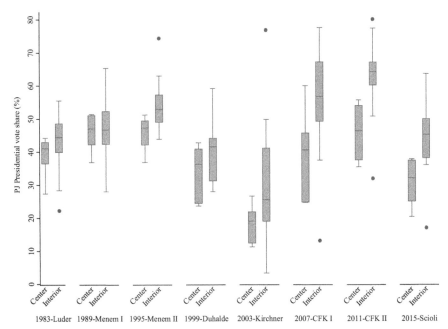

1983-Luder 1989-Menem I 1995-Menem II 1999-Duhalde 2003-Kirchner 2007-CFK I 2011-CFK II 2015-Scioli

FIGURE 9.4 Boxplots of Provincial PJ Vote Share in Presidential Elections by Region, 1983–2015
Notes: The horizontal lines within each box represent the median provincial electoral support for the PJ, while the lower and upper borders of the boxes are the first and third quartile, respectively.
"CFK" stands for Cristina Fernández de Kirchner. Circles represent outliers, i.e., provinces in which the PJ candidate did especially well or especially poorly.
Source: Author's calculations based on official electoral results.

alliances in different provinces and elections, most of them largely or totally local: over the last few elections the UCR has lost its "top two" status, for example, to PRO in the city of Buenos Aires, the PS and PRO in Santa Fe, the *Frente Cívico* in Córdoba, and to several parties in the critical province of Buenos Aires.

Factionalization and Personalization

Factionalization and personalization refer to a transition from parties that behave as relatively unitary organizations with routinized formal procedures to manage internal conflict, to parties that are composed of very autonomous, splinter-prone factions led by high-profile leaders that overshadow the organization.

Factionalism has a long history in Argentina. However, it has become more important in several respects over the last couple of decades. As in many parts of the world, Argentine politics has experienced a turn toward personalization, a process that has gone hand in hand with an erosion of party brands (Lupu 2013;

Chapter 12 of this volume). Moreover, parties have often purposively chosen to run under new labels that make no reference to traditional names (as well illustrated by the PJ, which since 2005 has run in most elections and provinces under the *Frente para la Victoria* label).[20] In such a context, heuristics citizens commonly used to make electoral decisions change: party labels were the main informational shortcuts until the 1980s, but more recently the most easily available heuristic has been the reputation of individual candidates. It is increasingly rare to hear voters say things such as "*voy a votar por el Radicalismo/Peronismo*" or "I'm voting for the *Radicalismo/Peronismo.*" Instead, taking as an example the 2011 presidential election, one may have more often heard "*yo la voto a Cristina*" or "*yo voto a Duhalde,*" or "I'm voting for Cristina/for Duhalde." The fact that these two candidates were very prominent Peronist leaders competing under different labels illustrates the point.[21]

Factions have been increasingly relevant also because they have tended to split from their parties to field their own candidates (forming new parties or "hiring" existing ones). The practice of "*ir por afuera*" (compete in elections from outside the original party) has been relatively common in the last couple of decades, especially in the PJ (Galván 2010). However, it became much more prevalent with the Kirchners' ascent to power (Galván 2011): During the presidencies of Alfonsín, Menem, De la Rúa, and Duhalde (1983–2003), there were an average of 3.4 Peronist dissident lists per year competing with official PJ lists for national offices (president, deputy, and senator) and provincial executives (governor). During the presidencies of Néstor Kirchner and his wife, this average jumped to 18.3 per year.[22] They sponsored many of these dissidences to take control of the party and marginalize governors and other party leaders who refused to be subordinate.[23] This anticipates a point I elaborate below: much of the recent destructuring of the party system has

---

[20] In previous presidential elections the PJ either used its name or it ran under alliances that contained the word "Justicialista," for example: *Frente Justicialista de Liberación* (1973), *Frente Justicialista Popular* (1989), and *Concertación Justicialista para el Cambio* (1999).

[21] In fact, in all the presidential elections since 1995 there have been more than one Peronist candidate. Menem's main rival in 1995 was a ticket made up of two PJ politicians, José Octavio Bordón and Carlos "Chacho" Álvarez. In 1999, the PJ had a single candidate, but Menem's former Minister of Economy Domingo Cavallo ran on a new party obtaining 10% of the vote. In 2003, the PJ allowed its three pre-candidates to run using the party label, but in different alliances (i.e., with dubious legality, the PJ competed against itself): former president Menem (24% of the vote), governor Néstor Kirchner (22%), and former interim president Adolfo Rodríguez Saá (14%). In 2007, Cristina Kirchner (45%) faced her husband's former Minister of Economy Roberto Lavagna (17%), and Alberto Rodríguez Saá (8%). In 2011, she competed against Alberto Rodríguez Saá (8%) and Duhalde (6%). Finally, Daniel Scioli was the official PJ candidate in 2015, but faced Peronist candidates Sergio Massa (14% in the primaries, or PASO), José Manuel de la Sota (6%), and Adolfo Rodríguez Saá (2%).

[22] Author's calculations based on Galván 2011, Figure 5. Data available until 2009.

[23] Notable among these was the aforementioned legislative dissident list headed by Cristina Kirchner in the province of Buenos Aires in 2005, successfully used by President Kirchner to defeat the official PJ list headed by former President Duhalde's wife.

been "from above," that is, due to the strategic actions of rulers, and in particular of the very active intervention by the Kirchners. The parallel process of personalization is surely part of a more general trend in contemporary politics, where the mass media and other factors have contributed to increase the power of popular leaders *vis-à-vis* party organizations. In Argentina, however, the growing complexity of the party system has furthered the centrality of individuals. Voters are not only faced with a more fragmented and denationalized system, but also with a highly volatile one, in which parties often change ideologies, political alignments, and labels. Not surprisingly, and contrary to countries such as Brazil, Chile, and Uruguay, politics in Argentina is talked about largely in terms of personal names: *menemismo, kirchnerismo, macrismo, massismo*, and so forth.

A clear symptom of the increasing importance of factions and leaders is that their behavior has grown more and more independent from party loyalties. They now frequently cross political lines that were practically unbridgeable in the past. A very prominent illustration of this phenomenon is that of the aforementioned Julio Cobos, the "Radical K" governor of Mendoza (2003–07). In the 2007 election, he left his party to become Cristina Kirchner's running mate, which implied competing against the ticket supported by his own UCR. After falling out with *kirchnerismo* in 2008 over a tax hike on agricultural exports (an episode that gave him much visibility and popularity), Cobos was readmitted to the UCR and soon became (again) one of its main leaders. Likewise, during the 2013–15 electoral period, several mayors of large cities (for example, Gustavo Posse of San Isidro) changed allegiances from one presidential candidate to another several times, with little regard for the party to which they belonged. The political logic of this "maverick" trajectory seems clear (see Tavits 2009 for a similar argument for legislators): these mayors enjoy firm personal (as opposed to party) command of their municipality and use that asset to negotiate candidacies with national parties, which present better chances for career progress than their original parties.

The same can be said of many mayors, governors, deputies, senators, and politicians in general: Radicals migrated to the PJ (for example,Tucumán's governor José Alperovich) or PRO (for example, Hernán Lombardi), *Coalición Cívica* leaders switched to the *Frente Renovador* (for example, Adrián Pérez), politicians who were identified with *kirchnerismo* suddenly became strong opponents (including former Chiefs of Cabinet Alberto Fernández and Sergio Massa), while some alleged opponents of *kirchnerismo* inexplicably found themselves liking it once elected (for example, senators Samuel Cabanchik and Roxana Latorre, and deputy Lorenzo Borocotó). Argentina still has real parties, but over the last few years it has moved in the direction of a system in which ambitious politicians often run with no significant party organization behind them, creating their own personalistic electoral vehicles, either from scratch (as illustrated by businessmen Francisco De Narváez and Salta's Alfredo Olmedo) or from pieces of their former parties (for example, Elisa Carrió and Sergio Massa).

If Argentina's party politics in the 1980s and 1990s was mostly about organizations which contained factions and leaders in tension, over recent years it has become more about leaders and factions that leave their parties, join other parties, and/or create new parties, thus making the system less stable and predictable. The elite loyalty to parties that characterizes institutionalized party systems (Mainwaring and Scully 1995a: 16) has eroded significantly in the last two decades.

Increasing Fluidity

The final characteristic trend of Argentina's recent party system – partly anticipated in the previous paragraphs – has been increasing fluidity. By this expression, I mean that the behavior of this larger and ever-more complex set of actors – parties, factions, leaders – has become more volatile and less predictable: parties change programs and allies, factions break away from their parties to join others or form new ones (often to return to the original party after a short time; see Galván 2010), and leaders switch, split, and found parties. To make things even more fluid, parties often change their labels (typically entering alliances whose names do not include any recognizable party labels, such as *Frente para la Victoria* or *Frente Amplio-UNEN*), adopt different labels in different provinces, and, more substantively, make different alliances in different provinces: often the provincial branches of a party ally with parties that are competitors in other provinces or at the national level (Clerici 2015; Jones and Micozzi 2013).

Take the 2013 legislative elections. The UCR competed alone in provinces such as Córdoba, Mendoza, and Misiones, allied with the center-left Socialist Party (and others) in the city and province of Buenos Aires and in Santa Fe, and allied with the center-right PRO in the provinces of Catamarca, Corrientes, and Neuquén. The PJ competed with small allies under the FpV label in most districts, but (a) these allies varied from province to province, (b) in some provinces the FpV did not include the PJ and competed against it (for example, in Córdoba and Santa Cruz, where the PJ governors opposed the national government), and (c) in two provinces it competed without allies under its traditional PJ label (La Pampa and Salta). In San Luis, the PJ did not compete formally, although the winning party (Adolfo Rodríguez Saá's *Compromiso Federal*) is clearly Peronist. Finally, in two provinces the FpV (including the PJ) competed (unsuccessfully) against a ruling local force clearly identified with the national FpV administration (Santiago del Estero and Misiones). This "crazy-quilt pattern of conflicting alliances" has often "ruptured the boundaries of ideological coherence" (Jones and Micozzi 2013: 45) – the allegedly progressive FpV, for example, has allied in some elections with the supposedly conservative UCeDé, the *Partido Liberal*, and the *Partido Renovador de Salta*.

If the reader feels confused, the point has been made. Not even scholars of Argentine parties thoroughly grasp this extremely complex scenario. Voters are understandably even more confused, and simple operations such as determining "who won" an election are complex: *kirchnerismo* claimed it won the 2013 legislative contest because the FpV was the single party with the most votes at the national level (true). But it was defeated in the five largest provinces (which include 68% of voters) and in half of the smaller ones, hardly a victory. The apparent inconsistency is resolved noting that the forces that defeated the FpV varied by province.

In sum, since the mid-1990s Argentina has had an increasingly complex and volatile party system. If at the outset of the current democratic period the party system had two main players that were strong across most provinces and that were relatively unitary actors with distinguishable brands and predictable strategies, by the beginning of the new century it had many players, most of them with uneven territorial strength, often with factional leadership struggles that made the "unitary actor" assumption risible, and with a level of fluidity in labels, alignments, and alliances unknown before. True, the system still has an "anchor" – the continuous centrality of the PJ, especially in the interior provinces – but this party has itself undergone a number of changes, including its own share of fragmentation, denationalization, factionalization, and personalization. In addition, it has been highly fluid, as illustrated by its abrupt changes in leadership, allies, and ideologies: The spectacular policy turnaround that Menem successfully imposed on the PJ during the 1990s and the similarly abrupt change led by the Kirchners after 2003 have few precedents in world politics. Oddly, a prime target of Néstor Kirchner's harsh rhetoric was a previous administration of his own party in which he had occupied an important office (he was a deferent PJ governor, who supported many of Menem's neoliberal policies).

If "institutionalization" is about "a stable party system that generates a sense of future predictability" (Mainwaring, Bizzarro, and Petrova, Chapter 1 of this volume), the sharp increase in complexity and fluidity that I have described implies that Argentina's current party system is no longer well institutionalized. This point is elaborated in the next section.

PARTY SYSTEM INSTITUTIONALIZATION: DECAY WITHOUT COLLAPSE

In *Building Democratic Institutions*, Argentina was seen as belonging (if barely) to the "institutionalized" group, along with Costa Rica, Chile, Colombia, Venezuela, and Uruguay. By the mid-2010s, it can more properly be described as having an intermediate to low level of institutionalization. Below, I assess the performance of the country in terms of the four dimensions of the concept proposed by Mainwaring and Scully (1995a): (1) the extent to which the rules and nature of inter-party competition are stable, (2) the extent to which major parties have stable roots in society, (3) the extent to which major political actors accord legitimacy to elections and parties, and (4) the extent to which party organizations are solid, independent from groups and individuals, and valued on their own terms. I stress the first of these dimensions, as per the emphasis of Chapter 1 of this volume.

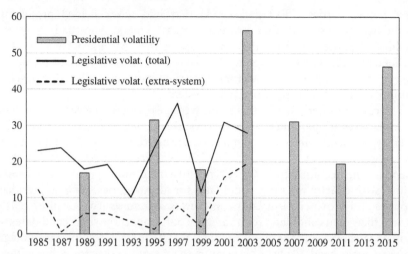

FIGURE 9.5 Electoral Volatility, Presidential and Lower Chamber Legislative Elections
Source: Author's elaboration on official electoral results and data from Mainwaring *et al.*
2016.

Dimension one (regularity in patterns of party competition) was measured in the 1995 volume through the Pedersen Index (1983) of electoral volatility for both congressional (lower chamber) and presidential elections. Argentina had moderate levels of volatility in the first years of democracy, but they have tended to grow since then, as shown in Figure 9.5. Even more telling is the recent increase in "extra-system" volatility, that is, in the share of the vote captured by new parties in legislative contests (Mainwaring *et al.* 2016). Similar trends have characterized presidential races. If the PJ and UCR candidates obtained most of the votes in the 1983 and 1989 elections, since 1995 and, especially, since 2003, things have become much more volatile. The UCR first lost its national "top-two status" to the newly born FREPASO in 1995. In 1999, there is a brief return to competition dominated by UCR and PJ candidates, but in fact the former ran and won in an alliance with FREPASO. In the 2003 elections, volatility soared to around 56%.[24] This is to a large extent explained by the fact that two Radical candidates, Carrió and López Murphy, ran and did well on splinter UCR successor parties (while the official UCR candidate, Leopoldo Moreau, got just 2% of the vote). Volatility in the presidential elections of 2007 was considerably lower but still high. It took a further step down in 2011 because of the anchoring effect of the FpV, which obtained large and comparable shares of the vote in both elections. This decreasing trend since 2003 may suggest a "normalization" of electoral competition, but it mainly reflected the effect of a strong incumbent party and a popular reelectable president. Volatility shot up again in 2015: two of the three main contenders

---

[24] A figure obtained when considering Kirchner, Menem, and Rodríguez Saá as PJ candidates.

were young parties (PRO and UNA) that had never fielded presidential candidates before and that attracted many voters who had supported established parties in 2011 (the vote share of the FpV and UCR candidates declined by 12% and 8%, respectively). That a young party won the presidency after decades of PJ and UCR victors is a strong indication of the low levels of stability of the current Argentine party system.

The rules of inter-party competition were also volatile. Several formal and informal institutional innovations of questionable legality were introduced or extensively used, mainly by incumbents, during the 2000s (Mustapic 2013). The most important were sudden and unexpected changes in the electoral calendar, the recourse to *listas espejo*[25] (two or more parties that present ballots with exactly the same candidates for all categories, such as president, deputies and provincial legislators) and *listas colectoras* (two or more parties present their own candidates for a category but support the same candidates for another category), and the use of *candidatos testimoniales* (popular incumbents who run as the head of a list of legislators to maximize votes for it, but without the intention of assuming the new position). These institutional manipulations had the effect of facing voters with "an electoral supply that is increasingly voluminous, complex, lacking transparency and confusing" (Mustapic *et al.* 2011: 1).[26] A major electoral reform was passed in 2009 introducing open and mandatory primaries (or PASO),[27] public financing for audiovisual publicity and more demanding requirements for establishing parties and presenting candidates. One important goal of the reform was to reduce party proliferation and fragmentation, but it also contributed to the instability of the electoral legal framework. All in all, since the mid-1990s the system has become considerably less institutionalized in terms of the first dimension: higher electoral volatility, less clear and less stable identities of the main actors, and less stability in the rules of the electoral game.

Dimension two, regarding parties' stable roots in society, was proxied by parties' longevity in *Building Democratic Institutions*. Using the share of the lower-chamber seats held by parties born before 1950 as a measure, Argentina experienced a significant decline, from 82.4% in 1989 (Mainwaring and Scully 1995a: 13) to approximately 65% and 56% in the 2013–15 and 2015–17 Congresses, respectively.[28] This change is mostly due to the decay of a pre-1950 party (the UCR) and its replacement by legislators of younger parties. Showing the same trend, the proportion of Argentines who declare to pollsters that they are members of a party or sympathize with one has declined from around two thirds

---

[25] The *listas espejo* were forbidden by the 2009 electoral reform (Mustapic, *et al.* 2011).
[26] My translation.
[27] Acronym in Spanish for "Primarias abiertas, simultáneas y obligatorias" (open, simultaneous, and compulsory primaries).
[28] Author's calculations based on data from www.diputados.gov.ar/secparl/dclp/bloques/index.html.

in the 1980s to roughly one fifth in the late 2000s (Mora y Araujo 2011: 117). The 2010 and 2012 waves of the LAPOP's AmericasBarometer surveys (LAPOP 2016) confirm the latter figure: averaging out both years, approximately 22.5% of the population sympathized with a political party (and of these 62% mentioned the PJ or FpV and 14% the UCR, with no other party reaching 5%). All evidence indicates that traditional Peronist and, especially, Radical identities have significantly eroded since 1983, and that they have not been replaced by new identities (a conclusion buttressed by the failure of most new parties to survive for more than a few elections). The prominence of PRO during the 2015 campaign appears to have brought about a significant change: the proportion of party sympathizers who preferred PRO was 13% in the June–July first wave of the Argentine Panel Election Study (Lupu *et al.* 2015), and grew to 21% in the second wave, conducted immediately after Macri's victory in November. These significant figures (still well under those for the FpV-PJ but above those for the UCR) are probably due to short-term effects of the campaign and the elections. Depending on many factors, they may or may not consolidate into a durable party identity.

There was no specific metric in 1995 to assess dimension three (that "citizens and organized interests perceive parties and elections as legitimate and as means of deciding who governs"). However, an informed analysis of Argentine politics shows that elections have remained in high regard as the only way to achieve high office. On the other hand, polls show that parties have lost popular support, reaching an all-time low around the 2001 crisis, and not recovering after that. According to the AmericasBarometer surveys conducted in 2008, 2010, and 2012, political parties have been consistently the institutions that Argentines trust the least. Moreover, the personalization of politics mentioned in the previous section means that parties are less important than they used to be: voters, donors, and interest groups made political decisions in the 1980s taking parties seriously, but now they are much more likely to think largely in terms of specific leaders.

Dimension four (party organizations must be solid, independent, and valued on their own, not just the instruments of ambitious leaders) implies that political elites are loyal to their parties and that there is party discipline in the legislature (Mainwaring and Scully 1995a: 16). The description of the Argentine party system in the previous section makes it clear that the country has not performed well in this area. If the PJ became more personalistic and more marginal as an organization during the Menem presidencies, these trends only deepened during the following years: the PJ did not even present a unique presidential candidate in the 2003 elections and after that year, it became an irrelevant organization, largely subordinated to the goals of presidents Néstor and Cristina Kirchner. The UCR was in an even worse state of disarray during the years of *kirchnerismo* (2003–15), with legislative leaders opposing the FpV administration, most governors and many mayors supporting it, several UCR officials leaving the party to join or start other parties, and with the remaining ones quite divided on ideological and strategic grounds. Moreover, the two traditional parties have weak central decision-making bodies and bureaucracies; most actual organizational life takes place at the level of the provincial branches of each party. The PJ and the UCR are consensually seen as loose confederations of provincial parties with modest levels of national coordination.

On the other hand, both the UCR and the PJ official legislative delegations command reasonable levels of party discipline in Congress, and are still organizations with their own value, independent of specific leaders. The third parties that have come to prominence in recent times vary from those that are relatively well organized and not fully dependent on the fate of a single politician (the PS and increasingly the PRO) to those that are essentially rubber-stamp organizations created to further the ambitions of its leader.

As the title of this section anticipates, the empirical evidence suggests Argentina's party system eroded over the last twenty years or so but it did not collapse. Argentina seems to have slid into a zone that was empty in *Building Democratic Institutions* (Mainwaring and Scully 1995a): less institutionalized than Mexico and Paraguay in 1995 but more so than Bolivia, Ecuador, Brazil, and Peru. Despite several parallels with the Colombian case, particularly in terms of fragmentation and denationalization (see Albarracín, Gamboa and Mainwaring in Chapter 8 of this volume), one of Argentina's traditional parties (the PJ) remains at the center of electoral and legislative politics in most provinces and at the national level, moderating the deinstitutionalizing tendencies highlighted above. Moreover, the UCR is still the second most important party in legislative and territorial-organizational terms. This is in contrast to Colombia, where both the Conservative and the Liberal parties lost their former dominance to the electoral vehicles that served Álvaro Uribe and Juan Manuel Santos to obtain the presidency, and where no party dominates the sub-national arenas. Argentina's party system, then, has lived in a limbo since the 2001–02 crisis: neither relatively well institutionalized like those of Chile (see Valenzuela, Somma and Scully in Chapter 5 of this volume) and Uruguay, nor collapsed like those of Peru and Venezuela (see Jana Morgan's chapter in this volume, and Seawright 2012).

An additional factor that seems to have prevented a further destructuring of the party system has been the anchoring effect of several small, electorally uncompetitive provinces. If the large districts such as Buenos Aires, Córdoba, or Santa Fe have been dynamic cradles of new parties and venues of intense electoral contestation, many small but strongly over-represented provinces have been impervious to such changes. They have typically been under the rule of a dominant incumbent party (generally the PJ) since 1983, and for the most part the UCR remains the main opposition. The third parties that at times successfully entered politics in the large districts have been absent or weak in provinces such as Catamarca, Formosa, La Rioja, San Luis, Santa Cruz, and Santiago del Estero. These and other districts are "shelters of partisan stability" (Calvo and Escolar 2005), in part because of the pro-majoritarian biases embedded in their small sizes, in part because of electoral reforms implemented by powerful provincial incumbents to benefit themselves (Calvo and Micozzi 2005), and in part – further back in the causal chain – because of the generous federal transfers they enjoy. These transfers have been shown to protect established provincial parties (Benton 2001) and to allow the rulers of these "subnational rentier states" to restrict democratic contestation (Gervasoni 2010). From this point of view, it is not so surprising that three of the key PJ leaders of the period, former presidents Kirchner, Menem, and Rodríguez Saá, had been governors of small and hegemonic provinces before they achieved national prominence.

EXPLAINING INCREASING COMPLEXITY AND DECREASING INSTITUTIONALIZATION

Changes in party systems are relatively common, and they have been more the norm than the exception in the region. Writing before the collapse or decay of several party systems in the region, Coppedge (1998: 550) documented that "[m]ost Latin American party systems are changing, and changing often in several dimensions at once," adding that "party systems as diverse and dynamic as these will not be easily explained" (p. 563), and certainly not explained by slow-moving structural factors such as level of development or ethnic cleavages. That the Argentine party system did not collapse can perhaps be explained by the type of long-term, historical factors emphasized by Kitschelt *et al.* (2010), such as the level of development in the early twentieth century (very high for Argentina), the length of democratic electoral competition after World War II (moderate in Argentina), and the extent to which the urban working class was mobilized in a context of generous social policies and import-substituting industrialization (a very large extent in Argentina). The recent deinstitutionalization trends, on the other hand, are almost certainly the consequence of less structural, more proximate explanatory factors.

The case evidence presented above, the literature on Argentine parties, and the theoretical literature on party systems suggest several explanations of this type. One important consideration is that the three long decades that have passed since 1983 provided the first opportunity for the country's party system to develop since 1930. All the electoral periods between the coup of that year and 1983 were either too short (1958–62; 1963–66; 1973–76) or too undemocratic (1932–43; 1946–55) to allow for the full development of the causal forces that may have been embedded in the system. For example, Argentina showed fragmentation and denationalization tendencies in the 1960s and 1970s that may have well advanced further if military coups had not interrupted democratic politics.

Table 9.2 summarizes a few theoretical approaches, and several explanatory factors derived from them that can plausibly account for the recent decline in PSI. The first approach is theoretically institutionalist. It emphasizes the legal framework that regulates party politics. According to this view – Mustapic

TABLE 9.2 *Plausible Explanations for Argentina's Party System Increasing Complexity and Decreasing Institutionalization*

	Explanations		Outcomes				
Theoretical approach	Explanatory Factor	Specific explanatory variable	Fragmentation	Denationalization	Factionalization	Personalization	Fluidity
Institutionalism	Party legal framework	Lax rules for party creation and maintenance	XX	XX	X	X	XX
		"*Listas colectoras*" and "*espejo*" (until 2009) permit small parties to survive and discourage aggregation	XX	X	X	X	X
		80% of public funding for parties goes to provincial branches		X	X	X	
	Electoral rules	District (provincial) parties are allowed to exist and to compete in national legislative elections	X	XX	X	X	X
		Provinces are districts for the election of national senators and deputies	X	XX			
		Rules allowing different alliances in different districts		X			X
		Majoritarian election of president (post 1994)	X		X	X	X
	Internal party rules	Decentralized structure of UCR and PJ		X	X	X	
	Federalism and decentralization	Political importance of provincial offices (e.g. governorship) and national offices elected in provincial districts (senators and deputies)	X	XX	X	X	

Strategic choices of political leaders	Abrupt changes in party ideology and alliances (PJ and UCR)	Erosion of party brand (in interaction with economic crisis)	X	X	X	X	XX
		Programmatic heterogeneity and inconsistency of parties	X	X	X	X	X
		Little or no programmatic differentiation among main parties	X	X	X	X	X
	Presidential strategy to reshape party system from above	Presidential cooptation of parts of opposition parties (UCR, PS)	X	X	XX	X	X
		Alliance with non PJ local forces (Misiones, Santiago del Estero)	X	X	X		X
		Sponsoring of dissident *kirchnerista* lists against rebellious PJ leaders	XX	XX	X	X	X
		Reshaping of PJ through appointments of cronies	X		XX	XX	
Exogenous shocks	2001–2 crisis	Crisis (in interaction with diluted party brands) contributed to collapse of UCR, thus opening up spaces for third forces	XX	X	X	X	

Note: an X signals a plausible causal connection between an explanatory variable and an outcome. Two Xs indicate a causal effect that is considered strong.
Source: Author's elaboration.

(2013) and Benton (2001) – lax rules and jurisprudence regarding parties and elections, the fact that provinces are the districts in which national legislators are elected, and regulations (including the parties' own internal rules) that make Argentine parties very decentralized all contribute to fragmentation in the sense of creating incentives and opportunities. This approach seems also to help explain the other outcomes analyzed here (denationalization, factionalization, personalization, and fluidity). They can be seen as a natural development of the permissiveness of the relevant rules.

What does the Argentine legal framework permit that is not common in other countries? Among other things, (a) there are modest requirements to create new parties, (b) local (provincial) parties are not only allowed but can compete in elections for national authorities (deputies and senators),[29] (c) parties have great leeway to make different alliances for different levels of government and districts (Clerici and Scherlis 2014), and (d) they can make de facto alliances by presenting the same candidates as other parties for one, some, or all the categories in a given election (the aforementioned *listas colectoras* and the now outlawed *listas espejo*; see Mustapic 2013: 266–72). The autonomy of the provincial branches *vis-à-vis* the national parties is reinforced by public financing rules that assign 80% of funds to the former and 20% to the latter.

A recent institutional change that may account for increasing fragmentation is the presidential electoral system established by the 1994 constitutional reform. Before that year, Argentina had an indirect plurality system, which fostered strategic voting and few candidates. Since 1994, presidents are elected in a majoritarian, two-round system that discourages strategic voting. The resulting increase in electoral fragmentation is transmitted down to legislative contests through coattail effects (Calvo and Escolar 2005: 52). The new system also fostered factionalization and personalization, as both Peronist and Radical politicians have taken advantage of it to run independent candidacies in recent elections.

Federalism is also a plausible explanatory factor, especially when combined with other institutional features such as provincial districts for the election of senators (common in federations) and deputies (uncommon in federations), and with the legality of provincial parties. Such federal structure creates favorable conditions for territorial fragmentation and, therefore, for denationalization (Jones and Mainwaring 2003: 159; Mustapic 2013: 259). In the same vein, federalism provides the basis for territorially defined factions. Many of the competing factions in the PJ and UCR are organized around a governor or other powerful provincial politician. Historically, the key role of autonomous provinces in the formation of the Argentine state and in the writing of its very federal constitution may explain much of the decentralized legal framework emphasized by institutional accounts (for instance, the use of provinces as districts for the election of national legislators dates back to the 1853

---

[29] As of 2014, 12 out of 72 senators (16.7%) belonged to provincial parties.

Constitution). A cousin of federalism, decentralization, has been argued to lead to denationalization (Chhibber and Kollman 2004) and for the Argentine case – a quite decentralized country in fiscal, administrative, and political terms – it has been considered as a facilitating condition for its decreasing nationalization (Leiras 2010).

A second theoretical approach belongs to the "agency-based" family of explanations that emphasize the causal powers of political factors (as opposed to societal or structural factors) and, in particular, "the capacity of the state and of political elites to reshape party systems from above" (Mainwaring 1999: 22). I present two plausible "agency" explanations. The first stresses the causal effects of programmatic inconsistency and diluted party brands (Lupu this volume, 2013, 2014; Roberts 2013; Scherlis 2008). The sharp shifts and inconsistencies in programmatic orientations[30] and pattern of alliances that major parties showed in the 1990s and 2000s made party brands less informative and more difficult to distinguish from other brands. Roberts identifies a critical juncture in the 1980s and 1990s related to the way Latin American parties faced the pressures towards market liberalization, arguing that where established left or populist forces in power adopted the neoliberal agenda, the party system dealigned. Voters became confused about what these parties actually stood for, and the party system left a large open space for the emergence of radical challengers on the left. Voter attachments to established parties weakened and, as a consequence, these were more likely to decline.

Argentina has been an extreme case of this type of ideological inconsistencies and abrupt policy switches. The notorious programmatic vagaries of the PJ over the last three decades and the very ambiguous behavior of the UCR described above should make these parties vulnerable.[31] Unlike the PJ, the UCR had to face two sharp economic crises during this process of brand erosion; it is likely that its strong decline after the mid-1990s was due to the interaction of poor performance in government with an increasingly diluted party brand (Lupu 2014). The PJ's good health in spite of its programmatic volatility could be partly explained by its great adaptive capacity (Levitsky 2003), that is, by "its unique ability to lead the process of market liberalization in the 1990s and then channel societal resistance to it" (Roberts 2013: 1440), and partly explained by the fact that, unlike the UCR, it has been able to navigate its terms in office without major crises.

Sharp ideological changes can impact parties through different pathways. They provide incentives for dissident factions to leave parties. Both the PJ's

---

[30] D'Alessandro (2013) analyzes party platforms for all presidential elections between 1983 and 2011 and shows some significant inconsistencies in terms of (state vs market) economic orientations, both for the PJ and the UCR.

[31] Scherlis (2008) notes that the UCR administrations of Alfonsín and De la Rúa "betrayed" some of their key campaign promises, and links such disregard for the party program directly to the deinstitutionalization of the Argentine party system.

neoconservative turn in the 1990s and its neopopulist turn in the 2000s pushed significant leaders out of the party and into new or existing forces. Weak programmatic brands also make it less costly for a person or faction to switch parties, as this does not imply an obvious ideological inconsistency. Furthermore, because of parties' programmatic inconsistencies, voters have trouble understanding what parties stand for, but they may still trust or distrust certain politicians on the grounds of their charisma, track record, or even ideology. This fosters personalization.

As with federalism, historical legacies are important here too. The main Argentine parties have never been very programmatic. The PJ was born in the mid-1940s as a complex combination of military officers, unions, dissident Radicals, aristocratic provincial elites, and Catholic intellectuals. Its ideological makeup was not less haphazard, mixing elements of nationalism, fascism, laborism, anti-communism, and social Christian doctrine. The UCR was not as ideologically disparate, but its programmatic profile was never very well defined beyond a vague centrist position and commitment to valence values such as clean elections and republican institutions. If stable and clear programmatic cleavages are conducive to institutionalized party systems (Kitschelt *et al.* 2010; Mainwaring and Torcal 2006), the historical ideological diffuseness of the Argentine main parties is likely a cause of the trends described above. The contrast with Brazil is instructive: whereas the opposing stances of the PSDB and the PT with respect to free-market economic reforms likely helped institutionalize the previous inchoate Brazilian party system (Hagopian *et al.* 2009; Mainwaring, Power, and Bizzarro in Chapter 6 of this volume; Roberts 2013), the ideological heterogeneity and inconsistency of the PJ, and the UCR are probably related to the decline of institutionalization in Argentina.

Another causal mechanism through which programmatic vagueness may fuel fragmentation, factionalization, and personalization is related to the type of politicians parties attract. Non-ideological parties that control attractive offices tend to lure careerist politicians (Greene 2007a). When such parties falter, their ambitious office-seeking leaders will be likely to leave them for a more promising one. In contrast, politicians more motivated by ideology will join programmatic parties and will find it harder to leave them. Much of the exodus of UCR leaders described above appears to respond to this factor.

The second agency-based explanation I present is derived empirically from the Argentine case, and stresses the political strategies of leaders, in particular of Néstor Kirchner. From the beginning of his presidency, he coopted leaders and factions of several opposition parties (notably the UCR's *"Radicales K"*) and sponsored dissident FpV lists where the official PJ did not go along with his leadership (Galván 2010). This seems to have been a general strategy, as similar cooptations of parts of political actors (as opposed to the whole actor) also took place among unions, *piqueteros*, human rights organizations, and so forth. Between 2003 and 2015, almost every relevant part of the Argentine political system had a *kirchnerista* faction. By the second half of the 2000s, the main political cleavage in Argentina was not class-, ideology-, or region-based, it was not even Peronism vs anti-peronism. It was kirchnerism vs anti-kirchnerism. Much case evidence indicates that the Kirchners were more than willing to weaken the PJ (and the UCR, and other parties and groups) to achieve their political goals. It seems that they were successful, and that the decline of Argentina's party system was a price paid for the consolidation of their personalistic rule. The phenomenon is not new, as already in 1995 Mainwaring and Scully (1995a) noted that "political leaders for decades intentionally weakened party organizations" in Argentina (p. 16).

This high level of personalization of politics – certainly much higher than in Brazil, Chile, or Uruguay, where "lulismo," "bacheletismo," and "vazquismo" are not relevant political concepts – coupled with the ideological heterogeneity and volatility of the main parties, make the programmatic structuration of the party system almost impossible. Many Argentines cannot place the PJ and the UCR on an ideological scale, and those who can put them both on average at the center, but with a very large variance. Unlike their Chilean counterparts, Argentine voters do not differentiate the main parties on ideological grounds (Calvo and Murillo 2013), even in the context of kirchnerism's intense leftist rhetoric. Argentina, then, tends to confirm the idea that recent populist, personalistic backlashes against market reforms in Latin America have hindered programmatic competition rather than promoted it (Kitschelt *et al.* 2010: 329).

A last explanatory factor which surely contributed to deinstitutionalization was the 2001–02 crisis. The economic, social, and political collapse the country suffered then was unlikely to leave the system, and especially the incumbent parties, untouched. The UCR and the FREPASO (the original members of the *Alianza*) and *Acción por la República* (incorporated into the government in 2001) paid extremely high prices for their incumbent status at such dire times. The two latter parties essentially disappeared, and the former was critically weakened. It is not clear, however, that crises have the "mechanical" effect of destroying whatever party happens to be in power when they hit. The US Republican party survived 1929–30, and the UCR itself weathered the "lost decade" of the 1980s and the 1989 hyperinflationary crisis. The fact that the second blow (2001) hurt the Radicals more than the first might be understood just as an additive effect, but it can also be interpreted as an interactive one: it was the combination of the crisis *and* a diluted party brand that made the UCR decline sharper than in 1989 (Lupu, Chapter 12 this volume). The Argentine evidence is consistent with the hypothesis that parties may be able to endure crises and brand dilution (as the very diluted PJ clearly has), but not both.

CONCLUSION

The post-1993 deinstitutionalizing trends described above are best assessed in comparative perspective. Over the last couple of decades, Argentina has not had the type of stable party system with well-defined players and predictable patterns of competition that has characterized some rich democracies or, in the region, Chile and Uruguay. At the same time, it has stayed clear of the party system collapse experiences of Peru and Venezuela. Of the cases analyzed in this book, Argentina's recent evolution comes closest to that of Colombia, but with a lesser level of decay largely due to the continuous centrality of one of its traditional parties, the PJ. In historical perspective, the system is significantly less institutionalized than that of the 1980s and early 1990s, but probably not too different from the short-lived party systems that existed in between military coups after 1930, or even from the older systems that revolved around the dominant UCR (1916–30) and *Partido Autonomista Nacional* (before 1916). From this perspective, the recent trends described above may just represent a return to normality.

Two and a half "anchors" seem to have prevented Argentina from sliding further into deinstitutionalized party politics. The first one is the persistent strength of the PJ. However inconstant programmatically, this party of careerist politicians dominated the presidency, both legislative chambers, and most of the governorships for most of the past three decades. In fact, the PJ is difficult to distinguish from the government offices it controls. The party leaders are de jure or de facto its highest elected officials. These leaders change, but not so much. Menem was a governor in the 1980s, president in the 1990s, and a (Peronist dissident) senator now. Kirchner was a provincial official and mayor in the 1980s, a governor in the 1990s, and president in the 2000s. The main Peronist presidential candidates in 2015, Daniel Scioli and Sergio Massa, both served in appointed and/or elected positions under Menem, Duhalde, and the Kirchners. Lower down, a dense network of provincial and municipal governments, unions, clientelistic networks, *unidades básicas* and *agrupaciones* provides material resources, connections to traditional lower-class constituencies, and, ultimately, electoral support. Coupled with comparatively decent performance in government and a legendary adaptive capacity, the party founded by Colonel Perón has managed to stay in good health and to provide some stability to the system – at least until its defeat in the 2015 elections, which deprived it of the presidency, the key governorship of Buenos Aires, and of several other significant provincial and municipal governments.

The second anchor has been the quite stable party systems in most small provinces. Even when the main parties lost power at the national level, they were able to remain alive as the ruling or main opposition parties in many provinces and municipalities. The remaining "half" anchor comes precisely from there: even when the UCR has performed very poorly in presidential elections since 2003, it has still been able to keep the executive (or a good chance at it) in several sub-national governments and to elect a significant number of national representatives and senators, especially in small but over-represented provinces such as Catamarca, Chaco, Jujuy, La Pampa, and Santa Cruz.

This partial process of deinstitutionalization bodes ill for democracy. One problem is that "weak institutionalization is inimical to electoral accountability," because to hold parties accountable "voters must be able to identify – in broad terms – what the main parties are and what they stand for" (Mainwaring and Torcal 2006). Consistent with this view, a recent analysis of Argentina's party system highlights "the virtual inability of Argentine voters to hold transient electoral alliances with widely varying names and partisan composition accountable as both reinvent themselves annually while their deputies join delegations in Congress that often bear little resemblance in name or programmatic goals to the electoral alliances supported by voters at the ballot box in congressional elections" (Jones and Micozzi 2013: 72).

A second problem for democracy is related to the "asymmetrical" decay of the UCR *vis-à-vis* the PJ. The combination of a dominant party in government with a fragmented and denationalized opposition has created a very imbalanced political game. During the menemist years, and more clearly under the Kirchners, PJ presidents have tended to abuse their power, partly as a consequence of the difficulties that the many parties in the opposition have had to coordinate a credible electoral threat. The 1997 *Alianza* was an (electorally) successful coordination effort, but one that is harder to achieve under the current, more fragmented, and denationalized conditions. None of the opposition parties individually has a national machine, a significant number of legislators, or a safe enough level of popular support across the country as to represent a significant electoral challenge to the PJ. The opposition parties' state of disarray was certainly in part responsible for the setbacks that liberal democracy suffered under the Kirchners (Gervasoni 2015). Their problems of coordination have been partly due to cross-cutting cleavages: the traditional left–right ideological divide (weak but present in Argentina) was orthogonal to the kirchnerism–antikirchnerism cleavage. Parties that were on the same side on the latter (say the center-right PRO and the center-left PS) were at odds on the former.

It took an alliance of several of these weak non-Peronist parties, and a number of conducive contingent events, for the *Cambiemos* alliance to (barely) defeat the PJ in the 2015 presidential elections. Four years of stagflation, several corruption scandals, the term-limit on the incumbent president, and the choice of a very unpopular candidate for the governorship of Buenos Aires (former Chief of Cabinet Aníbal Fernández) all contributed to a particularly weak showing of the FpV candidate Scioli, who nevertheless won the PASO and first-round elections, and lost the run-off election narrowly. Even after this defeat, the PJ controls, as of 2016, thirteen of the twenty-four provinces, more than half of the senators, and the largest bloc of legislators in the lower house of Congress.

Because of the precedents of "movementist" tendencies in Argentina's history (mainly by Presidents Yrigoyen and Perón), McGuire (1995: 237) was concerned about "erosion from within by an incumbent president." He was thinking about Menem's hegemonic inclinations. Fifteen years later, a new Peronist government had many Argentines worried, again, about "erosion from within." The Kirchners tried and failed to establish themselves as the leaders of a hegemonic movement, but they were closer to the goal than Menem for several reasons, the two most important of which were the commodity boom that provided them with plentiful fiscal resources, and a fragmented, denationalized, factional, and personalistic party system that was hardly effective at producing the checks and balances a liberal democracy critically needs.

10

Deterioration and Polarization of Party Politics in Venezuela

Jana Morgan[1]

For the second half of the twentieth century, party organizations dominated politics in Venezuela. Two main parties, the social democratic Acción Democrática (AD) and Christian democratic COPEI, alternated control of government, shaped policy making, distributed resources, and monopolized state–society relations. Several left parties also maintained small, dedicated followings. Unlike many other countries in the region where low PSI has been a steady feature of politics, the Venezuelan party system was considered highly institutionalized and frequently lauded throughout the 1970s and 1980s (Kornblith and Levine 1995).

However, by the late 1980s AD and COPEI faced fundamental challenges that undermined their ability to link society and the state. As a result, the parties decayed. Over the 1990s, partisan identification with AD and COPEI declined by half, and the parties lost control of the presidency and legislature. In 1998, the two parties did not support their own candidates for president, and left-leaning outsider Hugo Chávez Frías swept to victory. Chávez's ascent signaled the complete collapse of the Venezuelan party system, as the traditional parties lost control of government and the system fundamentally changed its structure from an institutionalized 2.5-party system toward greater fragmentation, personalism, and instability (Morgan 2011; Seawright 2012). These two processes of major party decay and party system transformation together define party system collapse.

With the traditional system's collapse, party politics and the political system more broadly have experienced traumatic and fundamental shifts. Rather than being dominated by two structured, well-established party organizations engaged

[1] I appreciate comments from Michael Coppedge, Gustavo Flores-Macías, Laura Gamboa, Sam Handlin, Steve Levitsky, Scott Mainwaring, Jim McGuire, David Myers, Iñaki Sagarzazu, and Jason Seawright as well as participants at the Kellogg Institute conference on Party Systems in Latin America: Institutionalization, Decay and Collapse. Funding was provided by Fulbright-Hays Doctoral Dissertation Research Abroad fellowship and the University of Tennessee Chancellor's Professional Development Award. Interpretations and any errors are my own. Final revisions were made in spring 2017; any subsequent developments are not reflected here.

in institutionalized patterns of democratic competition, the contemporary system features a multitude of comparatively weak parties. These parties compete in two coalitions, each encapsulating diverse interests unified primarily by support for or opposition to the polarizing project of political and economic transformation advanced by Chávez. The old party system exhibited broad agreement on fundamental rules of the political game together with moderate ideological differences between parties. In contrast, the current context features conflict over foundational issues such as the nature of political competition, the legitimacy of elections, and the value of democracy. Where individual leaders had traditionally faced strong incentives to work within the framework of existing national party organizations, today party organizations have limited influence. Instead, personalism and regionalism are central features of the political landscape. *Chavismo* anchors a highly bifurcated partisan environment that has generated a governance crisis amid intractable economic and security concerns, and the movement has increasingly focused its energies toward consolidating power through any means necessary rather than building effective representative institutions. Despite the pivotal role parties once played, political parties and the system of competition they form are no longer defining facets of politics in polarized, conflict-ridden Venezuela.

This chapter explores these shifts in Venezuelan party politics. I briefly describe the level of institutionalization and nature of state–society linkages under the old party system. Then I explain its collapse, discussing how challenges to the parties' core linkage strategies together with constraints that limited appropriate adaptation produced fundamental failures of representation leading to collapse. I follow by analyzing the contours of contemporary competition that emerged in response to the traditional system's failures, and I discuss the defining facet of Venezuelan politics – the *chavista*–opposition divide in which contestation centers on fundamental differences concerning the rules of the game and control of the state. Then I detail the uneven institutionalization of the current party system. I conclude by discussing potential future trajectories for Venezuelan party politics in a context where violations of liberal democratic norms and procedures have become commonplace and high stakes conflict abounds.

DEVELOPMENT AND CONSOLIDATION OF AN INSTITUTIONALIZED PARTY SYSTEM

When Venezuela transitioned to democracy in 1958, parties were instrumental in establishing the new regime. To limit destabilizing conflict and alleviate the fears of domestic elites and foreign interests, the parties formulated pacts encouraging compromise and cooperation (Levine 1973). The pacted transition empowered the participating parties, including AD and COPEI, solidifying their role as primary intermediaries between state and society

(Martz 1966). Immediately following the transition, multi-party competition characterized the system. But by 1973, a 2.5-party system consolidated, and the effective number of parties (ENP) in legislative elections hovered around three for the next fifteen years.[2] AD and COPEI were the main players, but small left parties regularly won legislative representation as well, with Movimiento al Socialismo (MAS) the most significant third party.

This 2.5-party system manifested a high level of institutionalization and employed multifaceted strategies for linking society and the state. The system's institutionalization has been well documented. Most importantly, inter-party competition was stable with power alternating between two major parties that received consistent vote shares and electoral volatility below the regional average (Roberts and Wibbels 1999). The system also displayed the three major features of embeddedness that promote party system stability: parties with roots in society, legitimacy of parties, and strong party organizations (see Chapter 1, this volume). First, AD and COPEI maintained close and long-standing ties with important social groups and had bases of committed partisans. Second, parties had legitimacy in the eyes of both ordinary citizens and elites. Venezuelans joined parties at unusually high rates (Coppedge 1994), and politicians typically built their careers within existing parties. Third, party organizations manifested high levels of party discipline, routinized internal procedures, and nationwide reach (Kornblith and Levine 1995).

During its heyday, the party system also employed a diverse portfolio of linkage strategies – mechanisms by which parties connect society and the state (Kitschelt 2000; Lawson 1980). In terms of programmatic representation, the system provided policy responses to citizen concerns as well as moderate but distinct ideological options (Karl 1997; Morgan 2011). The system also incorporated the most significant group-based interests in Venezuelan society by maintaining close ties to major functional groups, including business, organized labor, peasants, and middle-class professionals. Offering policies and material benefits that were sectorally targeted, representation in party organizations, and direct participation in policy making, the parties integrated interests corresponding to the traditional class cleavage (Crisp 2000; Martz 1966; Martz and Myers 1994; McCoy 1989), which encapsulated a substantial majority of the population at the system's peak (Morgan 2011). The traditional parties also employed clientelist appeals, primarily to reach those not linked through programmatic representation or incorporation of functional interests.

Thus, while the party system was imperfect, in the 1970s and early 1980s it seemed stable, structured, legitimate, and effectively linked to society. However, over the next decade the system entered a period of crisis, which culminated in major party decay and transformation of the system, first toward

---

[2] ENP provides an estimate of the number of parties competing in a party system, weighting each party according to their share of the vote (or seats). See Laakso and Taagepera (1979) for the formula.

fragmented multi-party competition and now highly polarized contestation featuring two coalitions competing across the *chavista*–opposition divide. Because the old system's weaknesses have structured post-collapse party politics in fundamental ways, understanding the post-collapse system requires explaining why the old system failed, a task to which I now turn.

VENEZUELAN PARTY SYSTEM COLLAPSE

Support for AD and COPEI deteriorated dramatically during the 1990s, and by the end of the decade, the traditional party system ceased to exist. While over 70% of Venezuelans identified with AD and COPEI as late as 1988, affiliation with these parties underwent drastic decay beginning in 1989 and declined to less than 20% by the turn of the century (Morgan 2007). By 1998, the major parties also lost electoral support and governing power, together holding less than 50% of seats in Congress and losing the presidency in two consecutive elections. At the same time, party system dynamics underwent fundamental transformation, with an institutionalized 2.5-party system giving way to a more fluid, polarized multi-party system. This transformation of the established system together with the decay of its major component parties marked the collapse of the once venerated and seemingly stable Venezuelan party system.

Linkage Failure and Party System Collapse

What caused the collapse of this institutionalized party system? The answer lies in the entire system's progressive failure to provide adequate linkage for the majority of Venezuelans. At its peak, the old system appealed to citizens through programmatic representation, interest representation based on incorporating major societal groups, and clientelism. However, beginning in the late 1980s, each of these strategies decayed, leaving many Venezuelans disconnected from the traditional system and in search of alternatives.

Using data from a national survey conducted in 1998,[3] I assess how loss of linkage affected partisan affiliation and electoral support for AD, COPEI, and MAS. Multinomial logit analyses of partisanship, vote choice in the November 1998 congressional elections, and intended vote in the December 1998 presidential election back the argument that Venezuelans without linkage were less likely to support the traditional parties. These analyses provide evidence that the deterioration of programmatic representation, group-based interest representation, and clientelism each played a central role in Venezuelans' decisions to abandon the traditional parties. Table 10.1 details the analysis of respondents' reported partisan identification, comparing supporters of the traditional parties to independents and those backing new parties on the right

---

[3] RedPol98 data collected November 13–28, 1998. Venezuelan survey firm DATOS carried out the nationally representative, face-to-face survey.

TABLE 10.1 *How Linkage Failure Contributed to Party Decay: Multinomial Logit Analysis of Partisanship during Venezuelan Party System Collapse*

	New left	New right	Independents
Programmatic representation			
Negative evaluations of economic policy responsiveness[a]	0.38**	0.22	0.16
	(0.13)	(0.13)	(0.14)
Left ideology[b]	0.33**	0.11**	0.19**
	(0.03)	(0.03)	(0.04)
Interest incorporation			
Outside incorporated groups[c]	0.82**	0.95**	1.37**
	(0.22)	(0.24)	(0.26)
Clientelism			
Clientelist demanding constituency[d]	0.50*	0.16	0.49*
	(0.20)	(0.21)	(0.21)
Constant	2.54**	1.19*	0.27
	(0.52)	(0.55)	(0.60)
N (Model significance)	1500 (0.00)		
Log Likelihood	−1454.49		
Likelihood Ratio (d.f.)	299.6 (30)		
Pseudo R-squared	0.09		

Standard errors in parentheses, $*p \leq 0.05$; $**p \leq 0.01$.
[a]Question: "What do you think about the economic policy of the current government? Would you say that this economic policy has been very good, good, bad or very bad?" Higher values indicate more negative assessments.
[b]Question: "In politics, people talk about 'left' and 'right.' Thinking in general terms, where would you locate yourself on this scale from left to right?" 1 = right; 10 = left.
[c]Question: "Do you belong to a union, guild or professional association?" Non-members coded as being outside traditionally incorporated groups.
[d]Measured by identifying groups of respondents most likely to lack economic certainty and therefore to seek clientelist exchanges. Frustrated clients are thus people who were unemployed or who possessed unskilled or unstable employment, such as street vendors, chauffeurs, taxi drivers, etc.
Note: Data are from the 1998 RedPol survey (RedPol 1998). Question wording for dependent variable: "With which party do you sympathize?" Reference category is respondents affiliated with AD, COPEI, or MAS. New left includes MVR, PPT, and LCR. New right includes Convergencia, Movimiento IRENE, and Proyecto Venezuela. Analysis conducted using the Amelia multiple imputation program (King *et al.* 2001) with the Clarify package in STATA 10. The analysis also included sociotropic and pocketbook economic evaluations, which had no significant effects, as well as controls for class, education, age and sex.

and the left. The analysis includes four independent variables to capture different facets of linkage failure, and all are significantly associated with reduced support for the traditional parties.[4] As the parties converged ideologically on the center-right, those on the left found little programmatic representation among the traditional parties and instead turned to new options, even favoring new parties of the right over the status quo. Likewise, those who rejected the system's performance on economic policy making abandoned the traditional parties, as they failed to offer responsiveness on the country's most pressing concerns. With regard to interest incorporation, those outside traditional functional groups turned toward options outside the system. Lastly, people likely to pursue clientelist forms of linkage and experience unmet demands did not support the old parties. Those who did not find programmatic representation, fell outside of incorporated sectors, or saw clientelist demands go unfulfilled withdrew support and looked elsewhere for representation.

Explaining Linkage Failure

But why did linkage fail? How did a party system with a rich array of established linkage strategies experience devastating incapacity to maintain these ties? System-wide linkage deteriorated because structural challenges, stemming from the exhaustion of the statist economic model and the advent of neoliberalism (Roberts 2014), threatened the system's core linkage strategies and because organizational and resource constraints limited parties' successful adaptation in the face of these challenges (Morgan 2011). Given that different linkage strategies are vulnerable to distinct risks, understanding the dynamics of Venezuelan collapse requires specifying the precise kinds of challenges and constraints that undermined each linkage type and made programmatic representation, interest incorporation, and clientelism broadly ineffective, not just for one party, but across the entire system.

Programmatic Decay

At its peak, the Venezuelan party system provided programmatic representation, both by offering policy responses that addressed salient, widely held concerns and by providing ideological differentiation between parties in the system (Bolívar 2001; Morgan 2011). But in the 1980s, the country entered a period of severe economic crisis characterized by inflation, unemployment, and plummeting and then stagnant oil prices (Karl 1997; OPEC 2003). By the late 1990s, average wages had fallen to one-third their 1982 level (ECLAC 2016) and poverty had more than doubled, surpassing 60% (CISOR 2001). The parties needed to intensify their efforts to resolve these issues, but because the crisis was rooted in exhaustion of the oil-based development model, conventional policy tools were ineffective, making innovation simultaneously necessary and difficult.

---

[4] See Table 10.1 for measurement details. For robustness checks, see Morgan (2011: Chapter 8).

As conditions deteriorated, the parties encountered mounting constraints on policy making imposed by the depletion of foreign reserves, debt crisis, and the international neoliberal consensus. Presidents Carlos Andres Pérez (1989–93) and Rafael Caldera (1994–99) both signed IMF agreements, which restricted policy making to options that were unpopular and at odds with the parties' traditional stances favoring state intervention and social protection.

While both presidents accepted neoliberalism, contradictions between the parties' ideals and neoliberal policies created confusion and inaction for the party organizations (Corrales 2002; interviews conducted by the author).[5] As a result, the parties took few steps to address the deteriorating situation. Although overall policy activity increased in the 1990s, policy responsiveness on the country's most pressing problems declined to half that experienced during the party system's height in the mid-1970s (Morgan 2011: Figures 5.2 and 5.3). Rather than stepping up their efforts to confront the crisis, the parties "had no answer for the people. There was no response to their problems" (author interview with former cabinet minister and presidential candidate). Public opinion surveys clearly indicated rising frustration with this policy unresponsiveness – nearly 90% of Venezuelans held negative evaluations of party efforts to solve the country's problems by the time the system collapsed.[6]

At the same time that valence responsiveness evaporated, the major system parties failed to offer ideological options to voters, eliminating any potential within-system alternative. By the late 1990s, AD and COPEI were ideologically indistinguishable (Morgan 2011; Seawright 2012), and inter-party agreements created the appearance of collusion within the political establishment (Lupu 2014; Morgan 2011). Instead, a neoliberal consensus emerged among the traditional parties. Despite initial resistance among some sectors of AD to the economic reform agenda of their co-partisan President Pérez (Corrales 2002), by the late 1990s the party supported President Caldera in his turn toward the IMF (Interviews). Thus, AD came to occupy the same ideological space as COPEI (Morgan 2011; Seawright 2012),[7] and 70% of Venezuelans saw AD and COPEI as indistinguishable.[8] Moreover, historical patterns of pact-making (Navarro 1995) and intra-party conflict (Coppedge 1994) created incentives for party leaders to form inter-party alliances during the crisis years of the 1990s. By the end of Caldera's presidency, AD, COPEI, and many smaller parties had collaborated in formal or informal cross-party agreements (de los Ángeles 2001).

---

[5] The author interviewed eighty-nine party leaders, politicians, and other experts during May 2001, April–December 2003, and June–July 2006.

[6] Data from Consultores21 quarterly public opinion surveys based on national urban samples of about 1,500 respondents. Question: "How much do you think that political parties are working to resolve the principle problems of the country; a lot, somewhat, a little, not at all?" Over 1994 to 1998, 86–90% of respondents fell into the bottom two categories (Consultores21 various years).

[7] Based on public opinion data from Baloyra 1973, Batoba 1983, and RedPol 1998, which asked Venezuelans to place the parties on the left–right spectrum.

[8] Data from IVAD (1993).

These alliances obscured the parties' ideological positions, creating the perception that no traditional party offered an alternative to neoliberalism (Lupu 2014; Morgan 2011: 116–20). Even parties typically associated with the left, including MAS and *La Causa R*, joined alliances with AD, COPEI, and/or Caldera's *Convergencia* during the five years preceding collapse, minimizing their credibility as meaningful alternatives (Morgan 2011: 118–19). As a result of ideological convergence and apparent collaboration among established parties, dissatisfied voters, particularly those on the left, had to look outside the system to find distinct programmatic appeal. Together the crisis of the economic model, international pressures that conflicted with established policy strategies, and inter-party agreements undermined valence responsiveness and limited programmatic options across the system.

Narrowing Incorporation

The parties had also traditionally maintained strong ties to major functional groups by offering them an array of benefits, including sectorally targeted policies and resources, descriptive representation within party organizations, and privileged influence in policy making. But the utility of these ties deteriorated as society transformed during the 1990s when Venezuela endured economic crisis and neoliberal reform. Incorporated groups, such as public sector employees and unionized workers, shrank, while excluded sectors, including informal and unemployed workers, expanded. The share of the workforce in unions declined by over 50% between the early 1980s and late 1990s, and the public sector shrank by one-third. Meanwhile, the informal and unemployed workers grew to 60% of the labor force (Table 10.2). In fact, Venezuela experienced one of the most dramatic increases in informality across the developing world (ILO 2001). These changes reflected fundamental societal restructuring away from the traditional worker–owner divide and toward a formal–informal one that pitted comparatively privileged formal sectors against growing masses living in economic uncertainty. This restructuring threatened the entire system of incorporation as none of the old parties could easily appeal to the expanding informal sector through established mechanisms of group-based representation, demanding significant adaptation to accommodate these groups through interest incorporation (as opposed to resorting to clientelism).

Two organizational constraints incentivized maintenance of established incorporation strategies and impeded successful adaptation. First, the diffuse structure and heterogeneity of the informal sector (Roberts 2014) did not fit entrenched patterns of incorporation, which were adapted to accommodate hierarchically organized traditional class-based interests (Buxton 1999; Crisp 2000). Second, informal sector interests frequently conflicted with those of incorporated formal sector groups, forcing parties to choose between maintaining established ties and building new ones (Roberts 2003). These organizational features made informal sector integration through group-based

TABLE 10.2 *Transformation of Venezuelan Society between 1980 and 1998*

	Early 1980s	Late 1990s
	Percentage of total labor force	
Traditionally incorporated groups		
Union members	40%	15%
Public sector	22%	16%
Traditionally unincorporated groups		
Informal sector	34%	49%
Unemployed	6%	11%

Sources: Union members: ILO (1987: 11) and ILO (1997); the estimate for the 1980s is conservative, as some sources place unionization as high as 45% (Díaz 2000). Public sector, informal sector, and unemployed: 1980s data for 1980; 1990s data for 1998, both from OCEI, Encuesta de Hogares (IESA 2003).

mechanisms of incorporation challenging and risky, because such incorporation would require innovation and could alienate traditional supporters. Rather than risk losing their base for an uncertain return, the parties and their formal sector allies largely ignored the burgeoning sectors without stable sources of income and instead relied on clientelist exchanges to provide linkage to these groups (Salamanca 1995; author interviews). As one former AD leader explained, the parties had "no tactic to incorporate [the growing informal sector] and never tried to organize or include them" (author interview). In fact, all but one of the former AD, COPEI, and MAS leaders I interviewed were unable to identify a single strategy their party pursued to extend group-based linkage to the informal sector.

As a result, the portion of society integrated through interest incorporation narrowed considerably. The popular sector was left "without an effective voice" (Lander 1996: 67), and marginalized groups bore the brunt of the economic crisis, with the informal sector experiencing poverty at quadruple the rate of formal sector workers (Orlando 2001; Riutort 1999). This marginalization pushed those in excluded groups to abandon the traditional parties at a considerably higher pace than incorporated sectors (Morgan 2011: 145–7). By the mid-1990s, poor Venezuelans were much more critical of party performance than the rich,[9] and the share of public sector workers supporting AD and COPEI was nearly twice that of unemployed or self-employed workers.[10]

---

[9] $p < 0.05$. A statistically significant class divide was not evident in evaluations of other institutions, including Congress, Supreme Court, and military.

[10] $p < 0.01$. Calculation based on nationwide public opinion surveys conducted by DATOS (various years). Measuring informality using surveys from this time period is not feasible, but

Clientelist Exhaustion

Clientelist capacity also deteriorated in the years preceding party system collapse. Traditionally, clientelism linked the poor and otherwise excluded to the state, but as programmatic representation and incorporation decayed, the parties relied increasingly on clientelist exchanges to provide linkage. Clientelism involves delivery of immediate tangible benefits in exchange for political support. As a result, clients typically look for parties to meet some basic need and frequently lack long time horizons. Therefore, clientelism is particularly susceptible to situations in which demands for benefits outstrip supply (Piattoni 2001).

During the 1990s, social changes and political decentralization heightened clientelist demands at the same time as the economic crisis and state reforms constrained the parties' ability to deliver. Venezuela experienced the most dramatic increase in poverty of any Latin American country between the early 1980s and late 1990s (ECLAC 2016), and the once-sizeable middle class lost half its purchasing power (Baptista 1997). Heightened poverty and uncertainty drove more Venezuelans to seek immediate, tangible clientelist exchanges (author interviews; Durán 1998). At the same time, decentralizing reforms established separate sub-national elections, requiring parties to invest more clientelist resources to compete in hundreds of new municipal and regional contests (Lalander 2004; Morgan forthcoming). Moreover, as sub-national elites gained autonomy, they demanded control over resources to support their own ambitions rather than using them to build support for the central party (author interviews; Grindle 2000; Morgan forthcoming; Sabatini 2003).

As clientelist demand expanded, resources dried up. In the face of precipitous drops in state revenue and escalating debt obligations, total government spending per capita declined by 74.7% and overall social spending dropped by 77.0% between 1981 and 1996 (Fernández 2003; Saínz 2005). These reductions in state resources, particularly in social programs frequently used for clientelist distribution, undermined the parties' capacity to furnish benefits (author interviews; Fernandes 2010: 74–9). Moreover, neoliberal reforms and efforts to promote technocratic decision making reduced public sector employment and restricted partisan manipulation of state funds, stripping parties of much-needed resources (author interviews; Baptista 2005; Brando 1990). Given the mismatch between clientelist demand and capacity, the parties' last remaining vestige of linkage was insufficient to shoulder the burden left by deteriorating programmatic representation and group-based incorporation.

Structural challenges to all three linkage strategies together with constraints on appropriate adaptation produced significant decay in the system's linkage capacity. As a result, Venezuelans' commitment to the political establishment frayed, and many who lacked linkage looked elsewhere for representation, producing party system collapse. Similar patterns of linkage decay caused by

the great majority of Venezuelan informal sector workers are self-employed, making self-employment a reasonable proxy for informality.

fundamental structural changes and constraints on adaptation also explain party system decay in places as diverse as Italy, Bolivia, and Colombia (Morgan 2011: 205–40).

Some explanations of party system collapse in Venezuela and elsewhere argue that frustration with corruption was instrumental in causing collapse (for example, Seawright 2012). In Venezuela, however, the popular attitude toward corruption was "soft and tolerant" until the economic crisis became acute and linkage deteriorated (Romero 1997: 19). In the absence of benefits from the state, more and more people became critical of clientelism as serving the interests of a select few. As a former AD leader explained, "there came a time when resources were not sufficient, and the party could not satisfy demands, but the people thought the money just stayed at the top in the hands of the politicians" (author interview). Because the parties did not fulfill linkage expectations, frustration grew, and accusations of corruption, real and imagined, mounted. Public opinion surveys confirm the view that significant frustration with corruption emerged only after linkage decay was well underway. In surveys conducted from the 1970s through the 1990s, Venezuelans identified the most important problem confronting the country, and corruption did not emerge as a top issue in these surveys until the onset of economic crisis and linkage decay in the 1990s. In a 1994 survey conducted by *Consultores21*, a majority of Venezuelans evaluated President Caldera's anti-corruption efforts positively, but by 1997, 87% thought he was failing to combat corruption. Escalating perceptions of corruption were a symptom not a cause of linkage decay, intensifying the implications of representational failures for the party system (Consultores21 various years).

Other accounts have focused on the significance of economic dependence on oil (Karl 1997) and rigid organizations (Burgess and Levitsky 2003; Coppedge 1994) in understanding Venezuelan party dynamics. My account here views these factors as relevant indirectly via their effects on the system's capacity to maintain linkage. The fluctuations of Venezuela's oil-based economy created important challenges for programmatic representation and clientelist linkages, while organizational inflexibility limited the parties' capacity to incorporate the interests of rapidly growing, but traditionally excluded social groups. However, the core cause of collapse was linkage decay, which weakened Venezuelans' commitment to existing parties and motivated them to abandon the system.

POST-COLLAPSE PARTY POLITICS: POLARIZATION AND PERSONALISM

The implications of party system collapse for the nature of inter-party competition and for politics more broadly have been profound. Conflict, volatility, and uncertainty characterized Venezuelan party politics following collapse. At the old system's zenith, parties effectively managed diverse interests, but as linkage deteriorated, conflict increased. After collapse, Venezuela lacked organizations

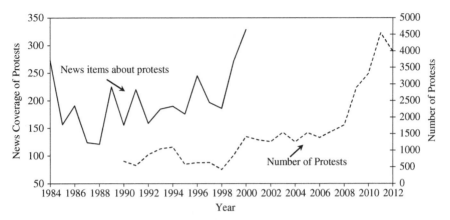

FIGURE 10.1 Protest Activity in Venezuela, 1984–2012
Note: Each year corresponds to October of the preceding year through September of the year indicated. In other words, the number of protests reported here for 1999 corresponds to the period October 1998 through September 1999.
Source: Protests from *Situación de los derechos humanos* (PROVEA, various years). News items from El Bravo Pueblo Database (López Maya and Lander 2005: 95).

able to channel disputes effectively, and contentious conflict became commonplace. As displayed in Figure 10.1, protest activity escalated following collapse and then plateaued before surging again in 2009. Political contestation no longer focused on ordinary policy differences debated within established institutions, and instead turned toward absolutist goals pursued through extraordinary strategies. For instance, Hugo Chávez and his allies rewrote the constitution in 1999, restructuring many institutions, and the opposition (unsuccessfully) sought to unseat Chávez through drastic methods, including the 2002 coup, 2002–03 general strike, and 2004 recall referendum. Heightened conflict and adversarial interactions continue to characterize Venezuelan politics more than fifteen years after party system collapse, as new waves of protest and repression frequently erupt.

Collapse also heightened party system fragmentation and volatility. At its peak, the traditional system consistently featured about 2.5 effective presidential parties and three legislative parties. By the 1990s, the effective number of parties ballooned to more than five and remained elevated for over a decade. Electoral instability also spiked in 1998, as presidential volatility approached 75 (on a 100-point scale) and legislative volatility surpassed 40.[11] Volatility stayed high through the mid-2000s, with levels far exceeding the pre-collapse average of 20 (see Figures 10.2 and 10.3 below). However, by 2010 the parties coalesced into

[11] Volatility is the sum of the absolute values of the change in seat shares won by each party from one election to the next, divided by two (Pedersen 1983).

two coalitions, with one alliance on each side of the pro/anti-Chávez divide. The effective number of electoral coalitions (rather than parties) in the most recent presidential and legislative elections was 2.4 and 2.2, respectively. Thus, while conflict continues to achieve new extremes in both level and intensity, the struggle occurs between two poles that maintain steady support.

Major Competitors in the Post-Collapse System

Chavistas

While the nature of the post-collapse system has fluctuated over time, one component has remained constant – *chavismo*. Hugo Chávez Frías and his *Movimiento Quinta República* (MVR) emerged in 1998 as the primary alternative to the failed party system. Much of Chávez's initial success can be attributed to his ability to attract support from those who saw their ties to the traditional parties deteriorate in the decade preceding collapse. In effect, Chávez offered linkage in areas where the old parties had failed (Morgan 2011).

As the old parties did not resolve pressing economic and social ills, including cost of living, unemployment, crime, and corruption, Chávez pledged to address these very issues. His commitments resonated with voters critical of the traditional parties' performance (Morgan 2007). Once in power, Chávez endeavored to follow through on his commitments, and in his first five years in office, legislation focusing the positions citizens identified as their most important concerns increased four-fold relative to during the final decade of the old system (Morgan 2011).

Moreover, while the old system converged ideologically and in the end failed to offer meaningful alternatives to a center-right consensus, Chávez presented a viable option on the left. This position gave him an edge over his main opponent in 1998, Henrique Salas Romer of the right-leaning *Proyecto Venezuela*. In the 1998 RedPol survey conducted immediately preceding Chávez's victory, respondents gave MVR an average score of 3.78 on a 10-point ideology scale where 1 indicates left and 10 right (RedPol 1998). This score placed MVR significantly to the left of AD, COPEI, and *Proyecto Venezuela*, which averaged statistically indistinguishable scores of 6.47, 6.51, and 6.62, respectively. Chávez's ideological positioning appealed to those on the left frustrated with the evaporation of programmatic options from the party system, and 76% of people with left ideologies voted for Chávez in 1998 (Molina 2002).

Chavismo, now under the banner of MVR's successor the *Partido Socialista Unido de Venezuela* (PSUV – United Socialist Party of Venezuela), continues to stake out a position on the left. In the 2012 AmericasBarometer survey,[12] PSUV

---

[12] Survey conducted by the Latin American Public Opinion Project (LAPOP). Nationwide samples are gathered through face-to-face interviews in the respondent's preferred language. I am

identifiers averaged a score of 3.55 on the 10-point ideology scale (LAPOP 2012). Likewise, in the Democracy and Accountability Project's (DALP) expert survey, PSUV scored an average of 3.42 on the same 10-point scale (Altman n.d.).[13] The presence of a significant left marks a major shift in the structure of Venezuelan party competition.

Substantively, although the ideology and composition of *chavismo* reflect varied influences, it has a clear statist orientation opposing the neoliberalism that ultimately dominated policy making in the old system (Corrales 2010). Initially, the party's ideals seemed quite reminiscent of the state-led model of growth advanced by AD during the oil boom years. But as Chávez fought off adversaries, consolidated power, and then announced a shift toward "twenty-first century socialism" in January 2005, leftist tendencies in MVR and later PSUV intensified (López Maya 2011). Since Chávez's death in March 2013, Chávez's successor Nicolás Maduro has not reversed this tendency.

In addition to filling the opening available on the ideological left, Chávez built support appealing to those increasingly marginalized by the old system's incorporation strategies. As the class cleavage restructured around the formal–informal divide and the traditional parties failed to maintain linkage with the growing numbers of Venezuelans falling into poverty and informality, Chávez and MVR catered to these groups. MVR leaders saw how the old parties' inability to adapt their linkage strategies and integrate these groups gave Chávez an opening and provided critical support (author interviews). Public opinion surveys corroborate that the poor and informal sectors are core *chavista* constituencies. As Chávez rose to power, poor Venezuelans were consistently more enthusiastic than the wealthy (Canache 2002; Molina 2002). Although Chávez enjoyed support from wide swaths of society when he was first elected in 1998, including segments of the upper-middle-class and even some business elites, he captured the votes of the poor and lower-middle sectors by the widest margins (Hellinger 2003). Moreover, when Chávez faced challenges from a coup attempt in 2002, an extended general strike in 2002–03, and a recall referendum in 2004, the poor and informal sector provided an important reservoir of support preserving Chávez's tenure (author interviews; Ciccariello-Maher 2013: 166–79; López *et al.* 2007; McGuire 2014).

Those marginalized due to the old system's inflexible incorporation strategies continue to form an integral part of the *chavista* base (García-Guadilla 2005; Valencia Ramírez 2005: 95). In the 2012 AmericasBarometer survey, Venezuelans who identified with PSUV had levels of household wealth and income significantly lower than those of opposition identifiers (LAPOP

grateful to LAPOP and its major supporters (United States Agency for International Development, United Nations Development Program, Inter-American Development Bank, and Vanderbilt University) for making the data available.
[13] Venezuela expert data were gathered between May 2007 and December 2008.

2012). PSUV supporters also had darker skin and fewer years of education than opposition supporters. In a recent region-wide analysis of class voting, Venezuelans outside traditionally incorporated groups clearly favored the *chavista* option, and the country manifested one of the widest income gaps in Latin American voting behavior, with poor Venezuelans more likely by 42 percentage points than the rich to support Chávez in 2006 (Mainwaring *et al.* 2015).

The geographical distribution of votes provides additional evidence concerning the class divide in Venezuelan politics. Chávez, and now Maduro, have consistently won by wide margins in poor neighborhoods and regions, while the opposition has fared better in wealthy areas (CNE 2013; López *et al.* 2007: 283–84). For instance, in the 2013 presidential election, Maduro received 50.6% of the vote nationally, but in Portuguesa, one of the poorest states, his vote share was 65.4%. Alternatively, in the wealthy oil state of Zulia, he won only 47.7% of the vote (CNE 2013). This pattern of disproportionate support persists if we compare poor and wealthy neighborhoods within urban centers (García-Guadilla 2005). In Caracas' 23 *de Enero* parish, one of Latin America's oldest housing projects, 62.5% of voters supported Maduro, while his vote share in wealthy Chacao was just 17% (CNE 2013). Likewise, in the 2015 legislative elections PSUV and its allies garnered only 40.9% of the vote nationwide, but won comfortable majorities in poor states such as Portuguesa (53.7%) and Delta Amacuro (58.6%). Of course, the poor, informal sector, and victims of racial/ethnic discrimination are not the only elements of the PSUV base; the party has also received electoral support from small but vibrant elements of the traditional working and middle classes (Cyr 2013; Ellner 2013) and from new economic elites who have benefited from affiliation with the government. But the distinctive and by far the largest component of the party's base comes from those who bore the brunt of the economic crisis and fell into poverty and informality, placing them outside groups traditionally incorporated by the old system.

Chavismo carefully cultivated support from the previously marginalized through social policies aimed at historically excluded groups (Fernandes 2010: 82–86). For instance, the extensive set of programs developed under the general label *Misiones* targeted the poor through benefits such as job training, health care, literacy programs, and affordable foodstuffs (Penfold-Becerra 2007). These programs often do not involve overt conditional exchanges and are therefore not explicitly clientelist in nature (Handlin 2013; Hawkins 2010). However, when oil revenues were high there was a significant expansion of discretionary spending channeled toward these programs (Corrales 2010: 36), which were designed to target likely supporters, prioritizing the impact on elections over social outcomes (Hawkins 2010; McGuire 2014: 13–14; Penfold-Becerra 2007).[14] Linkage for those ignored by the entrenched

---

[14] This pattern is similar to the traditional parties targeting spending toward core constituencies in organized labor, peasant, professional, and business associations.

political elite together with *chavismo's* left ideology provided a major
alternative to the old system, which not only enabled Chávez's rise to power
but have also helped sustain the movement even after his death.

In addition to these programmatic and group-based appeals capitalizing on
linkage gaps left by the old system, Chávez built a personal following, employing
his populist discourse, charisma, and his position as a political outsider. His
powerful persona drew many to support *chavismo*, and his approach
fundamentally altered the content and structure of political contestation in
Venezuela, although these tactics made the party and the entire movement
dependent upon his influence and shaped by his whims (López Maya 2011;
Pereira Almao 2004). His populist discourse promised to disrupt established
patterns of competition, upend the policy status quo, and advance popular will –
claims appealing to voters frustrated with the representational failures of the
ossified party system (Hawkins 2010). Once in power, *chavista* policy making
followed a populist logic, designed to circumvent established structures and build
support for the movement and especially its leader (Hawkins 2010).

Thus, *chavismo* possesses a complex and effective linkage portfolio based on
the charismatic legacy of its founder as well as substantive appeals that facilitated
a strong base of core supporters and prolonged control of the state. *Chavismo's*
linkage effectiveness is apparent in the strength and magnitude of support for the
movement. At its peak, the PSUV boasted more than 7 million members, which
represents nearly a quarter of the Venezuelan population (Kutiyski and Krouwel
2014). While this estimate likely overstates the number of truly committed party
activists, it represents a notable degree of partisan identification, particularly in a
region and country that have experienced so much party decay in recent decades.
Public opinion data support the conclusion that the party attracts considerable
amounts of support in comparison to other parties in Venezuela and across Latin
America. In the 2012 AmericasBarometer, nearly 10 times as many Venezuelans –
27.4% of the sample – identified with PSUV than with any other party (LAPOP
2012).[15] From an historical perspective, this ranks the PSUV around the same
level of support AD enjoyed when the traditional 2.5-party system was
consolidating in the early 1970s and consistently above rates of identification
with COPEI throughout the peak years of the system. Within Latin America, only
three parties found greater levels of partisan support than the PSUV in 2012
(FSLN in Nicaragua, *Frente Amplio* in Uruguay, and the PLD in the Dominican
Republic).[16]

Even after Chávez's death, as oil prices plummeted and the economy
unraveled, 19.3% of Venezuelan respondents in the 2014 AmericasBarometer
identified with the PSUV, which still placed the party among the top ten in the
region (LAPOP 2014). In comparison, the opposition party with the largest

---

[15] Identification with all *chavista* parties was 29.2%. *Primero Justicia* was second, with just 3.1%
of the sample, and all opposition partisans combined constituted 8.9% of respondents.
[16] I am grateful to Sam Handlin for this observation.

partisan base was *Primero Justicia* at 2.7%, and the MUD alliance and all its constituent parties attracted 18.2% of Venezuelans.[17] These data suggest that the PSUV has retained a significant core base even while inflation has escalated beyond control, shortages are commonplace, and Venezuela's social and political fabric frays.

However, party organizational development lags behind the strength of the *chavista* linkage and identity, despite recent efforts to build up the movement in this regard. Chávez did not initially invest in developing or institutionalizing a party (Hawkins 2003) and instead utilized various organizational vehicles. The PSUV's origins are in the *Movimiento Bolivariano Revolucionario 200* (MBR 200), a group within the military established in 1983 by several junior officers, including Chávez who was the most influential and charismatic. The organization grew gradually and built ties to civilian allies on the left, eventually attempting a coup against Carlos Andrés Pérez in February 1992. While this effort was unsuccessful, it formed the foundation for Chávez's eventual ascendance and provided him a platform to criticize the establishment. When Chávez decided to enter the electoral arena, the MVR[18] was founded as a political party to launch his 1998 candidacy (Hawkins 2010: 16–18; López Maya 2011: 214–16; Pereira Almao 2004). Given its origins as an electoral vehicle, the MVR never overcame its "electoral and personalist logic" (López Maya 2011: 217). The party remained weak and Chávez retained decisive influence over the organization (Hellinger 2005). This centralization and personalization of power helped control internal conflict and suited the movement's populist orientation, which relies heavily on direct ties between leader and supporters (López Maya 2011; Hawkins 2010). Chávez's candidacies in 1998, 2000, and 2006 were also supported by an array of left parties under the *Polo Patriótico* alliance, which included *Patria Para Todos* (PPT), *Partido Comunista de Venezuela* (PCV), *Movimiento Electoral del Pueblo*, and even MAS (Pereira Almao 2004).[19]

To counter the institutional weaknesses of MVR and the scattered nature of the movement, Chávez announced the creation of a new political party, PSUV, in December 2006 (Handlin 2013). This new organization was intended to replace MVR and subsume the diverse array of parties that supported the government (Hawkins 2010: 24). While many small parties dissolved and joined PSUV, several of the most important coalition partners, including PCV and PPT, chose to retain separate identities, initially drawing Chávez's ire before being welcomed back into the alliance (Álvarez 2007; López Maya 2011). Although the PSUV has made efforts to strengthen its organizational

[17] Excluding those identifying with the generic MUD alliance, only 6.7% of Venezuelans identified with an opposition party in 2014.
[18] Election law prohibits use of national symbols in party names, necessitating the change from MBR to MVR, which in Spanish are pronounced identically.
[19] Following the 2000 election, MAS joined the opposition, although a remnant calling itself PODEMOS remained with Chávez until 2007. PPT also left *chavismo* briefly in 2001, returned in 2002, and remained until a 2012 split when one faction left.

structure, the routinization of party operations remains low, and formal rules and procedures often lack sway in the face of internal power struggles between influential personalities.

Additionally, the heterogeneity of the *chavista* movement imposes significant challenges to strengthening the PSUV, which must compete with *chavista* organizations outside the party (for example, Bolivarian circles, 2001–04; *Comando Maisanta*, 2003–04; community councils, 2006–10) (Ellner 2013; Hawkins 2010; Pereira Almao 2004). Grassroots organizations, such as community radio stations and local cooperatives, also operate independently of the party and often pursue different goals (Fernandes 2010). These extra-party alternatives, both those originating from grassroots efforts and those initiated by *chavista* elites, lend vitality and complexity to the movement and facilitate mobilization (Handlin 2016). However, because the party often exists in tension not harmony with these groups, such groups have not enabled the organization to develop deep roots in society (Hawkins 2010; Pereira Almao 2004).

The PSUV also suffers from internal divisions. One major divide pits the militarist branch, which primarily emphasizes nationalism, against civilian leftists, who are more ideologically motivated (Pereira Almao 2004). Another fissure, which partially cuts across the first, sets movement hardliners against moderates favoring dialogue with the opposition. While alive, Chávez used his personal power to bridge these divides, a strategy that minimized outright conflict but also enervated party-building efforts. Since Chávez's death, the party has weathered these latent conflicts despite the absence of his powerful persona, due in large part to electoral incentives and the threat posed by the anti-Chávez opposition. But, in the long term, power struggles within the movement pose challenges for the party.

The Opposition

Since party system collapse, politics has polarized around the persona and now the legacy of Chávez, and the country is sharply divided between supporters and opponents of the *chavista* goal of transforming Venezuelan economic, social, and political power structures. People left outside the established hierarchy for whom traditional party linkages failed have tended to support the MVR/PSUV or one of the smaller parties in the *Polo Patriótico*. Alternatively, the broad coalition comprising the anti-*chavismo* opposition draws support from those who reject *chavismo's* perceived hegemony and fear its efforts to upend conventional power structures and liberal democratic norms (Valencia Ramírez 2005). Rejection of *chavismo* is the opposition's most important feature and its unifying force.

Significant diversity coexists within the opposition. The mélange includes all the surviving parties from the pre-collapse system, including AD, COPEI and MAS, as well as many newcomers. The parties span a wide ideological space, ranging from *Bandera Roja* on the left, *Un Nuevo Tiempo* near the center, and *Proyecto Venezuela* on the right. Individual opposition parties have niches in particular regions of the country or among certain types of supporters. For instance, COPEI is influential in Táchira state, *La Causa R* (LCR) in Amazonas, and *Proyecto Venezuela* in Carabobo (Sagarzazu 2011), and while *Primero Justicia* draws much of its support from middle-class professionals (Pérez Baralt 2004), LCR tends to represent sectors of the organized working class. However, no opposition party is particularly effective at appealing to the poor or informal sector, and the opposition fares better in urban areas than rural ones (Corrales 2010). Overall, the opposition is best understood not by who or what it stands for, but by what it stands against.

Despite the shared objective of defeating *chavismo*, the opposition has experienced persistent infighting regarding time horizons and strategies for achieving this goal. A radical faction favors immediate results and advocates more dramatic, often extra-institutional tactics. The moderate wing has shown more patience, is typically amenable to dialogue, and is more willing to operate within regime-established rules. In the years immediately following Chávez's ascendance, the radical faction had the upper hand in setting the opposition's agenda (Gamboa 2017). During this period, elements of the opposition staged a coup in April 2002, participated in a general strike that shut down much of the economy from December 2002 through February 2003, organized more than 150 protest marches from 2001 to 2003, petitioned for a referendum to recall Chávez, dismissed the referendum's results as fraudulent, and boycotted the 2005 legislative elections (Álvarez 2007; García-Guadilla 2005; Hsieh *et al.* 2009: 3–4; López Maya and Lander 2007: 5–6). However, following the failed recall referendum and the strategic miscalculation of boycotting the 2005 elections, which left the opposition without any legislative representation, many began to reconsider these tactics. As a result, power shifted toward moderate opposition voices, who advocated dialogue with *chavismo*, participating in elections and accepting the outcomes as legitimate (Cyr 2012; López Maya and Lander 2007). With the opposition's unsuccessful efforts to win a majority of the national vote in presidential and sub-national elections held after Chávez's death, frustrated radicals began to take independent actions that contradicted the mainstream opposition's more conciliatory tone and undermined dialogue with the government.

Most recently, anti-*chavistas* have employed a two-pronged strategy, by pursuing influence through elections and by seeking to destabilize the regime through protests and other efforts to force President Maduro's recall or resignation. Thus far, the electoral strategy has yielded the most tangible results, producing a decisive electoral victory for the opposition in the December 2015 legislative election, which gave them control of the National Assembly. However, as *chavismo* has blocked institutional channels for legislative influence and has effectively dissolved the opposition-controlled National Assembly, the government's position has appeared increasingly precarious amid escalating insecurity and economic uncertainty. As a result, the protest/recall route has gained many adherents among opposition leadership and the rank-and-file. Thus, at the same time many opposition leaders continue to call for elections as the appropriate exit from the mounting political and economic crisis, they have also gone to the streets, joining new waves of protest against the regime.

In light of the opposition's incongruous composition and often contradictory strategies, coordination has been difficult, leading to indecision, vague positions, and internal discord. To confront these challenges, the opposition has engaged in two major collaboration efforts since Chávez's rise to power. The first, *Coordinadora Democrática* (CD – Democratic Coordinator), was founded in 2001 and brought together more than two dozen parties as well as representatives from private media, business, organized labor, dismissed oil professionals, and other anti-Chávez elements (García-Guadilla 2005; López Maya and Lander 2007). The group played a major role in efforts to remove Chávez, including the 2002–03 general strike and the 2004 recall. However, the CD lacked influence apart from its components, and its organizational structure, which gave more influence to individual leaders and non-party actors than to parties, was unable to bridge internal divisions (Cyr 2012; López Maya and Lander 2007). Following the failed recall referendum, the CD disbanded, and there was little coordination of opposition efforts until the *Mesa de la Unidad* (MUD) was formed in 2008. MUD, while still quite expansive, includes only parties and has established clearer procedures concerning internal decision making (Cyr 2012: 109). The organization has been particularly successful at synchronizing electoral strategies among parties, including organizing primaries to select the opposition candidate for the 2012 presidential election and coordinating candidate selection for sub-national offices and single-member district seats in the National Assembly. These efforts have helped prevent the opposition from dividing its votes among multiple candidates, but electoral coordination has not resolved other conflicts over ideology, policy, and strategies. As a result, the opposition has yet to offer a clear alternative to the *chavista* project, relying instead on vague campaigns calling for the end to the *chavista* monopoly on power. Thus, most of the support garnered by the opposition stems primarily from mounting frustration with the government's failure to address escalating inflation, scarcity, and insecurity as opposed to the opposition's own policy offerings (Cyr 2013; López Maya and Lander 2007).

Within the opposition, the two most important party organizations are *Acción Democrática* and *Primero Justicia* (PJ – Justice First).[20] Although AD has been eviscerated electorally and organizationally, it retains nationwide reach, which contrasts with PJ as well as UNT, which find their support concentrated around Caracas and in the Zulia region, respectively (Cyr 2012; Sagarzazu 2011). Based on Sagarzazu's (2011: 132–33) calculations of party nationalization, AD is the

[20] Voluntad Popular, the party of imprisoned opposition politician Leopoldo López, has an important presence in opposition (social) media and protest activities, but has not yet demonstrated significant capacity as a party organization.

opposition party with the broadest national range, and AD offers the opposition its most effective electoral machine, giving it an important role during campaigns and influence within MUD (Cyr 2012). This capacity has helped AD demand placement on MUD electoral lists and allowed its leader, Henry Ramos Allup, to ascend to the presidency of the National Assembly in 2016.

However, AD has not engaged in much renewal since the party system collapsed; in fact, many of the same figures (including Ramos Allup) have controlled its apparatus since 2000. As a result, AD lacks leaders with national appeal and has been unable to put forth serious contenders for the opposition's presidential nomination (Cyr 2013). Ideologically, AD is located in much the same position as it was at the time of collapse, significantly right of PSUV but slightly left of the other major opposition party, Primero Justicia.[21] The party's base is aging, but the party retains strong ties to Venezuela's original peak union organization, *Confederación de Trabajadores de Venezuela* (CTV – Venezuelan Worker's Confederation), giving it a modicum of influence among organized workers despite some government successes in strengthening alternative *chavista* unions (Iranzo and Richter 2006).

Primero Justicia is the most influential new opposition party. While it has been more successful than most at attaining national reach and a clear identity, it lags behind AD in this regard (Álvarez 2007: 16; López Maya and Meléndez 2007; Sagarzazu 2011). PJ originated in 1992 as a civil society organization established by young, middle-class professionals, many with ties to COPEI (Pérez Baralt 2004; Sagarzazu 2011). The organization became a party in 2000 to compete in the state of Miranda, where its most important support base remains, and became a national party in 2002. PJ – the party of Henrique Capriles, the opposition's presidential nominee in 2012 and 2013 – has been ascendant within the opposition, and the party controlled the presidency of the National Assembly up until the 2017 Constituent Assembly elections, which displaced the National Assembly.[22] However, while the party has made recent organizational gains (Cyr 2012), it remains institutionally weak. Decision making is centralized in the hands of a few leaders, and the party relies on the media as much as grassroots campaigning to connect to voters (López Maya and Meléndez 2007; Pérez Baralt 2004).

PJ falls on the right ideologically, a position fitting its origins in COPEI (Álvarez 2007; Cyr 2012). The party espouses values of justice, liberty, and participation, but with little clear programmatic content. And while PJ leaders see themselves as promoting social justice, the party's base, which has been concentrated among the educated, urban, upper-middle class, suggests that this message carries little credibility among the poor (Pérez Baralt 2004). In the

---

[21] The small number of AmericasBarometer respondents identifying with AD in the most recent surveys makes using the ideological self-placement of partisans as a proxy for party ideology somewhat unreliable. Grouping together all AD supporters from 2008–12 suggests AD is right-of-center but left of PJ (LAPOP 2014).

[22] The position was/is occupied by Julio Borges, one of PJ's founders.

2012 AmericasBarometer survey, respondents who identified with the PJ averaged twelve years of schooling, significantly higher than the national average, and the modal PJ supporter fell into the highest quintile on the measure of household wealth (LAPOP 2012). As with much of the opposition, PJ's vision of society and politics can be defined in primarily negative terms – as opposition to *chavismo* without a clear alternative policy model (Pérez Baralt 2004: 266).

Beyond AD and PJ, the opposition is composed of numerous smaller parties with mainly regional or personalist bases, with COPEI, UNT, *Proyecto Venezuela*, and *Voluntad Popular* (Popular Will) among the most significant. COPEI leaders remain important actors within MUD even while the party itself is significantly debilitated (Cyr 2012: 117–18). UNT was founded by former AD leader Manuel Rosales to support his bid for governor of Zulia in 2000. Although Rosales was the opposition candidate for president in 2006 and other prominent opposition figures have since joined the party, UNT remains a regional party with personalist tendencies (Sagarzazu 2011; UNT 2014). Proyecto Venezuela, the electoral vehicle established by former COPEI member Henrique Salas Romer to support his 1998 presidential run, has lost significant ground since that time and is now largely confined almost to his home state of Carabobo. Voluntad Popular, which formed in a break with Primero Justicia, has staked out a more hard line position than other opposition parties, and its principle leader Leopoldo López is currently serving a sentence for fomenting anti-government protests in 2014.

Contestation in the Post-Collapse Party System

As the preceding discussion suggests, the primary axis of competition in post-collapse Venezuela is the *chavista*-opposition divide (Cyr 2013; García-Guadilla 2005; Hawkins 2010). But while this division is easily summarized with reference to Chávez's polarizing legacy, competition is not purely personalist in nature. There is substantive content to the intense conflict. However, the most important substantive divides are not the standard programmatic differences concerning economic and social policy or the role of the state. Of course, there are some differences between government and opposition on these issues. *Chavistas* generally favor more state intervention, with certain elements even advocating a socialist economic transformation; the opposition is generally more favorable toward market-based economic prescriptions. However, the opposition's ideological diversity makes pinpointing its policy positions difficult. Thus while *chavistas* are more toward the left and the opposition more toward the right, the extreme polarization in the Venezuelan party system cannot be attributed solely to differences concerning ordinary economic and social issues.[23]

[23] Comparing attitudes on these issues across opposition and MVR/PSUV identifiers supports this conclusion. The 2012 AmericasBarometer asked respondents five questions concerning various

Rather the most salient facets of Venezuelan polarization pertain to fundamental contestation over rules of the game and over who has the power to control the state. Core questions on which the government and opposition have deep disagreements include: (1) the importance of formal, procedural democracy versus substantive democratic values such as social equality, and (2) the priority of civil rights and liberties versus the tangible interests of the majority (Hawkins 2010). In survey data, these kinds of issues consistently and significantly divide MVR/PSUV partisans and opposition supporters (LAPOP 2012). Those who identified with one of the opposition parties were significantly more likely to support values traditionally associated with liberal, representative democracy, including political tolerance, respect for civil rights and liberties, accepting the need for parties in democracy, and agreement that democracy is the best form of government. Alternatively, MVR/PSUV supporters were more willing to accept violations of liberal democratic norms and focused instead on the goal of assuring that substantive political outcomes benefit the people. For instance, *chavistas* were more supportive of direct rule by the people without elected representatives, more concerned about violations of the majority's interests, and more accepting of alternatives to electoral democracy. It is important to emphasize that these views are likely shaped by each side's relative position within the current political landscape. *Chavismo* holds the power, and its supporters are therefore less nervous about potential violations of democratic norms, which would likely impose few tangible costs and might be to their benefit. Conversely, the opposition does not control the levers of the state and is consequently interested in protecting democratic procedures to defend their rights as regime opponents. Whether this alignment of democratic attitudes between *chavistas* and anti-*chavistas* would persist if the opposition came to control the state is difficult to judge.

Data from the DALP expert survey provide additional evidence concerning the significance of this divide between opposition support for democratic *procedures* and *chavismo*'s concern with substantive *outcomes* (Altman n.d.). Experts were asked to place the parties on a 10-point scale ranging from "instrumental valuing of democracy for its substantive achievements" (1) to "valuing democracy independent of its substantive achievements" (10). MVR's placement averaged 2.33 on this scale, while UNT averaged 8.33 and PJ 7.0. The gap between government and opposition on this issue was much larger than for items focused on the traditional left–right divide, such as the state's role in the economy, pro-poor social spending, and left–right ideology.

---

dimensions of state involvement in the economy and social policy (LAPOP 2012). While there were significant differences between *chavista* (MVR/PSUV) and opposition (UNT, PJ, COPEI, AD, PV and *Bandera Roja*) identifiers concerning state efforts to reduce inequality and state ownership of business/industry, there were no statistically significant differences concerning the state's role in providing for citizen's wellbeing, in job creation, or in healthcare.

Another important division concerns the parties' social bases, with *chavistas* drawing support from those excluded by the traditional party system and opposition parties protecting previously incorporated groups now marginalized under *chavismo*. The preceding discussion describing each of the major parties points to the significance of this cleavage. MVR/PSUV and other pro-Chávez parties draw support primarily from the poor, less educated, and otherwise marginalized, while the opposition speaks for groups successfully incorporated into the old system, including middle-class professionals, organized labor, and the traditional political elite. Experts in the DALP survey also identified the significance of this class-based divide in Venezuelan politics (Altman n.d.). When asked to list the most important sociopolitical divisions in the country, responses frequently identified this cleavage, pitting the marginalized against the powerful. In fact, there were more mentions of a divide between classes or between the people and oligarchy than mentions of the *chavista/anti-chavista* divide. These features of partisan divisions, which do not center around specific policy tools but instead focus on divergent priorities concerning who should control the levers of the state and how that power should be exercised, help explain how such strange bedfellows can coexist within each side of the government–opposition divide.

PARTY SYSTEM DEINSTITUTIONALIZATION

With the collapse of the traditional party system, party politics in Venezuela experienced extensive deinstitutionalization. While the new system has made uneven gains, institutionalization remains well below the levels attained at the height of the old system. Here I analyze institutionalization in the current system first by discussing stability in patterns of inter-party competition and then by assessing three dimensions of party systems posited in Chapter 1 of this volume to promote institutionalization: the legitimacy of parties, the presence of stable partisan ties to society, and the importance of party organizations. Patterns of inter-coalition competition have stabilized somewhat in recent years despite continued inter-party fluidity, but the factors needed to promote stability over the long term are less evident. While both government and opposition have begun to develop stable social roots, perceptions regarding the legitimacy of parties and elections are highly polarized, and party organizations often lack significance.

Inter-Coalition Stability Despite Inter-Party Fluidity

With collapse of the old party system, decades of stability in inter-party competition evaporated. Volatility in presidential and legislative elections reached levels unmatched throughout Venezuela's democratic history. But while inter-party volatility remains high, stability has returned to the patterns of competition between the system's two major coalitions.

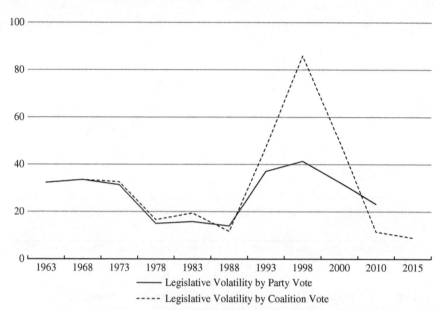

FIGURE 10.2 Volatility in Venezuelan Legislative Elections, 1963–2015
Note: The 2005 legislative election results are excluded because the opposition chose to boycott those elections, leaving the electoral playing field for pro-Chávez forces to dominate. As a result, election returns from that election do not reflect the nature of competition within the party system. If the 2005 data were included the volatility during the first decade of the twenty-first century would be much higher. For 2015, it is not possible to calculate legislative volatility by party because votes accrued to coalitions only, not individual parties.
Source: Author calculations based on election returns.

To explore temporal variation in stability, I calculated electoral volatility to assess the extent to which vote shares shift between parties from one election to the next. Typically, scholars use volatility to assess changes in *party* vote shares. However, in the Venezuelan party system, where competition is polarized between coalitions rather than individual parties, *coalition* volatility is an important indicator. Figures 10.2 and 10.3 present volatility for party and coalition vote in presidential and legislative elections. Solid lines present party-based volatility; dashed lines depict inter-coalition changes.

The most obvious pattern is the dramatic increase in all four volatility measures between 1988 and 1998. After decades of moderate and declining volatility, instability escalated swiftly with the collapse of the party system, and all four indicators reach their highest level in 1998. In the aftermath of collapse as new competitors vied for electoral space, volatility remained elevated through the mid-2000s. Moreover, if we consider individual party volatility, instability has persisted through the 2013 presidential elections and 2010

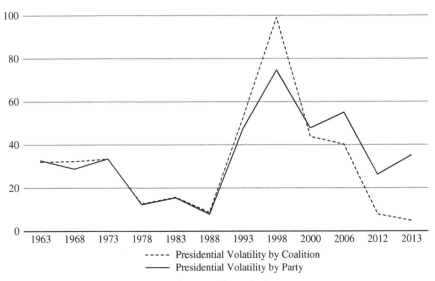

FIGURE 10.3   Volatility in Venezuelan Presidential Elections, 1963–2013
Source: Author calculations based on election returns.

legislative elections, which are the last legislative contests for which individual party vote shares are available. These high levels of fluctuation in individual party performance suggest that a party's vote share in the last election offers little insight into its ability to secure support in the next. Considering inter-party competition alone suggests that Venezuelan party system dynamics have remained unstable since the party system collapse.

However, if we analyze competition between major coalitions, a different pattern emerges. Preceding and immediately succeeding collapse, coalition volatility largely mimics party volatility. However, the two indicators diverge after the 2000 elections as coalition-based volatility declines more steadily and more rapidly than the party-based measures. Inter-coalition volatility dropped to 11.5 and then 8.9 in the 2010 and 2015 legislative contests, fell below 8 in the 2012 presidential election, and declined to less than five in the 2013 election to select Chávez's replacement after his death. These volatility scores are *lower* than those experienced during the peak years of the institutionalized 2.5-party system and are reminiscent of stability more often found in European systems. Much of the gap between party and coalition volatility is driven by instability within the opposition coalition. While MVR and its successor PSUV consistently receive the bulk of *chavista* votes, opposition votes have vacillated dramatically between coalition members.

These volatility data align with the general contours of current party competition discussed above. There is remarkable stability around the government–opposition divide, but substantial fluidity between individual parties within each coalition. The opposition camp is especially volatile with vote shifts depending on the party affiliations of the coalition's current presidential nominee and of other influential spokespeople as well as internal negotiations concerning nominations for key sub-national contests. Overall, patterns of inter-party dynamics create uncertainty within the opposition and to a lesser extent within *chavismo*, which suggests that deinstitutionalization still plagues the *party* system. However, the stability that increasingly characterizes inter-coalition competition suggests a certain routinization that supersedes the party system and instead centers on the alternative visions offered by *chavistas* and the opposition.

Polarization in the Legitimacy of Parties and Elections

Beginning in the 1990s, Venezuelan parties and elections have suffered a crisis of legitimacy. Although Venezuelans on average maintain some of the most positive attitudes regarding parties and elections in Latin America,[24] this general pattern masks considerable polarization in assessments of parties and elections, which divide government and opposition at the mass and elite levels.

Among the public, government supporters view parties as effective agents of representation and maintain high levels of trust in the electoral authority (CNE). In fact, Venezuelans who identified as *chavistas* in the 2012 AmericasBarometer survey held more favorable assessments of their national election authority than any other group of partisans in all of Latin America, with scores averaging 5.69 on a 7-point scale measuring institutional trust (LAPOP 2012). On the other hand, opposition identifiers were significantly more skeptical of the quality of representation provided by parties and more likely to hold the CNE in low esteem. From a regional perspective, Venezuelan opposition supporters had some of the lowest trust in their electoral authority, averaging 3.15 on the 7-point scale. In most countries, pro-incumbent partisans are more trusting of the election authority than opposition supporters, but Venezuela's government–opposition divide is remarkable – wider than any other country in the region. For most countries, this gap is less than 1 point on the 7-point scale. In Venezuela, the gap is 2.54; the only other country in Latin America that surpasses a 2-point gap is Nicaragua, where contestation over rules of the game is also acute. While this legitimacy gap may have closed somewhat following the 2015 legislative elections, which gave the opposition a resounding victory with 65% of seats in the National Assembly, lack of trust continues to color opposition partisans' views of the CNE. Moreover, recent decisions by the government to block efforts at a recall referendum aimed at President Maduro, to suspend regional elections scheduled for 2016, and to

---

[24] Source: LAPOP (2012). Venezuelans possess high trust in parties and elections, relatively positive assessments of party-based representation, and support the idea that parties are important for democracy.

hold widely discredited elections for a new Constituent Assembly to rewrite the constitution are likely to have further undermined the legitimacy of electoral processes among regime opponents.

Conversely, *chavistas* are much *less* positive than opposition partisans when asked about diffuse support for parties as important democratic institutions. MVR/PSUV identifiers are significantly more likely than opposition supporters to agree that democracy could function without parties. Thus, *chavistas* are pleased with the functioning of elections and parties, while opposition supporters are more abstractly convinced that parties are significant for the maintenance of democracy. These contrasting beliefs reveal deep polarization about the legitimacy of parties and elections, which coincides with a core divide between the two camps concerning the value and meaning of democracy as discussed above.

At the elite level, politicians often behave in ways that suggest low esteem for parties, eschewing the constraints parties impose and largely neglecting the development of effective party organizations. Consequently, many parties serve primarily electoral functions, and, as I discuss further below, few of the non-traditional parties have territorial reach, routinized intra-party procedures, or autonomy from the whims of individual leaders or social groups, which Riedl (2008) expects of institutionalized party organizations. Additionally, when rifts between co-partisans emerge, individual politicians are quick to form a new party, calculating that existing party organizations offer them few advantages. As a result, the political landscape is littered with parties like PODEMOS, *Alianza Bravo Pueblo*, and *Voluntad Popular* that formed when individuals or small groups broke with existing parties. Moreover, competition does not revolve around parties, but occurs either at the level of individual politicians (e.g. Maduro vs Capriles) or inter-party coalitions (*chavismo* vs opposition).

Additionally, elite views about election legitimacy are bifurcated like those of the mass public. *Chavistas* point to much progress, particularly since 2005, in professionalizing Venezuelan electoral administration, including introducing electronic voting, automating vote counting, extensive auditing of vote tallies, and updating voter rolls (Carter Center 2013; Von Bergen 2013). The CNE has at times invited international observers to lend legitimacy and transparency to the election process, although robust international observation has not been permitted since 2007 (McCoy 2015).[25] Additionally, in 2015 the CNE oversaw legislative elections that permitted a decisive victory for the opposition, temporarily bolstering claims about electoral transparency. However, the substantive effects of this victory have been essentially neutralized by *chavismo's* efforts to use other institutions under its control (for example, the Supreme Court, the Presidency, the Constituent Assembly, etc.) to circumvent the legislature.

---

[25] International observers were regularly invited between 1998 and 2006. After a brief period in which the government declined to invite observers, some were permitted to return in 2012, 2013, and 2015, although these efforts were more limited.

Despite efforts to strengthen the professionalism and credibility of elections, loyal *chavistas* dominate the CNE, press coverage of opposition campaigns is restricted, and the government leverages public resources to support its candidates. As a result, opposition leaders are often skeptical, frequently questioning the fairness of electoral processes, protesting election outcomes, and occasionally refusing to participate altogether. For instance, the opposition contested the 2004 recall referendum results as fraudulent (Kornblith 2005) and boycotted the 2005 legislative elections amidst claims the process was not free or fair (Álvarez 2007: 16).[26] Following the first post-Chávez presidential election in which Nicolás Maduro narrowly defeated opposition candidate Henrique Capriles, the opposition raised accusations of fraud and unsuccessfully pressured the CNE to nullify the results (Carter Center 2013). The opposition's concerns regarding the validity of election results and the independence of the CNE were initially fueled by the government's well-documented efforts to retaliate against those who signed recall petitions in 2004 (Hawkins 2010; Hsieh *et al.* 2009) and by extensive use of state resources to support incumbent party candidates, control the press, and disqualify leading opposition politicians (Carter Center 2013). More recently, government decisions to quash opposition efforts to invoke a recall referendum against President Maduro and to oversee highly controversial Constituent Assembly elections have undermined CNE independence and further discredited the regime's claims of electoral legitimacy.

In sum, the opposition is more acceptant of parties as inherently valuable, but points to multiple instances of electoral irregularities, an unfair playing field for competition, and the latest government attempts to avoid or manipulate electoral processes. *Chavistas* have more favorable views of how parties and elections function, extolling the quality of electoral administration and their willingness in 2015 to accept defeat. Overall, views of parties and elections are polarized, and the party system therefore lacks a firm base of legitimacy.

Stable Roots in Society

Like legitimacy, societal rootedness has the potential to facilitate party system stability. Often, measures of parties' ties to society use party age as a proxy (Mainwaring and Scully 1995a; Riedl 2008). However, the reality of party system collapse prohibits the Venezuelan system from demonstrating rootedness through age-based heuristics because collapse means that parties with considerable longevity lose their positions and are supplanted by new competitors. With the exception of the surviving traditional parties, most Venezuelan parties are less than twenty years old.

While younger parties may face challenges in establishing strong ties to society, building such ties is not impossible, particularly in intensely polarized, politicized contexts like contemporary Venezuela. Despite the constraints new

---

[26] In both instances, international observers declined to support the opposition's claims.

parties face in establishing roots and the time required to test the durability of these bonds, many Venezuelan parties have begun to develop strong ties to specific social groups and/or regions. Moreover, the social divide between the *chavistas* and opposition is one of the most salient features of contemporary political contestation, with the traditionally marginalized and formerly incorporated sectors facing off in repeated skirmishes for control of the state. Therefore, while the relatively young Venezuelan party system still lacks the deeply established ties between parties and major social organizations that characterized the pre-collapse system, both the *chavistas* and the opposition have clear constituencies that create continuity in their social bases.

As discussed above, the most distinctive element of the *chavista* constituency is strong support from those previously excluded by the traditional party system. The poor, the less educated and the racially marginalized are much more likely to support *chavismo* than the opposition, and the PSUV has performed particularly well in poor, rural areas and marginalized urban barrios. This social base is a defining element of the movement. These groups provided a critical base for *chavismo*, facilitating Chávez's initial rise to power and guaranteeing reliable and vocal support when the movement has faced attacks. Some in these sectors continue to back the party despite Chávez's death and Maduro's poor management of increasingly severe economic, social, and political challenges, and those who have abandoned Maduro are still reluctant to embrace the opposition with its rhetoric focused mostly on regime change and political rights rather than resolving the concrete challenges facing the poor (Casey and Torres 2017; Kurmanaev 2017).

The ties between PSUV and its base are not deeply ingrained through organizational linkages nor are they the product of routinized, carefully constructed interactions. Despite some efforts to establish more institutionalized ties through social organizations, such as developing a *chavista* labor movement (Ellner 2013; Iranzo and Richter 2006), links to the *chavista* base tend to be direct and personalist, typically occurring outside traditional organizational intermediaries (Handlin and Collier 2011). Most attempts by the party to organize the base have been illusory efforts spearheaded by presidential initiatives, like the Bolivarian circles and community councils, which rely on government funding and do not often survive when presidential attention shifts toward other concerns (Hawkins 2010; López Maya 2011; McGuire 2014; Pereira Almao 2004). Such state-sponsored efforts at grassroots mobilization are unlikely to serve as an organizational base for *chavismo* absent public funds acquired through control of the presidency (Handlin 2016; McGuire 2014). The movement's most vibrant social organizations, including local cooperatives, community radio stations, and other grassroots organizations have largely operated outside or perhaps alongside the party. Occasionally, the party and these social groups have coordinated their efforts, but they frequently work toward different, albeit not inherently incompatible, goals (Fernandes 2010). Moreover, while the party has enjoyed widespread activist networks, they are largely focused on electoral mobilization as opposed to enduring organization. Grassroots movements and activist networks provide an organizational foundation upon which the party might build enduring group-based ties, but this potential remains largely unrealized. Thus, while grassroots networks and deeply held *chavista* identities point to an underlying strength for *chavismo*, the party organization has not yet emerged as pivotal for amalgamating these interests or amplifying their influence.

On the opposition side, key supporters include those traditionally incorporated by the old system, such as organized labor, middle-class professionals, and business interests. Within the coalition, individual parties have niches that are sectorally or geographically defined. For instance, *Primero Justicia* appeals to middle-class professionals, while AD maintains strong ties to CTV, the original centralized labor organization. The varied party options within the opposition allow typically divergent interests to coexist as they coalesce around the goal of dethroning *chavismo*. Of course, this diversity also obscures the ideological positions of opposition candidates and undermines their ability to construct coherent and clear programmatic appeals. Moreover, most of the opposition parties are even weaker than PSUV in terms of maintaining established organizational ties that structure their constituency linkages in routinized ways. AD stands as a partial exception to this pattern, having sustained institutionalized incorporation strategies that facilitate preservation of the party's ties to core supporters (Cyr 2012). Thus, clear social bases and identities divide the supporters of pro- and anti-*chavista* parties, but organizational efforts to institutionalize these ties have been limited.

Uneven Institutionalization of Party Organizations

In Venezuela, the institutionalization of party organizations is uneven across parties and across various indicators of organizational strength, including degree of party structure, routinization of internal procedures, territorial reach, and lack of personalism and factionalism. In recent years, PSUV leadership has invested in organizational development by inaugurating offices throughout the country, implementing an extensive set of party statutes, holding three party congresses since 2010, and establishing internal commissions to promote a variety of tasks such as communications, ideological formation, and social movement relations (PSUV 2010, 2014a, 2014b). The party has also sought to mobilize party activists through civilian oversight committees and get-out-the-vote efforts like *"uno por diez"* (Espinoza 2012). These efforts set PSUV apart from new opposition parties, which have made more limited organizational investments.

However, PSUV's formal institutions are often without weight in party operations and decisions. Within both PSUV and new opposition parties, decision-making procedures lack routinization, and party rules are frequently victims of internal power struggles. For instance, candidate selection processes are unpredictable, and nominations often occur centrally without consulting party members or sub-national leaders (Lugo-Galicia 2013). The opposition used primaries to identify Capriles as its 2012 presidential nominee and to specify some candidates for the 2013 regional and 2015 legislative contests; PSUV employed primaries for the 2015 legislative election and a combination of primaries and centralized selection to nominate candidates for the 2010 parliamentary and 2008 sub-national elections (Lugo 2010a, 2010b; Lugo-Galicia 2008; Vásquez and Rivera 2013). However, such consultation has been haphazard and inconsistent, and the parties grant considerable autonomy to their central executive committees and feature highly centralized decision making (López Maya and Meléndez 2007). As a result, they tend to react impulsively to the pressures of idiosyncratic events, rather than making carefully deliberated decisions. *Chavista* initiatives have frequently been launched and then abandoned or replaced, and individual leaders across the political spectrum often announce major shifts in strategy or policy without consulting their party organizations (Hawkins 2010). These patterns permit flexibility (a feature the traditional parties sorely lacked), but also subject the parties to the whims of powerful individuals, create uncertainty for voters, activists, and party leaders, and may undermine democratic stability. AD offers a partial contrast to the new parties in terms of organizational routinization. But while AD retains many of its established guidelines governing internal decision making, the same small set of leaders has controlled the party since the early 2000s, and many formal rules have been jettisoned in favor of autonomy for these leaders.

Given these low levels of routinization, it is not surprising that personalism is a major feature of Venezuela's new parties. As president, Chávez exercised the ultimate authority within PSUV, and his wishes continue to carry important weight even after his death (Hawkins 2010; Morgan 2011). As Margarita López Maya (2011: 236) has noted, "the sustained mobilization of popular sectors and their direct relationship with the president, without need for intermediaries, weakened still more the already weak role of parties in the political regime." While the post-Chávez PSUV is not dominated by a single personality, individual leaders continue to act independently of the organization and at times in contradiction with each other. Personalism likewise characterizes the opposition, with UNT, Voluntad Popular (PV), and many smaller parties closely tied to one or a handful of influential leaders (López Maya and Meléndez 2007). AD and to a lesser extent COPEI and PJ maintain some organizational patterns and identities that manifest more, but still limited, independence from powerful personalities (Pérez Baralt 2004).

Factionalism and internal divisions also characterize Venezuelan parties, a feature largely consistent with the traditional parties' intra-party dynamics (Coppedge 1994). As detailed above, PSUV suffers from several axes of internal conflict between militarists and civilians and ideological moderates and hardliners. Likewise, the opposition features numerous divisions both between and within its component parties. Individual opposition leaders have frequently broken with their parties either to form new organizations or to join other parties in the coalition.

Finally, many Venezuelan parties are highly regionalized. The new opposition parties, in particular, lack territorial reach, with UNT centered in Zulia, PV in Carabobo, and COPEI in Táchira. Even PJ, which has had more success in establishing national appeal, has struggled to extend its reach beyond urban centers in the middle of the country (Cyr 2013; Sagarzazu 2011). MUD's candidate selection strategies reflect this pattern, with nominees for each state or locality typically hailing from regionally influential parties. Among the opposition, AD offers the most effective nationwide apparatus (Cyr 2012), yet its reach and viability as a national party has been significantly enervated since the system's collapse. Among the major competitors, PSUV has the greatest national appeal, but it has relied heavily on regional leaders to build support and still lacks the sub-national organizational penetration that characterized the traditional parties in their heyday (Sagarzazu 2011). In general then, party organizations in the post-collapse system are plagued by factionalism and are less routinized, more personalistic, and more spatially confined than the traditional parties were at their peaks. Among the new parties, PSUV has made the most organizational investments, but the impact of these efforts on actual party operations remains largely unrealized.

In sum, PSI as well as the dimensions that promote it are uneven in Venezuela across indicators and across parties. Despite continued volatility at the party level, particularly within the opposition, inter-coalition stability is high and compares favorably to neighboring countries with more established party systems like Chile and Mexico. Parties across the spectrum have stable roots in society, *chavistas* and anti-*chavistas* alike manifest strong identities, and before the onset of the current crisis the PSUV enjoyed levels of support that eclipsed those of many other parties discussed in this volume, including the PRI and PAN in Mexico and the PT in Brazil. But the organizational bases of these social ties remain weak (opposition) or uninstitutionalized (PSUV). Patterns of party and election legitimacy vary in predictable ways between the two coalitions. The opposition supports the preservation of their democratic rights but not the current regime's electoral institutions or partisan representation, while *chavistas* evaluate the system's electoral and representational achievements positively but are less enthusiastic about liberal democratic institutions in the abstract. The institutionalization of party organizations is also uneven. New opposition parties are nearly uniform in their weakness on all dimensions of party organizational strength. PSUV and to a lesser extent AD manifest greater territorial reach and more structured organizations, despite suffering from lack of routinization as well as personalism and factionalism.

Overall, the *chavistas* have taken more steps that might lay the foundation for an enduring party organization. However, the ability of the party to persist without control of the state remains uncertain, and the movement's indifference regarding liberal democratic norms and its willingness to violate democratic procedures raise serious concerns about the kind of party organization an institutionalized PSUV might be. Its extensive machinations to remain in power in the face of plummeting oil revenues and declining popularity have laid bare authoritarian tendencies within the movement and suggest that elements within *chavismo* likewise question the party's ability to survive without a grip on state power. Opposition parties, on the other hand, have focused on unseating Chávez and his successors, without much attention to building strong organizations or deeply rooted social ties that go beyond rejection of *chavismo*. Distinctions between the two camps may be partially explained by *chavista* use of the state apparatus for partisan ends, which has privileged PSUV's institutionalization and limited the opposition. But the frequently reactionary posture of the opposition, which positions itself primarily as the anti-*chavista* option instead of being pro-something else, also contributes to asymmetry in institutionalization.

THE FUTURE OF VENEZUELAN PARTY POLITICS

The collapse of the traditional party system in Venezuela has had dramatic consequences for the nature and structure of partisan competition and politics more broadly. While previously marginalized groups have found new voice and parties offer distinct ideological options for voters, collapse has also aggravated social and political conflict, heightened personalism, disrupted the predictability and routinization of party organizations, and undermined liberal democratic institutions. As *chavismo* has encountered run-away inflation, serious shortages, escalating violence, and depleted resources due to evaporating oil revenues, mismanagement and corruption, the movement's once unassailable position appears increasingly tenuous, and overt power grabs that go decidedly beyond the bounds of liberal democratic procedures tarnish its image.

Moving forward, the party system is likely to develop along one of three trajectories. First, the system could maintain the status quo with two polarized coalitions that command loyalty from core supporters alongside a substantial group of unaligned voters. The coalitions would remain internally fragmented between competing factions and personalities, and party organizations across the board would persist as primarily electoral machines with PSUV manifesting greater organizational complexity but not much internal routinization. Given the latest developments in government–opposition conflict, including a turn to extra-institutional strategies by both sides and the mounting economic and security crises, this first path of stasis seems the least likely of the three.

Second, PSUV could deepen its institutionalization, by establishing stronger organizational ties to grassroots *chavista* movements, strengthening the routinization of party decision-making procedures, and limiting the influence of personalities and factions within the party. If this process develops while the opposition remains organizationally weak and/or effectively repressed by the government and the PSUV maintains an ambivalent or hostile stance toward liberal democratic rules of the game, a hegemonic party system could solidify and likely promote development of an institutionalized authoritarian regime.

Finally, mounting frustration with the government's poor performance on economic and security issues could drive unaligned voters and weak *chavista* identifiers to back opposition efforts to force *chavismo* out of power, eventually granting state control to the opposition. This process could occur via recall referendum, ordinary election schedule, regime collapse, or even forceful removal. But recent moves by Maduro and his allies to close off electoral options and the opposition's return to the streets suggest that the path toward an ordinary transition from government to opposition is exceedingly narrow. A power transfer from government to opposition, be it through regular institutional channels or otherwise, would prove a considerable test for *chavismo*. While PSUV weathered the challenge posed by Chávez's death, its continued reliance on the state apparatus and public resources to motivate and mobilize supporters creates serious vulnerabilities for the party. The party's organization would be put to a significant test if it lost power, particularly if an opposition government opted not for a conciliatory tone but a scorched earth approach toward the dethroned *chavistas*. Under such circumstances, PSUV might forge a more robust party apparatus in order to survive, or it could fail to adapt to the new reality and lose its potency. While this third option would require a combination of effective opposition strategies and mistakes by the government, the prospect serves as a significant motivating factor for the *chavistas* to consolidate power and strengthen their organization in ways that resemble the second path outlined above.

As of this writing, the Venezuelan party system and the regime itself appear to be at a tipping point. Whether *chavismo* endures the profound crisis with its grasp on power intact or the opposition manages to unseat the government will have significant implications not only for the development of the party system but also for the nature of the regime and the procedural norms and substantive goals the regime promotes.

I I

Peru: The Institutionalization of Politics without Parties

Steven Levitsky

Of the twelve countries examined in Mainwaring and Scully's seminal analysis of PSI in Latin America, Peru ranked last (1995a: 17). Peruvian parties had long been weak (Cotler 1995), and when *Building Democratic Institutions* was published, the party system had just collapsed, permitting the rise of outsider-turned-autocrat Alberto Fujimori.

Two decades later, Peruvian parties are even weaker. Party system decomposition continued throughout the post-Fujimori period, resulting in levels of fragmentation and fluidity rarely seen in Latin America.[1] Established parties such as the Popular Christian Party (PPC), Popular Action (AP), and even the American Popular Revolutionary Alliance (APRA) became marginal actors.[2] At the same time, every new party created after 1990 collapsed,[3] failed to achieve national electoral significance,[4] or remained a strictly personalistic vehicle.[5] Increasingly, politicians operated outside of parties, either creating their own personalistic vehicles or negotiating candidacies with different parties at each election. In effect, parties were replaced by "coalitions of independents," or short-lived alliances of political "free agents" who come together on candidate slates for a single election cycle (Zavaleta 2014).

[1] Guatemala exhibits similar characteristics (Sánchez 2009).
[2] Although APRA and the PPC performed well in the 2001 and 2006 elections, triggered hopes of an electoral comeback (Kenney 2003), this performance was rooted almost entirely in the electoral appeal of the parties' presidential candidates, Alan García (APRA) and Lourdes Flores (PPC).
[3] Examples include Union for Peru (UPP), We are Peru (SP), and the Independent Moralizing Front (FIM).
[4] Examples include the Socialist Party (PS), the New Left Movement (MNI), and Social Force (FS).
[5] Examples include Popular Force (*Fujimorismo*), National Solidarity, the Nationalist Party, Alliance for Progress, and Possible Peru. A possible exception to this pattern is the Broad Front (FA), a new leftist coalition that won 19% of the presidential vote in 2016. At the time of this writing, however, FA remained a loose coalition whose prospects for institutionalization were uncertain.

This chapter examines the causes and consequences of party system decomposition in Peru. It first asks why parties were not rebuilt after Fujimori's fall from power. It argues that party collapse generated a self-reinforcing dynamic: post-Fujimori politicians developed alternative strategies and technologies that enabled them to succeed without parties, thereby weakening incentives for party building. The difficulties of party rebuilding were exacerbated by state weakness, which limited parties' ability to both govern well and implement their programs. The chapter then turns to the consequences of party collapse for democracy. It argues that although party collapse permitted the emergence of a more socially representative political elite, it also had clear negative effects on the quality of democracy. The amateur politicians who occupy a disproportionate number of elected offices are inexperienced and weakly socialized into democratic politics. Crucially, moreover, they operate with narrow time horizons, which limits their capacity for collective action, weakens their incentive to invest in democratic institutions, and strengthens incentives to engage in corrupt behavior. Amateur politics has thus reinforced public disaffection toward politicians and representative democratic institutions, leaving Peru vulnerable to populism.

THE DECOMPOSITION OF THE PERUVIAN PARTY SYSTEM

The Peruvian party system collapsed in the late 1980s and early 1990s in a context of deep socioeconomic crisis and a mounting Shining Path insurgency.[6] Party collapse permitted the election of outsider Alberto Fujimori and facilitated his authoritarian turn (1992–2000) (Cameron 1994; Levitsky and Cameron 2003). Fujimori effectively governed without a party, relying on state institutions as substitutes (Roberts 1995; Rospigliosi 2000). He created a new personalistic vehicle at nearly every election (Change 90 in 1990, New Majority in 1992 and 1995, Let's Go Neighbor in 1998, and Peru 2000 in 2000), only to discard it afterward.

Party decomposition accelerated under Fujimori (Lynch 1999; Tanaka 1998). Established parties fell into terminal crisis. The four parties that dominated Peruvian politics in the 1980s, APRA, AP, the PPC, and the United Left (IU), declined from 97% of the vote in 1985 to just 6% *combined* in 1995. As the established parties weakened, scores of politicians abandoned them and declared themselves "independents" (Planas 2000; Tanaka 1998). At the same time, new parties failed to take root. For example, the newly created Union for Peru (UPP) finished second in the 1995 presidential election (behind the candidacy of UN Secretary General Javier Pérez de Cuéllar) but declined precipitously thereafter (Meléndez 2007: 231). Likewise, We Are Peru (*Somos*

---

[6] On the collapse of the Peruvian party system, see Cameron (1994); Cotler (1995); Levitsky and Cameron (2003); Lynch (1999); Planas (2000); Seawright (2012); Tanaka (1998, 2005); and Vergara (2009).

Peru, or SP), which was created by Lima mayor (and presidential aspirant) Alberto Andrade, briefly emerged as a national force in the late 1990s, finishing second to *Fujimorismo* in the 1998 municipal elections. However, Andrade's subsequent decline in the polls triggered a wave of defections that reduced SP to minor party status. By 2000, party building efforts had largely ceased. Indeed, the five top finishers in the 2000 presidential race – Fujimori, Andrade, Alejandro Toledo, Federico Salas, and Luis Castañeda – headed personalistic vehicles.

Peru's redemocratization in 2000 raised expectations of a party system rebirth. Scholars viewed the strong electoral performance of APRA's Alan García and the PPC's Lourdes Flores in the 2001 presidential election and García's victory in the 2006 election as evidence of a traditional party comeback (Cyr 2012; Kenney 2003; Schmidt 2003). Party system "rebirth" proved illusory, however. The revival of APRA and the PPC was driven almost entirely by the presidential coattails of García and Flores, respectively. Whenever García and Flores were not on the ballot, both parties performed poorly. In 2011, when García could not stand for reelection and Flores opted not to run, neither party fielded a presidential candidate, and APRA and the PPC won a mere four and seven seats, respectively, in the 130-member Congress.

The most successful national parties to emerge in the post-Fujimori era – Toledo's Possible Peru (PP), Castañeda's National Solidarity Party (PSN), Ollanta Humala's Nationalist Party (PNP), and Pedro Pablo Kuczynski's Peruvians for Change (PPK) – were personalistic vehicles, or electoral labels created by, and exclusively for, a single presidential aspirant. Indeed, every new party that won at least 4% of the national vote between 1995 and 2011 was a personalistic vehicle,[7] and in the 2011 presidential election, all five major candidates either led personalistic vehicles (Humala, Keiko Fujimori, Toledo, Castañeda) or had no party at all (Kuczynski).[8]

Personalism generates extreme party system fluidity.[9] Most personalistic parties persist as long as their founding leaders' political careers. These careers may span multiple elections (for example, Toledo was a presidential candidate in 1995, 2000, 2001, and 2016), thereby creating the appearance of partisan stability. Individual careers eventually end, however, and when they do, most personalistic parties collapse or decline into obscurity.

The decomposition of the Peruvian party system is even more far-reaching than it appears. National parties survive in a nominal sense because they enjoy a legal monopoly over national candidacies: by law, candidates for president and

[7] These include PP, We Are Peru, PSN, the PNP, Humberto Lay's National Restoration, and César Acuña's Alliance for Progress. In 2016, a non-personalistic leftist coalition, the Broad Front, won 19% of the vote.
[8] Kuczynski was backed by an alliance of parties. He created PPK, a personalistic party, to run for president in 2016.
[9] Electoral volatility is reinforced by the ban on presidential reelection. Personalistic parties that win the presidency almost invariably suffer a steep decline in the subsequent election, in which the dominant leader cannot stand. Indeed, incumbent parties did not even field presidential candidates in 2006 (PP), 2011 (APRA), and 2016 (PNP).

Congress must be nominated by a registered party. Increasingly, however, they survive only on paper. National parties' linkages to local politics eroded almost completely during the 1990s and 2000s. Established party organizations evaporated at the local level, and new parties failed to establish a grassroots presence.[10] In effect, national parties were reduced to empty vessels, without the capacity to attract candidates or channel their careers. For one, they lacked useful labels. With the partial exception of *Fujimorismo* (discussed below) and APRA in a few northern regions, partisan identities have largely evaporated, and, consequently, national party labels have little value (De Gramont 2010).[11] National parties also lacked financial and organizational resources. Gutted of their local structures and activist bases, most parties offer little, if any, patronage, campaign infrastructure, or financial support to local candidates.[12]

Lacking either attractive labels or organizational resources, contemporary parties are, as PPC leader Lourdes Flores put it, "completely unable to recruit good candidates. The good ones all want to go it alone."[13] Although local aspirants to Congress must, by law, join national party tickets, most of them prefer to join new tickets sponsored by emergent personalistic candidates rather than those of established parties.[14]

Increasingly, then, national parties have been transformed into empty shells, without local linkages or grassroots-level existence. As Table 11.1 shows, national parties have been increasingly displaced by local or regional "movements," or parties that compete exclusively at the provincial and regional levels (De Gramont 2010; Zavaleta 2014). Whereas in the 2002 local elections national parties captured more than 70% of the vote and a majority of regional and provincial governments, by 2010 the national party vote had fallen to 34% and provincial and regional parties captured more than two thirds of local governments.[15]

Although emerging regional movements could, in theory, provide a foundation for party rebuilding, this has not occurred, for at least two reasons. First, regional movements remain localized. Efforts to coordinate across regions or to scale up into national organizations have consistently failed (De Gramont 2010; Muñoz and Dargent 2016). Second, the regional movements that emerged

---

[10] There exist a few exceptions. For example, APRA maintains an organized presence in parts of the north, and the PPC maintains an organized presence in Lima.

[11] As PPC leader Lourdes Flores put it, local office seekers "prefer their own label." Author's interview, March 30, 2011.

[12] Author's interview with PPC President Lourdes Flores, Lima (March 30, 2011), AP legislator Víctor Andrés García Belaúnde (May 5, 2011), ex-Congressperson José Barba Caballero (May 4, 2011), and Possible Peru leader Juan Sheput (May 5, 2011).

[13] Author's interview with PPC President Lourdes Flores, Lima (March 30, 2011). Also author's interviews with AP legislator Víctor Andrés García Belaúnde (Lima, May 5, 2011) and PP leader Juan Sheput (Lima, May 5, 2011).

[14] Author's interview with PPC President Lourdes Flores (Lima, March 30, 2011) and AP legislator Víctor Andrés García Belaúnde (May 5, 2011).

[15] Taken from Remy (2010); Tanaka and Guibert (2011); and Vera (2010).

TABLE 11.1 *Provincial and Regional Governments Won by National Parties and Regional Movements, Peru, 2002–14*

	2002		2006		2010		2014	
	Regions	**Provinces**	**Regions**	**Provinces**	**Regions**	**Provinces**	**Regions**	**Provinces**
National parties	17	110	7	109	6	68	6	47
Regional/provincial movements	8	84	18	86	19	126	19	147

Sources: Levitsky and Zavaleta (2016).

in the post-Fujimori period were, with few exceptions,[16] just as loosely organized, personalistic, and ephemeral as the national parties they displaced (Tanaka and Guibert 2011; Zavaleta 2014). Thus, not only has the national party system fragmented into twenty-five distinct regional party systems, but regional party systems are themselves highly fragmented and fluid. An average of twelve parties contested each regional election in 2010 (Seifert 2014: 53–54), and few of them endured beyond a single election or two. Manuel Seifert (2011) measured regional party volatility by dividing the number of new parties by the overall number of parties participating in each regional election. In 2006, the average level of party volatility was 62.5, meaning that most of the parties competing in that year's regional election were new (Seifert 2014: 45). In 2010, the figure increased to 68.3 (Seifert 2014: 52).

Far from experiencing a rebirth in the 2000s, then, Peru's party system decomposed. Not only were established parties displaced by personalistic vehicles, but, at the local level, national parties of all types were displaced by ephemeral candidate-centered "movements." The result was a level of partisan fragmentation and fluidity that was unparalleled in Latin America.

The Peruvian case thus scores unambiguously low on Mainwaring, Bizzarro, and Petrova's three dimensions of PSI (Chapter 1). First, in terms of stability of membership, the Peruvian party system is the second most unstable in Latin America after Guatemala (see Chapter 2, Table 2.6). Few parties remain major electoral contenders for more than a decade. For example, none of the three leading parties in the 2001 election (PP, APRA, PPC) finished in the top three in 2011. Likewise, none of the three leading parties in the 2006 election (PNP, APRA, PPC) finished in the top three in 2016.

Peru also scores very low on the dimension of inter-party electoral competition. In terms of mean electoral volatility, Peru scores second highest in Latin America in presidential elections (1990–2015) (Chapter 2, Figure 2.4) and highest in the region in legislative elections (Chapter 2, Figure 2.5). Consider the fate of Peru's three governing parties between 2001 and 2016: Toledo's Possible Peru fell from a forty-five seat plurality in 2001 to just two seats in 2006; APRA fell from thirty-six seats in 2006 to four seats in 2011; and Humala's Nationalist Party, which won a forty-seven seat plurality in 2011, failed to even run candidates in 2016.

Finally, Peru scores low on the dimension of the stability of parties' ideological positions. Mainwaring's finding that Peruvian parties are the most ideologically volatile in Latin America (Chapter 2, Figure 2.7) is not surprising. Many of Peru's leading parties have undergone dramatic programmatic change since 1990. Alberto Fujimori, who was elected in 1990 on a vaguely left-of-center platform, governed on the right. APRA positioned itself on the center-left in the 1980s but has been unambiguously conservative since García's return to the presidency in

---

[16] Exceptions include the Chim Pum Callao machine in Callao and the New Amazon Regional Movement in San Martín.

2006. Humala ran as a left-wing populist in 2006, ran a more moderate center-left campaign in 2011, and then abandoned much of that platform after winning the presidency.

Peru's party system thus scores as unambiguously "low" on all three of Mainwaring, Bizzarro, and Petrova's dimensions of institutionalization. Peru's overall PSI score (–1.16) (see Chapter 2, Table 2.6), is second lowest in Latin America, behind Guatemala.

THE CONTEMPORARY PARTY SYSTEM: THE FORMAL PLAYERS

This section provides a snapshot of the main actors in Peru's national party system during the 2006–16 period.[17] These include three established but minor parties: APRA, the PPC, and AP; three personalistic parties: PP, PSN, and PNP; and a mixed case: *Fujimorismo*.

ESTABLISHED BUT MARGINAL PARTIES

Three Peruvian parties may be described as minimally institutionalized but marginal. APRA, AP, and the PPC were all established prior to the third wave of democratization. Along with the now extinct United Left (IU), these three parties undergirded Peru's post-1980 party system (Cameron 1994; Tanaka 1998). They won more than 70% of the vote in the 1980 and 1985 legislative elections. All three parties weakened dramatically after the 1980s. Nevertheless, they survived as national organizations, effectively becoming minor parties.

APRA

APRA was Peru's first and only mass party.[18] Founded in 1924 by Víctor Raúl Haya de la Torre, APRA built a "powerful party organization at the national, departmental, and local level" (Sulmont 1975: 126), especially along Peru's northern coast. Its mass base was reinforced by close ties to the emerging labor movement (Sulmont 1975). Intense polarization and repression during the 1930s and 1940s crystalized *Aprista* identities and consolidated the party's roots in society (Cotler 1978: 246–47; North 1973). Notwithstanding years of electoral proscription, APRA became Peru's largest party, winning about a third of the vote whenever it was allowed to compete. The party survived the death of Haya de la Torre in 1979, and under the leadership of Alan García, it captured the presidency in 1985.

---

[17] This discussion excludes the leftist Broad Front (FA), a coalition that formed prior to the 2016 election and won 19% of the presidential vote.

[18] See Hilliker (1971); North (1973); and Sulmont (1975).

The poor performance of the first García government (1985–90) weakened APRA. The party finished third, with 22.5% of the vote, in 1990, and with García in exile, its vote share fell to 4.1% in 1995 and 1.4% in 2000. García's return revived APRA's electoral fortunes somewhat: the party won 19.7% of the legislative vote in 2001 and 20.6% (when García won the presidency) in 2006. Although this performance was interpreted as a comeback for APRA (Cyr 2017; Kenney 2003), it was almost entirely a product of García's presidential coattails. Whenever García was not on the ticket, APRA's electoral fortunes plummeted. Thus, despite presiding over a booming economy, APRA performed poorly in the 2010 local and regional elections, winning only one of twenty-five regional presidencies, and in 2011, when García could not stand for reelection, it fell to 6.4% of the legislative vote. The party's decline continued in 2014, when it failed to win a single regional presidency, and in 2016, when García himself finished fifth, with only 5.8% of the vote.

Relative to other Peruvian parties, APRA remains somewhat institutionalized, with a national structure that survived into the post-Fujimori era (Cyr 2017). Outside of its stronghold in the "solid north," however, *Aprismo's* societal roots have withered. *Apristas* now constitute a small share of the national electorate – smaller, in fact, than *Fujimorismo* (Meléndez 2014: 176). According to survey research undertaken by Carlos Meléndez, only 2% of Peruvian voters can be characterized as hardcore *Apristas*, while another 6% "lean APRA."[19] Thus, although APRA survives, it is a minor party.

The Popular Christian Party (PPC)

A conservative party founded by Lima mayor Luis Bedoya Reyes in 1966, the PPC was always an elite, Lima-centered party (Conaghan 2000). It developed a solid, if narrow, support base in Lima, which allowed Bedoya Reyes to come third in the 1980 (9.6% of the vote) and 1985 (with 11.9%) presidential elections. The PPC was quite institutionalized, surviving Bedoya Reyes's retirement in 2003 and maintaining a relatively vibrant internal life under his successor, Lourdes Flores.

However, the PPC suffered a steep decline beginning in the 1990s. The party achieved just 3% of the vote in the 1995 legislative elections, and many of its most talented politicians (including future Lima mayor Alberto Andrade and future Callao regional president Alex Kouri) abandoned it. Like APRA, the PPC appeared to make a comeback after 2000, as Lourdes Flores won 24% of the vote in the 2001 and 2006 presidential elections. However, this success was driven almost entirely by Flores's coattails. Whenever Flores was not on the ballot, the PPC barely registered in the polls. In 2014, for example, PPC candidate Jaime Zea won a mere 2% of the vote in the Lima mayoral race. Indeed, the PPC did not win a single regional or major mayoral election during the 2000s, and it did not field a presidential candidate in 2011 or 2016.

---

[19] Carlos Meléndez, personal communication.

The PPC has little organization outside of Lima.[20] The party launched a rebuilding effort in the 2000s, but it "lacked resources and *mística*," and, as a result, it failed to expand beyond a "small inner core."[21] As of 2016, then, the PPC survived, but as an increasingly minor political actor.

Popular Action (AP)

Founded in 1956 by Fernando Belaúnde, AP became Peru's second largest party, with a national organization and activist base. However, the party depended heavily on Belaúnde, who won the presidency in 1963 and 1980. While he lived, Belaúnde was AP's only leader and, prior to 1985, its only presidential candidate.

AP collapsed in the 1980s and 1990s. Its share of the presidential vote fell from 45% in 1980 to 7% in 1985 and just 2% in 1995, and many of its leaders, including Juan Carlos Hurtado Miller and Luis Castañeda Lossio, abandoned it for the Fujimori government. Having never broken its dependence on Belaúnde, AP "aged with its leader,"[22] and its organization and activist networks decomposed over time (Cyr 2017). By the time of Belaúnde's death in 2002, AP's national organization was "skeletal."[23] It could only field candidates in half of Peru's provinces in the 2010 local elections,[24] and it did not field a presidential candidate in 2011. In 2016, AP won a surprising 7% of the vote after drafting Alfredo Barnechea, an ex-*Aprista*, as its presidential candidate. This performance was driven almost exclusively by Barnechea, however – there is little evidence that AP had strengthened as a party.

PERSONALISTIC PARTIES

Three personalistic parties emerged as major national contenders in the post-Fujimori period: Toledo's Possible Peru (PP), Castañeda's National Solidarity Party (PNP), and Humala's Peruvian Nationalist Party (PNP). All three parties were organized by, and exclusively for, individual politicians in pursuit of the presidency, and none of them developed even a minimum of autonomy from their founding leaders.

Possible Peru (PP)

PP (originally *País Posible*, or Possible Country) was created by Alejandro Toledo in 1994 in anticipation of the 1995 presidential election. The party

---

[20] Author's interview with PPC President Lourdes Flores (Lima, March 30, 2011).
[21] Author's interview with PPC President Lourdes Flores (Lima, March 30, 2011).
[22] Author's interview with AP leader Víctor Andrés García Belaúnde (May 5, 2011).
[23] Author's interview with AP leader Víctor Andrés García Belaúnde (May 5, 2011).
[24] Author's interview with AP leader Víctor Andrés García Belaúnde (May 5, 2011).

took off in 2000, when Toledo emerged as serious presidential contender, and especially in 2001, when Toledo won the presidency. PP finished first in the 2001 legislative election, winning forty-five of 120 seats.

Yet PP failed to consolidate. In part, this failure was rooted in the poor performance of the Toledo government. Toledo's approval rating fell into single digits in 2003 and 2004, tarnishing the PP brand. More importantly, however, the PP was a thoroughly personalistic organization (Vera 2011). Toledo "wasn't interested in party building,"[25] and, as a result, the PP never built a territorial organization or established linkages to the local level (Vera 2011: 163). Indeed, the party organization remained dormant whenever Toledo was not a candidate.[26]

The PP was "orphaned" after Toledo left the presidency (Vera 2011: 164). It did not field a candidate in the 2006 presidential election and won a mere two seats in Congress. With Toledo living in the United States, the PP "practically disappeared" after 2006 (Vera 2011: 161–62). It participated only marginally in the 2006, 2010, and 2014 regional elections, fielding candidates in fewer than half the regions and winning none of them (Vera 2011: 164–65). Following Toledo's failed 2011 presidential bid, most of PP's leading politicians abandoned the party. Toledo finished eighth in the 2016 presidential election, winning a mere 1.3% of the vote; as a result, the party that had governed Peru only a decade earlier lost its legal status.

The National Solidarity Party (PSN)

PSN is a personalistic vehicle created by Luis Castañeda Lossio in 1999 in anticipation of a 2000 presidential bid. It attained national prominence during the 2000s, as Castañeda's success as mayor of Lima (2002–10) positioned him as a front runner in the 2011 presidential race. He finished fifth, with 10% of the vote, and PSN won nine of 130 seats in Congress.

The PSN is so personalistic that "to call it a party is an exaggeration" (Meléndez 2011: 180). The party has never fielded a candidate for executive office other than Castañeda, and its leadership "meets in Mr. Castañeda's living room."[27] The PSN organization has been described as "three offices in Lima that don't speak to one another" (Meléndez 2011: 181), and which is "held together with spit."[28] Although Castañeda's victory in the 2014 Lima mayoral election kept the PSN alive, there is little reason to think it will survive Castañeda's departure from politics.

[25] Author's interview with PP leader Juan Sheput (May 5, 2011).
[26] Author's interview with PP leader Juan Sheput (May 5, 2011).
[27] Author's interview, May 5, 2011.
[28] Author's interview with former congressman Guido Lombardi (May 4, 2011).

The Peruvian Nationalist Party (PNP)

The PNP is a personalistic vehicle created by Ollanta Humala and his wife, Nadine Heredia, in anticipation of the 2006 presidential race.[29] Although the party performed well in the 2006 and 2011 elections, capturing the presidency and a legislative plurality in 2011 (forty-seven of 130 seats), this vote was driven entirely by Humala's presidential coattails.

Notwithstanding its programmatic-sounding name, the PNP was a thoroughly personalistic organization (León 2011). The party accepted Humala's transformation from radical populist to centrist without internal debate (León 2011). When a group of Nationalist Youth activists sent Humala a letter questioning the conservative turn of his government, he responded, "I founded the Nationalist Party with two other people, and I can go back and do it again if necessary."[30] Humala's wife, Nadine Heredia, became party president in 2014.

Whenever Humala is not a candidate, the PNP has been dormant. It fielded few candidates in the 2006 and 2010 local and regional elections and virtually none in 2014. Unable to find a viable presidential candidate and barely registering in the polls, the PNP withdrew from the 2016 election.

FUJIMORISMO: A MIXED CASE

Fujimorismo, which was renamed Popular Force (FP) in 2012, is a mixed case. *Fujimorismo* was originally a personalistic vehicle – called Change 90 – created by Alberto Fujimori in anticipation of a presidential bid in 1990. Fujimori did not invest in party building (Roberts 2006a). He closed down the Change 90 headquarters after winning the presidency (Planas 2000: 251), opting instead for a new party, the NM, which had no members and "scarcely any organizational presence outside the national congress" (Roberts 2006b: 94–95); Fujimori created a third party, Let's Go Neighbor, for the 1998 municipal elections but abandoned it after the election; and he created a fourth one, Peru 2000, "out of thin air" just prior to the 2000 election (Cameron 2000: 10).

Given this extreme personalism, *Fujimorismo* was widely expected to collapse after Fujimori's fall from power. However, it reemerged as a potent electoral force in the 2000s. Under the leadership of Fujimori's daughter, Keiko, *Fujimorismo* won 13% of the legislative vote in 2006. In 2011, it won 23% of the legislative vote, and Keiko Fujimori nearly captured the presidency. In 2016, *Fujimorismo* again narrowly lost the presidency but captured an absolute majority in Congress. *Fujimorismo* has taken on some characteristics of an established party, developing a solid, if modest, partisan base (Meléndez 2010, 2014). Based on a survey experiment carried out in 2011, Meléndez classified 6% of Peruvian voters as "core" *Fujimorista* supporters and an additional 10% as *Fujimorista* "leaners" (Meléndez 2012c: 12). The figures exceed those of any other Peruvian party,

---

[29] Quoted in *La República*, July 8, 2012.   [30] Quoted in *La República*, July 8, 2012.

including APRA. *Fujimorismo* has also built a national organization (Urrutia 2011a, 2011b). By 2013, Popular Force (FP) had offices in a majority of provinces,[31] and in 2016 it was widely viewed as the best-organized party in the country. Indeed, *Fujimorismo* won an outright majority of the seats (73 of 130) in that years's legislative election – the first time any Peruvian party had achieved such a feat in democratic elections in more than thirty years. Although *Fujimorismo*'s future remains uncertain, its development of strong partisan attachments and a relatively robust organization suggests the potential for institutionalization.

THE WORLD UNDERNEATH: FREE AGENTS AND COALITIONS OF INDEPENDENTS

A focus on national party labels overstates the strength of Peruvian parties. In reality, post-Fujimori Peru is a democracy without parties (Levitsky and Cameron 2003; Tanaka 2005). Anthony Downs (1957: 25) defined parties as "team[s] of men seeking to control the governing apparatus by gaining office in a duly constituted election." It is debatable whether most contemporary electoral organizations in Peru meet even this minimalist definition.

Post-Fujimori politics is organized around individual candidates, not parties. Most politicians are partisan free agents. New politicians do not expect to build careers within a single party. Rather, they operate on their own, either creating their own parties or negotiating temporary partisan affiliations at each election. Higher-level politicians – those who aspire to be president of the republic, regional president, or mayor of a big city – generally create their own vehicles. Examples include Presidents Fujimori (multiple parties), Toledo (PP), and Humala PNP), former Lima mayors Alberto Andrade (We are Peru) and Luis Castañeda (PSN), former Prime Ministers Federico Salas (Let's Advance), Pedro Pablo Kuczynski (PPK), Yehude Simon (Humanist Party), businessman César Acuña (Alliance for Progress), evangelical leader Humberto Lay (National Restoration), and technocratic outsider Julio Guzmán (Purple Party).

Secondary politicians – those running for Congress, regional legislatures, smaller mayoralties, and city council – generally do not create their own parties. Yet few of them *join* parties in any meaningful sense. Rather, they negotiate, at each election, temporary positions on other parties' tickets. With the exception of well-known personalities with clear vote-winning potential (for example, media figures, athletes, artists), most secondary politicians purchase their candidacies, with payments reportedly ranging from $20,000 to $120,000.[32] Politicians acknowledge that legislative candidacies are "auctioned off,"[33] and that

---

[31] Author's interview with Keiko Fujimori, July 25, 2013.
[32] Author's interviews with ex-legislator José Barba Caballero (May 4, 2011); PP politician Juan Sheput (May 5, 2011); Mauricio Zavaleta's interviews with PNP legislator Sergio Tejada (May 23, 2013), and PSN legislator Heriberto Benítez (May 27, 2013).
[33] Author's interview with PP politician Juan Sheput (May 5, 2011).

candidates' position on party lists "hinge on how much money they pay."[34] Rather than work their way up through a party's ranks, then, politicians "rent" spots on legislative lists. Although they may formally affiliate with the party whose list they join, such affiliations represent nothing more than short-term contacts that cover a single election cycle.

The short-term nature of partisan affiliations is a product of extreme electoral volatility. Because parties that perform well in one electoral cycle often suffer marked decline in subsequent ones, politicians seeking to sustain a career must constantly renegotiate their partisan affiliations. Partisan loyalty exposes politicians to a high risk of defeat. To avoid going down with the ship, then, politicians must reevaluate their partisan affiliation – and often jump ship – at each electoral cycle.

The practice of party switching – known as *transfuguismo* – first gained notoriety in 2000, when Fujimori's spymaster, Vladimir Montesinos, bribed eighteen opposition legislators (known as *tránsfugas*, or "turncoats") to join the *Fujimorista* ranks. Although the original *tránsfugas* were disgraced after Fujimori's fall from power, the practice of *transfuguismo* diffused widely – indeed, became routinized – in the post-Fujimori era. Politicians no longer expect to develop stable partisan ties. Rather, they know that political survival requires constant party switching, via the negotiation of short-term contracts prior to each election. As a result, many contemporary Peruvian politicians have been affiliated with four, five, and even six or seven parties.

An example is Máximo San Román, a Cusco businessman who was elected Vice President on Fujimori's Change 90 ticket in 1990. San Román broke with Fujimori after the 1992 coup, and, in 1995, he was elected to Congress with Lima mayor Ricardo Belmont's party, Public Works. By 2000, Belmont was in political decline, so San Román jumped to the UPP, becoming its presidential candidate; a year later, when new elections were held after Fujimori's fall, he joined Castañeda's National Solidarity ticket as vice presidential candidate. In 2006, San Román ran as the vice presidential candidate of National Restoration, and later that year, he ran for Cusco's regional presidency with the Inka Pachakútec Movement. In 2010, he ran for the Cusco regional presidency with his own vehicle, the National Alternative Party, and in 2011, he joined Pedro Pablo Kuczynski's Alliance for the Big Change coalition, again as a vice presidential candidate. Between 1990 and 2011, San Román participated in eight elections with *eight different parties*.

San Román is by no means exceptional. *Transfuguismo* has become a routinized practice at all levels of Peruvian politics. In Congress, for example, deputies who were elected after 2000 had, on average, run for office under two party labels. Given that a quarter of these legislators were first time candidates, this figure is strikingly high. An analysis of legislative candidates in 2011 found that 63% had no prior affiliation with the party that nominated them.[35] And of

[34] Author's interview with ex-legislator José Barba Caballero (May 4, 2011).
[35] *Diario 16*, February 26, 2011, p. 8.

the ninety-eight elected legislators who had previously run for office, forty had switched parties since the last election.

Similar patterns can be seen at the local and regional levels. Of the forty-two district-level mayors elected in Lima in 2010, 31 had belonged to at least two parties, and nearly half had belonged to at least three parties. Likewise, an examination of the partisan trajectories of the ninety-three candidates who finished first or second in regional presidential elections between 2002 and 2010 found that candidates had belonged to an average of 2.3 parties. Five regional presidents elected in 2010 had belonged to four or more different parties during their career,[36] while four others had belonged to at least three parties.[37]

If an increasing number of politicians have become *free agents*, parties increasingly take the form of what Mauricio Zavaleta (2014) calls "coalitions of independents." Politicians who create personalistic vehicles in pursuit of executive office fill their legislative slates with free agents (either *tránsfugas* or amateurs without partisan backgrounds), most of whom lack any previous ties to the party. Party leaders recruit individuals who can contribute either votes (for example, well-known personalities) or money to the campaign (Rozas 2012). Partisan ties are secondary criteria.

Individual politicians seek to join tickets with the greatest electoral potential, which are those headed by the front-running candidates for executive office. Thus, they identify potential "locomotives," or top-of-the-ticket candidates with powerful coattails, and seek to negotiate their way aboard the train they are pulling.[38] Although most candidates nominally affiliate with the party they run with (by law, only 20% of parties' legislative candidates may be independents), such affiliations are essentially one-shot deals that cover a single election cycle: after the election, coalitions of independents disintegrate and candidates regain their free-agent status.

An example of a coalition of independents is Radical Change (CR), a Lima-based party created by former congressman José Barba Caballero. The party has no membership or activist base, but rather is (in Barba's words) merely a "platform in search of candidates."[39] When CR participated in the 2010 municipal election in Lima, it awarded all of its candidacies – including the Lima mayoral candidacy – to outsiders and free agents, using polling and candidates' ability to make financial contributions as selection criteria.[40] As Barba put it, "It doesn't matter who the [candidates] are or which party they

[36] These are Elías Segovia of Apurimac, Luis Picón of Huánuco, Klever Meléndez of Pasco, Tito Chocano of Tacna, and Gerardo Viñas of Tumbes.
[37] These are César Álvarez of Ancash, Jorge Acurio of Cusco, Maciste Díaz of Huancavelica, and César Villanueva of San Martín.
[38] Author's interviews with Lourdes Flores (March 30, 2011), José Barba Caballero (May 4, 2011), and Villa El Salvador District Councilor Genaro Soto (July 20, 2013).
[39] Author's interview with José Barba Caballero (May 4, 2011).
[40] Author's interview with José Barba Caballero (May 4, 2011).

come from, as long as they can win."⁴¹ Thus, CR's slate of district-level mayoral candidates was composed almost entirely of *tránsfugas*, most of whom abandoned the party after the election.

Coalitions of independents have become the predominant form of electoral organization in post-Fujimori Peru. Levitsky and Zavaleta (2016: 422–23) examined all political organizations that finished first or second in Peru's twenty-five regional elections in 2006 and 2010. Organizations in which at least 50% of mayoral candidates had previously run for office under the same label were scored as parties, while organizations in which a majority of mayoral candidates were either outsiders (i.e., did not previously belong to a party) or *tránsfugas* (i.e., defected from another party) were scored as coalitions of independents. By this measure, 70% of first and second place finishers in the 2006 and 2010 regional elections led coalitions of independents (Levitsky and Zavaleta 2016: 422). Only 16% of candidates represented parties; another 14% were pure independents who did not sponsor any mayoral candidacies.

In post-Fujimori Peru, then, party politics decomposed to the most basic unit: the individual candidate. Politicians became free agents, renegotiating their partisan affiliation at each election, and short-lived coalitions of independents became the primary mechanism through which politicians organized to compete in elections. Thus, coalitions of independents only meet Downs' minimalist definition of parties on election-day. Once the election-day snapshot is taken, many Peruvian teams break up into individual free agents.

EXPLAINING THE ABSENCE OF PARTY REBUILDING IN PERU

Why, a quarter of a century after party system collapse and more than a decade after redemocratization, has virtually no party building occurred in Peru? The Peruvian case suggests that democracy and electoral competition are, by themselves, insufficient to trigger party building. It also raises questions about the impact of electoral design. The 2001 transition gave rise to a series of electoral reforms aimed at strengthening parties, including a lower district magnitude, a 5% minimum threshold for entry into Congress, and a new Parties Law that banned independent candidacies, granted national parties a monopoly over legislative representation, and established an array of organizational requisites for new parties: to be legalized, new parties would need 135,000 signatures and a minimum of sixty-seven provincial branches – each with at least fifty activists – in two thirds of the country's regions (Tanaka 2005; Vergara 2009: 23). The reforms had no discernible effect on party building (Tanaka 2005; Vergara 2009).

One reason why parties have not reemerged in Peru is that party building is difficult.⁴² Durable party building requires the construction of robust organizations and strong partisan identities, neither of which come easily.

---

⁴¹ Author's interview with José Barba Caballero (May 4, 2011).   ⁴² See Levitsky *et al.* (2016b).

Because organization building is a "difficult, time-consuming, costly, and often risky enterprise" (Kalyvas 1996: 41), politicians who can win elections without investing in organization – for example, by using mass media as a substitute – are likely to do so (Hale 2006; Mainwaring and Zoco 2007).

Successful party building is most likely to occur during or after periods of intense polarization and conflict (Levitsky *et al.* 2016b). Violent conflict strengthens partisan identities and creates incentives for organization building. Politicians are more likely to invest in organization when they pursue extra-electoral goals or face severe threats (Kalyvas 1996; Roberts 2006b), as in the case of guerrilla movements (e.g., the FMLN, FSLN) or conservative parties created in the face of a revolutionary threat (e.g., ARENA in El Salvador, UDI in Chile). Moreover, a "higher cause" such as civil war, revolutionary struggle, or anti-authoritarian resistance mobilizes ideologically committed activists, which, given the time, labor, and uncertain payoffs associated with the construction of a territorial organization, are often essential to party building (Levitsky *et al.* 2016b). Many of Latin America's most robust parties were born or consolidated during periods of violent conflict. Major parties in Colombia, Costa Rica, Uruguay, and El Salvador emerged out of civil war. The largest parties in Mexico and Nicaragua were born out of revolution. Mass parties such as Argentine Peronism, Venezuela's Democratic Action, Peru's APRA, and Uruguay's Broad Front were born during periods of intense popular mobilization, and were consolidated during periods of violent repression.

Polarization and conflict have been largely absent – at least at the national level – in post-Fujimori Peru. Opposition mobilization against Fujimori was limited – it was an internal crisis, not popular mobilization, that ultimately brought down the regime (Cameron 2006). During the 2000s, radical movements were weak and national-level popular mobilization was virtually absent. Although Peru experienced important local-level conflicts (for example, the 2002 *Arequipazo*; the 2009 Bagua violence; the 2011 mining conflict in Cajamarca), these crises did not scale up into national-level conflicts (Meléndez 2012b). Given these relatively low levels of national-level mobilization or conflict, the absence of robust party building is perhaps not very surprising.

Arguably, however, two additional factors reinforced party system decomposition in the post-Fujimori era: the diffusion of non-party strategies and technologies (or party) substitutes and the weakness of the Peruvian state.

ALTERNATIVE STRATEGIES AND PARTY SUBSTITUTES

The Peruvian case suggests that party system collapse may be self-reinforcing. In the aftermath of party collapse, politicians may develop expectations, strategies, norms, and technologies that allow them to succeed in a context of elections without parties. Politicians who learn how to win public office without parties have little incentive to invest in them. Over time, the strategies, norms, and technologies of non-party politics diffuse (and even institutionalize), as electoral competition selects for politicians with the will, know-how, and resources to "go it alone."

Peruvian politicians learned during the 1990s that they could succeed without parties (Levitsky and Cameron 2003). The learning process arguably began with radio personality Ricardo Belmont's victory in the 1989 Lima mayoral race and was reinforced by Fujimori's success in 1990. The crisis of the so-called "traditional" parties had reduced the perceived value of established party labels, and Fujimori demonstrated that party organization was not necessary to win the presidency. Fujimori's success triggered a bandwagoning dynamic, as politicians abandoned established parties and declared themselves "independents" (Planas 2000). Many of these politicians were successful. Alberto Andrade (ex-PPC) and Luis Castañeda (ex-AP) were elected mayor of Lima and emerged as major presidential contenders; Alex Kouri (ex-PPC) was elected regional president of Callao. At the same time, new politicians – such as Toledo and Humala – eschewed existing parties and launched successful careers as outsiders. Similar patterns can be observed at the local and regional levels.

The post-Fujimori period saw the diffusion of three strategies that underlie (and reinforce) party-less politics. The first is *partisan free agency*. Outside of APRA, post-Fujimori politicians no longer expect to pursue careers within an individual party. Rather, it is widely known that politicians will act as partisan free agents, pursuing their career outside of established parties and adopting partisan labels on a temporary basis in order to compete in elections.

A second strategy that diffused widely after 2000 is *transfuguismo*. It is widely expected that politicians will routinely switch partisan affiliations, often renegotiating their party ties at each election cycle. This strategy of constant *transfuguismo* is viewed as necessary for political survival. During the 1990s, politicians learned that loyalty to one's original party could derail a career. Thus, sustained political success required that individuals, at each election, secure a position on a ticket headed by a viable candidate for executive office. By the mid-2000s, the logic of *transfuguismo* had achieved taken-for granted status among politicians.

A third strategy that diffused widely during the post-Fujimori era was the formation of "coalitions of independents" (Zavaleta 2014). Thus, the "parties" led by national and regional presidential candidates are not expected to nominate longtime activists or "careerists" for lower-level candidacies. Rather, they select the candidates – outsiders or *tránsfugas* – who can deliver the most votes or the largest financial contribution. These candidacies are expected to be short-term contracts that effectively expire after the election.

The turn away from parties has been reinforced by the deployment of what Henry Hale (2006) calls party substitutes (see Zavaleta 2014). One such substitute is private firms. Many private entrepreneurs have mobilized their firms' resources, employees, and infrastructure for electoral purposes, effectively transforming them into campaign organizations.[43] For example, César Acuña used his consortium of private universities as the basis for Alliance for Progress (APP), which he created prior to the 2002 local elections.[44] Acuña's universities were APP's principle source of finance (Barrenechea 2014). University profits were used to finance campaigns, and the universities themselves provided printing presses, media outlets, and meeting space (Barrenechea 2012: 21–25). The universities were also a major source of selective incentives for party members (Barrenechea 2014; Meléndez 2011). Most APP leaders and candidates held university positions, and many lower-level cadres held university scholarships (Barrenechea 2012: 26–30). Finally, Acuña's Clementina Peralta Foundation, a charity funded by university profits, operated a vast network of child care centers, health clinics, and other social services, which served as the bases for clientelist distribution (Barrenechea 2014; Meléndez 2011). Acuña's strategy was successful; he was elected mayor of Trujillo in 2006 and president of La Libertad in 2014, and his brother Humberto captured the regional presidency of Lambayeque in 2010.[45]

The number of "business parties" increased markedly in the 2000s.[46] In Ayacucho's 2010 regional presidential race, for example, both winner Wilfredo Oscorima and runner up Rofilio Neyra were successful entrepreneurs who used their business empires to finance lavish campaigns (Zavaleta 2014: 104–5). Likewise, Maciste Díaz (Huancavalica), Luis Picón (Huánuco), and Martín Vizcarra (Moquegua) used their firms as springboards to win or retain the regional presidency, while several other business-based candidates (e.g., Máximo San Román in Cusco, Fernando Martorell in Tacna) finished second. Other business-based candidates (e.g., José Luna, Julio Gagó) were elected to Congress.

A second type of substitute is media outlets. As Zavaleta (2014) shows, local radio station owners and prominent radio hosts frequently use radio as a means to mobilize votes in the absence of on-the-ground organization. In Puno, for example, outsider Hernán Fuentes used his Juliaca-based radio station, Radio Peru, as a springboard to the regional presidency in 2006 (Zavaleta 2014: 94–95). Fuentes' party, *Avanza País*, had no grassroots organization, but he gained name recognition by using Radio Peru to repeatedly attack Regional President David Jiménez. Fuentes won with less than 20% of the vote, nearly all of which was concentrated in areas covered by Radio Perú (Zavaleta 2014: 94). In 2010, Fuentes was succeeded by Mauricio Rodríguez, the founder of Radio Pachamama, the most successful station in Puno. Rodríguez had no real party organization, but Radio Pachamama allowed him to mobilize votes across the

[43] See Muñoz (2010) and Zavaleta (2010, 2014).
[44] On Acuña's party building project, see Barrenechea (2014) and Meléndez (2011).
[45] APP ran candidates for 12 of 25 regional presidencies in the 2010 local and regional elections. It won 7.7% of the national vote, second only to APRA's 10.6% (Barrenechea 2012: 13–14).
[46] See Ballón and Barrenechea (2010); Meléndez (2011); Muñoz (2010); Muñoz and García (2011); and Zavaleta (2014).

region (Zavaleta 2014: 94–95). Radio-based candidates also proliferated at the municipal level. In Puno region alone, Zavaleta identified ten radio owners or journalists who finished either first or second in the 2010 mayoral elections (2014: 95). Indeed, the use of media outlets as electoral springboards became so widespread that one Puno-based politician observed that "if you want to be a candidate, you don't create a party. You open a radio station."[47]

Media-based candidates succeeded in other regions as well. Journalists Carlos Cuaresma and Hugo Gonzales Sayán used their broadcast media presence to capture Cusco's regional presidency in 2002 and 2006, respectively (Muñoz 2010). In Madre de Dios, the winner of the 2010 regional presidential election, Luis Aguirre, was a radio journalist, while the runner-up, Simón Horna, was a local television broadcaster (Vilca 2011: 203).

Third, politicians hire freelance "operators" as a substitute for party organization (Zavaleta 2014). Operators are independent agents who undertake the grassroots campaign activities that are normally carried out by local party activists. Thus, they recruit lower-level candidates, build ties to local business, farmer, or neighborhood associations, organize meetings and rallies, oversee the distribution of clientelist goods, and recruit and coordinate personnel to carry out key campaign activities, such as painting graffiti, putting up posters, and distributing fliers (Zavaleta 2014: 98–102). Many operators are former leftist activists who, following the collapse of their parties, began to contract out their services at election time (Zavaleta 2014: 99). Like sub-contractors, they maintain small networks of clients or hired hands which they can mobilize for activist work during campaigns (Zavaleta 2014: 101). This enables local politicians to "rent" the organization that in most democracies is supplied by parties. When the election is over, the contracts expire and the organizations dissolve.

In sum, post-Fujimori politicians developed a set of organizational substitutes that enabled them to win elections in the absence of parties. The diffusion of these new electoral technologies makes it easier for individual politicians to opt for partisan free agency rather than join existing parties or invest in new ones.

Non-party politics may be reinforced by the fact that electoral competition selects for individuals who can win on their own. Thus, individuals who can deploy their firms or media outlets as substitutes for party structures, as well as celebrity candidates who can substitute their own "brand" for that of a party, appear to have an electoral advantage over professional politicians. Because party politicians lack organizational resources, they have difficulty competing against outsiders wielding substitutes: they are outspent by business people; they cannot reach voters as efficiently as radio-based candidates; and they lack the name recognition of celebrities and local notables.

[47] Efraín Pinazo, quoted in Zavaleta (2014:94).

Electoral competition may, therefore, generate a selection effect that reinforces party decomposition. Candidates who win election via substitutes are particularly unlikely to invest in party building. The ascendance of such politicians, together with the institutionalization of norms of partisan free agency, *transfuguismo*, and coalitions of independents may thus have a self-reinforcing effect, diminishing the probability of party rebuilding over time.

THE ROLE OF STATE WEAKNESS

Another factor that has inhibited party building in post-Fujimori Peru is state weakness. As Scott Mainwaring (2006a) has argued, state weakness undermines government performance, which can be a major source of public discontent. In the absence of minimally effective state agencies, even well-meaning governments routinely fail to deliver the (public) goods. Security, justice, education, and other basic services are under-provided, resulting in widespread perceptions of government corruption, unfairness, ineffectiveness, and neglect. In such a context, it is difficult for *any* party to govern well. Poor government performance erodes public support, making it difficult for new parties to consolidate an electoral base.

Party building is thus most likely to succeed where state capacity is high. Where states possess a minimum level of tax capacity and bureaucratic effectiveness, parties that win public office have an opportunity to govern well and carry out policies that strengthen their brands. Indeed, seven of the eleven new parties that successfully took root in Latin America after the onset of the third wave did so in countries with relatively effective states: Chile, Brazil, and Mexico (Levitsky *et al.* 2016b). Where states are weak, then, new parties are more likely to fail. In countries like Bolivia, Ecuador, and Guatemala during the 1980s and 1990s, weak states contributed to widespread perceptions of corruption and/or ineffective government performance, which eroded public support for new or emerging governing parties.

The Peruvian state has long been one of the weakest in Latin America (Soifer 2015). Tax capacity is limited, and the state's low regulatory capacity manifests itself in a sprawling urban informal sector in housing, commerce, and transportation (Soifer 2015). Throughout much of the interior, state authorities are "unable to enforce rules or regulations" (Mauceri 1997a: 156), police and judicial authorities are often absent; schools, health clinics, state bureaucracies are barely operative; and local officials are widely viewed as corrupt or ineffective (Soifer 2015). During the 1980s, the Shining Path insurgency and a profound economic crisis triggered the "rapid disintegration of the state" (Burt 2004: 250–51; Mauceri 1997a: 152). Although the Fujimori government restored a minimum of order in the 1990s (Burt 2004), widespread state deficiency persists, as is seen in the persistence of widespread coca production, the expansion of drug trafficking, and frequent incidents of lawlessness, such as the 2004 lynching of the mayor of Ilave, Puno. Indeed, according to an IDB-sponsored report published in 2006, Peru's "bureaucratic functional capacity" ranked near the bottom in Latin America, below Bolivia, Guatemala, and Nicaragua (Stein *et al.* 2006: 69).

State weakness has undermined party building in Peru in at least two ways. First, it has undermined government performance and, consequently, public support for governing parties. Despite unprecedented GDP growth, all three post-Fujimori governments were plagued by consistently low approval ratings: Toledo's approval rating fell into single digits in 2004 and 2005, triggering calls for his resignation; García's approval rating rarely exceeded 30%, despite GDP growth rates of nearly 10% in 2007 and 2008; and Humala's approval rating descended to 13% in 2015. Unpopular presidents generate perverse coattails effects for new parties. Thus, widespread public discontent under presidents Toledo and Humala prevented PP and the PNP from consolidating support bases, while widespread dissatisfaction under García limited APRA's capacity to rebuild its base.

Weak states also undermine parties' linkages to voters. For example, they inhibit the development of partisan brands, which Lupu (2016) and others have identified as critical to successful party building. A party brand is the image of it that voters develop by observing its behavior over time. Parties with strong brands "stand for" something in the eyes of their supporters. Thus, voter attachments are thus based on a sense of "comparative fit": in other words, "individuals identify with a party to the extent that they consider themselves similar to the party brand" (Lupu 2013: 50–51). According to Lupu (2016), brand development requires programmatic differentiation and consistency. If a party becomes indistinguishable from others, or if its programmatic profile changes markedly from one election to the next, the perceptions of "comparative fit" will diminish and its brand will be diluted.

Weak states undermine parties' ability to differentiate themselves or maintain programmatic consistency. Where states are weak, parties' ability to implement their programs – to deliver the programmatic goods they promise during campaigns – is limited. With limited tax capacity and ineffective and corrupt bureaucracies, even well-intentioned governments often fail to deliver policies that correspond to their programs. This has clearly been the case in Peru. The Toledo government's failure to break with the orthodox neoliberalism of the Fujimori period undermined the PP's brand; the García government's failure to implement its center-left campaign platform further eroded APRA's brand; and Humala's abandonment of not only his original radical populist platform but also his moderate center-left second round platform almost certainly undermined the PNP's incipient brand.

In sum, it is difficult to build strong parties upon weak states. In a context of widespread state deficiency, new parties generally fail to govern well or maintain a consistent programmatic profile, which limits their capacity to build stable electoral bases. Indeed, all post-Fujimori governing parties (PP in

2001–06; APRA in 2006–11, PNP in 2011–14) weakened during their period in power.

IS FUJIMORISMO AN EXCEPTION?

Paradoxically, *Fujimorismo* may constitute an exception to Peru's contemporary pattern of non-party building. Even though Alberto Fujimori never invested in a party (in fact, he openly disparaged them), several factors may facilitate *Fujimorismo's* consolidation in the post-Fujimori era. One is its condition as an authoritarian successor party, which, as Loxton (2016b) argues, facilitated right-wing party building in Chile, El Salvador, and elsewhere. Fujimori's authoritarian regime left several legacies that may facilitate party building. One is an established brand. Due to his government's success in stabilizing the economy and defeating the Shining Path, Fujimori retained considerable public support throughout his presidency (Carrión 2006). Indeed, this support persisted even after revelations of massive corruption and abuse triggered Fujimori's fall from power. In a 2006 survey, for example, 48% of respondents expressed a positive view of his presidency (Ipsos Apoyo 2006) and a 2013 survey found that 42% of Peruvians viewed the Fujimori government's performance as "good" or "very good" (GFK 2013).

Fujimori's authoritarian regime also left behind a patchwork of patronage and clientelist networks that could be used for organization building. Most notably, the Fujimori government's use of politicized social programs engendered extensive clientelist networks (Roberts 1995; Schady 2000). The government built strong ties to soup kitchens *(comedores)*, mothers' clubs, and squatters' associations, particularly in the lower-income districts surrounding Lima.[48] Many of these networks survived Fujimori's fall from power, and many of the activists who led them remained *Fujimoristas*.[49] These soup kitchens provided *Fujimorismo* with an organizational platform that was not available to other parties.[50]

Perhaps most importantly, *Fujimorista* party building was facilitated by polarization and conflict. For *Fujimoristas*, the 2000 transition ushered in a period of conflict and struggle that they describe as the "era of persecution" (see Urrutia 2011a). Fujimori supporters were treated as pariahs, scorned by much of the media, and occasionally insulted in public.[51] More than 200 *Fujimorista*

---

[48] Author's interviews with ex-*Fujimorista* legislator Martha Moyano (May 6, 2011), and *Fujimorista* parliamentary adviser Guido Lucioni (June 16, 2011).

[49] Author's interviews with ex-*Fujimorista* legislator Martha Moyano (May 6, 2011), and *Fujimorista* parliamentary adviser Guido Lucioni (June 16, 2011).

[50] Author's interviews with *Fujimorista* parliamentary adviser Guido Lucioni (June 16, 2011), ex *Fujimorista* legislator Martha Moyano (May 6, 2011), and Keiko Fujimori (July 25, 2013).

[51] As Keiko Fujimori put it, "the media ignored us ... We practically did not exist. And that created more solidarity among us" (author's interview, July 25, 2013). Also author's interview with ex-*Fujimorista* legislator Martha Moyano (May 6, 2011).

officials were prosecuted for corruption and/or human rights violations in the early 2000s (Urrutia 2011a: 102). In 2002, three prominent *Fujimorista* legislators, including former President of Congress Martha Chávez, were expelled from Congress. Finally, Fujimori himself was tried and convicted in 2007. Although Fujimori's conviction was deemed legitimate in international legal circles, *Fujimoristas* viewed it as an act of political persecution.[52] The perceived persecution of 2001–07 helped to unify and revitalize *Fujimorismo* (Navarro 2011; Urrutia 2011a, 2011b).

Fujimorismo initially reemerged as a social movement seeking Fujimori's return. The movement organized protests against the prosecution of Fujimori government officials and against transitional justice measures such as the Truth and Reconciliation Commission.[53] Though relatively small, the movement was characterized by a strong identity and sub-culture (Navarro 2011; Urrutia 2011b), as well as a shared ideology rooted in the experience of the 1990s counter-insurgency.

Fujimorismo began to take on a more party-like form in 2005, when the exiled Fujimori formed *Sí Cumple* (He Delivers) in the hope of returning to Peru to run for president.[54] After Fujimori was detained in Chile, *Sí Cumple* ran Martha Chávez as its presidential candidate. Although Chávez won only 7.4% of the vote, Keiko Fujimori was elected to Congress with more votes than any other candidate, which established her as a viable presidential candidate. *Fujimorista* mobilization against Fujimori's extradition, trial, and conviction in 2006 and 2007 strengthened the movement, and by the time Keiko Fujimori nearly captured the presidency in 2011, *Fujimorismo* was arguably Peru's strongest party (Urrutia 2011a, 2011b; Meléndez 2014). By 2016, it was unambiguously so.

Whether *Fujimorismo* will institutionalize remains uncertain. Its fate could parallel that of ex-dictator Manuel Odría's Odriísta National Union, which remained strong in the decade following his 1956 fall from power but weakened and eventually disappeared after his death. However, *Fujimorismo's* strong brand and organization, rooted in years of conflict during the Fujimori and post-Fujimori periods, suggests that it has the potential to consolidate.

THE CONSEQUENCES OF PARTY SYSTEM COLLAPSE

What consequences does the disappearance of parties have for democracy? There exists a near consensus among political scientists that democracy cannot function well without parties (Aldrich 1995; Mainwaring and Scully

---

[52] Also author's interviews with Jorge Morelli, Lima (June 18, 2011), Martha Moyano (May 6, 2011), and Santiago Fujimori, Lima (March 24, 2011). Also Navarro (2011: 53–54) and Urrutia (2011a, 2011b).

[53] Author's interviews with Jorge Morelli (Lima, June 18, 2011), Martha Moyano (May 6, 2011), Guido Lucioni (June 16, 2011), Santiago Fujimori (Lima, March 24, 2011); and Keiko Fujimori (July 25, 2013).

[54] Author's interview with Keiko Fujimori (July 25, 2013).

1995a; Schattschneider 1942: 1). The Peruvian case provides a test for these claims. This section examines how party decomposition has shaped how democratic institutions work in post-Fujimori Peru.

Governability without (Good) Governance

A major consequence of party collapse has been to shift the locus of decision making to individual politicians, which reduced political actors' time horizons and limited their capacity to coordinate or act collectively (Levitsky and Cameron 2003). Because institutionalized parties are collective and enduring organizations, they create incentives for more public-oriented and far-sighted behavior. Individual party politicians may be self-interested, but they are constrained by their parties, which must serve the needs of politicians across multiple electoral districts and multiple generations. Institutionalized parties thus impose a degree of coordination and far-sightedness on individual politicians that they would not otherwise achieve. Where parties collapse, these organizational incentives disappear. On their own, individual politicians have little incentive to think about anything beyond their own immediate electoral goals. Where personalistic vehicles predominate, then, cooperation becomes difficult: parties created to advance the short-term electoral goals of their founders are less likely to coordinate around collective or long-term goals.

What are the implications of this hyper-individualism? Weakly institutionalized party systems are widely viewed as a threat to governability, particularly in presidential systems. In Latin America, fragmented, inchoate party systems have been associated with executive–legislative conflict, institutional crises, and democratic breakdown (Mainwaring 1993; Mainwaring and Scully 1995a).

In Peru, however, party collapse has not undermined governability in the ways we might have expected. Although divided government became a permanent feature of post-Fujimori politics, hyper-individualism and short time horizons have not led to severe problems of executive–legislative conflict. Rather, they have enhanced the executive's capacity to govern by facilitating the cooptation of individual legislators. Because most parties cannot credibly offer their legislators the prospect of reelection, incentives for partisan loyalty are minimal. Thus, many legislators become free agents. Rather than creating problems for governability, however, free-agent legislators facilitate it. On their own, and with dim prospects for reelection, individual legislators operate with short time horizons and limited bargaining capacity, which makes them "easy to coopt."[55] Through a mix of patronage jobs, petty perks, cash bribes, and judicial protection from investigation of corruption, executives are able to forge working legislative majorities at relatively low cost.[56]

---

[55] Author's interview with ex-legislator Guido Lombardi (May 4, 2011).
[56] Author's interviews with ex-legislators Guido Lombardi (May 4, 2011) and Lourdes Flores (March 30, 2011).

Indeed, executive–legislative conflict was limited between 2001 and 2016. Despite his inexperience and unpopularity, President Toledo had relatively few problems with Congress. Carlos Ferrero, who served as President of Congress and Prime Minister under Toledo, was so effective in coopting legislators that opposition leaders spoke of a "Pax Ferrerino."[57] Likewise, although APRA controlled only thirty-six of 130 seats in Congress, the García administration used a variety of perks to induce opposition legislators to vote with the government. For example, one group of legislators, known as "the Romans," abandoned the opposition after receiving trips to Italy.[58] APRA retained control of Congress throughout the 2006–11 period, winning all leadership elections and nearly all votes of importance. Although the *Fujimorista* opposition's capture of a legislative majority in 2016 resulted in more difficult executive–legislative relations, this outcome was rooted in *Fujimorismo*'s *strength*, not party weakness. Moreover, it is likely to prove exceptional. In terms of executive–legislative relations, then, party weakness and minority presidencies have not undermined governability in post-Fujimori Peru. In the absence of stable parties, coopting individual legislators into working majorities has proven strikingly easy.

Yet governability based on party weakness is costly in terms of democratic governance. For one, legislative cooption undermines horizontal accountability. Congress had little effective oversight of the executive during the post-Fujimori period, and opposition initiatives to investigate executive abuse or censure cabinet ministers repeatedly failed. Under García, for example, APRA blocked a legislative committee report on the 2008 "Petroaudios" corruption scandal that implicated top government and party officials, and instead approved a report that effectively cleared those officials of wrongdoing. And following the tragic June 2009 violence in Bagua, opposition-led votes of censure against Prime Minister Yehude Simon and Interior Minister Mercedes Cabanillas fell short.

More broadly, a legislature filled with single-term, free-agent legislators is likely to be extraordinarily weak. Career legislators are critical of the development of a strong Congress. Not only do they possess the experience necessary to effectively oversee executive power, but they have the incentives and time horizons to do so as well. Because professional legislators devote their career to the Congress, their own power and prestige is closely linked to that of the Congress, which creates strong incentives to invest in it (Morgenstern and Manzetti 2003). By contrast, amateur legislators with little prospect for reelection have few incentives to invest in legislative capacity. In a Congress in which nearly 80% of legislators are novices and fewer than one in five are reelected, investment in institutional capacity will be limited.

[57] Author's interview with ex-legislator Lourdes Flores (March 30, 2011).
[58] Author's interviews with PP leader Juan Sheput (Lima, May 5, 2011) and ex-legislators Lourdes Flores Lima (March 30, 2011), Guido Lombardi (Lima, May 4, 2011), and José Barba Caballero (Lima, May 4, 2011).

THE RISE OF AMATEUR POLITICS

Another consequence of party collapse has been the rise of amateur politics. Party disintegration dramatically changed the nature of political careers. When national party linkages to local and regional politics evaporate, as in Peru, politicians can no longer rise up "through the ranks," from the local to the national level. With the partial exception of APRA, "the ranks" no longer exist. At the same time, electoral volatility makes it difficult for politicians to secure reelection. Between 1995 and 2008, Peru's legislative reelection rate was 20%, compared to 51% in Brazil, 52% in Argentina, and 63% in Chile (Tanaka and Barrenechea 2011). Likewise, only 20% of regional presidents were reelected between 2002 and 2010 (Muñoz and García 2011: 13). In the absence of national parties to provide mechanisms for career advancement, low reelection rates make it extremely difficult to sustain a political career.

With the collapse of partisan career paths, professional politicians have become an endangered species. Nearly all of the career politicians who were influential during the post-Fujimori period (APRA leaders Alan García and Jorge del Castillo, PPC leader Lourdes Flores; AP leader Víctor Andrés García Belaúnde; ex-PPC politician Alex Kouri; ex-IU leader Javier Diez Canseco) rose up through partisan ranks during the 1970s and 1980s. Very few stable political careers were launched after 1990.

The post-Fujimori period thus saw the ascendance of amateur politicians, or individuals who entered politics as a second career. Because aspiring politicians cannot rely on national parties for either resources or a useful label, they must either make a name for themselves or accumulate resources *prior to* entering the electoral arena. In other words, they must have a successful prior career. Many of these new politicians were successful business people (Muñoz and García 2011); others were prominent technocrats, media figures, religious leaders, well-known athletes, or leaders of other local institutions (e.g., university rectors, local police, or military commanders). Due to the uncertainty generated by low reelection rates, most of these new politicians remained active in other professions, allowing them to exit the political arena as quickly as they entered it. Examples include Guido Lombardi, a popular television host who was recruited onto the National Unity legislative ticket in 2006, and Humberto Lay, a prominent evangelical pastor who founded National Restoration and ran for president in 2006 and was later elected to Congress. Likewise, several former members of Peru's national women's volleyball team – including Cecilia Tait, Cenaida Uribe, Leyla Chihuán, and Gabriela Pérez del Solar – were elected to Congress.

Amateur politicians dominated Peruvian politics in the 2000s. Three of the four presidents elected after 2000 (Toledo, Humala, and Kuczynski) had never held elected office at any level. In the legislature, more than 80% of the congress people elected in 2006 and 2011 were new, and of the legislators elected in 2011, 70% had never held elected office (Tanaka and Barrenechea 2011). At the regional level, a study of the winners and runners up in the 2006 regional elections found that only twenty-eight of fifty had previously held elected office (Muñoz and García 2011: 11). In another study, Levitsky and Zavaleta (2016: 431–32) found that the number of amateur politicians who finished first or second in regional presidential elections increased from twenty-one (of fifty) in 2002 to thirty-one (of fifty) in 2010. Likewise, the number of amateur politicians elected to Congress increased from fifty-four (of 120) in 2001 to seventy-four (of 130) in 2011. In 2010–11, then, 57% of elected legislators and 62% of the top candidates for regional president were businessmen, media figures, or other celebrities who had recently jumped into politics.

The demise of the old political elite opened up Peruvian politics. Party collapse lowered the barriers to entry in the electoral arena, permitting the election of a diverse set of individuals who are more socially representative than in the past. The relatively narrow (and predominantly white-skinned) elite that dominated politics prior to 1990 has been displaced, and politicians from diverse socioeconomic, geographic, racial, and cultural backgrounds are now routinely elected to office. Presidents Fujimori (the son of working-class Japanese immigrants) and Toledo (who emerged from an impoverished and indigenous background) are but the most prominent examples of a pattern that has taken hold across the country.

Yet if the collapse of the political class and the rise of amateur politics have had an inclusionary effect, they also appear to have had several negative consequences for the quality (if not the stability) of Peruvian democracy. Several of these consequences are worth noting.

Making Democratic Institutions Work

The most obvious effect of amateur politics is limited experience in working with democratic institutions. Virtually by definition, amateur politicians are inexperienced with the nuts and bolts of democratic institutions. Compared to professional politicians, they tend to lack skills in bargaining and negotiation, coalition building, dealing with opponents, handling media, and other areas that are critical to governing and legislating. Widespread inexperience has several implications. For one, amateur-filled governments are more prone to make mistakes, squander political capital, fail to build or sustain coalitions, and respond poorly to crises. The Toledo and Humala governments both weakened themselves through costly political blunders. Likewise, Peru's amateur-dominated Congress was marred by a series of individual and collective missteps. Individual-level scandals include the revelation that a bill proposed by governing party legislator Natali Cordori had been plagiarized from Wikipedia (La República 2012). Among the most notorious collective blunders was the 2013 *Repartija*, in which the government and major opposition parties negotiated the nomination of several questionable justices for the Constitutional Tribunal, only to then reverse course in the face of widespread public repudiation.

Blunders and petty scandals erode public support and squander political capital, producing a more rapid and thorough *desgaste* (political deterioration) than is usual in democracies. More importantly, however, they may erode public confidence in democratic institutions. Indeed, the Peruvian Congress is among the least-trusted institutions in the country. According to the 2010 Latinobarometer survey, only 14% of Peruvians said they had confidence in Congress. The figure was the lowest in Latin America – less than half the regional average (34%). Likewise, Peruvian public trust in government was just 25%, compared to 45% in Latin America as a whole and more than 50% in Brazil and Chile (Latinobarometer 2010: 73).

Beyond avoiding blunders, political experience is critical to the development of shared norms, practices, and know-how that help make cabinets and legislatures work, facilitate the construction of multi-party coalition, and facilitate smooth executive–legislative relations. For example, the informal institutions that underlie coalitional presidentialism in Brazil and Chile developed over time, as a result of a sustained process of experimentation and learning by career politicians (Power 2010; Siavelis 2006). Such norms are less likely to emerge in a Congress with an 82% turnover rate.

Commitment to Democratic Institutions

Amateur politics may also reduce political actors' commitment to core democratic institutions. Mainwaring and Pérez-Liñán (2013) highlight the importance of actors' normative commitment to democratic regimes. Amateur politicians are less likely to be socialized into basic democratic norms such as mutual toleration and civility, winning graciously, and accepting defeat. Many of them have less patience for the negotiations and compromise that are inherent to democratic politics. (Accordingly, a former aide to Alberto Fujimori stated that he "couldn't stand the idea of inviting the President of the Senate to lunch in the Presidential Palace every time he wanted to pass a law").[59] And because they have not spent their careers working with democratic institutions (unlike professional politicians, democratic institutions are not their livelihood), amateur politicians may have less of a stake in their preservation.

Amateur politicians are also less likely to invest in *building* democratic institutions. Because the construction of strong institutions such as parties and legislatures is a costly, difficult, and often time-consuming process, it requires actors with long time horizons. Because amateurs do not work their way up through the political ranks and often do not expect to remain in politics for very long, their time horizons tend to be short. Such politicians are unlikely to invest in long-term institution building.

Corruption

Amateur politicians may be especially prone to corruption. Outsiders who do not expect to sustain a political career have little incentive to invest in their own

---

[59] Quoted in McClintock (1996: 65).

reputations and may have a stronger incentive to maximize their short-term gains – in effect, to "take the money and run" (see Muñoz 2014). Indeed, post-2000 legislatures were plagued by personal corruption scandals. For example, the legitimacy of the 2006–11 Congress was undermined by a string of widely publicized scandals involving individual legislators. The legislators involved in the most notorious scandals – nearly all of whom were first termers – became household names, with monikers such as "electricity thief," "foot washer," "chicken eater," and "dog killer." Overall, a whopping eighty-two of 130 legislators were accused of corruption *at least once* between 2006 and 2009.[60] The 2011–16 Congress was equally scandal-ridden: eighty of 130 legislators were formally accused of wrongdoing between 2011 and 2014.[61] At the same time, nineteen of Peru's twenty-five regional presidents were under investigation for corruption in 2014 (at the year's end, four regional presidents were in prison and a fifth was a fugitive).[62]

Political Weakness and Limited Capacity for Reform

Finally, there is evidence that the absence of professional politicians weakens democratic governments and limits their capacity to undertake reform. In an analysis of the surprising level of policy continuity in post-Fujimori Peru, Vergara and Encinas (2016) show how the inexperience of government officials left them unable to impose a policy agenda upon the cohesive and experienced class of free-market-oriented bureaucrats that had operated within the Peruvian state since the 1990s. The Humala government was almost completely devoid of politicians. In 2014, Humala's cabinet included only two politicians (Pedro Cateriano and Ana Jara); the rest were technocrats with little or no experience in politics. According to Vergara and Encinas (2016), Humala's politically inexperienced ministers were no match for the experienced and ideologically committed bureaucrats who occupied the upper ranks of the ministries they (nominally) ran. As a result, many of their reform initiatives were derailed.

It is unclear how sustainable Peru's contemporary democracy without parties (or, increasingly, professional politicians) is. On the one hand, the post-2001 regime is the longest-lived democracy in Peruvian history, and the economy has boomed for more than a decade. For some observers, the weakness of post-Fujimori politicians has permitted the policy continuity and limited state intervention necessary for Peru's economy to flourish, and, over time, sustained economic growth is the best guarantor of democratic stability.

On the other hand, there is reason to think that politics without parties or politicians will be difficult to sustain. Peru's democratic institutions function poorly. Vertical accountability is undermined by the fact that governments do not govern with the platforms upon which they are elected; horizontal

[60] *La República*, October 1, 2009.   [61] *El Comercio*, March 24, 2014.
[62] *La República*, May 28, 2014.

accountability is undermined by the fact that legislatures do not effectively oversee or check the power of the executive. And whereas the collapse of the old party system was rooted in widespread public discontent toward the political elite, the amateur politicians are equally despised by Peruvians. According to the 2010 Latinobarometer survey, Peruvians' trust in parties and Congress was the lowest in Latin America, and the percentage of Peruvians who believed that politicians "govern for the public good" (16%) was the second lowest in the region (Latinobarometer 2010: 73, 33). And crucially, only 28% of Peruvians were satisfied with their democracy – again, one of the lowest levels in Latin America (Latinobarometer 2010: 40). These numbers suggest that Peruvian democracy remains vulnerable.

CONCLUSION

Peru is an extreme case of party decomposition. Nearly three decades after the collapse of the party system, Peruvian politicians have neither rebuilt pre-existing parties nor constructed new ones. The Peruvian case thus suggests that democracy and electoral competition alone are by themselves insufficient to create incentives for party building. Rather, strong parties are most likely to emerge out of structural conditions – such as periods of intense social and political conflict – that have been absent in post-Fujimori Peru.

The Peruvian case also suggests that there may be a self-reinforcing dynamic to party collapse. Politicians learned how to win elections without parties and developed a set of informal norms and organizational substitutes to facilitate such efforts. Indeed, electoral competition appears to be selecting for partisan free agents, or politicians with the skills and resources needed to win elections in the absence of parties. To the extent that free agents and "coalitions of independents" displace party politicians, the prospects for a "return to parties" are likely to decline. Such an outcome does not bode well for democratic institutions. Although Peruvian democracy may survive in the absence of parties and professional politicians, it is unlikely to perform well.

PART III

COMPARATIVE ANALYSES

12

Party Brands, Partisan Erosion, and Party Breakdown

Noam Lupu*

The dramatic and sudden decline in the staying power of established political parties is one of the most puzzling features of Latin American democratic politics since the third wave of democratization. Between 1978 and 2007, one quarter of the region's established parties broke down, meaning that they suddenly became uncompetitive for national executive office. Parties that had only recently been major competitors were relegated to an average vote share of merely 6%. Their breakdowns severely deinstitutionalized these party systems, upending and fragmenting once stable systems (Mainwaring, Bizzarro, and Petrova, this volume; Roberts 2014).[1]

How might we explain these deinstitutionalizing breakdowns? Scholars of comparative politics often attribute party breakdowns to poor performance by incumbent parties. Corruption scandals or poor economic stewardship, they argue, cause voters to reject the incumbent party *en masse*, leading the party to break down (for example, Coppedge 2005; Dietz and Myers 2007; Kenney 2004). But bad performance is far more widespread than party breakdown, and established parties have survived some major economic crises. In the 1980s in Peru, for instance, President Alan García's economic policies led to some of the worst hyperinflation in world history, peaking in 1989 at 12,378%. Still, at the end of García's term, his Popular American Revolutionary Alliance (APRA) party received nearly a quarter of the vote and fell just 10 percentage points shy

* For their comments and suggestions, I thank Allen Hicken, Geoffrey Layman, Scott Mainwaring, and participants at the conference on "Party Systems in Latin America: Institutionalization, Decay, and Collapse" at the University of Notre Dame. This chapter draws in part on my work in Lupu (2016).

[1] In some cases, these breakdowns were associated with system-wide collapse (Morgan 2011; Seawright 2012), but such instances are rare. I focus on individual party breakdown because it is more frequent and because I think we can develop theories that travel across cases. A remaining open question is why individual party collapse is associated with different system-level outcomes across countries (see Roberts 2014).

of the winner. Bad performance is undoubtedly important, but it is not the whole story.

Classic theories of party politics also offer little traction in explaining these cases. Cleavage-based theories expect parties and party systems to change when the politically salient social cleavage shifts (for example, Dalton *et al.* 1984; Sundquist 1983). Theories such as these are helpful in explaining long-term trends of party decline and evolution, but they are difficult to apply to rapid shifts in a party's electoral fortunes. The slow shifting of social cleavages is unlikely to explain the sudden breakdown of a party.

Other aspects of the electoral environment, however, may change more quickly. Established parties – organizations that have remained competitive over decades – have adapted to existing environments (Cox 1997). Major changes could therefore threaten their survival. Making institutional arrangements, such as the rules governing elections, more permissive could have dramatic effects on parties that had adapted specifically to the old arrangements (Benton 2001; Centellas 2009; Kenney 2004; Remmer 2008; Tuesta Soldevilla 1996). They could also ease the entry of competitor parties that threaten established ones (Van Cott 2005). Or decentralizing political or fiscal authority – reforms that swept the developing world in the 1990s – could undermine national parties by strengthening local politicians (Morgan 2011; Penfold 2009).

Parties might also confront new social environments, especially in the economically volatile developing world. The debt crisis that swept Latin America in the 1980s, for instance, dramatically altered the socioeconomic environment for politicians. Default and economic stagnation meant high unemployment and shrinking government budgets. For parties that relied on state resources to fund patronage machines, these changes could pose serious obstacles (Benton 2001; Cameron 1994; Golden 2004; Morgan 2011; Roberts 2003, 2014).

Those parties that can adapt effectively will survive these institutional or social changes, whereas those too rigid to evolve may disappear. If party organizations are too institutionalized, if they privilege entrenched groups, or if their activist base is too extreme, they may fail to accommodate changing voter preferences (Coppedge 2005; Seawright 2012). In the Latin American context, those that relied most heavily on patronage might have found it particularly hard to mobilize support without access to state resources (Levitsky and Way 1998; Morgan 2011). Alternatively, those that relied on clientelism might have been able to cushion themselves against the forces of electoral decline (Kitschelt and Wilkinson 2007b; Levitsky 2003).

The crises and reforms of the 1980s and 1990s in Latin America undoubtedly challenged established parties. But politics is always dynamic; these same parties had adapted to dramatic social and institutional changes in the past. They had survived economic depressions, military dictatorships, even major revolutions. Indeed, established parties across the region – even some of those considered most institutionalized – did adapt to new and changing contexts. Some reneged on campaign promises and completely reversed their historic policy positions (Campello 2014; Stokes 2001), often forcing entrenched labor groups to swallow painful economic reforms (Burgess 1999; Murillo 2001). Others implemented more flexible internal procedures, severed links to certain interest groups, or adopted open primary elections, all in an effort to address changing public expectations.

Clientelism helped many Latin American parties maintain their local bases of support over decades. But parties that relied on patronage to drum up voter support also based their decades of electoral appeals on far more. Established parties, in fact, generated deep-seated loyalties that went far beyond any quid pro quo. In much of the region, supporters went to war for these parties or faced imprisonment and torture when they were banned by military regimes. In fact, clientelist parties often target many voters who already identify with the party (Nichter 2008; Stokes *et al.* 2013). And patterns of partisanship across Latin America suggest clientelism is not the basis for most voters' attachments to parties (Lupu 2015a). Moreover, clientelism alone, or the lack of it, is unlikely to account for the massive changes in the national electoral fortunes of established parties. The difference between parties that survived and those that broke down was millions of votes, and even the region's most efficient political machines are unlikely to sway so many voters, particularly as clientelism also entails electoral costs (Weitz-Shapiro 2013).[2]

The institutional reforms and social transformations of the period were also not uniform enough across the region to explain the varied fortunes of established parties in different countries (see Eaton and Dickovic 2004; Tulchin and Selee 2004). Parties broke down in countries that did not decentralize at all, whereas others survived despite changes to the electoral rules.

Within countries, many of these changes should have affected all parties more or less equally. After all, it is countries that reform their electoral rules, and whole party systems that should be affected by decentralization. Yet it is individual parties that broke down. Arguments that focus on system-wide transformations have a hard time explaining why one established party collapses whereas others in the same country live to fight another day. One could argue that system-level changes affected some parties more than others,[3] but these kinds of explanations would need to specify what made some parties more susceptible than others. An

---

[2] My evidence also contradicts claims that clientelism maintains partisan attachments. For instance, voter attachment to the PJ in Argentina declined in the 1990s, even though the party ramped up its clientelistic efforts during this period (Levitsky 2003).

[3] For instance, one could argue that parties that historically relied more heavily on patronage were more likely to break down as a result of declining state resources. But many patronage-based parties in the region survived the neoliberal era, whereas those far less reliant on state resources broke down.

adequate explanation of party breakdown needs to grapple with the different outcomes both across and within countries.

Party breakdown is also fundamentally about the attitudes and choices of voters. It is individual voters who decide to reject an established party they themselves had just recently supported (see Morgan 2011; Seawright 2012). In fact, party breakdowns are preceded by declines in partisan attachments (Lupu 2016). Something more than anti-incumbency was at work. We need to know why individual attachments to the parties erode and why, and when, that erosion leads them to abandon their party at the polls.

This chapter builds on the general explanation of party breakdown offered by Lupu (2014, 2016) by expanding its scope and testing its congruity across a broad range of cases. During the 1980s and 1990s, politicians across Latin America implemented policies that were inconsistent with the traditional positions of their party, provoked internal party conflicts, and formed strange-bedfellow alliances with traditional rivals. I argue that these actions blurred voters' perceptions of parties' brands – the kinds of voters the parties represent – eroding voters' attachments to them. Without the assured support of a partisan base, parties became more susceptible to voters' short-term retrospective evaluations. Voters who now had no party attachments deserted incumbent parties when they performed poorly. What looked like erratic voters suddenly abandoning the established parties they used to support was actually the result of a process of brand dilution. In this chapter, I examine whether the expectations of this theory are congruent with the outcomes for three parties: Argentina's Radical Civic Union (UCR), Bolivia's Nationalist Revolutionary Movement (MNR), and Chile's *Concertación*.

PARTY BRANDS, PARTISANSHIP, AND PARTY BREAKDOWN

Why did some parties in Latin America break down whereas others, even within the same country, did not? And why have partisan attachments for some Latin American parties eroded precipitously in recent decades? Party attachments are group identities, akin to the attachments people form to social groups. They are based on the stereotypes people have about each group. People have an idea about what the prototypical poor person looks like, or how the prototypical banker behaves, and they categorize themselves into group identities by comparing themselves to the group prototype. Individuals identify as a poor person or a banker if they think they resemble, or *fit*, that prototype (Hogg *et al.* 1995; Turner *et al.* 1987). And they also feel closest to a group when they think other groups' prototypes look very different from theirs – a concept social psychologists call *comparative fit* (Hogg *et al.* 2004; Turner 1999).

We can think of these prototypes as representing points on a continuum. For some, class may be the important dimension of political identity. Some parties will be seen as pro-poor, whereas others are seen as favoring the interests of the affluent. In many instances that class dimension correlates highly with the standard left–right ideological dimension that orients politics in much of the world (Huber and Inglehart 1995; Lijphart 1994). Parties that pursue redistribution to the poor will be seen as representing the poor; those that limit regulation on businesses will be seen as favoring the interests of the affluent. In the Latin American context, the most salient political dimension appears to be the economic left–right (for example, Altman *et al.* 2009; Colomer and Escatel 2005; Wiesehomeier and Doyle 2012).[4]

As with other social identities, an individual feels closest to the party whose prototype s/he thinks s/he most resembles, relative to all other parties (Green *et al.* 2002). Over the course of their lives, citizens form perceptions of party prototypes based on what they see the parties say and do over time.[5] They learn what to associate with the prototypical partisan by observing what politicians say and do, and they use these prototypes to inform their identity. These prototypes comprise what I call a *party brand*. Individuals repeatedly update their perceptions of parties' brands, incorporating new observations into their prior beliefs about the parties (Achen 1992).

Party brands can also be weak or strong, depending on how precisely citizens can pinpoint them. When people see a party sending clear signals, they develop a clearer image of its prototypical partisan, and the brand becomes stronger. As their uncertainty about the party's position increases, the party appears to be more heterogeneous, perhaps containing multiple prototypes, and the brand becomes diluted.

These learned party brands form the basis of mass attachments. A citizen will feel the greatest affinity with the party whose prototypical partisan s/he thinks s/he most resembles, relative to all other parties. As with other social identities, partisan identity is determined partly by the resemblance, or fit, between the individual's self-image and his/her image of the party prototype. Party attachments, therefore, increase as citizens perceive they more closely fit with the party. Moreover, the more ambiguous the party brand, the weaker that attachment, because an individual will perceive less fit with the party prototype.

Crucially, the degree of identification also depends on comparative fit, the degree to which a citizen feels s/he resembles the prototype of one group and differs from that of another group. Thus, a person will feel most attached to a party when its prototype most resembles him/her and the prototypes of other parties seem very different.

This conception of partisanship implies that the behaviors of parties can affect mass attachments (Lupu 2013). In particular, parties can dilute their

---

[4] I focus on the left–right dimension because it tends to be the most salient in Latin America and therefore offers substantial explanatory power. Nevertheless, the left–right need not be the only salient dimension in every case, and future studies could easily apply this theory to a context in which a different dimension matters more.

[5] Recent studies have found clear evidence that voter perceptions indeed respond to party behavior (for example, Fortunato and Stevenson 2013; Pope and Woon 2009).

brands through inconsistency or convergence. Inconsistency increases citizens' uncertainty about the party brand when parties suffer from internal conflicts (see also Grynaviski 2010). Citizens observe conflicting signals from the party and find themselves more uncertain about the party brand. Inconsistency also confuses citizens when a party shifts its position. They may, particularly in Latin America, observe a party they thought was statist suddenly support free-market economic policies (Stokes 2001).[6]

Party brands will also dilute when parties converge (e.g., Lupu 2015b). As they do, citizens become unable to distinguish one party brand from another.[7] They may observe that different party brands are effectively indistinguishable because elites from different parties support the same policies. Or they may see different parties entering into formal or informal alliances, which signals that they are willing to agree on a political agenda (Fortunato and Stevenson 2013). Even when people are certain about two party brands, their substitutability means that citizens fail to form strong attachments with either party.

Partisanship thus erodes in response to party inconsistency and convergence. But the erosion of partisanship also has electoral implications. Voters evaluate parties both in terms of their partisan attachments and in terms of performance. As voters become more attached to a party, they will forgive bad performance. But as they become less attached, performance will become an increasingly important determinant of vote choice (Kayser and Wlezien 2011). Party breakdown, therefore, occurs when two conditions are met: (1) the party's brand is diluted, leading partisan attachments to erode, and (2) the party performs poorly in office.

Partisan attachments eroded in Latin America because of growing confusion among citizens about party brands, or what a party stands for. Few established parties in Latin America had the strong, consistent brands of many Western European parties. But in earlier periods, citizens had fairly clear notions about what it meant to be a Peronist in Argentina or an *aprista* in Peru. That changed when incumbents were confronted with the economic crises and international policy consensus of the 1980s and 1990s.

The debt crisis that swept the region beginning in 1982 raised borrowing costs and forced governments to either cut spending or increase inflation. The Washington Consensus that emerged by the 1990s among economic policy

---

[6] Kitschelt and Wilkinson (2007b) suggest that parties lose votes when they are inconsistent. That contrasts with evidence that voters favor ambiguous candidates (Tomz and Van Houweling 2009) and that economic policy shifts sometimes get rewarded electorally (Stokes 2001; Tavits 2007). Still, my focus here is on partisanship, not vote choice. I argue that policy shifts blur party brands and weaken partisanship, even if they sometimes also increase electoral support.

[7] Morgan (2011) similarly highlights the effect of inter-party agreements, along with bad performance, on party system collapse. Her argument focuses on formal alliances and vote choice, whereas I highlight the effect of inter-party convergence of varying kinds on mass partisanship. By distinguishing partisanship from vote choice, my theory explains instances of party convergence eroding partisanship that do not lead to party collapse.

makers focused international attention on lowering debt levels, retrenching governments, and opening domestic markets. As a result, politicians across the region knew that they risked inflationary crises, massive capital flight, and debt default if they did not adopt economic reforms. The new economic circumstances posed a particular challenge to established parties of the left, which traditionally espoused precisely the kinds of economic interventions threatened by the new economic constraints. So politicians from leftist parties across the region implemented market-oriented economic policies that were inconsistent with their party's statist and labor-based brands. Doing so regularly provoked intense internal conflicts and often required forming surprising alliances with traditional rivals on the right.[8] That inconsistency and convergence with competitors eroded partisan attachments and made parties susceptible to voters' short-term valence evaluations. Voters who now had no party attachments deserted incumbent parties when they performed poorly, causing established parties to collapse.

In previous work, I focused on exogenous economic shocks that hit incumbent parties after their brands had been diluted and their partisan base eroded (Lupu 2014, 2016). In this chapter, I expand the operational definition of performance to include social conflict. My theory suggests that when voters do not identify with a particular political party, they will give more weight to valence evaluations. The most widely studied valence issue is economic performance, but we know that voters also care about other valence issues: they prefer clean government, competence, and social peace (Stokes 1992). This chapter thus expands and builds upon my prior theoretical framework.[9]

EVIDENCE FROM THREE CASES

If party brands matter in this way, we should observe their effects on both political attitudes and voter behavior. In the realm of attitudes, we would expect to see party inconsistency and convergence weaken voters' partisan attachments. When looking at voter behavior, we should see the combination of brand dilution and bad performance, broadly defined, lead to party breakdown.

I examine both implications by comparing three very different parties from three very different country contexts. These case studies explore the degree to

---

[8] I take these actions by parties as exogenous here. This seems reasonable: in this period, exogenous international conditions generated electoral incentives and induced presidents to take actions that dilute their party brand, such as policy switches (Burgess and Levitsky 2003; Stokes 2001). Elsewhere I specify the conditions under which political elites choose to take these actions (Lupu 2016). Note, though, that brand dilution need not be electorally damaging in the short term. Brand dilution only makes parties more susceptible to valence evaluations; as long as those evaluations are not bad, brand dilution may not hurt parties at the polls.

[9] Note that my theory focuses on incumbent parties. Although one could potentially extend it by theorizing how voters form valence evaluations about non-incumbent parties, the current theory does not explain cases in which parties collapse while in opposition.

which party brands help to explain the deinstitutionalization of party systems in the region. My aim is not to select cases that hold constant confounding variables or address alternative explanations, something I have done elsewhere (Lupu 2016). In this chapter, I use George and Bennett's (2005) congruence method to evaluate how consistent the theory is with the actual outcomes in a varied set of cases. Inevitably, both large-N analyses and small-N case studies beg questions about how well the theory fits other cases. This chapter takes up precisely those questions.

Since my goal here is not to engage in controlled comparisons across cases, I selected three cases that were representative of the deinstitutionalization we have seen in Latin America in the period covered by this volume (see Mainwaring and Bizzarro, Chapter 4 in this volume): party collapse as part of system-wide collapse (Bolivia's MNR), individual party collapse (Argentina's UCR), and partisan erosion (Chile's *Concertación*).[10] This approach – which follows "typical case" selection criteria laid out by Gerring (2007) – consciously selects on the dependent variable. But doing so offers a useful contribution about the generality of the theoretical argument to the broader region.

In each case, I use the available individual-level data as well as primary and secondary sources to study whether brand dilution had the effects my theory predicts: partisan erosion and, when combined with bad performance, party breakdown. The electoral trajectories of these parties is shown in Figure 12.1.

Unfortunately, quantitative measures of party behavior that are comparable across countries and over time are not available across these cases. The data that come closest are measures of party convergence based on representative surveys of national legislators conducted by researchers at the University of Salamanca (USAL). These surveys asked legislators to place their own party on a standard left–right dimension. Unfortunately, even these data start in the mid-1990s, after convergence had occurred in Argentina and had begun in Bolivia. Figure 12.2 reports the average response for the major parties I discuss in Bolivia and Chile.[11] Both cases demonstrate substantial party convergence. These figures are a useful first step, but we need to better trace the process of convergence – and, to the extent possible, voter perceptions of convergence – in each case to evaluate its congruence with the theoretical expectations.

---

[10] Note that in Chile, I focus on a coalition rather than an individual party. This is because of the uniquely institutionalized and stable nature of electoral coalitions in Chile, the result of Chile's peculiar electoral rules (Agüero 2003; Carey 2002). There is also good reason to think that voters' attachments in this context are directed to the coalitions (González *et al.* 2008), so my discussion will mostly focus on them as the unit of analysis.

[11] The question asked, "In speaking about politics, it is common to use the terms *left* and *right*. This card shows a scale of values that go from left to right [card with 1–10 scale is shown]. At which point would you situate your own party?"

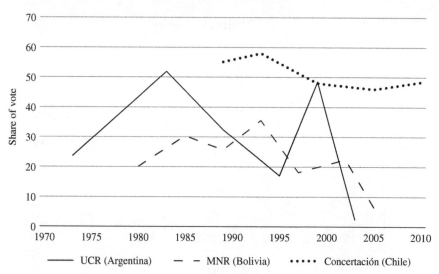

FIGURE 12.1 Electoral Strength of the UCR, MNR, and Concertación
Notes: Lines represent share of the vote for each party in the first round of presidential elections.
Sources: Payne *et al.* (2007) and author's updates.

Argentina's UCR

When democracy returned to Argentina in 1983, so too did the two political parties that had contested elections in prior periods of democracy, the UCR and PJ. Since its emergence in the1940s, the PJ drew its electoral support from the rural poor and urban working classes while the UCR was the party of the middle and upper classes (Lupu and Stokes 2009). Both parties were heterogeneous, but they nevertheless maintained some brand identities. In a September 1986 survey, nearly 50% of survey respondents named the UCR as "the party most bound to privileged sectors;" only 8% named the PJ. In contrast, 54% thought the PJ offered "the most concrete solutions for neediest sectors," and 73% thought it the party that "best represented workers," compared with 25% and 14%, respectively, for the UCR.[12]

The two parties relied on patronage to maintain internal discipline and to mobilize sectors of the electorate (Calvo and Murillo 2004; Snow 1971). But both also worked assiduously to build and maintain partisan attachments (Lupu and Stokes 2010). Already in 1965, 46% of Argentines identified with a party, of which 35% identified with the UCR and 30% with the PJ (Kirkpatrick 1971: 87). By October 1984, 58% of Argentines identified with

---

[12] Author's calculations from Aresco survey of 1,000 adults in Greater Buenos Aires. The series of questions began, "Could you signal which of the political parties active in the province is . . . " The options offered were: Radicalism, Peronism, PI, UCD, FREPU, or none.

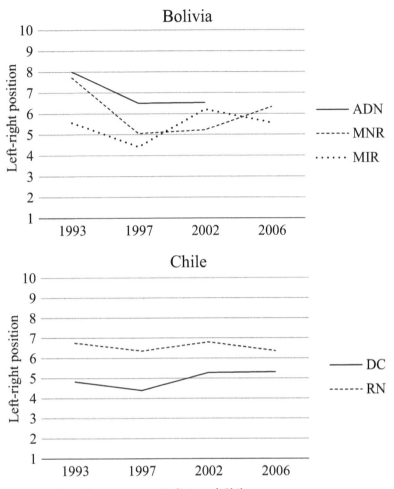

FIGURE 12.2 Party Convergence in Bolivia and Chile
Notes: Lines represent changes over time in parties' left–right positions.
Sources: USAL surveys.

a party, 52% of them with the Peronists and 33% with the Radicals (Catterberg 1989: 63).

During the 1980s, both the UCR and PJ maintained those partisan bases by hewing to their traditional brands. Radical president Raúl Alfonsín (1983–89) managed to maintain discipline within the UCR around his various economic proposals. Even some of his most controversial policy initiatives – dealing with the crimes of the 1976–83 military regime – achieved near-unanimous UCR support (Mustapic and Goretti 1992). On the other side of the aisle, the PJ demonstrated disciplined opposition to the administration's agenda. Along with its labor backers, the PJ staunchly opposed – and often blocked – Alfonsín's economic proposals. It rejected both Alfonsín's initial heterodox economic plan and his later, more market-oriented proposal. PJ-backed unions remarkably led thirteen general strikes during Alfonsín's administration, all with public support and the participation of PJ leaders. Anything short of opposition to Radical proposals was seen by Peronists as "illicit unions" (Mustapic and Goretti 1992: 268).[13] The result was a fairly steady base of Radical partisans: a consistent 20% of Argentines identified with the UCR throughout the 1980s.

All that changed when the PJ's Carlos Menem took over the presidency amid a hyperinflationary crisis in 1989. Menem was elected on a statist economic platform, promising to reverse the decline of the Argentine economy. But upon taking office, he shocked Argentine voters and his own party by pursuing both a staunchly neoliberal set of economic policies and a series of alliances with anti-Peronist elites and former opponents.

The UCR also found itself unprepared for the Peronist president's policy switch. With Menem offering policies nearly identical to those proposed by the Radical presidential candidate, Eduardo Angeloz, during the campaign, the UCR found itself in the strange position of agreeing with the Peronist president. Menem immediately opened talks with UCR leaders about forming a unity government. Although a formal pact never materialized, the repeated attempts and negotiations received widespread media coverage and were far more serious than Alfonsín's half-hearted attempts. Particularly noteworthy were two nearly successful rounds of negotiations with Angeloz himself aimed at persuading the former presidential candidate to join Menem's cabinet. As late as November 1991, Menem made serious public overtures for a pact among political parties.

UCR leaders attempted to maintain the nuanced position of opposing some administration proposals while supporting the broad thrust of Menem's economic program. Alfonsín himself oscillated between criticizing the speed of the economic reforms and offering his party's support. In Congress, the UCR proved far less obstructionist than the PJ had been during the 1980s. Then, in late 1993, Alfonsín and Menem emerged from the presidential residence in Olivos to announce their agreement to a pact for the general framework of a constitutional reform. The Pact of Olivos represented renewed convergence by the two parties, with the UCR effectively conceding to Menem's reelection. Coverage of the pact promoted the perception that the two parties had become indistinguishable: cartoons, for instance, fused Menem and Alfonsín into a single figure.[14] The convergence of the two parties significantly affected partisan attachments. By October 1995, less than 10% of Argentines

---

[13]   The PJ did suffer an important internal conflict in the 1980s. But unlike the intra-party conflicts that would emerge in the early 1990s, the conflict with the Renovation faction centered on organizational, rather than ideological, issues (Levitsky 2003).

[14]   *Clarín*, December 13, 1993, page 5.

identified with the UCR.[15] Still, Menem was reelected on positive public assessments of his stewardship of the economic crisis.

In his second term, the UCR began to reposition itself as a center-left alternative to Menem's neoliberal PJ. In 1997, it formalized an alliance with the left-wing FREPASO to solidify its anti-neoliberal credentials. FREPASO leaders – themselves defectors from the ranks of the PJ – had emphasized the social costs of neoliberal policies on unemployment, poverty, and inequality, and promised to work to address them. In 1999, the Alliance for Work, Justice, and Education (commonly called the *Alianza*) successfully elected the UCR's Fernando de la Rúa president with FREPASO leader Carlos Álvarez as vice president.

But the *Alianza's* electoral success did not translate into successful governing. Relations between the two parties strained quickly. On taking office, Economy Minister José Luis Machinea announced tax increases and austerity measures, including cuts in education and social services, the very areas the *Alianza* had promised to reinforce. The cuts were deeply criticized by FREPASO legislators and cabinet members. Although the *Alianza* held a majority in the lower chamber of Congress, the dissent of some FREPASO legislators made it difficult for the administration to pass legislation (Jones and Hwang 2005). So De la Rúa resorted to governing by decree (Mustapic 2005) and ceased consulting with Álvarez and FREPASO. Hostilities between the coalition partners came to a head in June 2000, when reports that the administration had bribed senators led Álvarez to resign suddenly.

In early 2001, De la Rúa appointed a neoliberal Radical as Minister of the Economy and announced new spending cuts to education, a direct contradiction of one of the foundations of FREPASO's program. The reaction from FREPASO and De la Rúa's own UCR was swift. Party leaders spoke out against the administration with unrestrained vehemence. Three Radical cabinet members resigned in protest. Alfonsín soon added his own criticism. Within weeks, the Radical president decided he could no longer govern with FREPASO and began to rely instead on the architect of Menem's neoliberal reforms, Domingo Cavallo, and his backers in the PJ. One prominent UCR deputy, Elisa Carrió, denounced fellow Radicals who voted for Cavallo's proposals as "traitors" (La Nación 2001); she soon left the UCR to form a new party.

The Radical party brand had become so meaningless and so indistinguishable from the PJ that politicians now preferred to form their own parties. In the ensuing months, other FREPASO and UCR politicians followed Carrió. With the credibility of the De la Rúa administration in decline, economic uncertainty soared. By the end of 2001, economic pressures forced De la Rúa to default on Argentina's loans and resign the presidency (Levitsky and Murillo 2003).

---

[15] Author's calculations from a national survey of 1,811 adults conducted by Romer & Associates. The question asked, "With which party do you identify more? Which party best represents your way of thinking?" This wording likely even overstates actual identification.

De la Rúa's resignation forced the PJ-controlled Senate to choose his successor. After some false starts, the Senate appointed Eduardo Duhalde, the former vice president who had lost the 1999 election to De la Rúa. His selection received the support of the PJ, UCR, and FREPASO. Duhalde called for a government of national unity and negotiated with both PJ and UCR governors, promising not to run in the 2003 elections. Two Radicals and one FREPASO leader joined his cabinet. And both the UCR and FREPASO supported granting Duhalde emergency decree powers, something they had denied De la Rúa. During his seventeen months in office, Duhalde repeatedly relied on UCR and FREPASO support in Congress. FREPASO even joined the administration's legislative bloc.

By the time of the 2003 election, Argentina's political parties were in disarray. The UCR's inconsistencies and internal conflicts during the De la Rúa administration had so diluted its brand that few voters still identified with the party. In the months leading up to the election, less than 5% of Argentines said they identified with the UCR.[16] At the same time, perceptions of De la Rúa's economic performance were dismal. In a November 2001 survey, fewer than 3% of Argentines said the De la Rúa administration was managing things well or very well.[17]

Blamed for disastrous performance in office and lacking a partisan base, the UCR was doomed. A party that only four years earlier had garnered 48% of the vote now attracted a mere 2%.[18] The 2003 election thus dealt the death blow to the UCR, which has since been uncompetitive in national elections. The Argentine party system had gone from a stable two-party system to a fragmented system of competing personalities with no clear party brands. Even the PJ, which muddled through its own brand's dilution during the economic crisis, would need to reconstruct its brand to recover the level of partisan attachments it had once enjoyed.

Bolivia's MNR

Bolivia's transition to democracy was one of the most chaotic in the region (Dunkerley 1984), the result of an economic crisis that led to labor unrest and peasant mobilization against the military regime. The result was a temporarily stable three-party system (Gamarra 2003). On the left, the Revolutionary Left Movement (MIR) was formed in 1970 to unite the disparate leftist and labor groups across the country. In the center was the historic MNR, born of the 1952

---

[16] Author's calculation from various surveys of adults in Greater Buenos Aires conducted by Carlos Fara & Associates.

[17] Author's calculations from a national survey of 1,200 adults conducted by Mora y Araujo & Associates. The question asked, "How do you believe the national government is managing things?"

[18] The UCR had performed dismally before, in 1989. But back then, it still had a loyal base of partisans supporting its candidate. Only in 2003, when bad performance was combined with brand dilution that eroded voter attachments, did breakdown occur.

popular revolution that had incorporated labor groups and mobilized rural peasants in favor of land reform. The political and economic right, led by the military dictator Hugo Banzer, formed the Nationalist Democratic Action party (ADN).

For both institutional and political reasons, the parties needed to join forces in order to govern. Bolivia's constitution provided that if no candidate received a majority of the vote, Congress would select the president. In a stable three-party system, no single candidate attracted an electoral majority until 2005, so the parties in Congress would need to form coalitions to select a president (Gamarra 1997). And since no party held a majority in Congress, those alliances would also be designed to persist so that the selected president could successfully pursue a legislative agenda.

Initially, Bolivia's coalition governments were broadly consistent with the historical traditions and origins of the three parties. In 1980, the centrist MNR and leftist MIR coalesced behind the candidacy of Hernán Siles Zuazo, a leftist defector from the MNR, in an effort to prevent Banzer, ADN's candidate, from retaking office.[19] Consistent with his campaign promises, Siles Zuazo pursued a series of economic policies aimed at stemming the government's growing export and debt crises. But in the midst of hyperinflation and massive popular protests, he agreed to step down ahead of schedule. As in 1980, the MNR and MIR coalesced to select the new president, the MNR's Víctor Paz Estenssoro, even though he had come in second (to Banzer) in the election.

Rather than govern with the MIR, Paz Estenssoro decided to ally his administration with the right-wing ADN and pursue the market-oriented economic reforms being prescribed by international financial institutions (Malloy 1991). Through an informal "Pact for Democracy," Paz Estenssoro provided Banzer's party with access to government jobs in exchange for legislative support (Gamarra 1994). The new administration reversed many of the economic policies of Siles Zuazo – and some of Paz Estenssoro's own campaign promises – but the three-party system made a center-right coalition just as palatable as a center-left one. Indeed, the ability of the parties to successfully select and support a president seemed to many observers to be a sign of the system's consolidation (Malloy 1991; Mayorga 1997; Whitehead 2001).

It was not until 1989 that the Bolivian parties began to engage in what Slater and Simmons call "promiscuous powersharing" (Slater and Simmons 2013). Following a fierce election campaign, the left-wing MIR and right-wing ADN agreed to jointly select the third-place MIR candidate Jaime Paz Zamora as president. The alliance between the two diametrically opposed parties, known as the "Patriotic Alliance," and the selection of the third-place candidate

---

[19] A subsequent military coup prevented Siles Zuazo from taking office until 1982 (Whitehead 1986).

shocked voters (Gamarra 1994).[20] Paz Zamora, moreover, abandoned his party's core constituency of workers and peasants, instead adopting the Paz Estenssoro administration's neoliberal economic agenda (Conaghan and Malloy 1994). As a result, it soon became clear to voters that the party of the left and the party of the right were in fact quite similar in terms of the kinds of policies they would be willing to support (Centellas 2007).

For those who still held out hope of differentiable party brands, the parties cemented their convergence over the course of the ensuing decade. As the economy grew and inflation stabilized, the three parties continued to alternate in an array of alliances. As fewer and fewer Bolivians identified with the parties, the volatility of the vote increased. The three historic parties also lost electoral ground to emerging new parties, some of which had started to build distinguishable brands and partisan followings. But even many of these parties, eager for the resources of office, entered into the governing coalitions. A notable exception was the Movement toward Socialism (MAS).

In 1993, ADN and MIR cemented their coalition by putting forward only one presidential candidate under the banner of the Patriotic Alliance. But MNR's Gonzalo Sánchez de Lozada, who for the second time came in first place in terms of votes, forged a coalition of small parties for a congressional majority. He even offered the vice presidency to the leader of the Revolutionary Liberation Movement Tupac Katari (MRTKL), an emerging indigenous party. And he passed several electoral and political reforms not only to deepen democratic consolidation and market reforms (Grindle 2003), but also to forestall further deinstitutionalization and to protect the electoral strength of his party (O'Neill 2005). But the reforms could not undo the fact that all three parties – MIR, ADN, and MNR – had espoused the same basic economic agenda. Like both his predecessors, Paz Zamora and Paz Estenssoro, Sánchez de Lozada continued to implement market-oriented economic reforms.

Following Sánchez de Lozada's lead, MIR and ADN similarly cobbled together an alliance of small parties – including some of the parties that had backed Sánchez de Lozada – to bring Banzer himself back to power in 1997. The so-called "mega-coalition" showed the Bolivian public that the parties had not only converged substantially on the neoliberal economic agenda, they were also now pursuing many of the same economic policies put forward by the pre-1982 military regime. By 2001, Banzer was seventy-five years old and his health was declining precipitously. He resigned, passing the presidency, and leadership of the ADN, to Jorge Quiroga, and died shortly thereafter.

With protests emerging in the countryside against neoliberalism (Arce and Rice 2009; Barr 2005), Sánchez de Lozada convinced MIR and Banzer's

[20] Gamarra and Malloy (1995) recount a joke circulating in the aftermath of the 1989 election: "Before the election the three candidates visited the *Virgen de Urkupiña*, who offered them one wish each. [MNR candidate] Sánchez de Lozada wished to win the elections; Paz Zamora, to be president; and Banzer, to run the country. The generous Virgin granted all three wishes" (p. 413).

coalition partners to back him for a second presidency in 2002 (Singer 2004). The historic parties, having all converged on center-right economic policies, were staging a last-ditch effort to keep the runner-up, left-wing Evo Morales and his MAS out of national office (Van Cott 2003).[21] The gambit worked temporarily, until MAS-led protests and marches on the capital destabilized the country (Gingerich 2009; Mayorga 2005). The "Gas War," as the social conflict over Sánchez de Lozada's plans to export natural gas through Chile became known, came to a head in 2003 when the countrywide protests and roadblocks were met with violent government repression. After sixty protesters were killed by government forces, Sánchez de Lozada resigned and fled the country. By the time of the scheduled 2005 elections, the MNR had collapsed; its candidate received a paltry 6% of the vote.

The MNR had not just severely diluted its brand by converging with its rivals again and again, it had also failed to quell the extraordinary social unrest. Like the UCR in Argentina, it likely had no partisan base to rely on at a time when voters uniformly blamed the party for dismal performance.[22] In Bolivia, that dismal performance came in terms of the government's incapacity to maintain social order and its violent response to the protests, whereas in Argentina it centered on the combination of a deep economic crisis and the De la Rúa government's violent handling of subsequent protests.

Chile's Concertación

In the 1990s, the Chilean party system was widely regarded as being among the most stable and most institutionalized in Latin America (see, for example, Dix 1992; Mainwaring and Scully 1995b). And yet, individual attachments to the country's political parties have eroded since the return to democracy in 1990. Despite the persistence of its historic political parties and continued competition among two main political coalitions (Valenzuela and Scully 1997), levels of voter partisanship in Chile are today among the lowest in the region (Lupu 2015a).[23] The reason has partly to do with the behaviors of those coalitions over the course of the 1990s and 2000s.

When the government of General Augusto Pinochet organized a plebiscite on his continuation in office, Chile's historic parties of the left and center joined forces in the campaign for democratization, eventually forming the *Concertación (Concertación de Partidos por la Democracia)* (Siavelis 2009). The left and right in Chile had fought vehement political and military battles

---

[21] This gambit is reminiscent of the last-ditch effort in 1998 by the two historic parties in Venezuela to coalesce around a single candidate in order to forestall the election of Hugo Chávez.

[22] Data on mass partisanship is not publicly available for this period in Bolivia, so in this case I am unable to document the intermediate step of partisan erosion between party convergence and breakdown.

[23] See also Luna and Altman (2011).

throughout the 1960s and 1970s, and polarization between the two sides was seen as an important contributor to the breakdown of democracy (Valenzuela 1978). Even during the Pinochet era, leftist leaders repeatedly failed to compromise and join forces with the centrist Christian Democrats (Siavelis 2014).

After winning the plebiscite, the *Concertación* then succeeded in getting its presidential candidate, the Christian Democrat Patricio Aylwin elected to the presidency. The centrist Aylwin oversaw significant increases in social spending, but without dismantling the neoliberal foundations of macroeconomic stability put in place by Pinochet and his "Chicago Boys." More radical socioeconomic or political reforms were opposed by many Christian Democrats within the coalition and would also have proved difficult to legislate given the system's "authoritarian enclaves," institutions like lifetime or designated Senate appointments inserted in the 1980 constitution by Pinochet to perpetuate the power of the regime (Siavelis 2000). In the post-transition context, Aylwin chose to pursue policies like tax and judicial reform that would gain support from segments of the right-wing Alliance for Chile (*Alianza*) rather than provoke hostility (Boylan 1996; Fuentes 2014). His successor, Eduardo Frei, a fellow Christian Democrat, took a similar tack of centrist compromise. Indeed, ideological questions were almost completely absent from the 1993 presidential campaign (Angell 2007). By the end of the 1990s, the *Concertación* was widely viewed as a very moderate center-left coalition (Agüero 2003),[24] in stark contrast to the once-radical positions held by some of its member parties (Portes 1970).

Throughout this period, the opposition *Alianza* found it difficult to soften its hardline right-wing image and association with the Pinochet regime. It was particularly hampered by conflicts between the coalition's two main parties and the fact that Pinochet himself remained head of the military (Navia and Godoy 2014). But his resignation and arrest in 1998 empowered those within the *Alianza* who wanted to moderate the coalition's stances. During the 1999 presidential campaign, the *Alianza's* Joaquín Lavín, associated with the hardline right wing of his coalition, moderated many of his positions, and came closer than expected to winning the election (Silva 2001). As Fontaine Talavera (2000) notes, "what began as merely tactical postures ended up becoming commitments" (p. 73).

Those commitments became even more pronounced when Sebastián Piñera became an *Alianza* candidate in opposition to Lavín in the presidential election of 2005. Unlike prior *Alianza* candidates, Piñera positioned himself as a moderate "Christian humanist," appealing to centrist supporters of the Christian Democratic Party (PDC), a member of the *Concertación* (Morales Quiroga 2008). Unlike Lavín, he had no ties to the military regime of Augusto Pinochet and its

---

[24] The coalition's electoral losses in 1997 were widely interpreted as resulting from defections on the left by sectors unhappy with the *Concertación's* moderate economic stances (Posner 1999).

neoliberal economic policies,[25] and he promised to govern not only with the right but in a 'New Coalition' with the center, a promise he sought to make more concrete by including former members of the PDC on his campaign team (Gamboa and Segovia 2006). The result, notes Angell (2007), was that the "emphasis of both candidates of the right on poverty and exclusion seemed to represent a shift from their free-market economic doctrine to one resembling the left of the *Concertación*" (p. 119).

By the end of the 2000s, the differences between the *Concertación* and *Alianza* on major economic issues had declined substantially. Indeed, by 2009, those who still identified with one or the other coalition scarcely differed in terms of their preferences over socioeconomic policies (Castillo *et al.* 2013). Consistent with my expectations, this convergence among the parties also eroded mass partisanship. The black lines in Figure 12.3 track the longitudinal trends in voter attachments to the *Concertación* and *Alianza* over the two decades of the current democratic period.[26] The trends show some decline in attachments to the *Concertación* during the 1990s, followed by a second decline in the latter half of the 2000s. The *Alianza* appears to gain partisans during the 1990s, but suffers a similar decline in the latter 2000s.

The USAL survey data in Figure 12.2 show some convergence between the PDC and RN during some of this period, but it only goes up to 2006. Moreover, those surveys ask only about individual parties, not about the coalitions. As an alternative, the grey line in Figure 12.3 plots a different measure of the ideological distance between the *Concertación* and *Alianza* over the same period. To construct this distance, I use a measure of party positions developed by Gamboa *et al.* (2013), using the electoral manifestos of the coalitions. They follow the methods employed by the Comparative Manifesto Project for mapping party positions in advanced democracies on a left–right ideological scale (Budge *et al.* 2001).[27] Although electoral manifestos are primarily internal party documents that few voters ever read, they may reflect the general positions of the parties and could therefore serve as reliable proxies of relative party positions.[28]

---

[25] In fact, Piñera had publicly voiced his intention to vote against Pinochet in 1988.

[26] The data come from nationally representative surveys conducted by the Centro de Estudios Públicos. The specific studies used here were conducted around the presidential elections of 1989, 1993, 1999, 2005, and 2009. The surveys were conducted in May–June 1990 (No. 14), November–December 1994 (No. 29), December 1997–January 1998 (No. 35), October–November 1999 (No. 38), June–July 2006 (No. 52), and June–July 2010 (No. 62).

[27] There is some debate among Chile scholars about whether the salient dimension of political competition in Chile is a left–right ideology or a democratic-authoritarian dimension held over from historical support or opposition for the Pinochet regime (Alcántara Sáez and Luna 2004; Alvarez and Katz 2009; Tironi and Agüero 1999; Torcal and Mainwaring 2003; J. S. Valenzuela 1999b).

[28] There is considerable debate about the appropriateness of using manifesto data to measure party positions (see, for example, Benoit and Laver 2006). Although I recognize the limitations of these

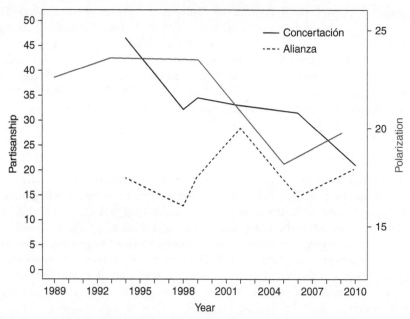

FIGURE 12.3 Partisanship and Party Polarization in Chile, 1990–2009
Notes: Black lines represent proportions of respondents from national surveys who said they identified with each coalition. The grey line represents the ideological distance based on party manifestos between the *Concertación* and *Alianza*.
Sources: Centro de Estudios Públicos surveys, and Gamboa *et al.* (2013).

Taken together, the two trends – convergence between the two coalitions and declining mass partisanship – seem to correlate as expected. As the *Concertación* shifted to the center during the 1990s and the *Alianza* did the same in the 2000s, mass attachments to both coalitions declined. This is consistent with the notion that as these coalitions diluted their brands by diminishing the differences between them, fewer and fewer Chileans formed long-standing attachments to one over the other. Party convergence in Chile also appears to have weakened other political identities (Bargsted and Somma 2016), as it has in other contexts (Evans and Tilley 2012).

Like the UCR in Argentina and MNR in Bolivia, though to a lesser degree, Chile's *Concertación* converged with its competitor over the course of the 1990s and 2000s. And, as in the other cases, this convergence eroded mass attachments to the coalition. But unlike the UCR and MNR, the *Concertación* remains a powerful electoral force in Chile. In part, the convergence of the Chilean coalitions has not been as dramatic – or as complete – as that of the

data, I consider them a reasonable choice given that few other options (such as reliable expert surveys over time) are available.

traditional parties in Argentina or Bolivia, as Figure 12.1 shows. The *Concertación*, therefore, maintains, a significant, though diminished, base of partisan supporters to this day. Moreover, the *Concertación's* performance in office has so far remained good, or average at worst.[29] Although its diminished partisan base has made it more susceptible to the performance evaluations of voters, it has yet to enter an election in which these evaluations are predominantly negative, as did the UCR in 2003 and the MNR in 2005.

PARTY BRANDS AND PSI

How parties behave affects how voters perceive them and, in turn, the attachments they will form. When parties are inconsistent, sending mixed signals to voters or shifting on issues voters care about, voters become uncertain about what the party stands for, and who it represents. Similarly, when parties converge, by allying with supposed rivals or simply by converging with major competitors, voters will feel less affinity with one over the other. As they see fewer and fewer differences in what parties stand for, and the types of voters they represent, voters will be less likely to form strong partisan attachments.

In Argentina, the UCR's inconsistency and its dramatic convergence with its historic rival, the PJ, severely eroded its partisan base. By the early 2000s, relatively few Argentines called themselves Radicals. In Bolivia, the three historic parties all converged in the midst of a deep economic crisis and severe international constraints. The MNR, once a deeply rooted fulcrum of Bolivian politics, no longer seemed to represent its peasant base. Though far less dramatically, even the stable Chilean coalitions have steadily moved closer on major economic issues, eroding voters' attachments to them.

These erosions are in and of themselves problematic for the institutionalization of these party systems. After all, stable bases of support are an important element of PSI (Mainwaring and Scully 1995b), and partisanship is a common way in which parties form stable bases. But in Argentina and Bolivia, partisan erosion also deinstitutionalized the party systems by contributing to the rapid collapse of major parties. The combination of an eroded partisan base and bad incumbent performance – the deep economic crisis in Argentina in 2001–02 and the destabilizing social conflicts in Bolivia in 2003 – caused two historic parties to go from winning the presidency to electoral irrelevance in a single term. Their collapse, and the rapidity with which it occurred, destabilized these party systems. Bolivia's

---

[29] Looking at all seventy-two of the national surveys conducted by Chile's Centro de Estudios Públicos since 1989, one finds that the only time in which a majority of voters held negative (as opposed to positive or neutral) evaluations of the economy was briefly at the beginning of Ricardo Lagos's term. But even those negative evaluations had dissipated by the time presidential elections were held again in 2005.

party system was already only weakly institutionalized, but whatever stability it had seen in the 1980s and 1990s was replaced by a fragmented and fluid party system. Only the MAS, the one party that had maintained a consistent and distinguishable brand, survived unscathed; indeed, it benefited enormously from the fragmentation of its opposition. Following the collapse of the UCR, Argentina's party system also fragmented dramatically (see Gervasoni, Chapter 9 of this volume). The political space formerly occupied by the UCR yielded to a dizzying array of parties, and the PJ, now effectively unchallenged, splintered. Party collapse rolled back whatever institutionalization the Bolivian party system had achieved and completely deinstitutionalized the once-stable Argentine one. Although Chile's party system has avoided these fates so far, further convergence among the coalitions would make it susceptible to these kinds of outcomes if an economic or social crisis arose.

What these cases suggest – and there are others like them across the region – is that two factors have played important roles in the deinstitutionalization of party systems across Latin America. The first is the particularly constrained economic policy environment in which many of these countries found themselves during the 1980s and 1990s, precisely during the consolidation of electoral democracies in much of the region. Because political leaders were severely constrained in the kinds of economic policies they could pursue, many had little choice but to dilute their parties' brands.[30] The second factor these cases, and others like them, highlight is the economic vulnerability of these developing democracies. Economic crises like those suffered in many countries in the region in the late 1990s and early 2000s led to the collapse of major parties that had been made vulnerable by brand dilution. Stronger economies less susceptible to crisis might have muddled through a period of diluted party brands and thin partisan bases to reconstruct distinguishable party brands and rebuild party attachments. What is also clear from these cases is that, in such contexts, even the most institutionalized party systems cannot be taken for granted.

More broadly, the emphasis here on party brands implies an important normative role for partisan conflict. Political moderation often seems normatively appealing; where extremism is dogmatic and polarization is conflictual, moderation is pragmatic and consensual. Hence the perennial calls in the United States for "bipartisanship." But if partisanship is necessary for the institutionalization of a party system, then voters need to be offered meaningfully different party choices rather than consensus. Too much polarization may well be destabilizing – as many scholars have argued (for example, Sartori 1976; Valenzuela 1978) – but too little may be just as harmful.

---

[30] On the one hand, international financial institutions often imposed economic policies on national leaders in this period. On the other hand, the international economic environment at the time also made pursuing market-oriented economic policies vastly more electorally attractive (in that they were far more likely to generate positive economic outcomes in the short term).

13

Roots in Society: Attachment between Citizens and Party Systems in Latin America

Jason Seawright

INTRODUCTION

Party systems are valuable at least in part because of their role in connecting citizens with the often elite-dominated politics of governance. Parties can represent voters in a Downsian sense of producing policy responsive to citizen preferences (Downs 1957) without incorporating citizens in any active, participatory sense – but such modes of representation foreclose opportunities for citizens to contribute to the process of representation in more creative, self-transformative, and potentially system-stabilizing ways. For these reasons, the study of party system institutionalization (PSI) must bring citizens into the discussion in a way that goes beyond their role as the demand side of the electoral market.

Mainwaring and Scully's concept of PSI (Mainwaring and Scully 1995b) brings citizens in by defining institutionalized systems as having roots in society. The first chapter in this volume instead sees stability as the defining feature of institutionalization, and suggests that a party system's roots in society contribute to institutionalization by facilitating stable identities, vote shares, and modes of voter linkages on the part of parties (Chapter 1 in this volume). This chapter examines party systems' roots in society as a window into institutionalization – a plausible cause of stability. I first propose a three-part conceptualization of party system/citizen attachment, in which a prototypical institutionalized party system will be one where many citizens have party identifications, work for parties and participate in their meetings, and hold supportive attitudes toward the party system as a democratic institution. I then demonstrate that existing theoretical and empirical literature on various components of this conceptualization provide an over-abundance of explanatory possibilities.

Using random forests (Breiman 2001), a machine learning tool for comprehensive description, I offer an exploratory descriptive analysis encompassing all of these candidate explanations, as well as virtually every other variable in use in cross-national statistical social science. While this analysis is at best a weak tool for causal inference, it provides empirically rich clues about domains for future investigation. The results are intriguing. In particular, social and economic development are negatively connected with rates of partisan identification and participation, but positively tied to attitudes of support for the party system as a democratic institution. Other factors, particularly several related to the structure of class and ethnic cleavages in society and the bureaucratic quality of the state, raise important issues for further research.

CONCEPTUALIZING THE SOCIETAL ROOTS
OF A PARTY SYSTEM

PSI is enhanced when the major parties have "somewhat stable roots in society" (Mainwaring and Scully 1995b: 5; Chapter 1 in this volume). This idea of roots in society includes the existence of organized connections between parties and interests, but it also requires attachment between citizens and the party system. Such attachment is relatively underdeveloped in the earlier work on institutionalization and its causes because of the scarcity of broadly comparable survey data for Latin America until recently. With the emergence of useful cross-national survey data, further work on this key contributor to institutionalization is timely.

Citizens can be attached to party systems in multiple, conceptually independent ways. In the first place, citizens may identify with one or another party. While party identification is not necessarily always a timeless, exogenous attribute that citizens inherit from their parents at birth,[1] there is substantial evidence that it is a relationship with more durability than vote choice. Parties with large groups of identifiers are more robust in times of crisis than those without this linkage, and indeed erosion of party identification is an almost necessary precursor of party breakdown and of party system collapse (Morgan 2011; Seawright 2012). For these reasons, party identification is an important element of PSI.

There are, however, other important sets of attachments between citizens and parties that do not involve identification. Consider first citizens' judgments about the systemic legitimacy of the parties as a collective (Dalton 2004). Some regard the existing parties as a necessary and legitimate component of a functioning democracy, and view them as trustworthy players in the country's political life. At the other extreme, some citizens see parties in general as corrupt, rapacious institutions that exist only to further the selfish personal

---

[1] Classic sources arguing that party identification is dynamic and responds to party performance include Fiorina (1981) and Achen (1992). A more recent statement from a similar perspective is Sanders *et al.* (2011). However, even the leading contemporary advocates of party identification as a stable long-term trait show in their discussion of Italy that such patterns can sometimes be disrupted (Green *et al.* 2002).

aims of the politicians, and the existing parties are viewed as discredited and untrustworthy players on the national stage. Many citizens obviously fall somewhere between these extremes, and some have mixed attitudes – for example, thinking of parties in general as necessary and legitimate but the existing parties as corrupt and unreliable. Nevertheless, the space defined by the two polar types is conceptually useful and is highly relevant for analyzing PSI.

Indeed, a claim that a particular party system was institutionalized when most of its citizens saw the parties as illegitimate and untrustworthy would be problematic. Citizens who oppose parties in general, or especially the existing set of parties in particular, are more likely than their more supportive peers to vote for candidates from outside the party system, to support new parties and movements, and to vote for personalistic campaigns without a party basis (Bélanger 2004). Thus, a society in which there is high systemic support for the parties as an institution is a society whose party system has a long life expectancy; low systemic support, by contrast, indicates a party system that is likely to change soon. For these reasons, systemic legitimacy and support for the parties is an important causal contributor to PSI.

The two prior contributors to linkage between party systems and society involved beliefs; the last to be considered here instead involves behavior. Citizens are connected to parties behaviorally when they work for those parties (as volunteers in elections, or perhaps in a more long-term and formal way) and when they attend party meetings and otherwise access the party organization. Such patterns of participatory action are the classic linkage mode of the mass party era (Duverger 1954), and as such remain potentially relevant and theoretically important in contemporary Latin America.

These categories clearly do not exhaust the conceptual universe of possible linkages between a party system and voters. Citizens might also be connected to a party system via, for example, the consumption of partisan media, wearing partisan shirts or hats, repeating party slogans to friends and coworkers, and so forth. There are limited empirical measures of most potential elements of party system/voter linkage, and so they are difficult to study systematically. Furthermore, it is reasonable to infer that a substantial proportion of citizens who are linked to the party system in one of these ways will also be involved in one or more of the linkage modes discussed above.

One more significant linkage pattern is left out here: when citizens vote repeatedly for the same party, they can be said to be meaningfully attached to the party system even if they do not identify with any party, evaluate the party system as a whole as an important institution, or work for a party. Unfortunately, there are significant obstacles to studying the extent of sustained party voting across the region. Few panel surveys have been carried out in Latin America. The best-known set of such surveys, the Mexican election studies (Lawson *et al.* 2007, 2008), have interviewed respondents repeatedly during the course of a single campaign and have not reinterviewed respondents across multiple campaigns. Hence, one cannot easily construct a viable measure

TABLE 13.1 *Correlations among Components of Citizen–Party System Attachment*

	Party identification	Party meetings	Work for party	Trust parties	No democracy without parties
Party identification	1.00	0.50	0.45	0.32	0.42
Party meetings	0.50	1.00	0.43	−0.02	−0.10
Work for party	0.45	0.43	1.00	−0.09	0.13
Trust parties	0.32	−0.02	−0.09	1.00	0.30
No democracy without parties	0.42	−0.10	0.13	0.30	1.00

Source: Prepared by the author based on LAPOP 2006, 2008, 2010, and 2012 datasets.

of the stability of vote choice over time from these data. Furthermore, even if such a measure were available from the Mexico surveys, there are very few comparable data sources from other countries in the region, making assessment across party systems problematic. Most work on this subject has instead focused on macro-level volatility of vote shares (Coppedge 2001; Madrid 2005; Roberts and Wibbels 1999), a variable that is obviously central to this volume's conception of PSI and will be explored below as a potential outcome of the kinds of factors considered here.

Hence, the discussion below will focus on a conceptualization of party system/citizen attachment as involving elements of identification, participation, and systemic evaluation. Are these categories empirically distinct at the analytical level of cross-national comparison? A simple way of examining the empirical structure of these concepts is to look at a correlation matrix (see Table 13.1).

The data presented in Table 13.1 draw on country–year averages from AmericasBarometer surveys in Latin America.[2] Identification-based attachment is the proportion of respondents for a given country in a particular wave of the survey who give an affirmative response to the question, "Do you currently identify with a political party?" Two variables measure rates of party organizational participation: the proportion of survey respondents who reported attending party meetings at least once a year, and the proportion who answered positively when asked, "There are people who work for some party or candidate during election campaigns. Did you work for any candidate or party during the recent elections of [election year]?" Finally, for evaluations of the party system as an institution, country–year means of two questions are used. The first asks respondents to respond, on a 7-point scale, to the question, "To what extent do you trust the political parties?" The second asks citizens to respond, again on

[2] LAPOP (2016). We thank the Latin American Public Opinion Project (LAPOP) and its major supporters (the United States Agency for International Development, the Inter-American Development Bank, and Vanderbilt University) for making the data available.

a 7-point scale, to the prompt, "Democracy can exist without political parties. To what extent are you in agreement or disagreement with this phrase?"

The results present descriptive patterns that conform to the conceptualization developed above. Party identification emerges as a uniquely pivotal mode of attachment between citizens and party systems, in that it is strongly associated with all other variables. Identification is a unique mode of attachment not because it is empirically separate from the others, but rather because it has relationships across the conceptual and empirical separation between attitude and behavior. The two partisan participation measures have a substantial correlation of 0.43; neither has any meaningful relationship with the two attitudinal variables. Finally, the two attitudinal variables have a reasonable correlation of 0.30. Thus, the data support the existence of conceptual clusters related to attitudes of attachment to the party system and to behavioral attachment via party organizational participation, with partisan identification a third concept that serves as a statistical pivot between the other two.

Finally, it is worth checking whether there is a connection between these modes of citizen attachment to the party system and the overall electoral stability that is pivotal to the concept of PSI. The Latinobarometer measures of party identification, trust, and work for parties are available as early as 1996; the correlation between these relatively early measures and countries' net electoral volatility between 1990 and 2014 is a useful test of whether there is evidence for the predictive relationship that is a necessary condition for a causal linkage.[3] In fact, all three variables show suggestive but statistically insignificant negative correlations with electoral volatility: −0.21 for party identification, −0.21 for work for parties, and −0.26 for trust in parties. Scatterplots reveal a triangular pattern: high scores on these variables correspond with low levels of volatility, while lower scores on the attachment variables are linked with scores across the volatility spectrum. This fits well with this volume's hypothesis that party system/citizen attachments represent one of several distinct causal pathways to overall party system institutionalization (Chapter 1 in this volume).

PATTERNS OF PARTY SYSTEM/CITIZEN ATTACHMENT
IN LATIN AMERICA

Given this conceptual framing of party system/citizen attachment, the next analytic task is to map these attitudes across Latin America. The data for this discussion come from country–year averages of survey responses from the AmericasBarometer survey used in the last section, as well as the

---

[3] Scott Mainwaring provided the data on electoral volatility. Given the limited data set of only sixteen countries and the comparatively strong interconnections among these attachment variables, multivariate analysis is unfortunately unhelpful here.

Latinobarometer survey (Latinobarometer 2015). Two major descriptive puzzles deserve consideration.

First, are the overall time trends in attachment, along the lines documented for the advanced industrial democracies? If a secular trend toward non-partisan orientations toward politics is a component of processes of modernization or post-materialism (Dalton 2014; Inglehart 1997), then it may be reasonable to expect a negative time trend for at least part of Latin America in the various components of party system/citizen attachment. After all, every country in the region has seen meaningful GDP growth during the period since 1995 covered by survey data; hence, it might be possible to detect a decline in attachment caused by this economic and related social change. If the relevant changes are part of the modernization process, a negative trend may well be widespread across the region, while if it instead involves post-materialism, it might instead be concentrated among the more advanced economies with larger middle classes.

However, if the relationship between economic development and party system/citizen attachment involves long-term processes connected with socialization, educational changes, and so forth, then there may well be little or no observable time trends in the data. Instead, for such long-term processes it would be more reasonable to expect contrasts across countries with different levels of development – or perhaps with different configurations of other conditions. Hence the second key descriptive question: are there systematic patterns of difference in attachment across country contexts within Latin America?

This section describes patterns across countries and over time in the various components of attachment. First, rates of individual partisanship are mapped over time and space. Attention then turns to measures of partisan participation. Finally, pro-party system attitudes are analyzed. The results are complex and show a variety of patterns in space and time. For some countries and some indicators, there are marked trends or instabilities over time, but these generally go in both positive and negative directions. Thus, for the attachment component of institutionalization, there is no clear evidence of a general region-wide time trend. Instead, most of the interesting patterns involve contrasts among countries.

In making this case, let us begin with the prototypical form of party system/citizen attachment: partisanship. Figure 13.1 shows the proportion of Latinobarometer respondents reporting a party identification in each country–year of the survey.[4] The results (for this figure as well as those that follow) are presented as a grid of scatterplots by country. Countries within a row of the grid share the same vertical axis, while countries within a column share the horizontal axis. Thus, comparisons across countries can be made by checking

---

[4] Venezuela is unfortunately excluded from all figures, as the country generated an unmanageable level of missing values.

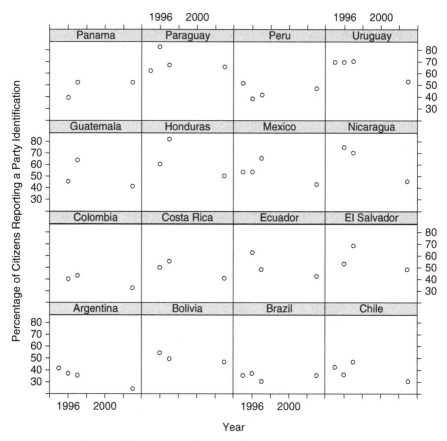

FIGURE 13.1 Partisanship Rates in the Latinobarometer Survey, 1995–2003
Source: Prepared by the author based on Latinobarometer 2015.

for patterns in which some scatterplots have points higher in the relevant cell than others.

The data show a few possible time trends. Partisanship rates seem to have declined meaningfully over time in Argentina and Nicaragua. Many other countries show a drop of partisanship to some degree at the last data point in the series, which might represent substantive change or, given the lack of a clear trend in most of these countries, some kind of methodological artifact of the survey process.

More frequently reported data on partisanship for most countries are available for recent years from the AmericasBarometer survey (LAPOP 2016), with results shown in Figure 13.2.[5] These data do not support any hypothesis of

---

[5] For the most part, these two data sources report similar figures for years of overlap.

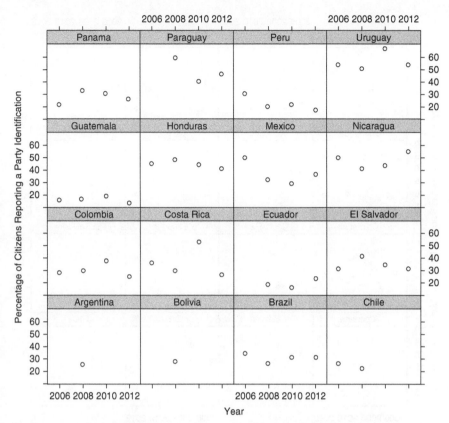

FIGURE 13.2 Partisanship Rates in the AmericasBarometer Survey, 2006–12
Source: Prepared by the author with data from LAPOP (2016).

a region-wide trend in terms of partisanship. While some countries such as Mexico and Costa Rica have quite volatile time series, only Peru and perhaps Chile show consistent decline.

While there is limited evidence for time trends, and thus no good reason to posit a decline in partisanship as a general mode of citizen attachment to the party system, there is substantial evidence in both data sources of variations across country contexts. Uruguay, Honduras, and Paraguay both have high levels of overall partisanship for the region, while Argentina, Brazil, Chile, and Colombia have consistently low levels. Ecuador, Bolivia, Peru, and Panama have moderate levels in the Latinobarometer data but fall to low levels in the AmericasBarometer data, while most other countries have volatile levels of partisanship in the moderate to high range.

Thus, some countries show patterns of variation over time that stand in need of explanation, but a greater proportion of the seemingly systematic variance is at the cross-country level.

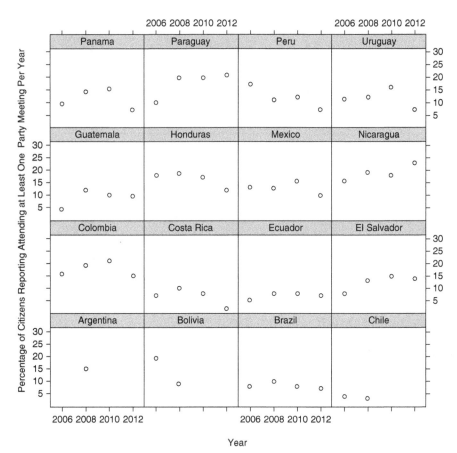

FIGURE 13.3 Participation Rates in Party Meetings in the AmericasBarometer Survey, 2006–12
Source: Prepared by the author with data from LAPOP (2016).

Turning from partisanship to party-centered modes of political participation, Figure 13.3 shows the proportion of AmericasBarometer respondents who report having attended at least one party meeting in the last year. Once again, some countries show evidence of change over time, to an extent in opposite directions. In Peru and Honduras, there appears to be a decline in participation in party meetings over the years covered; limited evidence in Bolivia also fits with a hypothesis of decline over time. On the other hand, there seems to be an increase in party meeting attendance over time in El Salvador, Nicaragua, and Paraguay. For the remaining countries, the pattern is one of fluctuation rather than clear trends. However, there are once again clear patterns of difference across countries, with Brazil, Chile, Costa Rica, Ecuador, El Salvador, and Guatemala having comparatively low levels of participation in party meetings.

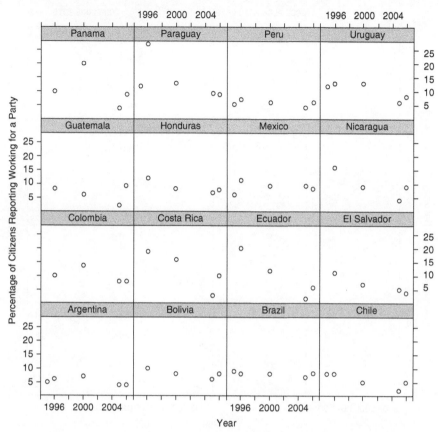

FIGURE 13.4 Participation Rates in Party Work in the Latinobarometer Survey, 1995–2006
Source: Prepared by the author with data from Latinobarometer 2015.

The rate at which citizens directly work for a party is the indicator for which there is the best evidence of a true regional trend over time. Data for this mode of party system/citizen attachment, shown in the Latinobarometer in Figure 13.4 and in the AmericasBarometer in Figure 13.5, is one for which many countries show a downward trend – and most of the countries with no trend have such low levels that a trend would be hard to detect were it present. Looking across the two data sources, there is simply no such thing as a country with a stable, even comparatively high rate of working for parties over time. Perhaps parties in the region are becoming more professionalized and relying less on volunteer labor, or perhaps on this one dimension attachment is simply eroding over time.

Turning from party-based modes of participation to attitudes about the party system taken as a whole, the pattern is once again one in which there

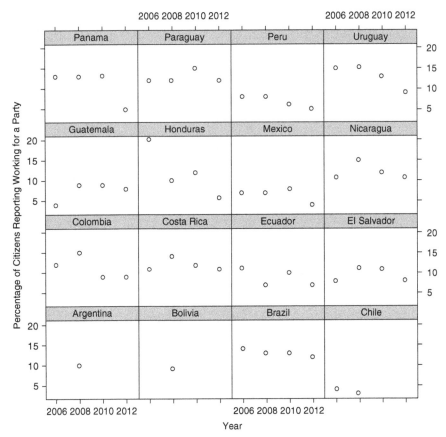

FIGURE 13.5 Participation Rates in Party Work in the AmericasBarometer Survey, 2006–12.
Source: Prepared by the author with data from LAPOP (2016).

are few signs of regional change over time and instead substantial evidence of patterns of difference across countries. This point holds both for trust in the parties as a system and for the belief that political parties are a necessary institution in a democracy.

With respect to trust in parties, shown in the Latinobarometer data in Figure 13.6 and for the AmericasBarometer in Figure 13.7, one important descriptive conclusion is that citizens everywhere in Latin America tend to distrust the political parties in their countries. For every country–year in the Latinobarometer data set, at least a majority and often a high majority of citizens distrust the political parties.

The AmericasBarometer data are somewhat different; respondents place themselves on a 7-point scale from distrust to trust. On that scale, there are

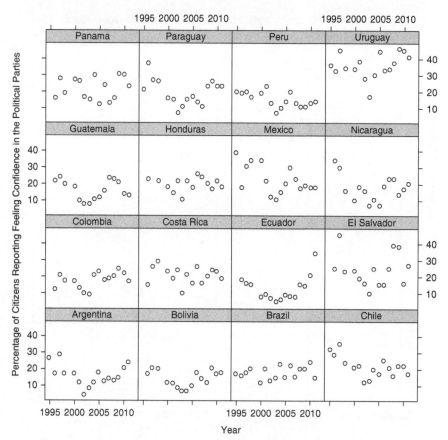

FIGURE 13.6 Rates of Confidence in Parties in the Latinobarometer Survey, 1994–2013
Source: Prepared by the author with data from Latinobarometer 2015.

only two country–years in the data set (one in Uruguay and one in Honduras) for which the average response is neutral or trusting toward the parties. Rather, for most years and most countries, the average opinion is significantly distrustful of the party system.

In both data sets, trends are generally difficult to discern. In Chile, Mexico, and Peru, there is some evidence of a noisy and inconsistent downward trajectory in the longer Latinobarometer series, although little or no similar movement in the AmericasBarometer data. Ecuador shows a dramatic upward trend from a very low starting point after about 2005 in both data sets. Other countries mostly show volatility rather than clear trends over time.

Looking at the data cross-sectionally, there are once again clearer groupings. Uruguay stands out in regional context as the country with the consistently highest level of trust in the party system. Ecuador before its late upward trend

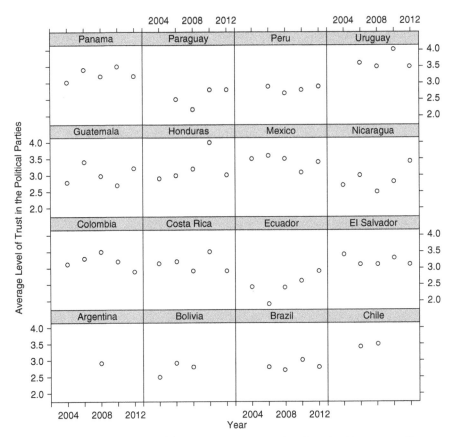

FIGURE 13.7 Rates of Confidence in Parties in the AmericasBarometer Survey, 2004–13
Source: Prepared by the author with data from LAPOP (2016).

had exceptionally low levels; widespread distrust in the party system is also common in Argentina, Bolivia, Brazil, Colombia, and Guatemala, particularly in the Latinobarometer data, and Peru. Thus, even though the region as a whole shows a pattern of marked distrust of existing party systems, there is important variation within that broader theme.

A related attitudinal form of party system/citizen attachment, support for the idea that democracy requires parties (Figure 13.8), shows similar patterns against a notably less negative regional background. The average response for most country–years in the data is above the mid-point of the scale, indicating regionwide agreement that parties are an indispensable democratic institution. At a finer level of detail, broader regional agreement conceals important variations. Costa Rica and Uruguay stand out as countries with high levels of support for parties as necessary democratic institutions. While most other

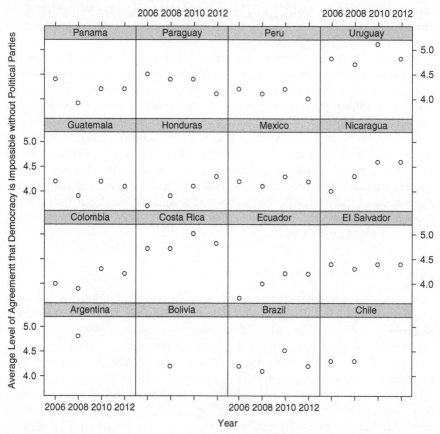

FIGURE 13.8 Average Level of Agreement that Democracy Requires Parties in the
AmericasBarometer Survey, 2006–12
Source: Prepared by the author with data from LAPOP (2016).

countries have lower levels of support, there are cross-national differences in
trends. Colombia, Ecuador, Honduras, and Nicaragua show steady rises over
time in this pro-party system attitude, while Paraguay and Peru show some
evidence of decline.

Thus, in general, it is impossible to characterize Latin America as having
undergone either a crisis or a growth in party system/citizen attachment.
Instead, patterns differ across countries. It is perhaps equally important to
recognize that patterns differ across components of party system/citizen
attachment. Paraguay and Costa Rica form an instructive comparison in this
regard. On most indicators of partisan identity and participation, Paraguay
ranks among the highest countries in the region, but the country has only a low
to moderate ranking on the three variables connected with attitudes of support

for the party system. Costa Rica, by contrast, has moderate to high levels of attitudinal support for the party system combined with low to middling levels of party-based participation and of partisanship.

As these two countries demonstrate, in conjunction with the overall descriptive analysis above, Latin American countries instantiate diverse configurations of the various components of party system/citizen attachment. The explanatory puzzle of party system/citizen attachment thus involves much more than explaining why some countries have a low overall level of attachment and others have a high level. Such combinations and contrasts do exist; Uruguay presents the best example of a country with a high level across all dimensions of attachment, while Ecuador is the purest contrasting case with a low level across all dimensions. Yet a theoretical approach to understanding and explaining party system/citizen attachment across Latin America must not only aim to account for these pure cases of high or low attachment but also the more numerous set of mixed cases.

EXPLANATORY HYPOTHESES

How, then, can we explain the existence of diverse configurations of attachment across space and to a lesser extent over time? Existing literature provides a plethora – indeed, a surplus – of possible hypotheses. Potentially relevant explanations can be drawn from literature about partisanship and its much discussed decline in advanced industrial democracies, anti-partisan and anti-political attitudes, changes in linkage patterns and in cleavage structures, retrospective and prospective evaluations of government competence and performance, elite strategies of mobilization and communication, and so forth. Looking synthetically across the literature, it is clear that a huge range of variables must be considered, as possible causes, or at least as possible confounders, in explaining party system/citizen attachment. This set includes measures of social and economic development, a variety of institutional and electoral patterns, government capacity and performance, inequality and economic polarization, the strength and scope of social welfare institutions, and ethnic and religious cleavage measures.

Social and economic development has been hypothesized to affect party system/citizen attachment in a variety of ways, most of them negative for institutionalization. Expanded access to education, for example, promotes the widespread development of the skills necessary for independent gathering and evaluation of political information, reducing citizens' need to identify with, participate in, and otherwise rely on parties in order to meet their goals in politics (Dalton 1984; Fuchs and Klingemann 1995). From a very different perspective, development by definition means that more citizens' basic needs are being met by private economic interaction or by stable, institutionalized state programs. As a result, patronage exchanges between parties and citizens are more costly, more difficult to supervise, and, as a consequence, less frequent

(Kitschelt and Wilkinson 2007b). Such an erosion of patronage removes a transactional, as opposed to cognitive resource-centered, basis for party system/citizen attachment. Drawing on these and related considerations, it is reasonable to expect social and economic development very broadly – including variables related to education and quality of life as well as raw economic production – to be a causally relevant domain for explaining a country's configuration of attachment.

Alongside the large literature positing a connection between development and elements of party system/citizen attachment, there are several arguments linking institutional features with aspects of attachment. Research on Latin America and other regions has emphasized the importance of institutions that give politicians an incentive to cultivate a personal vote (Carey and Shugart 1995). In brief, some electoral rules give politicians an incentive to develop a personally loyal electorate to ensure personal electoral success, while others reward politicians more collectively by awarding legislative representation in some sense to parties collectively rather than to candidates individually. When candidates emphasize personal connections to voters, it necessarily comes at the expense of the kinds of collective, partisan connections that are central to party system/citizen attachment. Other institutions, including patterns of legislative–executive relations, may also influence the relative strategic value of personalistic as opposed to partisan linkages between politicians and voters (Karvonen 2010). Thus, there are grounds to suppose that institutional factors quite generally may affect attachment.

A similarly vast literature has proposed that government capacity and performance affects attitudes about the party system. This includes the rich and long-standing literature on economic voting (Lewis-Beck and Paldam 2000), which presents evidence that voters consider past as well as expected future economic performance in voting and in adjusting their partisanship (Fiorina 1981; Lewis-Beck 1988) – although it is also likely that a causal process runs in the opposite direction, with partisan attachments altering economic evaluations (Evans and Pickup 2010; Gerber and Huber 2010); that voters pay attention to various aspects of the economy in different contexts, including inflation, unemployment, growth, and perhaps overall levels of development (Remmer 1991, 2003); and that there may well be causal interactions between evaluations of government performance and the political institutions mentioned in the previous paragraph (Duch and Stevenson 2008). Work on anti-partisan and anti-political attitudes shows that attachments to the party system as a whole, and not just to individual parties within it, can be affected by similar dimensions of government capacity and performance (Gidengil *et al.* 2001; Webb 1996). Once again, then, a host of factors connected with economic outcomes have prima facie credibility for inclusion in an explanation of overall levels of party system/citizen attachment.

As a final broad category, the configuration and salience of major social cleavages may well matter for the overall strength of citizen's party system attachments. That cleavage politics structure party systems is of course a classic hypothesis (Bartolini 2000; Lipset and Rokkan 1967). If this theoretical approach is right, then variation across countries and over time in the extent of citizen attachment to the party system should be due at least in part to variations in the cleavage system. Where the salience of class cleavages is high because of inequality, on the one hand, or strong class-based social welfare programs, it is reasonable to expect parties to have a strong class basis – and, as a consequence, strong and resilient ties to many voters. On the other hand, change in the class structure, due to informalization, or in the welfare state, as a result of globalization, may undermine such ties and reduce overall levels of attachment (Collier and Handlin 2009). Variations in ethnic cleavages may matter as well, particularly by altering elites' incentives regarding the use of partisan, populist, or more narrowly and explicitly ethnic mobilizing appeals (Chandra 2007; Madrid 2012; Van Cott 2005). Hence, variables measuring the salience and structure of ethnic divisions are relevant to the analysis in this chapter.

Of course, the theories connected with these various domains have varying degrees of logical rigor, empirical support, and intellectual appeal. One approach to the over-abundance of explanatory frameworks reviewed above would be to draw on such considerations in order to privilege some variables or explanatory categories and eliminate others. After such a simplification process, one or a few remaining hypothesized causes might then be subjected to statistical tests in the hope of making causal inferences.

Such a procedure is unlikely to be successful in the present context. Simply put, it is hard to imagine that there are enough legitimate theoretical considerations or existing causal findings to rule out so many different variables – to not just exclude them as primary causal factors, but also as possible confounders.[6] It is simply not obvious that the existing stock of theory and evidence is developed enough to accomplish this task, and hence some other approach is needed.

DATA AND METHODS

In a context where full-dress causal inference is an implausibly high goal, a useful alternative agenda is thorough multivariate description (Berk 2004). In the present analysis, such a description would answer the question: With which domains of society, economy, and politics are the various aspects of party system/citizen attachment most strongly connected? The nature of the connection as causal, reverse-causal, spurious, etc., cannot be sorted out via the kind of descriptive analysis used here. However, the analysis retains

---

[6] For discussions of the challenges involved in making such a case, as well as the consequences of error, see Clarke (2005) and Seawright (2010).

theoretical value as a source of heuristic guidance regarding the best starting places for causal theory and testing.

In light of the broad theoretical scope implied by the previous section, such a descriptive analysis should consider a long list of variables as possible predictors for each aspect of attachment. The analysis below includes each component of attachment as a predictor for every other component – with the exception that alternative indicators of the same concept are not used as predictors to avoid tautology. The analysis also includes every variable in the World Development Indicators data set (World Bank 2013), every variable in the Quality of Government standard time series data set (Teorell *et al.* 2013) (which is a large aggregation of standard and less common country-level indicators in the social sciences), and every variable in the updated Democratic Electoral Systems data set (Bormann and Golder 2013). Collectively, these data sets include most variables that have been used in the social sciences to measure various aspects of social and economic development, political institutions, economic performance, and class and ethnic cleavages, as well as a range of other less commonly analyzed phenomena. Hence, this collection casts a wide net. Each data set was matched to the country–years for which either Latinobarometer or AmericasBarometer data are available about one or more dimensions of citizen/party system attachment.[7]

The use of such a broad set of covariates creates two challenges. First, the number of possible predictor variables is substantially larger than the total number of country–year observations in the data. Hence, a regression-type analysis would be unidentified (Kellstedt and Whitten 2013: 181). Fortunately, however, random forests do generate the kind of information about the strength of descriptive relationships that are of interest here and are useful for data sets where the number of possible predictors is larger than the number of observations (Breiman 2001; for a social science example, see Jones *et al.* 2013). Second, across such a large number of variables, every single observation in the data set has at least one (and usually many) missing value. Thus, listwise deletion would result in an empty data set. Instead, multiple imputation is used, relying on a random-forest-based imputation technique that can simultaneously impute categorical and continuous variables (Stekhoven and Buhlmann 2012).

The output of such multiply imputed random forests is an importance score for each predictor variable in the data set. Although computational details involve a complicated process akin to cross-validation, in general terms this score measures the degree to which the outcome of interest can be better predicted by using the variable in question than by ignoring it. The following section reports the variables for each outcome that have a standardized

---

[7] Between missing questions on these surveys and widespread missing data in the above-mentioned data sets, the inclusion of Venezuela would have generated an unmanageable level of missing values. Hence, Venezuela is unfortunately excluded from the analysis.

importance greater than 3.0, which is heuristically regarded as a high level of importance. For working with a party, a threshold of 5.0 is instead used because the results at the 3.0 level were substantively similar but unhelpfully unparsimonious.

Importance scores capture the overall descriptive and predictive contribution of a given variable but do not provide information about the form of the relationship between that variable and the outcome (e.g., is the relationship positive, negative, non-linear, or interactive with some other variable). A full analysis of the form of each relationship would quickly become incredibly complex; as a simple indicator of the sign of the overall relationship, the analysis in the following section reports bivariate correlations between each reported variable and the outcome. An important interpretive point to bear in mind is that, given this methodological approach, positive findings are far more important than negative ones. A variable may show up in the list for one outcome and not for another simply because it by chance falls just below the cutoff for the second outcome.

EMBEDDING PARTY SYSTEM/CITIZEN ATTACHMENT

What, then are the domains of society with which each aspect of party system/citizen attachment has descriptive ties? This section will show that each element of party system/citizen attachment has substantial connections with a range of other major social, economic, and political domains. Attachment is deeply interwoven with issues of social and economic development, and has ties as well to patterns of state structure and bureaucratic quality. Further research is needed to decide whether these connections are causal or reflect other, perhaps more complicated, underlying structures. Even so, these results provide important initial insights and show that there are clearly some deep linkages between party system/citizen attachment and broader societal structures and trends.

This section demonstrates the existence of such linkages by showing the variables that are most important in a multiple imputed random forest analysis of outcomes connected to each of the three conceptual dimensions of attachment: overall rates of party identification, of party based political participation, and of attitudes supportive of the party system as a democratic institution.

Table 13.2 shows the predictor variables that are most important for a country's proportion of partisans, using the Latinobarometer data. Partisanship and confidence in parties are substantially and positively connected, a result that is hard to interpret causally but that is substantively unsurprising. A more complicated and less intuitively obvious set of results show connections involving development aid, liquid fuel use, and women in the workforce with only a basic education. These variables have a range of positive and negative correlations with partisanship and seem generally diverse. However, on closer inspection, in Latin America these variables all connect with social and economic

TABLE 13.2 *Important Predictors of Partisanship Levels, Latinobarometer Survey*

Predictor variable	Correlation with outcome
Confidence in parties	0.62
UN development-related cash flows	−0.59
Percent of CO2 emissions from liquid fuel	0.62
Road transportation-related fuel consumption	−0.23
Imports of goods and services	−0.27
Percent of women in the workforce with only primary education	0.53
Total exports	−0.28
Total trade	−0.25

Sources: Confidence in parties, from Latinobarometer (1995–2011 datasets); Total exports and Total trade, from Gleditsch (2013); UN development-related cash flows, Percent of CO2 emissions from Liquid Fuel, Road transportation-related fuel consumption, Imports of goods and services, and Percent of women in the workforce with only primary education, from World Bank (2013).

development: the least developed countries have low development-related transfers from the UN, high degrees of CO2 emissions from liquid fuel use other than for road-related transportation, and high numbers of working women with only a basic education. Hence, these results combine to suggest that partisanship is most common in countries with low levels of economic and social development.

The three trade-related variables are strongly interrelated. All three are raw quantities and are not adjusted by overall GDP. Thus, two interpretations are possible. Partisanship is either more common in smaller economies, or in economies that are less involved in international trade – or perhaps a combination of the two. Summing up, overall levels of partisanship are higher in Latin America among countries that have less developed economies, lower levels of education for working women, and perhaps less engagement with the global economy.

The same outcome variable is considered in Table 13.3, although the data here come from the AmericasBarometer survey. Less developed economies in Latin America have the highest overall stocks of public debt to the International Development Association, so that variable points here in the direction of poorer countries having higher levels of partisanship. Likewise, secondary private-school enrollment – which is an almost mandatory mark of middle- and upper-class status in the region – is negatively connected with partisanship, as is male progression to secondary school. These results in conjunction with the previous set support the finding that economic development tends to undermine personal partisan identities (Dalton 1984; Dalton and Wattenberg 2000).

TABLE 13.3 *Important Predictors of Partisanship Levels, AmericasBarometer Survey*

Predictor variable	Correlation with outcome
Largest opposition party's age	0.55
Career opportunities in the state bureaucracy	0.64
Number of tier 1 electoral districts	0.00
Largest minority share of the population	−0.70
Ethnolinguistic fractionalization, 1961	−0.69
Ethnolinguistic fractionalization, 1985	−0.61
Public debt to the International Development Association	0.50
Percent of secondary school enrollment that is private	−0.45
Progression Rate to Secondary School for Male Students	−0.59

Sources: Largest opposition party's age, from Beck *et al.* (2001, 2013); Number of tier 1 electoral districts, from Borman and Golder (2013); Career opportunities in the state bureaucracy, from Evans and Rauch (1999); Largest minority share of the population, from Fearon (2002); LAPOP (2016); Ethnolinguistic fractionalization, from Roeder (2001); Public debt to the International Development Association, Percent of secondary school enrollment that is private, and Progression rate to secondary school for male students, from World Bank (2013)

A second striking finding is that there is a strong negative connection between ethnic division and partisanship; countries that were coded in the 1960s and 1980s as more ethnolinguistically diverse have markedly lower levels of partisanship than those that were coded as more ethnically unified. Similarly, countries with at least one large minority group have substantially less partisanship than those without.

There is thus some reason to suspect that the structure of ethnic cleavages matters for partisanship in Latin America – and in fact that there may be a degree of rivalry between ethnic and partisan identity structures.

Furthermore, the results suggest that partisanship is higher in countries where bureaucratic jobs within the state apparatus are relatively desirable career trajectories for middle-class and highly educated individuals. This may suggest that partisanship in Latin America is bolstered by patronage politics; alternatively, it may also be another descriptive connection between lower levels of development and higher levels of partisanship.

While the positive findings above are more statistically powerful and substantively meaningful than negative findings, it is worth noting in passing that variables related to social and economic performance are entirely missing from Tables 13.2 and 13.3. While this certainly does not mean that partisanship is unconnected with performance evaluations in Latin America, it at least implies that longer-term factors related to cleavages and structural aspects of development deserve equal attention.

TABLE 13.4 *Important Predictors of Rates of Working for a Party, Latinobarometer Survey*

Predictor variable	Correlation with outcome
Rate of party identification	0.72
Total exports	−0.22
Total trade	−0.22
Population	−0.28
Seats in the upper house elected in national district	0.65

Sources: Total exports, Total trade, and Population, from Gleditsch (2013); Seats in the upper house, from Johnson and Wallack (2012); Rate of party identification, from Latinobarometer (1995–2011 datasets).

Turning from identification to measures of behavioral attachment, the results are equally supportive of a view that party system/citizen attachment is connected with major structures of society and the economy. Table 13.4 shows the most important variables connected with rates of working for a political party in the Latinobarometer data. Countries with higher rates of party identification unsurprisingly also have higher rates of citizens working for parties. Interestingly, there is also some hint that nationalized electoral institutions may somehow be connected with higher rates of working for parties. The remaining variables in this analysis suggest that smaller, less globalized countries have more citizens working for parties than larger countries that are more involved in international trade.

The AmericasBarometer results on working for parties, shown in Table 13.5, point toward a series of structural factors. To begin with, they show a pattern in which urbanized and industrialized countries have less party work while more rural, agricultural countries have a higher rate of citizens working for parties. The results also suggest a role for ethnic cleavage structures, with more culturally diverse countries having fewer citizens that report working for parties.

There is also evidence of a positive relationship between the percentage of government revenue that comes from social program taxes and the proportion of citizens engaged in party work. This is a distinctive finding that points toward issues of state fiscal structure, clientelism, and/or of the structure of welfare policy. One might, perhaps, suspect that the variable is strongly connected with economic development – as has been the case for some unusual variables previously in the analysis – but that does not appear to be the case. The highest scores for the region are in Costa Rica, Brazil, and Uruguay. Argentina and Mexico have moderately high scores as well, while Chile scores lower than much lower-income countries, such as Peru, Venezuela, and Bolivia. Thus, this result points toward a role for clientelism and the structure of fiscal or welfare-state policy in supporting participatory forms of party system/citizen attachment.

TABLE 13.5 *Important Predictors of Rates of Working for a Party,*
AmericasBarometer Survey

Predictor variable	Correlation with outcome
Percent of methane emissions from agriculture	0.71
Percent of methane emissions from energy production	−0.66
Percent of government revenue from social program contributions	0.45
Cultural diversity	−0.56

Sources: Cultural diversity, from Fearon (2002); LAPOP (2006, 2008, 2010, and 2012 datasets); Percent of methane emissions and Percent of government revenue from social program contributions, from World Bank (2013).

TABLE 13.6 *Important Predictors of Rates of Attending Party Meetings,*
AmericasBarometer Survey

Predictor variable	Correlation with outcome
Fertilizer consumption per hectare of arable land	−0.31
Percent of preprimary children enrolled in school	−0.49
Percent of preprimary girls enrolled in school	−0.49

Sources: LAPOP (2006, 2008, 2010, and 2012 datasets) and World Bank (2013).

Table 13.6 shows the most important variables in predicting another aspect of participatory attachment: a country's rate of attendance at party meetings, using AmericasBarometer data. The results fit several themes discussed earlier. The degree of development and modernization of the agricultural sector is negatively related to participation in party meetings, as are measures of early childhood education uptake – a set of variables strongly related to the overall quality of a country's educational system.

Jointly considering the set of outcomes related to partisan participation, the most noteworthy theme is that social and economic development, particularly related to rural modernization and education but perhaps also processes of integration into the global economy, is in statistical tension with participatory forms of party system/citizen linkage. This is consistent with the pattern for partisan identification, in which development broadly construed has a strong negative relationship with overall levels of partisanship.

Turning to attitudinal forms of linkage between the party system and citizens, the descriptive patterns are markedly different, although no less powerful in pointing to links between attachment and broader structural patterns in society and the economy. Table 13.7 shows the independent

TABLE 13.7 *Important Predictors of Trust in the Parties, Latinobarometer Survey*

Predictor variable	Correlation with outcome
Attendance at party meetings	0.08
Percent of the population included in social insurance programs	0.45
Percent of commercial sales lost to crime	−0.49
Social class equity of public resource use (6-point scale)	0.20
Quality of trade, financial sector, and business regulatory environment	0.47
Quality of public administration	0.50

Sources: Attendance at Party Meetings, from Latinobarometer (1995–2011 datasets); all other indicators, from World Bank (2013).

variables that are important predictors of trusting the parties as an institution, using the Latinobarometer data. Two major themes emerge in the list.

First, citizens trust the party system more in countries where state institutions are strong in a Weberian, bureaucratic, and perhaps economically neoliberal sense. Specifically, citizens trust the party system more when there is little shoplifting, and where the regulatory environment receives high evaluations from experts. If this proves upon further research to reflect a causal connection, the implication would be that patronage politics has a cost for PSI in terms of undermining public trust of the party system.

Second, states that are inclusive in their social programs and their use of public resources correspond with highly trusted party systems. Citizens are more likely to trust the parties in countries where a higher percentage of the population is included in state social insurance programs, and to a lesser extent in countries judged by experts to be equitable across social classes in the use of public resources. If this is causal, it represents the flip side of the pattern in the last paragraph: while corruption and clientelism might undermine attitudes that constitute PSI, inclusive and impersonal services and welfare institutions may enhance trust in the party system.

Finally, there is evidence of an interactive and non-linear relationship between attendance at party meetings and trust in the party system. The bivariate correlation is weak, suggesting that if there is a causal relationship here, it has diverse effects for different subsets of the population.

Looking at the same variable, trust in the party system, using the AmericasBarometer results shown in Table 13.8, adds additional details to the picture. It is worth noting another variable that fits with the theme of state institutional quality: trust in the party system is higher in countries where experts give high evaluations to legal institutions. Looking across these two sets of results, there is a strong suggestion that high quality state institutions are

TABLE 13.8 *Important Predictors of Trust in the Parties, AmericasBarometer Survey*

Predictor variable	Correlation with outcome
Percent of business expenses for dividends, rent, and other miscellany	0.51
Percent of roads that are paved	0.59
Total population labor force participation rate	−0.53
Legal institutional quality	0.61

Sources: Legal institutional quality, from Kuncic (2014); LAPOP (2006, 2008, 2010, and 2012 datasets); all other indicators, from World Bank (2013).

a fundamental ingredient for an attitudinally strong linkage between citizens and the party system.

Furthermore, there is evidence here of a positive descriptive relationship between economic development and trust in the party system. This is perhaps most self-evident in the paved roads variable, since such improvements to the transportation infrastructure are among the most visible components of economic development. Hence, the observed positive and important relationship between this variable and trust in the party system points to development as a potentially important explanatory domain for this contributor to institutionalization.

The labor force participation rate variable has the same overall implications, although the logic is perhaps less self-evident. Overall labor force participation can be low either because of an economic depression in which few jobs are available or because economic development allows high enough incomes that individuals and families can choose to leave the workforce – to retire, care for children, recover from illness, or otherwise pursue non-job-related goals. Because the period for which data are available in Latin America does not include major periods of economic disaster, lower labor force participation rates in these data correspond with higher levels of development. For this reason, the negative relationship between this variable and party system trust points in the same broad substantive direction as the roads variable.

Finally, there is a statistically important but substantively obscure result related to business expense categories. Specifically, countries where businesses spend relatively high amounts on dividends, rent, and a range of other minor and poorly documented expenses also have high levels of trust in the party system. This business expense variable correlates positively with per capita GDP and also with short-term economic growth, so it might represent a substantive connection between these domains and party system trust. Yet the variable is obscure enough that it may well have quite different implications.

TABLE 13.9 *Important Predictors of Belief that Democracy Is Impossible Without Parties, AmericasBarometer Survey*

Predictor variable	Correlation with outcome
Short-term external debt as a percentage of exports	0.46
Short-term external debt as a percentage of total external debt	0.52
Telephone lines per capita	0.52
Percent of rural population with improved sanitation facilities	0.44
Male unemployment rate	0.26
Percent of merchandise imports from developing economies in Europe and Central Asia	−0.28
Level of difficulty of governance	−0.64
Openness of the political system to participation	0.59
Female enrollment in tertiary education	0.66

Sources: Level of difficulty of governance and Openness of the political system, from Bertelsmann Stiftung (2014); LAPOP (2006, 2008, 2010, and 2012 datasets); Female enrollment in Tertiary education, from UNESCO Institute for Statistics (2014); all other indicators, from World Bank (2013).

Integrating the results from Tables 13.7 and 13.8, there is evidence of statistical relationships between citizens' overall level of trust in the party system, on the one hand, and the quality of state institutions, the class balance of state programs, and the overall level of economic development, on the other.

Variables related to economic development also appear repeatedly in the results for citizens' overall level of belief that democracy requires parties, shown for the AmericasBarometer data in Table 13.9. Prototypical development variables, including citizen's access to telephones and rural sanitation facilities, are positively related to the belief that parties are mandatory democratic institutions. Less intuitively, a country's overall mix of short- and long-term debt is also related to development; "as economies get richer and financial markets become deeper (through financial liberalization or other channels), the external debt profile gets tilted towards short-term liabilities" (Rodrik and Velasco 1999: 23). The results also show a strong connection between female rates of enrollment in higher education and support for parties as a necessary democratic institution, suggesting that social development also matters.

Two more complicated index variables appear to have strong descriptive relationships with citizens' support for parties as a democratic institution. The first, involving the level of difficulty of governance, aggregates education levels, economic development, quality of state institutions, and degree of ethnic and religious harmony. Thus, this variable contains most of the key explanatory themes that have appeared as statistically important throughout this analysis; the strong negative bivariate correlation suggests that country contexts, which score worse across this package of domains, also have low levels of support for parties as a required component of democracy, while more developed, institutionalized, and harmonious societies show higher support for parties in this sense.

The participation index includes standard measures of democracy: are elections free and fair, do elected officials have the power to rule, can citizens freely form parties and civil society associations, and is there freedom of expression? The data suggest that countries that score higher in these core democratic features also have more citizen support for the proposition that parties are needed in democracies.

In summary, there are important hints in the data of a positive connection between social and economic development, broadly conceptualized, and pro-party system attitudes. Stronger and more inclusive states may also support this attitudinal contributor to institutionalization.

While other variables show important and complex patterns of the relationship with elements of party system/citizen attachment, the discussion of variables connected with social and economic development throughout this section lays the groundwork for an intriguing theoretical possibility: development in a broad sense may undermine behavioral- and identity-related components of PSI while laying the groundwork for the replacement of such partisan attachments with more systemic support for parties as agents of democracy.

CONCLUSIONS

Institutionalized party systems are not just domains where elite politics is stable, predictable, and patterned over time, but also where large numbers of citizens are connected to the elite political world through stable linkages – a situation that is probably facilitated by patterns of partisan participatory behavior, pro-party system attitudes, and partisan self-concepts. The analysis above has shown that these components of party system/citizen attachment are not only conceptually but also empirically distinctive. At a first level, this differentiation appears in the fact that variables within each concept more closely correlate with each other than with variables in other concepts. More importantly, each component analyzed above has its own pattern of statistical interrelationships with social, economic, and political variables in its country–year context.

Thus there is good reason to think that the citizen-centered contributors to PSI are conceptually plural, and there are important initial clues that these concepts are causally distinctive. While variables connected to state capacity and performance appear with similar, positive relationships across domains, those connected with social and economic development have markedly different statistical roles. Development has a negative relationship with rates of partisan identification and participation but a positive relationship with attitudes of support for the party system as a democratic institution. If further work finds that these statistical relationships are causal, then we will see that citizen/party system attachment is more usefully conceptualized as having multiple qualitatively distinct configurations consistent with different modes of high institutionalization, rather than a unitary dimension from "high" to "low."

14

The Macroeconomic Consequences of PSI

Gustavo A. Flores-Macías*

What are the consequences of party system institutionalization (PSI) for economic policy making? Do stable patterns of inter-party competition have macroeconomic consequences? This chapter sets out to answer these questions by conducting a systematic study of the relationship between institutionalization and economic policy making based on a large-n study with evidence from Latin America. Consistent with earlier work that has pointed to the policy-making consequences of PSI, it finds that volatility in economic performance increases as institutionalization decreases. This relationship is important because, to the extent that economic volatility translates into decreased growth, PSI might have indirect consequences for a country's economic performance.

The remainder of this chapter proceeds as follows. In the first section, I present a brief overview of existing scholarship on the relationship between party systems and economic policy making, as well as the mechanism through which the two are related. Next, I outline the large-n research design based on a time series cross-section of seventeen Latin American countries since democratization, and discuss in detail the dependent and independent variables. The third section presents results, and the fourth discusses the indirect relationship between party systems and economic performance. The final section concludes.

PARTY SYSTEMS AND ECONOMIC POLICY MAKING

Most work on PSI has focused on the importance of PSI for democratic representation. Since Scott Mainwaring and Timothy Scully led the charge by first pointing to the importance of party systems for the process of democratic consolidation, it has become well established that institutionalized party

* I am grateful to Scott Mainwaring and Kenneth Roberts for generously sharing their party system volatility data, to David De Micheli for research assistance, and to Frances Hagopian, an anonymous reviewer, and the participants of Notre Dame Kellogg Institute's conference on Party Systems in Latin America for thoughtful feedback. All errors are my own.

systems are crucial for "sustaining modern mass democracy" (1995a: 1) based on four main functions. First, institutionalized party systems shape and moderate how different groups in society articulate their demands, therefore preventing street politics and making democracy less threatening for key actors. Second, they also make democracy work by establishing linkages between the government and the masses and providing voters with a sense of what politicians stand for, and whom to hold accountable. Third, institutionalized party systems contribute to governability because there are more established relations between the executive, the legislature, and political parties, and congressional coalitions therefore tend to be more stable. Fourth, they are conducive to reducing uncertainty, which allows actors to plan for the future and reduce the fear over whether their interests will be protected (Mainwaring and Scully 1995a: 23–27). A number of studies have since built on these insights, bringing nuance to this original characterization in specific Latin American countries (e.g., Levitsky 2003 on Argentina; Luna and Altman 2011 on Chile; Morgan 2011 and Seawright 2012 on Venezuela; Tanaka 1998 on Peru) and beyond (Kuenzi and Lambright 2001; Riedl 2014 on Africa; Hicken 2009; Hicken and Martinez Kuhonta 2011 on Asia).

However, comparatively little work has been done on another major area where PSI is also consequential: the policy-making arena.[1] To the extent that the relationship between party systems and policy making has been studied, most of the emphasis has been placed on fragmentation rather than institutionalization. For example, in their comprehensive study of the role of political institutions for market-oriented reforms during the 1980s and 1990s, Stephan Haggard and Robert Kaufman (1995) identified a role for party systems in the process of adoption of structural reforms, but point to the importance of fragmentation as a key factor hindering liberalization. Similarly, Mainwaring (1999) identified the significant fragmentation in the Brazilian system during the 1990s as an impediment to generating a minimum consensus behind the adoption of economic reforms in that country. More recently, in pointing to the general importance of strong institutions for good policy making, Ernesto Stein *et al.* (2006: 170) echo the detrimental effects of fragmentation for governability based on evidence from all of Latin America.

However, there is evidence that institutionalization plays an equally consequential role for economic policy making. Drawing on the Brazilian context, Mainwaring (1999: 286) first advanced the possibility that the party discipline that characterizes institutionalized party systems could decrease the extent of unpredictability in the policy-making process. Similarly, based on the adoption of tax and labor reforms during the 2000s in the Eastern European context, Conor O'Dwyer and Branislav Kovalcik (2007) found that,

---

[1] Naturally, the two consequences of party systems are related, since reducing uncertainty in policy making will have an effect on the stability of the democracy, but the emphasis on the latter has over-shadowed the former.

"underinstitutionalization insulates state reformers from social and political pressures, allowing them to undertake economic policies hard to envision in a more developed democracy" (p. 3). Further, work by Robert Kaufman (2011) and Hector Schamis (2006) suggested that PSI could explain the rise of populist governments in Latin America.

Building on these earlier studies and based on economic reforms in ten Latin American countries, I have argued elsewhere (2010; 2012) that PSI plays a role in explaining economic policies because of its consequences regarding: (1) the type of leaders that reach the presidency, and (2) the policy-making constraints that these leaders face once in office. First, the degree of institutionalization will shape the type of candidates that run for office. In institutionalized party systems, presidential candidates will tend to be the result of a process of accommodation within the party. This process, which often involves participation in local, regional, and then national politics, contributes to generating negotiation skills and provides incentives for politicians to accommodate different interests and party factions behind their campaigns. It also contributes to establishing a record of discipline and a reputation of honoring commitments with supporters. These incentives brought about by institutionalized party systems tend to both weed out political outsiders without a stake in the system and constrain presidents – through reputation and the commitments accumulated in their political trajectory – in their ability to adopt drastic changes to the status quo.

In contrast, weakly institutionalized party systems are conducive to the emergence of candidates with little experience in the political process and a brief if any record of interests accommodation. Owing their power to charismatic stardom, these candidates have few incentives for incorporating differing views behind a common government program and building consensus. Therefore, programmatic coherence and reputation become secondary concerns, and any association with the party establishment becomes an electoral liability. Without a stake in the system and therefore lacking incentives to engage in the political commitments that a trajectory in party politics requires, outsider politicians are more likely to adopt drastic reforms without broad consultation compared to the rank-and-file politicians that are bound by a trajectory of commitments within the party (Flores-Macías 2012: 62–64).

Second, the degree of institutionalization also shapes the constraints that leaders face in the policy-making process once they reach office. There are four main reasons behind this. First, the continuity of political parties over time lengthens actors' time horizons. As Guillermo O'Donnell (1994) noted, long time horizons are important because they generate incentives for negotiation and inter-temporal cooperation. The game theory literature on iterative games also highlights that actors' expectations of repeated interactions over time increase their tolerance for dissenting views and encourage consensus seeking (Mailath and Samuelson 2006). This is because the prospect of interacting with the same political parties – and often even the same politicians – in future legislatures involves the personal and party reputations of politicians and makes them relevant. Since politicians expect to have many interactions with their political opponents in the future as they alternate between majority and minority positions, finding common ground on the adoption of policies will be preferred to zero-sum arrangements. In other words, longer time horizons will encourage negotiation and be more conducive to compromise, because repeated interactions create constraints for conduct that are absent when time horizons are short. These dynamics result in piecemeal policy making rather than sweeping changes (Flores-Macías 2012: 63–64).

Second, the complex rules and organizational structures characteristic of institutionalized party systems lead to wide-ranging, collective interests that tend to prevail over individual leaders' views. As the overlapping generations literature (Alesina and Spear 1988; Stokes 1999) has noted, as parties become more established they increasingly function as a network of overlapping interests and cohorts. Since the policy positions of a politician in office affect the political prospects of other members of the party, party members in general have an interest in reining in maverick candidates and office holders. Such overlapping results in piecemeal reforms, or what Alesina and Spear (1988) have referred to as "far sighted policies." Thus, the complex selection mechanisms of institutionalized party systems, which tend to involve several layers of geographical and group-based membership in the process, such as primaries or assemblies, become particularly important for gradual economic changes because they tend to bring the positions of the party membership closer to a common ground acceptable to the party's core (Flores-Macías 2012: 64).

Third, the strong roots in society often associated with institutionalized party systems enable parties to obtain and mobilize resources in order to establish a consistent base of supporters. Enjoying strong roots in the electorate contributes to maintaining a reliable block of votes, resources, activists, and cadres. This is important for policy making because socially embedded parties will be more likely to consistently articulate constituents' demands in the legislative process. Compared to weakly institutionalized party systems, strong roots in society make it more difficult for parties to depart suddenly and significantly from their established record of policy making (Flores-Macías 2012: 64).

Fourth, the generalized sense of legitimacy typical of institutionalized party systems gives parties the necessary traction to shape the president's economic policies. When presidents seek to carry out drastic reforms by decree, the ample legitimacy of parties in an institutionalized system will make it politically costly because of parties' ability to translate popular support into political leverage. In contrast, in weakly institutionalized party systems, the cost of pushing parties aside to carry out drastic unilateral reforms is much lower (Flores-Macías 2012: 64–65). In short, these features of institutionalized party systems are conducive to finding common ground among relevant actors in the policy-making process. Naturally this does not mean that agreement will be reached on every issue. However, predictable, complex, established, and legitimate patterns of competition will encourage negotiation among the different forces because political parties matter. By eliminating extreme positions that are far from a common ground acceptable to a working majority, the result is piecemeal economic reforms rather than drastic transformations.

Conversely, the incentives present in weakly institutionalized systems are very different: they discourage cooperation and are conducive to extreme, unpredictable positions that result in significant policy changes. When parties are short-lived, with little guarantee that they will persist from one election to the next, actors' brief time horizons encourage extreme and intransigent positions in order to acquire quick, short-term gains. The prevalence of ephemeral electoral vehicles reduces incentives for compromise. Given the distinct possibility that concessions today will not be paid back in the future, the stakes in adopting the preferred policy decisions become higher. Moreover, the lack of complex rules and organizational structure, characteristic of weakly institutionalized party systems, results in parties' foregoing of the negotiation and accommodation skills that are often developed by the process of cadre formation and party socialization. Rather, the individual interests of a charismatic leader become the priority of electoral vehicles, with party-wide interests taking a back seat (Flores-Macías 2012: 64–66).

Additionally, weak roots in society give parties free rein to move away from their political positions and make sudden and considerable policy switches (Levitsky 2001). Lacking a clear government program, parties are more likely to oscillate back and forth between very different policy positions from one election to the next. Finally, parties' low levels of legitimacy weaken their legislative muscle, which undermines their bargaining power in Congress and their ability to shape policies in a way that might approach a common ground. Instead, due to a deficit of legitimacy among the electorate, presidents have every incentive to exclude parties from the decision-making process (Mainwaring and Scully 1995a) and, if necessary, take politics to the streets by appealing directly to the public to carry out their government program.

These features of weakly institutionalized party systems discourage legislative bargaining and inter-branch cooperation and favor the politics of confrontation and street mobilizations. Confrontation, in turn, raises the stakes in adopting a particular policy course and contributes to the radicalization of positions. In this context, the president has incentives to circumvent opposition to his or her project and push for extreme transformations by decree (O'Donnell 1998), contributing to the volatility of the policy process.

These stark differences between institutionalized and weakly institutionalized party systems matter for stability in the policy-making process and the policy outcomes that result. These differences arise from the existence or absence of constraints in the system: if decisions are made unilaterally by an outsider president facing few political constraints, the variance of policies and outcomes will tend to be greater than if decisions are forced to incorporate a large number of positions or even be reached by consensus.

It is not difficult to find examples in the region that correspond to the two types of dynamics described above: dramatic policy changes in weakly institutionalized party systems and gradual change in institutionalized systems. This is not to say that policy volatility does not take place in countries with institutionalized party systems, but that these instances take place more frequently and severely in those that are weakly institutionalized. For example, in the recent turn to the left in Latin America, the PT governments in Brazil, the *Concertación* governments in Chile, and the Broad Front governments in Uruguay have given remarkable continuity to the economic model in place when they reached power, and have only modified it at the margins by smoothing out the rough edges of the market-oriented economy (Flores-Macías 2010; Levitsky and Roberts 2011; Weyland *et al.* 2010). In all three cases, presidents overseeing moderate reforms have been political insiders with a long trajectory in party politics preceding their elections to office: Lula da Silva and Dilma Rousseff in Brazil, Ricardo Lagos and Michelle Bachelet in Chile,[2] and Tabaré Vázquez and José Mujica in Uruguay. In Brazil, although legislative party switching and the PMDB's ambiguous political position still undermine predictability in the policy-making process, the main political forces have been able to translate popular support into legislative strength, which has made them effective moderators of the president's initiatives for economic reforms, including in such areas as pensions reform, central bank autonomy, and tax reform. In Chile, economic policy making has been dominated by piecemeal reforms due to the incentives for political accommodation present in that country's institutionalized party system. The policy process has been characterized by both intra- and inter-coalition negotiations to moderate the content of such initiatives as free trade agreements, labor reform, and tax reform. In Uruguay, politicians' discipline and loyalty to party labels have characterized the party system (Lanzaro 2011), which has translated into Congressional forces' meaningfully shaping the president's initiatives to find common ground among the different positions. The fate of initiatives related to free trade agreements, tax reform, and central bank autonomy, which were successfully moderated by the different political forces, are cases in point.

In contrast, leftist governments in Bolivia, Ecuador, and Venezuela, with considerably less institutionalized party systems, have adopted major economic policy reforms. In these three countries, the presidents who carried out dramatic transformations reached power through movements transformed into electoral vehicles with anti-system platforms – Evo Morales with the *Movimiento al Socialismo*, Rafael Correa with *Movimiento País*, and Hugo Chávez with the *Movimiento V República*, respectively. Facing brief time horizons, lacking the constraints that come with a trajectory in party politics, and owing their popularity to the lack of legitimacy of the established political order, these leaders not only became feasible candidates in a national election but also had

[2] Although not from the left of center, Sebastián Piñera also had a trajectory in party politics by the time he reached the presidency.

few incentives to moderate their positions to implement gradual policy changes. Instead, they adopted drastic economic policy changes, including nationalizations in the energy and telecommunications industries, price controls, and exchange rate controls. Rather than incorporating relevant actors' views, they often pursued these reforms through decrees and even incorporated many of these policies into newly drafted constitutions. In these countries with party systems in disarray, the policy process has followed a path of election–contention–constitutional convention, in which outsider candidates reach office, clash with the existing order to carry out significant reforms, and draw new rules of the game that enable executives to make drastic changes.

Historically, the low levels of institutionalization in Peru have enabled very consequential decisions adopted with very little deliberation. With a volatility score of 50 and almost no actors informed of, let alone involved in, consequential decisions, the nationalization of the banking industry in Peru during Alan García's first presidency (1985–90) is a prominent case (Mauceri 1997b: 31), as were many of the drastic policies adopted by Alberto Fujimori (1990–2000), a political outsider who was a little-known agronomist when he ran for the presidency.

From a dynamic perspective, cases that have experienced variation over time in the degree of institutionalization have also experienced corresponding covariance on the policy-making front. In Brazil, for instance, the pace of economic reforms has slowed down as the party system has become progressively established since the return of civilian rule in the mid-1980s (Hagopian *et al.* 2009), whereas in Colombia the level of policy-making uncertainty has increased somewhat as the party system has deinstitutionalized since the early 1990s. In Argentina, drastic reforms have become more prevalent as the party system continues to deinstitutionalize. As a number of fronts emerge within the Peronist party, the Radicals steadily lose relevance, and new parties such as *Propuesta Republicana* gain ground (Levitsky and Murillo 2008), the prevalence of outsider politicians has increased and parties' legislative muscle has decreased. Instead, confrontation on economic issues and the president's reliance on executive decrees for economic policy making have become the norm.

In Venezuela, there has been an observable increase in policy-making volatility with deinstitutionalization. Although drastic policy shifts such as the nationalization of the oil industry during Carlos Andrés Pérez's first presidency (1974–79) took place in an institutionalized party system,[3] the contrast in the extent to which party politics has played a role in moderating the executives' policies before and after deinstitutionalization has been sharp. Before the early 1990s, when that country's system began to crack, parties meaningfully shaped relevant executive initiatives (Ellner 2008: 98). For example, Congress froze

---

[3] While Pérez's nationalization might have been predictable given his consistent nationalist stance, the measure is drastic in that it carries significant distributive consequences in a relatively short period of time.

Pérez's proposed reform to ease the burden on the severance payment system and privatize social security, and made significant changes to the president's fiscal reform package after two years of discussion (Villasmil *et al.* 2007: 273). Later on, in the aftermath of Pérez's impeachment, Congress negotiated a law that created a national VAT during the interim presidency of Ramón José Velásquez (Monaldi *et al.* 2006: 178). This type of meaningful shaping of the policy-making process to generate piecemeal reforms rather than drastic changes has all but disappeared since the collapse of the Venezuelan party system (Dietz and Myers 2007; Morgan 2011).[4] Instead, Venezuelan presidents have made rule by decree through Enabling Laws (*Leyes Habilitantes*) – comparable to a blank check for the president to carry out many of the legislative functions – the preferred way of conducting drastic reforms. These examples lend support to the view that policy volatility is more prevalent in weakly institutionalized party systems, and that volatility also co-varies with institutionalization within countries over time.

Although previous work has identified this relationship in the Latin American and Eastern European contexts, it has only been tested on a handful of cases in the contemporary period. A broad systematic study remains to be done to evaluate whether the relationship holds across more countries and longer periods of time and what the broader macroeconomic consequences might be. In the following paragraphs, I evaluate whether the volatility in economic policies that has been associated with weakly institutionalized party systems can be applied to the entire region since each country's return to democracy during the third wave.

RESEARCH DESIGN AND DATA

I test this hypothesis based on a time series cross-section for all Latin American countries from the time they most recently transitioned to democracy. The sample includes a panel of seventeen countries and the unit of analysis is the country–year. This large-n study complements the insights from previous small-n research by evaluating whether its findings travel to the whole region and extend to the realm of macroeconomic volatility.

Existing research has measured economic policy changes in different ways. O'Dwyer and Kovalcik (2007) rely on the adoption of reforms aimed at dismantling the existing social security programs. Flores-Macías (2010, 2012) focuses instead on the extent to which governments have departed from the status quo in both statist and pro-market directions, including privatizations, nationalizations, tax reform, trade, financial, and monetary liberalization.

Ideally, a comprehensive evaluation of the relationship between institutionalization and economic policy making in Latin America would take stock of each economic reform conducted in the region over the course of each

---

[4] By most accounts (for example, Corrales and Penfold 2011), Venezuela is no longer a representative democracy but a competitive authoritarian regime, as defined by Levitsky and Way (2010).

country's democratic period. To my knowledge, however, a systematic, historical dataset in this regard does not exist, in part because of the difficulty in settling on meaningful policy dimensions and identifying parameters for what constitutes drastic versus moderate change.[5] The index of reform that does exist – Escaith and Paunovic (2004), which updates Morley *et al.* (1999) – unfortunately has three main shortcomings for this purpose, namely that most of its coverage overlaps with authoritarian rule in many countries; it excludes important areas of reform, such as labor and social security; and it ends in 2000. Other indices, such as the Heritage Foundation's Index of Economic Freedom and Fraser Institute's Economic Freedom of the World Index have relatively short time series and score governments on a number of dimensions – such as corruption, rule of law, and maximum tax rates – related to the concept of economic freedom, but are not reflective of the policy transformations attributed to party systems.

An alternative indicator of volatility, however, is the degree to which economic performance fluctuates over time. The intuition behind using this indicator as a reflection of policy moderation is that piecemeal reforms are less likely to generate drastic jolts in economic performance. This does not mean that piecemeal reforms lead to economic stagnation or even a steady growth trajectory over time. Instead, piecemeal reforms lead to incremental changes in economic performance, whether positive or negative. For example, small changes to the prevailing tax rates or to the pensions system are likely to result in commensurate changes in economic performance. Conversely, big policy swings are likely to result in big changes, both positive and negative, in economic performance. For instance, the nationalization of the banking industry or the sudden elimination of currency controls is likely to result in significant changes in performance. This is in part because decisions made without political consensus are more likely to be prone to error, and, as the historical examples discussed earlier suggest, self-inflicted policy mistakes further contribute to macroeconomic volatility (Lederman and Xu 2009; Loayza *et al.* 2007). However, even in the absence of judgment errors, greater departures from the status quo can be expected to bring about significant jolts in performance.

Volatility is a relational concept, however, so the task then is to develop an indicator that captures volatility in economic performance with respect to an appropriate benchmark. Ideally, such an indicator would have to be broad to capture as many relevant policy areas as possible and free of components that correspond to normative or ideological considerations – e.g., corruption or high tax burdens. Therefore, indicators such as inflation, budget deficits, and government spending as a share of total output would not work because they represent fairly narrow policy areas. Not only is inflation a narrow indicator but in many countries monetary policy is beyond the competence of the president

---

[5] For a discussion, see Flores-Macías (2012: Chapter 2).

and in the hands of independent central banks. Similarly, changes in budget deficits and relative size of government expenditures would miss meaningful changes in other relevant dimensions, such as trade policy or labor policy. Further, such indicators as the share of government expenditures tend to record remarkably little variation over time and therefore do not capture the economic policy changes of interest.

Instead, I operationalize growth volatility as the absolute change in the GDP growth rate from one year to the next. I employ the absolute value to reflect swings in economic performance regardless of whether growth is positive or negative. For example, this measure would reflect a score of 9 for an economy that grows by 8% in one year (*t*–1) and contracts by 1% the following year (*t*). This indicator has the advantages of being broad – since changes in virtually any policy area can potentially influence overall economic performance – as well as normatively and ideologically neutral. At the practical level, another advantage is that data on GDP growth rates are available for the period of interest for all countries in the region.

Other work on economic volatility has used the standard deviation of GDP growth rates over a period of time, providing a single point estimate that is then regressed onto the averages of potential determinants for the period (for example, Mobarak 2004). However, while this approach would point to whether a correlation between the two exists, the direction of the causal arrow could go either way, since high growth volatility could very well be a determinant of deinstitutionalization. Further, by averaging data for the entire time series, this approach glosses over important variation within countries over time. This is especially problematic for countries with several decades of uninterrupted democratic rule, such as Colombia or Venezuela, and for whom the nature of the party system has changed. Given the dynamism of party systems in Latin America since the return of democracy, I favor the dynamic perspective that considers a time series cross-section.

Independent Variables

I rely on vote volatility as a measure of PSI,[6] both for the substantive reasons discussed in the introduction to this volume and as a practical matter. As Scott Mainwaring and Mariano Torcal (2006) note, "volatility is the easiest dimension of institutionalization to measure and perhaps the most important because institutionalization is very close conceptually to stability." In particular, I rely on the Pedersen Index (1983) reflecting net aggregate vote shifts from one election to the next. The index is calculated as the sum of individual party gains and losses, divided by two. The resulting score, on a scale of 0 to 100, corresponds to the net shift in percentage terms. This approach has the advantage

---

[6] An alternative would be to use seat volatility instead of vote volatility. Given issues of data availability for seat volatility, and the high correlation between the two, I employ vote volatility.

of considering institutionalization not as a dichotomous variable – whether institutionalized or not – but as a continuum.

Several factors have been associated with output volatility, including international business cycles, trade openness, levels of wealth, dependence on commodities, and number of veto players in the system. A first control variable is the average growth volatility for Latin America, which accounts for external crises and the region's economic business cycle. Including this variable is important because it captures volatility that originates from factors beyond country-specific characteristics (Aguiar and Gopinath 2004). For example, this measure would capture the volatility associated with the global recession in 2008 and 2009. The crisis originated in the United States as a result of financial institutions' over-exposure to mortgage-backed securities, but it had major adverse consequences for growth around the world regardless of that country's party system. I operationalize this control as the average of all Latin American countries' absolute change in the GDP growth rate from one year to the next year (i.e., from $t-1$ to t).

A different way to account for an underlying growth trend from which to evaluate growth volatility is to estimate predicted growth trends per country based on a regression for the period since the return of democracy, and then calculate the deviation in actual growth rates from the predicted trend. However, the slope of the trend line is fairly sensitive to outliers and to the length of the time period. An alternative would be to fit the predicted trend line based on a higher order polynomial, but each country would require an arbitrary decision as to what order polynomial provides the better underlying growth trend. Therefore, in light of the shortcomings of assuming an underlying growth trend per country, my preferred approach is to control for the volatility that the region is experiencing as a whole, which mirrors international business cycles and crises without having to make specific decisions for each country.

A second factor potentially affecting volatility is previous economic performance. Poor performance in previous years might affect growth volatility in future years because of lingering uncertainty among economic actors. In order to account for domestic performance beyond the effect of international business cycles and crises, I include the lagged GDP growth rate.

A third control is trade openness – a reflection of how integrated an economy is with others. More integrated economies have been found to be more prone to contagion whenever crises emerge elsewhere, generating unexpected, sudden shifts in economic performance (Rodrik 1998) This is because trade openness increases exposure to trade-transmitted volatility in international markets. However, recent work has cast doubt on the direction of the effect, suggesting that the net effect of greater commercial integration is one of more rather than less stability (Cavallo 2007). Regardless of the expected direction, trade openness has been found to have an effect on volatility. Therefore, and following convention, I include data on total trade (imports plus exports) as a share of GDP as a measure of trade openness in the economy.

The level of wealth is a fourth factor associated with volatility. Developed countries tend to experience lower levels of growth volatility than their less developed counterparts (Lucas 1998). For example, member countries of the Organization for Economic Cooperation and Development (OECD) tend to experience steady, smooth growth, whereas African countries tend to experience highly volatile economic performance (Mobarak 2004). Further, wealthier countries will have a greater capacity to estimate GDP growth with a smaller error, and therefore smaller variation, than less wealthy countries (Mobarak 2004: 14–15). I include data on per capita GDP (logged) to account for a country's levels of wealth.[7]

A fifth factor potentially having an effect on volatility is state capacity, which a number of scholars have argued has important consequences for economic development (Evans 1995; Evans and Rauch 1999; North 1989). Such a relationship might play out through growth volatility: low levels of state capacity could result in constantly changing and/or poorly designed policies, in turn affecting growth volatility. Conversely, higher levels of capacity could lead to better thought out policies, contributing to consistent economic stability. Since levels of state capacity are correlated with levels of wealth (Hendrix 2010: 277), GDP per capita is often used to proxy for "state administrative, military, and policy capabilities" (Fearon and Laitin 2003: 76). In addition to controlling for GDP per capita, I include a measure of infrastructural reach of the state (Mann 1986; Soifer 2008): telephone lines per 100 people, to account for the bureaucracy's ability to carry out reforms throughout the country (Morrison 2012). Further, differences in levels of state capacity across countries are captured in the model's fixed effects, which are discussed below.

A sixth potential driver of volatility is the extent to which countries' economies are dependent on commodities (Lederman and Xu 2009; Love 1986). Some scholars even attribute the perverse economic effects associated with the resource curse to the volatility that comes with commodity dependence rather than abundance of resources per se (Cavalcanti *et al.* 2012). Given the historical volatility of commodity prices, countries whose commodities' output represents a greater share of GDP are likely to experience greater fluctuations in growth rates than those with smaller shares. To capture the extent to which Latin American countries' economies depend on natural resources, I include a measure of total natural resource rents – or the sum of oil rents, natural gas rents, coal rents (hard and soft), mineral rents, and forest rents – as a share of GDP.[8]

---

[7] GDP per capita is measured in current US dollars.
[8] The World Bank estimates resource rents by calculating first "the difference between the price of a commodity and the average cost of producing it. This is done by estimating the world price of units of specific commodities and subtracting estimates of average unit costs of extraction or harvesting costs (including a normal return on capital). These unit rents are then multiplied by the physical quantities countries extract or harvest to determine the rents for each commodity as a share of gross domestic product" (World Bank 2016).

Finally, fragmented party systems have been found to make policy changes more gradual and therefore contribute to lower volatility (Nooruddin 2011). This is because the difficulty in departing from the status quo increases with the number of veto players in the decision-making process (Tsebelis 2002). In the context of Latin America, for example, Stephan Haggard and Robert Kaufman (1995) found that fragmentation was conducive to the preservation of the status quo in the context of the reforms of the 1980s and 1990s. Similarly, Scott Mainwaring (1999) suggested that party system fragmentation might have played a role hindering economic reforms in Brazil. I operationalize this variable by employing the Laakso and Taagapera Index (1979) of effective number of parties, which is a commonly used measure of party fractionalization.

In addition to these control variables, it is likely that unobserved, country-specific factors influence volatility. For instance, resource endowments are different across countries and they are likely to play a role in how volatile growth is. In order to account for these factors, I specify all models using fixed effects.

Another important consideration relates to the direction of the causal relationship. In addition to the relationship described above, in which party systems shape economic outcomes, a body of research suggests that economic factors also have an effect on the institutionalization of party systems (Morgan 2011; Roberts 1996, 2014; Roberts and Wibbels 1999; Seawright 2012). In particular, economic voting is advanced as a mechanism, such that retrospective evaluations of economic performance can lead voters to substantially change the share of the vote a party receives from one election to the next (Remmer 1991).[9] Thus, a challenge of the research design is to identify the effect of party systems on the economy, and not the other way around.

Econometric studies have dealt with endogeneity in different ways. One would be to employ an instrumental variable that is highly correlated with PSI but not with the error term (i.e., not related to economic performance in other ways). However, finding such a measure that also varies over time is a difficult proposition, particularly given our incipient knowledge of the dynamic determinants of PSI – indeed, expanding such understanding is one of the motivations behind this volume.[10] An alternative is to employ lagged values of the predictor variable, such that economic volatility during a period of government is explained by the institutionalization of the party system in a previous period (i.e., the party system volatility score for the election that led to that government). For example, the party system volatility recorded from changes between the 1988 and 1993 elections in Venezuela would predict economic volatility between 1994 and 1998. This way, party system volatility would be unaffected by the economic volatility of the subsequent period. While

[9] For research on how economic factors might affect the number of parties in the system, see Coppedge (1997).
[10] Even if an instrumental variable (IV) were available, it is worth noting IV estimation techniques are not without drawbacks.

not a perfect solution in that it does not entirely address the endogeneity problem, it increases our confidence that the results reflect the effect of party systems on economic growth volatility instead of the other way around. Given that the same considerations apply to fragmentation, I follow the same approach for this control variable.

RESULTS

Table 14.1 shows the results of OLS estimation of economic volatility. I estimate six models: the first three include seventeen countries in the region, whereas the rest include the seven main countries discussed in this volume. Models 1 and 4 include bivariate regressions showing the relationship between institutionalization and growth volatility. Models 2 and 5 include full models with control variables, with the exception of the measure of state capacity – telephone lines per 100 people – which is highly correlated (0.7) with per capita GDP. Models 3 and 6 include all control variables. In all cases, fixed effects are included to account for unobserved, country-specific factors.

The six models show that the effect of PSI on economic volatility is significant, whether controls are included or whether the sample is restricted to the seven countries discussed in this volume. However, the effect of institutionalization is about twice as large when the sample considers the seven countries. This is also the case for the magnitude of the effects and significance of some of the control variables, in spite of the loss of efficiency that results from fewer observations. The difference in effects could be due to a stronger relationship between institutionalization and economic volatility in the seven countries compared to the rest of the region, but it could also be due to greater noise in the data available among the smaller countries.

Regarding party system fragmentation, the models point to a positive relationship between fragmentation and economic volatility, such that greater fragmentation might lead to greater volatility. However, the standard errors are quite large and the coefficients are not significant at conventional levels. The coefficients of other control variables follow the expected direction when significant. As the region's average growth volatility increases, so does each country's volatility. As the GDP growth rate (lagged) increases, economic volatility decreases. The coefficients for levels of wealth, trade openness, state capacity, and ratio of resource rents to GDP are not significant, with the exception of resource rents in models 5 and 6.

Table 14.2 shows the effect on economic volatility resulting from changes in the independent variables based on Models 2 and 5.[11] It suggests that a change in party system volatility from the 25th to the 75th percentile results in an increase in GDP volatility of about half a percentage point when considering all

---

[11] Models 2 and 5 are the preferred models because of the high correlation between per capita GDP and Telephone lines per 100 people in Models 3 and 6.

TABLE 14.1 *OLS Estimation of Economic Volatility*

	(1)	(2)	(3)	(4)	(5)	(6)
Party system volatility	0.01**	0.02**	0.02**	0.03**	0.05**	0.05**
	(0.01)	(0.01)	(0.01)	(0.01)	(0.02)	(0.02)
Party system fragmentation		0.03	0.05		0.05	0.06
		(0.09)	(0.09)		(1.17)	(0.18)
Lat Am growth volatility		0.49***	0.49***		0.52*	0.51*
		(0.12)	(0.12)		(0.23)	(0.24)
GDP growth rate (lagged)		−0.19**	−0.2**		−0.23*	−0.24*
		(0.07)	(0.08)		(0.1)	(0.11)
Resource rents		0.03	0.02		0.09*	0.08*
		(0.03)	(0.03)		(0.05)	(0.05)
Trade openness		−0.01	0.0		−0.02	−0.01
		(0.01)	(0.01)		(0.07)	(0.06)
GDP per capita (log)		−0.45	−0.11		−1.14	−1.03
		(0.42)	(0.73)		(0.59)	(0.92)
Telephone lines per 100 people			−0.06			−0.03
			(0.06)			(0.07)
Constant	2.71***	5.95**	3.38	2.82***	11.03**	10.09
	(0.19)	(2.55)	(5.06)	(0.39)	(3.38)	(5.57)
Fixed effects	Yes	Yes	Yes	Yes	Yes	Yes
N	456	441	431	215	201	191

Note: Dependent variable is growth volatility, measured as the absolute value of change in the GDP growth rate from year t-1 to t. Robust SE reported in parenthesis. Significance indicated by * $p<0.1$, ** $p<0.05$, *** $p<0.01$.
Source: Prepared by the author.

countries. The change in volatility is over a full percentage point when considering the seven-country sample. This effect is larger than those of natural resource rents and trade openness for the full sample. Regional economic volatility had the largest effect, whereas the party system fragmentation had the smallest. When considering the restricted model, the change in party system volatility from the 25th to 75th percentiles had among the largest effects, along with the lagged GDP growth rate and GDP per capita.

As a robustness test, and further addressing endogeneity concerns, I replicated the analysis based on between-election averages so that the party system volatility scores from one election would predict subsequent *average* growth volatility for the years between that election and the next. For example, party system volatility recorded between 1988 and 1993 in Venezuela would predict *average* economic volatility between 1994 and 1998, when the next

TABLE 14.2 *Change in Economic Volatility when Predictor Variable Changes from 25th to 75th Percentile*

	All countries		Seven countries	
	25th to 75th percentile	Change in volatility	25th to 75th percentile	Change in volatility
Party system volatility	13.2 to 35.6	0.45**	12.56 to 34.8	1.11**
Party system fragmentation	2.75 to 5.67	0.12	3.18 to 6.66	0.17
Lat Am growth volatility	0.38 to 2.18	0.88***	0.38 to 2.11	0.87*
GDP growth rate (lagged)	1.85 to 5.84	−0.76**	1.44 to 6.37	−1.13*
Resource rents	2.62 to 9.78	0.21	4.08 to 14.45	0.93*
Trade openness	36.93 to 68.06	−0.31	27.14 to 50.6	−0.47
GDP per capita	1299 to 4621	−0.54	1928 to 5787	−1.22

Notes: Results based on Models 2 and 5. Significance indicated by * $p<0.1$, ** $p<0.05$, ***$p<0.01$.
Source: Prepared by the author.

election was held in that country. This approach evaluates the effect of institutionalization on medium-term economic volatility.[12] As Table 14.3 suggests, the relationship between party system volatility and growth volatility holds in models 7, 8, 9, and 11, in spite of the loss of efficiency in the estimates due to a considerable reduction in the number of observations. Models 10 and 12 miss significance at $p<0.1$. The magnitude of the effect of party system volatility remains unchanged.

PSI, VOLATILITY, AND GROWTH

Although I did not find a direct relationship between institutionalization and GDP growth, the evidence presented here is suggestive that an indirect or mediated relationship might exist. This is because the literature on the determinants of economic growth (for example, Hausman and Gavin 1996; Ramey and Ramey 1995) consistently points to economic volatility as a factor that hinders economic performance. It has also been established that the direction of causality is from volatility to lower growth and not the other way around (Kose *et al.* (2003) for growth. One mechanism is that volatility discourages investment, especially foreign investment (Eichengreen 1991). Additionally, volatility disproportionately affects poor sectors since "consumption patterns are much more sensitive to variations in income at low levels of income" (Mobarak 2004: 2). Moreover, macroeconomic volatility has been found to undermine subjective measures of wellbeing more generally (Wolfers 2003).

---

[12] The time frame for average growth volatility depends on how often elections have been held in each country.

TABLE 14.3   *OLS Estimation of Average Economic Volatility between Elections*

	(7)	(8)	(9)	(10)	(11)	(12)
Party system volatility	0.02*	0.02*	0.02*	0.04	0.04**	0.05
	(0.01)	(0.01)	(0.01)	(0.02)	(0.02)	(0.03)
Lat Am growth		0.63*	0.65**		0.13	0.16
volatility		(0.3)	(0.3)		(0.19)	(0.24)
Lagged GDP growth		−0.3**	−0.32**		−0.39***	−0.41***
rate		(0.11)	(0.11)		(0.05)	(0.07)
GDP PER		−0.47	0.12		−0.65	−0.05
CAPITA (LOG)		(0.37)	(0.64)		(0.52)	(0.8)
Telephone lines per			−0.09			−0.1
100 people			(0.06)			(0.09)
Resource rents		−0.02	−0.02		0.03	0.0
		(0.03)	(0.03)		(0.06)	(0.08)
Trade openness		−0.01	0.01		−0.03	0.01
		(0.01)	(0.01)		(0.06)	(0.06)
Party system		−0.02	0.0		−0.01	−0.02
fragmentation		(0.07)	(0.06)		(0.11)	(0.12)
Constant	2.56***	7.03**	2.51	2.66***	9.96**	4.98
	(0.25)	(2.21)	(4.46)	(0.50)	(3.18)	(5.48)
Fixed effects	Yes	Yes	Yes	Yes	Yes	Yes
N	131	125	123	65	59	57

Notes: Dependent variable is *average* growth volatility between one election and the next. Robust SE reported in parenthesis. Significance indicated by * $p<0.1$, ** $p<0.05$, *** $p<0.01$.
Source: Prepared by the author.

Although a study of the determinants of growth in Latin America is beyond the scope of this chapter, the data from the region bears out this relationship between volatility and growth. When considering between-election averages, for example, the relationship between volatility and growth is significant at $p<0.001$ both when including the entire region and when restricting the sample to our seven countries. Therefore, in light of the effect identified here between institutionalization and economic volatility, and the existing knowledge of the effect of economic volatility on growth, institutionalization might indirectly contribute to growth by reducing economic volatility.

CONCLUSION

This chapter evaluated the relationship between PSI and volatility in economic policy making. Based on a large-n study, it found support for the view that institutionalized systems are conducive lower growth volatility, whereas weakly institutionalized systems are conducive to higher growth volatility. First, it provided broad systematic evidence of the relationship between party systems and economic volatility at the regional level beyond the handful of cases that had been studied before. Second, it highlighted that this relationship exists not only based on a dichotomous understanding of institutionalization, but that it also holds when employing a continuous measure. Third, it supports the view that institutionalization and the nature of policy making co-vary not just across countries but across time, at least since the middle of the twentieth century for countries like Colombia and Venezuela and since the 1980s and 1990s for most other countries. Finally, this research is suggestive of a relationship between PSI and macroeconomic performance. Given the finding that PSI leads to lower growth volatility, this feature of party systems might have an indirect effect on growth.

15

From the Outside Looking In: Latin American Parties in Comparative Perspective

Allen Hicken and Rachel Beatty Riedl*

INTRODUCTION: THE DECLINE OF PSI

As comparative party scholars who work in other regions of the world, we offer observations on the points of similarity and contrast from a global perspective. One of the striking themes emerging in this volume is that the gap between party systems in Latin America and the rest of the developing world has closed considerably. For decades, an important point of contrast for scholars working in Sub-Saharan Africa/Southeast Asia has been the comparative lack of ideological differentiation across parties. In much of Sub-Saharan Africa and Southeast Asia it was impossible to credibly align parties along some sort of issue or policy dimension, which stood in contrast to Western Europe and parts of Latin American. But this gap has now closed considerably. After an initial intense period of polarization in most important cases of highly institutionalized party systems in Latin America (e.g. Colombia, Venezuela, Costa Rica and Uruguay) many party systems evolved over time to display very minimal differences between the main parties. Whereas in Western European states, the party systems remain more ideologically differentiable, in Asia and Sub-Saharan Africa, and now increasingly in Latin America, party programs, to the extent they can be identified, obscure more than they clarified.

The chapters in this volume make clear that there is little basis for a regional distinction for Latin America from other developing world regions based on ideological or programmatic differentiation. In many countries PSI has declined and the salience of left–right divisions has shifted over time and space – seemingly diminishing the connection between institutionalization and programmatic differentiation. This quote from the Philippines, for example, could now just as easily apply to Peru: "Far from being stable, programmatic organizations, the country's main political parties are nebulous entities that can be set up, merged with others, split, resurrected, regurgitated, reconstituted,

---

* Names are listed alphabetically.

renamed, repackaged, recycled or flushed down the toilet anytime" (Quimpo 2005).

This deinstitutionalization is an interesting and important development for a number of reasons. To begin with, deinstitutionalization contradicts what has been a common argument/assumption about increasing PSI over time. This argument was especially prevalent in work on Eastern Europe (for example, Tavits 2005; Tavits and Annus 2006). However, the work in this volume, consistent with the findings in much of the rest of the developing world, suggests the following three points. First, increasing system-wide institutionalization over time is extremely rare, particularly since the third wave. Brazil is the only example identified in this volume,[1] of increasing institutionalization over time, and even here recent electoral volatility and corruption scandals have raised challenges to sustaining the party system (see the Brazil chapter in this volume). Mexico's institutionalization is less a case of increasing institutionalization under democracy than of a party system inherited from a stable set of parties in the late authoritaritarian era. This trajectory actually fits more distinctly with the cases of authoritarian-led transitions in Asia and Africa (Hicken and Kuhonta 2011, Riedl 2014, Slater and Wong 2013). In Sub-Saharan Africa and Southeast Asia, Thailand is the only other partial example of increasing institutionalization, over time. Second, declines in institutionalization over time are common. And third, low levels of PSI can persist over long periods of time.

Widespread deinstitutionalization has the potential to reframe the kinds of questions we ask about party systems. The subtext of much of the work on PSI, and even some of the chapters in this volume, is that deinstitutionalization is an out of equilibrium state. It represents a transition period that should conclude with the realignment of the parties and voters in a new, stable pattern. The expectation is that political entrepreneurs will step into the breach and create new parties, or reinvigorate existing ones. We expect to see strong ties between voters and parties. That this is not happening in many cases seems puzzling. But from the view of the rest of the Global South, it is sustained high levels of PSI that seem anomalous and the deinstitutionalization we are observing in parts of Latin America looks like a fairly natural evolution of a modern party system – a reversion to the mean. Inchoate systems are the norm, rather than the exception in our regions of the world. Latin America is still, on average, more institutionalized than either of our regions (Hicken and Kuhonta 2011), but the gap, perhaps, is closing. At the very least, the deinstitutionalization and in some cases reinstitutionalization we see provides new points of comparison both within and across regions.

The material in this volume also reminds us that party systems are frequently asymmetrically institutionalized. This can happen in one of two ways. First, one (often dominant) party may be highly institutionalized while its competitors are not. The descriptions of the party systems in Bolivia, and to some extent in

---

[1] El Salvador is a second possible example from Latin America.

Ecuador and Venezuela, sound very similar to the party systems in Mozambique, Tanzania, and Thailand, where fairly institutionalized ruling parties compete against a less institutionalized opposition. Second, party systems may appear highly institutionalized along some dimensions but not others. In fact, our cases in Sub-Saharan Africa and East/Southeast Asia suggest that high electoral volatility can coexist with a variety of durable voter–party linkage mechanisms (and clientelist in particular) in which voters reliably support a particular party or group, but the parties themselves combine and compete at the national level in opposing forms from one election to the next. Likewise, low levels of volatility can sometimes persist, even where parties are programmatically indistinct and only loosely linked to voters.

To summarize, similar to the evolution of scholarly thinking about competitive authoritarian regimes (from transitional way stations to distinct regime types) the developments described in this volume underscore the need to adjust our approach to PSI in two ways. First, we should approach inchoate party systems as the norm rather than the exception. Second, we should recognize that partial, or asymmetric institutionalization can be a stable equilibrium under some conditions.

This suggests an interesting new question in addition to those already thoroughly explored in this volume: Why would we expect PSI to emerge in modern democracies? What are the channels through which stability is generated? How do varied *combinations* of programmatic differentiation, charismatic or populist appeals, and clientelism form the foundations for high, low, or asymmetric PSI? How do these forms of voter–party linkages undergird parties' stability, minimize electoral volatility, and generate a sense of future predictability? For example, it is striking that recent experiments with increasing voter information on individual politicians' performance in Sub-Saharan Africa have yielded few changes in voter behavior or activism (Lieberman *et al.* 2014). This is likely because voters are woven into a complex web of political party affiliations from the local to the national level that determine their expectations about the extent of resources they are likely to receive as a community. Programmatic differences and information about a particular individual can mean little when parties are deeply rooted through clientelistic distribution channels tied to identity group mobilization. Stability can be garnered despite programmatic indeterminacy in Sub-Saharan Africa, and in Latin America high levels of institutionalization coexisted with weak programmatic differentiation in many cases during the Cold War era,[2] whereas the contemporary deinstitutionalization has coincided with increasing programmatic differentiation and, in some cases, polarization.[3]

---

[2] Examples include Colombia and Uruguay until 1971, Costa Rica, and Venezuela from 1968 to 1988.

[3] Since 1999, the salience of left–right divisions has increased greatly in many Latin American countries (Venezuela, Bolivia, Ecuador, and Nicaragua, Chile, Brazil, Mexico, El Salvador,

Absent ideological or identity-based anchors, however, non-programmatic party systems tend to be less stable. This is the case in much of Southeast Asia, and, it appears now, in parts of Latin America. In the Philippines, pre-2001 Thailand, and to some extent post-2009 Indonesia, clientelist distribution is generally not tied to identity group mobilization. Party competition in these cases is impressively and stubbornly non-programmatic, but absent the identity anchor we see in parts of Sub-Saharan Africa, the party systems in these cases are more unstable.

The volume also explores a set of questions regarding party organization and investment in party construction – also salient questions in our regions. Under what conditions would modern politicians have an incentive to invest in party building? After all, parties in the modern era are not usually mobilization vehicles for suffrage, representational, or independence rights as were parties in the past (Mainwaring and Zoco 2007), and for parties that have descended from earlier mass mobilizers, those linkages and loyalties have faded and decayed. In the modern era, investing in party building is costly relative to other mobilization strategies. Perhaps it is something politicians pursue only when they have no better option. This is what makes cases like Brazil or Thailand so intriguing and worth studying further.

The deinstitutionalization described in many of these chapters also provides new opportunities to develop and test theories of party system development, stasis, and change. For example, comparing the experience of Latin America to Southeast Asia and Sub-Saharan Africa invites new theorizing about the importance of programmatic appeals and the development and maintenance of an institutionalized party system. In comparing the party systems historically found in Latin America with those found in Sub-Saharan Africa or Southeast Asia, no single point of contrast stands out more sharply than the lack of programmatic linkages in our respective regions. With few exceptions, strong leftist parties are absent in East and Southeast Asia and Sub-Saharan Africa and programmatic appeals based on non-class divisions are also rare.[4] Why is this the case? Answering this question goes beyond the scope of this volume, but whether the dearth of a partisan left in much of Sub-Saharan Africa and Southeast Asia is due to outright suppression or the distribution of political preferences, it has gone hand-in-hand with either inchoate party systems or alternative forms of party–voter linkage building.

This volume raises striking questions about the relationship between parties on the left and PSI. It is interesting that the decline in institutionalization was

Uruguay), accompanied by the growth of the partisan left in the last fifteen years (Levitsky and Roberts 2011; Mainwaring, Torcal, and Somma 2015).

[4] In Africa, almost all parties claim a leftist or socialist orientation, as a legacy of decolonization from the West and a contemporary pro-poor valence position. But, in reality, parties do not formulate economic policies or represent a clear class constituency that differentiates them along these lines (Collier 1982; Riedl 2014; Van de Walle 2003; Zolberg 1966). By contrast, overtly leftist parties faced enormous challenges in Cold War Southeast Asia.

associated with the decline of the partisan left in many countries – whether through the dilution of leftist party brands or the hollowing out of leftist parties organizationally. Does the increased salience of left–right divisions in recent years in many countries in Latin America presage greater institutionalization to come? What we yet lack are well-developed theories about the conditions under which the presence of leftist parties increases the probability of institutionalization and the conditions under which high PSI can exist in its absence. If there is a relationship between the presence/absence of leftist parties and institutionalization, we need to understand the underlying mechanisms that connect the two. Do parties on the left serve as an anchor to the party system? Do they facilitate programmatic differentiation and thus stability in the party system? Are they a competitive catalyst for party building by parties on the right? In the absence of a partisan left, are there viable alternatives that can serve as the catalyst for institutionalization? And can conservative parties – particularly authoritarian successor parties in other regions of the world – play a similar institutionalizing role (Hicken and Kuhonta 2015a; Riedl 2014)? Under what conditions could ethnic, tribal or religious divisions substitute for class divisions (more on this question below)? These are some of the questions that this volume provokes and about which we look forward to seeing more comparative work.

ECONOMIC CRISES, POPULISM AND PARTY SYSTEM CHANGE

Comparing the trajectories of party systems across regions one is struck by the differences in the role of political economy in party system change. In many Latin American cases severe economic shocks followed by radical, controversial reforms create the context for equally radical changes in the party system. But these globally relevant economic moments were experienced very differently in East/Southeast Asia and Sub-Saharan Africa. The global economic crises of the last three decades certainly contributed to government turnover (for example, Thailand in 1997, South Korea in 1998, and Mauritius in 1995), and contributed, in some cases, to the collapse of authoritarian regimes (for example, the Philippines in 1986, Indonesia 1998, and Benin in 1990). We will talk more about democratic transitions in the next section but, in democracies, the economic crises and subsequent response did not usually lead to a dramatic restructuring/destructuring of the party system. Perhaps this is not surprising. Where party brands were already weak, and voter–party ties tenuous to begin with, economic shocks *could* not lead to dealignment, and generally *did* not lead to realignment. To be sure, party incumbents were often punished by voters for their links to the crisis and/or unpopular reforms, but with low levels of institutionalization already the norm, there was little room for more systemic change in the level of institutionalization.

That said, one commonality across regions lies in the link between economic shocks and the rise of populism. Fujimori in Peru, Chávez in Venezuela, Morales in Bolivia, and Correa in Ecuador have certainly had counterparts in other regions. For example, economic crises contributed to the rise of populists in Thailand (Thaksin), Philippines (Estrada), Japan (Koizumi), and Zambia (Sata). The interaction of populism and PSI is one theme that emerges in many of the chapters in this volume, but the authors differ in how they view the relationship between the two variables. The issue is whether we see populism as a *symptom* of poor institutionalization, or a *cause* of deinstitutionalization. From the latter perspective, the rise of the populist politicians undermines existing party loyalties and makes existing partisan divisions increasingly obsolete. From the former perspective, low levels of PSI is the context that allows populists to rise and come to power (see the Flores-Macías and Levitsky chapters in this volume for examples). While the two of us tend to adopt the symptom approach in our own work, we sympathize with those who want to assign populism a causal role and seek to explore the conditions under which this is likely to occur. Populist politicians are often outsiders or mavericks from within their own parties. Backed by extra-party mobilization they often work to undermine existing ties between voters and their partisan rivals. But perhaps it is possible to reconcile both perspectives by understanding that populist politicians are more likely when party system institutionalization is low, while also acknowledging that the presence of populists can hasten the deterioration of institutionalized party systems.

STATE CAPACITY AND PARTY SYSTEM INSTITUTIONALIZATION

The dramatically limited role of the state may be a separate, independent factor driving party system deinstitutionalization. During the era of state retrenchment in the 1980s and 1990s, some significant portion of the citizenry experienced a decline in services provided by the state in Latin America, Sub-Saharan Africa, and Southeast Asia. When citizens perceive deterioration, this can create a feedback loop to declining citizen perceptions of parties and governance. If weak states limit parties' governing and implementation capacity across the board, citizens may well perceive ruling party performance failures in the economy as well as in security. This fuels public discontent. State weakness directly undermines government performance and service provision, and therefore makes it difficult for parties to consolidate or maintain their electoral base (Mainwaring 2006b). Although most of Latin America has reversed the neoliberal policies of the end of the twentieth century and many countries have dramatically expanded their public sectors, Sub-Saharan Africa and Southeast Asia continue to demonstrate the ongoing challenges associated with weak and/or minimal states and the potential effects on PSI. Does state weakness drive poor social service performance *and* a lack of policy differentiation, which then decreases PSI?

The comparison between Latin America and South-East Asia/Sub-Saharan Africa suggests that the relationship between a weak state and PSI is critical, but highly varied. While Latin American states certainly vary in terms of state capacity, the range of that variation appears to be much greater across the states in our regions of the world.[5] As a result state strength/state capacity stands out as an important variable in ways that are perhaps not as apparent from a focus on Latin America alone. There are two distinct issues surrounding a weak state. The first is whether citizens and parties experience a *contraction* of the state as an exogenous change. State contraction can be jarring, and create dissonance between parties' citizen linkage machinery and a state bureaucracy that is no longer capable of implementing their policies effectively. State contraction is thus a scenario that *creates* a disjuncture. Existing parties are no longer able to provide the goods and services they once did, and in the contemporary period of modern substitutes for parties – such as media, private firms, and local operators (Levitsky, this volume) – new parties are unlikely to invest in party building. Whereas when parties originally form and continually compete within a weak state environment, such as nationalist parties surrounding independence, their competitive practices and citizen linkage mechanisms may be more adapted to this context over the long term.

In Sub-Saharan Africa and much of Southeast Asia, parties do not generally exhibit economic policy differentiation from the start (Elischer 2013; Hicken and Kuhonta 2015a). Because many states are weak, they lack resources and effective bureaucracies to implement broad-reaching social programs to a large degree; but they also lack control over domestic economic policy to a significant extent. While electoral campaigns vigorously debate which party or candidate is *capable* of bringing about development and growth, the specific development policies are not the focus of debate (Bleck and van de Walle 2013). Macroeconomic policies are often scripted in collaboration with multilateral lending agencies as terms of continuing development aid. This is particularly true in Africa,[6] but was also the case at times in Indonesia, Thailand, and the Philippines. But whether due to proscribed structural adjustment reforms in aid-dependent countries, or domestic political bargains, there is significant stability in macroeconomic policy despite electoral transitions, even in the *most* institutionalized and differentiated party systems (Hill 1997; van de Walle *et al.* 2007). Therefore, competing parties lack the programmatic differentiation perhaps necessary to create a strong party brand (Lupu 2013). However, party brands can be built upon alternative mobilizing strategies – of ethnic leadership and brokers, for example. Indeed, dominant parties in Sub-Saharan Africa have anchored PSI in many weak states, such as Tanzania and Mozambique in particular.

[5] As an illustration, consider the World Bank's Government Effectiveness Indicator (http://info.world-bank.org/governance/wgi/). The GEI ranges from –2.5 to 2.5. Across this five-point scale, the difference between the most effective and least effective states in Latin America is 2.37, compared to 2.97 in Sub-Saharan Africa and 3.47 in Southeast Asia.

[6] Riedl interview, former Minister of Finance, Zambia 2006. Certainly there are exceptions and variation in the degree to which countries are directed by foreign donors versus able to implement their own economic policy, with Botswana, Rwanda, and Ethiopia maintaining significant control over their policy agenda (Fraser and Whitfield 2008; Young 2013).

As discussed above, because economic policy was not the organizing framework around which parties organized and identified in Africa and Southeast Asia, the countries in these regions did not experience dramatic partisan realignment with the wave of neoliberal reforms that required political and economic liberalization across the continent. While the state's role was indeed more limited, these neoliberal reforms offered a different type of disjuncture: they required the introduction of multi-party competition. The contracting role of the state and more limited state resources for patronage and civil servant salaries combined with the introduction of multi-party competition created an opening for authoritarian incumbent displacement. Party systems formed in the wake of this power–void transition were more volatile and resemble the inchoate equilibrium more recently established in Peru in the wake of party system collapse. That is, nascent party systems established in the wake of neoliberal reforms, in the shadow of a weak state, demonstrate similar characteristics: a lack of national territorial coverage, grand coalitions of alliances and power sharing among individual candidates, political elites cycling through on temporary party lists, and lack of differentiated party labels (Riedl 2014; Slater and Simmons 2013).

There are self-reinforcing mechanisms that sustain these strategies: successful personalist examples, partisan free agency, practices of party switching (*transhumance* in Francophone Africa; turncoatism in the Philippines), and pre- and post-electoral coalition building and bandwagoning that obviate the costs of party building for new politicians. As Levitsky (Chapter 11, this volume) suggests in the case of Peru, these are common practices across regions, and directly align with the strategies of electoral competition in Niger, Benin, Malawi, Zambia, the Philippines, Indonesia, and pre-2001 Thailand, among others at the low end of PSI.

The second issue surrounding the question of state capacity is that of territorial control and security. The Colombian case suggests that security performance failures may contribute to party system collapse or deinstitutionalization.[7] This is not surprising, perhaps, and is exemplified in other cases across regions. The territorial integrity of the state is likely a productive condition for greater PSI. Questions over the extent of state authority can lead to citizen disenchantment with the ruling party, with opposition party alternatives, and even distrust in accepting elections as the normalized route to gaining power.

For example, since the introduction of multi-party competition in Mali, state incapacity has complicated PSI. While hailed as a democratic over-achiever given its level of socioeconomic development and heterogeneous population, ongoing secessionist claims in the North indicated an underlying fragility in the state's capacity and ability to broadcast power over the national territory. Civic

---

[7] The Honduran and Venezuelan cases stand as potential counter examples. Honduras maintained an institutionalized party system through 2013, despite a severe security problem, and institutionalization has been increasing in Venezuela (albeit asymmetrically) despite security concerns.

abstention from the political realm and street protests were the main channels of addressing the situation: both were alternatives to voting for the available slate of political parties.[8] The weakly institutionalized party system remains volatile, and the security situation contributed to public acquiescence to alternatives to democratic party competition. We see very similar dynamics at work in the Philippines, a long-standing democracy with a stubbornly weak state (Hutchcroft and Rocamora 2003). As in Latin America, citizens engage in a range of alternatives to parties in a weak state context – from civic associations to mass mobilization.

But weak states, security threats, and political order performance failures do not *only* generate political party volatility and inchoate party systems. These conditions can, to the contrary, further relatively stable authoritarian rule (Riedl 2014; Slater 2010). Strong parties can be built around conflict, such as a civil war, revolution, or counter-revolution (LeBas 2011; Levitsky *et al.* 2016a). Threats to the ruling party can increase coherence of the inner circle around the need to thwart further political liberalization. Security threats can also increase domestic and international acceptance of ruling party strategies to maintain an authoritarian coercive apparatus to respond to such threats. Dominant parties in Indonesia, Malaysia, and Singapore were able to leverage real and existential threats to remain in, to build, and maintain their dominance for decades. The cross-regional comparisons beyond Latin America remind us of this potential for democratic backsliding and breakdown, overseen by a strongly institutionalized ruling party.

INSTITUTIONAL CHANGE AND CONTINUITY: PARTY SYSTEM STABILITY IN COMPARATIVE PERSPECTIVE

The cases examined in this volume suggest an important dialectic between institutional change and continuity of the party system. Overall party system stability – where it occurred – was undergirded by dramatic party adaptation and evolution by parties in the face of exogenous shocks. And by the same token, party system collapse and extreme institutional volatility were predicated on parties' internal institutional stasis and inability to adjust to the changing context around them.

This reality suggests that globally we might expect periodic cycles of instability based upon party lifecycles, which vary according to the parties' *raison d'être*. Revolutionary parties are rooted in grassroots mobilization and national territorial organization and, where successful, can create highly institutionalized political parties. But revolutionary parties and nationalist, independence parties have a declining lifecycle of citizen linkages (Levitsky and Way 2012). While they may have a territorial base and organization,

---

[8] Only approximately 20% of the electorate participated in the 1992 and 1997 elections, for example (Thiriot 2002).

their claim to represent the nation may decline over time and open new political space for opposition parties to emerge. South Africa's African National Congress (ANC) now faces the challenge of creating new channels for leadership selection and linkage mechanisms to the population. Zimbabwe's ZANU-PF has retained its dominance only by coercively constraining the opposition. India's Congress party shaped the nationalist independence movement; but over time the necessity of that role withered away (Kohli 1990). Alternative visions of what nationalism might entail have emerged, as have other issue domains and forms of voter mobilization (Chandra 2007). In Latin America, these lifecycles have been tied to neoliberal economic reforms and crises, which demonstrated the inability of sclerotic traditional parties to adapt and offer more plausible options to voters (see Chapters 10 and 13 of this volume).[9]

From a comparative perspective, Brazil's anomalous increasing PSI suggests a crucial lesson for perspectives on institutional change and continuity that relate well beyond Latin America. The only country to actually increase its level of institutionalization did so through complete institutional innovation. Brazil's party system became increasingly institutionalized because a new form of party institution developed, breaking with traditional modes of patronage organization.[10] The PT's innovation in party type and policy was firmly rooted in a partisan economic cleavage, which, while predating the reforms of the 1990s, became increasingly salient as those reforms took hold. The party's development and the salience of the economic cleavage were intimately linked: as the PT grew from a minor party to a national power, the salience of the economic cleavage became more evident. This path towards increasing PSI seems unlikely to be replicated in much of the developing world (Roberts 2014). But how likely are other catalysts of party innovation that would lead to increasing policy differentiation and PSI?

One challenge new opposition parties face is limited resources. However, where neoliberal economic reforms have stimulated more private capital, newly emergent business elite can finance opposition parties according to a variety of models (Arriola 2012). Therefore, a key factor driving the possibility of party system innovation and institutional change is the degree of privatization, and the diversification of resources away from state – and incumbent – control. New parties that form may attempt to follow the mold of existing, successful parties in order to compete on their terms and win over their voters. This may take the form of well organized, nationally coherent parties, particularly where the

---

[9] While the general global pattern appears to be one of declining support for revolutionary parties over time, Latin America has some revolutionary parties that have been able to adapt and survive (for example, the MNR in Bolivia, the FSLN in Nicaragua, and the FMLN in El Salvador), and these cases are worth further study.

[10] The PT in Brazil built local roots, created new partisan linkages, and solidified the party system through the process. Duvergerian logic then helped to further institutionalize the right and decreased electoral volatility.

incumbent has a dominant command (Riedl 2014). Traditional parties have even more difficulty to adapt to the environment than new, upstart parties, because once built according to a certain model, politicians and party leaders who have reached the top will work to protect their internal routes to power. However, where the existing mode of competition is centered around personalistic campaigns and temporary electoral vehicles or "movements" – as in Peru, and many countries across Sub-Saharan African and Southeast Asia – it is unlikely that newly financed opposition would endeavor to foster more deeply rooted citizen linkages through party building. The route to increasingly institutionalized party systems through party innovation seems improbable where electoral competition is already centered on valence issues rather than policy differentiation (Bleck and van de Walle 2013).

In a few cases in Latin America and beyond, an emerging equilibrium creates disincentives to party building. Inchoate party systems allow political elites to cycle "in" on different labels and form alliances with the best performing politicians at any given moment. The new political party system that is emerging in Peru following party system collapse mirrors those in other developing democracies across the world that emerge in the wake of incumbent displacement. Politicians develop strategies that allow them to succeed without parties; "over time, the strategies, norms, and technologies of non-party politics diffuse (and even institutionalize), as electoral competition selects for politicians with the will, know-how, and resources to 'go it alone'" (Levitsky, Chapter 11 of this volume). Voters and brokers even see parties as a negative attribute for some politicians, suggesting that the top layer of their patronage distribution is already predetermined to party loyalists. Party-less candidates, on the contrary, are viewed as being more available to broker deals attractive to local actors at any given moment because they lack those pre-established commitments.[11] Once politicians learn they can succeed without parties, they embrace partisan free agency and party switching practices to form pre-electoral and post-electoral coalitions of independents to bandwagon around frontrunners and winners for increased access to public resources (Hicken 2009).

These practices create new forms of institutional innovation, as candidates are increasingly selected for their ability to self-finance and mobilize their own voter base (Aspinall 2014). This short-term contracting rewards different types of candidates: amateur politicians, lacking ideological formation, but with financial resources to mobilize a following. A question for future research is whether these changes in the formal institutions of party system competition will ultimately create changes in the informal institutions of clientelism and party–broker linkages. If new candidates are increasingly self-financed independents, the long-term relationship

---

[11] Riedl interview; Presidential candidates Bruno Amoussou and Adrian Hounbedji. Cotonou, Benin (2006).

between political parties and traditional brokers may dissolve as local elite businessmen–candidates supplants it.

These cases demonstrate critical evolutionary changes across Latin America and beyond in the unequal adaptation of parties to the political environment. New parties may be able to emulate successful existing models, and also have more latitude to innovate where traditional models are discredited. Traditional parties are susceptible to decreasing public support when they govern badly, potentially impaired by the weakness of the state itself. Poor performance can create a downward cycle for PSI, as new upstart parties invest less in party building, and pre-existing parties are less able to adapt. The system's prior construction, in combination with external shocks, make some parties more able to thrive in a new (deinstitutionalized) equilibrium, whereas older parties cannot adjust and rapidly fade away. This asymmetric ability to adapt demonstrates that parties have unequal resources to draw upon (Grzymala-Busse 2002). Well-established parties may not benefit from their social rootedness and internal organization equally – some features constrain further party evolution, increase the likelihood of party system collapse, and the reestablishment of an entirely new, highly volatile, system.

As comparative party scholars, we find ourselves wondering whether we are witnessing the end of an era. Are institutionalized party systems increasingly going to become an endangered species? Is there a way to reverse the decline in institutionalization we have witnessed in much of Latin America, or spark its emergence in long-standing inchoate systems? Given changes over time in the salience of left–right divisions, what are alternative sources of mobilization and differentiation upon which to construct an institutionalized party system? The chapters in this volume suggest a few possibilities.

Social Service Provision Brazil is the most prominent example of increasing institutionalization in the region, though even here the future is less than certain. The Brazilian case suggests that social service provision can help parties differentiate themselves from their competitors while creating a cadre of loyal voters. The Workers' Party's *Bolsa Família* program helped the party expand its base into the country's populist Northeast. Indeed, it is not uncommon for parties to use social welfare/social services as a way to build support among poorer voters.

Outside of Brazil, El Salvador, and Thailand suggest that there is a possible pathway to increase party system institutionalization, even in a weak state context. In Thailand, the bundle of social welfare policies developed and delivered by the Thai Rak Thai party helped distinguish the party from its peers, and helped the party develop a base of voters who felt substantial loyalty to the party – a rare thing for Thailand. Similarly, India's Bharatiya Janata Party (BJP) emerged from a regionally based, Hindu nationalist party and developed into a nationally organized, deeply entrenched political party by serving as an *alternative* to the weak and insufficient state (Thachil 2015). The BJP developed a broad and deep grassroots base by providing disadvantaged voters with basic social services via local affiliates. The weak state context provided a pathway for an opposition party to create new linkages at the local level, stimulating demand for party organization across the national territory. Egypt's Muslim Brotherhood similarly built a strong organizational network across the local territory by first providing public services to constituents in need (Masoud 2014). Yet, it is clear from this comparative perspective that the path between service strategies and institutionalization is not always a straight line. For example, Thachil's work in India shows how using social services as side payments built a loyal cadre of BJP voters, but also obscured inter-party policy differences by allowing the party to simultaneously pursue a policy agenda supported by the economic elite.

Ethnic or Religious Divisions. If the salience of class as a marker of party difference has ebbed and flowed with time (Mainwaring *et al.* 2015), are there other social divisions that can fill the void and serve as the building blocks for institutionalized parties? Ethnic or religious divisions are one possibility. In parts of Latin America, particularly Bolivia and Ecuador, ethnicity/indigenity has emerged as a salient social division around which parties are organizing. Interestingly, the rise of MAS in Bolivia is generally viewed as a symptom of the collapse of the traditional party system – and it is true that the rise of Evo Morales and MAS was made possible by the weakness of Bolivia's previous party system (Flores-Macías 2012). But MAS also seems to be serving as a new focal point around which the Bolivian party system is stabilizing and perhaps institutionalizing. In the wake of the post-apartheid party system in South Africa, the rise of the Inkatha Freedom Party as a source of opposition to the African National Congress was constructed by mobilizing the Zulu population. Although the party's electoral support has waned in 2009 and 2014, it has contributed to building the opposition in the new South Africa.

Religious cleavages are another potential source of stability. In parts of South and Southeast Asia religious cleavages help inform the programmatic differences among parties, and provide the organizational capital necessary to link voters to candidates. There are fewer examples of this from Latin America, but they are not absent. For example, Trejo and Bizzarro (2014) suggest that while organized labor played a role in the creation and growth of the Workers' Party in Brazil, it was the organizational capacity and networks of the Catholic Church that enabled the party to develop into a mass-base political party.

Institutional Engineering. Given the strength of the institutionalist tradition among political scientists who work on Latin America, it is surprising that institutions and institutional reform receive little attention in the discussion of party system change. With the exception of Colombia, institutional changes seem to play no role in the deinstitutionalization of Latin American party systems,[12] nor do institutional variables appear to be the most important explanatory factor for the increasing institutionalization in Brazil. This is in

---

[12] In Colombia, institutional list changes fed into brand dilution, although the new rules were led by traditional parties strategizing to gain more seats in the short term (Albarracín, Gamboa, and Mainwaring, Chapter 8 of this volume).

contrast to work on Southeast Asian party systems where institutional factors feature prominently in explanations of increasing institutionalization in Thailand (Hicken 2006), deinstitutionalization in Indonesia (Aspinall 2014), and entrenched inchoateness in the Philippines. Institutional changes engineered by the authoritarian successor party in Senegal to gain short-term advantages have contributed to increasing deinstitutionalization of the party system over time.

Are institutions epiphenomenal or endogenous to the greater forces that shape de/institutionalization, or can they help hasten, arrest, or reverse deinstitutionalization? The question is a difficult one, in part because institutional change can be initiated by stable political parties attempting to maintain the status quo. Electoral rule change may then coincide with party system stability, as in Singapore, or in the early stages in Chile and Colombia.

But electoral rule change meant to assure stability can have unintended consequences over the long term and catalyze opportunities for dramatic reformulation. Rule change in Chile exposed traditional parties to new forms of electoral competition in a changing environment, particularly as voter–party linkages decay in the contemporary context. Rule changes in Thailand provided new rewards and new tools for party building but also presented new challenges for Thailand's traditional elite. Across world regions, reforms to decentralize governance have created new opportunities to run candidates at the local level. Some parties are more or less well positioned and internally organized to take advantage and adapt to these reforms; some parties will grow and reproduce whereas others will be challenged and potentially fade away, increasing party system volatility (Riedl and Dickovick 2014).

Polarizing Populism. Finally, as discussed earlier, many of the chapters in this volume link the rise of populism with party system deinstitutionalization. But the chapters also raise an intriguing question. Can populism serve as a catalyst for (re) institutionalization? Based on our read of the evidence presented in this volume, we suggest that populism can be catalytic under two conditions. First, populist politicians must also invest in organizational party building in order to produce a momentum for institutionalization. In other words, populist parties must transcend personalism and move beyond the appeal of charismatic leaders in order to serve as a foundation for party system institutionalization. The comparison between Morales in Bolivia and Chávez in Venezuela is instructive here. The former has worked from the very beginning to create a robust, nationwide party organization. By contrast, Chávez initially assiduously cultivated a cult of personality, before investing in serious party building beginning in 2007 with the formation of the PSUV. Similarly, in other regions, when populists have invested in party building they have brought increased stability to the party system (Thaksin Shinawatra/Thai Rak Thai being the most prominent example), but where populist politicians have eschewed party building we see stagnation (Philippines) or deinstitutionalization (Indonesia).

Second, populists must be polarizing. One lesson that can be drawn from the Latin American cases and pursued with further cross-regional research is that some degree of polarization seems beneficial for party system stability. To the extent that populists are also polarizing, they can be catalysts for new political cleavages that then serve as the basis for greater institutionalization. Yet revolutionary, nationalist, or regime-cleavage polarization has the potential to either disrupt democratic stability *or* fade away over time as an organizing and relevant cleavage. Polarization over different types of ideas and identities can contribute to institutionalization of the party system, but the content of polarization itself may challenge the territorial integrity of the state and the democratic regime.

CONCLUSION

In sum, while the Latin American cases increasingly resemble party systems from the global South, their sequential process of institutionalization and subsequent deinstitutionalization has much to teach us as students of political parties. The contemporary era continues to feature high economic uncertainty, which can catalyze a turn to populism, further break down traditional party–voter ties, and lead parties to adopt particularly transient strategies of mobilization (Lupu and Riedl 2013). And while the Latin American cases lead us to focus on the role of leftist parties and policy differentiation, a global comparison shifts the focus from policy to other forms of identification and affiliation: service provision, ethnic identities, and partnerships with existing social organizations (from unions to churches). These factors also loom large in Latin America, and their salience is increasingly apparent as politicians search for new ways of connecting with voters.

Bibliography

Abal, Medina, and Juan Manuel. 2009. "The Rise and Fall of the Argentine Center-Left: The Crisis of *Frente Grande.*" *Party Politics* 15(3): 357–75.

Achen, Christopher H. 1992. "Social Psychology, Demographic Variables, and Linear Regression: Breaking the Iron Triangle in Voting Research." *Political Behavior* 14(3): 195–211.

Agüero, Felipe. 2003. "Chile: Unfinished Transition and Increased Political Competition." In Jorge I. Domínguez and Michael Shifter, eds., *Constructing Democratic Governance in Latin America*, 2nd edn, pp. 292–320. Baltimore, MD: The Johns Hopkins University Press.

Aguiar, Mark, and Gita Gopinath. 2004. "Emerging Market Business Cycles: The Cycle is the Trend." NBER Working Paper No. 10734, September.

Aguilar, Héctor, and Lorenzo Meyer. 1993. *In the Shadow of the Mexican Revolution: Contemporary Mexican History, 1910–1989.* Austin, TX: University of Texas Press.

Albarracín, Juan. 2013. "Ideological Self-Placement and Issue Attitudes in Colombian Public Opinion." Presented at the 2013 Conference of the Latin American Studies Association, May 30–June 1, Washington, DC.

Albarracín, Juan, and Juan Pablo Milanese. 2012. "The Impact of Electoral Reform in Colombia: Congressional and Subnational Elections." Presented at the 2012 Conference of the Latin American Studies Association, May 23–26, San Francisco, CA.

2016. "Exploring Intra-Party Competition and the Effects of Electoral Reform: A Look at Colombia's Local Elections, 1997–2011." Presented at the 2016 Conference of the Latin American Studies Association, May 27–30, New York, NY.

Alcántara Sáez, Manuel, and Juan Pablo Luna. 2004. "Ideología y competencia partidaria en dos transiciones: Chile y Uruguay en perspectiva comparada." *Revista de Ciencia Política* 24(1): 128–68.

Aldrich, John. 1983. "A Downsian Spatial Model with Party Activism." *American Political Science Review* 77(4): 974–90.

1995. *Why Parties? The Origin and Transformation of Political Parties in America.* Chicago, IL: The University of Chicago Press.

Alesina, Alberto, and Stephen Spear. 1988. "An Overlapping Generations Model of Electoral Competition." *Journal of Public Economics* 37(3): 359–79.

Allamand, Andrés. 1999. *La travesía del desierto*. Santiago: Aguilar.

Altman, David. n.d. DALP Survey Data. Personal communication.

Altman, David, Juan Pablo Luna, Rafael Piñeiro, and Sergio Toro. 2009. "Partidos y sistemas de partidos en América Latina: Aproximaciones desde la encuesta a expertos 2009." *Revista de Ciencia Política* 29(3): 775–98.

Álvarez, Ángel E. 2007. "Venezuela 2007: Los motores del socialismo se alimentan con petróleo." *Revista de Ciencia Política* 27: 265–89.

Alvarez, R. Michael, and Gabriel Katz. 2009. "Structural Cleavages, Electoral Competition and Partisan Divide: A Bayesian Multinomial Probit Analysis of Chile's 2005 Election." *Electoral Studies* 28(2): 177–89.

Angell, Alan. 2007. *Democracy after Pinochet: Politics, Parties and Elections in Chile*. Washington, DC: Brookings Institution Press.

Arce, Moisés, and Roberta Rice. 2009. "Societal Protest in Post-Stabilization Bolivia." *Latin American Research Review* 44(1): 88–101.

Archer, Ronald P. 1990. *The Transition from Traditional to Broker Clientelism in Colombia: Political Stability and Social Unrest*. Notre Dame, IN: University of Notre Dame, Helen Kellogg Institute for International Studies.

Archila, Mauricio. 1991. *Cultura e identidad obrera: Colombia 1910–1945*. Bogotá: Cinep.

Arriola, Leonardo Rafael. 2012. *Multi-Ethnic Coalitions in Africa: Business Financing of Opposition Election Campaigns*. New York: Cambridge University Press.

Aspinall, Edward. 2014. "Parliament and Patronage." *Journal of Democracy* 25(4): 108–9.

Avetikian, Tamara. 1986. "Acuerdo Nacional y transición a la democracia." *Estudios Públicos* 21: 1–93.

Baker, Andy, Barry Ames, and Lucio R. Renno. 2006. "Social Context and Campaign Volatility in New Democracies: Networks and Neighborhoods in Brazil's 2002 Elections." *American Journal of Political Science* 50(2): 382–99.

Baker, Andy, Barry Ames, Anand E. Sokhey, and Lucio Rennó. 2016. "The Dynamics of Party Identification When Party Brands Change: The Case of the Workers' Party in Brazil." *Journal of Politics* 78(1): 197–213.

Baker, Andy, and Kenneth F. Greene. 2015. "Positional Issue Voting in Latin America." In Ryan Carlin, Matthew Singer, and Elizabeth Zechmeister, eds., *The Latin American Voter*, pp. 173–94. Ann Arbor, MI: University of Michigan Press.

Ballón, Eduardo, and Rodrigo Barrenechea. 2010 "Especial Poder Regional: El poder desde las regiones." *Revista Poder* 22 (December).

Baloyra, Enrique. 1973. *Encuesta Nacional*. Caracas: Universidad Simón Bolívar, Banco de Datos Poblacionales.

Baptista, Asdrúbal. 1997. *Bases cuantitativas de la economía venezolana, 1830–1995*. Caracas: Fundación Polar.

    2005. "El capitalismo rentístico: Elementos cuantitativos de la economía venezolana." *Cuadernos del Cendes* 22(60): 95–111.

Bardi, Luciano, and Peter Mair. 2008. "The Parameters of Party Systems." *Party Politics* 14(2): 147–66.

Bargsted, Matías A., and Nicolás M. Somma. 2016. "Social Cleavages and Political Dealignment in Contemporary Chile, 1995–2009." *Party Politics* 22(1): 105–24.

Barr, Robert R. 2005. "Bolivia: Another Uncompleted Revolution." *Latin American Politics and Society* 47(3): 69–90.

Barrenechea, Rodrigo. 2012. "Representación clientelar en el Perú: El caso de Alianza para el Progreso." Working Paper, Instituto de Estudios Peruanos. Lima, Peru.

2014. *Becas, bases, y votos: Alianza para el Progreso y la política subnacional en el Perú*. Lima: Instituto de Estudios Peruanos.

Bartels, Larry M. 2000. "Partisanship and Voting Behavior, 1952–1996." *American Journal of Political Science* 44(1): 35–50.

Bartolini, Stefano. 2000. *The Political Mobilization of the European Left, 1860–1980: The Class Cleavage*. Cambridge: Cambridge University Press.

Bartolini, Stefano, and Peter Mair. 1990. *Identity, Competition and Electoral Availability. The Stabilization of European Electorates 1885–1985*. Cambridge: Cambridge University Press.

Bartra, Roger. 1989. "Changes in Political Culture: The Crisis of Nationalism." In W. Cornelius, J. Gentleman and P. Smith, eds., *Mexico's Alternative Political Futures*, pp. 55–86. San Diego: Center for US–Mexican Studies.

Basabe Serrano, Santiago, Simón Pachano, and Andrés Mejía Acosta. 2010. "Ecuador: Democracia inconclusa." In Maxwell A. Cameron, and Juan Pablo Luna, eds., *Democracia en la región andina: Diversidad y desafíos*, pp. 165–95. Lima: Instituto de Estudios Peruanos.

Basedau, Matthias, and Alexander Stroh. 2008. "Measuring Party Institutionalization in Developing Countries: A New Instrument Applied to 28 African Political Parties." German Institute of Global and Area Studies Working Paper No. 69.

Batlle, Margarita, and José Ricardo Puyana. 2011. "El nivel de nacionalización del sistema de partidos colombiano : Una mirada a partir de las elecciones legislativas de 2010." *Colombia Internacional* (74): 27–57.

Batoba. 1983. *Encuesta Nacional, 1983*. Caracas: Universidad Simón Bolívar, Banco de Datos Poblacionales.

Becerra, Ricardo, Pedro Salazar, and José Woldenberg. 2000. *La mecánica del cambio político en México: elecciones, partidos y reformas*. Mexico City: Cal y Arena.

Beck, Nathaniel. 2001. "Time-Series Cross-section Data: What Have We Learned in the Past Few Years?" *Annual Review of Political Science* 4: 271–93.

Beck, Thorsten, George Clarke, Alberto Groff, Philip Keefer, and Patrick Walsh. 2001. "New Tools in Comparative Political Economy: The Database of Political Institutions." *World Bank Economic Review* 15(1): 165–76.

2013. "New Tools in Comparative Political Economy: Database of Political Institutions 2012." Available at: http://go.worldbank.org/2EAGGLRZ40 [accessed October 19, 2016].

Bejarano, Ana María. 2011. *Precarious Democracies: Understanding Regime Stability and Change in Colombia and Venezuela*. Notre Dame, IN: University of Notre Dame Press.

Bejarano, Ana María, Laura Zambrano Robledo, Felipe Botero Jaramillo, Laura Wills Otero, and Francisco José Quiroz. 2001. "¿Qué hace funcionar al Congreso? Una aproximación inicial a las fallas y los aciertos de la institución legislativa." *Estudios Ocasionales* (CIJUS–Universidad de los Andes, Bogotá).

Bélanger, Eric. 2004. "Antipartyism and Third-Party Vote Choice: A Comparison of Canada, Britain, and Australia." *Comparative Political Studies* 37(9):1054–78.

Bendel, Petra. 1993. "Partidos políticos y sistemas de partidos en Centroamérica." In Dieter Nohlen, ed., *Elecciones y sistemas de partidos en América Latina*, pp. 315–53. San José: Instituto Interamericano de Derechos Humanos/CAPEL.

Benoit, Kenneth, and Michael Laver. 2006. *Party Policy in Modern Democracies*. New York: Routledge.

Benton, Allyson Lucinda. 2001. "Patronage Games: Economic Reform, Political Institutions, and the Decline of Party Stability in Latin America." PhD dissertation, University of California, Los Angeles.

Berk, Richard A. 2004. *Regression Analysis: A Constructive Critique*. Thousand Oaks, CA: Sage Publications, Inc.

Berman, Sheri. 1998. *The Social Democratic Movement: Ideas and Politics in the Making of Interwar Europe*. Cambridge, MA: Harvard University Press.

Bernhard, Michael, Allen Hicken, Chris Reenock, and Staffan Lindberg. 2015. "Institutional Subsystems and the Survival of Democracy: Do Political and Civil Society Matter?" The Varieties of Democracy Institute Working Paper No. 4 (April). Available at: https://v-dem.net/media/filer_public/62/8e/628e4e08-ffb4-45ee-84c5-a25032d1b0dc/v-dem_working_paper_2015_4.pdf [accessed September 2016].

Bernhard, Michael, and Ekrem Karakoç. 2011. "Moving West or Going South? Economic Transformation and Institutionalization in Postcommunist Party Systems." *Comparative Politics* 44(1): 1–20.

Bertelsmann Stiftung. 2014. "Transformation Index BTI 2014." Available at: www.bti-project.org/btihome/ [accessed October 2014].

Birnir, Johanna. 2007. *Ethnicity and Electoral Politics*. New York: Cambridge University Press.

Bizzarro, Fernando, John Gerring, Allen Hicken, Carl-Henrik Knutsen, Michael Berhard, Sven-Erik Skaaning, Michael Coppedge, and Staffan Lindberg. 2015. "Party Rule and Economic Growth." V-Dem Institute Working Paper No. 21.

Blackwell, Matthew, James Honaker, and Gary King. 2015. "A Unified Approach to Measurement Error and Missing Data: Overview and Applications." *Sociological Methods and Research*, June 22, DOI 10.1177/0049124115589052.

Bleck, Jaimie, and Nicolas Van de Walle. 2013. "Valence Issues in African Elections Navigating Uncertainty and the Weight of the Past." *Comparative Political Studies* 46(11): 1394–421.

Bolívar, Adriana. 2001. "Changes in Venezuelan Political Dialogue: The Role of Advertising during Electoral Campaigns." *Discourse and Society* 12(1): 23–46.

Bormann, Nils-Christian, and Matt Golder. 2013. "Democratic Electoral Systems around the World, 1946–2011." *Electoral Studies* 32: 360–69.

Botero, Felipe, and Juan Carlos Rodríguez-Raga. 2008. *Grande no es sinónimo de fuerte: Los partidos y la reforma política*. Bogotá: PNUD/IDEA.

Boylan, Delia M. 1996. "Taxation and Transition: The Politics of the 1990 Chilean Tax Reform." *Latin American Research Review* 31(1): 7–31.

Braga, Maria, and Jairo Pimentel Jr. 2011. "Os partidos políticos brasileiros realmente não importam?" *Opinião Pública* 17(2): 271–303.

Braga, Maria, Pedro Ribeiro, and Oswaldo E. do Amaral. 2016. "El sistema de partidos en Brasil: estabilidad e institucionalización (1982–2014)." In Flavia Freidenberg, ed., *Los sistemas de partidos de América Latina (1978–2015)*, Vol. II, pp. 69–134. Mexico DF: INE; UNAM.

Brando, Jesús Eduardo. 1990. "AD quiere ministros de acción social." *El Nacional*, December 15, D-1.

Breiman, Leo. 2001. "Random Forests." *Machine Learning* 45(1): 5–32.

Brownlee, Jason. 2007. *Authoritarianism in an Age of Democratization*. Cambridge and New York: Cambridge University Press.

Bruhn, Kathleen. 1997. *Taking on Goliath: The Emergence of a New Left Party and the Struggle for Democracy in Mexico*. College Park, PA: Pennsylvania State University Press.

Bruhn, Kathleen, and Kenneth F. Greene. 2009. "The Absence of Common Ground between Candidates and Voters." In Jorge Domínguez, Chappell Lawson, and Alejandro Moreno, eds., *Consolidating Mexico's Democracy: The 2006 Presidential Campaign in Comparative Perspective*, pp.109–128. Baltimore, MD: Johns Hopkins University Press.

Budge, Ian, Hans-Dieter Klingemann, Andrea Volkens, Judith Bara, and Eric Tanabaum. 2001. *Mapping Policy Preferences: Estimates for Parties, Electors, and Governments, 1945–1998*. New York: Oxford University Press.

Burgess, Katrina. 1999. "Loyalty Dilemmas and Market Reform: Party-Union Alliances under Stress in Mexico, Spain, and Venezuela." *World Politics* 52(1): 105–34.

Burgess, Katrina, and Steven Levitsky. 2003. "Explaining Populist Party Adaptation in Latin America." *Comparative Political Studies* 36(8): 881–911.

Burt, Jo-Marie. 2004. "State Making against Democracy: The Case of Fujimori's Peru." In Jo-Marie Burt and Philip Mauceri, eds. *Politics in the Andes: Identity, Conflict, Reform*, pp. 247–268. Pittsburgh: University of Pittsburgh Press.

Buxton, Julia. 1999. "Venezuela: Degenerative Democracy." *Democratization* 6(1): 246–70.

Calvo, Ernesto. 2014. *Legislator Success in Fragmented Congresses in Argentina: Plurality Cartels, Minority Presidents, and Lawmaking*. Cambridge and New York: Cambridge University Press.

Calvo, Ernesto, and Marcelo Escolar. 2005. *La nueva política de partidos en la Argentina: crisis política, realineamientos partidarios y reforma electoral*. Buenos Aires: Prometeo/Pent Fundación para la Integración de la Argentina en el Mundo.

Calvo, Ernesto, and Juan Pablo Micozzi. 2005. "The Governor's Backyard: A Seat-Vote Model of Electoral Reform for Subnational Multiparty Races." *Journal of Politics* 67(4): 1050–74.

Calvo, Ernesto, and María Victoria Murillo. 2004. "Who Delivers? Partisan Clients in the Argentine Electoral Market." *American Journal of Political Science* 48(4): 742–57.

2013. "When Parties Meet Voters: Assessing Political Linkages Through Partisan Networks and Distributive Expectations in Argentina and Chile." *Comparative Political Studies* 46(7): 851–82.

Cameron, Maxwell A. 1994. *Democracy and Authoritarianism in Peru: Political Coalitions and Social Change*. New York: St. Martin's Press.

2000. "Elections in a Hybrid Regime: Civil–Military Relations and Caesarism in Peru." Prepared for the 2000 meeting of the Latin American Studies Association, Miami, Florida, March 16–18.

2006. "Endogenous Regime Breakdown: The Vladivideo and the Fall of Peru's Fujimori." In Julio Carrión, ed., *The Fujimori Legacy: The Rise of Electoral*

Authoritarianism in Peru, pp. 268–93. University Park, PA: Pennsylvania State University Press.

Campello, Daniela. 2014. "The Politics of Financial Booms and Crises: Evidence from Latin America." *Comparative Political Studies* 47(2): 260–86.

2015. "¿Es importante la institucionalización de los sistemas de partidos? Ataques especulativos y receptividad democrática en Latinoamérica." In Mariano Torcal, ed., *Sistemas de partidos en América Latina: Causas y consecuencias de su equilibrio inestable*, pp. 241–60. Barcelona: Anthropos/Siglo XXI.

Campos, Javiera. 2009. "El sistema electoral binominal: Duro de matar." In Patricio Navia, Mauricio Morales, and Renato Briceño, eds., *El genoma electoral chileno: dibujando el mapa genético de las preferencias políticas en Chile*, Chapter 1. Santiago: Universidad Diego Portales.

Canache, Damarys. 2002. "From Bullets to Ballots: The Emergence of Popular Support for Hugo Chávez." *Latin American Politics and Society* 44(1): 69–90.

Cárdenas, Mauricio, Roberto Junguito, and Mónica Pachón. 2006. "Political Institutions and Policy Outcomes in Colombia: The Effects of the 1991 Constitution." Inter-American Development Bank, Washington, February. Available at: www.iadb.org/res/publications/pubfiles/pubr-508.pdf [accessed July 19, 2016].

Carey, John M. 1996. *Term Limits and Legislative Representation*. New York: Cambridge University Press.

2002. "Parties, Coalitions, and the Chilean Congress in the 1990s." In Scott Morgenstern and Benito Nacif, eds., *Legislative Politics in Latin America*, pp. 222–53. Cambridge: Cambridge University Press.

Carey, John M., and Matthew Soberg Shugart. 1995. "Incentives to Cultivate a Personal Vote: A Rank Ordering of Electoral Formulas." *Electoral Studies* 14(4): 417–40.

Carr, Barry. 1992. *Marxism and Communism in Twentieth-Century Mexico*. Lincoln, NE: University of Nebraska Press.

Carreras, Miguel J. 2012. "The Rise of Outsiders in Latin America, 1980–2010: An Institutionalist Perspective." *Comparative Political Studies* 45(12): 1451–82.

2014. "Outsiders and Executive–Legislative Conflict in Latin America." *Latin American Politics and Society* 56(3): 70–92.

Carrión, Julio. 2006. "Public Opinion, Market Reforms, and Democracy in Fujimori's Peru." In Julio Carrión, ed., *The Fujimori Legacy: The Rise of Electoral Authoritarianism in Peru*, pp. 126–49. University Park, PA: Pennsylvania State University Press.

Carter Center. 2013. *Preliminary Report Study Mission of the Carter Center: Presidential Elections in Venezuela, April 14, 2013*. Atlanta: The Carter Center.

Casal Bértoa, Fernando. 2014. "Party Systems and Cleavage Structures Revisited: A Sociological Explanation of Party System Institutionalization in East Central Europe." *Party Politics* 20(1): 16–36.

Casal Bértoa, Fernando, and Peter Mair. 2012 "Party System Institutionalisation across Time in Post-Communist Europe." In Ferdinand Müller-Rommel and Hans Keman, eds., *Party Government in the New Europe*, pp. 85–112. London: Routledge.

Casey, Nicholas, and Patricia Torres. 2017. "At Least 3 Die amid Venezuela Protests against Maduro." *New York Times*. April 19, 2017.

Castañeda, Jorge. 1999. *La Herencia. Arqueología de la sucesión presidencial en México*. México City: Extra Alfaguara.

Castillo, Juan Carlos, Ignacio Madero-Cabib, and Alan Salamovich. 2013. "Clivajes partidarios y cambios en preferencias distributivas en Chile." *Revista de Ciencia Política* 33(2): 469–88.

Castro Cornejo, Rodrigo. 2017. "Campaign Effects and Party System Institutionalization." PhD dissertation, University of Notre Dame.

Catterberg, Edgardo. 1989. *Los argentinos frente a la política: Cultura política y opinión pública en la transición argentina a la democracia.* Buenos Aires: Planeta.

Cavalcanti, Thiago, Kamiar Mohaddes, and Mehdi Raissi. 2012. "Commodity Price Volatility and the Sources of Growth." Working Paper No. 12/12, International Monetary Fund.

Cavallo, Eduardo. 2007. "Output Volatility and Openness to Trade: A Reassessment." Research Department Working Paper No. 604. Inter-American Development Bank. Washington, DC.

Centellas, Miguel. 2007. "Democracy on Stilts: Bolivia's Democracy from Stability to Crisis." PhD dissertation, Western Michigan University.

2009. "Electoral Reform, Regional Cleavages, and Party System Stability in Bolivia." *Journal of Politics in Latin America* 1(2): 115–31.

Centro de Investigación Social (CISOR). 2001. "Procesamiento especial: Encuesta de hogares por muestreo, primer semestre 2001." Unpublished manuscript.

Centro de Memoria Histórica. 2013. "¡Basta ya! Colombia: Memorias de guerra y dignidad." *Centro de Memoria Histórica*, Bogotá. Available at: www.centrodememor iahistorica.gov.co/micrositios/informeGeneral/descargas.html [accessed July 19, 2016].

CERC. 2013. *Barómetro CERC: A cuarenta años del golpe militar.* Available at: http:// radio.uchile.cl/wp-content/uploads/2013/09/Revise-el-Barometro-de-CERC-aqu% C3%AD.pdf [accessed November 2016].

Chandra, Kanchan. 2007. *Why Ethnic Parties Succeed: Patronage and Ethnic Head Counts in India.* Cambridge: Cambridge University Press.

Charlesworth, James. 1948. "Is Our Two-Party System Natural?" *Annals of the American Academy of Political and Social Science* 259: 1–9.

Cheng, Tun-jen, and Teh-fu Huang. 2015. "Political Endurance and Resilience of the Legacy Parties in South Korea and Taiwan." Paper presented at the Conference Life after Dictatorship: Authoritarian Successor Parties Worldwide. University of Notre Dame, April 17–18.

Chhibber, Pradeep K. 1999. *Democracy without Associations: Transformation of the Party System and Social Cleavages in India.* Ann Arbor, MI: University of Michigan Press.

Chhibber, Pradeep, and Ken Kollman. 2004. *The Formation of National Party Systems: Federalism and Party Competition in Canada, Great Britain, India, and the United States.* Princeton, NJ: Princeton University Press.

Chhibber, Pradeep K., and Mariano Torcal. 1997. "Elite Strategy, Social Cleavages, and Party Systems in a New Democracy: Spain." *Comparative Political Studies* 30(1): 27–54.

Chong, Dennis. 1991. *Collective Action and the Civil Rights Movement.* Chicago, MI: University of Chicago Press.

Ciccariello-Maher, George. 2013. *We Created Chávez.* Durham, NC: Duke University Press.

Clarke, Kevin A. 2005. "The Phantom Menace: Omitted Variable Bias in Econometric Research." *Conflict Management and Peace Science* 22(4): 341–52.

Clerici, Paula. 2015. "La creciente importancia de las alianzas electorales en un escenario de competencia territorializada. El caso argentino." *Revista SAAP* 9(2): 313–41.

Clerici, Paula, and Gerardo Scherlis. 2014. "La regulación de las alianzas electorales y sus consecuencias en sistemas políticos multi-nivel en América Latina." *Revista Electrónica del Instituto de Investigaciones Ambrosio L. Gioja* 8(12): 79–98. Available at: www .derecho.uba.ar/revistagioja/articulos/R0012A008_0006_investigacion.pdf [accessed September 2016].

Collier, Ruth Berins. 1982. *Regimes in Tropical Africa: Changing Forms of Supremacy, 1945–1975*. Berkeley, CA: University of California Press.

  1992. *The Contradictory Alliance: State–Labor Relations and Regime Change in Mexico*. Berkeley, CA: International and Area Studies, University of California.

Collier, Ruth Berins, and David Collier. 1991. *Shaping the Political Arena: Critical Junctures, the Labor Movement, and Regime Dynamics in Latin America*. Princeton, NJ: Princeton University Press.

Collier, Ruth Berins, and Samuel Handlin, eds. 2009. *Reorganizing Popular Politics: Participation and the New Interest Regime in Latin America*. University Park, PA: Pennsylvania State University Press.

Colomer, Josep M., and Luis E. Escatel. 2005. "La dimensión izquierda-derecha en América Latina." *Desarrollo Económico* 45(177): 123–36.

Conaghan, Catherine M. 2000. "The Irrelevant Right: Alberto Fujimori and the New Politics of Pragmatic Peru." In Kevin J. Middlebrook, ed., *Conservative Parties, the Right, and Democracy in Latin America*, pp. 255–84. Baltimore, MD: Johns Hopkins University Press.

Conaghan, Catherine M., and James M. Malloy. 1994. *Unsettling Statecraft: Democracy and Neoliberalism in the Central Andes*. Pittsburgh, PA: University of Pittsburgh Press.

Consejo Nacional Electoral (CNE). 2013. *Resultados electorales: Divulgación Presidencial 2013*. Available at: www.cne.gob.ve/resultado_presidencial_2013/r/1/reg_000000.html [accessed March 10, 2014].

Consultores21. Various years. *Estudio de opinión pública*. Caracas: Consultores21.

Converse, Philip E. 1964. "The Nature of Belief Systems in Mass Publics." In David Apter, ed., *Ideology and Discontent*, pp. 206–261. New York: The Free Press.

  1969. "Of Time and Partisan Stability." *Comparative Political Studies* 2(2): 139–71.

Converse, Philip E., and Roy Pierce. 1986. *Political Representation in France*. Cambridge, MA.: Harvard University Press.

Coppedge, Michael. 1994. *Strong Parties and Lame Ducks: Presidential Partyarchy and Factionalism in Venezuela*. Stanford, CA: Stanford University Press.

  1997. "District Magnitude, Economic Performance, and Party System Fragmentation in Five Latin American Countries." *Comparative Political Studies* 30(2): 156–85.

  1998. "The Dynamic Diversity of Latin American Party Systems." *Party Politics* 4(4): 547–68.

  2001. "Political Darwinism in Latin America's Lost Decade." In Larry Diamond and Richard Gunther, eds., *Political Parties and Democracy*, pp. 173–205. Baltimore, MD: Johns Hopkins University Press.

  2005. "Explaining Democratic Deterioration in Venezuela through Nested Inference." In Frances Hagopian and Scott Mainwaring, eds., *The Third Wave of*

Democratization in Latin America: Advances and Setbacks, pp. 289–316. Cambridge: Cambridge University Press.

Coppedge, Michael, John Gerring, Staffan I. Lindberg, Svend-Erik Skaaning, Jan Teorell, David Altman, Michael Bernhard, M. Steven Fish, Adam Glynn, Allen Hicken, Carl Henrik Knutsen, Kyle Marquardt, Kelly McMann, Farhad Miri, Pamela Paxton, Daniel Pemstein, Jeffrey Staton, Eitan Tzelgov, Yi-ting Wang, and Brigitte Zimmerman. 2016a. "V-Dem Country–year Dataset v6.2." Varieties of Democracy (V-Dem) Project. [accessed July 2016].

Coppedge, Michael, John Gerring, Staffan I. Lindberg, Svend-Erik Skaaning, Jan Teorell, with David Altman, Michael Bernhard, M. Steven Fish, Adam Glynn, Allen Hicken, Carl Henrik Knutsen, Kelly McMann, Pamela Paxton, Daniel Pemstein, Jeffrey Staton, Brigitte Zimmerman, Rachel Sigman, Frida Andersson, Valeriya Mechkova, and Farhad Miri. 2016b. "V-Dem Codebook v6." Varieties of Democracy (VDem) Project.

Corrales, Javier. 2001. "Strong Societies, Weak Parties: Regime Change in Cuba and Venezuela in the 1950s and Today." *Latin American Politics and Society* 43(2): 81–113.

  2002. *Presidents without Parties: The Politics of Economic Reform in Argentina and Venezuela in the 1990s.* University Park, PA: Pennsylvania State University Press.

  2010. "The Repeating Revolution: Chávez's New Politics and Old Economics." In Kurt Weyland, Raúl L. Madrid, and Wendy Hunter, eds., *Leftist Governments in Latin America: Successes and Shortcomings*, pp. 28–56. New York: Cambridge.

  2014. "Constitutional Rewrites in Latin America, 1987–2009." In Jorge I. Domínguez and Michael Shifter, eds., *Constructing Democratic Governance in Latin America*, 4th edn, pp. 13–47. Baltimore, MD: Johns Hopkins University Press.

Corrales, Javier, and Michael Penfold. 2011. *Dragon in the Tropics: Hugo Chávez and the Political Economy of Revolution in Venezuela.* Washington, DC: Brookings Institution Press.

Cortez, Rafael. 2009. "Eleições majoritárias e entrada estratégica no sistema partidário-eleitoral brasileiro (1990–2006)." PhD dissertation, University of São Paulo.

Cotler, Julio. 1978. *Clases, estado y nación en el Perú.* Lima: Instituto de Estudios Peruanos.

  1995. "Political Parties and the Problems of Democratic Consolidation in Peru." In Scott Mainwaring and Timothy Scully, eds., *Building Democratic Institutions: Party Systems in Latin America*, pp. 323–53. Stanford, CA: Stanford University Press.

Cox, Gary W. 1990. "Centripetal and Centrifugal Incentives in Electoral Systems." *American Journal of Political Science* 34(4): 903–35.

  1997. *Making Votes Count: Strategic Coordination in the World's Electoral Systems.* Cambridge: Cambridge University Press.

Cox, Gary W, and Matthew Soberg Shugart. 1995. "In the Absence of Vote Pooling: Nomination and Vote Allocation Errors in Colombia." *Electoral Studies* 14(4): 441–60.

Crabtree, Charles, and Matt Golder. 2016. "Party System Volatility in Post-Communist Europe." *British Journal of Political Science* 47(1): 229–34.

Crisp, Brian F. 2000. *Democratic Institutional Design: The Powers and Incentives of Venezuelan Politicians and Interest Groups.* Stanford, CA: Stanford University Press.

Crisp, Brian, and Rachell Ingall. 2002. "Institutional Engineering and the Nature of Representation: Mapping the Effects of Electoral Reform in Colombia." *American Journal of Political Science* 46(4): 733–48.

Croissant, Aurel, and Philip Völkel. 2012. "Party System Types and Party System Institutionalization: Comparing New Democracies in East and Southeast Asia." *Party Politics* 18(2): 235–65.

Crow, David. 2010. "The Party's Over: Citizen Conceptions of Democracy and Political Dissatisfaction in Mexico." *Comparative Politics* 43(1): 41–61.

Cyr, Jennifer. 2017. "The Fates of Political Parties: Institutional Crisis, Continuity, and Change in Latin America." New York: Cambridge University Press.

2013. "Que veinte años no es nada: Hugo Chávez, las elecciones de 2012 y el continuismo político venezolano." *Revista de Ciencia Política* 33(1): 375–91.

D'Alessandro, Martín. 2013. "Las plataformas electorales en la Argentina moderna." *América Latina Hoy* 65: 107–39.

Daalder, Hans. 1987. *Party Systems in Denmark, Austria, Switzerland, the Netherlands, and Belgium*. New York: St. Martin's Press.

Dalton, Russell J. 1984. "Cognitive Mobilization and Partisan Dealignment in Advanced Industrial Democracies." *Journal of Politics* 46(1): 264–84.

2004. *Democratic Challenges, Democratic Choices: The Erosion of Political Support in Advanced Industrial Democracies*. Oxford and New York: Oxford University Press.

2014. *Citizen Politics: Public Opinion and Political Parties in Advanced Industrial Democracies*. Thousand Oaks, CA: CQ Press.

Dalton, Russell, David Farrell, and Ian McAllister. 2011. *Political Parties and Democratic Linkage: How Parties Organize Democracy*. New York: Oxford University Press.

Dalton, Russell J., Scott C. Flanagan, Paul Allen Beck, and James E. Alt. 1984. *Electoral Change in Advanced Industrial Democracies: Realignment or Dealignment?* Princeton, NJ: Princeton University Press.

Dalton, Russell J., and Martin P. Wattenberg. 2000. *Parties without Partisans: Political Change in Advanced Industrial Democracies*. Oxford and New York: Oxford University Press.

Dalton, Russell J., and Steven Weldon. 2007. "Partisanship and Party System Institutionalization." *Party Politics* 13(2): 179–96.

Dargent, Eduardo, and Paula Muñoz. 2011. "Democracy against Parties? Party System Deinstitutionalization in Colombia." *Journal of Politics in Latin America* 3(2): 43–71.

DATOS. Various years. *Estudio Opinión Nacional*. Caracas: DATOS, IR

Dávila, Andrés, and Natalia Delgado. 2002. "La metamorfosis del sistema político colombiano: ¿Clientelismo de mercado o nueva forma de intermediación?" In Francisco Gutiérrez, ed., *Degradación o cambio: evolución del sistema político colombiano*, pp. 321–55. Bogotá: Grupo Editorial Norma.

De Gramont, Diane. 2010. "Leaving Lima Behind? The Victory and Evolution of Regional Parties in Peru." Undergraduate Honors thesis, Harvard University.

De la Torre, Carlos. 2013. "Technocratic Populism in Ecuador." *The Journal of Democracy* 24(3): 33–47.

Dell, Melissa. 2015. "Trafficking Networks and the Mexican Drug War." *American Economic Review* 105(6): 1738–79.

De los Ángeles Fernández, María. 2001. "Venezuela: de la 'ilusión de armonía' a la cuasianomia social." *Estudios Avanzados Interactivos* 1(1): 1–4.

Delpar, Helen. 1981. *Red against Blue: The Liberal Party in Colombian Politics, 1863–1899*. Tuscaloosa, AL: University of Alabama Press.

Del Pozo, Belén, Camilo Fernández, Mauricio Morales, and Javier Torres. 2012. "El PDC en caída libre. Votos y escaños en las elecciones locales, 1992–2008." In Mauricio Morales and Patricio Navia, eds., *Democracia municipal en Chile, 1992–2012*, pp. 135–66. Santiago: Ediciones Universidad Diego Portales.

Díaz, Rolando. 2000. "Sindicatos y nuevo escenario político en Venezuela." *Nueva Sociedad* 169: 153–61.

Dietz, Henry A., and David J. Myers. 2007. "From Thaw to Deluge: Party System Collapse in Venezuela and Peru." *Latin American Politics & Society* 49(2): 59–86.

Dinas, Elias. 2014. "Does Choice Bring Loyalty?" *American Journal of Political Science* 58(2): 449–65.

Dix, Robert H. 1992. "Democratization and the Institutionalization of Latin American Political Parties." *Comparative Political Studies* 24(4): 488–511.

Downs, Anthony. 1957. *An Economic Theory of Democracy*. New York: Harper and Row.

Duch, Raymond M., and Randolph T. Stevenson. 2008. *The Economic Vote: How Political and Economic Institutions Condition Election Results*. Cambridge: Cambridge University Press.

Dugas, John C. 2000. "The Conservative Party and the Crisis of Political Legitimacy in Colombia." In Kevin J Middlebrook, ed., *Conservative Parties, the Right and Democracy in Latin America*, pp. 81–109. Baltimore, MD: Johns Hopkins University Press.

Dunkerley, James. 1984. *Rebellion in the Veins: Political Struggle in Bolivia, 1952–82*. London: Verso.

Durán, Milagros. 1998. "Sostiene Pedro Pablo Aguilar, en vez de renegar de Irene COPEI debe fortalecerla." *El Nacional*, October 30, D–2.

Duverger, Maurice. 1954. *Political Parties, Their Organization and Activity in the Modern State*. New York: Wiley.

Eaton, Kent. 2004. *Politics beyond the Capital: The Design of Subnational Institutions in South America*. Stanford, CA: Stanford University Press.

Eaton, Kent, and J. Tyler Dickovic. 2004. "The Politics of Re-Centralization in Argentina and Brazil." *Latin American Research Review* 39(1): 90–122.

Echandía Castilla, Camilo, and Eduardo Bechara Gómez. 2006. "Conducta de la guerrilla durante el gobierno Uribe Vélez: De las lógicas de control territorial a las lógicas de control estratégico." *Análisis Político* 19(57): 31–54.

Economic Commission for Latin America and the Caribbean (ECLAC). 2016. *Estadísticas e indicadores sociales. CEPALSTAT: Bases de Datos y Publicaciones Estadísticas*. Santiago, Chile: División de Estadística y Proyecciones Económicas, CEPAL. Available at: http://estadisticas.cepal.org/cepalstat/WEB_CEPALSTAT/Portada.asp?idioma=i [accessed September 13, 2016].

Eichengreen, Barry. 1991. "Historical Research on International Lending and Debt." *Journal of Economic Perspectives* 5(2): 149–69.

Elischer, Sebastian. 2013. *Political Parties in Africa: Ethnicity and Party Formation*. New York: Cambridge University Press.

452 Bibliography

Elites Parlamentarias de América Latina (PELA). *Base de datos*. Instituto de Iberoamérica, Universidad de Salamanca. Available at: http://americo.usal.es/oir/elites/bases_de_datos.htm [accessed July 2015].

Ellner, Steve. 2008. *Rethinking Venezuelan Politics: Class, Conflict, and the Chávez Phenomenon*. Colorado: Lynne Rienner.

2013. "Social and Political Diversity and the Democratic Road to Change in Venezuela." *Latin American Perspectives* 40(3): 63–82.

Epperly, Brad. 2011. "Institutions and Legacies: Electoral Volatility in the Post-Communist World." *Comparative Political Studies* 44(8): 829–53.

Escaith, Huber, and Igor Paunovic. 2004. *Structural Reforms in Latin America and the Caribbean, 1970–2000: Indexes and Methodological Notes*. Netherlands: UN Economic Commission for Latin America and the Caribbean.

Espinoza, Ocarnia. 2012. "Uno por diez." *El Universal*, May 30. Available at: www.eluniversal.com/nacional-y-politica/120530/uno-por-diez [accessed March 14, 2016].

Esquivel, Gerardo. 2015. "Desigualdad extrema en México: concentración del poder económico y político." Oxfam Mexico. Available at: www.oxfammexico.org/desigualdad-extrema-en-mexico-concentracion-del-poder-economico-y-politico/#.VsIabmtinIA [accessed June 28, 2016].

Evans, Geoffrey, and Mark Pickup. 2010. "Reversing the Causal Arrow: The Political Conditioning of Economic Perceptions in the 2000–2004 US Presidential Election Cycle." *Journal of Politics* 72(4): 1236–51.

Evans, Geoffrey, and James Tilley. 2012. "How Parties Shape Class Politics: Explaining the Decline of the Class Basis of Party Support." *British Journal of Political Science* 42(1): 137–61.

Evans, Peter. 1995. *Embedded Autonomy: States and Industrial Transformation*. Princeton, NJ: Princeton University Press.

Evans, Peter, and James E. Rauch. 1999. "Bureaucracy and Growth: A Cross-National Analysis of the Effects of 'Weberian' State Structures on Economic Growth." *American Sociological Review* 64(5): 748–65.

Falleti, Tulia G. 2005. "A Sequential Theory of Decentralization: Latin American Cases in Comparative Perspective." *The American Political Science Review* 99(3): 327–46.

Fearon, James. 2002. "Ethnic Structure and Cultural Diversity around the World: A Cross-National Data Set on Ethnic Groups." Presented at the Annual Meeting of the American Political Science Association, August 29–September 1, Boston.

Fearon, James, and David Laitin. 2003. "Ethnicity, Insurgency, and Civil War." *American Political Science Review* 97(1): 75–90.

Fernandes, Sujatha. 2010. *Who Can Stop the Drums? Urban Social Movements in Chávez's Venezuela*. Durham, NC: Duke University Press.

Fernández, Yajaira. 2003. "Gasto público social en Venezuela: Respuestas institucionales a las funciones del gasto público y una revisión empírica del gasto social en Venezuela." Working Paper. Caracas: PNUD.

Ferree, Karen E. 2010. "The Social Origins of Electoral Volatility in Africa." *British Journal of Political Science* 40(4): 759–79.

Ferreira, Denise Paiva. 2002. *PFL x PMDB: marchas e contramarchas (1982–2000)*. Goiânia: Editora Alternativa.

Ferreira, Denise Paiva, Carlos Marcos Batista, and Max Stabile. 2008. "A evolução do sistema partidário brasileiro: número de partidos e votação no plano subnacional 1982–2006." *Opinião Pública* 14(2): 432–53.

Figueiredo, Argelina, and Fernando Limongi. 1999. *Executivo e legislativo na nova ordem constitucional*. Rio de Janeiro: Editora FGV.

Fiorina, Morris P. 1981. *Retrospective Voting in American National Elections*. New Haven: Yale University Press.

Fish, M. Steven. 2006. "Stronger Legislatures, Stronger Democracies." *Journal of Democracy* 17(1): 5–20.

Flores-Macías, Gustavo. 2010. "Statist vs Pro-Market: Explaining Leftist Government's Economic Reforms in Latin America." *Comparative Politics* 42 (4): 413–33.

　　2012. *After Neoliberalism? The Left and Economic Reforms in Latin America*. New York: Oxford University Press.

　　Forthcoming. "Mexico's PRI: Explaining the Resilience of an Authoritarian Successor Party." In James Loxton and Scott Mainwaring, eds., *Life After Dictatorship: Authoritarian Successor Parties World Wide*.

Fontaine Talavera, Arturo, ed. 1991. "El miedo y otros escritos: el pensamiento de Jaime Guzmán." *Estudios Públicos* 42: 251–570.

Fontaine Talavera, Arturo. 2000. "Chile's Elections: The New Face of the Right." *Journal of Democracy* 11(2): 70–77.

Fortunato, David, and Randolph T. Stevenson. 2013. "Perceptions of Partisan Ideologies: The Effect of Coalition Participation." *American Journal of Political Science* 57(2): 459–77.

Fraser, Alastair, and Lindsay Whitfield. 2008. "The Politics of Aid: African Strategies for Dealing with Donors." Global Economic Governance Programme Working Paper No. 42. Available at: www.globaleconomicgovernance.org/geg-wp-200842-politics-aid-african-strategies-dealing-donors [accessed May 2015].

Freedom House. 2016. *Individual Country Ratings and Status, FIW 1973–2016 (EXCEL)*. Available at: https://freedomhouse.org/sites/default/files/Country%20Ratings%20and%20Status%2C%201973–2016%20%28FINAL%29_0.xlsx [accessed June 8, 2016].

Fuchs, Dieter, and Hans-Dieter Klingemann, eds. 1995. *Citizens and the State*. Oxford: Oxford University Press.

Fuentes, Carlos A. 2014. "Democratizing Chile Through Constitutional Reforms." In Kirsten Sehnbruch and Peter M. Siavelis, eds., *Democratic Chile: The Politics and Policies of a Historic Coalition, 1990–2010*, pp. 69–101. Boulder, CO: Lynne Rienner Publishers.

Fuentes, Claudio. 2011. "Financiación de partidos políticos en Chile." In International Institute for Democracy and Electoral Assistance, ed., *Evaluer la qualité de la démocratie: guide pratique*, pp. 135–83. Stockholm: IDEA.

Galván, Facundo. 2010. "Afuera del partido, dentro del Peronismo. Faccionalismo y disidencias electorales en el PJ (1983–2007)." MA thesis. Departamento de Historia, Universidad Torcuato Di Tella.

　　2011. "'Donde manda marinero'. El enfrentamiento entre ejecutivos nacionales y provinciales mediante listas peronistas disidentes (1983–2011)." Presented at the X Congreso Nacional de Ciencia Política de la Sociedad Argentina de Análisis Político. Córdoba, July 27–30.

Gamarra, Eduardo A. 1994. "Crafting Political Support for Stabilization: Political Pacts and the New Economic Policy in Bolivia." In William C. Smith, Carlos H. Acuña, and Eduardo A. Gamarra, eds., *Democracy, Markets, and Structural Reform in Latin America: Argentina, Bolivia, Brazil, Chile, and Mexico*, pp. 105–27. New Brunswick: Transaction Publishers.

  1997. "Hybrid Presidentialism and Democratization: The Case of Bolivia." In Scott Mainwaring and Matthew Soberg Shugart, eds., *Presidentialism and Democracy in Latin America*, pp. 363–93. Cambridge: Cambridge University Press.

  2003. "Political Parties Since 1964: The Construction of Bolivia's Multiparty System." In Merilee S. Grindle and Pilar Domingo, eds., *Proclaiming Revolution: Bolivia in Comparative Perspective*, pp. 289–317. London: Institute of Latin American Studies.

Gamarra, Eduardo A., and James M. Malloy. 1995. "The Patrimonial Dynamics of Party Politics in Bolivia." In Scott Mainwaring and Timothy R. Scully, eds., *Building Democratic Institutions: Party Systems in Latin America*, pp. 399–433. Stanford, CA: Stanford University Press.

Gamboa, Laura. 2012. "Campaigning with Empty Pockets: Why the Liberal Party Wins Regional Elections in Colombia." Presented at the XXX International Congress of the Latin American Studies Association, May 23–26, San Francisco, CA.

  2016. "Opposition in the Margins: The Erosion of Democracy in Latin America." PhD. dissertation, University of Notre Dame.

  2017. "Opposition at the Margins: Strategies against the Erosion of Democracy in Colombia and Venezuela." *Comparative Politics*.

Gamboa, Ricardo, Miguel Angel López, and Jaime Baeza. 2013. "La evolución programática de los partidos chilenos, 1970–2009: de la polarización al consenso." *Revista de Ciencia Política* 33(2): 443–67.

Gamboa, Ricardo, and Carolina Segovia. 2006. "Las elecciones presidenciales y parlamentarias en Chile, diciembre 2005 – enero 2006." *Revista de Ciencia Política* 26(1): 84–113.

Garay, Candelaria. 2016. *Social Policy Expansion in Latin America*. New York: Cambridge University Press.

García-Guadilla, María Pilar. 2005. "The Democratization of Democracy and Social Organizations of the Opposition: Theoretical Certainties, Myths and Praxis." *Latin American Perspectives* 32(2): 109–23.

Garrido, Luis. 1982. *El partido de la revolución institucionalizada: la formación del nuevo estado en México (1928–1945)*. México City: Siglo Veintiuno.

  1993. *La ruptura: la corriente democrática del PRI*. México City: Grijalbo.

Geddes, Barbara. 1999. "What Do We Know about Democratization after Twenty Years?" *Annual Review of Political Science* 2: 115–44.

Geddes, Barbara, and Erica Frantz. 2007. "The Legacy of Dictatorship for Democratic Parties in Latin America." Presented at the Annual Meeting of the American Political Science Association, Chicago, Il., August 30–September 2.

George, Alexander L., and Andrew Bennett. 2005. *Case Studies and Theory Development in the Social Sciences*. Cambridge, MA: MIT Press.

Gerber, Alan S., and Gregory A. Huber. 2010. "Partisanship, Political Control, and Economic Assessments." *American Journal of Political Science* 54(1): 153–73.

Gerring, John. 2007. *Case Study Research: Principles and Practice*. Cambridge: Cambridge University Press.

Gerring, John, Strom C. Thacker, and Rodrigo Alfaro. 2012. "Democracy and Human Development." *The Journal of Politics* 74(1): 1–17.

Gervasoni, Carlos. 1998. "El impacto de las reformas económicas en la coalición electoral justicialista (1989–1995)." *Boletín de la SAAP* 4(6): 67–96.

2010. "A Rentier Theory of Subnational Regimes: Fiscal Federalism, Democracy, and Authoritarianism in the Argentine Provinces." *World Politics* 62(2): 302–40

2015. "Libertades y derechos políticos, 2003–2014: El kirchnerismo evaluado desde siete modelos de democracia." In Carlos Gervasoni, and Enrique Peruzzotti, eds., *¿Década ganada? Evaluando el legado del kirchnerismo*, pp. 19–60. Debate, Buenos Aires.

GfK. 2013. "Evaluación de la gestión pública. Indulto a Fujimori." National urban survey (June). Available at: http://gfk.pe/wp-content/uploads/2013/06/GfK_Pulso_Peru_Junio_2013-Evaluacion_del_gobierno5.pdf [accessed September 22, 2016].

Gibson, Edward, and Ernesto Calvo. 2000. "Federalism and Low-Maintenance Constituencies: Territorial Dimensions of Economic Reform in Argentina." *Studies in Comparative International Development* 35(3): 32–55.

Gidengil, Elisabeth, Andre Blais, Neil Nevitte, and Richard Nadeau. 2001. "The Correlates and Consequences of Anti-Partyism in the 1997 Canadian Election." *Party Politics* 7(4): 491–513.

Gilbert, Alan. 2006. "Good Urban Governance: Evidence from a Model City?" *Bulletin of Latin American Research* 25(3): 392–419.

Gingerich, Daniel W. 2009. "Corruption and Political Decay: Evidence from Bolivia." *Quarterly Journal of Political Science* 4(1): 1–34.

Gleditsch, Kristian Skrede. 2013. "Expanded Trade and GDP Data." Available at: http://privatewww.essex.ac.uk/~ksg/exptradegdp.html [accessed October 2014].

Godoy Arcaya, Óscar. 1999. "La transición chilena a la democracia pactada." *Estudios Públicos* 74: 79–106.

Golden, Miriam. 2004. "International Economic Sources of Regime Change: How European Integration Undermined Italy's Postwar Party System." *Comparative Political Studies* 37(10): 1238–74.

Gómez Calcaño, Luis, Carlos Aponte, Nelly Arenas, Magally Huggins, Consuelo Iranzo, Thais Maingon, and Thanalí Patruyo. 2010. "Venezuela: Democracia en crisis." In Maxwell A. Cameron, and Juan Pablo Luna, eds., *Democracia en la región andina: Diversidad y desafíos*, pp. 31–99. Lima: Instituto de Estudios Peruanos.

González, Lucas. 2014. "Unpacking Delegative Democracy: Digging into the Empirical Content of a Rich Theoretical Concept." In Daniel Brinks, Marcelo Leiras, and Scott Mainwaring, eds., *Reflections on Uneven Democracies: The Legacy of Guillermo O'Donnell*, pp. 240–68. Baltimore, MD: Johns Hopkins University Press.

González, Roberto, Jorge Manzi, José L. Saiz, Marilynn Brewer, Pablo de Tezanos-Pinto, David Torres, María Teresa Aravena, and Nerea Aldunate. 2008. "Interparty Attitudes in Chile: Coalitions as Superordinate Social Identities." *Political Psychology* 29(1): 93–118.

Green, Donald P., Bradley Palmquist, and Eric Schickler. 2002. *Partisan Hearts and Minds: Political Parties and the Social Identities of Voters*. New Haven, CT: Yale University Press.

Greene, Kenneth F. 2007a. *Why Dominant Parties Lose: Mexico's Democratization in Comparative Perspective*. New York: Cambridge University Press
  2007b. "The Median Voter and the Plurality President in Mexico." *Política y Gobierno* 14(1): 203–13.
  2011. "Campaign Persuasion and Nascent Partisanship in Mexico's New Democracy." *American Journal of Political Science* 55(2): 398–416.
  2013. *The Mexico 2012 Panel Study* [Data file]. Available at: http://mexicopanelstudy.mit.edu/ [accessed June 28, 2016].
  2015. "Campaign Effects since Mexico's Democratization." In Jorge Domínguez, Kenneth F. Greene, Chappell Lawson, and Alejandro Moreno, eds., *Mexico's Evolving Democracy: A Comparative Study of the 2012 Elections*, pp. 128–152. Baltimore, MD: The Johns Hopkins University Press.
  2016. "The Niche Party: Authoritarian Regime Legacies and Party-Building in New Democracies." In Jorge Domínguez, Steven Levitsky, James Loxton, and Brandon Van Dyck, eds., *Challenges of Party-Building in Latin America*, Chapter 6. New York: Cambridge University Press.
Grindle, Merilee S. 2000. *Audacious Reforms: Institutional Invention and Democracy in Latin America*. Baltimore, MD: Johns Hopkins.
  2003. "Shadowing the Past? Policy Reform in Bolivia, 1985–2003." In Merilee S. Grindle and Pilar Domingo, eds., *Proclaiming Revolution: Bolivia in Comparative Perspective*, pp. 318–44. London: Institute of Latin American Studies.
Grynaviski, Jeffrey D. 2010. *Partisan Bonds: Political Reputations and Legislative Accountability*. Cambridge: Cambridge University Press.
Grzymala-Busse, Anna M. 2002. *Redeeming the Communist Past: The Regeneration of Communist Parties in East Central Europe*. New York: Cambridge University Press.
  2007. *Rebuilding Leviathan: Party Competition and State Exploitation in Post-Communist Democracies*. Cambridge: Cambridge University Press.
Gunther, Richard. 2005. "Parties and Electoral Behavior in Southern Europe." *Comparative Politics* 37: 253–75.
Gutiérrez, Francisco. 2002. "Fragmentación electoral y política tradicional en Colombia: piezas para un rompecabezas en muchas dimensiones." *Perfiles Latinoamericanos* 20: 53–77.
  2006. "Estrenando sistema de partidos." *Análisis Político* 57: 106–25.
  2007. *¿Lo que el viento se llevó?: Los partidos políticos y la democracia en Colombia 1958–2002*. Bogotá: Grupo Editorial Norma.
Guzmán Errázuriz, Rosario. 2008. *Mi hermano Jaime*, 4th edn. Santiago: Editorial JGE.
Haggard, Stephan, and Robert Kaufman. 1995. *The Political Economy of Democratic Transitions*. Princeton, NJ: Princeton University Press.
Hagopian, Frances, Carlos Gervasoni, and Juan Andrés Moraes. 2009. "From Patronage to Program: The Emergence of Party-Oriented Legislators in Brazil." *Comparative Political Studies* 42(3): 360–91.
Hale, Henry. 2006. *Why Not Parties in Russia? Democracy, Federalism, and the State*. New York: Cambridge University Press.
Handlin, Samuel. 2013. "Social Protection and the Politicization of Class Cleavages during Latin America's Left Turn." *Comparative Political Studies*. 46(12): 1582–1609.

2016. "Mass Organization and the Durability of Competitive Authoritarian Regimes: Evidence from Venezuela" *Comparative Political Studies* 49(9): 1238–69.

Handlin, Samuel, and Ruth Berins Collier. 2011. "The Diversity of Left Party Linkages and Competitive Advantages." In Steven Levitsky and Kenneth M. Roberts, eds., *The Resurgence of the Latin American Left*, pp. 139–61. Baltimore, MD: Johns Hopkins University Press.

Hanson, Stephen E. 2010. *Post-Imperial Democracies: Ideology and Party Formation in Third Republic France, Weimar Germany, and Post-Soviet Russia.* Cambridge: Cambridge University Press.

Hartlyn, Jonathan. 1988. *The Politics of Coalition Rule in Colombia.* Cambridge and New York: Cambridge University Press.

Hausman, Ricardo, and Michael Gavin. 1996. "Securing Stability and Growth in a Shock Prone Region: The Policy Challenge for Latin America." Research Department Working Paper No. 315. Inter-American Development Bank, Washington, DC.

Hawkins, Kirk A. 2003. "Populism in Venezuela: The Rise of *Chavismo.*" *Third World Quarterly* 24(6): 1137–60.

2010. *Venezuela's Chavismo and Populism in Comparative Perspective.* New York: Cambridge.

Hellinger, Daniel. 2003. "Political Overview: The Breakdown of *Puntofijismo* and the Rise of *Chavismo.*" In Steve Ellner, and Daniel Hellinger, eds., *Venezuelan Politics in the Chávez Era: Class, Polarization and Conflict*, pp. 27–53. Boulder, CO: Lynne Rienner.

2005. "When 'No' Means 'Yes to Revolution': Electoral Politics in Bolivarian Venezuela." *Latin American Perspectives* 32(3): 8–32.

Helmke, Gretchen, and Steven Levitsky. 2006. *Informal Institutions and Democracy: Lessons from Latin America.* Baltimore, MD: Johns Hopkins University Press.

Hendricks, Cullen. 2010. "Measuring State Capacity: Theoretical and Empirical Implications for the Study of Civil Conflict." *Journal of Peace Research* 47(3): 273–85.

Hicken, Allen. 2006. "Party Fabrication: Constitutional Reform and the Rise of Thai Rak Thai." *Journal of East Asian Studies* 6(3): 381–408.

2009. *Building Party Systems in Developing Democracies.* Cambridge: Cambridge University Press.

2015. "Party and Party System Institutionalization in the Philippines." In Allen Hicken, and Erik Martinez Kuhonta, eds., *Party System Institutionalization in Asia: Democracies, Autocracies, and the Shadows of the Past*, pp. 307–27. New York: Cambridge University Press.

Hicken Allen, and Erik Martinez Kuhonta. 2011. "Shadows from the Past: Party System Institutionalization in Asia." *Comparative Political Studies* 44(5): 572–97.

Hicken, Allen, and Erik Martinez Kuhonta, eds. 2015a. *Party System Institutionalization in Asia: Democracies, Autocracies, and the Shadows of the Past.* New York: Cambridge University Press.

Hicken, Allen, and Erik Martinez Kuhonta. 2015b. "Introduction: Rethinking Party System Institutionalization in Asia." In Allen Hicken and Kuhonta, eds., *Party System Institutionalization in Asia: Democracies, Autocracies, and the Shadows of the Past*, pp. 1–24. New York: Cambridge University Press.

Hill, Hal. 1997. "Towards a Political Economy Explanation of Rapid Growth in ASEAN: A Survey and Analysis." *ASEAN Economic Bulletin* 14(2): 131–49.

Hilliker, Grant. 1971. *The Politics of Reform in Peru: The Aprista and other Mass Parties of Latin America.* Baltimore, MD: The Johns Hopkins University Press.

Hinich, Melvin J., and Michael C. Munger. 1994. *Ideology and the Theory of Political Choice.* Ann Arbor, MI: University of Michigan Press.

Hofstadter, Richard.1969. *The Idea of a Party System: The Rise of Legitimate Opposition in the United States, 1780–1840.* Berkeley, CA: University of California Press.

Hogg, Michael A., Dominic Abrams, Sabine Otten, and Steve Hinkle. 2004. "The Social Identity Perspective: Intergroup Relations, Self-Conception, and Small Groups." *Small Group Research* 35(3): 246–76.

Hogg, Michael A., Elizabeth A. Hardie, and Katherine J. Reynolds. 1995. "Prototypical Similarity, Self-Categorization, and Depersonalized Attraction: A Perspective on Group Cohesiveness." *European Journal of Social Psychology* 25(2): 159–77.

Hormazábal, Ricardo. 2015. "El aborto, la DC y la libertad de conciencia." *El Mostrador*, February 10. Available at: www.elmostrador.cl/noticias/opinion/2015/02/10/el-aborto-la-dc-y-la-libertad-de-conciencia/ [accessed October 2016].

Hoskin, Gary. 1990. "Los partidos tradicionales, ¿Hasta dónde son responsables de la crisis?" In Francisco Leal and León Zamosc, eds., *Al filo del caos: crisis política en la Colombia de los años 80,* pp. 145–74. Bogotá, Colombia: Instituto de Estudios Políticos y Relaciones Internacionales: Tercer Mundo Editores.

Hoskin, Gary, and Gerald Swanson. 1974. "Political Party Leadership in Colombia: A Spatial Analysis." *Comparative Politics* 6(3): 395–423.

Howard, Marc, and Phillip Roessler. 2006. "Liberalizing Electoral Outcomes in Competitive Authoritarian Regimes." *American Journal of Political Science* 50(2): 365–81.

Hoyos, Diana. 2007. "Evolución del sistema de partidos en Colombia 1972–2000. Una mirada a nivel local y regional." In Diana Hoyos, ed., *Entre la persistencia y el cambio: reconfiguración del escenario partidista y electoral en Colombia,* pp. 21–48. Colombia: CEPI.

Hsieh, Chang-Tai, Edward Miguel, Daniel Ortega, and Francisco Rodriguez. 2009. "The Price of Political Opposition: Evidence from Venezuela's Maisanta." NBER Working Paper No. 14923 (April).

Huber, John D., and Ronald Inglehart. 1995. "Expert Interpretations of Party Space and Party Locations in 42 Societies." *Party Politics* 1(1): 73–111.

Hug, Simon. 2001. *Altering Party Systems: Strategic Behavior and the Emergence of New Political Parties in Western Democracies.* Ann Arbor, MI.: University of Michigan Press.

Huneeus, Carlos. 2000. *El régimen de Pinochet.* Santiago: Editorial Sudamericana.

Hunter, Wendy. 2010. *The Transformation of the Workers' Party in Brazil, 1989–2009.* Cambridge: Cambridge University Press.

Hunter, Wendy, and Timothy J. Power. 2007. "Rewarding Lula: Executive Power, Social Policy, and the Brazilian Elections of 2006." *Latin American Politics and Society* 49(1): 1–30.

Huntington, Samuel P. 1968. *Political Order in Changing Societies.* New Haven, CT: Yale University Press.

Hutchcroft, Paul, and Joel Rocamora. 2003. "Strong Demands and Weak Institutions: The Origins and Evolution of the Democratic Deficit in the Philippines." *Journal of East Asian Studies* 3(2): 259–92.

IESA. 2003. "'Empleo' Indicadores Macroeconómicos." Mimeo. IESA, Caracas.

Illera, Jorge A., and Lina F. Buchely. 2015. "Las fugas de la democracia. Análisis económico del derecho sobre las normas de transfuguismo político en Colombia (2003–2011)." *Colombia Internacional* 85(September–December): 17–52.

Inglehart, Ronald. 1990. *Culture Shift in Advanced Industrial Society.* Princeton, NJ: Princeton University Press.

1997. *Modernization and Postmodernization: Cultural, Economic, and Political Change in 43 Societies.* Princeton, NJ: Princeton University Press.

Instituto Nacional Electoral (INE). 2016. *Histórico de Resultados Electorales* [Data file]. Available at: www.ine.mx/archivos3/portal/historico/contenido/Historico_de_Resultados_Electorales/ [accessed September 16, 2016].

Inter-American Commission on Human Rights (IACHR). 2015. "Situación de los derechos humanos en México." Available at: http://www.oas.org/es/cidh/informes/pdfs/Mexico2016-es.pdf [accessed June 28, 2016].

International Labour Organization (ILO). 1987. *World Labour Report,* vols. 1–2. New York: Oxford University Press.

1997. *World Labour Report: Industrial Relations, Democracy and Social Stability.* Geneva: ILO.

2001. *Key Indicators of the Labour Report: 2001–2002.* Geneva: ILO.

International Monetary Fund (IMF). 2012. "World Economic Outlook, Database October 2012." Washington, DC: World Bank. Available at: https://www.imf.org/external/pubs/ft/weo/2015/02/weodata/index.aspx [accessed January 2016].

Ipeadata. 2016. Available at: http://www.ipeadata.gov.br/Default.aspx [accessed November 2016].

IPSOS APOYO. 2006. "La elección se polariza." *Resumen de Encuestas a la Opinión Pública* 6(65).

Iranzo, Consuelo, and Jacqueline Richter. 2006. "La política laboral en la Venezuela de Hugo Chávez Frías." *Revista Latinoamericana de Estudios de Trabajo* 11(18): 5–32.

IVAD. 1993. *Estudio Nacional, Mayo 1993.* Caracas: IVAD.

Jaramillo, Juan, and Beatriz Franco-Cuervo. 2005. "Colombia." In Dieter Nohlen, ed., *Elections in the Americas: A Data Handbook,* Vol. 2, South America, pp. 295–364. Oxford: Oxford University Press.

Johnson, Joel W., and Jessica S. Wallack. 2012. "Electoral Systems and the Personal Vote." Available at: http://hdl.handle.net/1902.1/17901 [accessed October 2014].

Joignant, Alfredo, and Miguel Ángel López. 2005. "Le comportement électoral au Chili: paradoxes et présomptions sur la continuité ou la rupture de l'orientation du vote." *Problèmes d'Amérique Latine* 56: 63–80.

Jones, Jason J., Jamie E. Settle, Robert M. Bond, Christopher J. Fariss, Cameron Marlow, and James H. Fowler. 2013. "Inferring Tie Strength from Online Directed Behavior." *PLOS One* 8(1): e52168. doi: 10.1371/journal.pone.0052168.

Jones, Mark P., and Wonjae Hwang. 2005. "Party Government in Presidential Democracies: Extending Cartel Theory Beyond the US Congress." *American Journal of Political Science* 49(2): 267–82.

Jones, Mark P., Wonjae Hwang, and Juan Pablo Micozzi. 2009. "Government and Opposition in the Argentine Congress, 1989–2007: Understanding Inter-Party Dynamics through Roll Call Vote Analysis." *Journal of Politics in Latin America* 1(1): 67–96.

Jones, Mark P., and Scott Mainwaring. 2003. "The Nationalization of Parties and Party Systems: An Empirical Measure and an Application to the Americas." *Party Politics* 9(2): 139–66.

Jones, Mark P., and Juan Pablo Micozzi. 2013. "Argentina's Unrepresentative and Unaccountable Congress under the Kirchners." In Moira MacKinnon and Ludovico Feoli, eds., *Representation and Effectiveness in Latin American Democracies: Congress, Judiciary and Civil Society*, pp. 40–74. New York: Routledge.

Jones, Mark P., Sebastián Saiegh, Pablo T. Spiller, and Mariano Tommasi. 2002. "Amateur Legislators, Professional Politicians: The Consequences of Party-Centered Electoral Rules in a Federal System." *American Journal of Political Science* 46(3): 656–69.

Kalyvas, Stathis. 1996. *The Rise of Christian Democracy in Europe*. Ithaca: Cornell University Press.

Karl, Terry Lynn. 1997. *The Paradox of Plenty: Oil Booms and Petro-States*. Berkeley, CA: University of California Press.

Karvonen, Lauri. 2010. *The Personalization of Politics: A Study of Parliamentary Democracies*. Wivenhoe Park: ECPR Press.

Katz, Richard, and Peter Mair. 1995. "Changing Models of Party Organization and Party Democracy: The Emergence of the Cartel Party." *Party Politics* 1(1): 5–28.

Kaufman, Robert. 2011. "The Political Left, the Export Boom, and the Populist Temptation." In Steven Levitsky and Kenneth Roberts, eds., *The Resurgence of the Latin American Left*, pp. 93–116. Baltimore, MD: Johns Hopkins University Press.

Kayser, Mark Andreas, and Christopher Wlezien. 2011. "Performance Pressure: Patterns of Partisanship and the Economic Vote." *European Journal of Political Research* 50(3): 365–94.

Keck, Margaret E. 1992. *The Workers' Party and Democratization in Brazil*. New Haven: Yale University Press.

Kellstedt, Paul M. and Guy D. Whitten. 2013. *The Fundamentals of Political Science Research*. 2nd edn. Cambridge: Cambridge University Press.

Kenney, Charles D. 1998. "Outsiders and Anti-Party Politicians in Power: New Conceptual Strategies and Empirical Evidence from Peru." *Party Politics* 4(1): 57–75.

  2003 "The Death and Re-birth of a Party System, Peru 1978–2001." *Comparative Political Studies* 36(10): 1210–39.

  2004. *Fujimori's Coup and the Breakdown of Democracy in Latin America*. Notre Dame, IN: University of Notre Dame Press.

Key, Valdimer O. 1964. *Southern Politics in State and Nation*. New York: Knopf.

King, Gary, Joseph Honaker, Anne Joseph, and Kenneth Scheve. 2001. "Analyzing Incomplete Political Science Data: An Alternative Algorithm for Multiple Imputation." *American Political Science Review* 95(1): 49–69.

Kinzo, Maria D'Alva Gil. 2005. "Parties in Electorate: Public Perceptions and Party Bindings in Brazil." *Revista Brasileira de Ciências Sociais* 20(57): 65–81.

Kirkpatrick, Jeane. 1971. *Leader and Vanguard in Mass Society: A Study of Peronist Argentina.* Cambridge, MA: MIT Press.
Kitschelt, Herbert. 1994. *The Transformation of European Social Democracy.* Cambridge: Cambridge University Press.
  2000. "Linkages between Citizens and Politicians in Democratic Polities." *Comparative Political Studies* 33(6–7): 845–76.
Kitschelt, Herbert, Kirk A. Hawkins, Juan Pablo Luna, Guillermo Rosas, and Elizabeth J. Zechmeister. 2010. *Latin American Party Systems.* New York: Cambridge University Press.
Kitschelt, Herbert, and Daniel Kselman. 2013. "Economic Development, Democratic Experience, and Political Parties' Linkage Strategies." *Comparative Political Studies* 46(11): 1453–84.
Kitschelt, Herbert, and Steven Wilkinson, eds. 2007a. *Patrons, Clients, and Policies: Patterns of Democratic Accountability and Political Competition.* New York: Cambridge University Press.
  2007b. "Citizen-Politician Linkages: An Introduction." In Herbert Kitschelt and Steven I. Wilkinson, eds., *Patrons, Clients, and Policies: Patterns of Democratic Accountability and Political Competition*, pp. 1–49. Cambridge: Cambridge University Press.
Kohli, Atul. 1990. *Democracy and Discontent: India's Growing Crisis of Governability.* New York: Cambridge University Press.
Kornblith, Miriam. 2005. "The Referendum in Venezuela: Elections versus Democracy." *Journal of Democracy* 16(1): 124–37.
Kornblith, Miriam, and Daniel Levine. 1995. "Venezuela: The Life and Times of the Party System." In Scott Mainwaring and Timothy Scully, eds., *Building Democratic Institutions: Parties and Party Systems in Latin America*, pp. 37–71. Stanford, CA: Stanford University Press.
Kose, Ayhan, Eswar Prasad, and Marco Terrones. 2003. "Financial Integration and Macroeconomic Volatility." IMF Working Paper WP/03/50. International Monetary Fund, Washington, DC.
Kuenzi, Michelle, and Gina Lambright. 2001. "Party System Institutionalization in 30 African Countries." *Party Politics* 7(4): 437–68.
Kuncic, Aljaz. 2014. "Institutional Quality Dataset 1990–2014." *Journal of Institutional Economics* 10(1): 135–61.
Kurmanaev, Antony. 2017. "Many Poor Venezuelans Are Too Hungry to Join Anti-government Protests" *Wall Street Journal.* April 20, 2017.
Kutiyski, Yordan K., and André Krouwel. 2014. "Narrowing the Gap: Explaining the Increasing Competitiveness of the Venezuelan Opposition." *Latin American Politics and Society* 56(4): 71–97.
Laakso, Markku, and Rein Taagepera. 1979. "'Effective' Number of Parties: A Measure with Application to Western Europe." *Comparative Political Studies* 12(1): 3–27.
Lagos, Ricardo. 2013. *Mi vida. De la infancia a la lucha contra la dictadura. Memorias I.* Santiago: Penguin Random House.
Lalander, Rickard O. 2004. *Suicide of the Elephants? Venezuelan Decentralization between Partyarchy and Chavismo.* Helsinki: Renvall Institute for Area and Cultural Studies; Stockholm: Institute of Latin American Studies.

La Nación. 2001. "Carrió denunciará a sus pares como 'traidores a la patria.'"[Online] March 26. Available at: http://www.lanacion.com.ar/57453-carrio-denunciara-a-sus-pares-como-traidores-a-la-patria [accessed September 26, 2016].

Lander, Edgardo. 1996. "The Impact of Neoliberal Adjustment in Venezuela, 1989–1993." *Latin American Perspectives* 23(3): 50–73.

Langston, Joy. 2003. "Rising from the Ashes? Reorganizing and Unifying the PRI's State Party Organizations after Electoral Defeat." *Comparative Political Studies* 36(3): 293–318.

Lanzaro, Jorge. 2011. "Uruguay: A Social Democratic Government in Latin America." In Steven Levitsky and Kenneth Roberts, eds., *The Resurgence of the Latin American Left*, pp. 348–74. Baltimore, MD: Johns Hopkins University Press.

LaPalombara, Joseph, and Myron Weiner. 1966. "The Origin and Development of Political Parties." In Joseph LaPalombara and Myron Weiner, eds., *Political Parties and Political Development*, pp. 3–42. Princeton, NJ: Princeton University Press.

La República. 2012. "Comisión de Ética cita a la 'Congresista Wikipedia.'" March 22. Available at: http://larepublica.pe/18-03-2012/comision-de-etica-cita-la-congresista-wikipedia [accessed September 20, 2016].

Latin American Public Opinion Project (LAPOP). Various dates. AmericasBarometer [Data files]. Vanderbilt University. Available at: http://datasets.americasbarometer .org/database-login/usersearch.php.

Latinobarometer 2010. "Informe 2010." Santiago, Chile. Available at: www .lat-inobarometro.org/documentos/LATBD_INFORME_LATINOBAROMETRO _2010.pdf [accessed September 2016].

2015. *Data Bank*. Corporación Latinobarómetro. Available at: www.latino-barometro.org/lat.jsp [accessed August and October 2016].

Various years. *Latinobarómetro Database*. Available at www.latinobarometro .org/lat.jsp

Latorre, Mario. 1974. *Elecciones y partidos políticos en Colombia*. Bogotá: Universidad de Los Andes, Departamento de Ciencia Política.

Lawson, Chappell, Andy Baker, Kathleen Bruhn, Roderic Camp, Wayne Cornelius, Jorge Domínguez, Kenneth Greene, Joseph Klesner, Chappell Lawson, Beatriz Magaloni, James McCann, Alejandro Moreno, Alejandro Poiré, and David Shirk. 2007. "The Mexico 2006 Panel Study." Available at: https://mexicopanelstudy.mit .edu/ [accessed June 28 and October 19, 2016].

Lawson, Chappell, Miguel Basañez, Roderic Camp, Wayne Cornelius, Jorge Domínguez, Frederico Estévez, Joseph Klesner, Beatriz Magaloni, James McCann, Alejandro Moreno, Pablo Parás and Alejandro Poiré. 2001. "The Mexico 2000 Panel Study." [Data file]. Available at: http://mexicopanelstudy.mit.edu/ [accessed June 28, 2016].

Lawson, Chappell, Miguel Basanez, Roderic Camp, Wayne A. Cornelius, Jorge Dominguez, Joseph Klesner, Federico Estevez, Beatriz Magaloni, James McCann, Alejandro Moreno, Pablo Paras, and Alejandro Poiré. 2008. "Mexican Election Panel Study, 2000." Available at: http://doi.org/10.3886/ICPSR03380.v1 [accessed October 2014].

Lawson, Kay, ed. 1980. *Political Parties and Linkage: A Comparative Perspective*. New Haven: Yale.

Leal Buitrago, Francisco, and Andrés Dávila. 1990. *Clientelismo: el sistema político y su expresión regional.* Bogotá, Colombia: Instituto de Estudios Políticos y Relaciones Internacionales.

LeBas, Adrienne. 2011. *From Protest to Parties: Party-Building and Democratization in Africa.* Oxford: Oxford University Press.

Lederman, Daniel, and L. Colin Xu. 2009. "Commodity Dependence and Macroeconomic Volatility: The Structural versus the Macroeconomic Mismanagement Hypothesis." The World Bank, Development Research Group.

Lehoucq, Fabrice. 2008. "Bolivia's Constitutional Breakdown." *The Journal of Democracy* 19(4): 110–24.

Leiras, Marcelo. 2010. "Los procesos de descentralización y la nacionalización de los sistemas de partidos en América Latina." *Política y Gobierno* 17(2): 205–41.

León, Carlos. 2011. "Nosotros nos equivocamos menos. Vida, muerte, y resurrección política de Ollanta Humala." In Carlos Meléndez, ed. *Post-Candidatos: Guía analítica de sobrevivencia hasta las próximas elecciones*, pp. 43–90. Lima: MITIN.

Lepsius, M. Rainer. 1978. "From Fragmented Party Democracy to Government by Emergency Decree and National Socialist Takeover: Germany." In Juan J. Linz and Alfred Stepan, eds., *The Breakdown of Democratic Regimes: Europe*, pp. 34–79. Baltimore, MD: Johns Hopkins University Press.

Levi, Margaret. 1997. "A Model, a Method, and a Map: Rational Choice in Comparative and Historical Analysis." In Mark I. Lichbach and Alan S. Zuckerman, eds., *Comparative Politics: Rationality, Culture, and Structure*, pp. 19–41. New York: Cambridge University Press.

Levine, Daniel H. 1973. *Conflict and Political Change in Venezuela.* Princeton: Princeton.

Levitsky, Steven. 2001. "Organization and Labor-Based Party Adaptation: The Transformation of Argentine Peronism in Comparative Perspective." *World Politics* 54(1): 27–56.

2003. *Transforming Labor-Based Parties in Latin America: Argentine Peronism in Comparative Perspective.* New York: Cambridge University Press.

Levitsky, Steven, and Maxwell Cameron. 2003. "Democracy without Parties? Political Parties and Regime Change in Fujimori's Peru." *Latin American Politics and Society* 45(3): 1–33.

Levitsky, Steven, James Loxton, Brandon Van Dyck, and Jorge Domínguez, eds. 2016a. *Challenges of Party Building in Latin America.* New York: Cambridge University Press.

Levitsky, Steven, James Loxton, and Brandon Van Dyck. 2016b. "Introduction: Challenges of Party-Building in Latin America." In Steven Levitsky, James Loxton, Brandon Van Dyck, and Jorge I. Domínguez, eds., *Challenges of Party-Building in Latin America*, pp.1–50. New York: Cambridge University Press.

Levitsky, Steven, and María Victoria Murillo. 2003. "Argentina Weathers the Storm." *Journal of Democracy* 14(4): 152–66.

2005. "Conclusion: Theorizing about Weak Institutions: Lessons from the Argentine Case." In Levitsky and Murillo, eds., *Argentine Democracy: The Politics of Institutional Weakness*, pp. 269–89. University Park, PA: Pennsylvania State University Press.

2008. "Argentina: From Kirchner to Kirchner." *Journal of Democracy* 19(2): 16–30.

2014. "Building Institutions on Weak Foundations: Lessons from Latin America." In Daniel Brinks, Marcelo Leiras, and Scott Mainwaring, eds., *Reflections on Uneven Democracies: The Legacy of Guillermo O'Donnell*, pp. 189–213. Baltimore, MD: Johns Hopkins University Press.

Levitsky, Steven, and Kenneth M. Roberts. 2011. *The Resurgence of the Latin American Left*. Johns Hopkins University Press.

Levitsky, Steven, and Lucan Way. 1998. "Between a Shock and a Hard Place: The Dynamics of Labor-Backed Adjustment in Poland and Argentina." *Comparative Politics* 30(2): 171–92.

2010. *Competitive Authoritarianism: Hybrid Regimes after the Cold War*. New York: Cambridge University Press.

2012. "Beyond Patronage: Violent Struggle, Ruling Party Cohesion, and Authoritarian Durability." *Perspectives on Politics* 10(4): 869–89.

Levitsky, Steven, and Mauricio Zavaleta. 2016. "Why no Party-Building in Peru?" In Steven Levitsky, James Loxton, Brandon Van Dyck, and Jorge I. Domínguez, eds., *Challenges of Party-Building in Latin America*, pp. 412–39. New York: Cambridge University Press.

Lewis-Beck, Michael S. 1988. *Economics and Elections: The Major Western Democracies*. Ann Arbor, MI: University of Michigan Press.

Lewis-Beck, Michael S., and Martin Paldam. 2000. "Economic Voting: An Introduction." *Electoral Studies* 19(2–3): 113–21.

Lieberman, Evan, Daniel Posner, and Lily Tsai. 2014. "Does Information Lead to More Active Citizenship? Evidence from an Education Intervention in Rural Kenya." *World Development* 60: 69–83.

Lijphart, Arend. 1994. *Electoral Systems and Party Systems: A Study of Twenty-Seven Democracies, 1945–1990*. New York: Oxford University Press.

Lima, Olavo, Jr. 1999. "Eleições presidenciais: centralidade, contexto e implicações." *Revista Brasileira de Ciências Sociais* 14(40): 11–30.

Limongi, Fernando, and Rafael Cortez. 2010. "As eleições de 2010 e o quadro partidário." *Novos Estudos Cebrap* 88: 21–37.

Lindberg, Staffan. 2007. "Institutionalization of Party Systems? Stability and Fluidity among Legislative Parties in Africa's Democracies." *Government and Opposition* 42(2): 215–41.

Linz, Juan J. 1978. "The Breakdown of Democracy in Spain." In Juan J. Linz and Alfred Stepan, eds., *The Breakdown of Democratic Regimes: Europe*, pp. 142–215. Baltimore, MD: Johns Hopkins University Press.

1994. "Presidential or Parliamentary Democracy: Does It Make a Difference?" In Juan J. Linz and Arturo Valenzuela, eds., *The Failure of Presidential Democracy*, pp. 3–87. Baltimore, MD: Johns Hopkins University Press.

Linz, Juan J., and Arturo Valenzuela, eds. 1994. *The Failure of Presidential Democracy*. 2 vols. Baltimore, MD: Johns Hopkins University Press.

Lipset, Seymour Martin, and Stein Rokkan. 1967. "Cleavage Structures, Party Systems, and Voter Alignments: An Introduction." In Seymour Martin Lipset and Stein Rokkan, eds., *Party Systems and Voter Alignments: Cross-National Perspectives*, pp. 1–64. New York: Free Press.

Loaeza, Soledad. 1999. *El Partido de Acción Nacional: La larga marcha, 1939–1994: Oposición leal y partido de protesta*. Mexico City: Fondo de Cultura Económica.

Loayza, Norman, Romain Ranciere, Luis Serven, and Jaume Ventura. 2007. "Macroeconomic Volatility and Welfare in Developing Countries: An Introduction." *The World Bank Economic Review* 21(3): 343–57

López, Claudia. 2010. "'La refundación de la patria', de la teoría a la evidencia." In Claudia López, ed., *Y refundaron la patria ... De cómo mafiosos y políticos reconfiguraron el estado colombiano*, pp. 29–79. Bogotá: Corporación Nuevo Arco Iris.

López, Miguel Ángel, and Mauricio Morales. 2005. "La capacidad explicativa de los determinantes familiares en las preferencias electorales de los chilenos." *Política* 45: 87–108.

López Maya, Margarita. 2011. "Venezuela: Hugo Chávez and the Populist Left." In Steven Levitsky and Kenneth M. Roberts, eds., *The Resurgence of the Latin American Left*, pp. 213–38. Baltimore, MD: Johns Hopkins.

López Maya, Margarita, and Luis Lander. 2005. "Popular Protest in Venezuela: Novelties and Continuities." *Latin American Perspectives* 32(2): 92–108.

2007. "Venezuela: Las elecciones presidenciales de 2006; ¿Hacia el socialismo del siglo XXI?" *Cuadernos del CENDES* 24(64): 1–21.

López Maya, Margarita, and Carlos Meléndez. 2007. "Partidos y sistema de partidos en Venezuela." In Rafael Roncagliolo and Carlos Meléndez, eds., *La política por dentro: Cambios y continuidades en las organizaciones políticas de los países andinos*, pp. 273–302. Lima: Asociación Civil de Transparencia/IDEA.

Losada, Rodrigo. 2005. "Los partidos políticos tradicionales en Colombia: Pasado, presente y futuro: Una perspectiva organizacional." In Clara Rodríguez and Eduardo Pizarro Leongómez, eds., *Los retos de la democracia: viejas y nuevas formas de la política en Colombia y América Latina*, pp.87–126. Bogotá: Fundación Foro Nacional por Colombia/IEPRI.

Love, James. 1986. "Commodity Concentration and Export Earnings Instability." *Journal of Development Economics* 24(2): 239–48.

Loxton, James. 2015. "Authoritarian Successor Parties." *Journal of Democracy* 26(3): 157–70.

2016a. "Authoritarian Successor Parties Worldwide: A Framework for Analysis." University of Sidney Working Papers, June.

2016b. "Authoritarian Successor Parties and the New Right in Latin America." In Steven Levitsky, James Loxton, Brandon Van Dyck, and Jorge I. Domínguez, eds., *Challenges of Party-Building in Latin America*, pp. 245–72. New York: Cambridge University Press.

Forthcoming. "Authoritarian Successor Parties Worldwide: A Framework for Analysis." In James Loxton and Scott Mainwaring, eds., *Authoritarian Successor Parties*.

Lucas, Kevin, and David Samuels. 2010. "The Ideological 'Coherence' of the Brazilian Party System, 1990–2009." *Journal of Politics in Latin America* 2(3): 39–69.

Lucas, Robert. 1998. "On the Mechanics of Economic Development." *Journal of Monetary Economics* 22(1): 3–42.

Lugo, Joaquín. 2010a. "Cúpula del PSUV elige candidatos por lista." *El Nacional*, March 2.

2010b. "PSUV va a primarias en medio de denuncias de ventajismo." *El Nacional*, May 2.

Lugo-Galicia, Hernán. 2008. "Chávez y dirección del PSUV definirán a candidatos en 8 estados." *El Nacional*, June 2.
    2013. "El PSUV descarta primarias y busca método unitario." *El Nacional*, June 7.
Lujambio, Alonso. 2001. "Dinero y democratización: El financiamiento y la fiscalización de los partidos políticos en la transición mexicana a la democracia, 1988–2000." *International Seminar on Money and Electoral Competition*, Federal Electoral Institute, Mexico City, June 5–8.
Luna, Juan Pablo. 2014. "Party System Institutionalization: Do We Need a New Concept?" *Studies in Comparative International Development* 49: 403–25.
Luna, Juan Pablo, and David Altman. 2011. "Uprooted but Stable: Chilean Parties and the Concept of Party System Institutionalization." *Latin American Politics and Society* 53(2): 1–28.
Luna, Juan Pablo, and Elizabeth J. Zechmeister. 2005. "Political Representation in Latin America. A Study of Elite-Mass Congruence in Nine Countries." *Comparative Political Studies* 38: 388–416.
    2010. *Cultura política de la democracia en Chile, 2010. Consolidación democrática en las Américas en tiempos difíciles*. Nashville, TN: Vanderbilt University.
Lupu, Noam. 2011. "Party Brands in Crisis: Partisanship, Brand Dilution, and the Breakdown of Political Parties in Latin America." Ph.D. dissertation, Princeton University.
    2013. "Party Brands and Partisanship: Theory with Evidence from a Survey Experiment in Argentina." *American Journal of Political Science* 57(1): 49–64.
    2014. "Brand Dilution and the Breakdown of Political Parties in Latin America." *World Politics* 66(4): 561–602.
    2015a. "Partisanship in Latin America." In Ryan Carlin, Matthew Singer, and Elizabeth Zechmeister, eds., *The Latin American Voter: Pursuing Representation and Accountability in Challenging Contexts*, pp.226–45. Ann Arbor, MI: University of Michigan Press.
    2015b. "Party Polarization and Mass Partisanship: A Comparative Perspective." *Political Behavior* 37(2): 331–56.
    2016. *Party Brands in Crisis: Partisanship, Brand Dilution, and the Breakdown of Political Parties in Latin America*. New York: Cambridge University Press.
Lupu, Noam, Carlos Gervasoni, Virginia Oliveros, and Luis Schiumerini. 2015. *2015 Argentine Panel Election Study*. Available at: http://noamlupu.com/data.html [accessed June 21, 2016].
Lupu, Noam and Rachel Beatty Riedl. 2013. "Political Parties and Uncertainty in Developing Democracies." *Comparative Political Studies* 46(11): 1339–65.
Lupu, Noam, and Susan C. Stokes. 2009. "The Social Bases of Political Parties in Argentina, 1912–2003." *Latin American Research Review* 44(1): 58–87.
    2010. "Democracy, Interrupted: Regime Change and Partisanship in Twentieth-Century Argentina." *Electoral Studies* 29(1): 91–104.
Lustig, Nora. 1992. *Mexico: The Remaking of an Economy*. Washington, DC: Brookings Institution Press.
Lynch, Nicolás. 1999. *Una tragedia sin héroes: la derrota de los partidos y el surgimiento de los independientes, Perú 1980–1992*. Lima: San Marcos.
Madrid, Raúl. 2005. "Ethnic Cleavages and Electoral Volatility in Latin America." *Comparative Politics* 38(1): 1–20.

2012. *The Rise of Ethnic Politics in Latin America*. Cambridge: Cambridge University Press.

2016. "Latin American Ethnicity Database." University of Texas at Austin. Available at: https://raulmadrid.org/ [accessed June 28, 2016].

Magaloni, Beatriz. 2006. *Voting for Autocracy*. New York: Cambridge University Press.

Mailath, George, and Larry Samuelson. 2006. *Repeated Games and Reputations: Long-Run Relationships*. New York: Oxford University Press.

Mainwaring, Scott. 1993. "Presidentialism, Multipartism, and Democracy: The Difficult Combination." *Comparative Political Studies* 26(2): 198–228.

1999. *Rethinking Party Systems in the Third Wave of Democratization: The Case of Brazil*. Stanford, CA: Stanford University Press.

2006a. "The Crisis of Representation in the Andes." *Journal of Democracy* 17(3): 13–27.

2006b. "State Deficiencies, Party Competition, and Confidence in Democratic Representation in the Andes." In Scott Mainwaring, Ana María Bejarano, and Eduardo Pizarro Leongómez, eds., *The Crisis of Democratic Representation in the Andes*, pp.295–345. Stanford, CA, California: Stanford University Press.

2015. "Party System Institutionalization: Reflections Based on the Asian Cases." In Allen Hicken and Erik Kuhonta, eds., *Party System Institutionalization in Asia: Democracies, Autocracies, and the Shadows of the Past*, pp. 328–48. New York: Cambridge University Press.

Mainwaring, Scott, Ana María Bejarano, and Eduardo Pizarro. 2006. *The Crisis of Democratic Representation in the Andes*. Stanford, CA: Stanford University Press.

Mainwaring, Scott, Carlos Gervasoni, and Annabella España-Nájera. 2016. "Extra- and Within-System Electoral Volatility." *Party Politics*. Published online before print January 11, 2016, doi: 10.1177/1354068815625229.

Mainwaring, Scott, and Aníbal Pérez-Liñán. 1997. "Party Discipline in the Brazilian Constitutional Congress." *Legislative Studies Quarterly* 22(4): 453–83.

2013. *Democracies and Dictatorships in Latin America: Emergence, Survival, and Fall*. New York: Cambridge University Press.

2015. "Cross-Currents in Latin America." *Journal of Democracy* 26(1): 114–27.

Mainwaring, Scott, and Timothy R. Scully. 1995a. *Building Democratic Institutions: Party Systems in Latin America*. Stanford, CA: Stanford University Press.

1995b. "Introduction: Party Systems in Latin America." In Scott Mainwaring and Timothy R. Scully, eds, *Building Democratic Institutions: Party Systems in Latin America*, pp.1–34. Stanford, CA: Stanford University Press.

Mainwaring, Scott, and Mariano Torcal. 2006. "Party System Institutionalization and Party System Theory After the Third Wave of Democratization." In Richard S. Katz and William Crotty, eds., *Handbook of Political Parties*, pp.204–27. London: Sage Publications.

Mainwaring, Scott, Mariano Torcal, and Nicolás Somma. 2015. "The Left and the Mobilization of Class Voting in Latin America." In Ryan E. Carlin, Matthew M. Singer, and Elizabeth J. Zechmeister, eds., *The Latin American Voter: Pursuing Representation and Accountability in Challenging Contexts*, pp.69–98. Ann Arbor, MI: University of Michigan Press.

Mainwaring, Scott, and Edurne Zoco. 2007. "Political Sequences and the Stabilization of Interparty Competition: Electoral Volatility in Old and New Democracies." *Party Politics* 13(2): 155–78.

Mair, Peter. 1997. *Party System Change: Approaches and Interpretations.* Oxford: Clarendon Press.

Malloy, James M. 1991. "Democracy, Economic Crisis and The Problem of Governance: The Case of Bolivia." *Studies in Comparative International Development* 26(2): 37–57.

Mann, Michael. 1986. *The Sources of Social Power,* Vol. I. New York: Cambridge University Press.

Marinova, Dani. 2016. *Coping with Complexity: How Voters Adapt to Unstable Parties.* Colchester, United Kingdom: ECPR Press.

Martínez Verdugo, Arnoldo. 1985. *Historia del comunismo en México.* Mexico City: Grijalbo.

Martz, John. 1966. *Acción Democrática: Evolution of a Modern Political Party in Venezuela.* Princeton, NJ: Princeton University Press.

Martz, John D., and David J. Myers. 1994. "Technological Elites and Political Parties: The Venezuelan Professional Community." *Latin American Research Review* 29 (1): 7–27.

Masoud, Tarek. 2014. *Counting Islam: Religion, Class, and Elections in Egypt.* New York: Cambridge University Press.

Mauceri, Philip. 1997a. "State Development and Counter-Insurgency in Peru." In Paul B. Rich and Richard Stubbs, eds., *The Counter-Insurgent State: Guerrilla Warfare and State Building in the Twentieth Century,* pp.152–74. London: Macmillan Press.

1997b. "The Transition to Democracy and the Failures of Institution Building." In Maxwell Cameron and Philip Mauceri, eds., *The Peruvian Labyrinth: Polity, Society, Economy,* pp.13–36. University Park, PA: Penn State University Press.

May, John. 1973. "Opinion Structures and Political Parties: The Special Law of Curvilinear Disparity." *Political Studies* 21: 135–51.

Mayorga, René A. 1997. "Bolivia's Silent Revolution." *Journal of Democracy* 8(1): 142–56.

2005. "Bolivia's Democracy at the Crossroads." In Frances Hagopian and Scott Mainwaring, eds., *The Third Wave of Democratization in Latin America: Advances and Setbacks,* pp. 149–78. Cambridge: Cambridge University Press.

Forthcoming. "State Weakness, Left Populism, and Erosion of Democracy in the Andean Region." Kellogg Institute for International Studies.

Mazzuca, Sebastián. 2014. "Natural Resources Boom and Institutional Curses in the New Political Economy of South America." In Jorge I. Domínguez and Michael Shifter, eds., *Constructing Democratic Governance in Latin America,* 4th edn, pp.102–126. Baltimore, MD: Johns Hopkins University Press.

McCann, James, and Chappell Lawson. 2003. "An Electorate Adrift? Public Opinion and the Quality of Democracy in Mexico." *Latin American Research Review* 38(3): 60–81.

McClintock, Cynthia. 1996. "La voluntad política presidencial y la ruptura constitucional de 1992 en el Perú." In Fernando Tuesta Soldevilla, ed., *Los Enigmas del Poder: Fujimori 1990–1996,* pp.53–74. Lima: Fundación Friedrich Ebert.

McConnell, Shelley. 1997. "Institutional Development." In Thomas W. Walker, ed., *Nicaragua without Illusions,* pp.45–63. Wilmington, DE: Scholarly Resources.

McCoy, Jennifer. 1989. "Labor and the State in a Party-Mediated Democracy: Institutional Change in Venezuela." *Latin American Research Review* 24(2): 35–67.

1999. "Chávez and the End of 'Partyarchy' in Venezuela." *The Journal of Democracy* 10(3): 64–77.

2015. Remarks at panel on "Venezuela's High-Stakes Legislative Elections. The December 6 Vote and What Comes Next." Washington, DC: Brookings Institution, November 9. Available at: www.brookings.edu/~/media/events/2015/11/09-venezuela/20151109_venezuela_election_transcript.pdf [accessed June 10, 2016].

McGuire, James 1995. "Political Parties and Democracy in Argentina." In Scott Mainwaring and Timothy Scully, eds., *Building Democratic Institutions: Party Systems in Latin America*, pp.200–47. Stanford, CA: Stanford University Press.

1997. *Peronism without Perón: Unions, Parties, and Democracy in Argentina.* Stanford, CA: Stanford University Press.

2014. "Sources of Populist Resistance: Peronismo, Getulismo and Chavismo." Presented at the conference A New Critical Juncture? Changing Patterns of Interest Representation and Regime Politics in Contemporary Latin America, Kellogg Institute for International Studies, University of Notre Dame, April 24–26.

McKelvey, Richard. 1986. "Covering, Dominance, and Institution-Free Properties of Social Choice." *American Journal of Political Science* 30(2): 283–314.

McMann, Kelly, Daniel Pemstein, Brigitte Seim, Jan Teorell, and Staffan I. Lindberg. 2016. "Strategies of Validation: Assessing the Varieties of Democracy Corruption Data." Varieties of Democracy Working Paper No. 23. Available at: www.v-dem.net/media/filer_public/aa/1c/aa1c7a54-db15-4d80-ae9f-075cf478957d/v-dem_working_paper_2016_23.pdf [accessed November 2016].

Meléndez, Carlos. 2007. "Partidos y sistema de partidos en el Perú." In Rafael Roncagliolo and Carlos Meléndez, eds. *La política por dentro. Cambios y continuidades en las organizaciones políticas de los países andinos*, pp.213–72. Lima: IDEA.

2010. "¿Cómo escapar del fatalismo de las estructuras? Marco para entender la formación del sistema de partidos en el Perú." In Carlos Meléndez and Alberto Vergara, eds. *La iniciación de la política. El Perú político en perspectiva comparada*, pp.161–82. Lima: PUCP.

2011. "Del Shambar al 'Sancochado:' El Proyecto Político de César Acuña." In Carlos Meléndez, ed., *Anti-Candidatos: Guía Analítica para unas Elecciones sin Partidos*, pp.173–86. Lima: Mitin.

2012a. "Partidos inesperados. La institucionalización del sistema de partidos en un escenario de post colapso partidario: Perú 2001–2011." *Análisis y Debate*, Fundación Friedrich Ebert. Available at: www.fes.org.pe/descargasFES/Partidos%20inesperados%20C.%20Melendez.pdf [accessed September 2016].

2012b. *La soledad de la política: Transformaciones estructurales, intermediación política y conflictos sociales en el Perú (2000–2012).* Lima: Mitin.

2012c. "Partisanship without Parties? Party Brands in Post-Party System Collapse: The Case of Fujimorismo in Peru." Paper Presented at the 71st Annual Meetings of the Midwest Political Science Association, Chicago, IL.

2014. "Is There a Right Track in Post-Party System Collapse Scenarios? Comparing the Andean Countries." In Juan Pablo Luna and Cristóbal Rovira Kaltwasser, eds.,

The Resilience of the Latin American Right, pp.167–93. Baltimore, MD: The Johns Hopkins University Press.

2015. "Transitional Partisanships and Political Linkages after Party System Collapse: The Case of Peru." PhD. dissertation, University of Notre Dame.

Melo, Carlos Ranulfo. 2010. "Eleições presidenciais, jogos aninhados e sistema partidário no Brasil." *Revista Brasileira de Ciência Política* 4(July–December): 13–41.

Mendes, Manuel, and Gustavo Venturi. 1994. "Eleição Presidencial: o Plano Real na sucessão de Itamar Franco." *Opinião Pública* 2(2): 39–48.

Meneguello, Rachel. 1989. *PT: A formação de um partido, 1979–1982*. São Paulo: Paz e Terra.

2011. "Las elecciones de 2010 y los rumbos del sistema de partidos brasileño: política nacional, fragmentación y lógica de coaliciones." In Manuel Alcántara Saéz and María Laura Tagina, eds., *América Latina: política y elecciones del bicentenario (2009–2010)*, pp. 449–88. Madrid: Centro de Estudios Políticos y Constitucionales.

Meneguello, Rachel, and Oswaldo Amaral. 2008. "Ainda uma novidade: uma revisão das transformações do Partido dos Trabalhadores no Brasil." Occasional Paper Number BSP-02-08, Brazilian Studies Programme, Oxford.

Meneguello, Rachel, Oswaldo Amaral, and Fernando Bizzarro. 2014. "A semelhança dos adversários: uma análise do perfil das elites intermediárias (middle-level elites) do PT e do PSDB." Paper presented at Latin American Studies Conference, Chicago May 21–24.

Meneguello, Rachel, and Fernando Bizzarro. 2012. "Contexto e competição na política paulista." *Dados* 55(1): 119–71.

Meyer, James. 1976. *The Cristero Rebellion: The Mexican People between Church and State, 1926–1929*. New York: Cambridge University Press.

Middlebrook, Kevin. 1986. "Political Liberalization in an Authoritarian Regime: The Case of Mexico." In Guillermo O'Donnell, Philippe Schmitter, and Laurence Whitehead, eds., *Transitions from Authoritarian Rule: Latin America*, pp. 123–47. Baltimore, MD: The Johns Hopkins University Press.

Milanese, Juan Pablo. 2011. "Participación, éxito y prioridad: un análisis macro de los equilibrios en las relaciones entre los poderes ejecutivo y legislativo en Colombia 2002–2006." *CS en Ciencias Sociales* (8): 111–45.

Milanese, Juan Pablo, Juan Albarracín, and Luis E. Jaramillo. 2014. "Patrones de competencia intrapartidaria. Análisis de la región suroccidental." Presented at the 2014 Meeting of the Latin American Studies Association, May 21–24, Chicago, IL.

Mobarak, Ahmed. 2004. "Determinants of Volatility and Implications for Economic Development. Research Program on Political and Economic Change."Working Paper No. PEC2004-0001, University of Colorado at Boulder.

Molina, José E. 2002. "The Presidential and Parliamentary Elections of the Bolivarian Revolution in Venezuela: Continuity and Change (1998–2000)." *Bulletin of Latin American Research* 21(2): 219–47.

Molinelli, Guillermo, Valeria Palanza, and Gisela Sin. 1999. *Congreso, Presidencia y Justicia en Argentina*. Buenos Aires: Temas.

Monaldi, Francisco, Rosa Amelia González, Richard Obuchi, and Michael Penfold. 2006. "Political Institutions, Policymaking Processes, and Policy Outcomes in Venezuela." IADB, Working Paper R-507 (January).

Mönckeberg, María Olivia. 2003. *El imperio del Opus Dei en Chile*. Santiago: Ediciones B.

Montecinos, Claudia, María José Pavlovic, and Gabriela Piergentili. 2001. *A diez años de su muerte: el legado político de Jaime Guzmán en la UDI de hoy*. Santiago: Tesis para el Grado de Comunicación Social, Universidad Diego Portales.

Mora y Araujo, Manuel. 1980. "Las bases estructurales del peronismo." In Manuel Mora y Araujo and Ignacio Llorente, eds., *El Voto Peronista*, pp.397–440. Buenos Aires: Editorial Sudamericana.

2011. *La Argentina bipolar: Los vaivenes de la opinión pública (1983–2011)*. Buenos Aires: Editorial Sudamericana.

Morales, Mauricio. 2015. "La UDI está enferma." *La Tercera*, March 15. Available at: http://voces.latercera.com/2015/03/12/mauricio-morales/la-udi-esta-enferma/ [accessed March 2015].

Morales Quiroga, Mauricio. 2008. "La primera mujer presidenta de Chile: ¿Qué explicó el triunfo de Michelle Bachelet en las elecciones de 2005–2006?." *Latin American Research Review* 43(1): 7–32.

Moreno, Erika. 2005. "Whither the Colombian Two-Party System? An Assessment of Political Reforms and their Limits." *Electoral Studies* 24(3): 485–509.

Moreno-Brid, Juan Carlos, and Jaime Ros. 2009. *Development and Growth in the Mexican Economy: A Historical Perspective*. New York: Oxford University Press.

Morgan, Jana. 2007. "Partisanship during the Collapse of the Venezuelan Party System." *Latin American Research Review* 42(1): 78–98.

2011. *Bankrupt Representation and Party System Collapse*. University Park, PA: Pennsylvania State University Press.

Forthcoming. "Decentralization and Party System Decay." *Latin American Research Review*.

Morgenstern, Scott, and Luigi Manzetti. 2003. "Legislative Oversight: Interests and Institutions in the United States and Argentina." In Scott Mainwaring and Christopher Welna, eds. *Democratic Accountability in Latin America*, pp.132–69. New York: Oxford University Press.

Morley, Samuel, Roberto Machado, and Stefano Petinatto. 1999. "Indexes of Structural Reform in Latin America." ECLAC, *Serie Reformas Económicas* 12.

Morris, Stephen. 2009. *Political Corruption in Mexico: The Impact of Democratization*. Boulder, CO: Lynne Rienner.

Morrison, Kevin. 2012. "Oil, Conflict, and Stability." Pittsburgh University, School of Public and International Affairs. Unpublished manuscript.

Moser, Robert. 2001. *Unexpected Outcomes: Electoral Systems, Political Parties, and Representation in Russia*. Pittsburgh: University of Pittsburgh Press.

Moser, Robert G. and Ethan Scheiner. 2012. *Electoral Systems and Political Context: How the Effects of Rules Vary Across New and Established Democracies*. New York: Cambridge University Press.

Muñoz, Paula. 2010. "¿Consistencia política regional o frágiles alianzas electorales? El escenario cuzqueño actual." *Revista Argumentos* 4(3).

2014. "An Informational Theory of Campaign Clientelism: The Case of Peru." *Comparative Politics* 47(1): 79–98.

Muñoz, Paula, and Eduardo Dargent. 2016. "Patronage, Subnational Linkages, and Party-Building: The Cases of Colombia and Peru." In Steven Levitsky, James

Loxton, Brandon Van Dyck, and Jorge I. Domínguez, eds. *Challenges of Party-Building in Latin America*, pp. 187–216. New York: Cambridge University Press.

Muñoz, Paula, and Andrea García. 2011. "Balance de las elecciones regionales 2010: tendencias, particularidades y perfil de los candidatos más exitosos." In María Ana Rodríguez and Omar Coronel, eds., *El nuevo poder en las regiones: análisis de las elecciones regionales y municipales 2010*, pp.8–17. Lima: Pontificia Universidad Católica del Perú.

Murillo, María Victoria. 2001. *Labor Unions, Partisan Coalitions, and Market Reforms in Latin America*. New York: Cambridge University Press.

Mustapic, Ana María. 2005. "Inestabilidad sin colapso: La renuncia de los presidentes: Argentina en el año 2001." *Desarrollo Económico* 45(178): 263–80.

2013. "Los partidos políticos en la Argentina. Condiciones y oportunidades para su fragmentación." In Carlos Acuña, ed., *¿Cuánto importan las instituciones? Gobierno, estado y actores en la política argentina*, pp.249–90. Buenos Aires: Siglo Veintiuno-Fundación OSDE.

Mustapic, Ana María, and Matteo Goretti. 1992. "Gobierno y oposición en el Congreso: La práctica de la cohabitación durante la presidencia de Alfonsín (1983–1989)." *Desarrollo Económico* 32(126): 251–69.

Mustapic, Ana María, Gerardo Scherlis, and María Page. 2011. "De colectoras, espejos y otras sutilezas. Claves para avanzar hacia una oferta electoral más transparente." *Documento de Políticas Públicas/Recomendación* N° 90, CIPPEC, Buenos Aires.

Navarro, Juan Carlos. 1995. "In Search of the Lost Pact: Consensus Lost in the 1980s and 1990s." In Jennifer McCoy, Andrés Serbin, William C. Smith, and Andrés Stambouli, eds., *Venezuelan Democracy under Stress*, pp. 13–29. Miami: University of Miami North-South Center and Transaction Publishers.

Navarro, Melissa. 2011. "La organización partidaria fujimorista a 20 años de su origen." Undergraduate thesis, Pontificia Universidad Católica del Perú.

Navia, Patricio, and Ricardo Godoy. 2014. "The Alianza's Quest to Win Power Democratically." In Kirsten Sehnbruch and Peter M. Siavelis, eds., *Democratic Chile: The Politics and Policies of a Historic Coalition, 1990–2010*, pp. 43–68. Boulder, CO: Lynne Rienner Publishers.

Navia, Patricio, Mauricio Morales, and Renato Briceño, eds. 2009. *El genoma electoral chileno: dibujando el mapa genético de las preferencias políticas en Chile*. Santiago: Universidad Diego Portales.

Navia, Patricio, and Rodrigo Osorio. 2015. "It's the Christian Democrats' Fault: Declining Political Identification in Chile, 1957–2012." *Canadian Journal of Political Science* 48(4): 815–38.

Navia, Patricio, and José Luis Saldaña. 2009. "Voto cruzado en las elecciones parlamentarias y presidenciales en Chile (1993–2005)." In Patricio Navia, Mauricio Morales, and Renato Briceño, eds. 2009. *El genoma electoral chileno: dibujando el mapa genético de las preferencias políticas en Chile*, Chapter 6. Santiago: Universidad Diego Portales.

Negretto, Gabriel L. 2013. *Making Constitutions: Presidents, Parties, and Institutional Choice in Latin America*. New York: Cambridge University Press.

Nichter, Simeon. 2008. "Vote Buying or Turnout Buying? Machine Politics and the Secret Ballot." *American Political Science Review* 102(1): 19–32.

Nicolau, Jairo Marconi. 1996. *Multipartidarismo e democracia: um estudo sobre o sistema partidário brasileiro, 1985–94*. Rio de Janeiro: Fundação Getúlio Vargas Editora.

Nohlen, Dieter. 2005. *Elections in the Americas: A Data Handbook*, Vol. 1. New York: Oxford University Press.

Nooruddin, Irfan. 2011. *Coalition Politics and Economic Development: Credibility and Strength of Weak Governments*. New York: Cambridge University Press.

North, Douglass. 1989. "Institutions and Economic Growth: A Historical Introduction." *World Development* 17(9): 1319–32.

1990. *Institutions, Institutional Change, and Economic Performance*. New York: Cambridge University Press.

North, Liisa, 1973. "The Origins and Development of the Peruvian Aprista Party." PhD dissertation, University of California, Berkeley.

O'Donnell, Guillermo. 1993. "On the State, Democratization, and Some Conceptual Problems: A Latin American View with Glances at Some Postcommunist Countries." *World Development* 21(8): 1355–69.

1994. "Delegative Democracy." *The Journal of Democracy* 5 (1): 55–69.

1998. "Horizontal Accountability in New Democracies." *Journal of Democracy* 9(3): 112–26.

1999. "Horizontal Accountability in New Democracies." In Andreas Schedler, Larry Diamond, and Marc Plattner, eds., *The Self-restraining State: Power and Accountability in New Democracies*, pp. 29–51. Boulder, CO: Lynne Rienner.

O'Dwyer, Conor. 2006. *Runaway State-Building: Patronage Politics and Democratic Development*. Baltimore, MD: Johns Hopkins University Press.

O'Dwyer, Conor, and Branislav Kovalcik. 2007. "And the Last Shall Be First: Party System Institutionalization and Second-Generation Economic Reform in Postcommunist Europe." *Studies in Comparative International Development* 41 (4): 3–26.

O'Neill, Kathleen. 2005. *Decentralizing the State: Elections, Parties, and Local Power in the Andes*. Cambridge: Cambridge University Press.

Olson, Mancur. 1965. *The Logic of Collective Action: Public Goods and the Theory of Groups*. Cambridge, MA: Harvard University Press.

Oppenheimer, Andrés. 1996. *Bordering on Chaos: Guerrillas, Stockbrokers, Politicians, and Mexico's Road to Prosperity*. Boston, MA: Little, Brown.

Organization of the Petroleum Exporting Countries (OPEC). 2003. *Annual Statistical Bulletin*. Vienna, Austria: OPEC.

Orlando, María Beatriz. 2001. "The Informal Sector in Venezuela: Catalyst or Hindrance for Poverty Reduction." Poverty Project Papers. Universidad Católica Andrés Bello, Caracas.

Ortega Frei, Eugenio. 1992. *Historia de una Alianza. El Partido Socialista de Chile y el Partido Demócrata Cristiano. 1973–1988*. Santiago: CED-CESOC.

Pachón, Mónica. 2003. "Explaining the Performance of the Colombian Congress: Electoral and Legislature Rules, and Interactions with the Executive." Presented at the Annual Latin American Studies Association Conference, March 27–29, Dallas, TX.

Pachón, Mónica, and Matthew S. Shugart. 2010. "Electoral Reform and the Mirror Image of Inter-Party and Intra-Party Competition: The Adoption of Party Lists in Colombia." *Electoral Studies* 29(4): 648–60.

Panebianco, Angelo. 1988. *Political Parties: Organization and Power.* Cambridge: Cambridge University Press.

Pavão, Nara. 2015. "Failures of Electoral Accountability for Corruption: Brazil and Beyond." PhD dissertation, University of Notre Dame.

Payne, J. Mark, Daniel Zovatto G., and Mercedes Mateo Díaz. 2007. *Democracies in Development: Politics and Reform in Latin America.* Washington, DC: Inter-American Development Bank.

Payne, Stanley G. 2006. *The Collapse of the Spanish Republic, 1933–1936.* New Haven, CT: Yale University Press.

Pécaut, Daniel. 2001. *Orden y violencia: evolución socio-política de Colombia entre 1930 y 1953.* Bogotá: Grupo Editorial Norma.

2006. *Crónica de cuatro décadas de política colombiana.* Bogotá: Editorial Norma.

Pedersen, Mogens N. 1983. "Changing Patterns of Electoral Volatility in European Party Systems, 1948–1977." In Hans Daalder and Peter Mair, eds., *Western European Party Systems: Continuity and Change,* pp. 29–66. Beverly Hills, CA: Sage.

Penfold, Michael. 2009. *Dos tradiciones, un conflicto: El futuro de la descentralización.* Caracas: Debate.

Penfold-Becerra, Michael. 2007. "Clientelism and Social Funds: Evidence from Chávez's Misiones." *Latin American Politics and Society* 49(4): 63–84.

Pennings, Paul, and Jan-Erik Lane. 1998. *Comparing Party System Change.* London: Routledge.

Pereira Almao, Valía. 2004. "Movimiento V República: Vocación de masas y atadura personalista." In José E. Molina and Ángel E. Álvarez, eds. *Los partidos políticos venezolanos en el siglo XXI,* pp. 57–108. Caracas: Vadell Hermanos Editores.

Pereira, Carlos, Frederico Bertholini, and Eric D. Raile (2016). "All the President's Men and Women: Coalition Management Strategies and Governing Costs in a Multiparty Presidency." *Presidential Studies Quarterly* 46(3): 550–68.

Pérez Baralt, Carmen. 2004. "Primero Justicia: Dificultades para la consolidación de un nuevo partido." In José E. Molina and Ángel E. Álvarez, eds. *Los partidos políticos venezolanos en el siglo XXI,* pp. 263–277. Caracas: Vadell Hermanos Editores.

Pérez, Hésper Eduardo. 1989. *Proceso del bipartidismo colombiano y Frente Nacional.* Bogotá: Universidad Nacional de Colombia.

Pérez-Liñán, Aníbal. 2007. *Presidential Impeachment and the New Political Instability in Latin America.* New York: Cambridge University Press.

Pérez-Liñán, Aníbal, and Scott Mainwaring. 2013. "Regime Legacies and Levels of Democracy: Evidence from Latin America." *Comparative Politics* 45(4): 379–97.

Piattoni, Simona, ed. 2001. *Clientelism, Interests, and Democratic Representation: The European Experience in Historical and Comparative Perspective.* New York: Cambridge University Press.

Pierson, Paul. 2004. *Politics in Time: History, Institutions, and Social Analysis.* Princeton, NJ: Princeton University Press.

Pinto, André. 2013. "Os enigmas da popularidade presidencial no Brasil: economia ou política?" MA thesis, Universidade Nacional de Brasília.

Pinzón de Lewin, Patricia. 1989. *Pueblos, regiones y partidos: la regionalización electoral,* 1st edn. Bogotá, Colombia: Ediciones Uniandes, CIDER, CEREC.

Pizarro Leongómez, Eduardo. 2002. "La atomización partidista en Colombia: el fenómeno de las microempresas electorales." In Francisco Gutiérrez, ed.,

Degradación o cambio: evolución del sistema político colombiano, pp. 359–90. Bogotá: Grupo Editorial Norma.

2006. "Giants with Feet of Clay: Political Parties in Colombia." In Scott Mainwaring, Ana María Bejarano, and Eduardo Pizarro Leongómez, eds., *The Crisis of Democratic Representation in the Andes*, pp.78–99. Stanford, CA: Stanford University

Planas, Pedro. 2000. *La democracia volátil: movimientos, partidos, líderes políticos y conductas electorales en el Perú contemporáneo*. Lima: Friedrich Ebert Stiftung.

Polga-Hecimovich, John, and Peter Siavelis. 2015. "Here's the Bias! A (Re-) Reassessment of the Chilean Electoral System." *Electoral Studies* 40: 268–79.

Polity IV Project. 2015. Polity IV. Political Regime Characteristics and Transitions, 1800–2010. Available at: www.systemicpeace.org/inscrdata.html [accessed August 2016].

Pope, Jeremy C., and Jonathan Woon. 2009. "Measuring Changes in American Party Reputations, 1939–2004." *Political Research Quarterly* 62(4): 653–61.

Pop-Eleches, Grigore. 2010. "Throwing Out the Bums: Protest Voting and Anti-Establishment Parties after Communism." World Politics 62(2): 221–60.

2014. "Communist Development and the Post-Communist Democratic Deficit." In Mark Beissinger and Stephen Kotkin, eds., *The Historical Legacies of Communism in Russia and Eastern Europe*, pp. 28–51. Cambridge University Press

Portes, Alejandro. 1970. "Leftist Radicalism in Chile: A Test of Three Hypotheses." *Comparative Politics* 2(2): 251–74.

Posada-Carbó, Eduardo. 1997. "Limits of Power: Elections under the Conservative Hegemony in Colombia, 1886–1930." *The Hispanic American Historical Review* 77(2): 245–79.

Posner, Paul W. 1999. "Popular Representation and Political Dissatisfaction in Chile's New Democracy." *Journal of Interamerican Studies and World Affairs* 41(1): 59–85.

Powell, Eleanor, and Joshua Tucker. 2014. "Revisiting Electoral Volatility in Post-Communist Countries: New Data, New Results, and New Approaches." *British Journal of Political Science* 44(1): 123–47.

Power, Timothy. 2000. *The Political Right in Postauthoritarian Brazil: Elites, Institutions, and Democratization*. University Park, PA: Pennsylvania State University Press.

2010. "Optimism, Pessimism, and Coalitional Presidentialism: Debating the Institutional Design of Brazilian Democracy." *Bulletin of Latin American Research* 29(1): 18–33.

Power, Timothy J., and César Zucco Jr. 2009. "Estimating Ideology of Brazilian Legislative Parties, 1990–2005: A Research Communication." *Latin American Research Review* 44(1): 218–46.

2012. "Elite Preferences in a Consolidating Democracy: The Brazilian Legislative Surveys, 1990–2009." *Latin American Politics and Society* 54(4): 1–27.

PROVEA. Various years. *Situación de los derechos humanos: reportes anuales*. Caracas: PROVEA.

Przeworski, Adam. 1986. "Some Problems in the Study of the Transition to Democracy." In Guillermo O'Donnell, Philippe Schmitter, and Laurence Whitehead, eds., *Transitions from Authoritarian Rule: Prospects for Democracy*, Part III, pp. 47–63. Baltimore, MD: Johns Hopkins University Press.

Przeworski, Adam, and John Sprague. 1986. *Paper Stones: A History of Electoral Socialism*. Chicago: University of Chicago Press.

Przeworski, Adam, Susan C. Stokes, and Bernard Manin, eds. 1999. *Democracy, Accountability, and Representation*. Cambridge and New York: Cambridge University Press.

PSUV. 2010. *Libro rojo: Documentos fundamentales*. Caracas: PSUV.

   2014a. *Comisiones de trabajo*. Available at: www.psuv.org.ve/psuv/comisiones-trabajo/ [accessed September 15, 2014].

   2014b. *III Congreso: Partido Socialista Unido de Venezuela*. Caracas: PSUV.

Quimpo, Nathan Gilbert. 2005. "Yellow Pad: Trapo Parties and Corruption." *BusinessWorld*, October 10.

Ragin, Charles C. 1987. *The Comparative Method: Moving Beyond Qualitative and Quantitative Strategies*. Berkeley, CA: University of California Press.

Ramey, Garey, and Valerie Ramey. 1995. "Cross-Country Evidence on the Link between Volatility and Growth." *American Economic Review* 85(5): 1138–51.

Raymond, Christopher, and Brian M. Barros Feltch. 2014. "Parties, Cleavages and Issue Evolution: The Case of the Religious-Secular Cleavage in Chile." *Party Politics* 20 (3): 429–43.

Rebello, Mauricio. 2012. "A fragmentação partidária no Brasil: visões e tendências." Paper presented at the 36th annual ANPOCS meeting, Águas de Lindóia, São Paulo.

RedPol. 1998. *Estudio Pre-Electoral*. Caracas: Universidad Simón Bolívar Banco de Datos Poblacionales.

Remmer, Karen. 1989. *Military Rule in Latin America*. Boston, MA: Unwin Hyman.

   1991. "The Political Impact of Economic Crisis in Latin America in the 1980s." *American Political Science Review* 85(3): 777–800.

   1993. "The Political Economy of Elections in Latin America, 1980–1991." *American Political Science Review* 97: 393–407.

   2003. "Elections and Economics in Contemporary Latin America." In Carol Wise and Riordan Roett, eds., *Post-Stabilization Politics in Latin America: Competition, Transition, Collapse*, pp. 31–55. Washington, DC: Brookings Institution.

   2008. "The Politics of Institutional Change: Electoral Reform in Latin America, 1978–2002." *Party Politics* 14(1): 5–30.

Remy, Marisa. 2010 "Crecientes distancias entre la política nacional y la política regional." *Revista Argumentos* 4(5).

Ribeiro, Pedro. 2014. "What Do These People Want? Membership and Activism in Brazilian Political Parties." ECPR Joint Sessions of Workshops 2014, University of Salamanca, Spain, April 10–15.

Ribeiro, Ricardo. 2014. "Decadência longe do poder: Refundação e crise do PFL." *Revista de Sociologia e Política* 22(49): 5–37.

Riedl, Rachel Beatty. 2008. "Institutions in New Democracies: Variations in African Political Party Systems." PhD dissertation, Princeton University.

   2014. *Authoritarian Origins of Democratic Party Systems in Africa*. New York: Cambridge University Press.

Riedl, Rachel Beatty, and J. Tyler Dickovick. 2014. "Party Systems and Decentralization in Africa." *Studies in Comparative International Development* 49(3): 321–42.

Riutort, M. 1999. "Pobreza, desigualdad y crecimiento económico." *Documentos del proyecto pobreza*. Caracas: Universidad Católica Andrés Bello.

Roberts, Kenneth. 1995. "Neoliberalism and the Transformation of Populism in Latin America: The Peruvian Case." *World Politics* 48(1): 82–116.

1996. "Economic Crisis and the Demise of the Legal Left in Peru." *Comparative Politics* 29(1): 69–92.

2002. "Social Inequalities without Class Cleavages in Latin America's Neoliberal Era." *Studies in Comparative International Development* 36(4): 3–33.

2003. "Social Correlates of Party System Demise and Populist Resurgence in Venezuela." *Latin American Politics and Society* 45(3): 35–57.

2006a. "Populism, Political Conflict, and Grass-Roots Organization in Latin America." *Comparative Politics* 38(2): 127–48.

2006b. "Do Parties Matter? Lessons from the Fujimori Experience." In Julio Carrión, ed., *The Fujimori Legacy: The Rise of Electoral Authoritarianism in Peru*, pp. 81–101. University Park, PA: Pennsylvania State University Press.

2013. "Market Reform, Programmatic (De)alignment, and Party System Stability in Latin America." *Comparative Political Studies* 46(11): 1422–52.

2014. *Changing Course in Latin America: Party Systems in the Neoliberal Era.* New York: Cambridge University Press.

Roberts, Kenneth M., and Erik Wibbels. 1999. "Party Systems and Electoral Volatility in Latin America: A Test of Economic, Institutional, and Structural Explanations." *American Political Science Review* 93(3): 575–90.

Rodríguez, Octavio, and Carlos Sirvent. 2005. *Instituciones Electorales y Partidos Políticos en México.* México City: Jorale.

Rodrik, Dani. 1998. "Why Do More Open Economies Have Bigger Governments?" *Journal of Political Economy* 106(5): 997–1032.

Rodrik, Dani, and Andrés Velasco. 1999. "Short-Term Capital Flows." NBER Working Paper No. 7364 (September). Available at: www.nber.org/papers/w7364.pdf [accessed October 19, 2016].

Roeder, Philip G. 2001. "Ethnolinguistic Fractionalization (ELF) Indices, 1961 and 1985." February 16. Available at: http://weber.ucsd.edu/proeder/elf.htm [accessed October 19, 2016].

Rohrschneider, Robert, and Stephen Whitefield. 2012. *The Strain of Representation: How Parties Represent Diverse Voters in Western and Eastern Europe.* Oxford: Oxford University Press.

Roll, David. 2002. *Rojo difuso y azul pálido. Los partidos tradicionales en Colombia: entre el debilitamiento y la persistencia*, 1st edn. Bogotá: Universidad Nacional de Colombia, Facultad de Derecho, Ciencias Políticas y Sociales.

Roma, Celso. 2009. "Organizaciones de partido en Brasil: El PT y el PSDB bajo perspectiva comparada." *América Latina Hoy* 44: 156–84.

Romero, Aníbal. 1997. "Rearranging the Deck Chairs on the Titanic: The Agony of Democracy in Venezuela." *Latin American Research Review* 32(1): 7–36.

Romero, Mauricio. 2003. *Paramilitares y autodefensas.* Bogotá, D.C: Instituto de Estudios Políticos y Relaciones Internacionales.

Rospigliosi, Fernando. 2000. *Montesinos y las fuerzas armadas: cómo controló durante una década las instituciones militares.* Lima: IEP.

Rozas, Lucila. 2012. "Trayectorias de postulación y carreras políticas en el Perú: un estudio comparado de Puno y La Libertad." Undergraduate thesis, Pontificia Universidad Católica del Perú.

Rubin, Donald B. 1975. "Bayesian Inference for Causality: The Importance of Randomization." In *The Proceedings of the Social Statistics section of the American Statistical Association*, pp. 233–39. Alexandria, VA: American Statistical Association.

Ruiz Rodríguez, Leticia. 2006. "El sistema de partidos chileno: ¿Hacia una desestructuración ideológica?" In Manuel Alcántara Sáez and Leticia Ruiz Rodríguez, eds., *Chile: política y modernización democrática*, pp. 73–110. Barcelona: Edicions Bellaterra.

Rustow, Dankwart A. 1955. *The Politics of Compromise: A Study of Parties and Cabinet Government in Sweden*. Princeton, NJ: Princeton University Press.

Sabatini, Christopher. 2003. "Decentralization and Political Parties." *Journal of Democracy* 14(2): 138–50.

Sagarzazu, Iñaki. 2011. "Nación vs región: Las tensiones del sistema de partidos venezolano postcolapso." *América Latina Hoy* 58: 121–42.

Sáinz, Pedro. 2005. "La equidad en Latinoamérica desde los años noventa." *Cuadernos del CENDES* 22(60): 63–93.

Salamanca, Luis. 1995. "The Venezuelan Political System: A View from Civil Society. In Jennifer McCoy, Andrés Serbin, William C. Smith, and Andrés Stambouli, eds., *Venezuelan Democracy under Stress*, pp. 197–214. Miami and New Brunswick: North-South Center Press and Transaction Publishers.

Samuels, David J., and Matthew S. Shugart. 2010. *Presidents, Parties, and Prime Ministers: How the Separation of Power Affects Party Organization and Behavior*. New York: Cambridge University Press.

Samuels, David, and Richard Snyder. 2001. "The Value of a Vote: Malapportionment in Comparative Perspective." *British Journal of Political Science* 31(4): 651–71.

Samuels, David J., and César Zucco Jr. 2014. "The Power of Partisanship in Brazil: Evidence from Survey Experiments." *American Journal of Political Science* 58(1): 212–25.

2015. "Crafting Mass Partisanship at the Grass Roots." *British Journal of Political Science* 45(4): 755–75.

Sánchez, Omar. 2008. "Guatemala's Party Universe: A Case Study in Underinstitutionalization." *Latin American Politics and Society* 50(1): 123–51.

2009. "Party Non-Systems: A Conceptual Innovation." *Party Politics* 15(4): 487–520.

Sanders, David, Harold D. Clarke, Marianne C. Stewart, and Paul Whiteley. 2011. "Downs, Stokes, and the Dynamics of Electoral Choice." *British Journal of Political Science* 41(2): 287–314.

Santoni, Alessandro. 2013. "Religión, política y Democracia Cristiana: Chile e Italia en perspectiva comparada." *Historia y Política* 29: 193–218.

Santos, Roberto. 2002. "A face de um partido: base política e comportamento eleitoral do PFL Pernambuco, 1985–2001." PhD dissertation, University of São Paulo.

Sartori, Giovanni. 1968. "The Sociology of Parties: A Critical Review." In Otto Stammer, ed., *Party Systems, Party Organizations, and the Politics of New Masses*, pp. 1–25. Berlin: Free University of Berlin.

1969. "From the Sociology of Politics to Political Sociology." In Seymour Martin Lipset, ed., *Politics and the Social Sciences*, pp. 65–95. Oxford: Oxford University Press.

1976. *Parties and Party Systems: A Framework for Analysis*. New York: Cambridge University Press.

1986. "The Influences of Electoral Systems: Faulty Laws or Faulty Method?" In B. Grofman and A. Lijphart, eds., *Electoral Laws and their Political Consequences*, pp. 43–68. New York: Agathon Press.

Schady, Norbert. 2000. "The Political Economy of Expenditures by the Peruvian Social Fund (FONCODES), 1991–95." *American Political Science Review* 94(2): 289–304.

Schamis, Hector. 2006. "A 'Left Turn' in Latin America? Populism, Socialism, and Democratic Institutions." *Journal of Democracy* 17(4): 20–34

Schattschneider, Elmer Eric. 1942. *Party Government*. New York: Farrar and Rinehart.

Schedler, Andreas. 1995. "Under- and Overinstitutionalization: Some Ideal Typical Propositions Concerning Old and New Party Systems." Kellogg Institute for International Studies Working Paper No. 213, University of Notre Dame, March. Available at: www3.nd.edu/~kellogg/publications/workingpapers/WPS/213.pdf.

2002. "The Nested Game of Democratization by Elections." *International Political Science Review* 23(1): 103–22.

2013. *The Politics of Uncertainty: Sustaining and Subverting Electoral Authoritarianism*. Oxford: Oxford University Press.

Scherlis, Gerardo. 2008. "Machine Politics and Democracy: The Deinstitutionalization of the Argentine Party System." *Government and Opposition* 43(4): 579–98.

2012. "Designaciones y organización partidaria: el partido de redes gubernamentales en el peronismo kirchnerista." *América Latina Hoy* 62: 47–77.

Schlesinger, Joseph. 1991. *Political Parties and the Winning of Office*. Ann Arbor, MI: University of Michigan Press.

Schlozman, Kay Lehman. 2002. "Citizen Participation in America: What Do We Know? Why Do We Care?" In Ira Katznelson and Helen Milner, eds., *Political Science: State of the Discipline*, pp. 433–61. New York: W.W. Norton.

Schmidt, Gregory D. 2003. "The 2001 Presidential and Congressional Elections in Peru." *Electoral Studies* 22: 344–51.

Schmitter, Philippe. 2001. "Parties Are Not What They Once Were." In Larry Diamond and Richard Gunther, eds., *Political Parties and Democracy*, pp. 67–89. Baltimore, MD: Johns Hopkins University Press.

Scully, Timothy R. 1992. *Rethinking the Center. Party Politics in Nineteenth and Twentieth Century Chile*. Stanford, CA: Stanford University Press.

Scully, Timothy R., and J. Samuel Valenzuela. 1993. "De la democracia a la democracia: continuidad y variaciones en las preferencias del electorado y en el sistema de partidos en Chile." *Estudios Públicos* 51(Winter): 195–228.

Seawright, Jason. 2010. "Regression-Based Inference: A Case Study in Failed Causal Assessment." In Henry E. Brady and David Collier, eds., *Rethinking Social Inquiry: Diverse Tools, Shared Standards*, 2nd edn. pp. 247–71. New York: Rowman and Littlefield.

2012. *Party System Collapse: The Roots of Crisis in Peru and Venezuela*. Stanford, CA: Stanford University Press.

Sehinkman, Diego. 2014. "José M. de la Sota: 'No hay teoría de dos demonios, hay dos crímenes'." La Nación, December 13. Available at: www.lanacion.com.ar/1752029-jose-m-de-la-sota-no-hay-teoria-de-dos-demonios-hay-dos-crimenes [accessed September 2016].

Seifert, Manuel. 2011. "Colapso de los partidos nacionales y auge de los partidos regionales. Las elecciones regionales 2002–2010." MA thesis, Pontificia Universidad Católica del Perú.

  2014. *Colapso de los partidos nacionales y auge de los partidos regionales. Las elecciones regionales y municipales 2002–2010.* Lima: Escuela de Gobierno y Políticas Públicas, Pontificia Universidad del Perú.

Servicio Electoral de Chile (SERVEL). 2014. *Resultados en Excel.* Available at: http://historico.servel.cl [accessed May 2014].

  2016. *Resultados en Excel.* Available at: http://servelelecciones.cl [accessed October 2016].

Shefter, Martin. 1994. *Political Parties and the State: The American Historical Experience.* Princeton, NJ: Princeton University Press.

Shirk, David. 2005. *Mexico's New Politics: The PAN and Democratic Change.* Boulder, CO: Lynne Rienner.

Shirk, David, and Joel Wallman. 2015. "Understanding Mexico's Drug Violence." *Journal of Conflict Resolution* 59(8): 1348–76.

Shugart, Matthew, Erika Moreno, and Luis E. Fajardo. 2007. "Deepening Democracy by Renovating Political Parties." In Christopher Welna and Gustavo Gallón, eds., *Peace, Democracy, and Human Rights in Colombia*, pp. 202–66. Notre Dame, IN: University of Notre Dame Press.

Siavelis, Peter. 2000. *The President and Congress in Post-Authoritarian Chile: Institutional Constraints to Democratic Consolidation.* University Park, PA: Pennsylvania State University Press.

  2005. "La lógica oculta de la selección de candidatos en las elecciones parlamentarias chilenas." *Estudios Públicos* 98(Fall): 189–225.

  2006. "Accommodating Informal Institutions and Chilean Democracy." In Gretchen Helmke and Steven Levitsky, eds. *Informal Institutions and Democracy: Lessons from Latin America*, pp. 33–55. Baltimore, MD: Johns Hopkins University Press.

  2009. "Enclaves de la transición y democracia chilena." *Revista de Ciencia Política* 29 (1): 3–21.

  2014. "From a Necessary to a Permanent Coalition." In Kirsten Sehnbruch and Peter M. Siavelis, eds., *Democratic Chile: The Politics and Policies of a Historic Coalition, 1990–2010*, pp. 15–42. Boulder, CO: Lynne Rienner Publishers.

Silva, Patricio. 2001. "Towards Technocratic Mass Politics in Chile? The 1999–2000 Elections and the 'Lavín Phenomenon'." *European Review of Latin American and Caribbean Studies* 70: 25–39.

Simmons, Joel W. 2016. *The Politics of Technological Progress: Parties, Time Horizons, and Long-term Economic Development.* New York: Cambridge University Press.

Simpser, Alberto. 2013. *Why Governments and Parties Manipulate Elections.* New York: Cambridge University Press.

Singer, Matthew M. 2004. "The 2002 Presidential and Parliamentary Elections in Bolivia." *Electoral Studies* 23(1): 172–82.

Slater, Dan. 2010. *Ordering Power: Contentious Politics and Authoritarian Leviathans in Southeast Asia.* New York: Cambridge University Press.

Slater, Dan, and Erica Simmons. 2013. "Coping by Colluding: Political Uncertainty and Promiscuous Powersharing in Indonesia and Bolivia." *Comparative Political Studies* 46(11): 1366–93.

Slater, Dan, and Joseph Wong. 2013. "The Strength to Concede: Ruling Parties and Democratization in Developmental Asia." *Perspectives on Politics* 11(3): 717–33.

Smith, Benjamin. 2005. "Life of the Party: The Origins of Regime Breakdown and Persistence under Single-Party Rule." *World Politics* 57(3): 421–51.

Smith, Brian. 1982. *The Church and Politics in Chile: Challenges to Modern Catholicism.* Princeton, NJ: Princeton University Press.

Snow, Peter G. 1971. *Political Forces in Argentina.* New York: Praeger.

Soares, Gláucio Ary Dillon, and Sonia Luiza Terron. 2008. "Dois Lulas: A geografia eleitoral da reeleição (explorando conceitos, métodos e técnicas de análise geoespacial)." *Opinião Pública* 14(2): 269–301.

Soifer, Hillel. 2008. "State Infrastructural Power: Conceptualization and Measurement in Empirical Analysis." *Studies in Comparative International Development* 43(3–4): 231–51.

　　2015. *State-Building in Latin America.* New York: Cambridge University Press.

Speck, Bruno Wilhelm, and Mauro Macedo Campos. 2014. "Incentivos para a fragmentação e a nacionalização do sistema partidário a partir do horário eleitoral gratuito no Brasil." *Teoria e Pesquisa* 23(2): 12–40.

Spiller, Pablo, and Mariano Tommasi. 2005. "The Institutional Foundations of Public Policy: A Transaction Cost Approach and Its Application to Argentina." In Steven Levitsky and María Victoria Murillo, eds., *Argentine Democracy: The Politics of Institutional Weakness*, pp. 269–289. University Park, PA: The Pennsylvania State Press.

　　2008. "Political Institutions, Policymaking Processes, and Policy Outcomes in Argentina." In Ernesto Stein and Mariano Tommasi, eds., *Policymaking in Latin America: How Politics Shapes Policies*, pp. 69–110. Washington, DC: Inter-American Development Bank and David Rockefeller Center for Latin American Studies, Harvard University.

Stein, Eduardo, Mariano Tommasi, Koldo Echebarría, Eduardo Lora, and Mark Payne. 2006. *The Politics of Policies: Economic and Social Progress in Latin America.* New York: Inter-American Development Bank

Stekhoven, Daniel J., and Peter Buhlmann. 2012. "MissForest – Non Parametric Missing Value Imputation for Mixed-Type Data." *Bioinformatics* 28(1): 112–18.

Stokes, Donald E. 1992. "Valence Politics." In D. Kavanagh, ed., *Electoral Politics*, pp. 141–64. New York: Oxford University Press.

Stokes, Susan C. 1999. "Political Parties and Democracy." *Annual Review of Political Science* 2: 243–67.

　　2001. *Mandates and Democracy: Neoliberalism by Surprise in Latin America.* New York: Cambridge University Press.

　　2007. "Political Clientelism." In Carles Boix and Susan Stokes, eds., *The Oxford Handbook of Comparative Politics*, pp. 604–27. Oxford and New York: Oxford University Press.

Stokes, Susan C., Thad Dunning, Marcelo Nazareno, and Valeria Brusco. 2013. *Brokers, Voters, and Clientelism.* Cambridge: Cambridge University Press.

Su, Yen-Pin. 2015. "Party Registration Rules and Party Systems in Latin America." *Party Politics* 21(2): 295–309.

Sulmont, Denis. 1975. *El movimiento obrero peruano (1890–1980)*, 5th edn. Lima: Tarea.

Sundquist, James L. 1983. *Dynamics of the Party System: Alignment and Realignment of Political Parties in the United States.* Washington, DC: Brookings Institution Press.

Tagina, María Laura. 2012. "Factores contextuales, predisposiciones de largo plazo y accountability electoral en Argentina en tiempos del kirchnerismo." *Política y Gobierno* 19(2): 343–75.

Tanaka, Martín. 1998. *Los espejismos de la democracia. El colapso del sistema de partidos en el Perú, 1980–1995, en perspectiva comparada.* Lima: IEP.

2005. *La democracia sin partidos. Perú 2000–2005: los problemas de representación y las propuestas de reforma política.* Lima: IEP.

2006. "From Crisis to Collapse of the Party Systems and Dilemmas of Democratic Representation: Peru and Venezuela." In Scott Mainwaring, Ana María Bejarano, and Eduardo Pizarro Leongómez, eds., *The Crisis of Democratic Representation in the Andes*, pp. 47–77. Stanford, CA: Stanford University Press.

Tanaka, Martín, and Rodrigo Barrenechea. 2011. "Evaluando la oferta de partidos: ¿Cuál es el perfil de los candidatos al próximo parlamento?" *Revista Argumentos* 5(1).

Tanaka, Martín, and Yamilé Guibert. 2011 "Entre la vaporización de los partidos y la debilidad de los movimientos regionales" In María Ana Rodríguez and Omar Coronel, eds. *El nuevo poder en las regiones: análisis de las elecciones regionales y municipales 2010.* Lima: Pontificia Universidad Católica del Perú.

Tarouco, Gabriela. 1999. "O Partido da Frente Liberal: trajetória e papel no sistema político." MA thesis, UNICAMP.

Tavits, Margit. 2005. "The Development of Stable Party Support: Electoral Dynamics in Post-Communist Europe." *American Journal of Political Science* 49(2): 183–98.

2006. "Party System Change: Testing a Model of New Party Entry." *Party Politics* 12 (1): 99–119.

2007. "Principle vs Pragmatism: Policy Shifts and Political Competition." *American Journal of Political Science* 51(1): 151–65.

2008. "Party Systems in the Making: The Emergence and Success of New Parties in New Democracies." *British Journal of Political Science* 38(1): 113–33.

2009. "The Making of Mavericks: Local Loyalties and Party Defection." *Comparative Political Studies* 42(6): 793–815.

2013. *Post-Communist Democracies and Party Organization.* Cambridge: Cambridge University Press.

Tavits, Margit, and Taavi Annus. 2006. "Learning to Make Votes Count: The Role of Democratic Experience." *Electoral Studies* 25(1): 72–90.

Teorell, Jan, Nicholas Charron, Stefan Dahlberg, Soren Holmberg, Bo Rothstein, Petrus Sundin, and Richard Svensson. 2013. *The Quality of Government Dataset, version 20Dec13.* University of Gothenburg, available at: www.qog.pol.gu.se [accessed October 2014].

Thachil, Tariq. 2015. *Elite Parties, Poor Voters: How Social Services Win Votes in India.* New York: Cambridge University Press.

The Maddison Project. 2013. *New Maddison Project Database.* Available at: www .ggdc.net/maddison/maddison-project/home.htm [accessed February 10, 2014].

Thiriot, Céline. 2002. "Rôle de la société civile dans la transition et la consolidation démocratique en Afrique: éléments de réflexion à partir du cas du Mali." *Revue International de Politique Comparée* 9(2): 277–95.

Thumala Olave, Angélica. 2010. "The Richness of Ordinary Life: Religious Justification among Chile's Business Elite." *Religion* 40(1): 14–26.

Tironi, Eugenio, and Felipe Agüero. 1999. "¿Sobrevivirá el nuevo paisaje político chileno?" *Estudios Públicos* 74: 151–68.

Tóka, Gábor. 1997. "Political Parties and Democratic Consolidation in East Central Europe." Studies in Public Policy Working Paper No. 279.

Tomz, Michael, and Robert P. Van Houweling. 2009. "The Electoral Implications of Candidate Ambiguity." *American Political Science Review* 103(1): 83–98.

Torcal, Mariano, ed. 2015. *Sistemas de partidos en América Latina: causas y consecuencias de su equilibrio inestable*. Barcelona: Anthropos de Siglo XXI.

Torcal, Mariano, and Ignacio Lago. 2015. "Volatilidad endógena y exógena: Una nueva medida de institucionalización." In Mariano Torcal, ed., *Sistemas de partidos en América Latina: Causas y consecuencias de su equilibrio inestable*, pp. 60–77. Barcelona: Anthropos Editorial.

Torcal, Mariano, and Scott Mainwaring. 2003. "The Political Recrafting of Social Bases of Party Competition: Chile, 1973–95." *British Journal of Political Science* 33: 55–84.

Toro Maureira, Sergio, Mauricio Morales Quiroga, and Rafael Piñeiro Rodríguez. 2011. "El efecto de las leyes electorales sobre la fragmentación partidaria en Chile, 1999–2008. Voto estratégico, barreras de entrada e información." *Política y Gobierno* 28(2): 331–58.

Tow, Andy. 2016. *Atlas Electoral de Andy Tow*. Available at: andytow.com/atlas/totalpais/indice.html [accessed June 28, 2016].

Trejo, Guillermo. 2012. *Popular Movements in Autocracies: Religion, Repression, and Indigenous Collective Action in Mexico*. Cambridge: Cambridge University Press.

Trejo, Guillermo, and Fernando Bizzaro. 2014. "Religious Competition and the Rise of the Workers' Party in Brazil." Equality Development and Globalization Studies (EDGS) Working Paper No. 21 (May 27), available at: www.edgs.northwestern.edu/wp-content/uploads/2014/05/Trejo_WP.pdf. [accessed November 2016].

Tribunal Superior Eleitoral. 2016. Available at: http://www.tse.jus.br/ [accessed November 2016].

Tsebelis, George. 2002. *Veto Players: How Political Institutions Work*. Princeton, NJ: Princeton University Press.

Tuesta Soldevilla, Fernando, ed. 1996. *Los enigmas del poder: Fujimori 1990–1996*. Lima: Fundación Friedrich Ebert.

Tulchin, Joseph S., and Andrew Selee, eds. 2004. *Decentralization and Democratic Governance in Latin America*. Washington, DC: Woodrow Wilson International Center for Scholars.

Turner, John C. 1999. "Some Current Issues in Research on Social Identity and Self-Categorization Theories." In Naomi Ellemers, Russell Spears, and Bertjan Doosje, eds., *Social Identity: Context, Commitment, Content*, pp. 6–34. Malden, MA: Blackwell.

Turner, John C., Michael A. Hogg, Penelope Oakes, Stephen Reicher, and Margaret Wetherell. 1987. *Rediscovering the Social Group: A Self-Categorization Theory*. New York: Blackwell.

UNESCO Institute for Statistics. 2014. "UNESCO Institute for Statistics Education Data." Available at: www.uis.unesco.org/datacentre/pages/BrowseEducation .aspx?SPSLanguage=EN [accessed October 2014].

United Nations High Commissioner for Refugees (UNHRC). 2016. *Global Trends. Forced Displacement in 2015.* Geneva: UNHRC.

UNT. 2014. "Nuestra historia." *Un Nuevo Tiempo.* Available at: http://partidounnuevotiempo.org/inicio/index.php/nuestro-partido [accessed April 13, 2014].

Urrutia, Adriana. 2011a. "Que la Fuerza (2011) esté con Keiko: el nuevo baile del fujimorismo. El fujimorismo, su organización y sus estrategias de campaña." In Carlos Meléndez, ed. *Post-Candidatos: Guía analítica de sobrevivencia hasta las próximas elecciones,* pp. 91–120. Lima: MITIN.

2011b. "Hacer campaña y construir partido: Fuerza 2011 y su estrategia para (re) legitimar al fujimorismo a través de su organización." *Argumentos* 5(2).

Valencia Ramírez, Cristóbal. 2005. "Venezuela's Boliviarian Revolution: Who are the Chavistas?" *Latin American Perspectives* 32(3): 79–97.

Valenzuela, Arturo. 1978. *The Breakdown of Democratic Regimes: Chile.* Edited by Juan J. Linz and Alfred Stepan, *The Breakdown of Democratic Regimes.* Baltimore, MD: Johns Hopkins University Press.

1985. "Orígenes y características del sistema de partidos en Chile: proposición para un gobierno parlamentario." *Estudios Públicos* 18(Fall): 1–69.

Valenzuela, Arturo, and J. Samuel Valenzuela. 1986. "Party Oppositions under the Chilean Authoritarian Regime." In J. Samuel Valenzuela and Arturo Valenzuela, eds., *Military Rule in Chile: Dictatorship and Oppositions,* pp. 184–229. Baltimore, MD: Johns Hopkins University Press.

Valenzuela, J. Samuel. 1985. *Democratización vía reforma. La expansión del sufragio en Chile.* Buenos Aires: Ediciones del IDES.

1995. "The Origins and Transformations of the Chilean Party System." Kellogg Institute Working Paper No. 215 (December). Available at: https://www3.nd.edu/~kellogg/publications/workingpapers/WPS/215.pdf.

1998. "La Constitución de 1980 y el inicio de la redemocratizatión en Chile." In Torcuato di Tella, ed., *Crisis de representatividad y sistemas de partidos políticos,* pp. 149–95. Buenos Aires: Nuevohacer, Grupo Editor Latinoamericano.

1999. "Respuesta a Eugenio Tironi y Felipe Agüero: Reflexiones sobre el presente y futuro del paisaje político chileno a la luz de su pasado." *Estudios Públicos* 75 (Winter): 273–90.

Valenzuela, J. Samuel, and Erika Maza Valenzuela. 2000. "The Politics of Religion in a Catholic Country: Republican Democracy, *Social Cristianismo,* and the Conservative Party in Chile, 1850–1925." In Austin Ivereigh, ed., *The Politics of Religion in an Age of Revival,* pp. 188–223. London: Institute of Latin American Studies, University of London.

Valenzuela, J. Samuel, and Timothy R. Scully. 1997. "Electoral Choices and the Party System in Chile: Continuities and Changes at the Recovery of Democracy." *Comparative Politics* 29(4): 511–27.

Valenzuela, J. Samuel, Timothy R. Scully, and Nicolás Somma. 2007. "The Enduring Presence of Religion in Chilean Ideological Positionings and Voter Options." *Comparative Politics* 40(1): 1–20.

2009. "Social and Political Effects of Religiosity and Religious Identities in Latin America." Kellogg Institute Working Paper No. 362 (December). Available at: https://kellogg.nd.edu/publications/workingpapers/WPS/362.pdf.

Van Biezen, Ingrid, Peter Mair, and Thomas Poguntke. 2012. "Going, going … gone? The Decline of Party Membership in Contemporary Europe." *European Journal of Political Research* 51: 24–56.

Van Cott, Donna Lee. 2003. "From Exclusion to Inclusion: Bolivia's 2002 Elections." *Journal of Latin American Studies* 35(4): 751–75.

2005. *From Movements to Parties in Latin America: The Evolution of Ethnic Politics.* Cambridge: Cambridge University Press.

Van de Walle, Nicolas. 2003. "Presidentialism and Clientelism in Africa's Emerging Party Systems." *The Journal of Modern African Studies* 41(2): 297–321.

Van de Walle, Nicolas, Todd Moss, and Gunilla Pettersson. 2007. "An Aid-Institutions Paradox? A Review Essay on Aid Dependency and State Building in Sub-Saharan Africa." In William Easterly, ed., *Reinventing Foreign Aid*, pp. 255–82. Cambridge, MA: MIT Press.

Van Dyck, Brandon. 2014. "Why Party Organization Still Matters: The Workers' Party in Northeastern Brazil." *Latin American Politics and Society* 56(2): 1–26.

2016. "The Paradox of Adversity: New Left Party Survival and Collapse in Brazil, Mexico, and Argentina." In Steven Levitsky, James Loxton, Brandon Van Dyck, and Jorge Domínguez, eds., *Challenges of Party-Building in Latin America*, pp. 133–58. New York: Cambridge University Press.

Varshney, Ashutosh. 1998. "Why Democracy Survives?" *The Journal of Democracy* 9 (3): 36–50.

Vásquez, Alex, and Adriana Rivera. 2013. "MUD aprobó tarjeta única para elecciones del 8 de diciembre." *El Nacional*, July.

Vera, Sofía. 2010. "Radiografía a la política en las regiones: tendencias a partir de la evidencia de tres procesos electorales (2002, 2006 y 2010)." *Revista Argumentos* 4(5).

2011. "Volar sin paracaídas : Alejandro Toledo y su re-elección frustrada." In Carlos Meléndez, ed. *Post-candidatos: Guía analítica de sobrevivencia hasta las próximas elecciones*, pp. 147–72. Lima: MITIN.

Vergara, Alberto. 2009. "El choque de los ideales: reformas institucionales y partidos políticos en el Perú post-fujimorato." Working Paper, International Institute for Democracy and Electoral Assistance (IDEA). Lima, Peru.

Vergara, Alberto, and Daniel Encinas. 2016. "Continuity by Surprise: Explaining Institutional Stability in Contemporary Peru." *Latin American Research Review* 51(1): 159–80.

Vilca, Paulo. 2011. "Por las rutas de la política regional." In Carlos Meléndez, ed., *Anti-Candidatos: Guía Analítica para unas Elecciones sin Partidos*, pp. 178–209. Lima: Mitin.

Villasmil, Ricardo, Francisco Monaldi, Germán Ríos, and Marino González. 2007. "The Difficulties of Reforming an Oil Dependent Economy." In José Fanelli, ed., *Understanding Market Reforms in Latin America*, pp. 266–318. Palgrave Macmillan.

Von Bergen, Franz. 2013. "76 municipios son vulnerables ante situación como la del 14-A." *El Nacional*, December 2. Available at: www.el-nacional.com/politica/ 8D-candidatos-Chavismo-elecciones-impugnacion-MUD-municipales_o_310769121 .html [accessed April 9, 2014].

486   *Bibliography*

Walker, Ignacio. 1990. *Socialismo y democracia: Chile y Europa en perspectiva comparada.* Santiago: CIEPLAN-Hachette.

Ware, Alan. 1996. *Political Parties and Party Systems.* Oxford: Oxford University Press.

Webb, Paul D. 1996. "A Partisanship and Anti-Party Sentiment in the United Kingdom: Correlates and Constraints." *European Journal of Political Research* 29(3): 365–82.

Weghorst, Keith R., and Michael Bernhard. 2014. "From Formlessness to Structure? The Institutionalization of Competitive Party Systems in Africa." *Comparative Political Studies* 47(12): 1707–37.

Weitz-Shapiro, Rebecca. 2013. "What Wins Votes: Why Some Politicians Opt Out of Clientelism." *American Journal of Political Science* 56(3): 563–83.

Welfling, Mary B. 1973. *Political Institutionalization: Comparative Analyses of African Party Systems.* Beverly Hills, CA: Sage Publications.

Weyland, Kurt. 2002a. *The Politics of Market Reform in Fragile Democracies: Argentina, Brazil, Peru, and Venezuela.* Princeton, NJ: Princeton University Press.

2002b. "Limitations of Rational Choice Institutionalism for the Study of Latin American Politics." *Studies in Comparative International Development* 37(1): 57–85.

2013. "Latin America's Authoritarian Drift: The Threat from the Populist Left." *Journal of Democracy* 24(3): 18–32.

Weyland, Kurt, Raul Madrid, and Wendy Hunter. 2010. *Leftist Governments in Latin America: Successes and Shortcomings.* New York: Cambridge University Press.

Whitehead, Laurence. 1986. "Bolivia's Failed Democratization, 1977–1980." In Guillermo O'Donnell, Philippe C. Schmitter, and Laurence Whitehead, eds., *Transitions from Authoritarian Rule: Latin America*, pp. 49–71. Baltimore, MD: The Johns Hopkins University Press.

2001. "High Anxiety in the Andes: Bolivia and the Viability of Democracy." *Journal of Democracy* 12(2): 6–16.

Wiesehomeier, Nina, and David Doyle. 2012. "Attitudes, Ideological Associations and the Left–Right Divide in Latin America." *Journal of Politics in Latin America* 4(1): 3–33.

Wilde, Alexander. 1978. "Conversations among Gentlemen: Oligarchical Democracy in Colombia." In Juan Linz and Alfred Stepan, eds., *The Breakdown of Democratic Regimes: Vol.3*, pp. 28–81. Baltimore, MD: Johns Hopkins University Press.

Wills Otero, Laura. 2014. "Colombia: Analyzing the Strategies for Political Action of Álvaro Uribe's Government, 2002–10." In Juan Pablo Luna and Cristóbal Rovira Kaltwasser, eds., *The Resilience of the Latin American Right*, pp. 194–215. Baltimore, MD: Johns Hopkins University Press.

Wolfers, Justin. 2003. "Is Business Cycle Volatility Costly? Evidence from Surveys of Subjective Wellbeing." NBER Working Paper 9619.

World Bank. 2013. *World Development Indicators.* Available at: http://data.worldbank.org/data-catalog/world-development-indicators [accessed October 2014].

2016. *World Development Indicators.* Online Resource. Available at: http://databank.worldbank.org/data/reports.aspx?source=world-development-indicators&preview=on [accessed July 2016].

Worldwide Governance Indicators. 2015. *Control of Corruption*. Available at: http://info.worldbank.org/governance/wgi/index.aspx#reports [accessed August 8, 2016].

Young, M. Crawford. 2013. *The Postcolonial State in Africa: Fifty Years of Independence, 1960–2010*. Madison, WI: University of Wisconsin Press.

Zavaleta, Mauricio. 2010. "¿Cómo se compite sin partidos? Política electoral en Cusco y Puno." *Revista Argumentos* 4(5).

2014. *Coaliciones de independientes: Las reglas no escritas de la política electoral en el Perú*. Lima: Instituto de Estudios Peruanos.

Zechmeister, Elizabeth. 2015. "Left–Right Identifications and the Latin American Voter." In Ryan Carlin, Matthew Singer, and Elizabeth Zechmeister, eds., *The Latin American Voter: Pursuing Representation and Accountability in Challenging Contexts*, pp. 69–98. Ann Arbor, MI: University of Michigan Press.

Zelaznik, Javier. 2011a. "Las coaliciones kirchneristas." In Andrés Malamud and Miguel De Luca, eds., *La Política en Tiempos de los Kirchner*, pp. 95–104. Buenos Aires: EUDEBA.

2011b. "Materiales para el estudio del sistema político argentino (1999–2011)." In Andrés Malamud and Miguel De Luca, eds., *La Política en Tiempos de los Kirchner*, pp. 277–327. Buenos Aires: EUDEBA.

Zielinski, Jacub, Kazimierz M. Slomczynski, and Goldie Shabad. 2005. "Electoral Control in New Democracies: The Perverse Incentives of Fluid Party Systems." *World Politics* 57(3): 365–95.

Zoco, Edurne. 2007. "The Collapse of Party Systems: Italy, Peru and Venezuela. PhD dissertation." University of Notre Dame.

Zolberg, Aristide. 1966. *Creating Political Order: The Party-States of West Africa*. Rand McNally.

Zucco, César, Jr. 2008. "The President's 'New' Constituency: Lula and the Pragmatic Vote in Brazil's 2006 Presidential Elections." *Journal of Latin American Studies* 40 (1): 29.

2011. "Esquerda, direita e governo. A ideologia dos partidos políticos brasileiros." In Timothy J. Power and Cesar Zucco, Jr., eds., *O congresso por ele mesmo: autopercepções da classe política brasileira*, pp. 37–60. Belo Horizonte: Editora UFMG.

2015. "Estabilidad sin raíces: la institucionalización del sistema de partidos brasileño." In Mariano Torcal, ed., *Los problemas de la institucionalización de los sistemas de partidos en América Latina*, pp. 78–107. Barcelona: Anthropos.

Index